MODERN BUSINESS ANALYTICS

McGraw Hill

MODERN BUSINESS ANALYTICS

Practical Data Science for Decision Making

Matt Taddy
Amazon, Inc.

Leslie Hendrix
University of South Carolina

Matthew C. Harding
University of California, Irvine

MODERN BUSINESS ANALYTICS

1 2 3 4 5 6 7 8 9 LKV 27 26 25 24 23 22

ISBN 978-1-264-07167-8 (SE)
MHID 1-264-07167-1 (SE)
ISBN 978-1-264-07165-4 (Loose leaf)
MHID 1-264-07165-5 (Loose leaf)

Portfolio Manager: *Rebecca Olson, Eric Weber*
Product Development Manager: *Michele Janicek*
Product Developer: *Christina Verigan*
Digital Product Developer: *Katherine Ward*
Marketing Manager: *Harper Christopher*
Content Project Managers: *Amy Gehl (Core), Emily Windelborn (Assessment)*
Buyer: *Susan K. Culbertson*
Design: *Matt Diamond*
Content Licensing Specialist: *Melissa Homer*
Cover Image Credit: *MirageC/Getty Images*
Compositor: *Straive*

Library of Congress Cataloging-in-Publication Data

Names: Taddy, Matt, author.
Title: Modern business analytics: practical data science for
  decision making / Matt Taddy, Amazon, Inc., Leslie Hendrix, University
  of South Carolina, Matthew Harding, University of California, Irvine.
Description: New York, NY: McGraw Hill Education, [2023]
Identifiers: LCCN 2021058431 | ISBN 9781264071678 (hardcover) | ISBN
  9781264071654 (Loose leaf)
Subjects: LCSH: Decision making—Econometric models. | Machine learning.
Classification: LCC HD30.23 .T3245 2023 | DDC 658.4/03—dc23/eng/20220125
LC record available at https://lccn.loc.gov/2021058431

ABOUT THE AUTHORS

Courtesy of Matt Taddy

Matt Taddy is the author of *Business Data Science* (McGraw Hill, 2019). From 2008–2018 he was a professor of econometrics and statistics at the University of Chicago Booth School of Business, where he developed their Data Science curriculum. Prior to and while at Chicago Booth, he has also worked in a variety of industry positions including as a principal researcher at Microsoft and a research fellow at eBay. He left Chicago in 2018 to join Amazon as a vice president.

Courtesy of Leslie Hendrix

Leslie Hendrix is a clinical associate professor in the Darla Moore School of Business at the University of South Carolina. She received her PhD in statistics in 2011 and a BS in mathematics in 2005 from the University of South Carolina. She has received two university-wide teaching awards for her work in teaching business analytics and statistics courses and is active in the research and teaching communities for analytics. She was instrumental in founding the Moore School's newly formed Data Lab and currently serves as the assistant director.

Courtesy of Matthew
C. Harding

Matthew C. Harding is a professor of economics and statistics at the University of California, Irvine. He holds a PhD from MIT and an M.Phil. from Oxford University. Dr. Harding conducts research on econometrics, consumer finance, health policy, and energy economics and has published widely in leading academic journals. He is the founder of Ecometricx, LLC, a big data and machine learning consulting company, and cofounder of FASTlab.global Institute, a nonprofit focusing on education and evidence-based policies in the areas of fair access and sustainable technologies.

BRIEF CONTENTS

CONTENTS

Appendix: R Primer 383

PREFACE

What Is This Book About?

The practice of data analytics is changing and modernizing. Innovations in computation and machine learning are creating new opportunities for the data analyst: exposing previously unexplored data to scientific analysis, scaling tasks through automation, and allowing deeper and more accurate modeling. Spreadsheet models and pivot tables are being replaced by code scripts in languages like R and Python. There has been massive growth in digitized information, accompanied by development of systems for storage and analysis of this data. There has also been an intellectual convergence across fields—machine learning and computer science, statistics, and social sciences and economics—that has raised the breadth and quality of applied analysis everywhere. This is the *data science approach to analytics*, and it allows leaders to go deeper than ever to understand their operations, products, and customers.

This book is a primer for those who want to gain the skills to use data science to help make decisions in business and beyond. The modern business analyst uses tools from machine learning, economics, and statistics to not only track what has happened but predict the future for their businesses. Analysts may need to identify the variables important for business policy, run an experiment to measure these variables, and mine social media for information about public response to policy changes. A company might seek to connect small changes in a recommendation system to changes in customer experience and use this information to estimate a demand curve. And any analysis will need to scale to companywide data, be repeatable in the future, and quantify uncertainty about the model estimates and conclusions.

This book focuses on business and economic applications, and we expect that our core audience will be looking to apply these tools as data scientists and analysts inside companies. But we also cover examples from health care and other domains, and the practical material that you learn in this book applies far beyond any narrow set of business problems.

This is not a book about *one of* machine learning, economics, or statistics. Rather, this book pulls from all of these fields to build a toolset for modern business analytics. The material in this book is designed to be useful for *decision making*. Detecting patterns in past data can be useful—we will cover a number of pattern recognition topics—but the necessary analysis for deeper business problems is about *why* things happen rather than what has happened. For this reason, this book will spend the time to move beyond correlation to causal analysis. This material is closer to economics than to the mainstream of data science, which should help you have a bigger practical impact through your work.

We can't cover everything here. This is not an encyclopedia of data analysis. Indeed, for continuing study, there are a number of excellent books covering different areas of contemporary machine learning and data science. For example, Hastie et al. (2009) is a comprehensive modern statistics reference and James et al. (2021) is a less advanced text from a similar viewpoint. You can view this current text as a stepping stone to a career of continued exploration and learning in statistics and machine learning. We want you to leave with a set of best practices that make you confident in what to trust, how to use it, and how to learn more.

GUIDED TOUR

This book is based on the *Business Data Science* text by Taddy (2019), which was itself developed as part of the MBA data science curriculum at the University of Chicago Booth School of Business. This new adaptation creates a more accessible and course-ready textbook, and includes a major expansion of the examples and content (plus an appendix tutorial on computing with R). Visit Connect for digital assignments, code, datasets, and additional resources.

Practical Data Science for Decision Making

Our target readership is anyone who wants to get the skills to use modern large-scale data to make decisions, whether they are working in business, government, science, or anywhere else.

In the past 10 years, we've observed the growth of a class of generalists who can understand business problems and also dive into the (big) data and run their own analyses. There is a massive demand for people with these capabilities, and this book is our attempt to help grow more of these sorts of people. You may be reading this book from a quantitative undergraduate course, as part of your MBA degree at a business school, or in a data science or other graduate program. Or, you may just be reading the book on your own accord. As data analysis has become more crucial and exciting, we are seeing a boom in people switching into data analysis careers from a wide variety of backgrounds. Those self-learners and career-switchers are as much our audience here as students in a classroom.

All of this said, this is not an *easy* book. We have tried to avoid explanations that require calculus or advanced linear algebra, but you will find the book a tough slog if you do not have a solid foundation in first-year mathematics and probability. Since the book includes a breadth of material that spans a range of complexity, we begin each chapter with a summary that outlines each section and indicates their difficulty according to a *ski-hill* scale:

● The easiest material, requiring familiarity with some transformations like logarithms and exponents, and an understanding of the basics of probability.

■ Moderately difficult material, involving more advanced ideas from probability and statistics or ideas that are going to be difficult to intuit without some linear algebra.

◆ The really tough stuff, involving more complex modeling ideas (and notation) and tools from linear algebra and optimization.

The black diamond material is not necessary for understanding future green or blue sections, and so instructors may wish to set their courses to cover the easy and moderately difficult sections while selecting topics from the hardest sections.

The book is designed to be self-contained, such that you can start with little prerequisite background in data science and learn as you go. However, the pace of content on introductory probability and statistics and regression is such that you may struggle if this is your first-ever course on these ideas. If you find this to be the case, we recommend spending some time working through a dedicated introductory statistics book to build some of this understanding before diving into the more advanced data science material.

It is also important to recognize that data science can be learned only by doing. This means writing the code to run analysis routines on really messy data. We will use the R scripting language for all of our examples. All example code and data is available online, and one of the most important skills you will get out of this book will be an advanced education in this powerful and widely used statistical software. For those who are completely new to R, we have also included an extensive R primer. The skills you learn here will also prepare you well for learning how to program in other languages, such as Python, which you will likely encounter in your business analysis career.

This is a book about how to *do* modern business analytics. We will lay out a set of core principles and best practices that come from statistics, machine learning, and economics. You will be working through many real data analysis examples as you learn by doing. It is a book designed to prepare scientists, engineers, and business professionals to use data science to improve their decisions.

An Introductory Example

Before diving into the core material, we will work through a simple finance example to illustrate the difference between data processing or description and a deeper *business analysis*. Consider the graph in Figure 0.1. This shows seven years of monthly returns for stocks in the S&P 500 index (a return is the difference between the current and previous price divided by the prior value). Each line ranging from bright yellow to dark red denotes an individual stock's return series. Their weighted average—the value of the S&P 500—is marked with a bold line. Returns on three-month U.S. treasury bills are in gray.

This is a fancy plot. It looks cool, with lots of different lines. It is the sort of plot that you might see on a computer screen in a TV ad for some online brokerage platform. *If only I had that information, I'd be rich!*

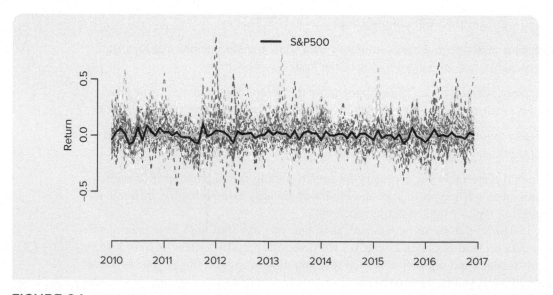

FIGURE 0.1   A fancy plot: monthly stock returns for members of the S&P 500 and their average (the bold line). *What can you learn?*

But what can you actually learn from Figure 0.1? You can see that returns do tend to bounce around near zero (although the long-term average is reliably much greater than zero). You can also pick out periods of higher volatility (variance) where the S&P 500 changes more from month to month and the individual stock returns around it are more dispersed. That's about it. You don't learn *why* these periods are more volatile or when they will occur in the future. More important, you can't pull out useful information about any individual stock. There is a ton of *data* on the graph but little useful information.

Instead of plotting raw data, let's consider a simple *market model* that relates individual stock returns to the market average. The capital asset pricing model (CAPM) regresses the returns of an individual asset onto a measure of overall market returns, as shown here:

$$r_{jt} = \alpha_j + \beta_j m_t + \varepsilon_{jt} \tag{0.1}$$

The *output* r_{jt} is equity j return at time t. The *input* m_t is a measure of the average return—the "market"—at time t. We take m_t as the return on the S&P 500 index that weights 500 large companies according to their market capitalization (the total value of their stock). Finally, ε_{jt} is an *error* that has mean zero and is uncorrelated with the market.

Equation (0.1) is the first regression model in this book. You'll see many more. This is a simple linear regression that should be familiar to most readers. The Greek letters define a line relating each individual equity return to the market, as shown in Figure 0.2. A small β_j, near zero, indicates an asset with low market sensitivity. In the extreme, fixed-income assets like treasury bills have $\beta_j = 0$. On the other hand, a $\beta_j > 1$ indicates a stock that is more volatile than the market, typically meaning growth and higher-risk stocks. The α_j is free money: assets with $\alpha_j > 0$ are adding value regardless of wider market movements, and those with $\alpha_j < 0$ destroy value.

Figure 0.3 represents each stock "ticker" in the two-dimensional space implied by the market model's fit on the seven years of data in Figure 0.1. The tickers are sized proportional to each firm's market capitalization. The two CAPM parameters—$[\alpha, \beta]$—tell you a huge amount about the behavior and performance of individual assets. This picture immediately allows you to assess market sensitivity and arbitrage opportunities. For example, the big tech stocks of Facebook (FB), Amazon (AMZN), Apple (AAPL), Microsoft (MSFT), and Google (GOOGL) all have market sensitivity β values close to one. However, Facebook, Amazon, and Apple generated more money independent of the market over this time period compared to Microsoft and Google (which have nearly identical α values and are overlapped on the plot). Note

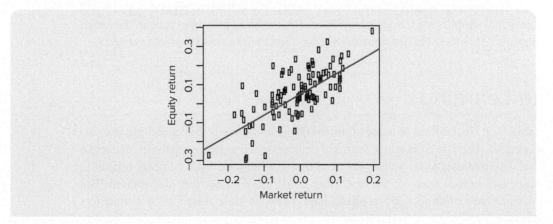

FIGURE 0.2 A *scatterplot* of a single stock's returns against market returns, with the fitted *regression line* for the model of Equation (0.1) shown in red.

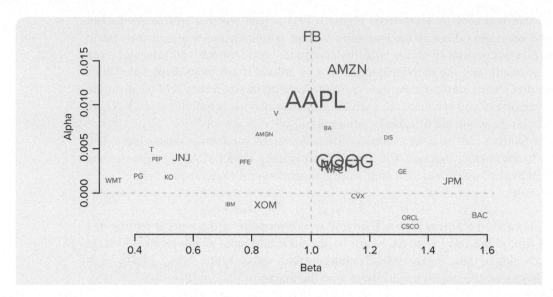

FIGURE 0.3   Stocks positioned according to their fitted market model, where α is money you make regardless of what the market does and β summarizes sensitivity to market movements. The tickers are sized proportional to market capitalization. Production change alpha to α and beta to β in the plot axis labels.

that Facebook's CAPM parameters are estimated from a shorter time period, since it did not have its IPO until May of 2012. Some of the older technology firms, such as Oracle (ORCL), Cisco (CSCO), and IBM, appear to have destroyed value over this period (negative alpha). Such information can be used to build portfolios that maximize mean returns and minimize variance in the face of uncertain future market conditions. It can also be used in strategies like pairs-trading where you find two stocks with similar betas and buy the higher alpha while "shorting" the other.

CAPM is an old tool in financial analysis, but it serves as a great illustration of what to strive toward in practical data science. An interpretable model translates raw data into information that is directly relevant to decision making. The challenge in data science is that the data you'll be working with will be larger and less structured (e.g., it will include text and image data). Moreover, CAPM is derived from assumptions of efficient market theory, and in many applications you won't have such a convenient simplifying framework on hand. But the basic principles remain the same: you want to turn raw data into useful information that has direct relevance to business policy.

Machine Learning

Machine learning (ML) is the field of using algorithms to automatically detect and predict patterns in complex data. The rise of machine learning is a major driver behind data science and a big part of what differentiates today's analyses from those of the past. ML is closely related to modern statistics, and indeed many of the best ideas in ML have come from statisticians. But whereas statisticians have often focused on *model inference*—on understanding the parameters of their models (e.g., testing on individual coefficients in a regression)—the ML community has historically been more focused on the single goal of maximizing *predictive performance* (i.e., predicting future values of some response of interest, like sales or prices).

A focus on prediction tasks has allowed ML to quickly push forward and work with larger and more complex data. If all you care about is predictive performance, then you don't need to worry about whether your model is "true" but rather just test how well it performs when predicting future values. This single-minded focus allows rapid experimentation on alternative models and estimation algorithms. The result is that ML has seen massive success, to the point that you can now expect to have available for almost any type of data an algorithm that will work out of the box to recognize patterns and give high-quality predictions.

However, this focus on prediction means that ML on its own is less useful for many *decision-making* tasks. ML algorithms learn to predict *a future that is mostly like the past.* Suppose that you build an ML algorithm that looks at how customer web browser history predicts how much they spend in your e-commerce store. A purely prediction-focused algorithm will discern what web traffic tends to spend more or less money. It will not tell you what will happen to the spending if you *change* a group of those websites (or your prices) or perhaps make it easier for people to browse the Web (e.g., by subsidizing broadband). That is where this book comes in: we will use tools from economics and statistics in combination with ML techniques to create a platform for using data to make decisions.

Some of the material in this book will be focused on pure ML tasks like prediction and pattern recognition. This is especially true in the earlier chapters on regression, classification, and regularization. However, in later chapters you will use these prediction tools as parts of more structured analyses, such as understanding subject-specific treatment effects, fitting consumer demand functions, or as part of an artificial intelligence system. This typically involves a mix of domain knowledge and analysis tools, which is what makes the data scientist such a powerful figure. The ML tools are useless for policy making without an understanding of the business problems, but a policy maker who can deploy ML as part of their analysis toolkit will be able to make better decisions faster.

Computing with R

You don't need to be a software engineer to work as a data scientist, but you need to be able to write and understand computer code. To learn from this book, you will need to be able to read and write in a high-level *scripting* language, in other words, flexible code that can be used to describe recipes for data analysis. In particular, you will need to have a familiarity with R (r-project.org).

The ability to interact with computers in this way—by typing commands rather than clicking buttons or choosing from a menu—is a basic data analysis skill. Having a script of commands allows you to rerun your analyses for new data without any additional work. It also allows you to make small changes to existing scripts to adapt them for new scenarios. Indeed, making small changes is how we recommend you work with the material in this book. The code for every in-text example is available on-line, and you can alter and extend these scripts to suit your data analysis needs. In the examples for this book, all of the analysis will be conducted in R. This is an open-source high-level language for data analysis. R is used widely throughout industry, government, and academia. Companies like RStudio sell enterprise products built around R. This is not a toy language used simply for teaching purposes—R is the real industrial-strength deal.

For the fundamentals of statistical analysis, R is tough to beat: all of the tools you need for linear modeling and uncertainty quantification are mainstays. R is also relatively forgiving for the novice programmer. A major strength of R is its ecosystem of contributed packages. These are add-ons that increase the capability of core R. For example, almost all of the ML tools that you will use in this book are available via packages. The quality of the packages is more varied than it is for R's core functionality, but if a package has high usage you should be confident that it works as intended.

The Appendix of this book contains a tutorial that is dedicated to getting you started in R. It focuses on the topics and algorithms that are used in the examples in this book. You don't need to be an expert in R to learn from this book; you just need to be able to understand the fundamentals and be willing to mess around with the coded examples. If you have no formal background in coding, worry not: many in the field started out in this position. The learning curve can be steep initially, but once you get the hang of it, the rest will come fast. The tutorial in the Appendix should help you get started. We also provide extensive examples throughout the book, and all code, data, and homework assignments are available through Connect. Every chapter ends with a *Quick Reference* section containing the basic R recipes from that chapter. When you are ready to learn more, there are many great places where you can supplement your understanding of the basics of R. If you simply search for *R* or *R statistics* books on-line, you will find a huge variety of learning resources.

ACKNOWLEDGMENTS

We are grateful for the reviewers who provided feedback on this first edition:

Sue Abdinnour, Wichita State University
Anil Aggarwal, University of Baltimore
Goutam Chakraborty, Oklahoma State University
Rick Cleary, Babson College
John Daniels, Central Michigan University
John Draper, Ohio State University
Janet Frasier, West Virginia University
Phillip C. Fry, Boise State University
Marina Girju, California Baptist University
Richard Hauser, East Carolina University
Kuo-Ting "Ken" Hung, Suffolk University
Aimee Jacobs, California State University, Fresno
Jaehwan Jeong, Radford University
Patrick Johanns, Univeristy of Iowa
Barry King, Butler University
Lauren Kleitz, Xavier University
Su "Sue" Kong, Kutztown University
Min Li, California State University, Sacramento
Jiajuan Liang, University of New Haven
Vic Matta, Ohio University
Ebrahim Mortaz, Pace University
Bob Myers, Georgia Tech University
Robert Nauss, University of Missouri-St. Louis

Arash Negahban, California State University, Chico
Yasin Ozcelik, Fairfield University
Brad Price, West Virginia University
Xingye Qiao, Binghamton University
Roman Rabinovich, Boston University
Bharatendra Rai, UMass-Dartmouth
Balaraman Rajan, California State University, East Bay
Rouzbeh Razavi, Kent State University
John Repede, Queens University of Charlotte
Thomas R. Robbins, East Carolina University
Wendy Swenson Roth, Georgia State University
Seokwoo Song, Weber State University
John R. Stevens, Utah State University
Jie Tao, Fairfield University
Vicar S. Valencia, Indiana University South Bend
Nikhil Varaiya, San Diego State University
Gang Wang, UMass-Dartmouth
K. Matthew Wong, St. John's University
Chase Wu, New Jersey Institute of Technology
Yajiong "Lucky" Xue, East Carolina University

Instructors: Student Success Starts with You

Tools to enhance your unique voice

Want to build your own course? No problem. Prefer to use an OLC-aligned, prebuilt course? Easy. Want to make changes throughout the semester? Sure. And you'll save time with Connect's auto-grading too.

65%
Less Time Grading

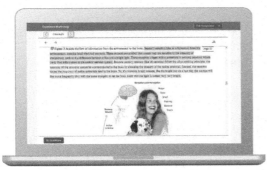

Laptop: McGraw Hill; Woman/dog: George Doyle/Getty Images

Study made personal

Incorporate adaptive study resources like SmartBook® 2.0 into your course and help your students be better prepared in less time. Learn more about the powerful personalized learning experience available in SmartBook 2.0 at **www.mheducation.com/highered/connect/smartbook**

Affordable solutions, added value

Make technology work for you with LMS integration for single sign-on access, mobile access to the digital textbook, and reports to quickly show you how each of your students is doing. And with our Inclusive Access program you can provide all these tools at a discount to your students. Ask your McGraw Hill representative for more information.

Padlock: Jobalou/Getty Images

Solutions for your challenges

A product isn't a solution. Real solutions are affordable, reliable, and come with training and ongoing support when you need it and how you want it. Visit **www.supportateverystep.com** for videos and resources both you and your students can use throughout the semester.

Checkmark: Jobalou/Getty Images

Students: Get Learning that Fits You

Effective tools for efficient studying

Connect is designed to help you be more productive with simple, flexible, intuitive tools that maximize your study time and meet your individual learning needs. Get learning that works for you with Connect.

Study anytime, anywhere

Download the free ReadAnywhere app and access your online eBook, SmartBook 2.0, or Adaptive Learning Assignments when it's convenient, even if you're offline. And since the app automatically syncs with your Connect account, all of your work is available every time you open it. Find out more at **www.mheducation.com/readanywhere**

> *"I really liked this app—it made it easy to study when you don't have your text-book in front of you."*
>
> - Jordan Cunningham,
>   Eastern Washington University

Calendar: owattaphotos/Getty Images

Everything you need in one place

Your Connect course has everything you need—whether reading on your digital eBook or completing assignments for class, Connect makes it easy to get your work done.

Learning for everyone

McGraw Hill works directly with Accessibility Services Departments and faculty to meet the learning needs of all students. Please contact your Accessibility Services Office and ask them to email accessibility@mheducation.com, or visit **www.mheducation.com/about/accessibility** for more information.

Top: Jenner Images/Getty Images, Left: Hero Images/Getty Images, Right: Hero Images/Getty Images

Proctorio
Remote Proctoring & Browser-Locking Capabilities

 Remote proctoring and browser-locking capabilities, hosted by Proctorio within Connect, provide control of the assessment environment by enabling security options and verifying the identity of the student.

Seamlessly integrated within Connect, these services allow instructors to control students' assessment experience by restricting browser activity, recording students' activity, and verifying students are doing their own work.

Instant and detailed reporting gives instructors an at-a-glance view of potential academic integrity concerns, thereby avoiding personal bias and supporting evidence-based claims.

ReadAnywhere

Read or study when it's convenient for you with McGraw Hill's free ReadAnywhere app. Available for iOS or Android smartphones or tablets, ReadAnywhere gives users access to McGraw Hill tools including the eBook and SmartBook 2.0 or Adaptive Learning Assignments in Connect. Take notes, highlight, and complete assignments offline–all of your work will sync when you open the app with WiFi access. Log in with your McGraw Hill Connect username and password to start learning–anytime, anywhere!

OLC-Aligned Courses

Implementing High-Quality Online Instruction and Assessment through Preconfigured Courseware

In consultation with the Online Learning Consortium (OLC) and our certified Faculty Consultants, McGraw Hill has created pre-configured courseware using OLC's quality scorecard to align with best practices in online course delivery. This turnkey courseware contains a combination of formative assessments, summative assessments, homework, and application activities, and can easily be customized to meet an individual's needs and course outcomes. For more information, visit https://www.mheducation.com/highered/olc.

Tegrity: Lectures 24/7

Tegrity in Connect is a tool that makes class time available 24/7 by automatically capturing every lecture. With a simple one-click start-and-stop process, you capture all computer screens and corresponding audio in a format that is easy to search, frame by frame. Students can replay any part of any class with easy-to-use, browser-based viewing on a PC, Mac, iPod, or other mobile device.

Educators know that the more students can see, hear, and experience class resources, the better they learn. In fact, studies prove it. Tegrity's unique search feature helps students efficiently find what they need, when they need it, across an entire semester of class recordings. Help turn your students' study time into learning moments immediately supported by your lecture. With Tegrity, you also increase intent listening and class participation by easing students' concerns about note-taking. Using Tegrity in Connect will make it more likely you will see students' faces, not the tops of their heads.

Test Builder in Connect

Available within Connect, Test Builder is a cloud-based tool that enables instructors to format tests that can be printed, administered within a Learning Management System, or exported as a Word document of the test bank. Test Builder offers a modern, streamlined interface for easy content configuration that matches course needs, without requiring a download.

Test Builder allows you to:

- access all test bank content from a particular title.
- easily pinpoint the most relevant content through robust filtering options.
- manipulate the order of questions or scramble questions and/or answers.
- pin questions to a specific location within a test.
- determine your preferred treatment of algorithmic questions.
- choose the layout and spacing.
- add instructions and configure default settings.

Test Builder provides a secure interface for better protection of content and allows for just-in-time updates to flow directly into assessments.

Writing Assignment

Available within Connect and Connect Master, the Writing Assignment tool delivers a learning experience to help students improve their written communication skills and conceptual understanding. As an instructor you can assign, monitor, grade, and provide feedback on writing more efficiently and effectively.

Application-Based Activities in Connect

Application-Based Activities in Connect are highly interactive, assignable exercises that provide students a safe space to apply the concepts they have learned to real-world, course-specific problems. Each Application-Based Activity involves the application of multiple concepts, allowing students to synthesize information and use critical thinking skills to solve realistic scenarios.

McGraw Hill create® Your Book, Your Way

McGraw Hill's Content Collections Powered by Create® is a self-service website that enables instructors to create custom course materials—print and eBooks—by drawing upon

McGraw Hill's comprehensive, cross-disciplinary content. Choose what you want from our high-quality textbooks, articles, and cases. Combine it with your own content quickly and easily, and tap into other rights-secured, third-party content such as readings, cases, and articles. Content can be arranged in a way that makes the most sense for your course and you can include the course name and information as well. Choose the best format for your course: color print, black-and-white print, or eBook. The eBook can be included in your Connect course and is available on the free ReadAnywhere app for smartphone or tablet access as well. When you are finished customizing, you will receive a free digital copy to review in just minutes! Visit McGraw Hill Create®—www.mcgrawhillcreate.com—today and begin building!

1 REGRESSION

This chapter develops the framework and language of regression: building models that predict response outputs from feature inputs.

- **Section 1.1 Linear Regression:** Specify, estimate, and predict from a linear regression model for a quantitative response y as a function of inputs $\mathbf{x}$. Use log transforms to model multiplicative relationships and *elasticities*, and use interactions to allow the effect of inputs to depend on each other.

- **Section 1.2 Residuals:** Calculate the residual errors for your regression fit, and understand the key fit statistics *deviance*, R^2, and *degrees of freedom*.

- **Section 1.3 Logistic Regression:** Build logistic regression models for a binary response variable, and understand how logistic regression is related to linear regression as a *generalized linear model*. Translate the concepts of deviance, likelihood, and R^2 to logistic regression, and be able to interpret logistic regression coefficients as effects on the log odds that $y = 1$.

- **Section 1.4 Likelihood and Deviance:** Relate likelihood maximization and deviance minimization, use the generalized linear models to determine residual deviance, and use the `predict` function to integrate new data with the same variable names as the data used to fit your regression.

- **Section 1.5 Time Series:** Adapt your regression models to allow for dependencies in data that has been observed over time, and understand time series concepts including seasonal trends, autoregression, and panel data.

- **Section 1.6 Spatial Data:** Add spatial fixed effects to your regression models and use Gaussian process models to estimate spatial dependence in your observations.

The vast majority of problems in applied data science require regression modeling. You have a *response* variable (*y*) that you want to model or predict as a function of a vector of *input features*, or covariates (**x**). This chapter introduces the basic framework and language of regression. We will build on this material throughout the rest of the book.

Regression is all about understanding the *conditional* probability distribution for "*y* given **x**," which we write as p(*y*|**x**). Figure 1.1 illustrates the conditional distribution in contrast to a *marginal* distribution, which is so named because it corresponds to the unconditional distribution for a single margin (i.e., column) of a data matrix.

A variable that has a probability distribution (e.g., number of bathrooms in Figure 1.1) is called a *random variable*. The *mean* for a random variable is the average of random draws from its probability distribution. While the marginal mean is a simple number, the conditional mean is a function. For example, from Figure 1.1b, you can see that the average home selling price takes different values indexed by the number of bathrooms. The data is distributed randomly around these means, and the way that you model these distributions drives your estimation and prediction strategies.

Conditional Expectation

A basic but powerful regression strategy is to build models in terms of *averages* and *lines*. That is, we will model the conditional mean for our output variable as a linear function of inputs. Other regression strategies can sometimes be useful, such as *quantile regression* that models percentiles of the conditional distribution. However for the bulk of applications you will find that *mean* regression is a good approach.

There is some important notation that you need to familiarize yourself with for the rest of the book. We model the conditional mean for *y* given **x** as

$$\mathbb{E}[y|\mathbf{x}] = f(\mathbf{x}'\boldsymbol{\beta}) \tag{1.1}$$

where

- $\mathbb{E}[\cdot]$ denotes the taking of the expectation or average of whatever random variable is inside the brackets. It is an extremely important operation, and we will use this notation to define many of our statistical models.

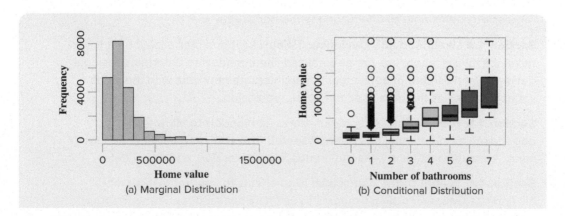

(a) Marginal Distribution   (b) Conditional Distribution

FIGURE 1.1   Illustration of marginal versus conditional distributions for home prices. On the left, we have the marginal distribution for all of the home prices. On the right, home price distributions are conditional on the number of bathrooms.

- The vertical bar | means "given" or "conditional upon," so that $\mathbb{E}[y|\mathbf{x}]$ is read as "the average for y given inputs $\mathbf{x}$."
- $f(\cdot)$ is a "link" function that transforms from the linear model to your response.
- $\mathbf{x} = [1, x_1, x_2, \ldots x_p]$ is the vector of covariates and $\boldsymbol{\beta} = [\beta_0, \beta_1, \beta_2, \ldots \beta_p]$ are the corresponding coefficients.

The *vector* notation, $\mathbf{x}'\boldsymbol{\beta}$, is shorthand for the sum of elementwise products:

$$\mathbf{x}'\boldsymbol{\beta} = [1 x_1 \, x_2 \cdots x_p] \begin{bmatrix} \beta_0 \\ \beta_1 \\ \beta_2 \\ \vdots \\ \beta_p \end{bmatrix} = \beta_0 + x_1\beta_1 + x_2\beta_2 + \ldots + x_p\beta_p \tag{1.2}$$

This shorthand notation will be used throughout the book. Here we have used the convention that $x_0 = 1$, such that β_0 is the intercept.

The link function, $f(\cdot)$, defines the relationship between your linear function $\mathbf{x}'\boldsymbol{\beta}$ and the response. The link function gives you a huge amount of modeling flexibility. This is why models of the kind written in Equation (1.1) are called *generalized linear models* (GLMs). They allow you to make use of linear modeling strategies after some simple transformations of your output variable of interest. In this chapter we will outline the two most common GLMs: linear regression and logistic regression. These two models will serve you well for the large majority of analysis problems, and through them you will become familiar with the general principles of GLM analysis.

1.1 Linear Regression

Linear regression is the workhorse of analytics. It is fast to fit (in terms of both analyst and computational time), it gives reasonable answers in a variety of settings (so long as you know how to ask the right questions), and it is easy to interpret and understand. The model is as follows:

$$\mathbb{E}[y|\mathbf{x}] = \beta_0 + x_1\beta_1 + x_2\beta_2 + \ldots + x_p\beta_p \tag{1.3}$$

This corresponds to using the link function $f(z) = z$ in Equation (1.1).

With just one input x, you can write the model as $\mathbb{E}[y|\mathbf{x}] = \beta_0 + x\beta_1$ and plot it as in Figure 1.2. β_0 is the intercept. This is where the line crosses the y axis when x is 0. β_1 is the

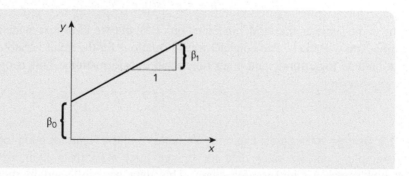

FIGURE 1.2 Simple linear regression with a positive slope β_1. The plotted line corresponds to $\mathbb{E}[y|x]$.

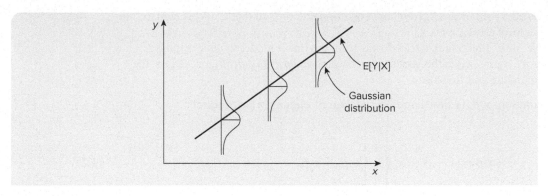

FIGURE 1.3 Using simple linear regression to picture the Gaussian conditional distribution for $y|x$. Here $\mathbb{E}[y|x]$ are the values on the line and the variation parallel to the y axis (i.e., within each narrow vertical strip) is assumed to be described by a Gaussian distribution.

slope and describes how $\mathbb{E}[y|x]$ changes as x changes. If x increases by 1 unit, $\mathbb{E}[y|x]$ changes by β_1. For a two predictor model, we are fitting a plane. Higher dimensions are more difficult to imagine, but the basic intuition is the same.

When fitting a regression model—i.e., when estimating the $\boldsymbol{\beta}$ coefficients—you make some assumptions about the conditional distribution beyond its mean at $\mathbb{E}[y|\mathbf{x}]$. Linear regression is commonly fit for Gaussian (normal) conditional distributions. We write this conditional distribution as

$$y \mid \mathbf{x} \sim \mathrm{N}(\mathbf{x}'\boldsymbol{\beta}, \sigma^2) \tag{1.4}$$

This says that the distribution for y as a function of $\mathbf{x}$ is normally distributed around $\mathbb{E}[y|\mathbf{x}] = \mathbf{x}'\boldsymbol{\beta}$ with variance σ^2. The same model is often written with an additive error term:

$$y = \mathbf{x}'\boldsymbol{\beta} + \varepsilon, \ \varepsilon \sim \mathrm{N}(0, \sigma^2) \tag{1.5}$$

where ε are the "independent" or "idiosyncratic" errors. These errors contain the variations in y that are not correlated with $\mathbf{x}$. Equations (1.4) and (1.5) describe the same model. Figure 1.3 illustrates this model for single-input simple linear regression. The line is the average $\mathbb{E}[y|x]$ and vertical variation around the line is what is assumed to have a normal distribution.

You will often need to transform your data to make the linear model of Equation (1.5) realistic. One common transform is that you need to take a *logarithm* of the response, say, "r," such that your model becomes

$$\log(r) = \mathbf{x}'\boldsymbol{\beta} + \varepsilon, \ \varepsilon \sim \mathrm{N}(0, \sigma^2) \tag{1.6}$$

Of course this is the same as the model in Equation (1.5), but we have just made the replacement $y = \log(r)$. You will likely also consider transformations for the input variables, such that elements of $\mathbf{x}$ include logarithmic and other functional transformations. This is often referred to as *feature engineering*.

Example 1.1 Orange Juice Sales: Exploring Variables and the Need for a log-log Model As a concrete example, consider sales data for orange juice (OJ) from Dominick's grocery stores. Dominick's was a Chicago-area chain. This data was collected in the 1990s and is publicly available from the Kilts Center at the University of Chicago's Booth School of Business. The data includes weekly prices and unit sales (number of cartons sold) for three OJ brands—Tropicana, Minute Maid, Dominick's—at 83 stores in the Chicago area, as well as an indicator, ad, showing whether each brand was advertised (in store or flyer) that week.

```
> oj <- read.csv("oj.csv",strings=T)
> head(oj)
  sales price      brand ad
1  8256  3.87  tropicana  0
2  6144  3.87  tropicana  0
3  3840  3.87  tropicana  0
4  8000  3.87  tropicana  0
5  8896  3.87  tropicana  0
6  7168  3.87  tropicana  0
> levels(oj$brand)
[1] "dominicks" "minute.maid" "tropicana"
```

Notice the argument strings=T in read.csv as shorthand for "stringsAsFactors = TRUE." This converts our brand column into a factor variable. This was the default behavior of read.csv prior to version 4.0.0 of R, but you now need to specify it explicitly. Otherwise you will get an error when you try to make the plots or fit the regression models below.

The code-printout above is our first example showing R code and output. We will include a ton of code and output snippets like this throughout the book: they are an integral part of the material. If this output looks unfamiliar to you, you should break here and take the time to work through the R-primer in the Appendix.

Figure 1.4 shows the prices and sales broken out by brand. You can see in Figure 1.4a that each brand occupies a different price range: Dominick's is the budget option, Tropicana is the luxury option, and Minute Maid lives between. In Figure 1.4c, sales are clearly decreasing with

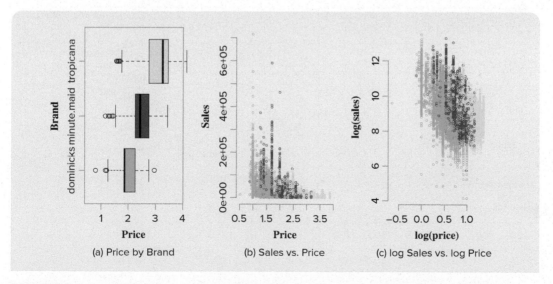

(a) Price by Brand   (b) Sales vs. Price   (c) log Sales vs. log Price

FIGURE 1.4   Dominick's OJ prices by brand and monthly sales, both raw and after a log transformation.

price. This makes sense: demand is *downward* sloping, and if you charge more, you sell less. More specifically, it appears that *log* sales has a roughly linear relationship with *log* price. This is an important point. Whenever you are working with linear (i.e., additive) models, it is crucial that you try to work in the space where you expect to find linearity. For variables that change *multiplicatively* with other factors, this is usually the log scale (see the nearby box for a quick review on logarithms). For comparison, the raw (without log) values in Figure 1.4b show a nonlinear relationship between prices and sales.

··

log-log Models and Elasticities

Another common scenario models against each other two variables that *both* move multiplicatively. For example, Figure 1.5 shows the national gross domestic product (GDP) versus imports for several countries. Fitting a line to the left panel would be silly; its slope will be entirely determined by small changes in the U.S. values. In contrast, the right panel shows that GDP and imports follow a neat linear relationship in log space.

Returning to our OJ example, Figure 1.4c indicates that this *log-log* model might be appropriate for the orange juice sales versus price analysis. One possible regression model is

$$\log(\texttt{sales}) = \beta_0 + \beta_1 \log(\texttt{price}) + \varepsilon \tag{1.7}$$

Here, $\log(\texttt{sales})$ increase by β_1 for every unit increase in $\log(\texttt{price})$. Conveniently, log-log models have a much more intuitive interpretation: sales increase by $\beta_1\%$ for every 1% increase in price. To see this, you need a bit of calculus. Write $y = \exp[\beta_0 + \beta_1 \log(x) + \varepsilon]$ and differentiate with respect to x:

$$\frac{dy}{dx} = \frac{\beta_1}{x} e^{\beta_0 + \beta_1 \log(x) + \varepsilon} = \frac{\beta_1}{x} y \quad \Rightarrow \quad \beta_1 = \frac{dy/y}{dx/x} \tag{1.8}$$

This shows that β_1 is the proportional change in y over the proportional change in x. In economics there is a special name for such an expression: *elasticity*. The concept of elasticity will play an important role in many of our analyses.

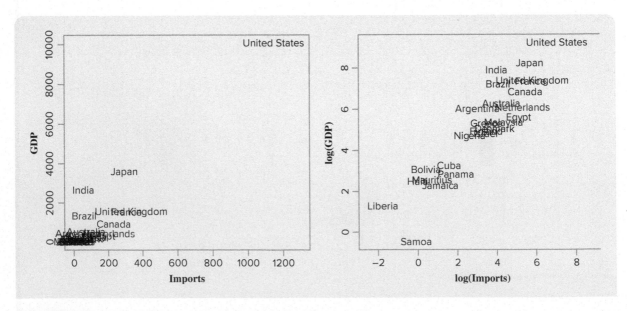

FIGURE 1.5   National GDP against imports, in original and log scale.

Logarithms and Exponents

Recall the logarithm definition:

$$\log(a) = b \Leftrightarrow a = e^b \tag{1.9}$$

Here, $e \approx 2.72$ is "Euler's number" and we refer to e^b as "e to the power of b" or, simply, 'b exponentiated.' We will sometimes write $\exp[b]$ instead of e^b; they mean the same thing. There are other types of logarithms (sometimes base 10 is used in introductory classes), but we will always use the *natural log* defined in Equation (1.9). The base e plays a central role in science and modeling of systems because e^x is its own derivative: $de^x/dx = e^x$ for those readers who know their calculus.

In a simple linear regression for $\log(y)$ on x, β_1 is added to the expected value for $\log(y)$ for each unit increase in x:

$$\log(y) = \beta_0 + \beta_1 x + \epsilon. \tag{1.10}$$

The fact that we are taking the log of y makes this model *multiplicative*. Recall some basic facts about logs and exponents: $\log(ab) = \log(a) + \log(b)$, $\log(a^b) = b \log(a)$, and $e^{a+b} = e^a e^b$. Thus, exponentiating both sides of Equation (1.10) yields

$$y = e^{\beta_0 + \beta_1 x + \epsilon} = e^{\beta_0} e^{\beta_1 x} e^{\epsilon} \tag{1.11}$$

Considering $x* = x + 1$, you get that

$$y* = e^{\beta_0 + \epsilon} e^{\beta_1 x*} = e^{\beta_0 + \epsilon} e^{\beta_1(x+1)} = e^{\beta_0 + \beta_1 x + \epsilon} e^{\beta_1} = y e^{\beta_1} \tag{1.12}$$

Therefore, each unit increase in x leads $\mathbb{E}[y|x]$ to be *multiplied* by the factor e^{β_1}.

Example 1.2 Orange Juice Sales: Linear Regression Now that we have established what a *log-log* model will do for us, let's add a bit of complexity to the model from (1.7) to make it more realistic. If you take a look at Figure 1.4c, it appears that the three brands have log-log sales-price relationships that are concentrated around three separate lines. If you suspect that each brand has the same β_1 elasticity but a different intercept (i.e., if all brands have sales that move with price the same way but at the same price some brands will sell more than others), then you would use a slightly more complex model that incorporates both `brand` and `price`:

$$\log(\texttt{sales}) = \alpha_{\text{brand}} + \beta \log(\texttt{price}) + \varepsilon \tag{1.13}$$

Here, α_{brand} is shorthand for a separate intercept for each OJ brand, which we could write out more fully as

$$\alpha_{\text{brand}} = \alpha_0 1_{[\text{dominicks}]} + \alpha_1 1_{[\text{minute.maid}]} + \alpha_2 1_{[\text{tropicana}]}. \tag{1.14}$$

The indicator functions, $1_{[v]}$, are one if v is the true factor level and zero otherwise. Hence, Equation (1.13) says that, even though their sales all have the same elasticity to price, the brands can have different sales at the same price due to brand-specific intercepts.

Fitting Regressions with `glm`

To fit this regression in R you will use the `glm` function, which is used to estimate the class of generalized linear models that we introduced in Equation (1.1). There is also a `lm` function that fits only linear regression models, so you could use that here also (it takes the same arguments), but we will get in the habit of using glm since it works for many different GLMs. The function is straightforward to use: you give it a data frame with the data argument and provide a formula that defines your regression.

```
> fit <- glm( y ~ var1 + ... + varP, data=mydata)
```

The fitted object fit is a list of useful things (type names(fit) to see them), and there are functions to access the results. For example,

- summary(fit) prints the model, information about residual errors, the estimated coefficients and uncertainty about these estimates (we will cover the uncertainty in detail in the next chapter), and statistics related to model fit.
- coef(fit) supplies just the coefficient estimates.
- predict(fit, newdata=mynewdata) predicts y where mynewdata is a data frame with the same variables as mydata.

The formula syntax in the glm call is important. The ~ symbol is read as "regressed onto" or "as a function of." The variable you want to predict, the y response variable, comes before the ~, and the input features, **x**, come after. This model formula notation will be used throughout the remainder of the book, and we note some common specifications in Table 1.1.

The R formula for (1.13) is log(sales) ~ brand + log(price). You can fit this with glm using the oj data, and then use the coef function to view the fitted coefficients. (More on this in Section 1.4.)

```
> fit<-glm( log(sales) ~ brand + log(price), data=oj)
> coef(fit) # fitted coefficients
    (Intercept) brandminute.maid    brandtropicana    log(price)
     10.8288216        0.8701747         1.5299428    -3.1386914
```

There are a few things to notice here. First, you can see that $\hat{\beta} = -3.1$ for the estimated coefficient on log price. Throughout this book we use the convention that $\hat{\theta}$ denotes the estimated value for some parameter θ. So $\hat{\beta}$ is the estimated "sales-price elasticity," and it says that expected sales drop by about 3% for every 1% price increase. Second, notice that there are distinct model coefficients for Minute Maid and Tropicana but not for Dominick's. This is due

y ~ x1	model by x_1
y ~ .	include all other columns
y ~ .-x3	include all except x_3
y ~ .-1	include all, but no intercept
y ~ 1	intercept only
y ~ x1*x2	include interaction for x_1 and x_2 and lower order terms
y ~ x1:x2	include interaction only
y ~ .^2	all possible 2 way interactions and lower order terms

TABLE 1.1 Some common syntax for use in formulas.

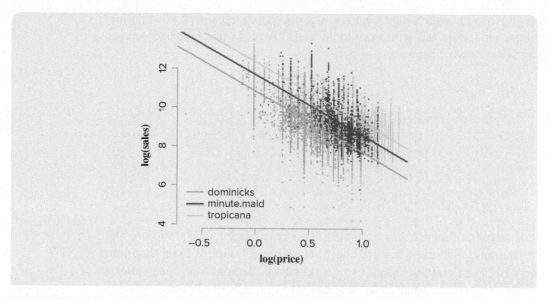

FIGURE 1.6 OJ data and the fitted regression lines (i.e., conditional expectations) for our model from (1.13) that regresses `log(sales)` on `log(price)` and `brand`.

to the way that R creates a numeric representation of the factor variables. It treats one of the factor levels as a 'reference level' that is subsumed into the intercept. For details, see the box on model matrices (i.e. design matrices).

The fitted values from the regression in Equation (1.13) are shown in Figure 1.6 alongside the original data. You see three lines shifted according to brand identity. *At the same price,* Tropicana sells more than Minute Maid, which in turn sells more than Dominick's. This makes sense: Tropicana is a luxury product that is preferable at the same price.

Model (Design) Matrices in R

When you regress onto a factor variable, `glm` converts the factor levels into a specific numeric representation. Take a look at rows 100, 200, and 300 from the `oj` data and notice that the `brand` column contains brand names, not numbers.

```
> oj[c(100,200,300),]
    sales price        brand ad
100  4416  3.19     tropicana  0
200  5440  2.79 minute.maid  0
300 51264  1.39     dominicks  1
```

The first step of `glm` is to create a *model matrix* (also called a *design matrix*) that defines the numeric inputs **x**. It does this with a call to the `model.matrix` function, and you can pull that step out to see what happens.

```
> x <- model.matrix( ~ log(price) + brand, data=oj)
> x[c(100,200,300),]
    (Intercept)  log(price) brandminute.maid brandtropicana
100           1   1.1600209                0              1
200           1   1.0260416                1              0
300           1   0.3293037                0              0
```

The `model.matrix` function has expanded these brand factor levels into a couple of binary, or "dummy," variables that are one when the observation is from that brand and zero otherwise. For example, `brandtropicana` is 1 for the Tropicana observation in row 100 and zero otherwise. There is no `branddominicks` indicator because you need only two variables to represent three categories: when both `brandminute.maid` and `brandtropicana` are zero, the *intercept* gives the value for Dominick's expected log sales at a log price of zero. Each factor's reference level is absorbed by the intercept and the other coefficients represent "change relative to reference" (here, Dominick's). To check the reference level of your factors, type `levels(myfactor)`. The first level is the reference and by default this will be the first in the alphabetized list of levels. To change this, you can do `myfactor = relevel(myfactor, "myref")`.

1.1.1 Interactions

All of the lines in Figure 1.6 have the same slope. In economic terms, the model assumes that consumers of the three brands have the same price sensitivity. This seems unrealistic: money is probably less of an issue for Tropicana customers than it is for the average Dominick's consumer. You can build this information into your regression by having log price *interact* with brand.

An interaction term is the product of two inputs. Including an interaction between, say, x_j and x_k inputs, implies that your linear regression equation includes the product $x_j x_k$ as an input.

$$\mathbb{E}[y|\mathbf{x}] = \beta_0 + \ldots + \beta_k x_k + \beta_j x_j + x_j x_k \beta_{jk} \tag{1.15}$$

Here, "..." just denotes whatever else is in your multiple linear regression model. Equation (1.15) says that the effect on the expected value for y due to a unit increase in x_j is $\beta_j + x_k \beta_{jk}$, such that it depends upon x_k.

Interactions are central to scientific and business questions. For example,

- How does drug effectiveness change with patient age?
- Does gender change the effect of education on wages?
- How does consumer price sensitivity change across brands?

In each case here, you want to know whether one variable changes the effect of another. You don't want to know the average price sensitivity of customers; you want to know whether they are more price sensitive for one product versus another.

Example 1.3 OJ Sales: Interaction In the OJ sales regression, to get brand-specific price elasticity terms you need to include an interaction between each of the brand indicator terms and the log price. We can write this as a model with a separate intercept and slope for each brand:

$$\log(\text{sales}) = \alpha_{\text{brand}} + \beta_{\text{brand}} \log(\text{price}) + \varepsilon \tag{1.16}$$

We can also expand this notation out to write the exact model that glm will be estimating:

$$\log(\text{sales}) = \alpha_0 + \alpha_1 \mathbb{1}_{[\text{minute.maid}]} + \alpha_2 \mathbb{1}_{[\text{tropicana}]} +$$
$$(\beta_0 + \beta_1 \mathbb{1}_{[\text{minute.maid}]} + \beta_2 \mathbb{1}_{[\text{tropicana}]}) \log(\text{price}) + \varepsilon \tag{1.17}$$

As before, dominicks is the reference level for brand and so it is absorbed into both the intercept and baseline slope on log price. For an observation from Dominick's, the indicator functions are all zero so that $\mathbb{E}[\log(\text{sales})] = \alpha_0 + \beta_0 \log(\text{price})$.

You can fit this model in glm with the * symbol, which is syntax for "interacted with." Note that * also adds the *main effects*—all of the terms from our earlier model in Equation (1.13).

```
> fit2way <- glm(log(sales) ~ log(price)*brand, data=oj)
> coef(fit2way)
                    (Intercept)                         log(price)
                    10.95468173                        -3.37752963
                brandminute.maid                     brandtropicana
                     0.88825363                         0.96238960
      log(price):brandminute.maid       log(price):brandtropicana
                     0.05679476                         0.66576088
```

The fitted regression is pictured in Figure 1.7.

In the glm output, the log(price):brand coefficients are the interaction terms. Plugging in 0 for both Tropicana and Minute Maid indicators yields the equation of the line for Dominick's:

$$\mathbb{E}[\log(\text{sales})] = 10.95 - 3.38 \log(\text{price})$$

Plugging in one for Minute Maid terms and zero for Tropicana terms yields the equation for Minute Maid:

$$\mathbb{E}[\log(\text{sales})] = 10.95 - 3.38 \log(\text{price}) + 0.89 + 0.06 \log(\text{price})$$
$$= 11.84 - 3.32 \log(\text{price})$$

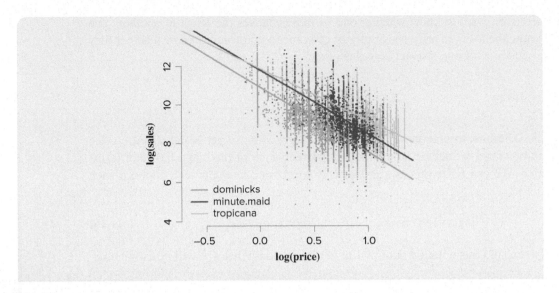

FIGURE 1.7 Fit for the model where we allow interaction between price and brand. Note that if you extrapolate too far, the linearity assumption implies Tropicana selling less than Minute Maid at the same price. This is a reminder that linear models are approximations and should be used with care away from the center of the observed data.

And plugging in one for Tropicana and zero for Minute Maid yields the regression line for Tropicana:

$$\mathbb{E}[\log(\texttt{sales})] = 10.95 - 3.38 \log(\texttt{price}) + 0.96 + 0.67 \log(\texttt{price})$$
$$= 11.91 - 2.71 \log(\texttt{price})$$

We see that Tropicana customers are indeed less sensitive than the others: they have a sales-price elasticity of -2.7 versus around -3.3 for both Dominick's and Minute Maid. This means, for example, that the store should expect a smaller sales increase for price cuts or coupons on Tropicana relative to use of the same promotion on the other brands. The price sensitivity that we estimated for model Equation (1.13), -3.1, was the result of averaging across the three distinct brand elasticities.

Advertising and Price Elasticity

We conclude this introduction to linear regression—and the study of orange juice—with a look at the role of advertising in the relationship between sales and prices. Recall that the OJ data includes an `ad` dummy variable, indicating that a given brand was promoted with either an in-store display or a flier ad during the week that sales and prices were recorded. The ads can increase sales at all prices, they can change price sensitivity, and they can do both of these things in a brand-specific manner. To model this, we specify a three-way interaction between price, brand, and `ad`:

$$\log(\texttt{sales}) = \alpha_{\text{brand, ad}} + \beta_{\text{brand, ad}} \log(\texttt{price}) + \varepsilon \qquad \textbf{(1.18)}$$

By subsetting on `brand, ad` we are indicating that there are different intercepts and slopes for each combination of the two factors. To fit this model with `glm`, you interact `brand`, `ad`, and `log(price)` with each other in the formula. Again, `glm` automatically includes the lower-level interactions and main effects—all of the terms from our model in (1.18)—in addition to the new three-way interactions.

```
> fit3way <- glm(log(sales) ~ log(price)*brand*ad, data=oj)
> coef(fit3way)
                      (Intercept)                         log(price)
                      10.40657579                        -2.77415436
                 brandminute.maid                      brandtropicana
                       0.04720317                         0.70794089
                               ad         log(price):brandminute.maid
                       1.09440665                          0.78293210
        log(price):brandtropicana                       log(price):ad
                       0.73579299                         -0.47055331
              brandminute.maid:ad                  brandtropicana:ad
                       1.17294361                          0.78525237
     log(price):brandminute.maid:ad      log(price):brandtropicana:ad
                      -1.10922376                         -0.98614093
```

The brand and ad specific elasticities are compiled in Table 1.2. We see that being featured always leads to more price sensitivity. Minute Maid and Tropicana elasticities drop from -2 to below -3.5 with ads, while Dominick's drops from -2.8 to -3.2. Why does this happen? One possible explanation is that advertisement increases the population of consumers who are considering your brand. In particular, it can increase your market beyond brand loyalists, to people who will be more price sensitive than those who reflexively buy your orange juice every week. Indeed, if you observe increased price sensitivity, it can be an indicator that your marketing efforts are expanding your consumer base. This is why Marketing 101 dictates that ad campaigns should usually be accompanied by price cuts. There is also an alternative explanation. Since the featured products are often also discounted, it could be that at lower price points the average consumer is more price sensitive (i.e., that the price elasticity is also a function of price). The truth is probably a combination of these effects.

Finally, notice that in our two-way interaction model (without including `ad`) Minute Maid's elasticity of -3.3 was roughly the same as Dominick's—it behaved like a budget product where its consumers are focused on value. However, in Table 1.2, you can see that Minute Maid and Tropicana have nearly identical elasticities and that both are different from Dominick's. Minute Maid is looking more similar now to the other national brand product. What happened?

	Dominick's	Minute Maid	Tropicana
Not featured	-2.8	-2.0	-2.0
Featured	-3.2	-3.6	-3.5

TABLE 1.2 Brand and ad dependent elasticities. Test that you can recover these numbers from the R output.

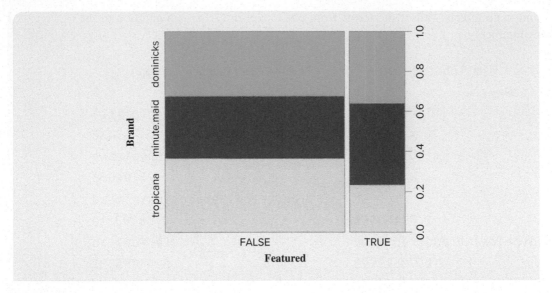

FIGURE 1.8   A mosaic plot of the amount of advertisement by brand. In a mosaic plot, the size of the boxes is proportional to the amount of data contained in that category. For example, the plot indicates that most sales are not accompanied by advertising (the featured=FALSE column is wider than for featured=TRUE) and that Minute Maid is featured (i.e., `ad=1`) more often than Tropicana.

The answer is that the simpler model in Equation (1.16) led to a *confounding* between advertisement and brand effects. Figure 1.8 shows that Minute Maid was featured more often than Tropicana. Since being featured leads to more price sensitivity, this made Minute Maid artificially appear more price sensitive when you don't account for the ad's effect. The model in Equation (1.18) corrects this by including `ad` in the regression. This phenomenon, where variable effects can get confounded if you don't *control* for them correctly (i.e., include those effects in your regression model), will play an important role in our later discussions of causal inference.

1.1.2 Prediction with `glm`

Once you have decided on a fitted model, using it for prediction is easy in R. The `predict` function takes the model you want to use for prediction and a data frame containing the new data you want to predict with.

Example 1.4 Orange Juice Sales: Predicting Sales We can use our fitted model, `fit3way`, to make predictions of sales of orange juice. Suppose you want to predict sales for all three brands when orange juice is featured at a price of $2.00 per carton. The first step is to create a data frame containing the observations to predict from. Be sure to specify a value for each predictor in the model.

```
> newdata <- data.frame(price=rep(2,3),
+     brand=factor(c("tropicana","minute.maid","dominicks"),
+          levels=levels(oj$brand)),
+     ad=rep(1,3))
> newdata #our data frame of 3 new observations
  price       brand  ad
1     2    tropicana   1
2     2 minute.maid   1
3     2    dominicks   1
```

Once you have your data frame specifying values for each variable in the model, simply feed it into the predict function and specify the model glm should use for prediction.

```
> predict(fit3way, newdata=newdata)
         1          2          3
10.571588  10.245901   9.251922
```

Of course, there is uncertainty about these predictions (and about all of our coefficient estimates above). For now we are just fitting lines, but in Chapter 2 we will detail how you go about uncertainty quantification.

Note that you can exponentiate these values to translate from log sales to raw sales:

```
> exp(predict(fit3way, newdata=newdata))
        1         2         3
39010.56  28166.85  10424.59
```

However, these raw sales predictions are actually *biased* estimates of the raw expected sales. Due to the nonlinearity introduced through log transformation, exponentiating the expected log sales will give you a different answer than the expected raw sales (the exponentiated expected log sales will tend to be lower than the expected sales). We will discuss this bias further in the next chapter and introduce a technique for bias correction.

● 1.2 Residuals

When we fit a linear regression model, we have estimated an expected value for each observation in our dataset. These are often called the *fitted values,* and they are written as $\hat{y}_i = \mathbf{x}_i'\hat{\beta}$ using our usual convention of putting hats on estimated values. Unless you have data with zero noise or as many input variables as observations (in either case you have no business fitting a regression with glm), then the fitted values will not be equal to the observed values.

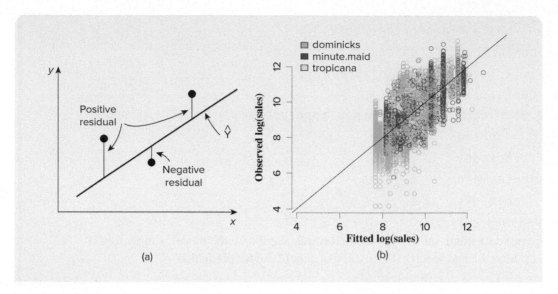

FIGURE 1.9   Panel (a) shows residuals in a simple linear regression, and panel (b) shows the fitted response $\hat{y}$ vs. observed response y for the Dominick's OJ example along with a line along $\hat{y} = y$. In both plots, the residuals are the vertical distance between each point and the fitted line.

The difference between them is called the *residual.* We will usually denote the residual as e_i, such that

$$e_i = y_i - \hat{y}_i = y_i - \mathbf{x}'_i \hat{\boldsymbol{\beta}} \tag{1.19}$$

Residuals play a central role in how linear regression works. They are our estimates of the error terms, ε_i, and they represent the variability in response that is not explained by the model.

Figure 1.9a illustrates residuals for a single-input regression. Points above the line have a positive residual and points below have a negative residual. Figure 1.9b shows the observed versus fitted y for our OJ example. The residuals are the vertical distance between each point and the fitted line. For observed y that are higher than the predicted response, $\hat{y}$, the residual is positive and for observed y that are lower, the residual is negative, that is, observed y that are higher than the predicted response $\hat{y}$.

The residuals tell you about your fit of the linear regression model. Recall our full model is $\log(\texttt{sales}_i) = \mathbf{x}'_i \boldsymbol{\beta} + \varepsilon_i$ where $\varepsilon_i \sim N(0, \sigma^2)$. The residuals are your estimates for the errors ε_i, and you can use them to evaluate the model $\varepsilon_i \sim N(0, \sigma^2)$. For example, one important consideration is whether we are correct to assume a *constant error variance*: the fact that σ^2 is the same for every ε_i. If you look at Figure 1.9b, you can see that this is probably not true. On the bottom side of the plot, there is a collection of large negative residuals for Dominick's. The model appears to have a floor on expected log sales. If you look at the results, the maximum price ever charged for Dominick's is \$2.69 and this leads to a floor on expected log sales of $\hat{y} = 7.66$ (when $\texttt{ad} = 0$). However, our residuals show that sometimes Dominick's sells far less than this floor. This is possibly driven by stock-outs, where the supply of Dominick's orange juice can't keep up with demand. Although the problem here appears isolated to a small number of observations, we could likely improve our model for the Dominick's OJ sales-price elasticity if we were able to remove observations where the store ran out of OJ. In Chapter 2 we will discuss strategies for dealing with this type of nonconstant error variance.

Error Variance

Another important use of the residuals is to estimate the error variance, σ^2. Notwithstanding the minor issue of the handful of large Dominick's errors just described, we can do this by looking at the variability of the residuals. When you call `summary` on the fitted `glm` object, R calls the `summary.glm` function that prints a bunch of information about the model estimates. Don't worry about all of this information; we will work through most of it in the coming two chapters. But near the bottom it prints out an estimate for the "dispersion parameter for gaussian family." This is what `glm` calls its estimate for the error variance, $\hat{\sigma}^2$.

```
> summary(fit3way)
...
(Dispersion parameter for gaussian family taken to be 0.4829706)
    Null deviance: 30079  on 28946  degrees of freedom
Residual deviance: 13975  on 28935  degrees of freedom
...
```

In the case of our three-way interaction model for OJ log sales, the estimated error variance is $\hat{\sigma}^2 = 0.4829706$. To understand how `glm` came up with this estimate, we need to dive deeper into the concepts in the bottom two lines shown here: deviance and degrees of freedom.

1.2.1 Deviance and Least Squares Regression

Deviance is the distance between your fitted model and the data. We will look at the specifics of deviance later, in the context of both linear and logistic regression. But for now you just need to know that deviance for linear regression is the sum of squared errors. The *null deviance* is calculated for the "null model," i.e. a model where none of the regression inputs have an impact on y. This is just the model $y_i \sim N(\mu, \sigma^2)$. Estimating μ with the sample mean response, $\bar{y}$, we can calculate this null deviance as $\Sigma_i(y_i - \bar{y})^2$. For our OJ regression, this produces the 30,079 value from the `summary` output.

```
> ( SST <- sum( (log(oj$sales) - mean(log(oj$sales)))^2 ) )
[1] 30078.71
```

The null deviance for linear regression is known as the *sum squared total* error, or SST. It measures how much variation you have in your response before fitting the regression.

The *residual deviance*, or more commonly *fitted deviance* or simply *deviance*, is calculated for your fitted regression model. It measures the amount of variation you have after fitting the regression. Given residuals $e_i = y_i - \hat{y}_i$, the residual deviance is just the sum of squared residuals $\Sigma_i e_i^2$. For our OJ regression, this gives us a residual deviance of 13,975.

```
> ( SSE <- sum( ( log(oj$sales) - fit3way$fitted )^2 ) )
[1] 13974.76
```

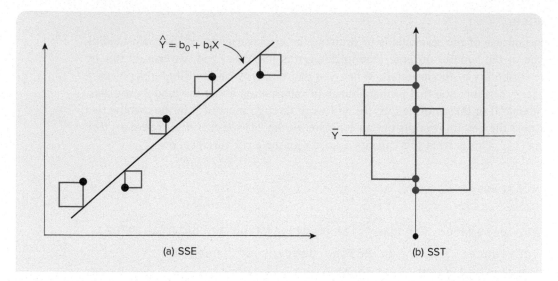

FIGURE 1.10   Figure 1.10a shows the squared residual errors. These are the components of the SSE, the quantity that linear regression minimizes and is output in glm as Residual deviance. Figure 1.10b shows the squared vertical distance for each observation to the overall mean, ȳ. The sum of these squared areas is the sum square total (SST) and is output as Null deviance.

This residual deviance for linear regression is known as the *sum squared residual error*, or SSE. It measures the tightness of your model fit. For example, a common metric for model fit takes the SSE and scales it by the number of observations to get mean squared error: $MSE = SSE/n$, where n is the sample size.

Proportion of Deviance Explained

The calculations behind SSE and SST are illustrated for simple linear regression in Figure 1.10. Comparison between these two deviances tells you how the variability has been *reduced* due to the information in your regression inputs. A common and useful statistic, one that we will use throughout the book, is the R^2 equal to one minus the residual deviance over the null deviance. In linear regression this is

$$R^2 = 1 - \frac{SSE}{SST} \tag{1.20}$$

The R^2 is the *proportion of variability explained by the regression*. It is the proportional reduction in squared errors due to your regression inputs. The name R^2 is derived from the fact that, for linear regression only, it is equal to the square of the correlation (usually denoted r) between fitted $\hat{y}_i$ and observed values y_i.

Example 1.5 Orange Juice Sales: R^2   We can calculate the R^2 a couple of different ways for our three-way interaction OJ regression.

```
# using the glm object attributes
> 1-fit3way$deviance/fit3way$null.deviance
```

```
[1] 0.5353939
# using the SSE and SST calculated above
> 1 - SSE/SST
[1] 0.5353939
# correlation squared
> cor(fit3way$fitted,log(oj$sales))^2
[1] 0.5353939
```

However you calculate it, the regression model explains around 54% of the variability in log orange juice sales. The interpretation of R^2 as squared correlation can help you get a sense of what this means: if $R^2 = 1$, a plot of fitted vs. observed values should lie along the perfectly straight line $\hat{y} = y$. As R^2 decreases the scatter around this line increases.

The residual, or "fitted," deviance plays a crucial role in how models are fit. The concept of deviance minimization is crucial to all model estimation and machine learning. In the case of linear regression, you are minimizing the sum of squared residual errors. This gives linear regression its common name: *ordinary least squares,* or OLS (the "ordinary" is in contrast to "weighted least squares" in which some observations are given more weight than others). Our readers coming from an economics or social sciences background might be more familiar with this terminology. We will use the terms OLS and linear regression interchangeably.

1.2.2 Degrees of Freedom

Reprinting the relevant summary output, we have one final concept to decipher.

```
> summary(fit3way)
...
(Dispersion parameter for gaussian family taken to be 0.4829706)
    Null deviance: 30079  on 28946  degrees of freedom
Residual deviance: 13975  on 28935  degrees of freedom
...
```

The *degrees of freedom* are crucial for mapping from your deviance to the estimated dispersion parameter, $\hat{\sigma}^2$. Unfortunately, the way that summary.glm uses this term is confusing because it doesn't differentiate between two different types of degrees of freedom: those used in the model fit, and those left for calculating the error variance. These concepts are important in statistics and machine learning, so we'll take the time to pull them apart.

To understand degrees of freedom, take a step back from regression and consider one of the most basic estimation problems in statistics: estimating the variance of a random variable.

Say you have a sample $\{z_1 \ldots z_n\}$ drawn independently from the probability distribution p(z). Recall your usual formula for estimating the variance of this distribution:

$$\text{var}(z) \approx \sum_{i=1}^{n} \frac{(z_i - \bar{z})^2}{n-1} \tag{1.21}$$

where $\bar{z} = (1/n) \sum_{i=1}^{n} z_i$ is the sample mean. Why are we dividing by $(n-1)$ instead of n? If we divide by n our estimate of the variance will be *biased low*—it will tend to underestimate var(z). To get the intuition behind this, consider an $n=1$ sample that consists of a single draw: $\bar{z} = z_1$, and thus $z_1 - \bar{z} = 0$ by construction. Since you are estimating the mean from your sample, you have the flexibility to fit perfectly a single observation. In other words, when $n=1$ you have zero opportunities to view any actual variation around the mean. Extending to a larger sample of size n, you have only $n-1$ opportunities to observe variation around $\bar{z}$.

To use the language of statistics, "opportunities to observe variation" are called degrees of freedom. In our simple variance example, we used one *model degree of freedom* to estimate $\mathbb{E}[z]$, and that leaves us with $n-1$ *residual degrees of freedom* to observe error variance. More generally:

- The **model degrees of freedom** are the number of random observations your model could fit perfectly. In regression models, this is the number of coefficients. For example, given a model with two coefficients (an intercept and slope) you can fit a line directly through two points.
- The **residual degrees of freedom** are equal to the number of opportunities that you have to observe variation around the fitted model mean. This is the sample size, n, minus the model degrees of freedom.

The model degrees of freedom are used for fitting the model and the residual degrees of freedom are what is left over for calculating variability after fitting the model. Throughout the rest of the book, we will follow the convention of using *degrees of freedom* (or df) to refer to the model degrees of freedom unless stated otherwise. Somewhat confusingly, the `summary.glm` output uses `degrees of freedom` to refer to the residual degrees of freedom, or $n - df$ in our notation.

Once we have the terminology straight, we can now complete our original mission to understand how `glm` has calculated $\hat{\sigma}^2$. In fitting the linear regression, the number of model degrees of freedom used is equal to the number of parameters in the regression line. For our model in `fit3way`, there are a total of 12 parameters in the model (use `length(coef(fit3way))` to verify). So we would say $df = 12$ for this model. And since there are 28,947 observations in the OJ dataset, the residual degrees of freedom for this model are $28{,}947 - 12 = 28{,}935$. This is the number that `glm` outputs next to the residual deviance. It is the number of opportunities that we have to view variation around the regression line. So, to estimate the residual variance, we take the sum of the squared residuals (the SSE) and divide by 28,935.

```
> SSE/fit3way$df.residual
[1] 0.4829706
```

This gives you $\hat{\sigma}^2$, or what `summary.glm` calls the "dispersion." The summary output also provides a `degrees of freedom` for the null deviance. Since the null model fits only a single mean value, $\mathbb{E}[y] = \bar{y}$, this is equal to $n-1$, the denominator in our simple variance equation (1.21). For the OJ example this is 28,946.

■ 1.3 Logistic Regression

Linear regression is just one instance of the general linear modeling framework. Another extremely useful GLM is *logistic regression*. This is the GLM that you will want to use for modeling a *binary* response: a *y* that is either 1 or 0 (e.g., true or false). While linear regression is probably the most commonly used technique in business analytics, logistic regression would come a close second in popularity. In machine learning, logistic regression and extensions of the framework are the dominant tools for prediction and classification.

Binary responses arise from a number of prediction targets:

- Will this person pay their bills or default?
- Is this a thumbs-up or thumbs-down review?
- Will the customer take advantage of the offer?
- Is the writer a Republican or Democrat?

Even when the response of interest is not binary (e.g., revenue), it may be that your decision-relevant information is binary (e.g., profit versus loss) and it is simplest to think in these terms. Logistic regression is also the stepping stone to more complex classification methodologies, which we will dive into in Chapter 4.

As you read through this section, it is important to keep in mind that logistic regression works very similarly to linear regression. It is easy to get wrapped up in the differences between logistic and linear regression, but the basics are exactly the same. In each case you are fitting a linear function of the input features and you are estimating the model by minimizing the deviance. The only difference is the choice of link function in your generalized linear model.

1.3.1 Logit Link Function

Recall our basic GLM specification of Equation (1.1) for expressing the expected value of response *y* given inputs $\mathbf{x}$: $\mathbb{E}[y|\mathbf{x}] = f(\mathbf{x}'\boldsymbol{\beta})$. The *link function*, *f*, is used to map from a linear function to a response that takes a few specific values. When the response *y* is 0 or 1, the conditional mean becomes

$$\mathbb{E}[y|\mathbf{x}] = \mathrm{p}(y = 1|\mathbf{x}) \times 1 + \mathrm{p}(y = 0|\mathbf{x}) \times 0 = \mathrm{p}(y = 1|\mathbf{x})$$

Therefore, the expectation you're modeling is a *probability*. This implies that you need to choose the link function $f(\cdot)$ to give values between zero and one.

Using the shorthand of $p = \mathrm{p}(y = 1|\mathbf{x})$, you need to choose a link function such that it makes sense to write

$$p = \mathrm{p}(y = 1|\mathbf{x}) = f(\beta_0 + \beta_1 x_1 \ldots + \beta_k x_k)$$

Logistic regression addresses this by using a *logit* link function, $f(z) = e^z / (1 + e^z)$. This function, which is also often called the "sigmoidal function," is plotted in Figure 1.11. Notice that the function asymptotes (approaches but does not cross) zero at large negative *z* values, and one at large positive *z* values.

To see how this link works, consider extreme values for *z*. At large negative values, say as $z \to -\infty$, then $f(z) \to 0/(1 + 0) = 0$ and the event $y = 1$ approaches zero probability. At large positive values, say as $z \to \infty$, then $f(z) \to \infty/(\infty + 1) = 1$ and $y = 1$ becomes guaranteed. Thus, the logit link maps from the "real line" of numbers to the [0,1] space of probabilities.

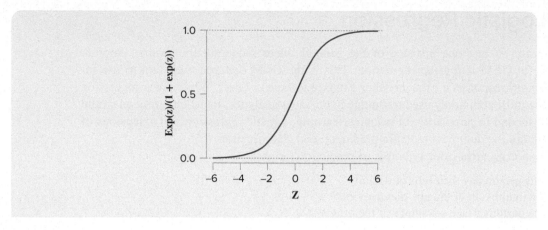

FIGURE 1.11   The logit link function, $f(z) = e^z/(1 + e^z)$.

Using a logit link, the GLM equation for $\mathbb{E}[y|\mathbf{x}]$ is defined as

$$\mathbb{E}[y|\mathbf{x}] = \mathrm{p}(y = 1|\mathbf{x}) = \frac{e^{\mathbf{x}'\beta}}{1 + e^{\mathbf{x}'\beta}} = \frac{e^{\beta_0 + \beta_1 x_1 \cdots + \beta_k x_k}}{1 + e^{\beta_0 + \beta_1 x_1 \cdots + \beta_k x_k}} \qquad \textbf{(1.22)}$$

A common alternate way to write (1.22) results from dividing the numerator and denominator by $e^{\mathbf{x}'\beta}$:

$$\mathbb{E}[y|\mathbf{x}] = \frac{e^{\mathbf{x}'\beta}}{1 + e^{\mathbf{x}'\beta}} = \frac{\dfrac{e^{\mathbf{x}'\beta}}{e^{\mathbf{x}'\beta}}}{\dfrac{1}{e^{\mathbf{x}'\beta}} + \dfrac{e^{\mathbf{x}'\beta}}{e^{\mathbf{x}'\beta}}} = \frac{1}{e^{-\mathbf{x}'\beta} + 1} \qquad \textbf{(1.23)}$$

How do we interpret the β coefficients in this model? We need to start with the relationship between probability and *odds*. The odds of an event are defined as the probability that it happens over the probability that it doesn't.

$$\text{odds} = \frac{p}{1 - p} \qquad \textbf{(1.24)}$$

For example, if an event has a 0.25 probability of happening, then its odds are 0.25/0.75, or 1/3. If an event has a probability of 0.9 of happening, the odds of its happening are 0.9/0.1 = 9. Odds transform from probabilities, which take values between zero and one, to the space of all positive values from zero to infinity.

Looking at (1.22), we can do some algebra and then take the log to derive an interpretation for the β_j coefficients. Using the shorthand $p = \mathrm{p}(y = 1|\mathbf{x})$, we have

$$p = \frac{e^{\mathbf{x}'\beta}}{1 + e^{\mathbf{x}'\beta}}$$
$$\Rightarrow p + pe^{\mathbf{x}'\beta} = e^{\mathbf{x}'\beta}$$
$$\Rightarrow \frac{p}{1 - p} = e^{\mathbf{x}'\beta}$$
$$\Rightarrow \log\left(\frac{p}{1 - p}\right) = \beta_0 + \beta_1 x_1 \cdots + \beta_k x_k$$

Thus, logistic regression is a *linear model for log odds.* Using what we know about logs and exponentiation, you can interpret e^{β_j} as the *multiplicative* effect for a unit increase in x_j on the odds for the event $y = 1$. For example, consider a logistic regression model with a single predictor x, such that $\text{odds}(x) = \exp[\beta_0 + \beta_1 x]$.

1.3.2 Fitting Logistic Regression in R

You can use `glm` to fit logistic regressions in R. The syntax is exactly the same as for linear regression, you just add the argument `family="binomial"`. Recall that the binomial distribution is the distribution for random trials with a binary outcome. The classic binomial distribution is a coin toss. Telling `glm` that you are working with a binomial distribution implies that you will be working with a binary response and want to estimate probabilities. The logit link is how `glm` fits probabilities. The response variable can take a number of forms including numeric 0 or 1, logical `TRUE` or `FALSE`, or a two level factor such as `win` vs. `lose`.

Example 1.6 Logistic Regression: Detecting Spam For our first logistic regression example, we'll build a filter for email spam—junk mail that can be ignored. Every time an email arrives, your email client performs a binary classification: is this *spam* or *not spam*? The email that is classified as spam gets automatically moved to a spam folder (like that in Figure 1.12), keeping your inbox free for important messages. We'll train our own spam filter by fitting logistic regression to previous emails.

Our training data `spam.csv` has 4601 emails, 1813 of which are spam. It contains 57 email features including indicators for the presence of 54 keywords or characters (e.g., `free` or `!`), counts for capitalized letters (total number and longest continuous block length), and a numeric `spam` variable for whether each email has been tagged as spam by a human reader (`spam` is one for true spam, zero for important emails). We read this data into R as a data frame named `spammy`.

```
> spammy<- read.csv("spam.csv")
> spammy[c(1,4000), c(16,56,58)]
      word_free capital_run_length_longest spam
1             1                         61    1
4000          0                         26    0
```

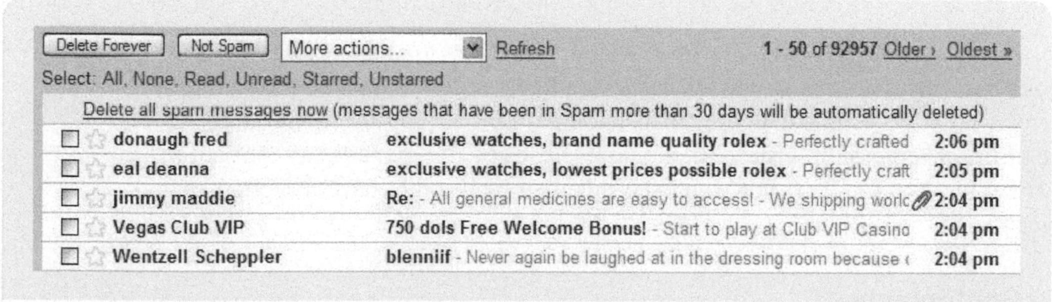

FIGURE 1.12 An email folder filled with spam.

Notice that the first email, which contained the word `free` and had a block of 61 capitalized letters, was tagged as spam. Email 4000, with its more modest sequence of 26 capital letters, is not spam.

Our logistic regression will use all of the features in `spammy` as inputs. The R formula "y ~ ." tells `glm` to regress onto all variables in the data frame except for the response.

```
> spamFit <- glm(spam ~ ., data=spammy, family='binomial')
Warning message:
glm.fit: fitted probabilities numerically 0 or 1 occurred
```

The warning message you get when you run this regression, `fitted probabilities numerically 0 or 1 occurred`, means the regression is able to fit some data points *exactly*. For example, a spam email is modeled as having a 100% probability of being spam. This situation is called *perfect separation*; it can lead to strange estimates for some coefficients and their standard errors. It is a symptom of *overfit*, and in Chapter 3 we show how to avoid it via regularization techniques.

The fitted object, `spamFit`, is a `glm` object that contains all the same attributes that we were able to access when doing linear regression. For example, you can use the `summary` function to get statistics about your coefficients and model fit.

```
> summary(spamFit)
...
 Coefficients:
                Estimate Std. Error  z value  Pr(>|z|)
(Intercept)    -1.9682470  0.1465703  -13.429  < 2e-16 ***
word_make      -0.5529572  0.2356753   -2.346  0.018963 *
word_address   -0.1338696  0.2217334   -0.604  0.546016
word_all       -0.4946420  0.1775333   -2.786  0.005333 **
word_3d         0.8301668  0.8244961    1.007  0.313994
...
(Dispersion parameter for binomial family taken to be 1)
    Null deviance: 6170.2  on 4600  degrees of freedom
Residual deviance: 1548.7  on 4543  degrees of freedom
...
```

The output looks basically the same as what you get for a linear regression. Note that in logistic regression there is no σ^2 to estimate as the "dispersion parameter" because there is no error term like the ε of linear regression. Instead, `glm` outputs `Dispersion parameter for binomial family taken to be 1`. If you don't see this, then you might have forgotten to put "type=binomial".

Interpreting Coefficients

Take a look at one of the large positive coefficients in your fit:

```
> coef(spamFit)["word_free"]
word_free
 1.542706
> exp(1.542706)
[1] 4.67723
```

The `word_free` variable is either one if the email contains the word `free`, and zero if it doesn't. Thus, the *odds* that an email is spam are about five times higher for emails that contain the word `free` than for those that do not. On the other hand, you can see next that if the email contains the word `george`, the odds of its being spam *decrease*.

```
> coef(spamFit)["word_george"]
word_george
  -5.779841
> exp(-5.779841)
[1] 0.003089207
> 1/exp(-5.779841)
[1] 323.7077
```

The odds of the email being spam when the word `george` is present are 0.003 of the odds of its being spam if it does not contain the word `george`. Or, taking the reciprocal, the odds of its being spam when the word `george` is *absent* are about 324 times higher than if the word `george` is *present*. This is an old dataset collected from the inbox of a guy named George. Spammers were not very sophisticated in the 1990s, so emails containing your name were most likely not spam.

Predicting Spam Probabilities

As with linear regression, prediction for logistic regression is easy after you've fit the model with `glm`. You call `predict` on your fitted `glm` object and provide some `newdata`, with the same variable names as the training data, at the locations where you'd like to predict. The output will be $\mathbf{x}'\hat{\beta}$ for each $\mathbf{x}$ row of `mynewdata`.

```
> predict(spamFit, newdata=spammy[c(1,4000),])
        1        4000
 2.029963   -1.726788
```

Of course, these are *not* probabilities. To get those, you need to transform to $f(\mathbf{x}'\hat{\beta})$ through the logit link as $e^{\mathbf{x}'\hat{\beta}}/(1 + e^{\mathbf{x}'\hat{\beta}})$, as in Eqn 1.22. The `predict()` function lets you add the `type="response"` argument to make this transformation and get predictions on the scale of the response (i.e., in [0,1] probability space).

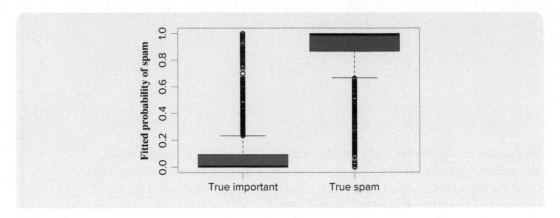

FIGURE 1.13 Fit plot of $\hat{y}$ versus y for the spam logistic regression. Since the true y is binary for spam, you get a boxplot rather than a scatterplot. As a test of your intuition, imagine what a *perfect* fit (i.e., $\hat{y} = y$) would look like for this regression.

```
> predict(spamFit,newdata=spammy[c(1,4000),],type="response")
        1        4000
0.8839073 0.1509989
```

The first email (true spam) has an 88% chance of being spam, while email 4000 (not spam) has a 15% chance of being spam—in other words, an 85% chance of being important email that George wants to read. Figure 1.13 shows predicted probabilities of spam by actual spam status for every email in the dataset. Note the long tails of small spam probabilities for true spam and of large spam probabilities for truly important mail: any spam classifier that you construct based on this model will occasionally make a mistake on how it treats the email. See Chapter 4 for material on designing and evaluating classification rules.

■ 1.4 Likelihood and Deviance

Earlier in this chapter, you learned that deviance is the distance between the *model* and the *data*. In the case of linear regression, the deviance is the sum of squared errors. Logistic regression also has a deviance, and this is the metric that `glm` minimizes to fit the model. But what is the deviance for logistic regression? It is not a sum of squared errors. Instead, the logistic regression deviance is derived from the assumed binomial distribution for the response.

How this works relies on two complementary concepts: the likelihood and the deviance. These concepts are a bit abstract, but they play a key role in the statistical learning algorithms that we will be working with throughout this book.

- *Likelihood* is the probability of your data given the estimated model. When you maximize the likelihood, you are fitting the parameters to "make the data look most likely."
- *Deviance* is a measure of the distance between the data and the estimated model. When you minimize the deviance, you are fitting the parameters to make the model and data look as close as possible.

Likelihood

To unravel these concepts we'll start with the likelihood function. Consider a dataset, say Z, with probability $p(Z|\Theta)$. This probability is a function of both the data Z and the parameters Θ. The likelihood function takes a given dataset as fixed and represents how this probability changes as a function of the parameters. Thus we write the likelihood as $\mathrm{lhd}(\Theta; Z)$, or sometimes just $\mathrm{lhd}(\Theta)$ for short, to indicate that it is a function of the parameters Θ. But there is nothing complicated going on: the likelihood is just a probability. In particular, $\mathrm{lhd}(\Theta) = p(Z|\Theta)$ in our imaginary setup here.

Consider a simple binomial example. You have a weighted coin with probability p of coming up heads. You have flipped the coin ten times: it has come up heads eight times and tails twice. We could write our dataset as $Z = \{\text{heads} = 8, \text{tails} = 2\}$. The probability of this dataset, and the likelihood, is written

$$p(Z|p) = \binom{10}{8} p^8 (1-p)^2 = \mathrm{lhd}(p) \tag{1.25}$$

We can evaluate and plot this likelihood in R (see Figure 1.14a).

```
> p <- seq(0,1,length=100)
> plot(p, dbinom(8, size=10, prob=p), type="l", ylab="Likelihood")
```

Every time glm fits a model, it is choosing the parameters to maximize the likelihood. This is a very common estimation strategy with many great properties. Although we will look at other techniques in the next chapter, in particular adding *penalties* on parameter size during estimation, everything will still be built around the foundation of likelihood maximization. In our coin-flipping example, the maximum likelihood estimate (the MLE) is $\hat{p} = 0.8$. This is marked with a vertical line in Figure 1.14a, and it corresponds to the highest point on the likelihood curve.

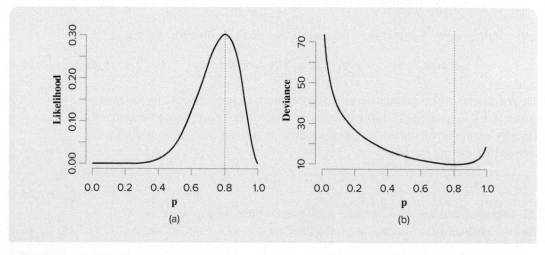

FIGURE 1.14 The likelihood (a) and deviance (b) for the probability of success, p, in a binomial trial with eight successes and two failures.

Deviance

The deviance—the distance between your model and the data—is a simple transformation of the likelihood. In particular,

$$\text{Deviance} = -2 \log[\text{Likelihood}] + C \qquad (1.26)$$

Here, C is a constant that you can ignore. The precise definition for deviance is -2 times the difference between log likelihoods for your fitted model and for a "fully saturated" model where you have as many parameters as observations. The term corresponding to this fully saturated model gets wrapped into the constant, C, but again you can ignore this in most situations. In practice, we will often use the $\propto$, or proportional to, symbol when working with the deviance and only keep track of the parts that change as a function of the parameters. For example, in our coin tossing example, the deviance is

$$\text{dev}(p) \propto -2 \log(p^8 (1-p)^2) = -16 \log(p) - 4 \log(1-p) \qquad (1.27)$$

This is plotted in Figure 1.14b, with the deviance minimizing solution marked at $\hat{p} = 0.8$. Deviance minimization is the mirror image of likelihood maximization. With `glm` you have been fitting models by minimizing the deviance, just the same as you have been fitting models to maximize the likelihood.

Example 1.7 **Gaussian Deviance** Let's work through an example with linear regression and Gaussian (normal) errors. The probability model is $y \sim N(\mathbf{x}'\beta, \sigma^2)$, where the Gaussian probability density function is

$$N(\mathbf{x}'\beta, \sigma^2) = \frac{1}{\sqrt{2\pi\sigma^2}} \exp\left[-\frac{(y - \mathbf{x}'\beta)^2}{2\sigma^2}\right] \qquad (1.28)$$

Recall that independent random variables have the property that $p(y_1, \ldots, y_n) = p(y_1) \times p(y_2) \times \ldots p(y_n)$. Given n independent observations, the likelihood (i.e., the probability density of the data) is

$$\prod_{i=1}^{n} p(y_i | \mathbf{x}_i) = \prod_{i=1}^{n} N(y_i; \mathbf{x}_i'\beta, \sigma^2) = (2\pi\sigma^2)^{-\frac{n}{2}} \exp\left[-\frac{1}{2\sigma^2} \sum_{i=1}^{n} (y_i - \mathbf{x}_i'\beta)^2\right] \qquad (1.29)$$

Taking a log and multiplying by -2 (and removing terms that don't involve β), you get

$$\text{dev}(\beta) = \frac{1}{\sigma^2} \sum_{i=1}^{n} (y_i - \mathbf{x}_i'\beta)^2 + C \propto \sum_{i=1}^{n} (y_i - \mathbf{x}_i'\beta)^2 \qquad (1.30)$$

Thus, for linear regression with Gaussian errors, the deviance is proportional to the sum of squared errors (the SSE). We stated this fact earlier in the chapter, but now you can derive it for yourself. This is why linear regression is also "least-squares" regression: deviance minimization is the same thing as minimizing the SSE.

Example 1.8 **Logistic Deviance** We can do a similar derivation for logistic regression. For binary response with probabilities $p_i = p(y_i = 1)$, the likelihood is

$$\prod_{i=1}^{n} P(y_i | \mathbf{x}_i) = \prod_{i=1}^{n} p_i^{y_i} (1 - p_i)^{1 - y_i} \qquad (1.31)$$

Using your logistic regression equation for p_i, this becomes

$$\text{lhd}(\boldsymbol{\beta}) = \prod_{i=1}^{n} \left(\frac{\exp(\mathbf{x}_i'\boldsymbol{\beta})}{1 + \exp(\mathbf{x}_i'\boldsymbol{\beta})}\right)^{y_i} \left(\frac{1}{1 + \exp(\mathbf{x}_i'\boldsymbol{\beta})}\right)^{1-y_i} \tag{1.32}$$

Taking log and multiplying by -2 gives you the logistic regression deviance:

$$\text{dev}(\boldsymbol{\beta}) = -2 \sum_{i=1}^{n} [y_i \log(p_i) + (1 - y_i) \log(1 - p_i)]$$

$$\propto \sum_{i=1}^{n} [\log(1 + \exp^{\mathbf{x}_i'\boldsymbol{\beta}}) - y_i \mathbf{x}_i'\boldsymbol{\beta}] \tag{1.33}$$

This is the function that `glm` minimizes for logistic regression.

Deviance in `summary.glm`

Returning to our output from `summary.glm` (which is the function that is called when you apply `summary` to a fitted `glm` object), we have deviances for each of the OJ and spam regressions. For the three-way interaction OJ linear regression:

```
> summary(fit3way)
...
    Null deviance: 30079  on 28946  degrees of freedom
Residual deviance: 13975  on 28935  degrees of freedom
...
```

And for the spam filter logistic regression:

```
> summary(spamFit)
...
    Null deviance: 6170.2  on 4600  degrees of freedom
Residual deviance: 1548.7  on 4543  degrees of freedom
...
```

From Equations (1.30) and (1.33), we now know how to calculate these residual deviance values. The null deviances come from the same models, and so have the same functional form, but they replace the regression fitted values for y with simple sample averages. With D_0 as the symbol for null deviance, we have

- $D_0 = \Sigma(y_i - \bar{y})^2$ in linear regression
- $D_0 = -2\Sigma[y_i \log(\bar{y}) + (1 - y_i) \log(1 - \bar{y})]$ in logistic regression

While some statistics texts restrict the concept of R^2 to linear regression, we find it useful to generalize it as *the proportion of deviance that is reduced due to the regression model.* Using the symbol D to denote the residual deviance, our R^2 formula is

$$R^2 = 1 - \frac{D}{D_0} \tag{1.34}$$

This R^2 formula is often called McFadden's Pseudo R^2 when it is used outside of linear regression.

In the case of our OJ example, we previously calculated an R^2 of 0.54. For the spam regression, we can apply (1.34) to calculate that $R^2 = 1 - 1549/6170 = 0.75$ such that around three-quarters of the variability in spam occurrence is explained by our logistic regression. We introduced R^2 in the context of linear regression, as a function of the SST and SSE, but expressing it in terms of deviance means that it applies to any model that we fit.

■ 1.5 Time Series

We close this chapter with an introduction to working with *dependent* data. The models we have looked at so far all assume that you have *independent* observations. However, events that occur one after the other in time, or say geographically near to each other, can be correlated. For example, lawn furniture sales are always higher in spring and summer, the weather today gives you information about what the weather will be tomorrow, or when a popular restaurant has a busy night its neighboring restaurants also gain traffic from those who couldn't get a table. In this section we'll figure out how to work with data that occurs in *time,* and in the next section we consider data that occurs in *space.*

Fortunately, the main tools for dealing with dependence all fit within a standard regression framework. For the most part, you simply include the variables that cause dependence in your set of inputs. By engineering the right input features, you can control for underlying trends (e.g., monthly trends or regional effects) and for *autoregression,* which is the dependence between neighboring outcomes. In this section we will focus on *time series* dependence. This is the sort of dependence that you get for data that are observed over time, and it is common in business analysis settings. The tools you learn for time series extend to other dependence settings, and we give some pointers on this at the end of the section.

The traditional statistics approach to time series emphasizes careful testing for different forms of time series structure. Through the regularization and machine learning material from later chapters in this book, we can avoid a lot of this manual feature selection. Although it won't work for all types of time series dependence, a powerful modeling strategy is to simply include a large set of time series features and rely on the data to tell you what works best. Thus, this section will focus on helping you understand how to construct the features that are useful for modeling time series data rather than on techniques for testing for time series dependence. If you have a good intuition about the ingredients of a time series model, you will be in good shape to use these features in your applied analysis work.

1.5.1 Regression for Time Series Data

A time series dataset contains observations of a response variable, and input features, taken over time. Typical time intervals are daily, weekly, monthly, quarterly, or yearly. In business settings, the response of interest is typically sales numbers, revenue, profit, active users, or prices. The response variables are almost always correlated over time.

Example 1.9 Airline Passenger Data: Regression for Time Series As an introductory example, consider a series of monthly total international airline passengers between the years 1949 and 1960.

```
> air<-read.csv("airline.csv")
> air[c(1,70,144),]
    Year Month Passengers
1     49    1        112
70    54    10       229
144   60    12       432
```

To work with time series data in R, your first step is to create a time variable. We can use the as.Date function to build a Date class vector. Note that if you are working on a finer time scale, R has the POSIXct class that can be used to represent dates and times down to fractions of a second. To create a Date variable in our air travel example, we need to translate from the Year and Month variables in our data frame. The first step is to paste these two variables into a single year-month string for each observation, and we then call as.Date to tell R that this is date information. The default format to read in dates is year-month-day, and that is what we will use here. We set the day to the first of each month for convenience; these are monthly counts so it doesn't matter what day we use.

```
> air$date<-paste("19",air$Year,"-",air$Month,"-01", sep="")
> air$date[c(1,70,144)]
[1] "1949-1-01" "1954-10-01" "1960-12-01"
> air$date<-as.Date(air$date)
> air$date[c(1,70,144)]
[1] "1949-01-01" "1954-10-01" "1960-12-01"
> class(air$date)
[1] "Date"
```

We now have the date variable, which R knows to treat as a calendar date. These dates are represented internally as days relative to January 1, 1970. You can convert them to numeric to see how R tracks the date.

```
> as.numeric(air$date[c(1,70,144)])
[1] -7670 -5571 -3318
```

```
> as.numeric(as.Date("1970-01-01"))
[1] 0
```

The two lines of code below produce plots of this data as in Figure 1.15.

```
> plot(Passengers ~ date, data=air, type="l")
> plot(log(Passengers) ~ date, data=air, type="l")
```

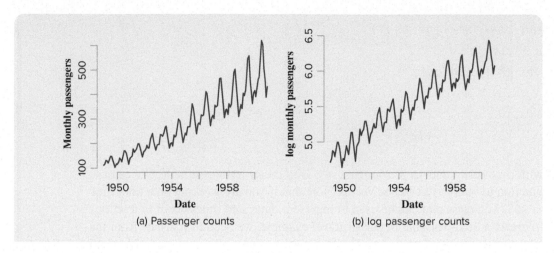

FIGURE 1.15 Time series data for 12 years of the monthly total count of international air passengers, 1949 through 1960.

Unlike our usual approach of plotting scatters of data points, here we have drawn a line plot (using the type="l" argument) to indicate dependence over time. In Figure 1.15a, you see an overall trend of an increasing number of passengers with time. In addition to this upward trend, you also see a repeated annual oscillation around the annual average. It is evident from Figure 1.15a that the oscillations around this upward trend are getting larger with time. This is a hallmark of a time series that is changing on a percentage scale with each observation. Recalling our work with sales data earlier in this chapter, that is an indication that you will want to be building a linear model on the log scale. Figure 1.15b shows the log monthly passenger volume. You can see that the log transformation yields consistently sized annual oscillations around a roughly linear-looking trend.

Linear Time Trend

We could fit a simple linear regression model to this data, say

$$\log(y_t) = \alpha + \beta t + \varepsilon_t$$

If you use the date variable as the input to glm to fit this regression, then from our as.numeric representations above you can see that the time trend will be counted in terms of days. This means that the impact of β on the monthly change will be a function of the number of the days of the month. This might be desirable in some applications, but to keep things simple here we will instead regress onto a simple index variable t that tracks the counts of months since the beginning of the dataset.

```
> air$t <- 1:nrow(air)
> fitAirSLR <- glm(log(Passengers)~t, data=air)
> coef(fitAirSLR)
```

```
(Intercept)               t
 4.81366828   0.01004838
> exp(coef(fitAirSLR)["t"])
        t
1.010099
```

The expected count of passengers increases by about 1% every month.

Seasonal Effects

This model just fits a line through the data in Figure 1.15b. It doesn't capture any of the oscillation around this line. This oscillating trend appears to be regular, trending up in summer months and down in winter. This is a classic *seasonal* pattern and we should account for it in the model. To do so, we can add *monthly* factor effects that encode the fact that, for example, people travel more in July than they do in November. The model is then

$$\log(y_t) = \alpha + \beta t + \gamma_{m_t} + \varepsilon_t \tag{1.35}$$

where γ_{m_t} denotes a separate seasonal effect for each month m_t (we are mixing in new greek letters beyond α and β here because the indexing gets complicated). To fit this in R, you need to encode Month as a factor and add it to your regression.

```
> air$Month <- factor(air$Month)
> levels(air$Month)
 [1] "1" "2" "3" "4" "5" "6" "7" "8" "9" "10" "11" "12"
> fitAirMonth <- glm(log(Passengers) ~ t + Month, data=air)
> round(coef(fitAirMonth),2)
(Intercept)        t    Month2      Month3       Month4       Month5
       4.73     0.01     -0.02        0.11         0.08         0.07
     Month6   Month7    Month8      Month9      Month10      Month11
       0.20     0.30      0.29        0.15         0.01        -0.14
    Month12
      -0.02
```

Noting that January is the reference month, absorbed into the intercept, we see that the highest months for travel are in the summer (June through August) and the lowest months are November through February. The fitted values for this regression are plotted in Figure 1.16 alongside the original data. The model appears to be doing a nice job of summarizing the passenger traffic (on log scale). To illustrate what each component is doing, Figure 1.17 shows the decomposition of this time series model into its two components: the fitted linear trend and the annual seasonal oscillations.

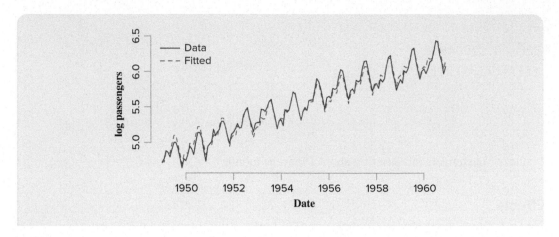

FIGURE 1.16   Airline passenger regression modeling using linear and monthly trends.

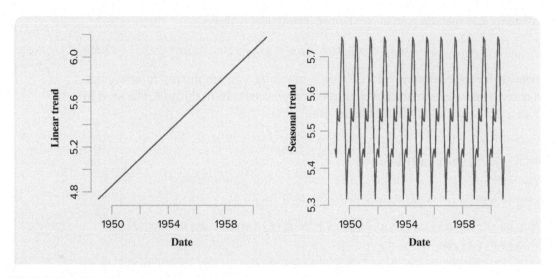

FIGURE 1.17   Decomposition of the fitted time series model for air travel.

Following the recipe we've just worked through, modeling the trends in time series data is easy. If your data include dates, then you should create indicator variables for, say, each year, month, and day. A best practice is to *proceed hierarchically:* if you are going to include an effect for May-1955, then you should also include broader effects for May and for 1955. This allows the model to use the broad effects as baselines, and the May-1955 effect will only summarize deviations from this base. In the language of Chapter 3, May-1955 is *shrunk* toward generic levels for May and 1955. The same logic applies for space: if you condition on counties, then you should also include state and region effects. This hierarchical approach is not strictly necessary when you are fitting OLS regressions via glm, but it will be crucial once we start to use the model regularization and selection techniques of Chapter 3.

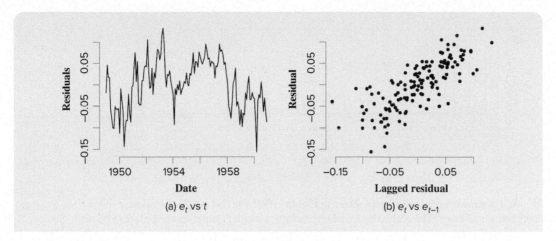

FIGURE 1.18   Residuals from the airline passenger regression including a linear time trend and monthly effects, plotted against time in (a) and against the lagged residuals in (b).

1.5.2 Autoregressive Models

Consider the air travel regression residuals shown in Figure 1.18a. That is a common approach to see what or how much is left unexplained by the model. When you look at this time series of residuals, you are looking for any patterns in how the residuals move over time. In this case, even though the combination of a linear trend and monthly effects did a decent job of predicting log passenger counts, there appears to be a stickiness in the residual time series: when they are high one month, they tend to be high the next month. More precisely, they appear correlated in time, such that $e_t = (y_t - \hat{y}_t)$ is dependent upon e_{t-1}. Diving deeper, Figure 1.18b plots the residuals e_t against their *lagged values,* e_{t-1}. There is a clear relationship between the current value and the one previous. This means that y_{t-1} can be used to predict y_t. It also implies that our regression residuals are now correlated, which violates the basic linear regression assumption of independence between residual errors.

This phenomenon is called *autocorrelation:* correlation between periods in a time series. Time series data is simply a collection of observations gathered over time. For example, suppose $y_1 \ldots y_T$ are weekly sales, daily temperatures, or five-minute stock returns. In each case, you might expect what happens at time t to be correlated with time $t - 1$. For example, suppose you measure temperatures daily for several years. Which would work better as an estimate for today's temperature:

- The average of the temperatures from the previous year?
- The temperature on the previous day?

In most cases, yesterday's temperature is most informative. That means you view the *local* dependence as more important than the broad annual pattern.

Autocorrelation Function

You can summarize dependence between subsequent observations with an autocorrelation function (ACF) that tracks 'lag-l' correlations.

$$\mathrm{acf}(l) = \mathrm{cor}(\varepsilon_t, \varepsilon_{t-l}) \tag{1.36}$$

Figure 1.19 shows the ACF for our airline regression residuals. You can produce this with the following command.

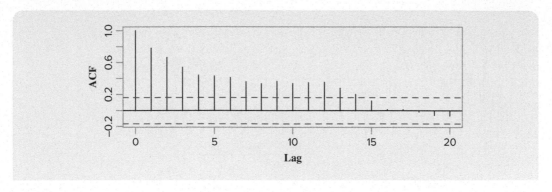

FIGURE 1.19 ACF for the residual time series shown in Figure 1.18. Note that acf(0) = 1 because this is the correlation between y_t and itself. The dashed horizontal line marks a rough calculation on the threshold for "significant" autocorrelations.

```
> plot(acf(fitAirMonth$residuals))
```

The plot confirms our visual inspection of the residual plots: there is significant correlation in the residuals. The correlation between y_t and y_{t-1} is around 0.8, which is pretty high. It indicates that 64% of the variation in e_t could be explained through a simple linear regression onto e_{t-1} (from 0.8^2 using our R^2 formula for linear regression).

How do you model this type of data? Consider a simple cumulative error process, where each ε_t is random with mean zero:

$$y_1 = \varepsilon_1,$$
$$y_2 = \varepsilon_1 + \varepsilon_2,$$
$$\vdots$$
$$y_t = \varepsilon_1 + \varepsilon_2 + \ldots + e_t$$

Each y_t is a function of every previous observation all the way back to the first observation. This implies

$$y_t = \sum_{s=1}^{t} \varepsilon_s = y_{t-1} + \varepsilon_t \tag{1.37}$$

such that you can define y_t in terms of y_{t-1} and ε_t. This means that $\mathbb{E}[y_t|y_{t-1}] = y_{t-1}$ and all you need to know to predict t is what happened at $t - 1$. The model in (1.37) is called a *random walk*. It is defined by the fact that the expectation of what will happen next is always what happened most recently.

Random walks are one type of a general class of *autoregressive* (AR) models. In an autoregressive model of order one, you have

$$AR(1) : y_t = \beta_0 + \beta_1 y_{t-1} + \varepsilon_t \tag{1.38}$$

This is just a simple linear regression model, where y_t is the response and lagged y_{t-1} is the input. The random walk of (1.37) corresponds to $\beta_1 = 1$, and in a random walk any nonzero β_0 is referred to as *drift*. But β_1 can take all sorts of values, and you can complicate (1.38) by adding in whatever covariates that are also useful to predict y_t. Or, to think about it another way, you can add an AR(1) term to any regression where you suspect correlation between residuals.

Example 1.10 Airline Passenger Counts: Accounting for Autocorrelation To fit an AR(1) model, all you need to do is to create lagged values of your response and then include them in the regressions. To do this with the airline passenger counts, you can create a new column called lag1 and fill it with the previous month's passenger counts.

```
> air$lag1 <- c(NA, air$Passengers[-nrow(air)])
> air[1:3,]
  Year Month Passengers        date t lag1
1   49     1        112 1949-01-01 1   NA
2   49     2        118 1949-02-01 2  112
3   49     3        132 1949-03-01 3  118
```

Notice that lag1 for the first observation is empty (set to NA) because we don't know the passenger counts for December 1948. When we run our regression with an AR(1) term, we will want to exclude this first observation from the training data; glm actually does this automatically, because it skips observations containing NA values. Fitting the model is straightforward: you just add this lagged variable to your R formula (on log scale, to match the response).

```
> fitAirAR1 <- glm(log(Passengers) ~ log(lag1) + t + Month,
data=air)
> coef(fitAirAR1)["log(lag1)"]
log(lag1)
0.7930716
```

The resulting coefficient on the AR(1) term is 0.79. That means that each month's log counts are expected to be about 80% of the previous month's, before you add the linear and monthly trend effects. Figure 1.20 shows the resulting residuals and their ACF plot. Now, the residuals appear

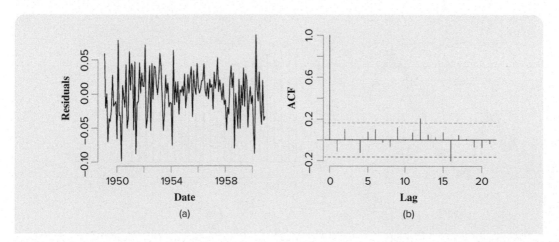

FIGURE 1.20   Residuals for the airline passenger regression that includes an AR(1) term and linear and monthly trends, showing them against time in (a) and their ACF in (b).

to be completely random from one month to the next (contrast with the residual time series in Figure 1.18). It appears the single lag term solved the bulk of our autocorrelation problems. For example, in Figure 1.20b there are no autocorrelations larger than 0.2 at any of the time lags.

Properties of AR Models

The AR(1) model is simple but hugely powerful. If you have any suspicion of autocorrelation, it is a good move to include lagged response as an input. The coefficient on this lag gives you important information about the time-series properties.

- If $|\beta_1| = 1$, you have a random walk.
- If $|\beta_1| > 1$, the series diverges and will move to very large or small values.
- If $|\beta_1| < 1$, the values are mean reverting.

Random Walk

In a random walk, the series just wanders around, and the autocorrelation stays high for a long time. See Figure 1.21. More precisely, the series is *nonstationary:* it has no average level that it wants to be near but rather diverges off into space. For example, consider the daily Dow Jones Average (DJA) composite index from 2000 to 2007, shown in Figure 1.22a. The DJA appears as though it is just wandering around. Sure enough, if you fit a regression model it looks like a random walk.

```
> dja <- read.csv("dja.csv")[,1]
> n<-length(dja)
> coef(ARdj <- glm(dja[-1] ~ dja[-n]))
(Intercept)      dja[-n]
   7.054185     0.997643
```

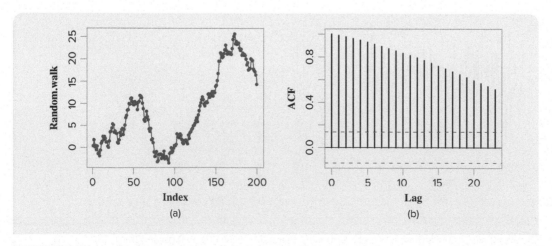

FIGURE 1.21 A simulated random walk and its ACF.

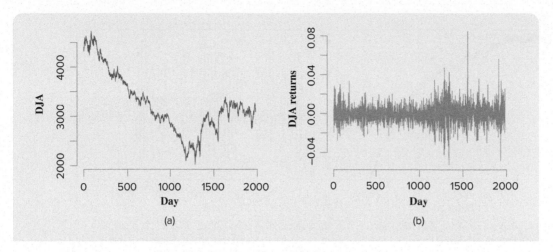

FIGURE 1.22 Dow Jones Average daily value (a) and returns (b) from 2000 to 2007.

The AR(1) term has a coefficient very near to one.

However, when we switch from prices to returns, $(y_t - y_{t-1})/y_{t-1}$, we get data that looks more like pure noise as shown in Figure 1.22b. Rerunning the regression on returns, we find that the AR(1) term is now very close to zero.

```
> returns <- (dja[-1]-dja[-n])/dja[-n]
> coef(glm(returns[-1] ~ returns[-(n-1)]))
     (Intercept) returns[-(n - 1)]
  -0.0001138386      -0.0144411430
```

This property is implied by the series being a random walk: the *differences* between y_t and y_{t-1} are independent. If you have a random walk, you should perform this "returns" transformation to obtain something that is easier to model. For example, it is standard to model asset price series in terms of returns rather than raw prices.

Diverging Series

For AR(1) terms larger than one, life is more complicated. This case results in what is called a *diverging* series because the y_t values move exponentially far from y_1. For example, Figure 1.23a shows how quickly the observations diverge even for $\beta_1 = 1.02$, very close to one. Since these series explode, they are useless for modeling and prediction. If you run a regression and find such an AR(1) term, you are likely missing a trend variable that needs to be included in your regression.

Mean Reverting Series

Finally, the most interesting series have AR(1) terms between −1 and 1. These series are called *stationary* because y_t is always pulled back toward the mean. These are the most common, and most useful, type of AR series. The past matters in a stationary series, but with limited horizon and autocorrelation drops off rapidly.

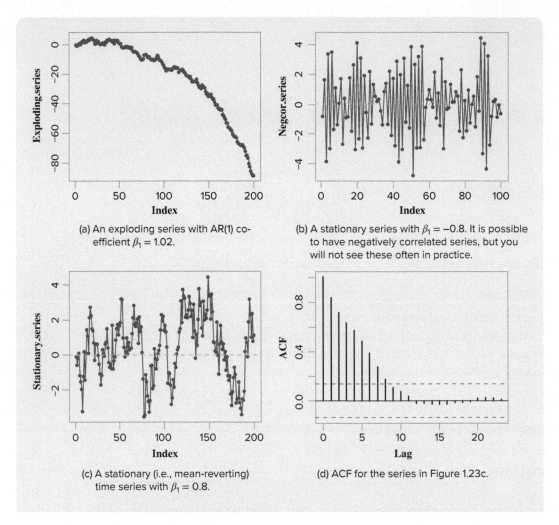

(a) An exploding series with AR(1) coefficient $\beta_1 = 1.02$.

(b) A stationary series with $\beta_1 = -0.8$. It is possible
to have negatively correlated series, but you
will not see these often in practice.

(c) A stationary (i.e., mean-reverting)
time series with $\beta_1 = 0.8$.

(d) ACF for the series in Figure 1.23c.

FIGURE 1.23   Various AR(1) time series examples.

An important property of stationary series is mean reversion. Think about shifting both y_t and y_{t-1} by their mean μ. A simple AR(1) model holds that

$$y_t - \mu = \beta_1 (y_{t-1} - \mu) + \varepsilon_t$$

Since $|\beta_1| < 1$, y_t is expected to be closer to the μ than y_{t-1}. That is, each subsequent observation is expected to be closer to the mean than the previous one. Mean reversion is common and if you find an AR(1) coefficient between -1 and 1 it should give you some confidence that you have included the right trend variables and are modeling the right version of the response. The AR(1) component of our regression for log passenger counts was mean reverting, with each y_t expected to be 0.79 times the response for the previous month.

It is also possible to expand the AR idea to higher lags.

$$AR(p) : y_t = \beta_0 + \beta_1 y_{t-1} + \dots \beta_p y_{t-p} + \varepsilon_t$$

The model selection and regularization methods of Chapter 3 make it straightforward to let the data choose the appropriate lags. Using those tools, you can feel free to consider bigger p in your $AR(p)$. The only problem is that the simple stationary versus nonstationary interpretations for β_1 no longer apply if you include higher lags. In addition, the need for higher lags sometimes indicates that you are missing a more persistent trend or seasonality in the data.

Before moving to the next section, it is worth emphasizing how we have been dealing with all sorts of time series dependence: we just engineer features to explain that dependence and include them in our regression models. It really is that easy. Some techniques based on data sampling, such as the bootstrapping or cross validation of next chapters, need to be adapted for dependent data. But with regression you have a great tool set for dealing with time dependence.

1.5.3 Panel Data

A common scenario for analysis has multiple time series together in a single dataset. You might have sales data over time for a number of different stores. Or, you might have a *longitudinal* survey where you ask a set of customers the same questions at a regular interval to see how their opinions change over time. This type of data—a stack of time series for multiple observation units—is called *panel data*. You have N units (e.g., stores or individuals) and a time series of length T_i for each unit. Your total number of observations is $n = \sum_{i=1}^{N} T_i$. When all of the time series are the same length, such that $Ti = T$ for all units, it is called a balanced panel; otherwise it is an unbalanced panel.

Panel data is especially common in economics applications, and econometricians have an extensive toolset for estimating models on this type of data. The literature in this area is pretty dense and jargon heavy, but the plm package for R (Croissant and Millo (2008)) is an extensively documented library of tools from econometrics for panel data analysis. Fortunately, with modern computing techniques (especially the regularization and sparse matrix tools from Chapter 3), you can do the state of the art of panel data analysis using standard regression models. As we've stated before in this chapter, time series analysis is just regression analysis where you have engineered and included some special features. The same holds true for panel data.

Example 1.11 **Hass Avocado Panel Data** We will introduce panel data analysis through an analysis of weekly sales by U.S. region for Hass avocados. Avocados have become enormously popular in recent years and the Hass variety is dominating the market. The Hass Avocado Board (HAB) was formed in 2002 to maintain and expand demand for avocados in the United States. The dataset hass.csv contains data from HAB. These data represent weekly retail sales of Hass avocados measured directly via cash register transactions. The data include sales from supercenters, club stores, national chains, regional chains, independent grocers, and the military. They do not reflect sales from farm stands, drug stores, or convenience outlets.

The data include unit sales and the average sales price per unit (ASP) aggregated by week and by region.

```
> hass<-read.csv("hass.csv",stringsAsFactors=TRUE)
> head(hass,3)
   region        date asp      units
```

```
1 Albany 12/27/2015 1.33  64236.62
2 Albany 12/20/2015 1.35  54876.98
3 Albany 12/13/2015 0.93 118220.22
```

The first things we will do are to convert the date into a `Date` variable, being careful to check the date formatting, and then *order* the data frame by region and date:

```
> hass$date <- as.Date(hass$date,format='%m/%d/%Y')
> hass<-hass[order(hass$region,hass$date),]
> head(hass,3)
    region       date asp    units
52 Albany 2015-01-04 1.22 40873.28
51 Albany 2015-01-11 1.24 41195.08
50 Albany 2015-01-18 1.17 44511.28
```

This step of ordering by unit and date is a good practice with panel data, since it helps you stay organized during data manipulation. It will be essential for our calculation of lagged variables below.

We will investigate the sales-price elasticity of avocados by regressing log units sold onto log ASP. The most basic panel data model doesn't include any real time series modeling: you just regress your response of interest (`log(units)`) on the explanatory variables interest (`log(asp)`). (Recall our earlier discussion of log-log models and price elasticity around Equation 1.8.) The key step is that you need to account for the fact that your data are *grouped* according to the panel units—in our case grouped by region. You will expect different average weekly avocado sales in Boise than you would get in Los Angeles. You deal with this by including the regions as factor effects in the regression. The model is then

$$\log(\text{units}_{it}) = \alpha_i + \beta \log(\text{asp}_{it}) + \varepsilon_{it} \tag{1.39}$$

The subscript indexing here is important: x_{it} indicates the value at the tth time series observation for the ith region. This double indexing references a unique row of the `hass` data frame. However, the region effects α_i are only indexed by region, such that every time series observation from the same region is fit as having this region-specific mean. These α_i are called *fixed effects* in a panel data setting. Including them is equivalent to removing the regional mean from your sales data before fitting the regression. With panel data it is important that you include these fixed effects; otherwise, the difference in baseline sales between, say, Boise and Los Angeles will be included in your estimate of β.

We'll fit this model with `glm`.

```
> fitHass <- glm(log(units) ~ log(asp) + region, data=hass)
> coef(fitHass)["log(asp)"]
   log(asp)
-0.7283443
```

This estimated elasticity implies that expected unit sales drop by 0.73% for every 1% increase in ASP. This is a fine result in the context of the model we have specified, but it is suspicious if you want to interpret β in terms of what grocers experience in terms of lost or gained sales when they change prices. In particular, elasticities greater than -1 indicate what economists call inelastic products. For such products, the grocers could increase *revenue* (i.e., total sales before costs) by increasing prices. Finding $\beta = -0.73$ as the sales-price elasticity for avocados, which suggests that they are an inelastic good, is surprising. If you are interested to learn more, see the nearby box on this topic. Regardless, we will find soon that if we control for additional influences on sales, then avocados no longer appear inelastic.

Pricing, Elasticities, and the Limits of log-log Regression

First, we note that the economics literature on pricing and sales-price elasticities is deep and complex. There is no single framework that describes to any degree of fidelity how firms set prices, and the prices you experience as a consumer are driven by a massive variety of influences. Simple log-log regression models like those we use throughout this chapter measure the *short-term* elasticity to *local* changes in price for a *single* product. This means that a number of price-demand effects are not included without further modeling.

- The long-term elasticity to prices can be different from the short term. If your store increases prices consumers may still buy the items out of convenience, but eventually they will shift their entire shopping trip to a store that offers better value across a broad range of items. Your log-log regression doesn't capture this long-term view, and a firm that optimizes too much for short-term profit risks losing customers in the long term.

- Our regression models measure the immediate customer sales variation as a function of relatively small price changes around the average price (i.e., within the range of observed price variation). If the average price increases by a large amount (e.g., if avocados suddenly doubled in average price) then the measured elasticities would likely change. You should view your measured elasticities from a simple log-log model as applicable only within the observed range of current prices.

- Stores sell many products. Some may be heavily discounted to get people into the store, or because they are "basket builders" that encourage people to buy other (more profitable) products. In a more sophisticated demand analysis, it is common to incorporate *cross-price* elasticities that measure how changes in price on one product (e.g., pasta) influence the sales on complementary products (e.g., pasta sauce).

Other issues include the impact of supply (if you have too many avocados you might discount them to avoid spoilage), temporal substitution (if you discount one day, then customers can stock up and buy less in the future), and product substitution (price changes on one product can cause people to switch to or from another item).

Despite these limitations, the log-log regressions of this chapter are a common and useful tool for understanding pricing and demand. To see why we say that -0.73 is a suspicious elasticity for avocados, consider that a sales-price elasticity greater than -1 implies that a grocer could raise total revenue by raising prices. To see this, take Equation (1.39) and do a bit of basic algebra to write

$$\log(\texttt{units}_{it}) = \alpha_i + \beta \log(\texttt{asp}_{it}) + \log(\texttt{asp}_{it}) - \log(\texttt{asp}_{it}) + \varepsilon_{it}$$
$$\Rightarrow \log(\texttt{units}_{it} \times \texttt{asp}_{it}) = \alpha_i + (\beta + 1) \log(\texttt{asp}_{it}) + \varepsilon_{it} \tag{1.40}$$

Now, `units × asp` is your total revenue (units sold times price). And if $\beta > -1$, then (1.40) leads to $\beta + 1 > 0$ and you have a *positive* revenue-price elasticity. If we apply this elasticity to set prices at each store, it implies that the grocers can increase *revenue* by increasing prices.

Grocers are not attempting to maximize short-term *profit* (revenue minus costs) on every item: they need to worry about long-term customer retention and the cross-price elasticities. However, it is a bit unusual to see average prices so low that they could be raised without negatively impacting revenue. Unless cheap avocados play an outsized role in basket building or attracting people to shop, then the inelastic demand implied by $\hat{\beta} = -0.73$ suggests that average prices might drift upward until consumers start to become more price sensitive. More likely, however, is that our elasticity here is "polluted" by effects on sales separate from price.

To learn more about pricing and demand, look to Chapter 6 where we discuss a higher dimensional log-log elasticity regression in the context of beer pricing.

Two-Way Fixed Effects

The likely issue here is that we are missing an underlying variable that is correlated with both prices and sales. Such "omitted variables" can make it difficult to interpret the estimated relationships in your regression (like the one between price and sales). In panel data, you can mitigate this issue by including *fixed time effects*. If we include fixed effects for each week then we will be controlling for events or seasonal effects that impact both the price and sales of avocados. For example, events such as the Super Bowl cause Americans to eat a lot of avocados (guacamole!) and grocers will want to increase prices on their limited supply, leading to a positive relationship between price and sales. If we include a fixed effect for the Super Bowl week, this positive relationship will be explained by that effect rather than being incorporated into our price elasticity estimate.

We have now talked about having a region fixed effect for each time series in our panel and having a week fixed effect for each time point across all series. The term "fixed effect" might be a bit confusing if you haven't seen it before. There is nothing complicated going on here: we are simply including additional factor variables into our regression (a factor for region and a factor for week). The "fixed" label is used in panel data analysis to differentiate from so-called random effects, where you allow for correlations between the error terms in your analysis. We consider this type of dependence between errors in the next chapter as part of our uncertainty quantification. However, this is not a replacement for including the proper fixed effects in your regression specification. These fixed effects play a crucial role in accounting for the influence of unobserved factors, such as different tastes or budgets across regions or the Super Bowl effect described above.

Getting back to our avocado sales analysis, an alternative model with week fixed effects is

$$\log(\texttt{units}_{it}) = \alpha_i + \delta_t + \beta \log(\texttt{asp}_{it}) + \varepsilon_{it} \tag{1.41}$$

Here, δ_t is the fixed effect for week t.

To fit this in R, you create a factor variable for *week* and add it to the R formula.

```
> hass$week <- factor(hass$date)
> fitHassDF <- glm(log(units) ~ log(asp) + region + week,
data=hass)
> coef(fitHassDF)["log(asp)"]
  log(asp)
-0.9465598
```

Sure enough, the elasticity is now close enough to -1 to seem plausible. At a sales-price elasticity of -1, the grocers can't make more revenue by raising prices.

Note that the model in Equation (1.41) is often referred to as the *two-way fixed effects model*. It is very common in economic analysis, since it allows you to control for unobserved influences in both time (t) and region (i). Since it is such a common model, we caution you to remember that it is not magic and you can still get bad estimates if, for example, the elasticities are different for each region or if there is an unmodeled time trend in each region (e.g., if sales are increasing at different linear rates in each region). As we've said before: panel data analysis is just applied regression, so you need to think about the process you are trying to model and not assume that you can just fit a common model and interpret the fitted values the way you want.

Adding AR Terms

We can further improve the model by including lagged variables. First, we can include lagged log unit sales to account for the autoregressive correlation across weeks in the same region. Just like the weather, this week's avocado sales in your city are almost certainly correlated with last week's sales (even after controlling for price and the major regional or weekly trends). But we can also include the *lagged log price effect*. Such lagged price effects are often a good idea to include because of *pull forward in demand*. If you have a deal on avocados, then customers will stock up, and the next week they won't buy avocados because their pantry is already full.

The full regression model is then

$$\log(\text{units}_{it}) = \alpha_i + \delta_t + \beta_1 \log(\text{units}_{i,t-1}) + \beta_2 \log(\text{asp}_{it}) + \beta_3 \log(\text{asp}_{i,t-1}) + \varepsilon_{it} \quad \textbf{(1.42)}$$

Calculating the lagged variables for panel data takes a bit of care. We need to group the data into its region-level time series and calculate the lags for each individual time series. We will use the `tapply` function to do this. `tapply` takes any vector as its first argument, splits the vector up according to the factor levels in its second argument, and then applies to the splits whatever function you give as its third argument. Hence, we can use it to calculate things like the maximum for each subgroup.

```
> tapply(c(1:5), c("a","b","a","b","c"), function(x) max(x))
a b c
3 4 5
```

Since we *ordered* the hass data frame in the beginning of this example (which is crucial for this to work), we can use `tapply` to split asp and units into their region-level time series and create lagged variables within each region (same as we did to create lagged passengers for the airline example).

```
> hass$lag.asp <- unlist(tapply(hass$asp, hass$region,
+                     function(x) c(NA,x[-length(x)])))
> hass$lag.units <- unlist(tapply(hass$units, hass$region,
+                     function(x) c(NA,x[-length(x)])))
> head(hass,3)
   region       date asp   units   lag.asp lag.units
52 Albany 2015-01-04 1.22 40873.28      NA        NA
51 Albany 2015-01-11 1.24 41195.08    1.22  40873.28
50 Albany 2015-01-18 1.17 44511.28    1.24  41195.08
```

The `unlist` command is necessary because `tapply` returns here a list of vectors, one for each lagged time series, and you want to collapse them into a single vector. You can confirm by inspection that we have things lined up properly. For example, the avocado ASP in Albany for the week of January 4 is $1.22, and this is also the lagged avocado ASP for the week of January 11.

Fitting the model with `glm`, you can see that the estimate of price sensitivity has increased:

```
> fitHassLags <- glm(log(units) ~ log(lag.units) + log(asp)
+                     + log(lag.asp) + region, data=hass)
> coef(fitHassLags)[2:4]
log(lag.units)      log(asp)   log(lag.asp)
     0.7734225    -1.4025468      1.2631973
```

The model estimate says that Hass unit sales decrease by about 1.4% per every 1% price increase. Notice that the AR(1) term on lagged units is 0.77, indicating a stationary and mean reverting autocorrelation process. Finally, the effect of lagged log ASP is positive. Interpreting this through the lens of pull forward in demand, expected unit sales in a given week *drop* by 1.3% per every 1% price *decrease* in the week prior. That is the effect of customers stocking up on those cheap avocados.

◆1.6 Spatial Data

We've shown that you can model all sorts of time series dependence using basic regression tools. This same lesson applies to spatial dependence: space is just like time but with another dimension. The same as you can include monthly or weekly factors in your regressions, you can include geographic factors like region or city. This approach of adding *spatial fixed effects* will be your main tool in managing dependence in spatial data. To see how this works in practice, consider the example of our next chapter: we will be modeling the listing price for used cars, and always include the `city` where a car is listed as a spatial fixed effect.

Modeling autocorrelation in spatial data is a bit more complicated than it is for time series. Whereas time series are *ordered,* spatial data is not. In AR models the current observation is regressed onto the previous observation, but with spatial data there is no simple notion of "previous." There do exist spatial autoregressive (SAR) models, where each observation is regressed onto the observations of its "neighbors." For example, when processing image data you can regress the value at one pixel onto the average of the neighboring pixels. These SAR models work fine for spatial data that is observed on a regular *grid,* such that each observation is evenly spaced from its neighbors. Unfortunately, most examples of spatial data that we encounter in practice do not live on a nice grid. Instead, you need models for autocorrelation that allow for the observations to be unevenly spaced from each other.

1.6.1 Gaussian Process Modeling

Gaussian processes (GPs) are the dominant modeling framework for spatially dependent data. GPs are models that smooth predictions across observations according to distances between their locations. They are a relatively simple example of the sort of *stochastic process* models that are commonly used for such purposes. However, to describe GPs we need to talk about multivariate distributions that describe the *joint* distribution for multiple observations.

Suppose that you have two response observations y_i and y_j observed at two different locations with coordinates $\mathbf{s}_i$ and $\mathbf{s}_j$. These can be latitude and longitude coordinates, or they can correspond to any other spatial coordinate system that makes sense for your data. A Gaussian process models the responses at two locations as draws from a Gaussian distribution:

$$\begin{bmatrix} y_i \\ y_j \end{bmatrix} \sim \mathrm{N}\left(\begin{bmatrix} \mu_i \\ \mu_j \end{bmatrix}, \sigma^2 \begin{bmatrix} 1 + \delta & \kappa(\mathbf{s}_i, \mathbf{s}_j) \\ \kappa(\mathbf{s}_i, \mathbf{s}_j) & 1 + \delta \end{bmatrix} \right) \tag{1.43}$$

Equation (1.43) is a *multivariate* distribution. It describes the expectation (μ_i and μ_j) and variance ($\sigma^2(1 + \delta)$) for each variable, as well as the covariance between the responses. The expectations can be functions of covariates, say $\mu_i = \mathbf{x}_i'\boldsymbol{\beta}$, or a simple mean such that $\mu_i = \mu_j = \mu$. The variance is determined by σ^2 and the *nugget* δ. This nugget term measures how much variance you will have for repeated observations *at the same location*. If you have two observations at the same spatial location, then δ represents the amount that they tend to differ from each other.

The covariance between observations is determined by $\kappa(\mathbf{s}_i, \mathbf{s}_j)$, the *kernel function*. It defines the correlation between the corresponding responses, such that

$$\mathrm{cor}(y_t, y_s) = \frac{\kappa(\mathbf{s}_i, \mathbf{s}_j)}{1 + \delta} \tag{1.44}$$

and the *covariance* between these responses is $\sigma^2 \kappa,(\mathbf{s}_i, \mathbf{s}_j)$. The form for this kernel function dictates how the GP models spatial correlation. For example, the common *exponential* kernel function is

$$\kappa(\mathbf{s}_i, \mathbf{s}_j) = \frac{1}{\exp\left[\left(\dfrac{(s_{i1} - s_{j1})^2}{\rho_1} + \dfrac{(s_{i2} - s_{j2})^2}{\rho_2} \right) \right]} \tag{1.45}$$

Here, correlation decreases with the exponentiated distance between locations. The *range* parameters, ρ_1 and ρ_2, allow for different units of distance in your two coordinates (say lat and long). The kernel from (1.45) results in smoothly decaying dependence between responses, y_i and y_j, as a function of distance between inputs, $\mathbf{s}_i$ and $\mathbf{s}_j$. Note that this $\kappa(\cdot, \cdot)$ produces values between zero and one, since $\kappa(\mathbf{s}_i, \mathbf{s}_j) = 1$ if $\mathbf{s}_i = \mathbf{s}_j$ and it approaches zero as the locations get further apart.

GP Predictions

Predictions from a GP combine information in the mean function with the information from observations at nearby locations. Consider prediction (forecasting) at a new location $\mathbf{s}_f$ given a single observation y_i at location $\mathbf{s}_i$. The conditional expectation for the response at the new location is

$$\mathbb{E}[y_f | y_i] = \mu_f + \frac{\kappa(\mathbf{s}_f, \mathbf{s}_i)}{1 + \delta}(y_i - \mu_i) \qquad (1.46)$$

This shows the prediction will be a combination of the mean for the new observation, μ_f, and the correlation between y_f and y_i multiplied by the residual error $y_i - \mu_i$. When the residual error is positive, then the residual at y_f is also expected to be positive. The strength of this relationship is determined by the kernel function and the distance between locations. When you have many observations, the analogue to (1.46) has that the prediction for y_f is a function of the *matrix* of correlations between y_f and those observations and the *vector* of residual errors.

Estimating and predicting from GP models is not a simple exercise. You need to consider the correlations between all pairs of locations in your data in order to estimate the range, variance, and mean parameters. And you need to do the matrix-vector calculations to calculate predictions that depend upon the correlations with residuals errors—that is, to calculate the n-observation analogue to (1.46). This gets computationally expensive when you have many observations (many locations) in your dataset. For big datasets, an efficient technique is to consider a subsample of neighboring observations for each location where you want to predict the response. That is, if you want to predict at new location $\mathbf{s}_k$, then you fit a *local* GP that only uses a fixed number of observations at locations near to $\mathbf{s}_k$.

Fitting GPs with `laGP`

To fit such local GPs in R, you can make use of the `laGP` package (Gramacy, 2015). It contains the `aGP` function which takes as arguments your observed locations and responses, and a set of new locations where you want to get predictions. The algorithm goes through each location where you want to predict, and fits a local GP model to the set of nearby locations. The argument `end` sets the number of observations used to estimate each local GP; if you set `end` bigger, the algorithm takes longer to run but will consider a wider set of neighbors for each location. The `aGP` function uses the efficient search algorithm described in Gramacy and Apley (2015) to choose the most useful neighbors for use in each local GP fit. Detailed examples are provided in the vignette of Gramacy (2015) and in the package documentation.

Example 1.12 **California Census Data: Gaussian Processes** To illustrate GP estimation, we will look at some (old) census data from California. In the `CalCensus.csv` dataset you have the longitude and latitude for the center of each census tract in the state, along with some statistics for that census tract. We will be focusing on the median values for income and home value within each census tract, and investigating the relationship between them. Note that each of these metrics has been *trimmed* to replace very large values with a threshold: income is thresholded at $150k and home value is thresholded at $500k.

```
> ca <- read.csv("CalCensus.csv")
> ca[1,]
  longitude latitude housingMedianAge population households
1  -122.23    37.88               41        322        126
  medianIncome medianHouseValue AveBedrms AveRooms AveOccupancy
1        83252           452600   1.02381 6.984127     2.555556
```

To understand the relationship between house prices and income, we can calculate the *elasticity* between them using a log-log regression.

```
> linc <- log(ca[,"medianIncome"])
> lhval <- log(ca[,"medianHouseValue"])
> summary(glm(lhval ~ linc))
...
Coefficients:
            Estimate Std. Error t value Pr(>|t|)
(Intercept) 3.569235   0.065110   54.82   <2e-16 ***
linc        0.814520   0.006221  130.92   <2e-16 ***
```

Using what we know about interpreting coefficients in log-log regression, the estimated coefficient on linc says that median home prices should increase by about 0.8% per every 1% increase in income.

We might want to be skeptical about that result, however. There is a likely dependence in the home values across neighboring census tracts: people can easily commute from their home in one census tract to their work in another one. Indeed, Figure 1.24 shows a strong pattern of spatial correlation in both incomes and home values across California (it also shows that the highest home prices are tightly concentrated in the SF Bay Area and along the coast—the color maps here are calculated on percentiles of the distributions—while incomes are more evenly distributed). Thus the estimated relationship between income and home values here might be *polluted* by the incomes and home values in neighboring census tracts. This is the same as how you can get polluted estimates for regression coefficients in time series if you do not control for autocorrelation.

To control for this spatial dependence, you can use a GP to model the error structure for log home value conditional upon log income. However, the laGP package doesn't allow for regression functions to specify the response mean; it applies a single fixed mean, such that $\mu_i = \mu_j = \mu$ in our notation of Equation (1.43). In a preview of Chapter 6, however, we can proceed by using GP predictions to first *residualize* both the income and home values against their predicted value given the spatial correlation between observations. That is, we'll use a GP model to obtain fitted values for income and home value, calculate the residuals (the

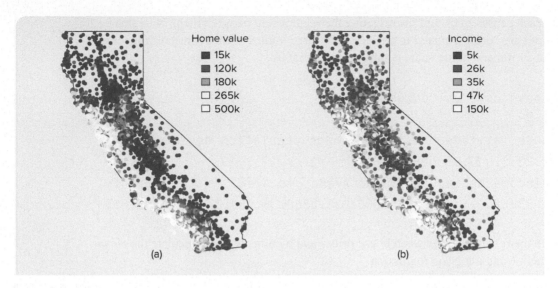

FIGURE 1.24 Median home value and income by census tract.

difference in the fitted and observed values), and then regress the residuals for home value onto the residuals for income. The regression relationship between these residuals then tells you the elasticity for home values on incomes *after* having controlled for spatial dependence across census tracts.

Say that y denotes log median home values (lhval) and d denotes the log median incomes (linc), and the full samples for each are **y** and **d**. Then we will use GP models to estimate $\hat{y}_i = \mathbb{E}[y_i|\mathbf{y}]$ and $\hat{d}_i = \mathbb{E}[d_i|\mathbf{d}]$. The residuals are calculated as $\tilde{y}_i = y_i - \hat{y}_i$ and $\tilde{d}_i = d_i - \hat{d}_i$ for each census tract i. The final regression for $\tilde{y}_i$ onto $\tilde{d}_i$ gives us an unpolluted estimate of the elasticity between incomes and home prices. Note that if you find this residualization confusing, you can ignore the motivation here and just think about fitting two GPs: one to predict income and the other to predict home values.

To fit the GPs with aGP, you pull out longitude and latitude as the spatial coordinates both for the current observations and the locations where you want to predict. We use end=20 here so that each fitted GP will use 20 local census tracts.

```
> library(laGP)
> s <- ca[,1:2] # long and lat
> gpinc <- aGP(s, linc, XX=s, end=20)
> gphval <- aGP(s, lhval, XX=s, end=20)
```

When you run this, it will take several minutes and print a lot of information. Recall that aGP is fitting a unique GP for each of the locations where you want to predict—in this case, 20,640 census tracts. The laGP package is actually very sophisticated under the hood, and if you "compile" (i.e., turn the code into an executable computer program) correctly it can execute each local GP in parallel across the many processors on your computer. However, this will be tricky if you are not familiar with these tools (it is not as easy as loading the parallel

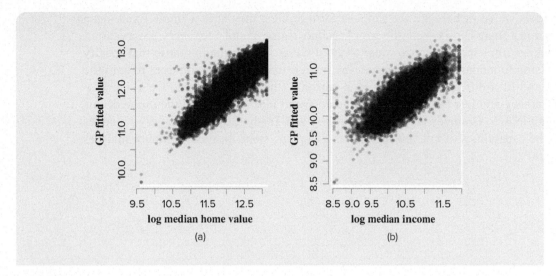

FIGURE 1.25   log median home value and income, fitted values from `laGP` plotted against the observed values.

library). You can run the code here without fancy parallel tricks and make yourself some coffee or tea while it runs.

The resulting predictions at `XX` are in the `mean` entry of the fitted `aGP` objects. The fitted values are plotted in Figure 1.25. Remember: these predictions are based on only the dependence between nearby census tracts. We use these fitted values to calculate residuals for each of *y* and *d* and regress the residuals onto each other. Note that you will get slightly different output since `aGP` is taking a random sample from the posterior distribution (refer to the Bayes section in the next chapter).

```
> rinc <- linc - gpinc$mean
> rhval <- lhval - gphval$mean
> summary(glm(rhval ~ rinc))
...
             Estimate Std. Error t value Pr(>|t|)
(Intercept) -0.001351   0.001427  -0.947    0.344
rinc         0.353034   0.004942  71.438   <2e-16 ***
```

The estimated elasticity is less than half of our previous estimate. Controlling for spatial dependence through the GP-based residualization leads us to conclude that home values rise by about 0.4% per every 1% increase in income. It is intuitive that controlling for spatial dependence reduces the elasticity. If incomes increase for jobs in one census tract then the influence on home price will be spread over a large regional area (people can commute and move) rather than concentrated in a single census tract. There will also be correlated spatial effects of, say, school districts and neighborhood appeal.

The models we've fit here are the simplest form of GPs: they have a single fixed mean parameter μ and a shared homoskedastic error structure (same σ^2 and δ for every observation). The tgp package implements a much wider array of GP models, including those that specify linear regression functions as the mean and even models that use regression trees to split the input space and fit a different GP within each partition (these are the Treed Gaussian Processes of Gramacy and Lee 2008). Although the code and ideas are beyond the scope of this book, you can look to Gramacy (2007) and Gramacy and Taddy (2010) for lengthy vignettes illustrating the capabilities of tgp and use that as a stepping stone for more complex analyses of spatial data.

QUICK REFERENCE

This chapter moves rapidly through the methods of linear and logistic regression, and explains how these methods are both applications of maximum likelihood estimation. The connection between likelihood maximization and deviance minimization will be important for future chapters where we consider the deviance as a part of more complex "loss functions" that are estimated as part of machine learning. We also introduce the basic concepts of time series analysis, with the main point being that regression techniques can be applied to analyze data that is correlated across time.

Key Practical Concepts

- To fit a linear regression in R, where your data frame `data` contains response `y` and inputs `1`, `x2`, etc, you use `glm`.

  ```
  fit <- glm( y ~ x1 + x2, data=data )
  ```

  Other formula options are in Table 1.2.

- To fit a logistic regression, for when your `y` is binary, logical, or a two-level factor, you just add `family="binomial"`.

  ```
  fit <- glm( y ~ x1 + x2, data=data, family="binomial" )
  ```

- Calling `summary(fit)` returns a summary of the model and coefficient estimation, and `coef(fit)` just returns the regression coefficients.

- For prediction, with new data in `newdata` with the same variable names as the `data` used to fit your regression, use the `predict` function.

  ```
  predict(fit, newdata=newdata)
  ```

  This returns the linear equation predictions $\mathbf{x}'\hat{\beta}$. If you have fit logistic regression and you instead want predicted probabilities (after logit transformation), then you need to add the argument `type="response"`.

- The `glm` object includes the residual `deviance` and null model `null.deviance`. The R^2 is then available as

  ```
  1-fit$deviance/fit$null.deviance
  ```

- To deal with time dependence, you can

  1. Create factor variables like `month` to represent time fixed effects.

  2. Add numeric variables like `day` to allow for time trends.

  3. Create lagged variables y_{t-1} as inputs to allow for autoregressive errors.

- Panel data has time series for many units together in the same dataset. You typically want to include fixed effects both for each unit and each time period. You can use `tapply` to calculate different lags for each time series.

- Use the `laGP` package to fit a Gaussian process (GP) that models spatial dependence in data. A useful strategy is to use the residuals from a GP as data for a downstream analysis—these residuals will have no spatial dependence on each other so you can use standard regression methods for analysis.

2 UNCERTAINTY QUANTIFICATION

This chapter gives you the tools to quantify uncertainty in your model estimates and predictions.

⬤ **Section 2.1 Frequentist Uncertainty:** Understand the thought experiment of repeated sampling for frequentist uncertainty, and be able to characterize uncertainty through the sampling distribution. Use standard errors to test hypotheses and build confidence intervals.

■ **Section 2.2 False Discovery Rate Control:** Use the Benjamini-Hochberg algorithm to keep your false discovery rate below a pre-defined threshold when testing multiple hypotheses at the same time.

■ **Section 2.3 The Bootstrap:** Use with replacement sampling to mimic a sampling distribution, and use the resulting bootstrap samples to estimate properties of the sampling distribution.

◆ **Section 2.4 More on Bootstrap Sampling:** Apply bootstrap samples to estimate bias in your estimates, and build bias-corrected confidence intervals. Simulate data from a parametric bootstrap when the standard bootstrap fails.

◆ **Section 2.5 Bayesian Inference:** Understand Bayesian inference as a formalization of how beliefs update with data, and apply Bayes' Rule for basic inference tasks.

This book is about turning data into decisions. In complex settings, there will always be uncertainty about what the data is telling you. Your goal with statistical analysis is not to eliminate uncertainty, but rather to reduce it where you can and quantify it always. With complex real world data, rigorous uncertainty quantification (or UQ for short) is what differentiates a sophisticated and useful analysis from one that can be hopelessly naive.

A regression model learned from data, say by applying the `glm` function, gives you an estimate of the average value of the response. You get an estimate of $\mathbb{E}[y|\mathbf{x}] = f(\mathbf{x}'\beta)$. How good is this estimate? Surely if you got a new random sample of data, your estimates for β would change. You need to be able to quantify how much they might change. This chapter introduces the frameworks that we use to quantify uncertainty in terms of probabilities. The tools you learn will allow you to make decisions that are optimal in the face of estimation noise.

We will start by reviewing the basics of *frequentist* uncertainty, which is the sort of uncertainty that is taught in most introductory statistics classes. This framework is characterized by a thought experiment: "If I were able to see a new sample of data, generated by the same processes and scenarios as my current data, how could my estimates change?" If you're familiar with *p*-values and confidence intervals, then you are already familiar with common statistical procedures for dealing with frequentist uncertainty. We will also introduce a number of more advanced tools, including the *bootstrap*, false discovery rate control, and aspects of Bayesian decision theory, which will be useful for situations where the usual assumptions of basic statistics don't apply. A theme of this chapter is that you need to work with robust UQ methods: tools that work even if your modeling assumptions are not completely correct, or that work for high-dimensional models (i.e., when you need to make a large number of decisions from a single dataset).

In this chapter, we describe how to avoid confusing signal with noise and to balance risks when making decisions from data. In future chapters we will explore techniques such as regularization and cross-validation that automate some of the questions we address here (e.g., whether a specific regression coefficient should or should not be set equal to zero). However, you can never fully automate away the need to think about uncertainty. The tools of this chapter will be useful for you throughout your data analysis career.

● 2.1 Frequentist Uncertainty

The label "frequentist" refers to a way of understanding uncertainty that is based on the concept of repeatedly drawing samples of data and counting the frequency that events happen. Consider a medical trial to measure the effectiveness of, say, a new vaccine. A treatment sample of patients get the vaccine, and a control sample of patients are given a placebo. These trial participants are drawn from the full population of people who need to be vaccinated. After this trial, you will have an estimate of the vaccine effectiveness: the percent reduction in the rate of patient illness between the treatment and control groups. If you were to run another trial, and sample a new group of participants, you would get a new estimate of effectiveness. A frequentist analysis of uncertainty imagines running many trials and quantifying the distribution of effectiveness estimates you get across those many trials. If the estimates are nearly all "good enough," say above some threshold like 50% effectiveness, then you can conclude that the vaccine is effective. But if a large portion of the distribution of estimates is below this "good enough" threshold, then you can't conclude that the vaccine is effective.

Frequentist thought-experiments like this allow us to map from data samples to *probabilities* about the underlying mechanism generating these samples (e.g., true underlying vaccine effectiveness). We refer generically to this underlying but unknown reality as the *data generating process* (often abbreviated as DGP). The trick of frequentist statistics is to be able to quantify probabilities about the DGP without actually running many trials (because in most circumstances you do not have the ability to run many trials). You need to be able to talk about a distribution of estimates when you have only one data sample, hence only one estimate. Fortunately, there are some basic tools of statistical theory that can be used to quantify how estimates will change from sample to sample. These tools all rely on assumptions about the underlying DGP, so you need to understand both the tools and the assumptions in order to do a good job of uncertainty quantification.

Example 2.1 **Used Car Prices: Sampling Distribution of the Sample Mean** To illustrate these ideas, we'll work with data on the market for used cars in California. We collected listings of cars available for sale through the Autotrader.com website. Autotrader is an online platform that allows individuals and dealers to sell new and used cars. The majority of the sellers are dealers.

The data were collected from the website in early 2020 and they consist of a number of listings for Southern California. It is common for dealers to repost the same listing many times in order to draw attention to their most recent listings, so when creating this dataset we first removed duplicate listings. We will restrict our attention to used cars built since 1970 with mileage between 10,000 and 150,000 miles, and with price less than $100,000. This leaves us with a sample of 2088 cars that is relevant for someone wanting to understand the market for used cars in Southern California.

```
> Cars <- read.csv("SoCalCars.csv", stringsAsFactors=TRUE)
> Cars <- subset(Cars,  Cars$type != "New"  &
+     Cars$year >= 1970 & Cars$mileage >= 10000 &
+     Cars$mileage <= 150000 & Cars$price <= 100000 )[,-1]
> # the [,-1] removed variable "type" which is all "Used"
> dim(Cars)
[1] 2088   13
```

For each listing record, we observe several features of the car such as the make (e.g. BMW), the model and trim (e.g. Z4 sDrive28i), and whether it is a certified pre-owned sale. We also observe the current mileage, price, and year of manufacture. For many of the listings we observe a rating and the number of reviews which gave rise to that rating. Finally, the data include the dealer selling the car and the city in which the dealer is located.

```
> # print the first row of data
> Cars[1,]
   type certified       body make model       trim
1  Used          0 Convertible  BMW    Z4  sDrive28i
   mileage price year                   dealer
1    64899 16891 2012    Audi Fletcher Jones
        city  rating reviews        badge
  Costa Mesa     4.9     368    Good Deal
```

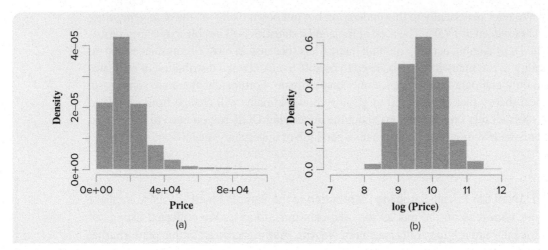

FIGURE 2.1   Histograms of the price and log price for used cars in Southern California on Autotrader. Notice that the distribution is roughly normal on the *log scale*.

Figure 2.1 shows the distribution of the price (measured in USD) observed in our sample. The bulk of cars are less than $40,000, with highest frequency between $10,000 and $20,000, but there is a tail of more expensive cars out toward our threshold of $100,000. As is often the case with price data, taking the logarithm produces a distribution that looks more normally distributed. The right panel of Figure 2.1 shows that the log price distribution is roughly symmetric around an average of log(price) $\approx$ 9.7. We'll work with the log distribution later. For now, we'll analyze the untransformed data.

Estimating an Expectation

Consider the expected price of a used car sold in Southern California (given our constraints: 10–150k miles, built since 1970, and price below $100k). You can estimate this mean, say $\mu = \mathbb{E}[\texttt{price}]$, with its *sample average*.

```
> mean(Cars$price)
[1] 19674.49
```

The average price of a used car in our sample is $\bar{x} = \$19,674.49$. Of course, we don't think that μ is *exactly* equal to $19,674.49$. The sample mean $\bar{x}$ is *unbiased* for the true population mean μ: if you draw many samples, then the expected value for $\bar{x}$ is equal to μ. However, in any single sample the sample mean will be lower or higher than μ due to random variation. Rather than being an exact match, the sample mean is a good guess and the true μ is hopefully *near* this value.

How near? Let's review some basic statistics. Suppose you have n *independent* random variables: $\{x_i\}_{i=1}^{n}$. In our current example, the assumption of independence says that the price of each car sold is determined by the buyer and seller without consideration of any other specific used car sale. The sample mean is then

$$\bar{x} = \frac{1}{n} \sum_{i=1}^{n} x_i \tag{2.1}$$

The variance of this statistic can be calculated as

$$\text{var}(\bar{x}) = \text{var}\left(\frac{1}{n}\sum_{i=1}^{n}x_i\right) = \frac{1}{n^2}\sum_{i=1}^{n}\text{var}(x_i) = \frac{\sigma^2}{n} \tag{2.2}$$

Here, $\sigma^2 = \text{var}(x_i) = \mathbb{E}\left[(x_i - \mu)^2\right]$ is the variance of a randomly drawn price. Thus the variance of the sample mean is the variance of the sample, divided by the number of observations in your sample.

Let's recall a few properties of the variance operator to make sure we understand how this expression was obtained. If a is a constant, then for any random variable x it is the case that $\text{var}(ax) = a^2\text{var}(x)$. Moreover, for a sum of *independent* random variables it is always the case that the variance of the sum is equal to the sum of the variances. Using these two properties yields Equation (2.2). Applying this in R gives the variance for $\bar{x}$ as 88,388.39.

```
> var(Cars$price)/nrow(Cars)
[1] 88388.39
```

Here, n is equal to the number of rows in the data frame. This implies an estimated standard deviation around $\sqrt{88388.39} \approx \$297.30$. The standard deviation tells you how much your sample mean would vary if you were to take multiple samples of the data and recalculate the sample mean each time.

Sampling Distribution

As we discussed above, the sample mean is an unbiased estimate of μ. We have also calculated the variance of realizations of the sample mean $\bar{x}$ around μ. To complete the picture we can use the ever-important *Central Limit Theorem* to describe the shape of the distribution of possible sample means. It states that the average of independent random variables becomes normally distributed if your sample size is large enough (greater than 60 is a rule of thumb). Given that $n = 2088$ (the number of used car listings in our sample) is certainly large enough, the end result is that the sample average price for used cars listed online in Southern California is estimated to have a normal distribution with a mean of \$19,674 and a standard deviation of \$297.30. Figure 2.2 plots the distribution, which you can write as $\bar{x} \sim \text{N}(19{,}674, 297^2)$.

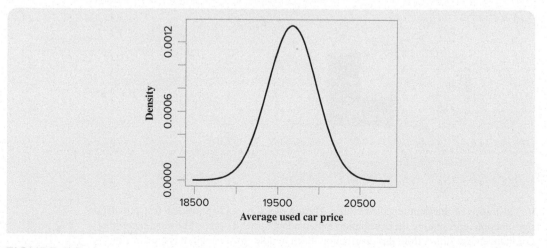

FIGURE 2.2   An estimated sampling distribution for $\bar{x}$. This picture tells you that if you got a new sample of 2088 cars, you would expect the new sample average price to be around \$19,674 ± 594 based on a range of plus or minus two standard errors.

What is this distribution? It is an estimate of the *sampling distribution*. It captures the uncertainty described by the thought experiment: "If I was able to get a *new* sample of observations from the same data generating process (DGP), what is the probability distribution of the new sample average?" See Figure 2.3 for an illustration. The sampling distribution is what you are working with when you quantify frequentist uncertainty. The standard deviation of this distribution is an especially important metric and it is given a special name: the *standard error*. It measures the amount of variation you should expect if you were to repeatedly draw new samples and calculate new sample averages.

Independence Assumption

The sampling distribution and standard error in our example are derived from statistical theory. We did not actually go out and collect many different samples of cars listed for sale in Southern California, but we believe that the distribution in Figure 2.2 is what would happen if we were to collect many samples. Given the assumptions we have made about how the data were generated, in particular the assumption of independence between observations, we are able to use mathematical results to derive this estimate of the sampling distribution.

Unfortunately, our main assumption is probably untrue here! Independence implies that the price of each car listed does not depend upon any other car listings. But what if the sellers look at similar cars that are currently listed before setting their price? That would introduce *dependence* between the observations. How would this change the sampling distribution? It is

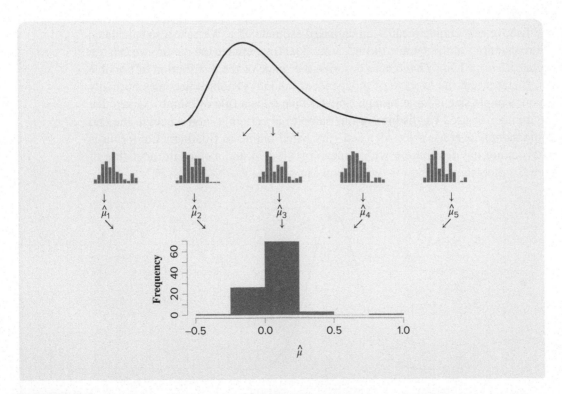

FIGURE 2.3   Illustration of the sampling distribution. The top plot shows a hypothetical true population probability density function representing the distribution for a random variable, say x. The *data generating process* consists of independent draws from this distribution. Each middle-row histogram is a sample of independent draws $\{x_1 \ldots x_n\}$ from the true data generating process (i.e., independent draws from the population distribution in the top plot). Each of these five middle histogram samples leads to a different estimated $\hat{\mu}_k = \bar{x}_k$, and the bottom histogram is the distribution of these estimates.

difficult to say precisely, but in general ignoring dependencies in the data leads you to *under-estimate* uncertainty. So long as the dependencies between observations are weak enough, this will not make a big difference in practice. That is why calculations like (2.2) are ubiquitous in practical data analysis. However, it is good to recognize the underlying assumptions and be aware that they may not be a perfect fit to your data.

2.1.1 Hypothesis Testing and Confidence Intervals

Many readers will be most familiar with frequentist statistics through its implementation as *hypothesis testing*. A hypothesis test is a tool for deciding between two qualitatively different realities. One option will be the null hypothesis, which should be considered your safe bet. It typically corresponds to setting a parameter equal to zero. The alternative hypothesis will be a set of possible values. When you "reject the null" in favor of the alternative, you will end up making decisions based upon the sample estimate for some parameter.

Shorthand notation for the null hypothesis is H_0 and the alternative can be denoted by H_1. A test of the null hypothesis $\beta = \beta_0$ versus the alternative $\beta \neq \beta_0$ can then be written as

$$H_0 : \beta = \beta_0$$
$$H_1 : \beta \neq \beta_0$$

where β_0 is the value of the null hypothesis. To choose between null and alternative hypotheses you make use of a *test statistic* that measures the distance (the difference measured in units of standard errors) between the null hypothesis and your parameter estimates:

$$z_\beta = \frac{\hat{\beta} - \beta_0}{\text{se}(\hat{\beta})} \tag{2.3}$$

where $\hat{\beta}$ denotes the sample estimate of β and $\text{se}(\hat{\beta})$ denotes its standard error (i.e., the standard deviation of the sampling distribution). This test statistic tells you how far away your sample estimate is from the null hypothesis value, *measured in standard errors.* Since the value for the null hypothesis is typically 0, your test statistic will often take the form $z_\beta = \hat{\beta}/\text{se}(\hat{\beta})$.

Example 2.2 Used Car Prices: Testing for a Difference in Car Price Means Our Autotrader data include the variable `certified`. This binary variable indicates whether or not the car is certified pre-owned, which means it has been inspected and refurbished by the original manufacturer. Certified cars often come with an extended warranty. We can ask whether certified used cars have a different average price than noncertified used cars. To formulate this as a hypothesis test, you specify the linear model

$$\text{price} = \alpha + \text{certified}\beta + \varepsilon \tag{2.4}$$

When `certified = 0`, the expected price is α, and when `certified = 1`, the expected price is $\alpha + \beta$. Our null hypothesis is $\beta = 0$, such that all cars have the same average price, against the alternative $\beta \neq 0$ such that certified car prices are distributed around a different average price.

Using glm to Test a Difference in Means

We can evaluate this model in R using the `glm` function.

```
> summary( glm(price ~ certified, data=Cars) )

  ...

Coefficients:
            Estimate Std. Error t value Pr(>|t|)
(Intercept)  18995.0      296.9   63.97   <2e-16 ***
certified    14331.0     1363.6   10.51   <2e-16 ***
---
Signif. codes:  0 '***' 0.001 '**' 0.01 '*' 0.05 '.' 0.1 ' ' 1
```

This should look familiar. All of the regressions you fit in Chapter 1 led to a similar table of coefficient estimates and statistics. For our simple linear model, we see that $\hat{\alpha} = \$18,995$ and $\hat{\beta} = \$14,331$ such that there is a roughly $14k average price premium for certified cars. The standard error on this price premium is $1363.60.

R automatically calculates test statistics for the hypothesis test of whether or not each coefficient is equal to zero. This is what is labeled as t value in the regression output. This test statistic is $z_\beta = \hat{\beta}/\text{se}(\hat{\beta}) = 10.51$ in our example, which says that $\hat{\beta} \approx \$14k$ is more than 10 standard errors away from zero. That means it is very far from zero! Notice that R uses the term *t*-value here because the test statistic has a Student's *t*-distribution. This distribution, (named after the pseudonym of the Guinness beer brewer W. S. Gosset who first characterized it), is similar to a Gaussian distribution but it has slightly fatter tails (higher probability of large absolute values). These fat tails account for the error you introduce when estimating σ with the sample variance as in Equation (2.2), and the fatness of the tails decreases with n. Even in small-sized samples, however, the t distribution becomes practically equivalent with a Gaussian distribution for most purposes and so you likely won't need to pay attention to this distinction. For example, with $n > 60$ you have more than 95% of the distribution within two standard deviations of the mean. Given the large sample sizes in this book, we will keep things simple by instead referring to such test statistics as z-values and treating them as having a Gaussian distribution.

The final column of the glm output, with the heading Pr(>|t|), translates the test statistic into a probability called a *p-value* that represents how rare your sample would be *if* the null hypothesis is true. This *p*-value gives you the probability of seeing a larger test statistic (larger absolute value) than what you've observed. In the output of glm, the *p*-value is $P(|Z| > |z_\beta|)$ where $Z \sim N(0,1)$ and z_β is the test statistic. The normality of Z comes from the Central Limit Theorem and large sample size, the standard deviation of 1 is because you've divided by the standard error, and the center at 0 is the null hypothesis assumption. As illustrated in Figure 2.4, the *p*-value measures the probability mass in the tails of the sampling distribution past your observed test statistic. In our example, the test statistic $z_\beta = 10.51$ is way out in the tails. The corresponding *p*-value is practically zero (2e-16 is $2/10^{16}$), such that you would conclude it is very likely that there is a nonzero price premium for certified pre-owned cars.

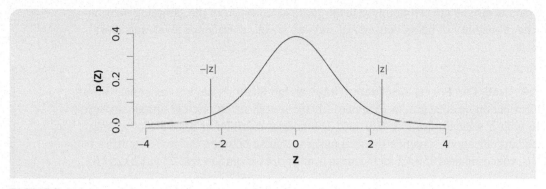

FIGURE 2.4 Illustration of a normal test statistic. For the two-sided alternative $\beta \neq 0$, the *p*-value is the area in the tails out past either |z| or −|z|.

Example 2.3 **Spam Filter: Tests for Coefficients in Logistic Regression** All estimators have sampling distributions. Although we have been working with a linear regression example, the same ideas apply for logistic regression. For example, if you revisit the spam filter example of Chapter 1 you can see that the output from `summary.glm` provides standard errors, test statistics, and *p*-values for the fitted logistic regression model.

```
> summary(glm(spam ~ ., data=spammy, family='binomial'))
...
Coefficients:
               Estimate Std.     Error   z value    Pr(>|z|)
(Intercept)    -1.9682470  0.1465703   -13.429     < 2e-16 ***
word_make      -0.5529572  0.2356753    -2.346     0.018963  *
word_address   -0.1338696  0.2217334    -0.604     0.546016
word_all       -0.4946420  0.1775333    -2.786     0.005333 **
...
```

Notice that the output uses the term `z value` rather than the `t value` that you get for a linear regression with `family="gaussian"`. This is because the theory behind Student's *t*-distributions applies only for linear regression, where you are estimating an error variance σ^2. For logistic regression, and any other nonlinear regression, you rely on the central limit theorem to derive the Gaussian sampling distribution.

An alternative to testing is to summarize the sampling distribution through a *confidence interval* (CI). This is a range of values that captures a specified percentage of the mass in your sampling distribution. Typically this range is centered on your sample estimate for the quantity of interest (although not always; we'll consider alternatives when we discuss the bootstrap). When built using standard errors, the confidence intervals take the form

$$\hat{\theta} \pm z \times \mathrm{se}(\hat{\theta})$$

where θ is the parameter you are estimating, z is the "critical value" from the sampling distribution such that the probability of being between $|z|$ and $-|z|$ is your confidence level, and $se(\hat{\theta})$ is the standard error.

Example 2.4 Used Car Prices: Confidence Interval for Mean Price For example, from the sampling distribution calculations in Example 2.1, the overall mean price of listed cars was $\hat{\mu} = \$19,674.96$ with a standard error of $\$297.30$. The normal distribution has 95% of its mass within 1.96 standard deviations (imagine the area under the curve between the two z-statistics in Figure 2.4). Thus, your estimated 95% CI for the mean listing price is from $\$19,092.25$ to $\$20,257.67$.

```
> 19674.49 + 1.96*297.3*c(-1,1)
[1] 19091.78 20257.20
```

This says there is a 95% probability that the true mean listing price is between these two values. Given the frequentist thought experiment underlying this probability, the implication is that, if you were able to sample more cars, 95% of the intervals that you construct using this recipe will include the true value of the population average price. Also, note that since 1.96 is close to 2, a common calculation is to round and simply look at a range of plus or minus two standard errors. We will often take this approach, and for example would say that a 95% CI for the price premium on certified cars is around $\$14,331 \pm 2 \times \$1363.6$, or roughly from $\$11,600$ to $\$17,100$.

The Pitfalls of Significance

Turning back to hypothesis tests and the `glm` output, notice the *** symbols next to the *p*-values. A common way to use *p*-values is to compare them to a significance threshold α, commonly $\alpha = 0.05$ or $\alpha = 0.01$, and conclude that the parameter of interest is significant (i.e., conclude $\beta \neq 0$) only if the *p*-value is smaller than this threshold. This procedure is designed to control your *false positive rate:* the proportion of parameters called significant that are in reality indistinguishable from zero. If you use a significance threshold of, say, 0.05, then it should be that you wrongly reject your safe null in no more than 5% of analyses where the null hypothesis is true. The symbols like *** or * that you see next to the *p*-value in the R output indicates whether each coefficient is significant at different thresholds (printed along the bottom of our code snippet).

This style of highlighting statistical significance is common in many research fields, including economics and medicine. Unfortunately, the convenience of quick significance checks has sometimes turned into an excessive preoccupation with *p*-values. In 2016, the American Statistical Association took the step of cautioning about the misuse of *p*-values (Wasserstein et al., 2016). The authors point out that the risk of false discovery for a given coefficient is a choice that we make. There is nothing special about common significance threshold values such as 0.05, and if you get enough data you will find that even tiny effects become significant. With big data, things can easily be statistically significant but practically insignificant.

Due to the way that science is actually practiced, there is also a worry that the true risk of a false positive is much higher than the stated *p*-values that are reported. This is due to the phenomenon of "*p*-hacking" where people look at many tests and report only those which have a *p*-value less than, say, 0.05. Reporting only the significant results and ignoring the rest will lead to a high proportion of false discoveries in the published literature. You can have *p*-hacking without individual scientist malfeasance if the journals accept only the 1 out of every 20 papers that managed to luck into a significant test statistic. For this reason, many major journals now require scientists to pre-register their experiments and they commit to publish the results regardless of the final *p*-values. But the issues remain, especially in media reporting of "interesting" scientific results.

2.1.2 Uncertainty about Regression Predictions

In regression analysis you are often using all of the elements of $\hat{\beta} = \left\{ \beta_0, \ldots, \beta_K \right\}$, for example in combination with some inputs **x** for prediction. For these applications, you need to understand the joint sampling distribution of the elements of $\hat{\beta}$: how they will all change together if you get new data and re-estimate the regression.

In a generalized linear model, such as logistic or linear regression, the expected response at inputs **x** will be

$$\mathbb{E}[y|\mathbf{x}] = f(\mathbf{x}'\boldsymbol{\beta}) \tag{2.5}$$

where $f(z) = z$ for linear regression and $f(z) = e^z/(1 + e^z)$ for logistic regression. Given a specific input vector **x** and a fitted coefficient vector $\hat{\beta}$, you can estimate the expected response as $\mathbb{E}[y|\mathbf{x}] \approx f(\mathbf{x}'\hat{\beta})$.

How accurate is this estimate of $\mathbb{E}[y|\mathbf{x}]$? It will have a standard error that depends upon the *joint* sampling distribution for all of the $\hat{\beta}_j$ coefficients. Also, it is important to recognize that we are conditioning on a specific value for the inputs **x** (i.e., the **x** here is treated as given and is not random). The standard error for $f(\mathbf{x}'\hat{\beta})$ will depend upon the value of **x** (for example, if $\mathbf{x} = \mathbf{0}$ then $\mathbf{x}'\hat{\beta} = 0$ with zero sampling variance). Recall the variance identity that for a constant c and random variable y, $\text{var}(cy) = c^2\text{var}(y)$. The formula for variance of a regression prediction uses the vector version of this same identity.

$$\text{var}(\mathbf{x}'\hat{\beta}) = \mathbf{x}'\text{var}(\hat{\beta})\mathbf{x} \tag{2.6}$$

Here, $\text{var}(\hat{\beta})$ is a *covariance matrix*. If β is a length-d vector, then $\text{var}(\hat{\beta})$ is a $d \times d$ matrix. The diagonal of this matrix is the sampling variance of each individual coefficient (the square of the standard error) and the off-diagonal elements are the covariances between the different $\hat{\beta}_j$ and $\hat{\beta}_k$.

For example, consider a simple linear regression $\mathbb{E}[y|x] = \alpha + \beta x$. Then

$$\text{var}([\hat{\alpha} \; \hat{\beta}]) = \begin{bmatrix} \text{var}(\hat{\alpha}) & \text{cov}(\hat{\alpha}, \hat{\beta}) \\ \text{cov}(\hat{\alpha}, \hat{\beta}) & \text{var}(\hat{\beta}) \end{bmatrix} \tag{2.7}$$

and

$$\text{var}(\hat{\alpha} + \hat{\beta}x) = [1 \; x]\text{var}\left([\hat{\alpha} \; \hat{\beta}]\right)[1 \; x] = \text{var}(\hat{\alpha}) + x^2\text{var}(\hat{\beta}) + 2x\,\text{cov}(\hat{\alpha}, \hat{\beta}) \tag{2.8}$$

which is your usual equation for the variance of a sum of two random variables that aren't necessarily independent. In multiple regression models the matrix algebra gets a bit more complicated but the intuition remains the same.

Using the `predict` Function

Fortunately, the `predict` function in R will do all this math for you. Recall how you used `predict` in Chapter 1: you pass it a fitted regression model and a data frame of new observations **x**, and it produces $\mathbf{x}'\hat{\beta}$ for each observation. Or if you set `response=TRUE`, it produces $f(\mathbf{x}'\hat{\beta})$ for nonlinear models like logistic regression. To get standard errors, you just add the argument `se=TRUE`.

Example 2.5 **Used Car Prices: Confidence Interval for** $\mathbb{E}[y|\mathbf{x}]$ Applying this to our car data, we can get the expected price and standard errors for a certified car.

```
> certreg <- glm(price ~ certified, data=Cars)
> ( certpred <- predict(certreg, data.frame(certified=1),
se.fit=TRUE) )
$fit
     1
33326

$se.fit
[1] 1330.901

$residual.scale
[1] 13242.3
```

The `se.fit` value is the standard error on the estimated expected log price. It is the square root of $\text{var}(\mathbf{x}'\hat{\boldsymbol{\beta}})$. Using our two standard error rule, a 95% CI for the price is then from \$30,664 to \$35,987.

```
> certpred$fit + c(-2,2)*certpred$se.fit
[1] 30664.2 35987.8
```

Prediction vs. Confidence Intervals

The confidence intervals we just calculated represent uncertainty about the predicted expectation—our estimate for $\mathbb{E}[y|\mathbf{x}]$ at a given $\mathbf{x}$. You can also calculate a prediction interval for a future realization of y given $\mathbf{x}$. This prediction interval will include uncertainty about the true $\mathbb{E}[y|\mathbf{x}]$ *and* random variation of y around $\mathbb{E}[y|\mathbf{x}]$.

Looking at the output from the `predict` function, notice that it also includes a value for the `residual.scale`. This term is specific to linear regression and it is the estimate of $\sigma = \text{sd}(\varepsilon)$, where ε is an error term that is independent from the input variables in $\mathbf{x}$. Recalling our linear model, $y = \mathbf{x}'\boldsymbol{\beta} + \varepsilon$, we can write the discrepancy between the estimated and true response as $\mathbf{x}'\boldsymbol{\beta} - \mathbf{x}'\hat{\boldsymbol{\beta}} + \varepsilon$. Since ε is independent by definition, we can calculate the variance of this "prediction error" as the sum of variances,

$$\text{var}(y - \mathbf{x}\hat{\boldsymbol{\beta}}) = \text{var}(\mathbf{x}\boldsymbol{\beta} - \mathbf{x}\hat{\boldsymbol{\beta}}) + \text{var}(\varepsilon) \tag{2.9}$$

The first term on the right-hand side is the square of `se.fit`, and the second term is the square of `residual.scale`.

Example 2.6 Used Car Prices: Prediction Interval for *y* given x For a certified car we can calculate the prediction standard error (the square root of the sampling variance) as follows.

```
> predvar <- certpred$se.fit^2 + certpred$residual.scale^2
> sqrt(predvar)
[1] 13309.01
```

This leads to a 95% prediction interval from $6,708 to $59,944.

```
> certpred$fit + c(-2,2)*sqrt(predvar)
[1]  6707.975 59944.025
```

Notice that this prediction interval for y given $\mathbf{x}$ is much wider than the earlier confidence interval for $\mathbb{E}[y|\mathbf{x}]$. This should make sense since there is more uncertainty about a single observation (the price of a single car) than for the average of many observations (the average price of cars with the same characteristics).

While prediction intervals of the sort derived here are common in statistic texts, we find that they are not heavily used in practice. They rely heavily on assumptions about the distribution of the independent error ε. As we will see in our next chapter, a better tool for quantifying predictive uncertainty is the routine of *cross-validation* where you use models trained on one dataset to predict responses on another dataset. The resulting record of "out of sample performance" gives you the most reliable measure of how a prediction model will perform in real world practice.

■ 2.2 False Discovery Rate Control

The problem of p-hacking is related to a deeper issue for hypothesis testing: the problem of multiplicity. The machinery of significance thresholds is built around controlling the error rate in a single test. But in most real world settings you will be considering many questions simultaneously. Suppose that you use a significance threshold (i.e., p-value cutoff) of α. If you repeat many tests, about $\alpha \times 100\%$ of the true-null signals (e.g., regression coefficients that correspond to nonexistent relationships) should erroneously pop up as significant. This leads to strange results when you are looking for rare true signals in a haystack of spurious noise.

Imagine a regression estimation problem where 5 out of 100 coefficients have a real relationship with the result. We would say here that the true coefficient set is *sparse:* most of the β_j are zero. In the best-case scenario, when you run hypothesis tests, you find all of these five true signals (i.e., there are no false negatives). Let's assume you do find all five and test the remaining 95 with $\alpha = 0.05$ significance cutoff. In that case, you expect that you will erroneously conclude significance for 5% of the useless 95 variables, leading you to include $4.75 \approx 5$ spurious regressors in the final model. The end result has you using a model with 10 inputs, but in truth 50% of them are junk that is unrelated to your response variable! Such false discoveries are worse than useless: they add noise to your model and reduce the quality of your predictions.

This situation, where a high proportion of discoveries are false positives, gets worse with decreasing signal-to-noise ratios. For example, if you have one true signal out of 1000 hypothesis tests with $\alpha = 0.05$ cutoff, then you will have around $0.05 \times 999 \approx 50$ false discoveries. Your false discovery proportion (FDP) will be around $50/51 \approx 98\%$. This might sound extreme, but having far fewer than 1/1000 true signals is the norm in applications like digital advertising, where a true signal is the rare existence of a website in browser history that indicates future purchasing intent, or in genetic analysis where you are looking for the correlations between DNA locations and high level information like disease prevalence.

False Discovery Rates

We need a framework for thinking about the aggregate risk due to false discovery across multiple tests. In general, you have

$$\text{FDP} = \frac{\text{\# false positives}}{\text{\# tests called significant}}$$

as a measure of the amount of spurious noise you have introduced into the model through false discovery. The false discovery proportion is a property of the fitted model. You can't know it: either you've made mistakes or you haven't. However, you can control its expectation, the *false discovery rate*.

$$\text{FDR} = \mathbb{E}[\text{FDP}] = \mathbb{E}\left[\frac{\text{\# false positives}}{\text{\# tests called significant}}\right]$$

This is the multiple-test analog of your probability of a false positive from the familiar single-test setting. You can see that the FDR for a single test is equal to the probability of falsely rejecting the null hypothesis.

FDR Control

The same as you can use a significance threshold (e.g., the common 0.05 cutoff) to control false positives in a single test, you can ensure that $\text{FDR} \leq q$ for any chosen q-cutoff between zero and one. This is achieved through the Benjamini-Hochberg (BH) procedure (Benjamini and Hochberg, 1995) which controls your FDR by defining a cutoff on a ranked list of p-values. See Algorithm 2.1 for the BH procedure. This algorithm introduces the notation of *order statistics* where $p_{(k)}$ denotes the kth ranked value in a set when ordering from smallest to largest.

Algorithm 2.1 **Benjamini-Hochberg (BH) FDR Control**

For N tests, with N p-values $\{p_1 \ldots p_N\}$:
- Order your N p-values from smallest to largest as $p_{(1)} \ldots p_{(N)}$.
- Set the p-value cutoff as $p^* = \max\left\{p_{(k)} : p_{(k)} \leq q\frac{k}{N}\right\}$.

The *rejection region* for an $\text{FDR} \leq q$ is the set of all p-values $\leq p^*$.

Example 2.7 Used Car Prices: Hedonic Regression and the BH Algorithm The BH procedure is easiest to understand visually. To illustrate, we'll look deeper at the Autotrader data. A common analysis task in business is to model the price of a product as the function of its characteristics. This is called a *hedonic* regression by economists. It is useful as a model that breaks the price of a good (e.g., a used car) into the prices of its constituent characteristics. Such models are useful to understand what features influence demand and to plan future pricing strategies. We will build a regression model for the logarithm of listed car price. As discussed in Chapter 1, changes to price are typically multiplicative as a function of input features. This means you want to fit your linear model on the log scale. In addition, we will use log mileage as an input such that you are estimating an *elasticity* between miles and price. We will also include the make, year, and body type of the car, whether it is certified pre-owned, and the city in which it is listed.

As a pre-processing step, you can set the default level for the `make`, `body`, and `city` factors to the most common levels in the dataset. These levels specify the regression intercept. In this case, the coefficients for other makes, body types, and listing cities will represent the expected price difference when compared to a Ford sedan listed in Costa Mesa.

```
> Cars$make <- relevel(Cars$make, "Ford")
> Cars$body <- relevel(Cars$body, "Sedan")
> Cars$city <- relevel(Cars$city, "Costa Mesa")
```

You can then fit the regression model using `glm`.

```
> carsreg <- glm(log(price) ~ log(mileage) + make +
+         year + certified + body + city, data=Cars)
> pvals <- summary(carsreg)$coef[-1,"Pr(>|t|)"]
> length(pvals)
[1] 116
```

After the model fit, we extracted the 116 p-values for each regression coefficient.

Plotting p-values

The p-values are plotted in Figure 2.5a. For comparison, Figure 2.5b plots 116 draws from a uniform distribution, defined as $p(U < u) = u$ for $u \in [0,1]$. This is the distribution for p-values corresponding to true null hypotheses. That is, if all of the true regression coefficients are zero (all of the null hypotheses are true), then the fitted p-values should be spread uniformly between zero and one. Comparing these two graphs, you will notice that the p-values from our regression are distributed with a big spike near zero. This spike is the evidence of signal in your data. It tells you that you have a bunch of coefficients that are many standard errors away from zero (since small p-values come from big test statistics).

The difference in shape between the two distributions in Figure 2.5 is key to how the BH algorithm works. It is measuring the amount of signal in your data, and the risk of false discovery, from how much the observed p-values differ from what you'd get from a uniform

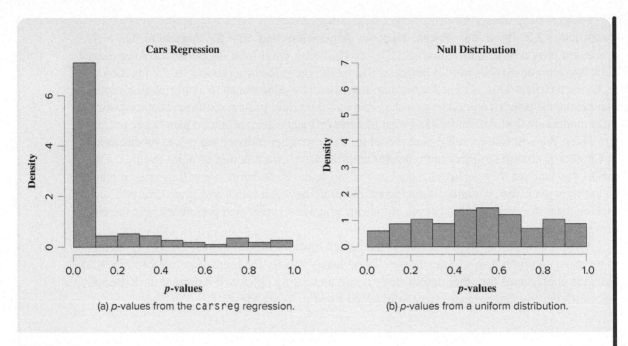

FIGURE 2.5 Histograms of *p*-values from (a) the Autotrader log price regression and (b) a null (i.e., uniform) distribution.

distribution. This distance is measured in the space of the *order statistics,* the ordered *p*-values from smallest to largest. Figure 2.6a shows the plotted order statistics for each of these distributions. Notice that, while the null *p*-values line up along 45 degrees, the observed *p*-values from our regression form a curve that lies largely along the horizontal axis.

The gap between observed *p*-value order statistics and the null 45 degree line gives a measure of how much non-null signal is in the data. The BH algorithm is equivalent to drawing a

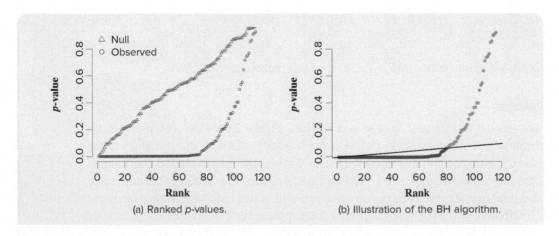

FIGURE 2.6 Panel (a) shows the ordered *p*-values from both the carsreg log price regression ("observed") and from a uniform distribution ("null"), plotted against their rank. Panel (b) shows the carsreg regression *p*-values along with the BH significance line for an FDR of 0.1. This line has slope 0.1/116. The *p*-values below this line are considered significant, and a procedure that defines significance in this way has an FDR of less than 10%.

line of slope q/N, where N is the number of p-values and q is your desired FDR. Everything below the last point where the p-values cross this line is called significant. The procedure is illustrated in Figure 2.6b for $q = 0.1$. All of the red points correspond to significant regression coefficients. Note that if $q = 1$, which leaves you with an FDR that is as high as 100%, the BH significance line has a slope of 1 and it will follow the null p-values along 45 degrees. As q decreases, the BH line gets closer to the horizontal axis and will cut off more of the curve of observed p-values.

A simple R function to implement the BH algorithm is given below. You can use it to find the p-value cutoff corresponding to a given FDR value. We've applied it here for $q = 0.1$ on our `carsreg` p-values.

```
> fdr_cut <- function(pvals, q){
+         pvals <- pvals[!is.na(pvals)]
+         N <- length(pvals)
+         k <- rank(pvals, ties.method="min")
+         max(pvals[ pvals<= (q*k/N) ])
+ }
> # 10% FDR
> cutoff10 <- fdr_cut(pvals,q=.1)
> print(cutoff10)
[1] 0.06544179
> print(sum(pvals<=cutoff10))
[1] 80
```

This yields a significance threshold of around 0.065 and 80 significant regression coefficients. With $q = 0.1$, we expect that no more than 8 of these are false discoveries.

....

BH and Independence between Tests

The validity of the BH algorithm relies on independence between tests. Unfortunately, independence between tests is usually an unrealistic assumption. For example, it doesn't hold in our regression example: if you remove a variable from the regression, the p-values for all other coefficients will change (try this). However, the BH algorithm will still give decent (if conservative) answers so long as the dependence between tests is not extremely high (Benjamini and Yekutieli, 2001). One of the main points of this chapter is that you make many decisions whenever you interact with data. Model uncertainty is not resolvable into single tests, and the problem of multiplicity will be ever-present. In later chapters, we will resort to alternative methods such as the lasso for variable selection. These methods don't rely on independence between coefficients, and they are much more robust and scalable than the BH algorithm. However, FDR is *the* way to summarize risk when you must perform many hypothesis tests and the BH algorithm is a useful tool to assess your FDR.

■ 2.3 The Bootstrap

The previous section used statistical theory to derive sampling distributions. In this section, we will introduce the bootstrap as an alternative algorithm that can simulate draws from the sampling distribution. Monte Carlo methods, such as the bootstrap, replace the mathematical derivation of probability distributions with sampling from close replicas of the distributions of interest. Instead of getting an equation for a specific probability distribution, say a Gaussian with some given mean and variance, you end up with a bunch of random draws from the distribution. Monte Carlo methods have become popular with increases in computing power, as they require weaker assumptions than traditional theoretical frameworks.

The bootstrap is a simple algorithm that can be used to estimate sampling distributions. The idea is that you resample from your existing data, and use these resamples to mimic draws from the sampling distribution. It is an extremely useful algorithm, with applications in machine learning (see "Random Forests" in Chapter 7) beyond its original purpose as a tool for uncertainty quantification. It is also useful for understanding the mechanics of frequentist statistics: by replacing theoretical derivations with a simple computational recipe, the analyst is able to build intuition about how sampling distributions are constructed. The bootstrap will be a key tool in your data science work.

Approximating the Sampling Distribution

Recall the definition of a sampling distribution: this is the distribution of statistics that you would get by drawing many repeated samples from the same DGP that generated your original dataset and computing the same statistic on each sample. For example, suppose that your statistic of interest is an estimated sample mean, $\hat{\mu}$. The sampling distribution for $\hat{\mu}$ is what you would get if you repeatedly drew new samples and calculated $\hat{\mu}$ for each new sample.

In practice, we observe only a single data sample. We saw in the previous section that you can make some assumptions about the DGP and derive a theoretical sampling distribution, such as the Gaussian in Figure 2.2. The bootstrap, which was first proposed and studied by Bradley Efron (e.g., see Efron 1982), instead uses *resampling with replacement* from your current sample to mimic the sampling distribution. It allows you to create a version of the sampling distribution on your computer, so that you can draw from it as needed to understand the properties of your analysis. The procedure is incredibly simple. As outlined in Algorithm 2.2, the bootstrap mimics the process in Figure 2.3 by replacing samples from the DGP with *resamples* from your observed data. See Figure 2.7 for the corresponding illustration of bootstrapping. The bootstrap replaces the population distribution with a histogram representing the *empirical data distribution*–the distribution that you get by placing probability $1/n$ on each observed data point.

Algorithm 2.2 **The Bootstrap**

Given data $\{x_i\}_{i=1}^n$, for $b = 1 \ldots B$:

- Resample n observations, *with replacement*: $\{x_i^b\}_{i=1}^n$.
- Calculate your estimate of the parameter of interest, say $\hat{\theta}_b$, using this resampled set of observations.

Then $\{\hat{\theta}_b\}_{b=1}^B$ is an approximation to the sampling distribution for $\hat{\theta}$.

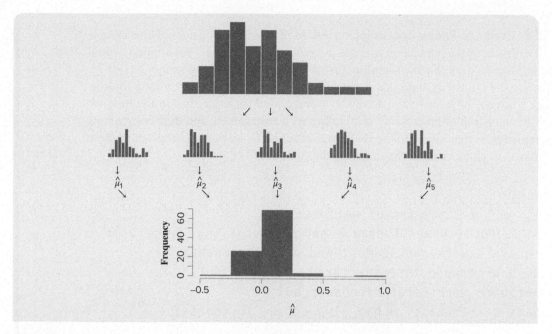

FIGURE 2.7   An illustration of the bootstrap approximation to a sampling distribution. Compare to Figure 2.3. Now, the top plot is a histogram of the original sample of data and each of the middle-row histograms is a with replacement resample from these observations. Each middle row resample implies a bootstrap draw of the sample mean, $\hat{\mu}_b = \bar{x}_b$, and the bottom histogram is the distribution of these estimates.

With Replacement Sampling

The "with replacement" is essential here. This means that each observation can be chosen more than once for inclusion in the resample. For example, if you are resampling with replacement five items from the set $\{1, 2, 3, 4, 5\}$, possible resamples would include $\{1, 1, 3, 3, 4\}$ and $\{2, 2, 2, 3, 5\}$. Using the common analogy of drawing balls out of a bucket, you are putting the ball back in the bucket after each draw. This type of resampling is necessary to introduce variability in your results: in this example, *without replacement* sampling would always yield the set $\{1, 2, 3, 4, 5\}$. To see this in R, you can mess around with the `sample` and `sample.int` functions.

```
# without replacement
> sort(sample(1:10, 10))
 [1]  1  2  3  4  5  6  7  8  9 10
 > sort(sample.int(10))
 [1]  1  2  3  4  5  6  7  8  9 10
# with replacement
> sort(sample(1:10, 10, replace=TRUE))
 [1]  2  3  5  7  7  7  7  8 10 10
> sort(sample.int(10, replace=TRUE))
 [1]  1  1  1  3  5  5  6 10 10 10
```

The `sample(set, size)` function draws `size` items from the given `set`. The `sample.int(n, size)` function is a shortcut for `sample(1:n, size)` and it defaults to `size=n` unless you specify otherwise. In either case, with `replace=TRUE` you can get a different resample each time.

Example 2.8 Used Car Prices: Bootstrapping Prices Earlier, we considered the sample mean ($\bar{x}$) as an estimate of the population average price of used cars, say μ. We applied central limit theorem arguments to derive the sampling distribution as a Gaussian, $\bar{x} = \hat{\mu} \sim N(19{,}674, 297^2)$. We can use the bootstrap to do this instead. Below, we use a simple for loop to draw 1000 bootstrap estimates of $\hat{\mu}$, our estimate of the average used car price. Inside the loop we construct each bth bootstrap estimate using resampling with replacement and then compute its mean. This sampled $\hat{\mu}_b$ is then stored in the vector muhats. Lastly, we plot a histogram of these 1000 sample means as an estimate of the sampling distribution.

```
> set.seed(1)
> muhats <- c() # empty set of estimates
> for(b in 1:1000){ # we'll draw B estimates
+     # resample with replacement and estimate mu.hat
+     samp_b <- sample.int(nrow(Cars), replace=TRUE)
+     muhat_b <- mean(Cars$price[samp_b])
+     muhats <- c(muhats, muhat_b) # append to the set
+ }
> hist(muhats, main="", xlab="average used car price", freq=FALSE)
```

* Note that, even with the same seed, you may get different results for different operating systems and versions of R. You should at least be able to replicate your own results by running the same code twice on your own machine.

The resulting distribution is shown as the histogram in Figure 2.8. The Gaussian sampling distribution that we derived earlier, using the central limit theorem, is also shown. They match up pretty well! This makes sense: you have a fairly large sample here ($n = 2088$) and are targeting a simple statistic ($\bar{x}$), so the assumptions of the CLT hold true and it gives a good approximation to reality. The advantage of the bootstrap is that it will work in many settings where this theory is unavailable or incorrect. The disadvantage of the bootstrap is that it often takes a lot longer to run, especially if you want to use a large number of bootstrap resamples (B) to make sure that your bootstrap estimate of the sampling distribution is precise (see below for the discussion on practical considerations when using the bootstrap).

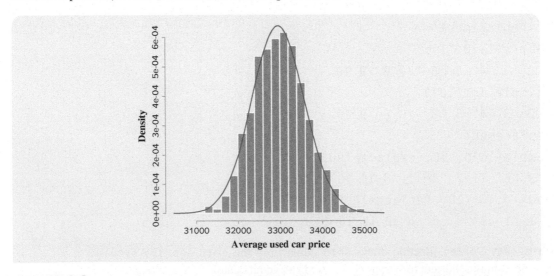

FIGURE 2.8   The bootstrapped sampling distribution (histogram) for the average price of used cars. The theoretical sampling distribution from Figure 2.2 is overlaid.

Your bootstrap estimates can be used for all of the same purposes as a theoretical sampling distribution. For example, a bootstrapped estimate of the standard error is simply the standard deviation of your sample of bootstrap estimates.

```
> sd(muhats)
[1] 291.5442
> sd(Cars$price)/sqrt(nrow(Cars))
[1] 297.3019
```

The estimated standard error is around 292. This is close to the theoretical standard error for the mean, calculated as $sd(x)/\sqrt{n} \approx 297$. Again, it makes sense that these are close because we have a large sample.

Random Seeds

In the beginning of the code to bootstrap the average car price, notice that we have the command `set.seed(1)`. This sets the "seed" for R's internal pseudorandom number generator: the algorithm that simulates random variables and samples on your computer. Since the bootstrap is based on *random* sampling, you will get different results every time you run it. If you want your answers to be *replicable,* such that someone can run the code and get the exact same results, then you need to set the seed using `set.seed` (you can give it any number as a seed). This then means that you will get the same answers for the sequence of random numbers generated afterwards. This might be necessary if, for example, you need to replicate the exact sample to test the impact of code changes. For example, see below for how setting the seed gives us a fixed set of five draws from the uniform distribution.

```
> set.seed(1867)
> runif(5)
[1] 0.01675051 0.43847434 0.32488533 0.44866848 0.59809451
> set.seed(1867)
> runif(5)
[1] 0.01675051 0.43847434 0.32488533 0.44866848 0.59809451
```

[*] Note that, even with the same seed, you may get different results for different operating systems and versions of R. You should at least be able to replicate your own results by running the same code twice on your own machine.

We won't often bother with setting a seed in this text, so if you run code that has random sampling in any part of the algorithm, you might get a slightly different answer.

Practical Considerations when Bootstrapping

How close is the bootstrap-estimated sampling distribution to the truth? In general, dimension matters: you can bootstrap a low-dimensional statistic (like $\hat{\mu} = \bar{x}$) but should be wary of bootstrapping high dimensional statistics (such as the joint distribution of a large set of regression coefficients). The bootstrap is not practically useful for approximating high dimensional sampling distributions because you need an enormous observed sample to get enough information to summarize all of the covariances between variables. For example, in our `carsreg` above we have 116 regression coefficients. The joint covariance matrix for these coefficients includes 116 variance terms and 6670 unique covariance terms (since $(116^2 - 116)/2 = 6670$). Our sample of 2088 cars is large enough for us to bootstrap low-dimensional statistics like $\bar{x}$, and for the CLT to give good theoretical sampling distributions on low-dimensional statistics, but it is not large enough to give a reliable estimate of a 116 dimensional joint distribution. To estimate large joint distributions, you will typically need to make some strong modeling assumptions. For example, you may make use of the sort of factor models that we introduce in Chapter 8.

Fortunately, even if your model is high dimensional you can still bootstrap low-dimensional functionals of that distribution. For example, in `carsreg` with 116 inputs you are perfectly safe using the bootstrap to approximate the sampling distribution for a few coefficients, or for a conditional expectation $f(\mathbf{x}'\hat{\beta}) \approx \mathbb{E}[y|\mathbf{x}]$. Most of your important decisions will occur in a low-dimensional space: you want to know the distribution for a single crucial $\hat{\beta}_j$ or you want to know the distribution of a projection like $\mathbf{x}'\hat{\beta}$. As a very rough rule of thumb, if you have at least 100 observations for each dimension of your statistic of interest then you should feel comfortable using the bootstrap.

The other variable to keep track of is the size of your sample of bootstrap estimates, B. We used 1000 in our first example here. This is enough to get within about $10 dollars of the true standard error. To see this, remove the `set.seed` line and run the bootstrap code a few times to observe the variability in `sd(muhats)`. This variability is your *Monte Carlo* variation. You can make it smaller by increasing the size of the sample of bootstrap estimates. When choosing this sample size, you are trading between computation time and precision. The precision you need will be application dependent. And the computation time can be reduced if you use efficient techniques like parallel computing (using multiple processors on your computer at the same time). If you are unsure whether you have enough bootstrap estimates, it is worth running the bootstrap a few times and seeing if you are comfortable with the amount of variability in results.

2.3.1 Robust Uncertainty Quantification

Bootstrapping can be applied for all of the frequentist analysis that we covered in the previous section. We have already seen how to derive standard errors: just bootstrap the statistic of interest, and the standard deviation of the resulting sample of bootstrap estimates is your standard error. You can use this standard error to calculate test statistics and p-values. For example, with our bootstrap standard error of 292 for the mean car price, you can calculate the test statistic for a test of whether the expected car price is significantly different from $20,000.

```
> (z <- (mean(Cars$price) - 20000)/292)
[1] -1.114774
> 2*pnorm(-abs(z))
[1] 0.2649475
```

The sample mean is just a bit over one standard error away from $20,000, for a p-value of 0.26. This is not enough evidence to reject the null hypothesis. If you like round numbers, then you can be comfortable saying that the average used car listing price in Southern California is around $20,000.

The advantage of using a bootstrap to calculate your standard errors, and the other derived test statistics, is that it is *robust* to some common model assumptions being incorrect. The bootstrap doesn't care if the model you are fitting doesn't represent the true DGP. So long as the observations that you are bootstrapping are independent, the bootstrap will provide a sampling distribution for your estimator that is derived from nothing other than your data. This is why the bootstrap of Algorithm 2.2 is often referred to as the *nonparametric* bootstrap. It doesn't assume a parametric model for how the data were generated. For this reason we say that the bootstrap provides robust standard errors: it estimates the sampling distribution for your estimator of interest, even if that estimator is derived from an incorrect model.

Example 2.9 **Used Car Prices: Bootstrap UQ for Price-Mileage Elasticity** To demonstrate how this robustness works, we will return to the `carsreg` regression and investigate the mileage elasticity of price: the coefficient β on log mileage in our model to predict log price. Recall from Chapter 1 that, as the coefficient in a log-log regression, this β is interpretable as the percentage change in expected price per 1% increase in mileage. From the fitted regression, we have an estimated $\hat{\beta} = -0.323$ such that we expect a 32.3% price drop for a doubling of mileage (i.e., per 100% increase in mileage).

```
> (betaStats <- summary(carsreg)$coef["log(mileage)",])
  Estimate Std.  Error     t value   Pr(>|t|)
 -0.322702    0.015715 -20.534860   4.50e-85
```

The standard error on this value is 0.016, so $\hat{\beta}$ is more than 20 standard errors away from zero and the *p*-value is vanishingly small.

We can re-evaluate this analysis using the bootstrap. Instead of writing our own `for` loop each time we want to bootstrap, we can make use of the `boot` package that wraps up the code from our loop above and provides a number of options to increase computational efficiency. This package was written to accompany the book by Davison and Hinkley (1997), which is a useful reference for extended reading on bootstrapping methodologies.

To use `boot`, you need to define a function that takes a data frame as the first input, takes an index of observations as the second input, and produces your statistic of interest as output. The function below runs `glm` using the same formula as `carsreg` and extracts the coefficient on `log(mileage)`.

```
> getBeta <- function(data, obs){
+     fit <- glm(log(price) ~ log(mileage) + make + year
+                 + certified + body + city, data=data[obs,])
+     return(fit$coef["log(mileage)"])
+ }
> getBeta(Cars, 1:nrow(Cars))
log(mileage)
  -0.3227021
```

Running on the Cars dataset returns the original estimate $\hat{\beta} = -0.323$.

To bootstrap this coefficient estimate, you pass to the boot function the full Cars data frame, your function to extract the coefficient estimate, and the desired size of the sample of bootstrap estimates. We will also take advantage of boot's capacity for parallel computing, asking it to use snow for socket-style parallelization across all of the processor cores available on your computer (see the box on parallel computing).

```
> library(parallel)
> library(boot)
> ( betaBoot <- boot(Cars, getBeta, 2000,
+                    parallel="snow", ncpus=detectCores()) )
ORDINARY NONPARAMETRIC BOOTSTRAP
...
Bootstrap Statistics :
      original          bias    std. error
t1* -0.3227021  0.005609681    0.03407489
```

The function outputs a boot-class object that contains the results of your bootstrap. Remember that these results will change when you run this bootstrap due to Monte Carlo variation. Component t is the vector of bootstrap realizations for your statistic and component t0 is the original sample estimate, $\hat{\beta}$. In the summary statistics printed above, original is the original sample $\hat{\beta}$ estimate.

```
> (bhat <- betaStats["Estimate"])
  Estimate
-0.3227021
> betaBoot$t0
log(mileage)
  -0.3227021
```

The std. error is the standard deviation of your sample of bootstrap estimates. This is your bootstrap estimate of the standard error for $\hat{\beta}$.

```
> sd(betaBoot$t)
[1] 0.03407489
```

The bias is the mean of your sample of bootstrap estimates minus $\hat{\beta}$.

```
> mean(betaBoot$t) - bhat
   Estimate
0.005609681
```

Estimation Bias

Recall that statistical bias is the difference between the expectation of your estimator and the expectation of the target that you are trying to estimate. An important function of the bootstrap, beyond estimating the sampling variance, is that the difference between the mean of your sample of bootstrap estimates and the original sample estimate gives you an estimate of the bias in your estimator. This will be useful when you apply the bootstrap to calculate confidence intervals. In the example here, the estimated bias of 0.0056 is small relative to the estimated elasticity −0.323. It is small because ordinary least squares regression is theoretically unbiased for the true linear coefficients–in this case, for the linear effect of changes in `log(mileage)` on the expected `log(price)`. The estimated bias here is Monte Carlo noise: if you run the same bootstrap multiple times it will just bounce around zero.

Parallel Computing

The idea behind parallel computing is to break algorithms up into components that can be run simultaneously on distinct computer processing units, or "cores." Scientific supercomputers have long used parallelism for massive speed, but since the early 2000s it has become standard to have many processor cores on consumer machines. Even small mobile devices, like a phone, will have two or more cores.

One of the advantages of R is that it has a robust and accessible framework for parallelization. The `parallel` library wraps together the basic tools, and the `boot` package uses these tools to enable parallel bootstrapping. You can call `detectCores()` to see how many independent processors are available on your computer (you might have more or less than the machine here).

```
> library(parallel)
> detectCores()
[1] 8
```

There are a couple of different methods for parallelization. Socket methods launch a new R environment on each core, whereas forking methods copy the current R environment to each processor. Forking tends to be faster and easier to work with. For example, with socket parallelization any object needed for execution must be copied to each core, usually as an argument to the function being executed in parallel. Socket parallelization also makes it complicated to set a seed for the random number generator in each parallel process. However, chances are that forking will not work if you are using a Windows machine. In the `parallel` library, you can choose between `snow` for socket and `multicore` for forking. In this book we will use `snow` because it works on Windows.

To see the benefits of parallelization, use the `system.time` function. This reports the elapsed time required for whatever process you pass it (it also reports `user` and `system` times, which are obscure statistics tracked by your OS).

```
> system.time( boot(Cars, getBeta, 2000) )
   user   system elapsed
113.772    5.515 119.660
> system.time( boot(Cars, getBeta, 2000,
+                     parallel="multicore", ncpus=8) )
   user   system elapsed
153.587    8.692  25.596
> system.time( boot(Cars, getBeta, 2000,
+                     parallel="snow", ncpus=8) )
   user   system elapsed
  0.724    0.177  29.565
```

Here, parallelization cuts the wait for 2000 bootstrap draws from two minutes to under 30 seconds (using either `snow` or `multicore`). The speedup is not 8× because of the overhead of launching and stopping the parallel processes.

The parallel computing routines involve copying data and communication between the different processors on your computer. When you are using `parallel=snow`, you need to pass any data or functions that you need as arguments to the function that you are bootstrapping (e.g., see how we pass `xpred` to the `getPrice` function in our block bootstrap later in this section). Moreover, if your computer operating system is not set up correctly for parallel computing (or not set up in a way expected by R) then you will get errors that are frustrating to debug. If you have trouble running `boot` using parallelization, then feel free to run your bootstraps without the `parallel` argument. They will take a bit longer to run but they will work fine.

Comparison between Bootstrap and Theoretical Standard Errors

Returning to the topic of robustness, notice that the bootstrap standard error is more than double the CLT-derived standard error from `glm`.

```
> sd(betaBoot$t)
[1] 0.03407489
> betaStats["Std. Error"]
Std. Error
0.01571484
```

There are a couple of reasons for this. First, the two standard errors are actually measuring different sampling distributions corresponding to different frequentist thought experiments. Let's think about the data at hand. For each observation we have response y (here, `log(price)`) and a vector **x** of input features (such as `log(mileage)`, `certified`, etc). For the theoretical standard errors provided by `glm`, the thought experiment is to sample new y values while keeping your current $\mathbf{x}$ values fixed. This is called a *fixed design* sampling model: only the output is treated as random. In the example here, it implies that for each new sample you have 2088 cars with the exact same characteristics as your current sample (same make, model, year, mileage, listing city, etc). You sample a new log price for each car from the conditional distribution $p(y|\mathbf{x})$.

The bootstrap instead corresponds to a *random design* sampling model where both the inputs and outputs are randomly drawn from their joint distribution $p(\mathbf{x}, y)$. That is, you are imagining a new sample of cars and their prices drawn from the population of cars in Southern California. It is much easier to derive theoretical standard errors for a fixed design, since you don't need to characterize the joint distribution for both inputs and outputs. That is why `glm`, and every other statistical regression software, gives standard errors under a fixed design model. However, unless you are in a lab setting where you get to set the inputs deterministically, the random design is a better representation of reality. If we want to draw a new sample of car prices from Autotrader.com it will involve a new set of cars.

The difference between fixed and random design sampling can have an impact on your standard errors, especially when the inputs $\mathbf{x}$ are high dimensional. However, it is not the main source of discrepancy in this `carsreg` example. Instead, the main problem with the standard errors from `glm` here is that they are sensitive to a false assumption: that the idiosyncratic errors (the ε_i for each observation) are *identically* distributed with a constant error variance, σ^2. This is often referred to as the assumption of *homoskedasticity,* as opposed to *heteroskedacticity* or nonconstant error variance. In reality, the error variance is likely larger for, say, older cars than for newer cars. Or we can imagine that the variance is smaller with mainstream brands than for luxury brands. You need a methodology for calculating standard errors that is *robust* to this potential model misspecification: one that gives accurate UQ even if you have heteroskedastic errors.

The assumption of constant error variance should not be surprising: it is front and center in our standard linear model specification, $y_i \sim N(\mathbf{x}_i'\boldsymbol{\beta}, \sigma^2)$ where σ is the same for all observations. However, ordinary least squares does a fine job of estimating coefficients even when this assumption is not true. So it is totally reasonable to use linear regression even if you suspect there is a nonconstant error variance. The problem is that if you do this then you can't rely on the the usual standard errors from `glm`. This is a common problem in linear regression analysis, and there are a number of approaches to building heteroskedactic-robust standard errors. They all involve some method of estimating a separate error variance for each observation, say σ_i^2 for ε_i. The most basic way to do this is to use the square of the fitted residuals to estimate the error variance: $\hat{\sigma}_i^2 = e_i^2$ where $e_i = y_i - \mathbf{x}_i'\hat{\boldsymbol{\beta}}$ are your fitted regression residuals. These $\hat{\sigma}_i^2$ are then passed into the formulas for estimating $\mathrm{var}(\hat{\boldsymbol{\beta}})$ instead of the usual constant $\hat{\sigma}^2 = \Sigma e_i^2/(n - df)$.

Heteroskedactic-Robust Standard Errors

To get heteroskedactic-robust standard errors in R, you can use the `sandwich` package (so named because formulas for $\mathrm{var}(\hat{\boldsymbol{\beta}})$ have the error variances multiplied on either side by—sandwiched between—functions of the design matrix $\mathbf{X}$). You can recalculate $\mathrm{var}(\hat{\boldsymbol{\beta}})$ using the `vcovHC` function, where the HC stands for "heteroskedastic consistent." In the code below, we use the `HC0` method of calculating HC standard errors, which implements the basic $\hat{\sigma}_i^2 = e_i^2$ rule described above. Note that it is fine to omit this `HC0` argument in which case a slightly different estimator is used but the basic idea is the same; type `vcovHC` for details.

```
> library(sandwich)
> VHC = vcovHC(carsreg, "HC0")
> dim(VHC)
[1] 117 117
```

The result is a 117 by 117 dimensional covariance matrix for the 116 coefficients and the intercept. The `coeftest` function from the `lmtest` package is useful to summarize the results into a familar format.

```
> library(lmtest)
> hcstats <- coeftest(carsreg, vcov = VHC)
> round(hcstats["log(mileage)",], 5)
   Estimate Std.    Error    z value    Pr(>|z|)
       -0.32270 0.03314   -9.73686    0.00000
```

The HC standard error, 0.033, is very close to the bootstrap standard error of 0.034. It seems that the (surely incorrect) assumption of homoscedastic errors explains the bulk of the attenuation in our original `glm` standard error of 0.016. See Figure 2.9 for the three different sampling distributions. As we've already discussed, the bootstrap doesn't make any parametric modeling assumptions and thus provides standard errors that are robust to nonconstant variance. Tools like `sandwich`'s `vcovHC` are useful if you have a specific known source of mis-specification and wish to correct your theoretical standard errors. If you get in the habit of using the bootstrap then your standard errors will be robust to many sources of mis-specification without you having to worry about the details. The only drawback is that the bootstrap takes more computation time. If your model is slow to fit and you can't wait for the bootstrap, then using `vcovHC` as we did here is a good fast option.

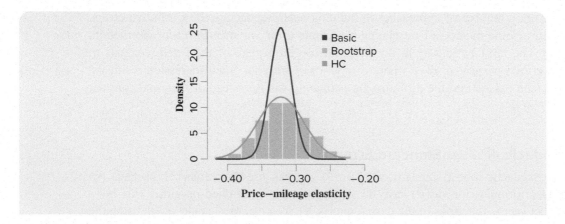

FIGURE 2.9 Estimated sampling distributions for the `log(mileage)` coefficient in the regression for `log(price)`. The histogram is the bootstrap sampling distribution and the lines are Gaussian densities centered at $\hat{\beta}$ and using different standard error calculations. "Basic" denotes the usual standard errors out of `glm` and HC denotes the heteroskedastic robust standard errors from `vcovHC`.

Dependence and the Block Bootstrap

The bootstrap makes no parametric modeling assumptions, but it does have an Achilles' heel: it relies on an assumption of independence between observations. There are plenty of situations where this might be a suspect assumption. Fortunately, there is an easy fix: instead of resampling individual observations, you resample *blocks* of observations that are potentially correlated with each other.

In regression analyses, you can reduce or eliminate dependence between observations by including the appropriate group-level factors as inputs. For example, perhaps car listing prices in the same city are correlated because that city's customers tend to be more or less price sensitive than elsewhere. By conditioning on the city factors as inputs to carsreg—creating so-called *fixed effects* for cities, such that each has a different mean price, we remove this dependence from the random errors. However, you may not want to include fixed effects for every group in your data. For example, we have 258 different car dealers in our Autotrader dataset. We can think of many reasons why listings for cars from the same dealer may not be independent of each other. Perhaps the dealer has a specific pricing strategy, or she looks at pricing cars relative to each other. But including 258 fixed effects would more than triple the number of degrees of freedom in our regression model, and with only a few cars from each dealer it is unlikely that we will do a good job estimating these fixed effects. Instead, we can fit the model without the dealer effects and then account for the potential dependencies when calculating the standard errors.

Example 2.10 **Used Car Prices: Dealer Dependence in Regression Errors** To build a block bootstrap, you first need to break your data up into blocks. The split command below breaks the Cars data frame into a list of data frames, one for each dealer.

```
> CarsByDealer <- split(Cars, Cars$dealer)
> length(CarsByDealer)
[1] 258
```

You then write a new function to run glm and extract the coefficient, one that allows you to specify which blocks are included in the training data.

```
> getBetaBlock <- function(data, ids){
+     data <- do.call("rbind",data[ids])
+     fit <- glm(log(price) ~ log(mileage) + make +
+                     year + certified + body + city, data=data)
+     return(fit$coef["log(mileage)"])
+ }
> getBetaBlock(CarsByDealer, 1:length(CarsByDealer))
log(mileage)
  -0.3227021
```

This is mostly the same as our earlier `getBeta` function, but it takes as inputs a list of data frames and a vector of block IDs. It also adds a code line to combine the selected blocks into a single data frame (see `?do.call`; this is a useful tool for applying an action to all elements of a list).

You then run the bootstrap using `boot`. Since `CarsByDealer` is now a list of 258 data frames, the function will sample with replacement on these dealer blocks rather than on the full set of 2088 observations.

```
> ( betaBootB <- boot(CarsByDealer, getBetaBlock, 2000,
+                      parallel="snow", ncpus=detectCores()) )
...
        original        bias      std. error
t1* -0.3227021  0.005769183    0.03587098
```

The resulting standard error of 0.036 is close to our earlier bootstrap estimate of 0.034, and to the standard error from the HC procedure. This suggests that most of the difference in error variances across cars is explained by allowing different error variances for each dealer. After you allow for a different error variance for each dealer, the correlation between prices from the same dealer does not appear to have a large impact on the results (it adds about 0.002 to the standard error relative to the original bootstrap results).

Clustered Standard Errors

There are also theoretical tools for dealing with dependence between observations. The `sandwich` package has the `vcovCL` function, which works similarly to the HC procedure but now allows for a different error variance and dependence within each designated block, or cluster, of observations. The results of this procedure are often referred to as "clustered standard errors." We will use the dealer factor to define our clusters, and again apply `coeftest` to summarize the results.

```
> Vblock <- vcovCL(carsreg, cluster=Cars$dealer)
> clstats <- coeftest(carsreg, vcov = Vblock)
> round(clstats["log(mileage)",], 5)
  Estimate Std. Error    z value    Pr(>|z|)
  -0.32270     0.03519   -9.16925     0.00000
```

The resulting standard error of 0.035 is less than 0.001 away from what we found with the block bootstrap. This 0.001 discrepancy includes Monte Carlo error (run the block bootstrap again too see the answer change a bit). Using `vcovCL` to estimate clustered standard errors is a good option if model fit is expensive and you don't want to wait for a bootstrap to run. In general, whether you use a block bootstrap or theoretical clustered standard errors, allowing for dependence between known groupings is usually a worthwhile step.

2.3.2 Bootstrap Confidence Intervals

Your most common representation of uncertainty will likely be through confidence intervals. In business applications, it is natural to use a range of parameter values as the input to decision making. Confidence intervals give you a range of values that capture the "true" value of your parameter of interest with some specified probability (e.g., 95%). The bootstrap gives you a few different ways to calculate confidence intervals, and this flexibility will help you to build more representative UQ and make better decisions.

Recall our standard approach to calculating confidence intervals. You get a standard error for your parameter of interest, say $se(\hat{\beta})$, and then you create an interval of standard errors around your estimate of that parameter, say $\hat{\beta} \pm 1.96se(\hat{\beta})$ for a 95% CI. The 1.96 here (see example 2.4) is due to the central limit theorem implying that your sampling distribution should be a Gaussian and the fact that 5% of the mass of a Gaussian distribution is more than 1.96 standard deviations from the mean (-1.96 is the 2.5th percentile of the standard normal distribution and 1.96 is the 97.5th percentile). You can apply this same approach after bootstrapping simply by plugging in the bootstrapped standard error. For example, we get an interval of $[-0.39, -0.25]$ for the price-mileage elasticity in our Autotrader regression.

```
> bhat + c(-1,1)*1.96*sd(betaBootB$t)
[1] -0.3930092 -0.2523950
```

Note that we are using the results of the block bootstrap here since it controls for potential dependence within dealer listings.

However, given a sample of bootstrap estimates you no longer need to assume that the sampling distribution is Gaussian. Instead, you have in your sample of bootstrap estimates a full estimate of the sampling distribution. It makes little sense to compress this distribution into a standard error and then plug it into a procedure built around the Gaussian distribution.

Percentile Bootstrap Confidence Intervals

A simple way to get a confidence interval after bootstrapping is to calculate the bounds directly on your sample of bootstrap estimates. This is called a *percentile* bootstrap confidence interval, as it is is based on the percentiles of the sample of bootstrap estimates rather than some theoretical distribution, like the Gaussian. For example, you can use the `quantile` function to get the 2.5th and 97.5th percentiles of the sampling distribution for the price-mileage elasticity.

```
> quantile(betaBootB$t,c(0.025, 0.975))
     2.5%       97.5%
-0.3898071 -0.2456626
```

And that's it! The percentile interval of $[-0.39, -0.25]$ is actually a bit narrower than the one found using ± 1.96 standard errors, but it is very close. You could also have calculated a noncentered 95% interval, say from the 1st to 96th percentiles, but the convention is to leave the same amount of probability in both upper and lower tails.

◆ 2.4 More on Bootstrap Sampling

This section considers two more advanced topics: the use of the bootstrap for estimating (and correcting) bias in our estimators, and the parametric bootstrap as an option for situations where the standard bootstrap doesn't work.

2.4.1 Biased Estimators

Recall our earlier discussion of bias: it is the difference between the expected value of your estimator and your target of interest. Ideally, you work with *unbiased* estimators so that the expected value of your estimator is the same as the target (the quantity being estimated). Indeed, ordinary least squares is provably unbiased for coefficients β so we know that $\mathbb{E}[\hat{\beta}] = \beta$. But this will not always be possible. Whenever you suspect bias in your estimators it is wise to look at the sampling distribution for errors, and use these errors to correct for any estimation bias.

Example 2.11 **Used Car Prices: Confidence Intervals for Biased Estimators** We will consider using our `carsreg` model from earlier to predict the price of a given Dodge Caravan minivan.

```
> Cars[1000,c("make","model","year","mileage")]
      make           model year mileage
2487 Dodge Grand Caravan 2018   33438
> ( pred <- predict(carsreg, Cars[c(1000),]) )
    2487
9.671831
> ( phat <- exp(pred) )
    2487
15864.38
```

The predicted log price for the van is 9.7, and exponentiating gives our price prediction of \$15,864.38. However, this is a *biased* estimate of the expected price. Jensen's inequality is one of the most important inequalities in probability and it says that, for any convex (i.e., curved upwards) function g and random variable z, $\mathbb{E}[g(z)] \geq g(\mathbb{E}[z])$. Exponentiation is a convex function and, since $\hat{\beta}$ is unbiased for true coefficients β,

$$\mathbb{E}[\exp(\mathbf{x}'\hat{\beta})] \geq \exp(\mathbb{E}[\mathbf{x}'\hat{\beta}]) = \exp(\mathbf{x}'\beta) \tag{2.10}$$

This implies that our estimate above will tend to *overestimate* the expected price of this Caravan. Say $\hat{p} = \exp(\mathbf{x}'\hat{\beta})$ is our estimate and $p = \exp(\mathbf{x}'\beta)$ is the target (the price $\hat{p}$ is estimating); then $\mathbb{E}[\hat{p}] > p$. The bootstrap allows you to estimate the size of the bias, $\mathbb{E}[\hat{p}] - p$. Recall that, when bootstrapping, we are using the original sample as a stand-in for the true unknown DGP. In this stand-in, the "true" expected price is the sample estimated expected price, $\hat{p} = \exp(\mathbf{x}'\hat{\beta})$. When predicting price using each bootstrap sample, the result will tend to be biased away from $\hat{p}$ the same way $\hat{p}$ is biased away from p. Thus we can use the sample of bootstrap errors, say $e_b = \hat{p}_b - \hat{p}$ for each bootstrap iteration b, to estimate the sampling distribution for the true error $\hat{p} - p$.

To see this in action, create a function to generate the predicted price for a given car in each bootstrap sample.

```
> getPrice <- function(data, ids, xpred){
+     data <- do.call("rbind",data[ids])
+     fit <- glm(log(price) ~ log(mileage) + make +
+                     year + certified + body + city, data=data)
+     return(exp(predict(fit,xpred)))
+ }
> getPrice(CarsByDealer, 1:length(CarsByDealer), Cars[1000,])
    2487
15864.38
```

Again, we are using dealer blocks to account for dependence. When we run `getPrice` on the full dataset and do prediction on our Dodge Caravan, we recover the original sample price estimate $\hat{p} = \$15,864.38$. Running the bootstrap for 2000 iterations, we get an estimated bias of $129.67.

```
> set.seed(101)
> ( priceBoot <- boot(CarsByDealer, getPrice, xpred=Cars[1000,],
+                 2000, parallel="snow", ncpus=detectCores()) )
...
    original      bias  std. error
t1* 15864.38  129.6696      815.0589
```

---

[*] Note that, even with the same seed, you may get different results for different operating systems and versions of R. You should at least be able to replicate your own results by running the same code twice on your own machine.

Note that we set a random seed here before the bootstrap, so that if you run this bootstrap after `set.seed(101)` you should get the exact same results. We set the seed here because this bootstrap can return errors in the random chance that one of our 2000 bootstrap estimates ends up including no cars from the same city as our Dodge Caravan (Montclair). You can remove the risk of errors like this by removing `city` as a variable in the regression or by using `model.matrix` to create a numeric design matrix in advance of the bootstrap and using that numeric matrix as your `data` and to define `xpred`.

Bias-Corrected Percentile Confidence Intervals

The bias term is the average error between bootstrap predicted price, $\hat{p}_b$, and the original sample estimate $\hat{p}$.

```
> priceErrors <- priceBoot$t - phat
> mean(priceErrors)
[1] 129.6696
```

This average error is an estimate for $\mathbb{E}[\hat{p} - p]$. An improved bias-corrected price prediction is then $\hat{p} - \mathbb{E}[\hat{p} - p]$, shifting our Dodge Caravan prediction down by \$129.67 to \$15,734.71.

```
> phat - mean(priceErrors)
     2487
15734.71
```

The sample of bootstrap errors, $\{e_b\}_{b=1}^{2000}$, gives us an estimated sampling distribution for the true error. This implies a recipe for calculating bias-corrected confidence intervals with the bootstrap, as detailed in Algorithm 2.3.

Algorithm 2.3 **Bias-Corrected CIs**

Given the bootstrap estimates $\left\{\hat{\theta}_b\right\}_{b=1}^{B}$ and original sample estimate $\hat{\theta}$

- Calculate the bootstrap estimation errors, $e_b = \hat{\theta}_b - \hat{\theta}$.
- Subtract these errors from your original sample estimate to create a sample of bias-corrected parameter estimates, $\hat{\theta} - e_b$.
- Calculate the percentile interval on this sample of bias-corrected estimates.

Then, for example, a 95% confidence interval is between the 2.5th and 97.5th percentiles of $\left\{\hat{\theta} - e_b\right\}_{b=1}^{B}$.

In our Dodge Caravan example, the bias-corrected sample of bootstrap parameter estimates is $\{\hat{p} - e_b\}_{b=1}^{2000}$. We get a confidence interval for the expected price by calculating percentiles on this sample.

```
> quantile(phat-priceErrors, c(.025,.975))
     2.5%      97.5%
13646.88 17002.44
```

The interval is shifted around \$1000 dollars to the left (lower price) than the percentile interval calculated on the original bootstrap sample of price predictions.

```
> quantile(priceBoot$t, c(.025,.975))
     2.5%      97.5%
14726.31 18081.87
```

This shift corrects for upward bias in our original price estimate (again, due to Jensen's inequality). This is a good reminder that even if the average bias might be small (in this case around \$130), applying nonlinear functions like exponentiation to your estimates can have a larger impact on the bounds of your confidence intervals.

Looking at Algorithm 2.3, a bit of algebra shows that $\hat{\theta} - e_b = 2\hat{\theta} - \hat{\theta}_b$, so that you can define the getCI function to get bias-corrected CIs from any boot object.

```
> getCI <- function(bo, p=c(.025,.975)) quantile(2*bo$t0 - bo$t, p)
```

For example, we can use this function to calculate the bias-corrected 95% CI for the price of our Dodge Caravan.

```
> getCI(priceBoot)
     2.5%      97.5%
13646.88 17002.44
```

This is the same as what we calculated above for the bias-corrected interval. This `getCI` function will be handy for you to use when calculating CIs from `boot` objects.

Bootstrap methods give you robustness to some incorrect modeling assumptions that can result in estimation bias. It takes some practice to get the hang of bootstrapping. You should experiment with different bootstrap sample sizes to understand Monte Carlo variation, target different parameters and functions of those parameters to understand how sampling distributions and standard errors work, and calculate samples of errors to understand bias. This will give you a much better practical intuition about how uncertainty works and how to best quantify it when making decisions.

2.4.2 The Parametric Bootstrap

The bootstrap has limitations. There are a variety of settings where it "breaks." This can happen due to a strange data-generating process. For example, if the population distribution has very heavy tails (i.e., it places nontrivial probability on extremely large values), you will have trouble bootstrapping because the extreme values have an outsize influence on your estimate of the sampling distribution. Another reason the bootstrap fails is that your estimation strategy involves some form of *model selection:* deciding among possible models, rather than getting a good estimate for a single model (see Chapter 3). This messes with the bootstrap because with replacement sampling, which leads to having repeats of the same observation in your sample, makes the data seem less noisy than it really is and causes you to select a more complicated model than you should (although we will see in Chapter 3 a way to mitigate this issue in the case that you are using cross-validation for model selection).

In these situations, you need to add some parametric structure to the procedure. The bootstrap of Algorithm 2.2 is completely nonparametric: it makes no assumptions about the model behind the DGP. An alternative is the *parametric* bootstrap where, instead of resampling from the original data, you generate new data for each bootstrap sample by drawing from a fitted model. The parametric bootstrap reintroduces model assumptions and your UQ will now be sensitive to these model assumptions. However, with parametric bootstraps your simulated samples are not restricted to the observed data and this can be useful if that restriction is getting in your way.

Example 2.12 Used Car Prices: Parametric Bootstrap for Mileage-Price Elasticity Turning again to our `carsreg` regression, a parametric bootstrap would take the fitted `carsreg` model and use it to simulate new samples of car prices. Our linear regression model has $y_i \sim \mathrm{N}(\mathbf{x}_i' \boldsymbol{\beta}, \sigma^2)$. You can plug in estimates for $\boldsymbol{\beta}$ and σ to turn this model into a data simulation machine.

```
> CarsSim <- function(data, mle){
+     n <- nrow(data)
+     Ey <- predict(mle, data)
+     data$price <- exp( rnorm(n, Ey, summary(mle)$dispersion) )
+     return(data)
+ }
> simcars <- CarsSim(Cars, carsreg)
> simcars[1,]
  certified       body make model   trim mileage      price year
1         0 Convertible  BMW  Z4 sDrive28i   64899   20425.79 2012
                dealer         city rating reviews       badge
1 Audi Fletcher Jones Costa Mesa      4.9     368 Good Deal
```

The output of `CarsSim` is a new data frame that is the same as `Cars` except that the `price` column is replaced by estimates from our fitted model (which we passed as `mle=carsreg`). For example, the first row's BMW had a sample price of \$16,891 and has a simulated price of \$20,425.79. Note the use of the `rnorm` function; R has convenient functions like this for generating draws from all sorts of random distributions.

The `boot` library can be used to turn this simulator into a parametric bootstrap. We will again be investigating the price-mileage elasticity. You need to define a function to generate estimates from data, as we did for the nonparametric bootstrap but without requiring the vector of data indices (since we will be simulating new data rather than resampling from the existing data). You then pass this function to `boot` as usual, along with `sim="parametric"` and your simulator as `ran.gen` and fitted model as `mle`.

```
> getBetaPar <- function(data){
+     fit <- glm(log(price) ~ log(mileage) + make +
+                     year + certified + body + city, data=data)
+     return(fit$coef["log(mileage)"])
+ }
> ( parboot <- boot(Cars, getBetaPar, 2000,
+     sim = "parametric", ran.gen = CarsSim, mle=carsreg,
+     parallel="snow", ncpus=detectCores()) )
...

       original          bias   std. error
t1* -0.3227021  -9.644334e-05  0.004972614
```

The estimated standard error for price-mileage elasticity, 0.005, is much smaller than our previous bootstrap estimates (and smaller than the original CLT-derived standard error). This is because our model assumptions make the simulated data have nice, independent, homoskedastic, normally distributed errors. Again: with parametric bootstrapping you are introducing a bunch of model assumptions. We are also back to a *fixed design* sampling model, where the car characteristics are fixed across draws and only the prices are treated as random.

We can eliminate one of these assumptions by allowing nonconstant error variance. The updated linear regression model is then $y_i \sim N(\mathbf{x}_i' \boldsymbol{\beta}, \sigma_i^2)$, with a different σ_i for each observation. You can use the absolute value of the residuals, $|\hat{y}_i - y_i|$, to estimate each σ_i (this is the same as saying $\hat{\sigma}^2 \approx e_i^2$).

```
> CarsSimNCV <- function(data, mle){
+     n <- nrow(data)
+     Ey <- predict(mle, data)
+     data$price <- exp( rnorm(n, Ey, abs(mle$residuals) ))
+     return(data)
+ }
> ( parbootNCV <- boot(Cars, getBetaPar, 2000,
+     sim = "parametric", ran.gen = CarsSimNCV, mle=carsreg,
+     parallel="snow", ncpus=detectCores()) )
...
t1* -0.3227021 0.0008738499  0.03445535
```

The standard error of 0.034 is now in the neighborhood of what we got with our nonparametric bootstraps. So, even though our assumptions of normality and independence remain suspect, our nonconstant variance simulator gets close enough to the truth to give realistic results. In general, when deploying a parametric bootstrap it pays to use as flexible as possible a model in your simulator.

◆ 2.5 Bayesian Inference

Our discussion of uncertainty until now has focused on *frequentist* uncertainty—that corresponding to the thought experiment of repeated draws from a fixed data generating process. This is only one of two main types of uncertainty. The other is *Bayesian uncertainty,* which characterizes probabilities over models and parameters by appealing to the idea of subjective beliefs rather than repeated trials.

One way to think about this is to imagine inferring probabilities from decisions. Consider two people gambling on the same sports game. Even if we assume that they are both rational and get the same utility from winning or losing money (i.e., they have the same risk tolerance), they might place different amounts of money on different outcomes. This variation in decisions is driven by each person's placing her own personal probabilities on possible outcomes. The probabilities can come from different mental models for incorporating information from previous games, or from prior beliefs that each person has about the underlying strength of the different teams. Bayesian statistics is the mathematics of how these beliefs are applied.

Decision making on this basis is referred to as *Bayesian inference.* In this book, we don't have scope for a full treatment of Bayesian methods and ideas. For that, we refer you to the now-classic reference from Gelman et al. (2014). However, although we will not deal in detail with explicit Bayesian inference, this way of thinking about uncertainty can be used to understand many of the techniques we cover in the rest of the book. Formal decision theory—quantification of risk and reward probabilities and their implications for decisions— is inherently Bayesian. A basic understanding of Bayesian statistics will help you understand how modern analytics methods are developed and why they work.

2.5.1 Formalizing Beliefs

Bayesian inference is the mathematical framework of rational beliefs. It formalizes the process of "If you believe *A* and you then observe *B*, you should update your beliefs to *C*." This is sometimes referred to as *subjective probability,* but you don't need anyone to hold these specific beliefs for the framework to be valid. Rather, Bayesian inference provides a framework for combining assumptions (and a degree of confidence in those assumptions) with evidence. When those assumptions are clear, then Bayesian inference is completely transparent: you know all of the inputs to your decision process and the relative weight placed on data versus prior knowledge is explicit.

Example 2.13 Medical Testing: Bayes' Rule We'll start with an example to understand the basic mathematics of Bayesian inference. Suppose that you need to get screened for a specific disease before you travel to your tropical vacation destination. If you test positive for the disease, you will have to quarantine for two weeks when you arrive. A quick search on the Internet shows that about 1 in 1000 people people have the disease in the area where you live. The disease can also be asymptomatic, such that it is common to have it without knowing. This information can be summarized as a probability that you have the disease, according to the information and beliefs that you have *prior* to getting the test.

$$\pi(disease) = 0.001$$

This probability is called the *prior* probability, and we use the special symbol (π) to highlight it as being your belief before you are able to gather new data (e.g., before getting tested). This prior summarizes a combination of the information you have on general prevalence of the disease and your understanding of how the disease symptoms work.

When you arrive at the testing location to get screened, you ask about the testing procedure and the disease and the physician tells you that the test is highly accurate. The *likelihood* of testing positive if you have the disease is 99.9% and the likelihood of testing negative for the disease if you don't have it is 99.8%.

$$p(test + \mid disease) = 0.999 \tag{2.11}$$
$$p(test - \mid no\ disease) = 0.998 \tag{2.12}$$

You take the test and when the results come back, unfortunately *you have tested positive for the disease.* The rules mean that you need to quarantine now.

While sitting in quarantine, you wonder: what is the probability that you actually have the disease? Sure, you tested positive, but very few people actually have this disease.

The probability in (2.11) is the probability of testing positive given you have the disease, not the probability of having the disease given that you tested positive. To get the probability that you want, you need to apply *Bayes' Rule*.

$$p(disease \mid test +) = \frac{p(disease \cap test+)}{p(test+)}$$

$$= \frac{p(test+ \mid disease)\pi(disease)}{p(test+)} \qquad (2.13)$$

We have everything we need to calculate this probability. For the numerator, the prior probability of having the disease is 0.001 from earlier, and we have the value for the likelihood as 0.999. The key to computing the value for the denominator is realizing that in this scenario, there are two ways to test positive: testing positive and actually having the disease or testing positive and not having the disease. Then p(*disease* | *test*+) in (2.13) becomes

$$\frac{p(test+ \mid disease)\pi(disease)}{p(test+ \mid disease)\pi(disease) + p(test+ \mid no\ disease)\pi(no\ disease)}$$

$$= \frac{0.999 \cdot 0.001}{0.999 \cdot 0.001 + 0.002 \cdot 0.999} = 0.3333$$

Here, it says that accounting for prior information (in the form of disease prevalence) and observed data (the test result), the probability you have the disease is 1/3.

Bayes' Rule defines how you can combine prior beliefs with data to update your beliefs. It is the mathematics that allows you to combine your prior beliefs about having the disease (you had this as 0.001, or 0.1%) with what you have learned from the data under your assumed likelihood model. All Bayesian inference works by using these same Bayes' Rule mechanics to combine prior distributions with observed data likelihoods. We can write the general version of Bayes' Rule as

$$p(\Theta|Z) = \frac{p(Z \mid \Theta)\pi(\Theta)}{p(Z)} \qquad (2.14)$$

where
- Z are your observed data,
- Θ are the parameters of your likelihood model,
- $p(Z \mid \Theta)$ is the likelihood of the data given the parameters,
- $\pi(\Theta)$ is the prior distribution on the parameters,
- $p(Z)$ is the *marginal likelihood* of the data, and
- $p(\Theta \mid Z)$ is the posterior distribution of your parameters.

For our medical example, Θ is the single binary variable indicating whether or not you have the disease. It takes two possible values — disease, or no disease. And Z is our observation of testing positive. Our marginal likelihood was p(*test*+) and we calculated it by *averaging over all possible values of the disease status variable*.

This marginal likelihood calculation is easy to see in this discrete example. In the case where Θ is more complicated, and includes continuous values, you would need to use calculus to get the marginal likelihood by taking an *integral* over all possible values of Θ. In general, the marginal likelihood is written

$$p(Z) = \int p(Z \mid \Theta)\pi(\Theta)d\Theta \qquad (2.15)$$

In practice, this marginal likelihood is usually a pain to calculate. So for most applications of Bayesian analysis we instead work only with the numerator in (2.14) and write

$$p(\Theta \mid Z) \propto p(Z \mid \Theta)\pi(\Theta) \tag{2.16}$$

Here, recall that $\propto$ stands for "proportional to." Since $p(Z)$ doesn't depend upon Θ, the parameters you want to estimate, it is mostly a nuisance for Bayesian inference. Indeed, the computational strategy of estimating Equation 2.14 via Markov chain Monte Carlo (MCMC; Gelfand and Smith 1990) is a successful attempt to circumvent the need to ever calculate $p(Z)$. This strategy is largely responsible for the explosion of Bayesian inference during the 1990s and 2000s. In the rest of this section, we'll focus on giving you a basic intuition for how Bayesian inference works and introduce a couple of basic applied examples.

2.5.2 Conjugate Models

A good way to get an intuition for Bayesian inference is to explore *conjugate models*. These are prior and likelihood combinations such that, as you accumulate data, the posterior distribution remains in the same family as the prior. Hence, the mechanics of posterior updating can be written out and made explicit.

One simple example is the *beta-binomial model:* you have binomial trials with constant success probability q, and the prior distribution for q is a beta distribution:

$$\pi(q) = \text{Beta}(q; \alpha, \beta) \propto q^{\alpha-1}(1-q)^{\beta-1} \mathbb{1}_{[q\in(0,1)]} \tag{2.17}$$

For example, the Beta(1, 1) prior yields $\pi(q) = \mathbb{1}_{[q\in(0,1)]}$, your familiar uniform probability density function. Again, note that the $\propto$ symbol means "is proportional to" and in Equation 2.17 we are ignoring a normalizing constant that ensures $\int_0^1 \pi(q)dq = 1$ for all $\alpha, \beta > 0$.

Each binomial realization can be viewed as a combination of Bernoulli trials (e.g., tosses of a weighted coin), where $x = 1$ with probability q and $x = 0$ with probability $1 - q$. Under a Beta(a, b) prior distribution on q, the posterior distribution for q after a single Bernoulli realization for x becomes

$$p(q|x) = \text{Beta}(a_1 = a + x, b_1 = b + 1 - x) \tag{2.18}$$

Thus the posterior is a beta distribution with parameters $a_2 = a + x$ and $b_2 = b + 1 - x$. Updating in this manner over n trials, a_n can be interpreted as the number of observed successes and b_n the number of observed failures out of n trials. As you run more trials (i.e., you flip the coin more times), these parameters grow and your uncertainty about q decreases.

For example, consider a situation where the true success probability is $q = 1/3$. When you don't know the true value of q, you can use a flat prior that has q uniformly distributed between zero and one, which is equivalent to the specification q Beta(1,1). Since the mean of a the mean of a Beta(α, β) distribution is $\alpha/(\alpha + \beta)$, under a Beta(1, 1) prior a single successful trial yields a mean of $\mathbb{E}[q|x_1] = 2/3$. An additional successful trial yields $\mathbb{E}[q|x_1,x_2] = 3/4$. As the number of simulations grows, the posterior probability distribution gets more focused around the true value of q, 1/3. Figure 2.10 illustrates beta-binomial posterior updating across a number of simulated binomial trials, from the flat uniform prior to a Gaussian-like peak around the true probability of 1/3 after 100 trials.

As this example illustrates, Bayesian inference is inherently *parametric*: you specify a model that depends upon a set of parameters, and the updating formula in Equation 2.14 defines how uncertainty about these parameters changes with observed data. This is in contrast to the ideas of *nonparametric* inference, such as the nonparametric bootstrap of Algorithm 2.2, where you quantify uncertainty on results of a given procedure without assuming

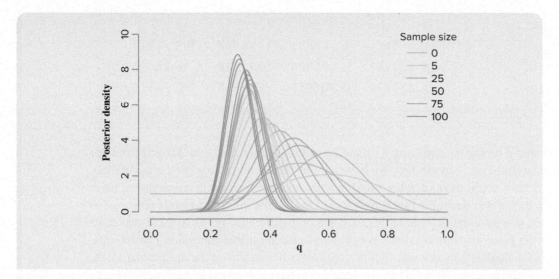

FIGURE 2.10 Posterior density functions for q, the success probability in a series of Bernoulli trials (coin tosses), as a function of the sample size (number of tosses) under a Beta(1, 1) prior. The "true" probability is 1/3.

the correctness of the models behind that procedure. There is a field of "nonparametric" Bayesian analysis, but this title is a misnomer. The field is closer to what we would call *semiparametrics:* it applies flexible models that can relax common assumptions (e.g., linearity) but still rely upon restrictive model structure to facilitate inference in high dimensions. During the 2000s there was a great cross-discipline communication between machine learning and nonparametric Bayesian statistics: both fields were working to build computationally feasible algorithms that give reasonable inferential results in ultra-high-dimensional models. Many people in the current deep learning community (see Chapter 10) have connections to research in Bayesian analysis.

2.5.3 Bayesian Regression Analysis

Implementing fully Bayesian analysis can be quite challenging and often requires computationally intensive simulation programs. Fortunately, there are quite a few R packages that implement specific Bayesian analysis routines. The arm package (Gelman and Hill, 2006) provides a command bayesglm which works similarly to our familiar glm but which estimates the regression model and quantifies uncertainty using Bayesian rather than frequentist methods.

Example 2.14 Used Car Prices: Bayesian Regression Turning again to our car price regression, and price-mileage elasticity, you can run bayesglm using the exact same syntax we used to run glm.

```
> library(arm)
> carsregBayes <- bayesglm(log(price) ~ log(mileage) + make +
+                   year + certified + body + city, data=Cars)
> summary(carsregBayes)
...
```

```
Coefficients:
                  Estimate Std.      Error   t value    Pr(>|t|)
(Intercept)       -56.691152   5.004094    -11.329    < 2e-16 ***
log(mileage)       -0.323290   0.015717    -20.569    < 2e-16 ***
...
```

The estimated $\hat{\beta}$ on log mileage, and its standard error, are essentially unchanged from our original `glm` analysis. This is by design. We have a lot of data here, relative to the complexity of the model. Both `glm` and `bayesglm` are working with the same linear regression model here, and for a given model it is desirable that Bayesian and frequentist inference results *converge* to each other when you get enough data. In this case, the only difference between these two analyses is due to the prior distribution that `bayesglm` has placed on the regression coefficients. This function uses Student's-*t* prior distributions that are calibrated from the design matrix, **X**, as described in Gelman et al. (2008). They are designed to have a minimal impact on the results beyond avoiding extreme coefficient estimates in cases where you have very little information (e.g., for fixed effects where you have only one or two observations for the corresponding factor level).

One nice feature of `bayesglm` is that it tracks the full posterior distribution for the regression coefficients. This is similar to how a bootstrap provides you with a full sampling distribution: you don't need to assume the posterior is Gaussian, you can just draw samples from it directly. Note that similar to the bootstrap, you will get a slightly different sample each time you draw samples. You access the posterior through the `sim` and `coef` functions as below.

```
> posterior <- coef(sim(carsregBayes))
```

The result here is a matrix, and `posterior[,"log(mileage)"]` is a sample of draws from the estimated posterior distribution for the price-mileage elasticity. A density estimate of this sample is shown in Figure 2.11, along with sampling distributions from `glm` and from the

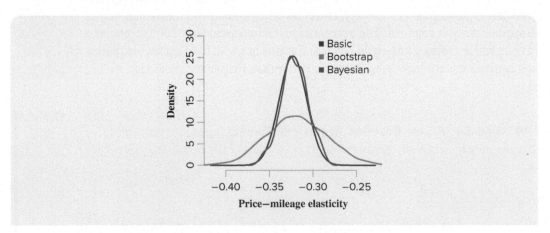

FIGURE 2.11   Density estimates for samples from the Bayesian posterior and frequentist sampling distributions for the `log(mileage)` coefficient in the regression for `log(price)`. "Basic" denotes the usual standard errors out of `glm`, bootstrap is the ordinary bootstrap from Figure 2.8, and the Bayesian density is the posterior sample from `bayesglm`.

ordinary bootstrap. The Bayesian posterior matches up closely with the basic sampling distribution derived through the Central Limit Theorem, and both are much less dispersed than the bootstrap sampling distribution.

2.5.4 Frequentist or Bayesian?

There has long been a debate in statistics between Bayesian and frequentist approaches to uncertainty quantification. The fascinating history by Hacking (1975) describes how subjective and frequentist characterizations of probability were both present in the earliest mathematical formulations of uncertainty. However, for the practical data scientist there should be no debate. You need both frequentist and Bayesian methods depending upon your application. Bayesian methods provide a formalism for incorporating prior or existing information into your uncertainty quantification and model estimation. Frequentist analysis provides an objective framework for evaluating uncertainty. These are complementary toolsets.

Ideally, when making business decisions, everything is nonparametric: you always accumulate enough data so that prior beliefs are no longer relevant, and you work in a way that is not sensitive to model assumptions. Unfortunately, model-free inference is possible only in information-rich settings, when you have many observations and a low-dimensional inference target. Robust frequentist inference becomes difficult in high dimensions, as you have already seen from our discussions on limitations of the bootstrap and on the challenges of multiple testing (where the best you can hope for is to control an average false discovery rate). Much of contemporary business analytics occurs in environments that are high-dimensional. In such settings, to get workable results you need to make assumptions about the model and give some reasonable *prior* guesses about the parameters of those models. Bayesian statistics is the formalism for building these models and incorporating prior information.

Throughout the rest of this book, we will encounter further Bayesian ideas without their being referred to as explicitly Bayesian. For example, the penalties that we use for regularization in the next chapter are interpretable as the effects of Bayesian priors on model estimation. Even if we don't do any uncertainty quantification, the influence of Bayesian statistics allows us to produce point estimates that perform well in noisy high-dimensional environments. This is the strength of thinking like a Bayesian. To build a learning algorithm that works when given only messy unstructured data, you need a framework that lets you bring prior experience to bear and that is transparent about how to combine data with beliefs.

QUICK REFERENCE

Uncertainty quantification is a big topic, but this chapter has introduced the core tools that you can apply throughout the remainder of the book. In future chapters we will use both theoretical standard errors and bootstrapping in our analyses.

Key Practical Concepts

- An estimated parameter $\hat{\theta}$ has a *standard error*. In frequentist statistics, you characterize uncertainty by imagining getting new samples from the same *data generating process*. The distribution of $\hat{\theta}$ values that you get from redoing your estimation on each new sample is the *sampling distribution* and the standard deviation of this distribution is the *standard error* $\text{se}(\hat{\theta})$.

- You can use the summary function to calculate standard errors on models estimated through glm. It produces a table for each of your regression coefficients β that includes
  Estimate $\hat{\beta}$ as the maximum likelihood estimate of the regression parameters.
  Std. Error $\text{se}(\hat{\beta})$ as the estimated standard error for this estimate.
  z value or t value as the test statistic, $\hat{\beta}/\text{se}(\hat{\beta})$ for the null hypothesis $\beta = 0$ vs. alternative $\beta \neq 0$.
  Pr(>|z|) or Pr(>|t|) as the *p*-value for this hypothesis test.
  A flag of significance, such as * for *p*-value below 0.05.

- The summary.glm standard errors assume that the residuals have a constant variance. This is usually not true. You can use the sandwich and lmtest packages to calculate *heteroskedastic robust* standard errors. Given a fitted glm object fit, you do this by calling
  ```
  coeftest(fit, vcov=vcovHC(fit, "HC0"))
  ```

- When you have multiple hypotheses to test you can use the BH algorithm to control your false discovery rate. Given a vector of N *p*-values pvals and an FDR of q, you set your significance threshold alpha as
  ```
  k <- rank(pvals, ties.method="min")
  alpha <- max(pvals[ pvals <= (q*k/N) ])
  ```

- You can use the boot library to obtain a bootstrap sample that approximates draws from the sampling distribution through *with replacement* sampling of the original data. With function getStat(data, obs) that returns statistic $\hat{\theta}$ when given your original data frame data and obs=1:nrow(data), then
  ```
  b <- boot(data, getStat, B)
  ```

  will return B bootstrap estimates of this statistic as b$t and the original sample estimate $\hat{\theta}$ as b$t0. You can use the results to calculate

The standard error of $\hat{\theta}$ as `sd(b$t)`.

The bias of $\hat{\theta}$ as `mean(b$t)-b$t0`.

The bias-corrected 95% confidence interval as
```
quantile(2*b$t0 - b$t, c(0.025, 0.975))
```

- You can pass the `ncpus` argument to `boot` to tell it to use parallel computing over multiple processor cores (CPUs). For Windows, you also specify `parallel="snow"` and for Mac you can use `parallel="multicore"`.

- When you have data that is dependent within clusters, use the `split` function to create a list of data frames (one for each cluster) and bootstrap by resampling clusters rather than individual observations. You can also use the `sandwich` and `lmtest` libraries to obtain clustered standard errors for `glm` object `fit` with data frame `data` and cluster IDs `id`.
```
coeftest(fit, vcov=vcovCL(fit, cluster=data$id))
```

- You can obtain Bayesian estimates and UQ for generalized linear models by running `bayesglm` from the `arm` package with the same syntax and inputs as you use for `glm`.

3 REGULARIZATION AND SELECTION

This chapter lays out the modern approach to building models from data: use regularization to obtain paths of candidate models, and use estimates of *out-of-sample* predictive performance to choose the best model.

- ● **Section 3.1 Out-of-Sample Performance:** Understand the concepts of overfitting and underfitting a model and how to avoid both situations. Run *cross-validation* experiments to test out-of-sample predictive performance of candidate models.

- ■ **Section 3.2 Building Candidate Models:** Estimate models to minimize a penalized deviance, introducing *regularization* that helps you avoid overfit by putting a price on model complexity. Build paths of models estimated under a sequence using Lasso penalties.

- ■ **Section 3.3 Model Selection:** Use cross-validation experiments and information criteria such as AICc to select the best model from a Lasso path.

- ◆ **Section 3.4 Uncertainty Quantification for the Lasso:** Adapt bootstrap algorithms to estimate sampling distributions for estimated parameters in models selected from a Lasso path.

When you are estimating a model from data, your goal is always to use as much of the true *signal* as possible to estimate your parameters. In doing this, you need to guard against the *noise* in the data introducing noise in your estimates. Noise here can be due to error terms or (in regression) the presence of spurious covariates that are not useful for predicting the response. You need to use methods that pull apart the signal from the noise.

This is especially important in the high-dimensional (many parameter) settings that you will encounter in data science. Today's companies—whether in services, technology, manufacturing, or any other sector—have the opportunity to collect data on a huge number of signals related to process improvement and product performance. Analyzing these signals requires the use of high-dimensional models. These models have the flexibility to recognize complex patterns, but they expose you to the risk of *overfit:* tuning the model to predict random errors in your current sample rather than to predict the signal that will persist in new samples.

This chapter introduces the tools of *regularization* and *model selection* that allow you to separate signal from noise and find the best model among many high-dimensional possibilities. The basic principle is that you want to build models that predict well *out-of-sample:* when you apply them to predict what will happen in the future, they give results that are accurate and robust. More specifically, using the language of Chapter 1, you want models that will have a low deviance when tested on data beyond your training sample. This chapter will give you the recipes for constructing such models.

● 3.1 Out-of-Sample Performance

To understand the need to separate signal from noise, consider the issues of *overfit* and *underfit* for regression on some simple simulated data. Figure 3.1 shows three different models fit to data generated from a quadratic model with Gaussian errors ($y = \beta_0 + \beta_1 x + \beta_2 x^2 + \varepsilon$). A simple linear model fit to this data is underfit: it misses the curvature in the underlying true mean

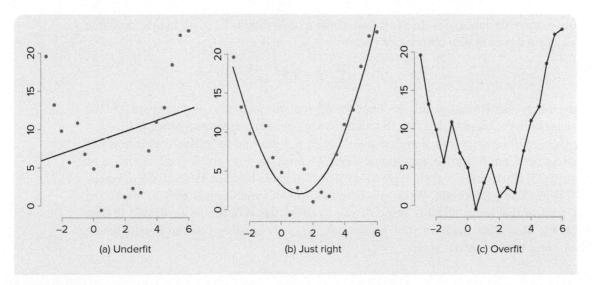

FIGURE 3.1 Data were generated from a quadratic model $y = \beta_0 + \beta_1 x + \beta_2 x^2 + \varepsilon$ where ε is the random noise (error) term generated from a Gaussian distribution. Panel (a) demonstrates *underfit* by fitting the simple linear regression $\mathbb{E}[y] = \beta_0 + \beta_1 x$, panel (b) shows the fit for the true quadratic model, and panel (c) demonstrates *overfit* when simply connecting the dots.

function. The model in Figure 3.1c interpolates each point exactly (i.e., connects the dots) and confuses the sample error (ε) for true signal. This model does a worse job predicting new observations than a simpler model.

In Chapter 1, we introduced *deviance* as a measure of how tightly your model fits your sample of data. The data that has been used to estimate the model is called the *training* sample, and the deviance you calculate on the training data is called the *in-sample* (IS) deviance. If we calculate the in-sample deviance for the model in Figure 3.1c, it will be zero: this interpolator fits the data perfectly. But when we want to use a model for prediction on *new data* (i.e., to predict the y for new x) the model fit will be no longer be perfect. The noise in new observations will be different from the noise in your training sample, and the jagged fitted surface in Figure 3.1c will lead to predictions that are far from the new observations. The underfit model in Figure 3.1a and the "just right" model in Figure 3.1b will also not have predictions that line up perfectly with new observations. When deciding which model is "best," we want to evaluate which model will have the lowest *out-of-sample* (OOS) deviance: the lowest deviance when evaluated against new data.

In-sample vs. Out-of-Sample Deviance

Recall from Chapter 1 that we defined the regression R^2 as one minus the ratio of the deviance for your fitted model over the deviance for a *null model* (i.e., the model with no input variables such that you are estimating $\mathbb{E}[y] = \beta_0$). This is our measure of "the proportion of deviance explained by your fitted model." The same as how we have both in-sample deviance (that calculated on the training data) and out-of-sample deviance (that calculated on new, or *test,* data), you have both in- and out-of-sample R^2. And the only R^2 you ever really care about in practice is the OOS R^2.

Suppose that you have data $[\mathbf{x}_1, y_1] \ldots [\mathbf{x}_n, y_n]$ and you use this data to fit $\hat{\beta}$ in a linear regression model $\mathbb{E}[y] = \mathbf{x}'\beta$. The in-sample deviance is then

$$\text{dev}_{IS}(\hat{\beta}) = \sum_{i=1}^{n} (y_i - \mathbf{x}_i'\hat{\beta})^2 \tag{3.1}$$

For out-of-sample deviance, $\hat{\beta}$ is the same (still fit with observations $1 \ldots n$), but the deviance is now calculated over m new observations (say $n + 1, \ldots, n + m$):

$$\text{dev}_{OOS}(\hat{\beta}) = \sum_{i=n+1}^{n+m} (y_i - \mathbf{x}_i'\hat{\beta})^2$$

Similarly, when calculating the null deviance for R^2 you will look at $(y_i - \bar{y})^2$ where $\bar{y}$ is the response mean in the training data; for IS null deviance you sum these errors over $i = 1, \ldots, n$ and for OOS null deviance you sum over $n + 1, \ldots, n + m$. And for other models you just swap out squared errors for the appropriate deviance function (e.g., the logistic deviance of Equation (1.33) when doing logistic regression). The distinction between IS and OOS deviance (and R^2) is massively important. When you have many input variables it is easy to *overfit* the training data so that your model is being driven by noise that will not be replicated in new observations. That adds errors to your predictions, and it is possible that the overfit model becomes worse than no model at all.

Example 3.1 **Semiconductor Manufacturing: OOS Validation** As a real data example, let's consider quality-control data from a semiconductor manufacturing process. This industrial setting involves many complicated operations with little margin for error. There are hundreds of diagnostic sensors along the production line, measuring various inputs and outputs in the process. The goal is to build a model that maps from this sensor data to a prediction for chip failure. On the basis of this model, chips at risk of failure can be flagged for further (expensive, human) inspection.

For training data we have 1500 observations of a length-200 vector **x** of diagnostic signals, along with binary data on whether the chip was a failure. Note that the x_j inputs here are actually independent from each other (i.e., orthogonal): they are the first 200 principal component directions from a bigger set (see Chapter 8 on factorization). The response `fail` is binary (0 or 1). We define a logistic regression model to predict failure probability from the diagnostics:

$$p(\texttt{fail}|\mathbf{x}) = \frac{e^{\mathbf{x}'\beta}}{1 + e^{\mathbf{x}'\beta}} = \frac{e^{\beta_0 + \beta_1 x_1 \ldots + \beta_k x_k}}{1 + e^{\beta_0 + \beta_1 x_1 \ldots + \beta_k x_k}} \tag{3.2}$$

You can fit this in R using `glm`.

```
> SC <- read.csv("semiconductor.csv")
> full <- glm(fail ~ ., data=SC, family="binomial")
Warning message:
glm.fit: fitted probabilities numerically 0 or 1 occurred
```

Note that you get the same perfect fit warning we had in the logistic regression of Example 1.6 in Chapter 1. This is symptomatic of overfit: it indicates that for some observations your fitted regression assigns probabilities $\hat{y} = y$ (1 or 0), similar to how our 18 degree polynomial interpolates points perfectly in Figure 3.1c.

The IS-deviances are available in the fitted `glm` object.

```
> full$deviance
[1] 320.3321
> full$null.deviance
[1] 731.5909
> 1 - full$deviance/full$null.deviance
[1] 0.5621432
```

Since this is logistic regression, these metrics are based upon the binomial deviance from Equation (1.33). We see that this regression has an R^2 of 56%—more than half of the variation in failure versus success is explained by the 200 diagnostic signals.

We can pull out the 200 p-values from `summary.glm`.

```
> pvals <- summary(full)$coef[-1,4] # -1 drops intercept
```

Figure 3.2a shows the distribution of the 200 p-values for tests of null hypothesis $\beta_k = 0$ in this regression. Recall from our FDR discussion in Chapter 2 that p-values from the null distribution have a uniform distribution; in contrast, here we see a spike near zero (indicating useful diagnostic signals), while the remainder sprawl out toward one (most likely useless signals for predicting failure). You can use the Benjamini-Hochberg algorithm to obtain a smaller model

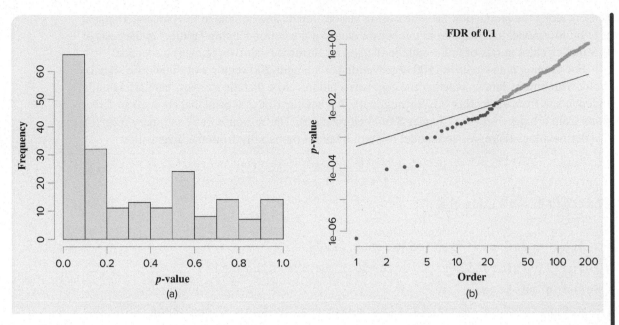

FIGURE 3.2 The distribution of *p*-values for the 200 coefficients from the semiconductor regression. Panel (a) shows the histogram of *p*-values, and (b) shows them ranked in increasing size. Red points in (b) are the 25 $\hat{\beta}_k$ that are significant using the BH algorithm for an FDR of 10%.

with controlled false discovery rate. Figure 3.2b illustrates the procedure for an FDR of 10% (q=0.1), as executed using the code below.

```
> pvals <- sort(pvals[!is.na(pvals)])
> J <- length(pvals)
> k <- rank(pvals, ties.method="min")
> q=0.1
> ( alpha <- max(pvals[ pvals<= (q*k/(J+1)) ]) )
[1] 0.01217043
> sum(pvals<=alpha)
[1] 25
```

This yields an $\alpha = 0.0122$ *p*-value rejection cutoff and implies 25 significant regression coefficients (of which you expect 22 to 23 are true signals). This is illustrated by the code fdr_cut(pVals).

We can identify these 25 significant signals and rerun glm on only those variables, yielding a much more parsimonious model.

```
> signif <- which(pvals < 0.0122)
> cut <- glm(fail ~ ., data=SC[,c("fail", names(signif))],
+            family="binomial")
> 1 - cut$deviance/cut$null.deviance # new in-sample R2
[1] 0.1811822
```

Notice that the *cut* model, using only 25 signals, has IS $R^2_{cut} = 0.18$. This is much smaller than the full model's $R^2_{full} = 0.56$. In general, the *IS R^2 always increases with more covariates*. This in-sample R^2 is exactly what the maximum likelihood estimate (MLE), $\hat{\boldsymbol{\beta}}$, is fit to maximize. If you give glm more knobs to turn (more β_k's), then it will be able to get you a tighter fit. This is exactly why we don't really care about IS R^2—it can be made to look arbitrarily good just by adding more variables to the design. The real question is, how well does each model predict *new* data?

Out-of-Sample Experiments

Of course, you can't know about performance on unseen data because you don't have it. However, you can mimic the experience of predicting on unseen data by performing an out-of-sample experiment to evaluate your models on data that was not used for training. You do this by breaking your data into several *folds* and then repeatedly training your model on all data except one fold and recording the deviance on the left-out fold.

We perform this OOS experiment for both the *full* and *cut* regression models. First, we randomly sample a fold ID for each observation in the semiconductor data set (we set a seed here so you can repeat the same experiment).

```
> n <- nrow(SC) # the number of observations
> K <- 10 # the number of 'folds'
> # create a vector of fold memberships (random order)
> set.seed(1)
> foldid <- rep(1:K,each=ceiling(n/K))[sample(1:n)]
> foldid[1:20]
 [1] 7 5 1 7 4 3 2 9 9 5 9 3 1 8 5 6 4 6 3 7
```

* Note that, even with the same seed, you may get different results for different operating systems and versions of R. You should at least be able to replicate your own results by running the same code twice on your own machine.

We set $K = 10$ folds, and now foldid contains the allocated random fold for each observation. The OOS experiment is then run using a for-loop.

```
> fulldev <- cutdev <- nulldev <- rep(NA,K)
> for(k in 1:K){
+     train <- which(foldid!=k) # train on all but fold 'k'
+
+     ## fit the two regressions
+     cuts <- c("fail",names(signif))
+     rfull <- glm(fail~., data=SC, subset=train,
+                   family="binomial")
+     rcut <- glm(fail~., data=SC[,cuts], subset=train,
+                   family="binomial")
+
+     ## predict (type=response for probabilities)
```

```
+        pfull <- predict(rfull, newdata=SC[-train,],
+                         type="response")
+        pcut <- predict(rcut, newdata=SC[-train,],
+                        type="response")
+
+        ## calculate OOS deviances
+        y <- SC$fail[-train]
+        ybar <- mean(y)
+        fulldev[k] <- -2*sum(y*log(pfull)+(1-y)*log(1-pfull))
+        cutdev[k] <- -2*sum(y*log(pcut)+(1-y)*log(1-pcut))
+        nulldev[k] <- -2*sum(y*log(ybar)+(1-y)*log(1-ybar))
+
+        ## print progress
+        cat(k, " ")
+ }
1  2  3  4  5  6  7  8  9  10
```

There is a lot going on here, but if you go through each step you'll find that we are simply (a) fitting each regression on the subset that excludes fold k via the subset argument, and (b) predicting and calculating deviances for observations in fold k.

Looking at the resulting OOS deviances, you will see that the cut model has much lower (better) deviance than the full model.

```
> round(fulldev)
 [1] 1838  306  284  198  455  221  263  301  822  158
> round(cutdev)
 [1] 98 50 40 81 68 59 67 57 87 53
> R2 <- data.frame(
+     full = 1 - fulldev/nulldev,
+     cut = 1 - cutdev/nulldev )
> colMeans(R2)
       full          cut
-5.24145031   0.08020355
```

The resulting R^2 values are especially striking: the full model has a *negative* R^2, indicating that its predictions are further from new observations than you get using the training sample mean as your predictor. In this case, the average OOS R^2 are −5.2 for the full model (or −520%) and a positive 0.08 for the cut model. So, while the cut-model's OOS R^2 is lower than its IS R^2, it still manages to do 8% better than the null.

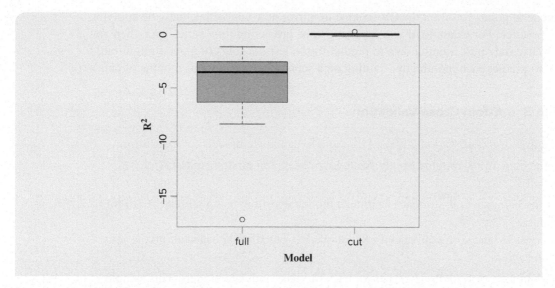

FIGURE 3.3 OOS R^2 for both full (200 signal) and cut (25 signal) semiconductor regressions.

Figure 3.3 shows the distribution of R^2 values across the folds: the full model has a negative R^2 for every fold of the OOS experiment. How can this happen? Look at the R^2 formula: $1 - \text{dev}(\hat{\beta})/\text{dev}(\beta = 0)$. The R^2 will be negative if your fitted model performs worse than the null model, that is, if your $\hat{y}$ estimates are further from the truth than the overall average, $\bar{y}$. Since $\bar{y} \approx 1/15$ here, you are better off simply auditing every 15th chip instead of using a quality control process based upon the overfit full model.

You may have never seen a negative R^2 before. If so, it is likely because you have been looking only at in-sample performance. Out-of-sample, negative R^2 are unfortunately more common than you might expect. Example 3.1 is a dramatic demonstration of the basic principle: *all that matters is out-of-sample R^2*. You don't care about in-sample R^2, because you can get better numbers simply by adding junk variables and inducing overfit.

3.1.1 Cross-Validation

The routine we introduced in Example 3.1—using OOS experiments to select the best model—is called *cross-validation*. The generic procedure is outlined in Algorithm 3.1. Note that we are folding the data into nonoverlapping subsets. Folding your data in this way guarantees that each observation is left out once for validation—each data point is given a chance to yield a large error in a prediction exercise. Doing this, rather than sampling overlapping subsets, reduces the variance of CV model selection.

Cross-validation will play a big role in this text, since using OOS performance in selection of "the best" model is at the core of practical data science. Note that, in the way we ran the OOS experiment in Example 3.1, we were actually violating one of the key rules of running a CV experiment. In our analysis, the full sample was used to choose the 25 variables that are in the cut model. A true OOS experiment would have done FDR control *inside* the for loop, such that the OOS results are a validation of the end-to-end selection procedure. Anything you do to the data, do it without the left-out fold if you want an accurate assessment of OOS performance.

As another general point, you want the CV scheme to mirror how you will actually be applying the model in practice. For example, if you are going to be predicting time series data, then you might want to use only past training data to predict future left-out folds (e.g., you might build a CV routine to predict each month after training on a set number of previous months of data).

Algorithm 3.1 *K*-fold Cross-Validation

Given a dataset of n observations, $\{[\mathbf{x}_i, y_i]\}_{i=1}^{n}$, and M candidate models (or algorithms),

- Split the data into K roughly evenly sized nonoverlapping random subsets (*folds*).
- For $k = 1 \ldots K$:

  Fit the parameters $\hat{\beta}^m$ for each candidate model/algorithm using all but the kth fold of data.

  Record deviance (or, equivalently R^2) on the left-out kth fold based on predictions from each model.

This will yield a set of K OOS deviances for each of your candidate models. This sample is an estimate of the distribution of each model's predictive performance on new data, and you can select the model with the best OOS performance.

■ 3.2 Building Candidate Models

We will revisit cross-validation and other model selection tools in Section 3.3. However, before we get there, we need to develop algorithms for constructing good *sets of candidate* models. The bulk of modern statistical analysis proceeds in two steps. First, you build a set of plausible candidate models. Second, you use a tool like cross-validation to choose among these candidates. This chapter is split into these two steps: building a set of candidate models, and then later selecting amongst the candidates. In this section we will introduce the twin ideas of regularization and model paths as the tools for constructing candidate sets of regression models.

Stepwise Selection

How do you build sets of candidate models? With any reasonable input dimension, it is impossible to simply catalog all possible models. For example, if you have a regression setting with J potential covariates, there are 2^J different possible models depending upon whether each covariate is included. With just 20 covariates, this implies already more than 1 million candidate models. In the previous section we used p-values on the most complex model as the basis for selecting a simpler model. However, this is generally a *bad idea* for a couple of reasons:

- When you have *multicollinearity*—correlation between inputs—the p-values for all of these variables will be large (they will look insignificant) even if any one of the variables provides a useful signal on the response. You will end up including none because you don't know which one of them should be included.
- The p-values are based on a likely overfit model, and this leads to an *unstable* foundation for model construction. You are choosing candidate models on the basis of a noisy regression fit, and small changes in the data can lead to big changes in the candidate models this implies. More dramatically, when you have more covariates than observations there is no full model because glm will fail to converge (it will give you an error or a warning and default some coefficient estimates to zero).

This general approach—estimating the most complex model and then using metrics like "significance" to cut it down to size—is sometimes called backward stepwise regression. It should be avoided.

A better solution is to proceed in the opposite direction, building from simplicity to complexity in a *forward stepwise regression*. The procedure is simple: you start by estimating all single input models (one for each dimension of **x**) and select the one that has the lowest in-sample deviance. You then estimate all two input models that include this first best covariate (the one that was best among all single input models), and then select the best two input model. This process repeats until you get to some maximum model dimension that you are willing to consider.

Example 3.2 Semiconductor Manufacturing: Forward Stepwise Regression The `step` function can be used to execute this stepwise routine. You give a starting point, called the `null` model, and a biggest possible model, called the `scope`. We can use forward stepwise regression on the semiconductor manufacturing data from Example 3.1. The null model is the model with only the intercept, denoted by 1 in the `glm` formulation. The code below takes a few minutes to run (notice we are timing it with the `system.time` function).

```
> null <- glm(fail~1, data=SC)
> system.time(
+ fwd <- step(null, scope=formula(full), dir="forward") )
...
Step:  AIC=92.59
FAIL ~ SIG2
...
   user  system elapsed
  82.55   16.75  128.93
> length(coef(fwd))
[1] 69
```

This procedure enumerated 69 models, ranging from a univariate model including only `SIG2` up to a model with 68 input signals (plus the intercept). The algorithm stopped at 68 because the AIC (Akaike Information Criterion) score for that model was lower (better) than any of the AIC scores for models with 69 inputs. AIC is a "model selection criteria" that attempts to predict how well the model will perform in OOS prediction (without actually running an OOS experiment). We will detail AIC and other information criteria in Section 3.3.1. The `step` function stopped when it thought it had found the best model, making the assumption that since the aic is not getting any better when moving from 67 to 68 inputs it will not improve with 70+ inputs. From this perspective, `step` has determined that the 68 input regression is "best" overall and this is the model that you should use for prediction.

Problems with Subset Selection

In general, forward stepwise regression has a lot of flaws. It can be improved upon dramatically using the regularization ideas that we will introduce in this section. But the general approach of proceeding forward in your search, from simplicity to complexity, is a common and useful approach to building sets—or paths—of candidate models. This is an example of a *greedy* search strategy. In a greedy search you proceed myopically, at each point adding the next iteration of complexity that seems most useful given the current search state. Despite not optimizing for *global* properties of the search path (i.e., each decision does not consider implications for future decisions), greedy algorithms are a useful way to reduce the complexity of your model search and they play a prominent role in many ML strategies.

The problems with forward stepwise selection are that it is *slow* (step took approximately 129 elapsed seconds) and *unstable*. These are going to be issues for any model selection procedure that is based on *subset selection*: choosing sets of inputs, and then using maximum likelihood estimation to fit a regression to each set of inputs. The slowness is because you need to estimate from scratch every model (every subset of inputs) that you want to consider, and because there will be a massive set of possible input subsets to consider (this is true even if you use a greedy search to reduce the number of candidate models). If you run the step function you will see the massive number of glm models that it fits during its greedy search. This is a waste of time.

The alternative to subset selection (and to slow tools like step) is to introduce the idea of regularization: replacing deviance minimization with *penalized* deviance minimization, where you are incorporating a "cost of complexity" in your model estimation. Then, instead of selecting subsets of inputs, you select the "price of complexity" as a tuning parameter. We will see that this yields fast construction of useful sets of candidate models.

3.2.1 Penalized Deviance Estimation

The key to modern statistics is *regularization:* penalizing complexity so as to depart from optimality and stabilize your set of candidate models. Incorporating the cost of complexity in your estimations, and considering different prices on complexity in this cost function, allow you to enumerate a list of promising candidate models that range from simple to complex.

Recall from Section 1.4 in the regression chapter that, in classical maximum likelihood estimation, you are fitting $\hat{\boldsymbol{\beta}}$ to minimize the in-sample deviance (which is just -2 times the likelihood). You are choosing the MLE $\hat{\boldsymbol{\beta}}$ to minimize $\text{dev}(\boldsymbol{\beta})$, for example, to minimize $\Sigma_i(y_i - \mathbf{x}_i'\boldsymbol{\beta})^2$ in linear regression (i.e., in OLS estimation). When you use glm to fit a regression model you are minimizing the deviance. A regularization strategy will instead involve minimizing *penalized* deviance. You are fitting $\hat{\boldsymbol{\beta}}$ to minimize

$$\frac{1}{n}\text{dev}(\boldsymbol{\beta}) + \lambda \sum_j c(\beta_j) \qquad (3.3)$$

where λ is your penalty and $c(\beta_j)$ is the *cost function*. The cost function determines how different magnitudes of β_j translate to a cost on complexity. For example, we will be largely working with the absolute value cost function, $c(\beta) = |\beta|$, which is the basis for the common and useful *Lasso* estimation framework.

Notice that we are dividing the deviance by n, the sample size, so that (3.3) is technically the *penalized average deviance*. We do this so that λ is on the scale of the average deviance and doesn't need to increase with n to yield similar results. To help with your intuition, consider the setting of linear regression where the deviance is the sum of squared errors. Equation (3.3) then becomes

$$\frac{1}{n}\text{MSE}(\boldsymbol{\beta}) + \lambda \sum_j c(\beta_j) = \frac{\sum_{i=1}^n (y_i - \mathbf{x}_i' \boldsymbol{\beta})^2}{n} + \lambda \sum_j c(\beta_j) \qquad (3.4)$$

This implies that the complexity penalty is on the same scale as your mean squared error, which should be roughly similar to the variance in additive errors (σ^2).

Putting a Cost on Complexity

Equation (3.3) adds a penalty—the $\lambda \sum_j c(\beta_j)$ term—to the deviance function that we were minimizing in our regression chapter. This penalty puts a *cost* on the magnitude of each β_j. That penalizes *complexity,* because the β_j coefficients are what allow your predicted $\hat{y}$ values to move around with different input $\mathbf{x}$ values. If you force all the $\hat{\beta}_j$ to be close to zero, then your $\hat{y}$ values will be *shrunk* toward $\bar{y}$ and when you jitter the data your predictions will not change as much as they would if you did not include a penalty term during estimation.

Another way to think about Equation 3.3 is through the lens of decision theory—a framework built around the idea that choices have costs. If you consider the decision-making process in classical statistics—focused on a two-stage process of estimation and hypothesis testing—what are the costs?

- *Estimation cost:* Deviance, i.e. the cost of distance between data and the model, and it is what you minimize to obtain the MLE.
- *Testing cost:* There is a fixed price placed on $\hat{\beta}_j \neq 0$. This is implicit in the hypothesis testing procedure, where you set $\hat{\beta}_j = 0$ unless you have *significant evidence otherwise*. The null is *safe* and you need to "pay" to decide otherwise.

Thus, in classical statistics, the cost of $\hat{\beta}$ is deviance plus a penalty for being away from zero. However, the cost of moving away from zero is hidden away inside the hypothesis testing procedure. Equation 3.3 makes both costs explicit.

Cost Functions

What should the penalty function look like? First, $\lambda > 0$ is the penalty weight that determines the "price" of complexity. It is a tuning parameter that needs to be selected in some data-dependent matter, and the later parts of this chapter are focused on how to do this. For now we will take λ as given. The rest of the penalty is determined by the shape of the cost function. In all cases, $c(\beta)$ will be lowest at $\beta = 0$, and you pay more for $|\beta| > 0$; that is, the penalization *shrinks* the coefficients toward zero. Otherwise, the variety of options is wide; Figure 3.4 shows a few.

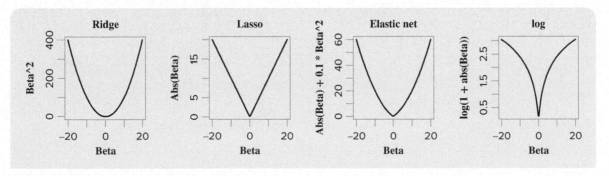

FIGURE 3.4 Common penalty functions: ridge β^2, Lasso $|\beta|$, elastic net $\alpha\beta^2 + |\beta|$, and a "nonconvex" penalty $\log(1 + |\beta|)$.

Each of these leads to different estimation results. The ridge penalty, β^2, places little penalty on small values of β but a rapidly increasing penalty on large values. This will be appropriate for scenarios where you believe each covariate has a small effect, with no big coefficients dominating the model. The Lasso's absolute value penalty, $|\beta|$, places a constant penalty on incremental deviations from zero. Moving β from 1 to 2 costs the same as a move from 101 to 102. And the "elastic net" is an elaborate name for the combination of ridge and Lasso penalties.

Penalties like the log penalty on the far right are special because they have *diminishing bias:* they place extreme cost on the move from zero to small values of β, but for large values the rate of penalty change is small. These penalties encourage lots of zeros in your fit while allowing large signals to be estimated without any bias (i.e., without shrinking large $\hat{\beta}_j$ toward zero). Such "nonconvex" penalties are sometimes favored by theoretical statisticians, but they need to be treated with care in practice because they introduce many of the instability and computational issues that you observe with subset selection. Indeed, you can interpret forward stepwise regression as solving for a penalized deviance under the extreme version of this where $c(\beta) = \mathbb{1}_{[\beta \neq 0]}$ such that $c(0) = 0$ and $c(\beta) = 1$ for any $\beta \neq 0$. The problems of subset selection—needing to refit a completely different model every time you add a variable—are extreme versions of the problems associated with any nonconvex penalty scheme.

An advantage of the Lasso is that it gives the least possible amount of bias on large signals while still retaining the stability of a convex penalty like the ridge (convex means that the penalty doesn't flatten out for large values). Another massive advantage of the Lasso, and of all the three right "spiky" penalties in Equation 3.4, is that it will yield *automatic variable screening*. That is, some of the solved $\hat{\beta}_j$ values will be exactly equal to zero—not close to zero, but zero as in "they are not in the model, so you don't need to store or think about them." The reason that this happens is illustrated in Figure 3.5: the deviance is smooth while the absolute value function is pointy, and the minimum of their sum can be at zero if the penalty dominates. Any penalty that involves a $|\beta|$ term will do this—for example, all but ridge in Figure 3.4.

In summary, there are *many* penalty options. As you will see, the Lasso is a common default. You can think of it as a baseline and consider others only if you have a strong reason to do so. There are certain settings where in theory you might prefer the elastic net (if the true regression relationship has many small coefficients) or a nonconvex log penalty (e.g., when model compression—having the fewest coefficients as possible—is the goal) but it is rare in practice that you can do much better than the Lasso.

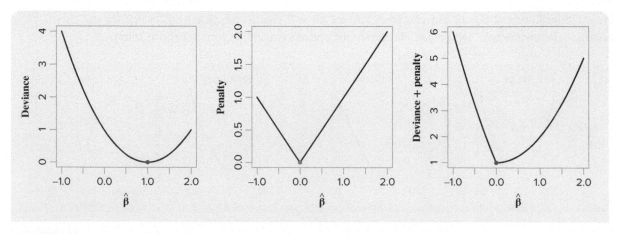

FIGURE 3.5   Illustration of penalized deviance minimization leading to $\hat{\beta} = 0$.

3.2.2 Regularization Paths

The Lasso alone does not select models. Rather, it provides a mechanism to *enumerate* a set of candidate models to choose among. A Lasso regularization path minimizes, for a *sequence* of penalties $\lambda_1 > \lambda_2 \ldots > \lambda_T$, the penalized deviance

$$\frac{1}{n}\mathrm{dev}(\boldsymbol{\beta}) + \lambda_t \sum_j |\beta_j| \qquad (3.5)$$

This yields a sequence of estimated regressions with coefficients $\hat{\boldsymbol{\beta}}_1 \ldots \hat{\boldsymbol{\beta}}_T$. Given this sequence, model selection tools (e.g., cross-validation) are used to choose the best $\hat{\lambda}_t$ and hence the best $\hat{\boldsymbol{\beta}}_t$.

Algorithm 3.2 outlines this recipe. You start with λ_1 just big enough that $\hat{\boldsymbol{\beta}}_1 = 0$. This is always possible: from Equation 3.5, you can set λ so that the cost of moving any $\hat{\beta}_j$ slightly away from zero is equal to the corresponding decrease in the deviance, and so the optimization keeps $\hat{\beta}_j = 0$. Most software will find this starting point automatically. You then iteratively shrink λ while updating the estimated $\hat{\boldsymbol{\beta}}$.

A crucial detail here is that the coefficient updates are smooth in λ; that is,

$$\hat{\beta}_t \approx \hat{\beta}_{t-1} \text{ for } \lambda_t \approx \lambda_{t-1}. \qquad (3.6)$$

This leads to both *speed* and *stability* for the Lasso algorithm. The speed comes from the fact that each update $\hat{\beta}_{t-1} \to \hat{\beta}_t$ is small and hence fast. Selection stability is the mirror image of this property: even if the "best" λ changes across data samples, it will remain in a local neighborhood and the selected $\hat{\beta}$ will thus also stay in a small neighborhood.

Algorithm 3.2 Lasso Regularization Path

Begin with $\lambda_1 = \min\{\lambda : \hat{\beta}_\lambda = 0\}$.
   For $t = 1 \ldots T$:

- Set $\lambda_t = \delta\lambda_{t-1}$ for $\delta \in (0, 1)$.
- Then find $\hat{\beta}_t$ to optimize Equation 3.5 under penalty λ_t.

Path Plots

The whole enterprise is easiest to understand visually. The *path plot* in Figure 3.6 illustrates Algorithm 3.2. The algorithm moves right to left with decreasing values of λ. The vertical axis here is $\hat{\beta}$, with each colored line a different $\hat{\beta}_j$ as a function of λ_t. Each vertical slice of the plot represents a candidate model. From right to left, the models become increasingly complex as the $\hat{\beta}_t$ include more and larger nonzero $\hat{\beta}_j$ values (the plot header marks the number of nonzero $\hat{\beta}_j$ at certain segments).

This picture and the underlying path estimation were executed using the `gamlr` package for R (Taddy, 2017). We will use this package heavily. It provides fast and reliable Lasso paths. The popular `glmnet` package (Friedman et al., 2010) is also an excellent option for Lasso estimation. Both `gamlr` and `glmnet` use similar syntax and use similar optimization routines (coordinate descent). The difference is in what they can do beyond the Lasso: `gamlr` offers diminishing bias penalization, like the log penalty in Figure 3.4, while `glmnet` provides for the elastic net of that same figure. We use the `gamlr` software because it was written to provide for

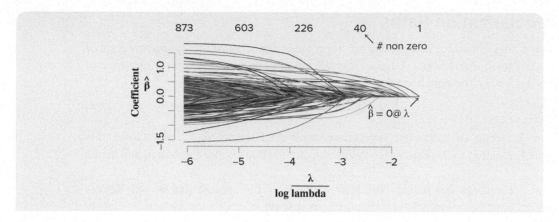

FIGURE 3.6 A Lasso regularization path plot from `gamlr`. Algorithm 3.2 proceeds from right to left, with decreasing λ_t.

useful features covered in this book (e.g., AICc selection, double ML for causal inference, and distributed multinomial regression).

Running a Lasso in `gamlr` is fairly straightforward, but there are some particularities, which we'll outline in the next section. The main difference from `glm` is that that you need to create the numeric model matrix yourself. There are some tricks to creating model matrices for Lasso regressions, and we will spend some time outlining those details before starting to fit our Lasso paths.

3.2.3 Sparse Model Matrices

To use `gamlr` you need to feed it the data in the correct format. Recall from Chapter 1 that converting a data frame to a numeric model matrix is one of the first steps done inside `glm`. The numeric model matrix contains a column for each continuous (`numeric`) variable and columns for *levels* of the categorical (`factor`) variables. In creating the model matrix, R will create a column for all but one level of a categorical variable. The level that is omitted is the reference level. When you fit `glm`, the coefficients for the other factor levels can each be interpreted as a comparison to the baseline expected response for this reference level.

In Chapter 1, we worked with data on orange juice sales. The `oj` data frame contains a continuous covariate `price` and a factor variable `brand` with three levels: `dominicks`, `minute.maid`, and `tropicana`. To create the model matrix that is used by `glm` for regression estimation, you pass a regression formula and the data to `model.matrix` the same way as you would to `glm` but without including the response variable. We do that here and print a row for each brand.

```
> oj<-read.csv("oj.csv",strings=T)
> modMat<-model.matrix(~log(price)+brand,data=oj)
> modMat[c(100,200,300),] #look at one row for each brand
    (Intercept) log(price) brandminute.maid brandtropicana
100           1  1.1600209                0              1
200           1  1.0260416                1              0
300           1  0.3293037                0              0
```

Notice the column of 1s for the intercept, the single column for the quantitative predictor, and a binary column for each of `minute.maid` and `tropicana`. The reference level for factor `brand` is `dominicks` and this reference level is subsumed into the intercept. Notice that the third printed row has zero for both the categorical columns: this observation is from `dominicks`, so it gets a zero for each of `brandminute.maid` and `brandtropicana` columns.

This is not the model matrix that you want to use with `gamlr` (or `glmnet`) for Lasso regression. You will want to make three changes:

1. Create a column for all factor levels (including `dominicks`).
2. Delete the column of 1s for the intercept (`gamlr` adds its own intercept).
3. Convert to a *sparse matrix* to reduce storage and increase efficiency.

We will work through these changes in turn.

Including All Factor Levels in the Model Matrix

For MLE regression with `glm`, it doesn't matter which brand of OJ is the baseline level for the `brand` factor. Even though one of them will get subsumed into the intercept, you end up with the same predicted $\hat{y}$ values. But when you start penalizing coefficients, *factor reference levels now matter*. Since the penalty rewards $\hat{\beta}_j$ values closer to (or at) zero, you are shrinking factor coefficients toward the intercept—toward the reference level. And it makes a difference which level is the baseline (i.e., whether you shrink Minute Maid toward Tropicana instead of Dominicks).

The solution is to simply get rid of the reference level. Once you add a penalty to the deviance, there is no reason to have only $K - 1$ coefficients for a K-level factor. If every category level is given its own dummy variable, then every factor level effect is shrunk toward a shared intercept. You are shrinking toward a shared mean, with only significantly distinct effects getting nonzero $\hat{\beta}_k$.

You can force R to create separate dummies for each level by creating an *extra* factor level. The `gamlr` package includes the utility function `naref` which makes NA ("not available," R's code for "missing") the reference level for every factor. Conveniently, `naref` has the extra advantage of providing a framework for missing data; we will introduce this functionality later in this chapter. Here we apply `naref` to create the new data frame `ojdf`.

```
> library(gamlr)
> ojdf <-naref(oj)
> ojdf[c(100,200,300),"brand"]
[1] tropicana    minute.maid dominicks
Levels: <NA> dominicks minute.maid tropicana
```

If you apply `naref` to your data frame before creating the model matrix, then it will lead to every factor level having its own column.

```
> modMatAllLevs<-model.matrix(~log(price)+brand,data=ojdf)[,-1]
> modMatAllLevs[c(100,200,300),]
     log(price) branddominicks brandminute.maid brandtropicana
100   1.1600209              0                0              1
200   1.0260416              0                1              0
300   0.3293037              1                0              0
```

Notice that we appended `[,-1]` when we created the model matrix here. This removed the intercept column, as desired because `gamlr` adds its own intercept. You can also add a `-1` term in the regression formula to get the same result.

Sparse Matrices

The model matrix we just created is in *dense* format: R stores the matrix as a rectangle of data. You can provide dense matrices to `gamlr`, however `gamlr` (along with `glmnet` and many other R packages) is able to take advantage of the `Matrix` library representation for *sparse matrices*. A sparse matrix is one with many zero entries, which is a common scenario in modern data analysis. For example, many interacting categorical variables will—when represented as 0/1 indicator variables—lead to sparse designs. It is then efficient to ignore zero elements in the matrix whenever you can. Packages like `gamlr` use sparse matrix structures for lower storage costs and faster computation. This will be essential for big data.

One common sparse representation is a simple triplet matrix (STM) with three key elements: the row `i`, column `j`, and entry value `x`. Everything else in the matrix is assumed zero. Here's an example:

$$\begin{bmatrix} -4 & 0 \\ 0 & 10 \\ 5 & 0 \end{bmatrix} \text{ is stored as } \begin{Bmatrix} i = & 1,3,\ 2 \\ j = & 1,1,\ 2 \\ x = & -4,5,10 \end{Bmatrix}$$

The `Matrix` library provides tools for creating and working with sparse matrices. After loading this library we can use `sparse.model.matrix` to create the same model matrix as before, but in efficient simple triplet format.

```
> xOJ<-sparse.model.matrix(~log(price)+brand,data=ojdf)[,-1]
> xOJ[c(100,200,300),]
3 x 4 sparse Matrix of class "dgCMatrix"
    log(price) branddominicks brandminute.maid brandtropicana
100  1.1600209              .                .              1
200  1.0260416              .                1              .
300  0.3293037              1                .              .
```

The zeros have been replaced by "." when we print the matrix. This is a hint that this is a sparse matrix. Under the hood, the `Matrix` library has created a special sparse matrix structure.

```
> class(xOJ)
[1] "dgCMatrix"
attr(,"package")
[1] "Matrix"
```

This specific matrix is of the `dgCMatrix` (compressed, sparse, column-oriented) format. The `Matrix` library has a variety of different structures that it uses for representing sparse matrices, and packages that are compatible with `Matrix`, like `gamlr`, are able to recognize and process all the different formats. You can ignore the details and just benefit from lower memory usage and faster optimizations. However, you will often need to remove the sparse matrix formatting and convert back to a dense representation. This happens, for example, if you are trying to use the output `gamlr` in another function that doesn't recognize sparse matrices. One way to do this is to apply the `as.matrix` function.

```
> as.matrix(xOJ[c(100,200,300),])
    log(price) branddominicks brandminute.maid brandtropicana
100  1.1600209              0                0              1
200  1.0260416              0                1              0
300  0.3293037              1                0              0
```

Alternatively, if you just want to pull a single vector out from the matrix (row or column) it will automatically be converted back to dense format.

```
> xOJ[100,]
      log(price) branddominicks brandminute.maid  brandtropicana
        1.160021       0.000000         0.000000        1.000000
```

3.2.4 Path Estimation with `gamlr`

Once you know how to build your sparse model matrix, running `gamlr` is easy. You simply supply the model matrix as x and the response as y and off you go. For example, we can regress log sales onto `xoj`.

```
> fitOJ <- gamlr(x=xOJ, y=log(ojdf$sales))
> plot(fitOJ)
```

Calling `plot` on the fitted `gamlr` object produces the path plot in Figure 3.7a. You can also add `family="binomial"` to fit a Lasso logistic regression, as we do here for the semiconductor data (note that the first column of SC is `fail`, the response).

```
> fitSC <- gamlr(x=SC[,-1], y=SC[,1], family="binomial")
> plot(fitSC)
```

The resulting path plot is shown in Figure 3.7b. We didn't bother to create a sparse model matrix for the semiconductor Lasso because the original data is all numeric and dense (it doesn't contain a bunch of zeros). In that case you can just give `gamlr` the raw data as x.

The default behavior of `gamlr` solves for a sequence of 100 penalties λ_t, ranging from the initial λ_1 (set just big enough so that $\hat{\boldsymbol{\beta}}_1 = \mathbf{0}$) down to $\lambda_T = 0.01\lambda_1$. You can change this default behavior by specifying `nlambda` to set the sequence length T, or `lmr` to set the minimum λ_T

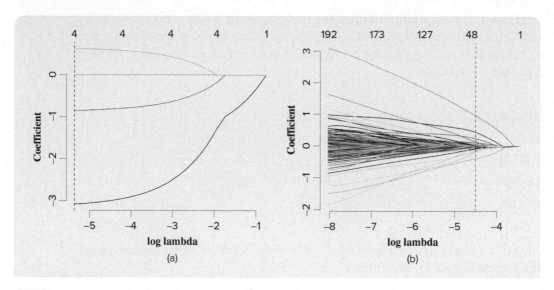

FIGURE 3.7 Lasso path plots for the orange juice (a) and semiconductor manufacturing (b) regression examples.

penalty size via the ratio lmr = λ_T/λ_1. This lmr argument is one you will use often; it is common that you will want to fit more complex models than you get for the default lmr=0.01 and then you need to set a smaller lmr.

Example 3.3 Orange Juice Sales: Lasso Paths You can print the fitted gamlr object to get a quick statement on what we fit above.

```
> fitOJ
gaussian gamlr with 4 inputs and 100 segments.
```

And you can call summary on it to get information about each path *segment* (the estimation at each λ_t).

```
> summary(fitOJ)
gaussian gamlr with 4 inputs and 100 segments.
           lambda par df          r2          aicc
seg1    0.465057217   1  1 0.00000000    1112.15134
seg2    0.443919649   2  2 0.01849065     573.89239
...
seg99   0.004872013   4  4 0.39390922  -13376.34842
seg100  0.004650572   4  4 0.39392573  -13377.13705
```

The information here includes the number of nonzero parameters (par) and degrees of freedom (df, which will be the same as par for the Lasso) and two measures of fit: in-sample R^2 and a corrected version of the AIC (we will work with this in the next section).

The gamlr object contains a number of attributes.

```
> names(fitOJ)
 [1] "lambda"    "gamma"    "nobs"     "family"   "alpha"    "beta"
 [7] "df"        "deviance" "iter"     "free"     "call"
 > dim(fitOJ$beta)
[1]    4 100
```

For example, lambda is the sequence of fitted λ_t penalties, alpha is the sequence of fitted intercept terms, and beta is the sequence of fitted regression coefficients. The intercept sequence is a vector of length nlambda (100 by default) and the coefficient sequence beta is an nlambda-column matrix with number of rows equal to the number of input variables (the number of columns in your model matrix). Each column of beta contains a segment of the path of estimated regression coefficients. Here we show the first two and last two segments.

```
> fitOJ$beta[,c(1:2,99:100)]
4 x 4 sparse Matrix of class "dgCMatrix"
                  seg1          seg2        seg99       seg100
log(price)        .     -0.07278185   -3.0761907   -3.0790315
branddominicks    .         .         -0.8468649   -0.8479243
brandminute.maid  .         .              .            .
brandtropicana    .         .          0.6376020    0.6386095
```

At λ_1 all of the coefficients are set equal to zero. As the penalty decreases to λ_2, the coefficient on log price enters the model with a nonzero elasticity. At the end of the path, at λ_{100}, all of the coefficients are nonzero except for the brandminute.maid coefficient. Sensibly, gamlr has determined that Minute Maid is the baseline OJ and that the economy Dominick's and luxury Tropicana can be represented through deviations from this baseline. Note that the intercept is *always unpenalized* in gamlr, so you have a nonzero intercept at every path segment.

```
> fitOJ$alpha[c(1:2,99:100)]
     seg1       seg2       seg99      seg100
 9.167864   9.224931   11.649609   11.651854
```

At the end of the Lasso path, the penalty is very small and our model fit is approaching that which you would get by using OLS to estimate this regression model. We can compare to the OLS results after re-leveling brand to have minute.maid as the reference level.

```
> oj$brand <- relevel(ojdf$brand, "minute.maid")
> glm(log(sales) ~ log(price) + brand, data=oj)
Coefficients:
   (Intercept)      log(price)   branddominicks   brandtropicana
       11.6990         -3.1387          -0.8702           0.6598
```

Another `gamlr` argument that we will encounter frequently is the `free` argument. You can pass `free` column indices (or names) for your design matrix and `gamlr` will leave the corresponding coefficients *unpenalized* in the regression fit. This is useful if there are some variables that you *know* need to be in the regression model, and you want their coefficients to be estimated without any bias (without any shrinkage toward zero). For example, we could have log price enter without a coefficient penalty in our simple OJ regression.

```
> fitOJfree <- gamlr(x=xOJ, y=log(ojdf$sales),free="log(price)")
> fitOJfree$beta[,c(1:2,99:100)]
4 x 4 sparse Matrix of class "dgCMatrix"
                     seg1         seg2      seg99      seg100
log(price)      -1.601307  -1.64724906  -3.1199089  -3.1207643
branddominicks          .  -0.04531381  -0.8612653  -0.8616711
brandminute.maid        .            .           .           .
brandtropicana          .            .   0.6508045   0.6512121
```

We now have a nonzero coefficient on `log(price)` even at λ_1. Of course, even though it is unpenalized, the coefficient on log price changes along the path as it adjusts to the influence of the estimated `brand` effects.

You may be confused at this point about what to do with this path of estimates. What use is a set of 100 model estimates if you don't know which one to use? Indeed, this path estimation is just the first step in model construction: once you have a path, you will need to use the selection tools of Section 3.3 to determine which model to deploy in practice.

Scaling the Penalty by Standard Deviations

A key thing to be aware of is that for Lasso regression the size of the covariates matters. Since the β_k values are all penalized by the same λ, you need to make sure they are on comparable scales. For example, $x\beta$ has the same effect as $(2x)\beta/2$, but $|\beta|$ is twice as much penalty cost as $|\beta/2|$. The common solution to this is to multiply β_j by $\mathrm{sd}(x_j)$ in the cost function to standardize across scales. That is, instead of Equation 3.5, you minimize

$$\frac{1}{n}\mathrm{dev}(\beta) + \lambda \sum_j \mathrm{sd}(x_j)\, |\beta_j|. \tag{3.7}$$

This implies that each β_j's penalty is now measured on the scale of 1 standard deviation change in x_j and, for example, switching from meters to feet or Fahrenheit to Celsius won't change your model fit.

This standardization scaling is the default in `gamlr` (and in `glmnet`) via the argument `standardize=TRUE`. There are some occasions where you instead want `standardize=FALSE`. Most commonly, you might want `standardize=FALSE` if you have all indicator variables indicating category membership (such as brand or geographic region). In this case, the standardization would put *more* penalty on common categories (since $\mathrm{sd}(x_j)$ will be higher) and less penalty on rare categories, which might be undesirable. However, unless you have clear reason to do otherwise, you should stick with the default `standardize=TRUE`.

In the remainder of this section, we will introduce two regression examples—one linear and one logistic—and work through them to illustrate `gamlr` Lasso regression.

Example 3.4 Ames Housing Data: Lasso Linear Regression The data in `amesHousing.csv` consist of information that the local government in Ames, Iowa, uses to assess home values. These data were compiled from 2006 to 2010 by De Cock (2011). They contain 2930 observations on 79 variables describing properties in Ames and their observed sale price.

```
> ames <- read.csv("AmesHousing.csv", strings=T)
> dim(ames)
[1] 2930   79
> ames[1:3,c(1:5,79)]
  MS.Zoning Lot.Frontage Lot.Area Street Alley SalePrice
1        RL          141    31770   Pave  <NA>    215000
2        RH           80    11622   Pave  <NA>    105000
3        RL           81    14267   Pave  <NA>    172000
```

Our prediction target here will be the log of `SalePrice`. We are working on log scale because, following the discussions in Chapter 1, prices tend to change with product characteristics in a multiplicative fashion. The sale price distribution is shown in Figure 3.8, both as a histogram and in a log-log scatterplot against lot size.

We will do some light processing on the raw data.

```
> ames$Yr.Sold <- factor(ames$Yr.Sold)
> ames$Mo.Sold <- factor(ames$Mo.Sold)
> ames$Lot.Area <- log(ames$Lot.Area)
```

Here we have converted the lot area to log scale, and converted the year and month of sale to factors. This is a rich data set and there is a ton of additional feature engineering that you can do to improve predictive performance. For example, you might want to use additional log

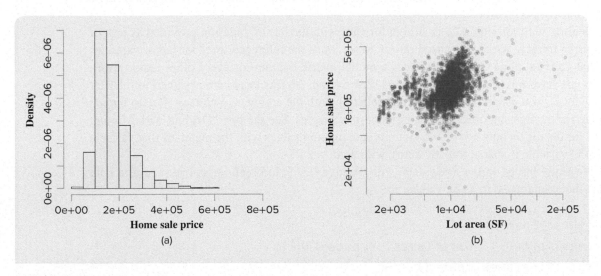

FIGURE 3.8 Home sale prices in Ames, Iowa. Panel (a) shows the marginal distribution of sale prices and (b) shows prices against the property lot size in square feet (note that this plot uses log scaling on the axes).

transforms or include factor representations of additional variables. There are also interesting interaction variables to consider (e.g., many of the variables are related to house condition and these can be interacted with the variables related to house size). For this illustration we will keep things simple, but we encourage you to explore the data further and try to engineer features that improve predictive performance. The regularization and selection tools of this chapter will allow you to build a really sophisticated prediction model.

Missing Data

Before we create our model matrix, we need to deal with a common issue: *missing data.* If you look at the data frame of observations, 13,960 of the entries are NA (this is R's code for "not available").

```
> sum(is.na(ames))
[1] 13960
```

This indicates that these entries are missing in the assessor's data. Looking at some individual variables, we see examples of missing entries in Pool.QC (a quality category for the swimming pool) and Lot.Frontage.

```
> summary(ames$Pool.QC)
   Ex   Fa   Gd   TA NA's
    4    2    4    3 2917
> ames$Lot.Frontage[11:15]
[1] 75 NA 63 85 NA
```

Presumably, Pool.QC is missing because most properties do not include a swimming pool. The Lot.Frontage variable—the feet of street connected to the property—could be missing for a variety of reasons. Perhaps it is because the property has zero frontage (although some of these missing values correspond to houses with large property areas) or perhaps it is just a variable that is not always recorded.

Dealing with missing data is straightforward with the naref function provided as part of the gamlr library. We already used naref to set NA as the reference level for factor variables (so that sparse.model.matrix creates a model matrix column for every other factor level). When you have missing data, the missing observations on this factor are assigned to this reference level. You can also call the naref function with the argument impute=TRUE to *impute* a value for the missing observations in numeric variables. See the box "Dealing with Missing Data" for details on how naref works to impute missing values with the mean for that variable or, if the variable is sparse (mostly zero), with zero.

We apply naref to the ames data, with impute=TRUE, to obtain amesImputed as a data frame that contains no missing values.

```
> library(gamlr)
> amesImputed <- naref(ames, impute=TRUE)
> sum(is.na(amesImputed))
[1] 0
```

The factors now all have <NA> as their reference level, and numeric variables with missing values have been replaced by var.x which has no missing values (these have been imputed) and var.miss that is 1 if the entry was imputed and 0 otherwise.

```
> summary(amesImputed$Pool.QC)
<NA>   Ex   Fa   Gd   TA
2917    4    2    4    3
> amesImputed$Lot.Frontage.x[11:15]
[1] 75.00000 69.22459 63.00000 85.00000 69.22459
> amesImputed$Lot.Frontage.miss[11:15]
[1] 0 1 0 0 1
```

Again, refer to the "Missing Data" box for detail on how we deal with missing data.

Dealing with Missing Data

Missing data is an issue that will occur repeatedly in practice. Incomplete observations occur for a variety of reasons. In some cases, data will be missing because the variable doesn't make sense for that observation (e.g., pool quality for a house without a pool). In survey data, you can have variables that are missing because people don't answer all of your questions. And in any telemetry data (e.g., for anything from tracking industrial processes to tracking online customer behavior) information is often missed or dropped in processing.

The naref function from gamlr is useful to prepare data with missingness for use in regression analyses. We will describe here how it deals with each of categorical (factor) and numeric (numeric or integer) variables.

For factor variables, you simply treat the missing observations as a separate category. As described earlier in this chapter, adding NA as a new reference level for each factor variable forces R to have a separate coefficient for each observed factor level. Recall that in Example 3.4 the original data frame is ames and amesImputed is the output from calling naref on this original data.

```
> summary(ames$Pool.QC)
  Ex   Fa   Gd   TA NA's
   4    2    4    3 2917
> summary(amesImputed$Pool.QC)
<NA>   Ex   Fa   Gd   TA
2917    4    2    4    3
```

In the original data, `Pool.QC` had mostly missing values. In `amesImputed`, the output from `naref`, these missing values are allocated to a new reference factor level called `<NA>`. When you build a model matrix using `amesImputed`, the impact on expected response from these missing values will be subsumed into the intercept (i.e., such that the `Pool.QC` factor level effects will be interpretable as being relative to a property with no swimming pool).

For numeric variables, you need to replace the missing values with a numeric value. This is referred to as *data imputation*. There are a bunch of different ways that you can do this—missing data imputation, or guessing what the missing values *would* have been, is an interesting regression problem in its own right. Two simple approaches that work well for most problems are *zero* and *mean* imputation. In the former, which we recommend for sparse variables (those that are mostly zero), you replace missing values with zero. In the latter, you replace the missing values with the mean of the nonmissing entries. Mean imputation has better theoretical properties because observations close to the mean have less impact on your fitted regression coefficients (they have low *leverage*). But zero imputation can be preferable if you have sparse data and you don't want to lose that convenient sparsity by imputing a bunch of close-but-not-quite-zero values (when variable is mostly zero, the mean tends to be near zero).

The `naref` function has the argument `pzero` which is used to decide between mean and zero imputation. If the proportion of zeros in the nonmissing entries is greater than `pzero`, then it does zero imputation. Otherwise it does mean imputation. The default is `pzero=0.5` so that you will impute zeros if more than half of the values are zero. If you want to force zero imputation, then you specify `pzero=0`.

Looking at our Ames housing data, the feet of property frontage is a numeric variable with missing values. After running `naref` with `impute=TRUE`, the missing entries have been replaced with the mean of the nonmissing values.

```
> ames$Lot.Frontage[11:15]
[1] 75 NA 63 85 NA
> amesImputed$Lot.Frontage.x[11:15]
[1] 75.00000 69.22459 63.00000 85.00000 69.22459
> amesImputed$Lot.Frontage.miss[11:15]
[1] 0 1 0 0 1
```

The single variable `Lot.Frontage` has been replaced with two columns, `Lot.Frontage.x` which contains the numeric values after imputation, and `Lot.Frontage.miss` which is a binary variable with 1 for those observations that were missing and are now imputed. Notice that the imputed value is around 69, indicating that the average feet of frontage is around 69 for properties where this is not missing.

For an example of zero imputation, consider the `Bsmt.Full.Bath` variable that counts the number of full bathrooms in the house basement. This variable is 58% zeros and has two `NA` values. Since this proportion of zeros is higher than the default `pzero=0.5`, `naref` has replaced the missing values with zero.

```
> mean(ames$Bsmt.Full.Bath==0, na.rm=TRUE)
[1] 0.5829918
> ames$Bsmt.Full.Bath[1341:1344]
[1]  1 NA  0  0
> amesImputed$Bsmt.Full.Bath.x[1341:1344]
[1] 1 0 0 0
> amesImputed$Bsmt.Full.Bath.miss[1341:1344]
[1] 0 1 0 0
```

Again, `naref` outputs both the `.x` imputed numeric variable and a `.miss` indicator for whether or not the original value was missing.

You should always include the missingness indicator (e.g., `Bsmt.Full.Bath.miss` and `Lot.Frontage.miss`) in your analysis because the fact that data were missing might itself be useful information. For example, the missing `Lot.Frontage` values might occur because those houses have no yard. The only situation where you can ignore the fact that data was missing is if it was missing completely at random: if the probability of data being missing is independent from the other characteristics of the observation. This is unlikely to be true in practice. And even if it is true, including the missingness indicator will make your analysis more robust to the accuracy of your missing data imputation procedure.

Finally, note that none of the observations of `SalePrice` were missing in the original `ames` data frame. When you are doing data imputation, you never want to impute missing values in your response variable. An observation with a missing response should simply be dropped from your analysis (although if you have a large number of missing responses you need to understand why that happened and how it impacts your interpretation of what you are predicting).

Building the Model Matrix

Once you have constructed the data frame `amesImputed`, which has imputed missing numeric values and created a `<NA>` reference level for all factors, you can proceed with Lasso estimation. The first step is to extract the response variable, *y*, as the log of the property sale price.

```
> yAmes <- log(ames$SalePrice)
> head(yAmes)
[1] 12.27839 11.56172 12.05525 12.40492 12.15425 12.18332
```

The next step is to create the numeric model matrix. We do that here using `sparse.model.matrix` and a formula that specifies regression onto every variable except the `SalePrice` column that we used to create our log sale price response.

```
> ycol <- which(names(amesImputed)=="SalePrice")
> xAmes <- sparse.model.matrix( ~ ., data=amesImputed[,-ycol])
[,-1]
> dim(xAmes)
[1] 2930  339
```

The result is a 339 column model matrix (note that we used `[,-1]` to remove the intercept). As mentioned earlier, you can create much more complex regression models here by combining and interacting variables. The "main effects only" model is a starting point but you can expand it yourself by changing the regression formula that defines x.

Fitting the Lasso Path

Now that we have x and y, we can apply `gamlr` to fit the Lasso regularization paths.

```
> fitAmes <- gamlr(xAmes, yAmes, lmr=1e-4)
```

Note that we have specified `lmr=1e-4` here to set a smaller than default (`lmr=1e-2`) ratio for the smallest λ_T relative to the starting λ_1. This tells `gamlr` to run the Lasso path down to a smaller level of penalization. The fitted path is shown in Figure 3.9b. For comparison, the path plot corresponding to a default specification with `lmr=1e-2` is shown in Figure 3.9a. While the default path stops at $\lambda_T \approx e^{-6}$, our specified path goes down to $\lambda_T < e^{-10}$. This allows for many more nonzero estimated coefficients at the end of the path (from the plot headers, 301 for `lmr=1e-4` vs 115 for `lmr=1e-2`) and these estimated coefficients are allowed to move further from zero.

Note that the vertical dashed lines on the plots in Figure 3.9 correspond to the "best" model as selected by the AICc selection rule introduced in the next section. By this rule, the "best" model is at the edge of the λ_t values evaluated using `lmr=1e-2`. Whenever your best model is at the lowest-penalty edge of the space of models you are considering (i.e., if your selection rule chooses the model at λ_T) you should consider re-running the path algorithm to consider smaller penalization levels.

The Fitted `gamlr` Object

The fitted `gamlr` object, which we've names `fitAmes`, contains the data behind the path plots shown in Figure 3.9. For example, we can see that `gamlr` fit 100 λ_t segments and that $\lambda_{100}/\lambda_1 = 1/10{,}000$.

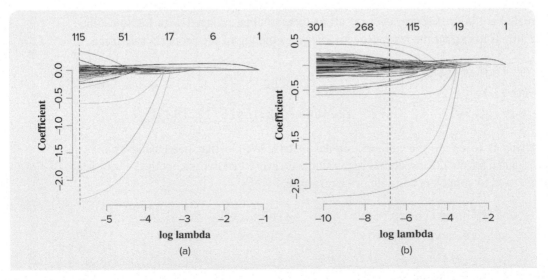

FIGURE 3.9 The Lasso regularization paths for Ames house sale price using `gamlr` with default `lmr=1e-2` in (a), and with `lmr=1e-4` in (b). In our analysis we use the specification in (b) such that $\lambda_T/\lambda_1 = 1/10{,}000$.

```
> length(fitAmes$lambda)
[1] 100
> fitAmes$lambda[100]/fitAmes$lambda[1]
seg100
 1e-04
```

The fitted coefficients for each segment, $\hat{\beta}_t$, are columns of the beta attribute.

```
> dim(fitAmes$beta)
[1] 339 100
> sum(fitAmes$beta[,100]!=0)
[1] 300
```

At the end of the path there are 300 nonzero $\hat{\beta}_{100,j}$ coefficients. This plus the intercept gives the 301 nonzero parameters marked on the left of the header in Figure 3.9b. We can pull out some coefficients from the first and last two segments.

```
> fitAmes$beta[
+ c("Overall.Qual","Lot.Area","Lot.Frontage.x","Lot.Frontage.
miss"),
+ c(1:2,99:100)]
4 x 4 sparse Matrix of class "dgCMatrix"
                   seg1        seg2        seg99        seg100
Overall.Qual       .     0.0211872   0.0497281614   0.0497218631
Lot.Area           .          .      0.0864251705   0.0864501758
Lot.Frontage.x     .          .      0.0001757198   0.0001758566
Lot.Frontage.miss  .          .      0.0049547699   0.0049655247
```

The first variable to enter the path with a nonzero coefficient is Overall.Qual, which rates the overall finish and construction of the house from 1 (very poor) to 10 (very excellent). Clearly the condition of your house has a major impact on its sale price. The lot size and frontage variables do not get nonzero coefficients until later in the path. Notice that the missingness indicator Lot.Frontage.miss has a positive estimated coefficient. The estimation has determined that the missing frontage entries tend to occur for more expensive properties.

Again, we emphasize that path estimation is just the first step of model construction. You don't know which path segment is most useful for prediction until you apply the model selection techniques of later sections.

Example 3.5 Telemarketing Data: Lasso Logistic Regression To illustrate Lasso logistic regression for a binary response, we will use the Telemarketing data from Moro et al. (2011). The telemarketing.csv data set consists of observations from the marketing campaign of a

Portuguese bank that was trying to get customers to subscribe to a term deposit product. Term deposits are basically loans to the bank: you deposit money that you will not be able to access for an agreed length of time, and in exchange the bank pays you a higher interest rate on this deposit than you would get on money that you can access at any time.

We read the data in as the tlmrk data frame.

```
> tlmrk <- read.csv("telemarketing.csv", strings=T)
> dim(tlmrk)
[1] 4521   15
> tlmrk[1,]
  age        job marital education default balance housing loan
1  30 unemployed married   primary      no    1787      no   no
   contact  campaign   durmin previous poutcome pweek subscribe
1 cellular         1 1.316667        0  unknown     0         0
```

The variables here include demographic information and finances such as their account balance and whether they have an existing housing or personal loan. We also have data about the marketing campaign for this customer, including

- campaign: number of contacts performed during this marketing campaign for this client.
- contact: the format of the most recent contact (land-line or cell phone).
- durmin: the length of time in minutes for the most recent phone conversation with the customer.
- previous: the number of previous contacts with this customer before the current marketing campaign.
- poutcome: the outcome of the previous marketing campaign for this customer.
- pweek: the weeks that have passed since the customer was last contacted during the previous campaign.

All of this data is important for designing marketing campaigns. People do not usually like getting calls from telemarketers. When designing a campaign, you want your sales agents calling only people who are likely to subscribe and not bothering those who are not. In addition, variables like durmin tell you how long it takes your agents to close the deal and when they are spending too much time on the phone. It is a waste of time and money for everyone to spend too long talking to a customer who will not be convinced to subscribe.

Our response of interest is the binary variable subscribe that indicates whether or not the customer ended up subscribing to a term deposit. We pull it out as the variable yTD.

```
> yTD <- tlmrk$subscribe
> mean(yTD)
[1] 0.11524
```

Roughly 11.5% of the customers end up subscribing to the term deposits.

There are no NA entries in this data, so we don't need to worry about missing data imputation. However, we will still run `naref` to create `<NA>` as the reference level for factor variables. Since the data contain the level `unknown` for many factors, we could have also gone through and set that as the reference level. However, it is convenient to simply call `naref` and you get the result that all factor effects will be interpretable as variations around an overall average intercept.

```
> sum(is.na(tlmrk))
[1] 0
> library(gamlr)
Loading required package: Matrix
> tlmrkX <- naref(tlmrk[,-15])
> levels(tlmrkX$job)
 [1] NA             "admin."       "blue-collar" "entrepreneur"
 [5] "housemaid"    "management"   "retired"      "self-employed"
 [9] "services"     "student"      "technician"   "unemployed"
[13] "unknown"
```

Notice that we removed column 15 when creating the `tlmrkX` data frame using `naref`. This was the column containing our response, `subscribe`, so that now `tlmrkX` contains only the input variables.

Building the Model Matrix

Now we are ready to build our numeric model matrix. This time, we will include all of the input variables interacted with each other and create a new variable as `durmin^2` to allow the probability of success to change quadratically (as a curve) during the phone call. We use `I(durmin^2)` in the regression formula to tell R to create a new variable named `I(durmin^2)` representing the square of `durmin`.

```
> xTD <- sparse.model.matrix(~.^2 + I(durmin^2), data=tlmrkX)
> dim(xTD)
[1] 4521   656
```

The resulting model matrix has $n = 4521$ observations on $J = 656$ columns.

Fitting the Logistic Lasso Regression Path

You can fit a logistic Lasso path with `gamlr` by specifying `family="binomial"`.

```
> fitTD <- gamlr(xTD, yTD, family="binomial")
```

The resulting Lasso path is shown in Figure 3.10a. We kept the default `lmr=1e-2` here such that $\lambda_{100}/\lambda_1 = 1/100$. As before, the fitted `gamlr` object contains all of the estimated $\hat{\beta}_t$ coefficients for each segment. You can pull out any specific segment, and Figure 3.10b shows the fitted $\hat{y}$

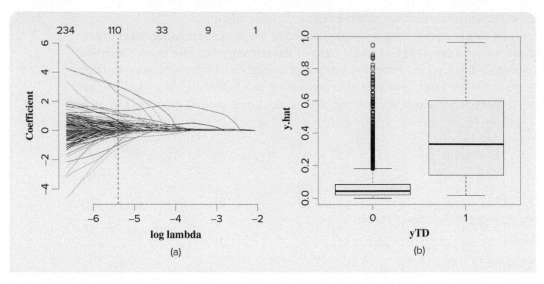

FIGURE 3.10   Panel (a) shows the Lasso regularization path for prediction of telemarketing call success, and (b) shows the fitted values corresponding to the AICc selected segment of coefficients at the dashed line in (a).

probabilities of success corresponding to the segment at the dashed line in Figure 3.10a (this is the AICc selected segment; see the next section for details). In the code below we pull out the first and last two segment coefficients on `durmin` and `I(durmin^2)`, the minutes and squared minutes spent on the phone call.

```
> fitTD$beta[c("durmin","I(durmin^2)"),c(1:2,99:100)]
2 x 4 sparse Matrix of class "dgCMatrix"
               seg1         seg2          seg99         seg100
durmin         .      0.01244651    0.338559757    0.340290880
I(durmin^2)    .         .         -0.009229655   -0.009359627
```

The minute length `durmin` is the first variable to enter the path with a nonzero coefficient, indicating that this variable has strong predictive signal on the outcome of the phone call.

■ 3.3 Model Selection

The Lasso is used to obtain paths of promising candidate variables. Running `gamlr` with the default `nlambda=100` gives us 100 vectors of fitted coefficients $\hat{\beta}_t$ based on 100 different penalties λ_t. Once you have this path, you need to do *model selection* to choose the best vector of coefficients to use for prediction. There are a number of different ways to do this, but all can be thought of as having the same motivation: select the model that does the best job predicting out of sample. The term "best job" will have different meanings in different applications. In some cases, you will simply want to get the best (lowest) average OOS deviance. In other cases, you might be motivated to trade some average performance for a more robust model—a simpler model that may have slightly higher OOS deviance but has less probability of producing the occasional really bad prediction. Regardless, you are always using some concept of predictive performance as the foundation for your model selection.

The benefit of the Lasso is that you have *indexed* your potential models with a single parameter: λ. This penalty weight is a *signal-to-noise filter*. It works like the squelch on a VHF radio (or, to be a bit more contemporary, the noise canceling level on a cellular phone). If you turn it all the way up, you don't hear anything. If you turn it all the way down, you hear only static. The key to being able to communicate on a radio is finding the sweet spot in the middle where you hear the other person's voice and none of the background noise. It is the same for good statistical prediction: you need to find the λ that gives you good signal with little noise. Looking at the Lasso path plots, "all the way up" is the far right where all coefficients are zero, and "all the way down" is the far left where most coefficients are nonzero.

When you do model selection on Lasso paths, you should think about what you are doing as *selecting the best* λ_t. In contrast to subset selection, where you need to consider all possible combinations of input variables (or a greedy search through possible combinations), with the Lasso you are considering selection only for this tuning parameter: the penalty weight that acts as your signal-to-noise filter. In this section we will introduce two different frameworks for selecting λ. The first framework is built on *information criteria* that combine in-sample deviance with the model degrees of freedom to estimate OOS predictive performance. The second framework is built around the sort of cross-validation experiments that we saw earlier in this chapter, where you split the data into folds and use OOS predictive performance across folds to get an estimate of future OOS performance.

3.3.1 Information Criteria

Information criteria (IC) are theoretical approximations to what OOS deviance you can expect when using your model to predict new data. Compared to running cross-validation experiments, IC estimates of OOS performance have the advantage of being fast (you need to fit the Lasso path only once, to your original dataset) and deterministic (there is no Monte Carlo variation due to random sampling). We use information criteria a lot in this book, especially the AICc that will be introduced below, and our practical experience is that this is a convenient and robust foundation for model selection.

There are many information criteria out there. We will look at Akaike's AIC, its corrected version AICc, and the Bayesian BIC. All of these IC attempt to approximate the distance between a fitted model and draws from the "true model" using different analytic approximations. That is, the IC are all attempting to approximate the OOS deviance (the distance between new data and the fitted model). Since the IC measure a distance, you can apply them in model selection by choosing the model with minimum IC.

The information criteria all take the form

$$\text{IC}(\hat{\boldsymbol{\beta}}) = \text{dev}(\hat{\boldsymbol{\beta}}) + \kappa \cdot df \tag{3.8}$$

where $\text{dev}(\hat{\boldsymbol{\beta}})$ is the *in-sample* deviance and *df* is the *model degrees of freedom*: the number of observations that the procedure you used to estimate $\hat{\boldsymbol{\beta}}$ should be able to fit exactly (refer back to Chapter 1 for more discussion on the model degrees of freedom). As we will describe below, *df* for the Lasso is equal to the number of nonzero estimated parameters.

Note that the deviance calculations used for Eqution (3.8) require you to use the full deviance formula that expands the constant *C* from Equation (1.26). This constant includes a bunch of negative log likelihood terms that don't change with $\hat{\beta}$. However, this will be taken care of by the R functions you use to calculate ICs.

The term κ in (3.8) is the IC *complexity penalty:* it is the price you pay for adding additional degrees of freedom to your model. Equation (3.8) looks similar to the penalized deviance equations, like (3), that we used to define our Lasso regression estimator. And it is similar! You are combining an in-sample deviance with a price on complexity. You apply the IC equation to evaluate models fit to optimize a penalized deviance, and the value of κ that you want to use is derived from theory rather than being a tuning parameter that you estimate from the data.

Recall the simulated data example that opened this chapter. We aplied models with 2, 3, and 19 parameters (linear, quadratic, and 18-degree polynomial regression) fit to a cloud of points. The model selection goal is to select the "just right" model in Figure 3.1 that fits the persistent pattern but doesn't overfit to noise. In this example, which used OLS to estimate the coefficients, the model degrees of freedom is equal to the number of parameters in each model (2, 3, and 19). The correct value of κ in our IC of Equation (3.8) should lead to the IC being lowest for the 3-parameter quadratic model. Even though the 18-degree polynomial fits the data perfectly (and has zero in-sample deviance), you should have that the complexity penalty $\kappa \cdot 19$ is large enough to compensate for this low in-sample deviance.

The AIC

A common IC is *Akaike's* information criterion, the AIC. The AIC is an attempt to approximate the average OOS deviance on new data. Through a lot of theoretical statistics work, Akaike (1973) determined that the "right" complexity penalty to approximate the OOS deviance is simply $\kappa = 2$.

$$\text{AIC}(\hat{\beta}) = \text{dev}(\hat{\beta}) + 2 \cdot df \tag{3.9}$$

This AIC score is an output of many standard statistical software routines. For example, in Example 3.1, in the semiconductor dataset, we used glm to fit the 25-input cut logistic regression model. The printed information from calling summary on the cut object includes the AIC.

```
> summary(cut)

...

    Null deviance: 731.59  on 1476  degrees of freedom
Residual deviance: 599.04  on 1451  degrees of freedom
AIC: 651.04
> 599.04 + 2*26
[1] 651.04
```

The AIC here is equal to the in-sample deviance, 599.04, plus two times the number of parameters in the model (26 for the 25 inputs plus the intercept). Recall that, confusingly, what R calls degrees of freedom here is actually the residual degrees of freedom: the number of opportunities to observe error variability around the fitted model, or $n - df$ in our notation. There are $n = 1477$ observations here, and $1477 - 26 = 1451$ as in the R output (note that the residual degrees of freedom for the null model is $n - 1$ since it just fits a single mean response parameter).

In maximum likelihood estimation, as applied inside glm, the *df* is simply the number of parameters in the model. More generally, the *df* measures the in-sample correlation between $\hat{y}$

and *y*—how much flexibility you have to make the model fit look like the observed data. For important theoretical reasons (Zou et al., 2007) the Lasso, like for MLE fitted models, has *df* simply equal to the number of nonzero $\hat{\beta}_j$ at a given λ. This is *not* true for any other penalization cost function. For example, if you use a ridge penalty in your penalized deviance minimization then all coefficients will be nonzero, but *df* will be less than the full model dimensions because the coefficients are shrunk toward zero.

It is a massive advantage for the Lasso that you have a simple measure of the number of degrees of freedom (the number of nonzero estimated parameters) at a given λ penalty weight. This fact lets you apply ICs to choose the best Lasso model. For example, R has the AIC function that you can apply to a fitted gamlr object. Here we apply it to the telemarketing example Lasso path from Example 3.5.

```
> AIC(fitTD)
     seg1      seg2      seg3      seg4
3233.000  3173.971  3123.801  3081.680
...
    seg97     seg98     seg99    seg100
2293.355  2297.469  2295.603  2296.141
> which.min(AIC(fitTD))
seg92
   92
> sum(fitTD$beta[,92]!=0)
[1] 185
> fitTD$lambda[92]
      seg92
0.001858245
```

The minimum AIC score occurs for the 92nd segment, with $\lambda_{92} \approx 0.00186$ and 185 nonzero coefficients in $\hat{\boldsymbol{\beta}}_{92}$.

The Corrected AICc

The AIC is the most commonly applied IC, but *you should not use the AIC.* We introduced the AIC only as a stepping stone to the superior corrected AIC that we now describe. When you have a lot of potential parameters in your model, the AIC will tend to overfit. The reason why this happens is worth understanding because it motivates the IC that you *should* use: the corrected AICc. The AIC overfits because the actual κ that Akaike derives as optimal for linear regression is

$$\kappa = 2\mathbb{E}\left[\frac{\sigma^2}{\hat{\sigma}^2}\right] \tag{3.10}$$

where σ^2 is the true error variance and $\hat{\sigma}^2$ is the variance of your fitted residuals. Akaike made the simplifying assumption that the variance of the residuals is a good approximation to the true error variance, such that $\hat{\sigma}^2 \approx \sigma^2$ and you can simplify Equation (3.10) to say $\kappa \approx 2$. However, an overfit model (e.g., our 18-degree polynomial from the chapter opening) will have very small residuals because the model is fitting the noise. That implies that σ^2 will be much bigger than $\hat{\sigma}^2$ and $\kappa = 2$ will be too small a complexity penalty.

It turns out that you can actually predict the ratio of variances in (3.10) as

$$\mathbb{E}\left[\frac{\sigma^2}{\hat{\sigma}^2}\right] \approx \frac{n}{n - df - 1} \tag{3.11}$$

This approximation comes from the theoretical definition of degrees of freedom. It leads to the *corrected AIC* (Hurvich and Tsai, 1989) with $\kappa = 2n/(n - df - 1)$,

$$\text{AICc}(\hat{\beta}) = \text{dev}(\hat{\beta}) + \frac{n}{n - df - 1} 2 \cdot df \tag{3.12}$$

You *should* use the AICc for IC-based model selection. Although motivated using a ratio of error variances in linear regression, it also works for logistic regression or any other generalized linear model (fit via likelihood maximization or with Lasso estimation). Notice that for big n/df, the AICc becomes similar to the AIC as the ratio $n/(n - df - 1)$ gets closer to one. Hence, the AIC will work well for large n/df (which is the classical statistics setting where it was developed) while the corrected AICc works for any n/df you encounter.

The `gamlr` package uses AICc for selection by default. The AICc selected segment is marked on the path plot with a vertical line (see Figures 3.9 or 3.10a, for example), and if you call `predict` or `coef` on a fitted `gamlr` object it will give you results corresponding to the AICc minimizing path segment.

The BIC

Before diving into AICc selection for our Lasso examples, we note one additional IC that you will sometimes encounter. The BIC, where B stands for Bayes, is motivated from the Bayesian inference ideas we outlined in Chapter 2. Instead of attempting to predict the average OOS deviance for candidate models, as the AIC and AICc do, the BIC is attempting to approximate the *posterior probability* that each model is best. This subtle difference leads it to select more simple (fewer parameter) models than you get from the AICc. A more complex model might have lower expected OOS deviance, but higher variation in OOS deviance around this expectation. For example, you have higher probability of getting a bad model fit from an unlucky training sample when you are working with more model complexity.

Schwarz et al. (1978) developed the BIC around the same time as Akaike's work on the AIC. The Schwarz complexity penalty is $\kappa = \log(n)$, such that

$$\text{BIC}(\hat{\beta}) = \text{dev}(\hat{\beta}) + \log(n) \cdot df \tag{3.13}$$

Although the BIC can be useful for model selection in small sample settings, for most applications the $\log(n)$ complexity penalty tends to be too large. That is, the BIC will tend to underfit and choose overly simple models. You can treat it as giving a lower bound on the amount of useful model complexity.

Example 3.6 Ames Housing Data: IC Model Selection Returning to the house price prediction of Example 3.2, we have `fitAmes` as our `gamlr` object containing the fitted Lasso path. Since `gamlr` uses the AICc as its default model selection rule, if you call `coef` on this object you will get the coefficients corresponding to the AICc-minimizing path segment.

```
> bAmes <- coef(fitAmes) ## coefficients selected under AICc
> head(bAmes)
6 x 1 sparse Matrix of class "dgCMatrix"
                      seg62
intercept          4.5352809
MS.ZoningA (agr)  -0.3664627
MS.ZoningC (all)  -0.1779210
MS.ZoningFV          .
MS.ZoningI (all)     .
MS.ZoningRH          .
```

The output is in a `Matrix` library sparse format. We will drop the intercept and convert it to a dense vector before exploring the selected $\hat{\beta}$ coefficients.

```
> bAmes <- bAmes[-1,]
> sum(bAmes!=0)
[1] 195
> tail(sort(bAmes),3) ## big increaser
Kitchen.QualPo Exterior.1stPreCast NeighborhoodGrnHill
     0.1132968          0.3267350          0.4425938
> bAmes[c("Lot.Area","Lot.Frontage.x","Lot.Frontage.miss")]
     Lot.Area     Lot.Frontage.x Lot.Frontage.miss
 7.525206e-02       9.585679e-05       0.000000e+00
```

The AICc selects a model with 195 nonzero coefficients. The largest positive coefficient is the effect of the property being in the Green Hill neighborhood, and we notice that in the selected model the missingness indicator for `Lot.Frontage` has a zero coefficient: the AICc has decided that the fact that this variable is missing is not a useful predictor of house price. You can call the `AICc` function on `fitAmes` to see the AICc values underlying this selection.

```
> which.min(AICc(fitAmes))
seg62
   62
> fitAmes$lambda[62]
      seg62
0.001154232
```

We find that the AICc has selected $\lambda_{62} \approx 0.00115$ as the best penalty weight.

The `predict` function also uses AICc selection by default. For example, if we call `predict` on `fitAmes` for the 1st and 11th observations we get (after exponentiating the predicted log price) expected sale price values of around $210k and $170k.

```
> ( yhat <- predict(fitAmes, xAmes[c(1,11),]) )
2 x 1 Matrix of class "dgeMatrix"
      seg62
1  12.25147
11 12.05597
> drop(yhat)
        1        11
12.25147 12.05597
> exp(drop(yhat))
        1        11
209289.1 172123.5
```

Notice that we applied `drop` to `yhat` to convert the predictions from special sparse `Matrix` format to a simple vector. You will often want to take this step when working with predictions from `gamlr`.

To use the other IC for model selection, you apply the appropriate function to the fitted `gamlr` object to get the set of IC scores and then find the segment with the minimum score. This segment can then be passed to `coef` (and to `predict`) with the `select` argument to get results for that specified path segment.

```
> (bicsel <- which.min(BIC(fitAmes)))
seg48
   48
> bAmesBIC <- coef(fitAmes, select=bicsel)[-1,] ## and BIC
> sum(bAmesBIC!=0)
[1] 95
```

We see here that the BIC selects λ_{48} which corresponds to 95 nonzero coefficients (about half of what the AICc selected). The AIC ends up selecting the same segment as the AICc: that with 195 coefficients at λ_{62}.

```
> (aicsel <- which.min(AIC(fitAmes)))
seg62
   62
```

The AIC and AICc give the same results here because n is much larger than the full potential df (we have 2930 observations on 339 input dimensions), such that the correction ratio is close to one: $2930/(2930 - 339 - 1) \approx 1.13$. All of the IC surfaces are plotted in Figure 3.11a. The AIC and AICc scores are very similar, again due to the high n/df ratio.

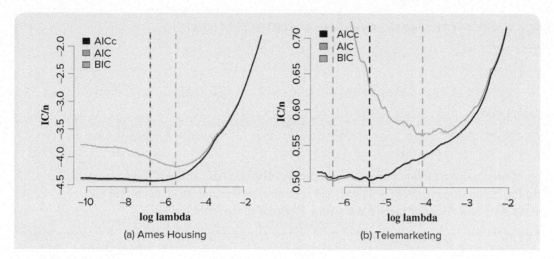

FIGURE 3.11 Information criteria scores as a function of the λ_t penalty weights for each of our Ames Housing (a) and Telemarketing (b) examples.

We are presenting all of the options here so that you can understand what to expect when you encounter AIC, AICc, or BIC model selection in practice. However, you should use the AICc as your default IC for model selection.

Example 3.7 Telemarketing Data: IC Model Selection Turning to logistic regression and our telemarketing example, recall that we have the fitted `gamlr` object `fitTD` for prediction of call success (getting the customer to subscribe to a term deposit) as a function of customer characteristics and campaign information.

The default AICc selection chooses a model with 90 nonzero coefficients.

```
> bTD <- coef(fitTD)[-1,] ## coefficients selected under AICc
> sum(bTD!=0)
[1] 90
```

Notice that we appended [-1,] on the exctracted coefficients to remove the intercept and drop the `Matrix` formatting. We can pull out the coefficients on the length of the phone call.

```
> bTD[c("durmin","I(durmin^2)")]
     durmin  I(durmin^2)
 0.276468974 -0.004644089
```

The AICc selected model has a positive coefficient on `durmin` and a negative coefficient on `durmin`^{2}, such that the odds of success will increase with the beginning of the phone call but eventually start to decrease as time progresses.

The BIC selects a much simpler model with only 20 nonzero coefficients and the AIC selects a much more complex model with 185 nonzero coefficients.

```
> bTDbic <- coef(fitTD, select=which.min(BIC(fitTD)))[-1,]
> sum(bTDbic!=0)
[1] 20
> bTDaic <- coef(fitTD, select=which.min(AIC(fitTD)))[-1,]
> sum(bTDaic!=0)
[1] 185
```

All three IC scores are shown as a function of λ in Figure 3.11b. The AIC and AICc match up at large λ, where the correction $n/(n - df - 1) \approx 1$, but then start to separate from each other at larger values. Both AIC and AICc surfaces have a very different shape from the BIC.

3.3.2 Cross-Validation for Lasso Paths

An alternative to IC model selection is to apply the sort of cross-validation (CV) experiment we described in Algorithm 3.1. For Lasso paths, you want to design a CV experiment to evaluate the OOS predictive performance of different λ penalty values. This is in contrast to CV for subset selection, where you evaluated different pre-set subsets of variables inside the CV experiment. To execute Algorithm 3.1 for Lasso paths, you need to

- Fit the Lasso path for the full dataset to get a grid of candidate λ_t penalties.
- Run a CV experiment where you split your data into K folds and apply these λ_t penalties in Lasso estimation on the training data excluding each fold. Record OOS deviances for prediction on each left-out fold.
- Select the λ_t with "best" OOS performance. Your selected model is defined by the corresponding $\hat{\beta}_t$ coefficients that were obtained through Lasso estimation on the full dataset with penalty λ_t.

How Many Folds?

A common question around CV is *How do I choose K?* The short answer is that more is better (it reduces the Monte Carlo variation due to random fold assignment) but only up to a point. Using too many folds gets computationally very expensive. Moreover, using too many folds (anything approaching $K = n$) gives bad results if there is even a tiny amount of dependence between your observations. Smaller values of K lead to CV that is more robust to this type of mis-specification.

To figure out how many folds is "enough," note that the variance on your CV estimate of *average* OOS deviance is the variance of the K OOS deviances on each left-out fold divided by $\sqrt{K}$ (recall from Chapter 2 that the variance on a mean is the variance of the observations divided by the square root of the number of observations). If you run your CV experiment and the uncertainty around average OOS deviance is larger than you want, then you can re-run the experiment with more folds. However, if adding a small number of folds doesn't significantly reduce the uncertainty then you are probably better off using the AICc for model selection.

CV Path Plots

Once again, this is all easiest to understand visually. The `gamlr` library provides the `cv.gamlr` function to run CV experiments for Lasso paths. This function uses the exact same syntax as the standard `gamlr` function, and you can pass it any arguments that you would pass to `gamlr`; these arguments are used for the full sample path and for the reduced-sample fits inside the CV

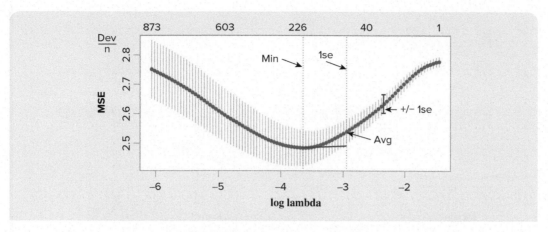

FIGURE 3.12 A cross-validated Lasso path plot from `cv.gamlr`. The blue dots are mean OOS deviances (here MSE, as this is from a linear regression) and the error bars mark ±1 standard error around the estimated average OOS deviance. The CV-min and CV-1se selection rules are marked with vertical dashed lines.

experiment. Figure 3.12 shows the results of `cv.gamlr` on a linear regression example. Just like the path plot, the CV plot has λ on the x axis and the degrees of freedom (number of nonzero coefficients) on the top. The average OOS deviances are marked with blue dots, and error bars are extended one standard error on each side of these estimates of the expected OOS deviance. From our discussion above, the standard errors are calculated as the variance of the K OOS deviances at each λ_t value, divided by $\sqrt{K}$. The default K for `cv.gamlr` is `nfold=5`. If this results in error bounds that are too large for you to decide which λ is best, then you can simply increase the number of folds to reduce the standard error on your expected OOS deviance estimates.

Given the results from `cv.gamlr`, there are two common options for how you select the optimal λ_t (and hence select your coefficients $\hat{\beta}_t$). The CV-min rule, shown as the leftmost dashed line in Figure 3.12, simply selects the λ_t corresponding to the smallest *average* OOS deviance. The CV-1se rule, shown as the rightmost dashed line in Figure 3.12, selects the *biggest* λ_t with average OOS deviance no more than one standard error away from the minimum. For most applications, we recommend using the CV-min rule. This is the best choice if you are focused on OOS predictive performance. The `1se` rule is more *conservative:* it hedges toward a simpler model. This can be used if you have a heightened worry about accidentally including useless coefficients in your model. The CV-1se rule is the default in `cv.gamlr` (and in `cv.glmnet`) but we will often specify that we want to use CV-min selection instead.

Example 3.8 Ames Housing Data: CV Lasso Selection To run a CV Lasso for the Ames house sale price regression, you can use the same model matrix `xAmes` and response `yAmes` that you previously used as input to `gamlr`. In Example 3.4 we specified `lmr=1e-4` to get smaller λ_t values than the default, and we will pass that same argument to `cv.gamlr`.

```
> ### cross validation
> set.seed(0)
> cvfitAmes <- cv.gamlr(xAmes, yAmes, verb=TRUE, lmr=1e-4)
fold 1,2,3,4,5,done.
```

[*] Note that, even with the same seed, you may get different results for different operating systems and versions of R. You should at least be able to replicate your own results by running the same code twice on your own machine.

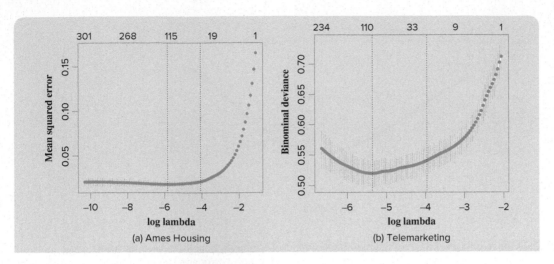

FIGURE 3.13 Cross-validated OOS deviance as a function of the λ_t penalty weights for each of our Ames Housing (a) and Telemarketing (b) examples.

The `verb=TRUE` argument leads `cv.gamlr` to output a progress report as it progresses through the folds. Notice that we set a random seed here so that if you run this code you should get the exact same results. The CV experiment results are plotted in Figure 3.13a. We can work through the attributes of the `cvfitAmes` object output from `cv.gamlr` to understand all of the pieces here.

```
> attributes(cvfitAmes)
$names
 [1] "gamlr"     "family"    "nfold"     "foldid"     "cvm"
 [6] "cvs"       "seg.min"   "seg.1se"   "lambda.min" "lambda.1se"
> cvfitAmes$gamlr
gaussian gamlr with 339 inputs and 100 segments.
$class
[1] "cv.gamlr"
> cvfitAmes$nfold
[1] 5
```

There is a `gamlr` object contained within `cvfitAmes`. This is the fitted Lasso path for the full data sample, and it is exactly the same as the `fitAmes` object that we estimated in Example 3.4. The `nfold` attribute here is *K,* the number of folds, and it is set to 5 by default.

The `cvm` attribute contains mean OOS deviances and `cvs` contains their standard errors. These are vectors with one value for each of the `nlambda` λ_t values used in the full sample path.

```
> cvfitAmes$cvm
  [1] 0.16532834 0.14703130 0.13104589 0.11777469
...
 [97] 0.02118427 0.02121335 0.02122546 0.02123655
> cvfitAmes$cvs
  [1] 0.004943823 0.004566041 0.003893101 0.003353137
...
 [97] 0.004669086 0.004688207 0.004690687 0.004694711
```

The `cvm` vector contains the blue dots marked on Figure 3.13a and `cvs` contains the half-length of the gray error bars. In this case the standard errors are small relative to the range of `cvm` deviance estimates, and you need to squint at the plot to see them. You can also use the `cvm` OOS deviance estimates to get estimates for the OOS R^2. We know that the null model corresponds to the first Lasso path segment where $\hat{\beta}_1 = 0$ by design. Thus an estimate of the OOS R^2 at any λ_t is available as one minus the corresponding mean OOS deviance over the first element of `cvm`.

```
> 1 - cvfitAmes$cvm[100]/cvfitAmes$cvm[1]
[1] 0.8715493
```

The OOS R^2 at the end of our Lasso path (at λ_{100}) is around 87%.

The λ penalties selected by CV-min and CV-1se rules (corresponding to the two vertical dashed lines in Figure 3.13a) are in attributes `lambda.min` and `lambda.1se` respectively. These correspond to the segment indices in `seg.min` and `seg.1se`.

```
> cvfitAmes$seg.min
[1] 52
> log(cvfitAmes$lambda.min)
[1] -5.833983
> cvfitAmes$seg.1se
[1] 33
> log(cvfitAmes$lambda.1se)
[1] -4.066342
```

The CV-min rule selects the 52nd segment with $\log(\lambda_{52}) \approx -5.8$, and the CV-1se rule selects the 33rd segment with $\log(\lambda_{33}) \approx -4.1$. You can pass `select="min"` or `select="1se"` to `coef` and `predict` functions to access coefficients and predictions corresponding to the models selected under each rule.

```
> bAmesCVmin <- coef(cvfitAmes, select="min")[-1,]
> sum(bAmesCVmin!=0)
[1] 127
> bAmesCV1se <- coef(cvfitAmes, select="1se")[-1,]
> sum(bAmesCV1se!=0)
[1] 35
> cbind(bAmesCV1se,bAmesCVmin)[c("Lot.Area","Lot.Frontage.x"),]
                bAmesCV1se bAmesCVmin
Lot.Area         0.0661714 0.07424132
Lot.Frontage.x   0.0000000 0.00000000
```

We see that the CV-min rule selects a model with 127 nonzero coefficients and the CV-1se model selects a model with 35 nonzero coefficients. Both selection rules lead to a nonzero coefficient on lot area and a zero coefficient on frontage. Note that the default for `cv.gamlr` is to use CV-1se so that if you don't specify `select` you will get the same results as for `select="1se"`.

....

Example 3.9 **Telemarketing Data: CV Lasso Selection** For the telemarketing logistic regression example, we apply `cv.gamlr` to our `xTD` model matrix and `yTD` binary response with `family="binomial"`. To illustrate the parallel computing capability of `cv.gamlr`, we also used the `parallel` library to create a parallel cluster and passed it as the `cl` argument. This will allow `cv.gamlr` to run each CV fold iteration in parallel across the processors on your computer (which is a handy speed-up if each Lasso path takes a while to fit).

```
> library(parallel)
> cl <- makeCluster(detectCores())
> set.seed(0)
> cvfitTD <- cv.gamlr(xTD, yTD, family="binomial", cl=cl)
```

[*] Note that, even with the same seed, you may get different results for different operating systems and versions of R. You should at least be able to replicate your own results by running the same code twice on your own machine.

The results of this CV experiment are plotted in Figure 3.13b. This time it is easier to see the error bars (from `cvfitTD$cvs`) around the mean OOS deviance values (from `cvfitTD$cvm`). To access select coefficients, we call the `coef` function and set the different CV selection rules via the `select` argument.

```
> betamin <- coef(cvfitTD, select="min")[-1,]
> sum(betamin!=0)
[1] 88
> beta1se <- coef(cvfitTD, select="1se")[-1,]
> sum(beta1se!=0)
[1] 18
```

The CV-min rule returns a model with 88 nonzero coefficients and the CV-1se rule returns a model with 18 nonzero coefficients.

To illustrate prediction, we will apply the `predict` function using each CV selection rule on the 1st and 100th observations. Note that, as was also necessary for `glm` fitted logistic regressions, we specify `type="response"` to get predicted probabilities rather than $\mathbf{x}'\hat{\beta}_t$. This outputs predicted probabilities that the campaign resulted in a successful subscription for each customer.

```
> yTD[c(1,100)]
[1] 0 1
>
drop(predict(cvfitTD,xTD[c(1,100),],select="min",type="response"))
         1           100
```

```
0.04862848 0.42464789
> drop(predict(cvfitTD,xTD[c(1,100),],select="1se",type="response"))
           1          100
0.05605473 0.36512179
```

Both methods give a probability less than 0.06 for $\hat{y}_1$ (true $y_1 = 0$) and above 0.36 for $\hat{y}_{100}$ (true $y_{100} = 1$). The CV-min selected predictions fit these observations a bit more tightly than the CV-1se selected predictions (CV-min $\hat{y}$ is lower for the true failure and higher for the true success).

The techniques of this chapter give you a diversity of tools for selecting from a path of candidate models. Figure 3.14 shows the segments selected under all of these different selection rules for both the Ames housing and telemarketing examples. For most applications, we recommend using either the AICc or CV-min selection rules. The results for the telemarketing example, in Figure 3.14b, are typical in that the AICc and CV-min rules select very similar λ values. Figure 3.14a shows that the rules give more varied selections in the Ames housing example, where the AICc selects $\log(\lambda) \approx -6.8$ and CV-min selects $\log(\lambda) \approx -5.8$. However, looking at the Ames housing CV plot in Figure 3.13a you can see that the OOS deviance is nearly flat between these two λ values and thus both are expected to yield similar average OOS deviance. In the case where the AICc selects a model that your CV experiment predicts will do poorly OOS, then it could indicate that something weird is going on and that neither is giving a good result (e.g., this can happen when you have dependence between observations that is not incorporated into your model).

The BIC and CV-1se rules can be used if you have a strong preference for simpler models, e.g., if you want your model to be portable enough to provide predictions on slightly different data generating processes than that which produced your training sample. You should never use the AIC when you could instead use the AICc.

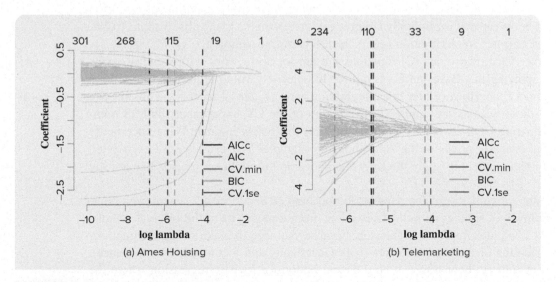

FIGURE 3.14 Path plots and the selected segments under all of our IC and CV selection rules, for each of the (a) Ames housing and (b) telemarketing examples.

◆ 3.4 Uncertainty Quantification for the Lasso

As a final topic for this chapter, we will touch on techniques for quantifying uncertainty *after* you have used model selection to choose a Lasso estimated regression. At the outset, we note that if you really care about the uncertainty for a set of parameters in your regression you should look to the purpose-built tools of Chapter 6. In that chapter, we introduce the techniques of "double ML" and "cross-fitting" that can be used to quantify uncertainty about treatment effects in the presence of high-dimensional controls—that is, to get uncertainty distributions for coefficients on specific input variables conditional on a larger set of other predictors.

That said, *if* you want to quantify uncertainty for functions or parameters of a fitted Lasso, then you can make use of some of the bootstrapping techniques that we introduced in Chapter 2. Unfortunately, the standard nonparametric bootstrap of Algorithm 2.2 does not work well for quantifying uncertainty of a Lasso path selection procedure. The issue with bootstrapping IC selection is that having repeated with-replacement samples of the same observations makes your dataset seem less noisy (easier to predict) than it actually is, and the theory behind the various IC selection rules implies that they will tend to select more complex models on the bootstrap resamples than they would on a true new sample from the original data generating process. For CV selection the issue is similar: if you naively bootstrap, then you can have the same observation repeated both in the kth CV training sample and in the left-out fold. This will make the OOS prediction seem easier than it actually is, and you will tend to select a more complex model inside the bootstrap than you would want for a true OOS prediction exercise.

You can adapt the bootstrap to work in this setting by replacing the random with-replacement sampling with a random re-weighting of the original observations. This is referred to as the *Bayesian bootstrap* (Rubin, 1981). In each bootstrap iteration, you generate n independent random weights from a *standard exponential* distribution. Draws from this distribution have the probability density function $p(w) = e^{-w}$, with $\mathbb{E}[w] = 1$ and $\text{var}(w) = 1$, and they are restricted to be positive ($w > 0$). The "Bayesian" moniker comes from how this is derived as the "right" distribution to use for the random weights under a specific prior model. Under this model, the standard exponential describes the posterior distribution for the prevalence of similar observations in new samples. However, you can think of it as simply a continuous extension of the standard bootstrap that is implicitly assigning discrete weights to the observations (0,1,2, etc; the number of times an observation occurs in each bootstrap sample).

Because the AICc (and other IC) functions are not set up to work with weights on the observations, applying this Bayesian bootstrap for IC selection would require you to write a bunch of custom R code. However, for linear regression only, `cv.gamlr` accepts the `obsweight` argument and these weights are applied at every step of the CV experiment (both in training and in evaluating OOS deviance). We will illustrate this below in quantifying uncertainty about predicted property prices in the Ames housing example. You can also use `cv.glmnet` with the `weights` argument to apply the Bayesian bootstrap for nonlinear models like logistic regression.

Another alternative is to use the parametric bootstrap of Section 2.4.2 where each bootstrap iteration involves simulating *new* observations from a model fit to the original sample. This is usually a bad idea for linear regression, because you need to make strong assumptions about the distribution of the random errors (e.g., Gaussianity and a constant error variance). However, the parametric bootstrap can be a decent option for logistic regression where the response distribution is a simple binomial. We will illustrate this approach for estimating the effect of phone call length on odds of success in the telemarketing example.

Example 3.10 Ames Housing Data: Bayesian Bootstrap We will consider uncertainty quantification for the expected sale price for two of the homes in our dataset. We are going to be studying the distribution for the CV-min selected sale price prediction.

First, calculate the original sample fitted predictions for sale price for these two properties.

```
> xnew <- xAmes[c(1,11),]
> yhat0 <- drop( predict(cvfitAmes, xnew, select="min") )
> exp(yhat0)
        1        11
204531.5 173117.9
```

Next, set the number of bootstrap estimates B and create a 2 by B matrix yhatB to fill with these estimates.

```
> B <- 100
> yhatB <- matrix(nrow=2, ncol=B)
```

We will also use the parallel library to create a parallel cluster cl that can be used by cv.gamlr to speed up each bootstrap iteration.

```
> library(parallel)
> cl <- makeCluster(detectCores())
```

We will now use a for loop to run through the bootstrap iterations. Note that the random weights are drawn in the first line inside this loop with a call to rexp. The other lines run cv.gamlr using these observation weights and then store the CV-min selected predictions in yhatB (and print a progress report, so you have something to watch while you wait).

```
> for(b in 1:100){
+     wb <- rexp(nrow(xAmes))
+     fitb <- cv.gamlr(xAmes, yAmes, obsweight=wb, lmr=1e-4,
cl=cl)
+     yhatB[,b] <- drop(predict(fitb, xnew, select="min"))
+     cat(b, " ")
+ }
1 2 3 4 5 ... 95 96 97 98 99 100
```

At the end of this loop, each column of yhatB contains a single bootstrap estimate of the expected log sale price for our two properties.

You can calculate a 95% probability interval for each house's sales price by exponentiating and looking at the 2.5th and 97.5th percentiles of the bootstrap sampled prices. We do this for each row of yhatB via the apply function.

```
apply(exp(yhatB), 1, quantile, probs=c(.025,.975))
           [,1]       [,2]
2.5%   190347.5 169952.7
97.5% 211883.9 175364.4
```

The expected sale price range for the first house is \$190k–\$212k and for the second house is \$170k–\$175k.

Alternatively, since we are exponentiating the predictions and introducing bias, you can apply the bias-corrected bootstrap of Algorithm 2.3 by taking percentiles on the distribution of bias-corrected sales prices, $e^{\hat{y}} - (e^{\hat{y}_b} - e^{\hat{y}}) = 2e^{\hat{y}} - e^{\hat{y}_b}$ where $\hat{y}$ is the original sample prediction and $\hat{y}_b$ is a bootstrap estimate.

```
> apply(2*exp(yhat0)-exp(yhatB),1,quantile,probs=c(.025,.975))
           [,1]       [,2]
2.5%   197179.1 170871.5
97.5% 218715.5 176283.1
```

The first house's expected sale price interval is now \$197k–\$219k and the second house's is \$171k–\$176k. Note that because of the randomness in our bootstrap procedure, your results will differ slightly when you replicate these procedures.

Example 3.11 Telemarketing Data: Parametric Bootstrap For our telemarketing example, we will consider uncertainty quantification for the effect of call duration in minutes (durmin) on the odds of success. Recall that we included both durmin and durmin^2 as inputs in our regression. We will use the parametric bootstrap to obtain a sampling distribution for the AICc selected estimates for these parameters.

To run a parametric bootstrap, you need to build a function that simulates data from a fitted model. You want to use a model that is low bias (corresponds to a small λ) for this simulator even if it is potentially overfit. We will use the fitted probabilities from our smallest penalty fit, at λ_{100}, as the basis for simulating new realizations of success and failure for the marketing campaign.

```
> p0 <- drop( predict(fitTD ,xTD, type="response", select=100) )
```

These probabilities, p0, are then used in the getBoot simulator function to draw a new random response vector yb from a binomial distribution with prob=p0. The rest of the getBoot function fits a gamlr path for the simulated responses and returns the AICc selected coefficients on durmin and durmin^2. Note that the argument b to getboot doesn't do anything, it is just there for our convenience when calling this function inside parSapply.

```
> getBoot <- function(b){
+      yb <- rbinom(nrow(xTD),size=1,prob=p0)
+      fitTDb <- gamlr(xTD, yb, family="binomial")
```

```
+        coef(fitTDb)[c("durmin","I(durmin^2)"),]
+ }
> getBoot(1)
       durmin   I(durmin^2)
 0.154883844 -0.003303299
 > bTD[c("durmin","I(durmin^2)")]
       durmin   I(durmin^2)
 0.276468974 -0.004644089
```

The last two lines show a random draw of the coefficients from `getBoot` and the original sample AICc selected estimates for these same coefficients.

We will use `parSapply` and the `parallel` library to distribute 100 runs of `getBoot` across multiple processors on our computer. Note that, to use `parSapply`, we need to call the `clusterExport` function that copies a list of objects we will need inside `getBoot` to each processor in the cluster.

```
> ## run the bootstrap
> library(parallel)
> cl <- makeCluster(detectCores())
> clusterExport(cl, c("gamlr", "xTD", "p0"))
> betaB <- parSapply(cl, 1:100, getBoot)
> plot(t(betaB))
```

The output `betaB` is 2 by 100 matrix containing a parametric bootstrap sample of 100 realizations from the sampling distribution for these two coefficients (as estimated via an AICc Lasso). The bootstrap sample is plotted in Figure 3.15a. This is a *joint* distribution: the two coefficients are correlated with each other in their sampling distribution. For a given call length, the implied impact on the log odds of call success is available as the first coefficient times `durmin` plus the second times $durmin^2$. We create a grid of `durmin` values and evaluate and plot this function for each bootstrap estimate.

```
> grid <- seq(0,max(tlmrk$durmin),length=200)
> dmy <- apply(betaB, 2, function(b){ b[1]*grid+b[2]*grid^2 } )
> matplot(grid, dmy, col=8, type="1")
```

The bootstrap sample of effect curves is shown in Figure 3.15b along with the original sample estimated curve. This is the additive effect on the log odds of success (getting a customer to subscribe to a term deposit). We see that the call success probability is increasing until around 1/2 hour, and then after that it becomes decreasingly likely that the customer will subscribe. However, there is considerable variability around the effect of `durmin` for long phone calls (in the right half of Figure 3.15b) since we have few observations of calls that take longer than 30 minutes.

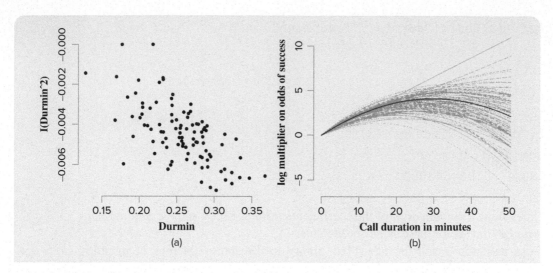

FIGURE 3.15 Parametric bootstrap sampling distribution for the coefficients on durmin and durmin^2, shown as a scatterplot in (a) and in terms of the implied effect on the log odds of success in (b). The original sample estimate is shown in (b) as the dark blue curve.

QUICK REFERENCE

This chapter presented many options for estimating paths of candidate models and for selecting among those candidates. We also introduced some key material for practical computational analysis, including sparse model matrices and dealing with missing data. There is a lot of content here, however we emphasize that the overall procedure is really simple:

- Fit a Lasso path to obtain multiple model estimates corresponding to different penalty values.
- Use CV or AICc to select the best model estimate from this path.

Everything else is context to help you adapt to practical difficulties and have a solid understanding of what is happening when you apply these techniques.

Key Practical Concepts

- Lasso regression models with coefficients β are estimated to minimize the penalized deviance

$$\frac{1}{n}\mathrm{dev}(\boldsymbol{\beta}) + \lambda_t \sum_j |\beta_j|$$

You fit the regression for a sequence of λ_t penalties and use model selection tools to choose the best.

- To build Lasso regression models, you need to create your own numeric model matrix for input. You can do this using the `sparse.model.matrix` function from the `Matrix` library to use efficient sparse matrix storage.

  ```
  x <- sparse.model.matrix( y ~ . , data=naref(data) )[,-1]
  ```

  The result will be a model matrix for regressing y on all the variables in `data`. We removed the intercept with `[,-1]`. You can use other formulas to add interactions or include specific variables.

- When fitting a Lasso regression, you typically want to include in your model matrix a separate binary indicator for each level of the factor variables in your `data`. In the above call to `sparse.model.matrix`, we applied the `naref` function from `gamlr` to set `NA` as the reference level for each factor so that all other levels are represented in the model matrix.

- When you have missing data, you can call `naref(data, impute=TRUE)` to impute missing values. For numeric variables `var` that include NAs, they will be replaced by `var.x` with no missing values and `var.miss` indicating which entries have been imputed.

- To run a path of Lasso regressions along a sequence of penalties, with input matrix x and response y, you call

  ```
  fit <- gamlr(x, y)
  ```

  and you can add family="binomial" for logistic regression.

- Add the argument lmr=1e-4 (or another small number) to run the path to smaller λ than the default $\lambda_{100}/\lambda_1 = 0.01$. You should run the path to small enough penalties such that when you look at the output of plot(fit) the AICc selection is not at the left edge of the figure.

- You can call coef and predict on the gamlr object fit exactly as you would for a fitted glm object, although you will need to apply the drop function to the output if you want to transform it to a simple array of predictions (rather than a sparse matrix). The resulting predictions and coefficients will correspond to the AICc-selected segment of the Lasso path.

- To run a CV experiment to select the optimal Lasso penalization, run

  ```
  cvfit <- cv.gamlr(x, y)
  ```

  and again you can add family="binomial" for logistic regression. When calling coef and predict on cvfit you can specify either select="min" for CV-min selection (choose the λ_t corresponding to lowest mean OOS deviance) of select="1se" for CV-1se selection (choose the largest λ_t with mean OOS deviance no more than 1 standard error larger than the minimum).

- To run CV experiments in parallel, create a parallel cluster and pass this to cv.gamlr as the cl argument.

  ```
  cl=makceCluster(detectCores())
  ```

4 CLASSIFICATION

This chapter describes how you can classify data into multiple classes, and how to use probability regression models to build a probability-based classifier.

- **Section 4.1 Nearest Neighbors:** Use K nearest neighbors to classify observations with unknown labels as a function of their neighbors with similar input features.

- **Section 4.2 Probability, Cost, and Classification:** Learn how to turn class probabilities into classification decisions, and understand that decisions have costs. Characterize your classifier by its success rates such as sensitivity (recall), specificity, and precision.

- **Section 4.3 Classification via Regression:** Use logistic regression to estimate class probabilities and build classification rules on top of your fitted logistic regression models.

- **Section 4.4 Multinomial Logistic Regression:** Extend logistic regression to multiclass problems, and use *distributed multinomial regression* for fast parallel estimation of multinomial logistic regression models.

M any of the prediction questions that we face are classification questions. You might want to predict a website user's intent among several options, a speaker's political affiliation among a few parties, or the subject of an untagged image. These examples fit in our usual regression framework, where the response y is a function of inputs $\mathbf{x}$. The difference is that y now represents membership in 1 of m categories: $y \in \{1, 2, ..., m\}$. The question we want to answer is, "Given a new $\mathbf{x}$, what is the best guess at the response category, $\hat{y}$?"

We have already worked with two-category classification via logistic regression, where $y \in \{0, 1\}$ and $p(y = 1|\mathbf{x})$ is modeled with a logit link. This *binary* logistic regression is a special case of general *multinomial* logistic regression for more than two classes. We'll return to that modeling approach (and our regularization and model selection tools) later in this chapter, but first we cover a simple and intuitive classifier: the K nearest neighbor algorithm.

● 4.1 Nearest Neighbors

The K nearest neighbor (K-NN) algorithm predicts the class for $\mathbf{x}$ by asking, "What is the most common class for observations around $\mathbf{x}$?" Figure 4.1 shows the K-NN algorithm for a simple illustrative example. We have a bunch of points in a two-dimensional coordinate system labeled as either a red star or green square. You want to classify as either red star or green square an unlabeled point marked as "?" that is located near labeled points. For a specified K, the K-NN algorithm looks at the K nearest labeled points to take a majority vote for what class (label) we should assign to "?". Figure 4.1a shows that using $K = 3$ yields a neighborhood of 2 green squares and 1 red star, so we'd classify the point as a green square. Figure 4.1b shows that $K = 5$ yields a neighborhood of 3 red stars and 2 green squares, so we'd classify the point as a red star.

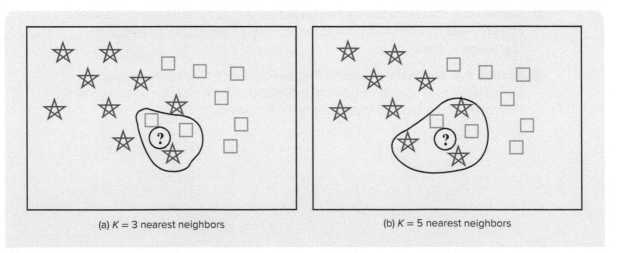

(a) $K = 3$ nearest neighbors   (b) $K = 5$ nearest neighbors

FIGURE 4.1 K nearest neighbor classification. Panel (a) shows the classification scheme for the unlabeled point based on $K = 3$, leading to its classification as a green square. Panel (b) demonstrates that for $K = 5$ the class assignment would be a red star since the majority of the 5 neighbors are red stars.

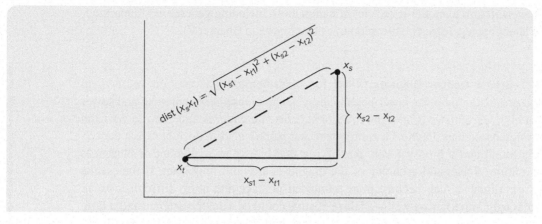

FIGURE 4.2   Visualization of the Euclidean distance formula in two dimensions.

Calculating Distances

You can think about every observation **x** as a point in the *space* of possible values for each variable. The *K*-NN algorithm counts nearest neighbors based upon the distance from an unlabeled point to other points in this space. The distance *K*-NN uses is *Euclidean distance:* the length of a straight line between two points in space. This intuitive measure of distance is quantified through the equation

$$\text{dist}(\mathbf{x}_t, \mathbf{x}_s) = \sqrt{\sum_{j=1}^{J}(x_{tj} - x_{sj})^2} \qquad (4.1)$$

where $\mathbf{x}_t$ and $\mathbf{x}_s$ are two vectors with J dimensions. For example, in two dimensions the distance between two points is given by the classic Pythagorean theorem from geometry that says the length of the hypotenuse of a triangle is the root of the sum of the squared lengths of each side. This is illustrated in Figure 4.2. If the equations seem a bit confusing, remember that Equation (4.1) simply calculates what you know intuitively as the straight-line distance between two points.

This distance is measured in the units of the dimensions of your inputs **x**, which means that you need to think carefully about what units you are using for these input variables. Unless you have a really good reason to do otherwise, you should convert your inputs to be measured in units of *standard deviations*. R's scale function can be used to transform from x_j to $\tilde{x}_i = x_i/\text{sd}(x_i)$, which can then be input to a *K*-NN algorithm.

K-NN in R

To run *K* nearest neighbors in R, you can load the class package (Venables and Ripley, 2002), which includes the function knn. You then need to create *numeric* matrices of training data **x** values (usually the output of scale), accompanied by labels *y*, and provide new test values that you want to classify. Unlike glm, for knn you must supply test data: there is no model being fit, knn is simply counting neighbors for each observation in test. Although there are efficient industrial applications of *K*-NN, this structure—where you need to calculate distances to the dataset of labeled points for each classification task—is a limitation on the scalability of *K*-NN algorithms.

For this reason we will turn to model-based classification tools, including generalized linear models, in this and later chapters (e.g., classification trees and forests in Chapter 7).

Example 4.1 Breast Cancer Biopsies: *K*-NN for Classification Automation in medical diagnostics is a promising path for lower health care costs, increased convenience, and lower error rates. Machine learning tools are used to recognize disease patterns and provide decision support for physicians such as diagnostic radiologists and pathologists. Consider breast cancer. Once a lump is found and a biopsy taken, classifying that biopsy as malignant or benign is a high-stakes venture. Speed and accuracy of the diagnosis are both important. If the results take too long, a malignancy can become more advanced in stage and more difficult to treat. Accuracy is obviously important as well—a false negative could be a death sentence and a false positive causes unnecessary physical and emotional harm and is very expensive financially.

We'll attempt to classify breast tumor biopsies as malignant cancer or not (benign) using the biopsy data from the MASS library in R which contains ratings for 9 categories (on a scale from 1 to 10) on 699 breast biopsies:

- ID - sample identifier
- V1 - clump thickness
- V2 - uniformity of cell size
- V3 - uniformity of cell shape
- V4 - marginal adhesion
- V5 - single epithelial cell size
- V6 - bare nuclei (16 values are missing)
- V7 - bland chromatin
- V8 - normal nucleoli
- V9 - mitoses
- class - benign or malignant

These observations are taken by human technicians, although image recognition technology (via deep learning; see Chapter 10) is getting to the point where the same measurements can be made based upon raw imaging data.

Loading the data into R, we can apply the str function to see that all of the values are numeric except for the ID and the response target class.

```
> library(MASS)
> data(biopsy)
> str(biopsy)
'data.frame':   699 obs. of  11 variables:
 $ ID   : chr  "1000025" "1002945" "1015425" "1016277" ...
 $ V1   : int  5 5 3 6 4 8 1 2 2 4 ...
 $ V2   : int  1 4 1 8 1 10 1 1 1 2 ...
 $ V3   : int  1 4 1 8 1 10 1 2 1 1 ...
 $ V4   : int  1 5 1 1 3 8 1 1 1 1 ...
```

```
$ V5    : int  2 7 2 3 2 7 2 2 2 2 ...
$ V6    : int  1 10 2 4 1 10 10 1 1 1 ...
$ V7    : int  3 3 3 3 3 9 3 3 1 2 ...
$ V8    : int  1 2 1 7 1 7 1 1 1 1 ...
$ V9    : int  1 1 1 1 1 1 1 1 5 1 ...
$ class: Factor w/ 2 levels "benign","malignant": 1 1 ...
```

Figure 4.3 shows the distributions of the 9 rating categories by malignancy status. You can see that most of the inputs are *discriminators:* their levels give you good information about whether the tumor is malignant or benign. For example, clump thickness (V3) is 1 for almost all benign examples and above 5 for the bulk of the malignant examples.

To prepare the data for use in knn we will first remove the 16 observations with missing entries. You could have also used, e.g., mean imputation for these values but since they are a small portion of the overall data we will drop them to keep things simple.

```
> biopsyNM<-na.omit(biopsy)
```

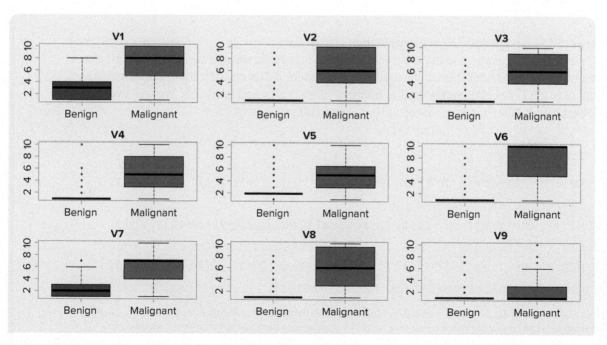

FIGURE 4.3 Distribution of biopsy measurements by malignancy status.

Next, we scale the inputs so that they all have a standard deviation of one (i.e., so that the measurements in x are in units of standard deviations from the mean).

```
> x <- scale(biopsyNM[,2:10]) # scale data
> apply(x,2,sd)
V1 V2 V3 V4 V5 V6 V7 V8 V9
 1  1  1  1  1  1  1  1  1
 > class(biopsy)
[1] "data.frame"
> class(x)
[1] "matrix" "array"
```

Note that the original biopsy object is a data frame and the output from scale, x, is a numeric matrix as required by knn. Finally, we pull out class as our response variable y.

```
> y <- biopsyNM$class
> table(y)
y

   benign malignant
      444       239
```

There are 444 benign and 239 malignant tumors in our data.

We are now ready to use the knn function. For illustration, we will create a random test index of 400 observations that can be used as test-cases for *K*-NN classification. The remainder of the data (283 observations) is used as training inputs train and labels cl. We will evaluate the results of *K*-NN for a *K* values of 1, 10, 50, and 100.

```
> set.seed(0)
> test <- sample(1:nrow(x),400)
> library(class)
> K1 <- knn(train=x[-test,], test=x[test,], cl=y[-test], k=1)
> K10 <- knn(train=x[-test,], test=x[test,], cl=y[-test], k=10)
> K50 <- knn(train=x[-test,], test=x[test,], cl=y[-test], k=50)
> K100 <- knn(train=x[-test,], test=x[test,], cl=y[-test], k=100)
```

*Note that, even with the same seed, you may get different results for different operating systems and versions of R. You should at least be able to replicate your own results by running the same code twice on your own machine.

The output of knn is a vector containing the predicted class for each observation in x[test,]. We can look at the first ten predictions for each *K* next to the true class.

```
> res<-data.frame(y[test],K1,K10,K50,K100)
> res[1:10,]
      y.test.           K1          K10          K50         K100
1   malignant    malignant    malignant    malignant    malignant
2      benign       benign       benign       benign       benign
3      benign       benign       benign       benign       benign
4   malignant    malignant    malignant    malignant    malignant
5      benign       benign       benign       benign       benign
6      benign       benign       benign       benign       benign
7      benign       benign       benign       benign       benign
8      benign       benign       benign       benign       benign
9      benign    malignant    malignant    malignant       benign
10  malignant    malignant    malignant    malignant    malignant
```

As we might have guessed from the clear discrimination between tumor classes in Figure 4.3, this is a pretty easy classification problem. For the 10 predicted classes that we printed above, the different K-NN runs mostly predict the correct true class, except in the 9th observation where only $K = 100$ leads to the correct classification (benign). We can calculate the *accuracy* for each K-NN algorithm as the rate at which it predicts the true class.

```
> apply(res[,-1], 2, function(c) mean(c==res[,1]))
    K1     K10     K50    K100
0.9425 0.9675 0.9475 0.9125
```

The different K all lead to accuracies above 90%, with $K = 10$ best at 96.75%.

K-NN is intuitive and simple to code, which is why we use it to introduce the topic of classification. However, it is not a great choice for large scale classification because, as already mentioned, it is computationally expensive to access the original data (rather than refer to a fitted model) whenever you want to make a prediction. Moreover, an important issue with K-NN is that it doesn't give you a good estimate of the uncertainty about your classifications. You *can* use the "votes" of the K neighbors to get approximate class probabilities. For example, in Figure 4.1 you can count the neighbors around our unlabeled point to estimate the probability that it is a green square under the different K:

$$K = 3 \Rightarrow \mathrm{p}(?\ is\ green\ square) \approx 2/3$$
$$K = 5 \Rightarrow \mathrm{p}(?\ is\ green\ square) \approx 2/5$$

Even if K-NN does a good job at classification, these are pretty crude probability estimates. For example, you likely want the points closest to your unlabeled observation to have more votes than those that are furthest away. That is precisely the sort of probability estimates you get when you instead use regression modeling as your foundation for classification.

■ 4.2 Probability, Cost, and Classification

Before diving deeper into modeling, we need to discuss the relationship between probabilities and classification. We'll introduce the ideas with binary classification problems where $y \in \{0, 1\}$, but all of these ideas extend to multiclass problems.

Classification Decisions

There are two ways to be wrong in a binary problem:

- False Positive (FP): predict $\hat{y} = 1$ when $y = 0$.
- False Negative (FN): predict $\hat{y} = 0$ when $y = 1$.

And there are two ways to be right:

- True Positive (TP): predict $\hat{y} = 1$ when $y = 1$.
- True Negative (TN): predict $\hat{y} = 0$ when $y = 0$.

In general, there will be different costs associated with each type of error and different benefits associated with each type of success. A doctor might place a lower cost on overtreatment than on a missed diagnosis, and a higher benefit on catching a true disease case than on correctly detecting an absence of disease.

More generally, *decisions have costs.* Suppose that you know the probabilities of each class in a classification problem, say p_m for potential classes $m = 1 \ldots M$, and that each outcome m yields payoff (or utility) $u(a, m)$ under action a. Then the expected utility if you take action a is

$$\mathrm{E}[\text{utility}(a)] = \sum_m p_m \, u(a, m) \tag{4.2}$$

For example, suppose that the action a is that you decide to loan \$100 to someone under the agreement that they pay you back \$125 next week. If you decide that there is a 10% chance that they *do not* pay you back, then there is a 10% chance of a \$100 loss and a 90% chance of a \$25 gain. Using dollars as utility, the expected utility is $0.9 \times 25 - 0.1 \times 100 = 12.5$. You expect to *make* \$12.50 on such a loan.

Once you know the probabilities of the various outcomes, then you can assess expected profits and losses and make optimal decisions. Suppose that you have a binary outcome y with the probability $\mathrm{p}(y = 1) = p$. A classification rule, or cutoff, is the probability threshold τ at which you predict $\hat{y} = 0$ for $p \leq \tau$ and $\hat{y} = 1$ for $p > \tau$. In our example above, say that $y = 1$ if the person *does not* pay you back (i.e., that they default) and $y = 0$ if they do pay you back. Then the expected payoff if you lend to them is

$$\mathrm{E}[\text{utility}(\textit{lend money})] = (1 - p)25 - p100 \tag{4.3}$$

since you get \$25 if they pay you back and lose \$100 if they default. For simplicity, say the expected payoff if you don't lend to them is zero (i.e., assuming you have nothing better to do with your \$100). Then you should make the loan if your expected utility in (4.3) is positive. This occurs if $(1 - p)25 - p100 > 0$, which implies that you will lend the money if

$$25 - 125p > 0 \Rightarrow p < \frac{25}{125} = \frac{1}{5} \tag{4.4}$$

Hence, you only lend the money if the probability of default p is less than 0.2. In general, for this simple setup where you have "interest" X and get $100 + X$ in the case of repayment, you will expect to profit if $p < X/(100 + X)$. That implies that you could reverse the decision process and, instead of treating the $25 interest as fixed, you could set the interest charge to be any $X > 100 \cdot p/(1 - p)$ to ensure a positive expected utility.

Confusion Matrix

Given the importance of understanding the consequences of classification predictions, there is a rich terminology for describing various classification success rates. Figure 4.4 shows a *confusion matrix* of true and false positive and negative outcomes. On the margins we have printed common terminology for different ways to measure the rate of *success* for a classifier. Recalling that $\hat{y}$ is the predicted class and y is the actual true class:

- *Negative predictive value* (NPV) is the proportion of cases with $\hat{y} = 0$ where true $y = 0$.
- *Precision* or *positive predictive value* (PPV) is the proportion of true positives among all predicted positives, so cases with $\hat{y} = 1$ where true $y = 1$.
- *Recall* or *sensitivity* is the proportion of cases with $y = 1$ where you have correctly predicted $\hat{y} = 1$.
- *Specificity* is the proportion of cases with $y = 0$ where you have correctly predicted $\hat{y} = 0$.

Notice that the denominators in the calculations here each correspond to a row or column total of the confusion matrix.

There are also corresponding terms to describe classification errors. For example, the false discovery rate is the proportion of cases with $\hat{y} = 1$ where where true $y = 0$, and this is equal to one minus the precision. All of these various rates are used to assess the performance of classification algorithms. Machine learning practitioners tend to favor tracking recall and precision, while in statistics it is more common to report sensitivity (i.e., recall) and specificity. In any case, you need to look at a couple of these rates in order to get a sense of your algorithm's performance. For example, you could guarantee a sensitivity of 1 by simply classifying $\hat{y} = 1$ for every observation. However this would lead to zero true negatives, and hence a specificity of zero.

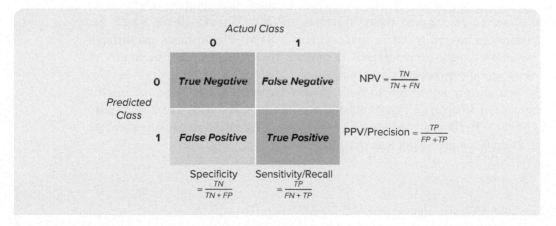

FIGURE 4.4   A confusion matrix with classification success rate calculations relative to the row and column totals. The actual biopsy outcome class (i.e., benign or malignant) changes left to right, and the predicted outcome class changes top to bottom.

Example 4.2 **Breast Cancer Biopsies: Confusion Matrix** It is simple to build the confusion matrix in R using the `table` function. Give the `table` function your row variable (the predictions) first, and your column variable (the actuals) second. Here we print the confusion matrix for our classification of breast cancer biopsy tumors from Example 4.1. We are using the predicted classes for the $K = 10$ knn fit K10.

```
> table(pred=K10,actual=y[test])
          actual
pred        benign malignant
  benign      246          8
  malignant     5        141
```

Using the table we see that the sensitivity (or recall) is $141/(141 + 8) \approx 0.946$, so the chance of getting a malignancy diagnosis if you really have a malignancy is 94.6%. The specificity is $246/(5 + 246) \approx 0.98$, so the chance of getting diagnosed as benign is 98% if it really is benign. And the precision is $141/(141 + 5) \approx 0.966$, so 96.6% of the diagnosed malignancies are actually malignant.

4.3 Classification via Regression

Doing classification based upon estimated probabilities is important because it allows you to set different classification rules (probability thresholds) depending upon the cost of false negatives or positives and the utility of true negatives or positives. It turns out that doing classification via probabilities also makes it easier to construct rich and robust models. Most modern classification methods are *probabalistic:* they are trained to minimize a deviance (or penalized deviance) that relates observed classes to fitted probabilities. The notable exception is the method of support vector machines (SVM) (Vapnik, 1996), which fits classification boundaries around points in space. However SVMs are unstable and difficult to tune, and they have mostly been replaced in practice by techniques like the forests of Chapter 7 and deep neural networks of Chapter 10.

Fortunately, you already know how to build models for probabilities using the logistic regression techniques of Chapters 1 (via likelihood maximization and `glm`) and 3 (via Lasso estimation and `gamlr`). To illustrate the use of a fitted probability model in classification, we will consider an example on predicting loan defaults.

Example 4.3 **Loan Defaults: Regression and Classification** To work through the steps of probability-based classification, we'll use a dataset on loans and defaults from a set of local lenders in Germany (from the UCI machine learning repository). Credit scoring—predicting the probability of default—is a classic problem of classification, and it remains one of the big application domains for ML: use previous loan results (default versus payment) to train a model that can predict the performance of loans that you currently have on the books (or new loans you are considering making).

We read the data into R as the `credit` data frame of borrower and loan characteristics alongside the binary `Default` outcome.

```
> credit <- read.csv("credit.csv", strings=T)
> credit[1,]
  Default duration amount installment age
1       0        6   1169           4  67
  history       purpose foreign  rent
1 terrible goods/repair foreign FALSE
> dim(credit)
[1] 1000    9
```

We'll run a Lasso logistic regression path for `Default` onto all of these inputs *interacted* with each other (i.e., you include all pairwise interactions). Following the steps of Chapter 3, you first call `naref` to create a new reference level for every factor. Then use `sparse.model .matrix` to create the model matrix.

```
> library(gamlr)
Loading required package: Matrix
> xcred <- sparse.model.matrix(Default~.^2, data=naref(credit))
[,-1]
> ycred <- credit$Default
```

Here we have also created `ycred` as the response variable (one for default, zero otherwise). Finally, call `gamlr` to fit the Lasso paths (note the `family="binomial"` argument for logistic regression).

```
> credscore <- gamlr(xcred, ycred, family="binomial")
> sum(coef(credscore)!=0)
[1] 18
> which.min(AICc(credscore))
seg46
   46
```

The AICc rule selects the 46th segment with 18 nonzero parameters.

We will use the AICc selected probabilities as the basis for classification. These are extracted as `pcred` using the `predict` function with `type` = "`response`" (and `drop` to convert to a vector).

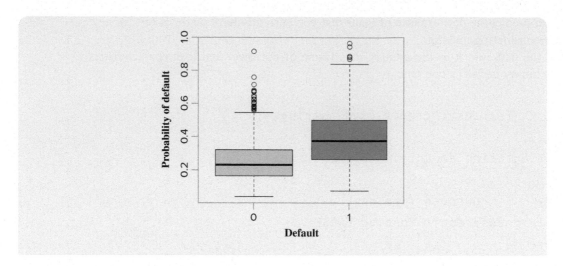

FIGURE 4.5 Fitted probabilities for the default-prediction AICc Lasso.

```
> pcred <- drop( predict(credscore, xcred, type="response") )
```

Figure 4.5 shows the resulting *in-sample* fit. This is a tough, noisy problem, and it appears that there is a lot of overlap between probabilities for the true defaults and the true nondefaults. This means that any classification rule you choose will induce a number of false negatives and false positives.

Consider a $\tau = 0.2$ classification cutoff, such that you predict all loans with $p > 0.2$ as defaulting and all those with $p \leq 0.2$ as nondefaulting. The resulting confusion matrix for this classification rule is printed here after calculating $\hat{y}$ values as a function of this $\tau = 0.2$ classification rule.

```
> rule <- 1/5
> yhat <- as.numeric(pcred>rule)
> table(yhat, ycred)
    ycred
yhat   0    1
   0 263   20
   1 437  280
```

In this case, we have a low number of false negatives (20) but a high number of false positives (437). This occurs due to our classification threshold that predicts default for any loan with greater than 1/5 chance of defaulting (and because these inputs are not particularly predictive of loan defaults). This might be a fine classification rule for a conservative lender who is mainly worried about managing the risk of loan default. This $\tau = 0.2$ rule results in a classifier that is sensitive ($280/(280 + 20) \approx 0.93$) but not specific ($263/(263 + 437) \approx 0.38$). Of course, this specificity and sensitivity are functions of the classification rule and we could get different values for a different rule applied to these same fitted Lasso probabilities.

ROC Curves

A nice visual summary of potential classification rules is the ROC curve that plots sensitivity against one minus specificity for a range of cutoff thresholds from 0 to 1. The name here comes from signal processing theory, where ROC stands for receiver operating characteristic. Figure 4.6a shows ROC curves for our fitted in-sample default probabilities. A tight regression fit (such that $\hat{p} \approx y$ for many examples) will lead to an ROC curve forced into the top-left corner since in that case you will be able to obtain high sensitivity while maintaining high specificity. If the ROC curve drops toward the diagonal, then classification based on these probabilities is not much better than random guessing.

As with any fit statistic or plot, you can obtain both in-sample and out-of-sample versions (and the latter is always the more interesting). Figure 4.6b shows the OOS ROC plot that corresponds to an AICc-selected Lasso model that was fit on half the data and evaluated for sensitivity and specificity on the left-out half. Notice that the OOS curve is slightly flatter (closer to diagonal) than the IS curve: the sensitivity/specificity trade-off for new predictions will be a bit worse than implied by in-sample fit.

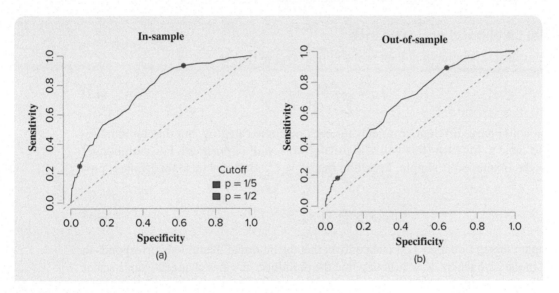

FIGURE 4.6   In-sample (a) and out-of-sample (b) ROC curves for the German credit example, with both $p = 0.2$ and $p = 0.5$ rules marked.

◆ 4.4 Multinomial Logistic Regression

Good classification starts from good probability models. For binary classification, you can use a binary logistic regression to build your probability models. In *multiclass* problems, where the response is one of M categories, you can build a similar generalized linear model formulation.

We'll start by defining the model. In contrast to binary logistic regression, we now have m vectors of regression coefficients—one for each class. It is useful to rewrite the multiclass response as the length-M vector $\mathbf{y}_i = [0, 1, \ldots, 0]$, where $y_{im} = 1$ if response i is class m. Then, following our generic linear model formulation from way back in Chapter 1, you are building a model to represent the probability of each class:

$$E[y_{im}|\mathbf{x}_i] = p(y_{im} = 1|\mathbf{x}_i) = f(\mathbf{x}_i'B) \text{ for } m = 1\ldots M \tag{4.5}$$

Here, $B = [\beta_1 \cdots \beta_M]$ is now a *matrix* with columns of coefficients for each outcome class. We will write β_{jm} for the coefficient on x_j in $\boldsymbol{\beta}_m$, the vector of coefficients for class m.

In *multinomial logistic regression,* we use a *multiclass logit link* function:

$$p(y_{im} = 1|\mathbf{x}_i) = p_m(\mathbf{x}_i) = \frac{e^{\mathbf{x}_i'\beta_m}}{\sum_{l=1}^{M} e^{\mathbf{x}_i'\beta_l}} \tag{4.6}$$

In ML, the link function in (4.6) is often called a *softmax* function, and it is a very commonly used function to translate from multiple linear functions (one for each class) to probabilities (again, one for each class). You might see it elsewhere specified with denominator $1 + \sum_m e^{\mathbf{x}_i'\beta_m}$, which corresponds to setting a reference outcome class where $\beta_m = \mathbf{0}$. As was the case for factor reference levels, this is an artifact of maximum likelihood estimation (where you need to restrict the space of variables to get a well-defined maximum) and setting a reference class is unnecessary if you are using Lasso penalization methods.

Multinomial Likelihood and Deviance

We write the estimated multinomial logit probabilities $p(y_{im} = 1|\mathbf{x}_i)$ as

$$\hat{p}_{im} = \frac{e^{\mathbf{x}_i'\hat{\beta}_m}}{\sum_{l=1}^{M} e^{\mathbf{x}_i'\hat{\beta}_l}} \tag{4.7}$$

Note that you could have different covariates for each outcome category, but that for simplicity we use the same $\mathbf{x}_i$ for each (this will also usually work well in practice). For multinomial distributions, the likelihood is simple. Recalling that $a^0 = 1$ and $a^1 = a$ (also, $\propto$ denotes "proportional to"),

$$\text{lhd}(\hat{B}) \propto \prod_{i=1}^{n} \prod_{m=1}^{M} \hat{p}_{im}^{y_{im}} \tag{4.8}$$

You can compare this to Equation 1.31 and confirm that the binomial likelihood corresponds to Equation 4.8 in the case where $M = 2$ (noting that the definition of y_i has changed from a scalar number to a length-2 vector).

Taking the log of Equation 4.8 and multiplying by -2 gives you the multinomial deviance

$$\text{dev}(\hat{B}) = -2 \sum_{i=1}^{n} \sum_{m=1}^{M} y_{im} \log(\hat{p}_{im}) \tag{4.9}$$

We will be working with Lasso multinomial logit regression estimation, where you fit the parameters $\hat{B}$ to minimize the penalized deviance

$$\text{dev}(\hat{B}) + \sum_{m=1}^{M} \lambda_m \sum_j |\beta_{jm}| \tag{4.10}$$

Notice that we have here a different penalty λ_m for each outcome class m. Some Lasso packages allow for this, others restrict $\lambda = \lambda_m$ as a single shared penalty weight for all classes.

You can also do maximum likelihood estimation for multinomial logit regression models; however, we will focus on the Lasso specification because it is faster to estimate and it simplifies things by avoiding the need to set a reference outcome class. If you want to fit the models with little penalty then you can focus on the smallest penalty segments of the Lasso path.

Estimation with `glmnet`

The `gamlr` package doesn't include the estimation routine in Equation 4.10. Instead, `gamlr` is used in an efficient parallel computing strategy called *distributed multinomial regression* that is described later in this section. In the meantime, you can fit your multinomial logistic regressions using the `glmnet` package with the `family="multinomial"` flag. `glmnet` and `gamlr` use almost the exact syntax with some small differences.

Example 4.4 **Heating Data: Multinomial Logistic Regression** We'll illustrate with data from Train (2009) on the choice of heating method for homes. The `Heating` data frame is available from the `mlogit` package (Croissant, 2020). The outcome classes are the type of heating system installed in houses built in California:

- `gc`: central gas furnace
- `gr`: room-specific gas furnace (gr)
- `ec`: central electric heat
- `er`: room-specific electric heat
- `hp`: a heat-pump system

The inputs include some demographic variables and, for each type of heating system, the *installation cost* (`ic.type`) and annual *operating cost* (`oc.type`).

```
> library(mlogit)
> data(Heating)
> dim(Heating)
[1] 900  16
> head(Heating,5)
  idcase depvar  ic.gc  ic.gr  ic.ec  ic.er   ic.hp  oc.gc
1      1     gc 866.00 962.64 859.90 995.76 1135.50 199.69
2      2     gc 727.93 758.89 796.82 894.69  968.90 168.66
3      3     gc 599.48 783.05 719.86 900.11 1048.30 165.58
4      4     er 835.17 793.06 761.25 831.04 1048.70 180.88
5      5     er 755.59 846.29 858.86 985.64  883.05 174.91
    oc.gr  oc.ec  oc.er  oc.hp income agehed rooms region
1  151.72 553.34 505.60 237.88      7     25     6 ncostl
2  168.66 520.24 486.49 199.19      5     60     5 scostl
3  137.80 439.06 404.74 171.47      4     65     2 ncostl
4  147.14 483.00 425.22 222.95      2     50     4 scostl
5  138.90 404.41 389.52 178.49      2     25     6 valley
```

There are 900 houses in the sample. Note that the `income` variable is a set of 7 increasing income levels rather than raw dollars.

We will use `model.matrix` to create a numeric model matrix xH. You could also have used `naref` and `sparse.model.matrix` following our usual practice, but we will skip those steps here for illustration. Note that our single factor variable `region` has reference level `valley` indicating California's Central Valley region (you could also treat `income` as a factor, which leads to similar results).

```
> xH <- model.matrix( depvar ~ ., data=Heating[,-1])[,-1]
> yH <- Heating$depvar
> table(yH)
yH
  gc  gr  ec  er  hp
 573 129  64  84  50
```

We pulled the response out as `yH`, and see that the classes are ordered by prevalence (gas is most common, then electric, then heat pumps).

To fit the multinomial logit with `glmnet`, you pass it the inputs and response (the same as you would to `gamlr`) and specify `family="multinomial"`.

```
> library(glmnet)
> netfit <- glmnet(xH, yH, family="multinomial")
```

The Lasso paths for the coefficients for each outcome class are shown in Figure 4.7. Notice that the λ values are the same on the horizontal axis of each plot; `glmnet` uses a single shared penalty weight for all classes.

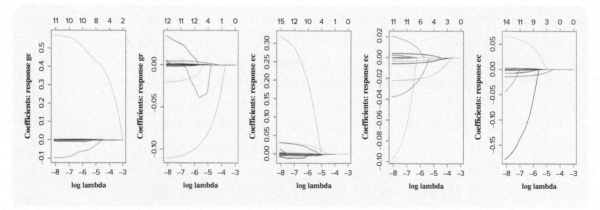

FIGURE 4.7 Lasso regularization paths for `glmnet` multinomial logistic Lasso regression on the heating data.

Predicting Probabilities

To get predictions from `glmnet`, you need to call `predict` with the "s" argument to specify the λ value corresponding to the segment that you want use. Here, we will use the smallest λ fit by `glmnet` to get the near-to-MLE (i.e., minimal penalization) model estimate.

```
> LMIN <- min(netfit$lambda)
> pnet <- drop( predict(netfit, xH, s=L100, type="response") )
```

For some reason glmnet gives back predictions as an $n \times M \times 1$ array. You use drop() to make it an $n \times M$ matrix. We look at some here.

```
> newi <- c(1,14,21,4,24)
> pnet[newi,]
          gc         gr         ec         er         hp
1   0.7275054 0.07639648 0.06384421 0.05701540 0.07523854
14  0.5381347 0.16562425 0.06730274 0.11120758 0.11773070
21  0.5185461 0.10670896 0.07992465 0.26581821 0.02900209
4   0.5398101 0.18774050 0.12046587 0.08788119 0.06410231
24  0.5760982 0.11706689 0.04933049 0.19495452 0.06254986
> yH[newi]
[1] gc gr ec er hp
```

Notice that the probability of the true classes here are along the diagonal of pnet[newi,]. The distribution of fitted probabilities for each true class (i.e., $\hat{p}_{im}$ where $y_{im} = 1$) is plotted in Figure 4.8. This is a difficult classification problem! There are far more central gas systems than cases of electric heating, and the inputs are not strong discriminators for the different classes. That leads to low fitted probabilities for true observations of every heating type other than central gas.

Classification

As we described earlier, probabilities can be combined with decision utilities to build classification rules. In the common setting where you have symmetric utilities for getting each class

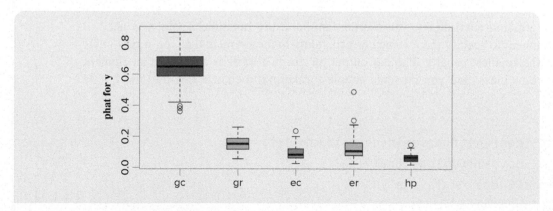

FIGURE 4.8   In-sample fit for the heating multinomial logistic Lasso regression. The width of each box is proportional to the sample size for that class.

correct or incorrect, you can just use a *maximum probability rule* and classify $\hat{m}$ to the class with the largest probability in each observation. You get this in R with apply(phat,1,which.max), which gives the maximizing column index for each row of a matrix of probabilities phat. Here, because of the dominance of central gas heating, that simply classifies gc for nearly every observation.

```
> head( levels(yH)[apply(pnet,1,which.max)] )
[1] "gc" "gc" "gc" "gc" "gc" "gc"
```

As a home builder, an alternative classification task might be to classify whether you think it is worth trying to convert the customer to, say, a heat-pump system. You could then apply a classification rule to the column of hp probabilities. For example, you might decide to pitch a heat pump if there is a more than 10% probability that a household would choose hp under the given installation and operating costs.

```
> hpHat <- pnet[,"hp"]> 0.1
> table(predHP=yH=="hp", trueHP=hpHat==1)
        trueHP
 predHP FALSE  TRUE
   FALSE   794    42
   TRUE     56     8
> 8/(8+56)
[1] 0.125
```

The resulting confusion matrix shows that this classification rule yields an in-sample *precision* of 0.125. If you use this rule then you will be correct 12.5% of the time that you predict a customer will install a heat-pump.

Interpreting Coefficients

To get the regression coefficients, you use the familiar coef function. Again, you need to use the s argument to specify the λ value corresponding to the segment that you want to use. We will use the smallest penalty. The raw output for coef.glmnet is a list with an element for each outcome class, and you do some simple formatting to change this into the $J \times M$ matrix $\hat{B}$.

```
> Bnet <- coef(netfit,s=min(netfit$lambda))
> Bnet <- do.call(cbind, Bnet)
> colnames(Bnet) <- levels(yH)
> round(Bnet, 4)
17 x 5 sparse Matrix of class "dgCMatrix"
```

	gc	gr	ec	er	hp
(Intercept)	−0.2427	−0.9859	0.0176	1.6922	−0.4812
ic.gc	−0.0024	−0.0016	0.0009	.	0.0029
ic.gr	.	0.0010	−0.0024	0.0041	−0.0019
ic.ec	0.0005	.	−0.0009	−0.0004	0.0024
ic.er	0.0001	.	0.0000	−0.0034	−0.0013
ic.hp	0.0005	−0.0007	.	0.0004	−0.0001
oc.gc	.	0.0021	0.0304	−0.0014	−0.0001
oc.gr	0.0012	.	−0.0024	0.0025	−0.0073
oc.ec	0.0017	0.0004	−0.0046	.	−0.0003
oc.er	.	0.0006	−0.0012	−0.0058	0.0024
oc.hp	0.0037	0.0046	−0.0085	.	−0.0074
income	.	−0.1104	0.0036	−0.0379	0.0659
...					

Interpreting the MN logit coefficients is not straightforward. In binary logistic regression, recall that you had a simple interpretation for the β_j values as linear effects on the log-odds of success. However, we're now comparing across M categories and the log-odds interpretation applies on the *difference* between coefficients for any *pair* of classes:

$$\log\left(\frac{p_a}{p_b}\right) = \log\left(\frac{e^{\mathbf{x}'\beta_a}}{e^{\mathbf{x}'\beta_b}}\right) = \mathbf{x}'[\beta_a - \beta_b]. \tag{4.11}$$

To interpret the effect of change in a single input variable, say Δx_j, the effect on the odds of class a over class b is

$$\frac{p_a}{p_b} = \exp\left[\Delta x_j \left(\beta_{ja} - \beta_{jb}\right)\right]. \tag{4.12}$$

For example, moving up a single income class increases the odds of choosing hp over gc by around 7%.

```
> exp( (Bnet["income","hp"] − Bnet["income","gc"]) )
[1] 1.068082
```

Beyond the complexity of interpreting multinomial logit coefficients, these interpretations are also notoriously misleading if you want to apply them to understand the causal impact of making changes to the inputs (e.g., here the causal impact of changing costs). Because the coefficient for one class affects all other class probabilities, any sort of correlation between inputs can lead to results that go against your intuition. Economists have a large literature on the best ways to estimate these models when you want to interpret the coefficients as causal effects (e.g., Train, 2009). Unless you have a variable that changes a lot independently from the other variables (e.g., as the result of running an experiment) you should be cautious in assigning too much interpretability to the fitted coefficients from a multinomial logit.

CV Lasso Estimation

You can also use `cv.glmnet` to run a cross-validation experiment for the multinomial logistic regression. This takes the same arguments as `glmnet`.

```
> cv.netfit <- cv.glmnet(xH, yH, family="multinomial")
```

When you call `predict` or `coef` on this `cv.netfit` object, you can pass either `s=lambda.min` or `s=lambda.1se` for CV-min and CV-1se selection, respectively. For example, we find that the CV-min selection rule chooses a sparse estimate of $\hat{B}$ corresponding to $\log(\lambda) \approx -4.3$. (Note that, since there is random sampling in the cross validation routine, this will return slightly different results when you run it).

```
> log(cv.netfit$lambda.min)
[1] -4.29475
> Bcv <- do.call(cbind, coef(cv.netfit,s="lambda.min"))
> colnames(Bcv) <- levels(yH)
> round(Bcv, 4)
17 x 5 sparse Matrix of class "dgCMatrix"
                  gc       gr       ec       er       hp
(Intercept)   0.2959  -0.1666   0.0326   1.0984  -1.2603
ic.gc            .        .        .        .        .
ic.gr            .       0.0000  -0.0008   .        .
ic.ec            .        .        .        .        .
ic.er         0.0002     .        .      -0.0011    .
ic.hp            .        .        .        .        .
oc.gc            .        .        .        .        .
oc.gr            .        .        .        .        .
oc.ec         0.0006     .      -0.0006    .        .
oc.er            .        .        .      -0.0008    .
oc.hp         0.0012   0.0003  -0.0001    .        .
income           .     -0.0495    .        .        .
...
```

4.4.1 Distributed Multinomial Regression

The `glmnet` we ran in the heating example was pretty fast to execute. However, for larger examples—especially examples with many observations on many outcome classes—the code will get very slow. This is because, compared to the linear and logistic Lassos, you now have M times more coefficients and every optimization step needs to be repeated M times (once for each class). A computational bottleneck occurs because the deviance for each $\hat{\beta}_m$ depends on all of the other category coefficients through the logit link in Equation 4.6.

Parallel Regressions for Each Class

Through a relationship between Poisson and multinomial distributions, it turns out that multinomial logistic regression coefficients for each class will be—for practical purposes and under some assumptions—similar to those that you get through *independent* estimation of a *Poisson* regression for each y_m (i.e., for the 0/1 outcome for each class m). Poisson regression is a useful model when your response y is a discrete count variable. The model is

$$y_{im} \sim \text{Poisson} \left(\exp[\mathbf{x}_i' \beta_m] \right) \tag{4.13}$$

which leads to the Poisson deviance function

$$\text{dev}(\beta_m) \propto \sum_{i=1}^{n} \exp(\mathbf{x}_i' \beta_m) - y_i(\mathbf{x}_i' \beta_m) \tag{4.14}$$

The `gamlr` function can be used to fit Lasso-penalized Poisson regression by specifying the argument `family="poisson"`. You can use it whenever your response is a discrete count (e.g., number of events).

When you have many outcome classes (or even a handful and want to save time) a good strategy is to replace multinomial logistic regression with a separate Poisson regression for each outcome class. This is called *distributed multinomial regression* (DMR) (Taddy, 2015). The computational advantage of using DMR is that you can estimate each $\hat{\beta}_m$ in *parallel*.

Fitting DMR with the `distrom` Library

As we've discussed elsewhere, `R`'s `parallel` library makes it easy to take advantage of multiple processor "cores" on your computer (in the code below we see the computer used had 4 cores; yours may have more or less). See the box on parallel computing in Chapter 2.

```
> library(parallel)
> detectCores()
[1] 4
> cl <- makeCluster(4)
> cl
socket cluster with 4 nodes on host 'localhost'
```

The `dmr` function in the `distrom` library implements distributed multinomial regression. You give `dmr` a `parallel` cluster object, and it will outsource `gamlr` runs for each outcome class's Poisson Lasso regressions to the available processor cores.

Since `dmr` is based on `gamlr`, the syntax will be familiar. You can call the function using `dmr(cl, covars, counts, . . . .)` where

- `cl` is a `parallel` cluster,
- `covars` is $\mathbf{x}$,
- `counts` is $\mathbf{y}$, and
- `. . .` are any additional arguments to `gamlr`

This gives you a fast alternative to `glmnet` for fitting (approximate) multinomial logistic regressions.

Example 4.5 Heater Data: Distributed Multinomial Regression Returning to our heating data, we can use the same `xH` and `yH` objects that we created in Example 4.4. Using a cluster `cl` created via `makeCluster` as in the code above, you can use `dmr` to fit parallel Poisson regressions.

```
> library(distrom)
> dmrfit <- dmr(cl, xH, yH)
> length(dmrfit)
[1] 5
> dmrfit[[1]]


poisson gamlr with 16 inputs and 100 segments.
```

The resulting object, `dmrfit`, is a list containing a `gamlr` object for each outcome class. The path plots for each Poisson regression Lasso are shown in Figure 4.9. Notice two things about this plot: there is a different set of λ values along each horizontal axis, and the AICc selected segment is also different for every outcome class. This is because `dmr` allows a different λ_m penalty weight for each class's coefficients and it does model selection on each individual Poisson regression. Note that you can call `dmr` with `cv=TRUE` if you want it to run `cv.gamlr` for each Poisson regression and use CV model selection.

You can call `coef` and `predict` directly on the `dmr` object to get AICc selected coefficients and predictions (or use the `select` argument to ask for any other segment choice).

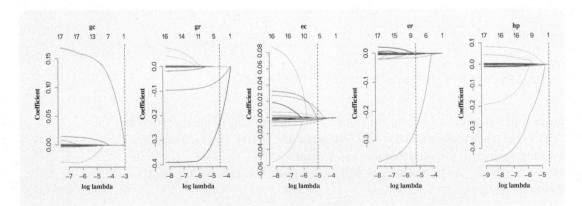

FIGURE 4.9 Lasso paths for the heating data distributed multinomial regression via `dmr`. Dashed lines show AICc selection.

```
> round(coef(dmrfit),4)
17 × 5 sparse Matrix of class "dmrcoef"
                 gc       gr       ec       er       hp
intercept   -0.4515  -1.6488  -0.7665   0.2433  -2.8904
ic.gc            .        .        .        .        .
ic.gr            .        .    -0.0014   0.0020     .
ic.ec            .        .        .        .        .
ic.er            .        .        .    -0.0023     .
ic.hp            .        .        .        .        .
oc.gc            .        .     0.0099     .        .
oc.gr            .        .        .        .        .
oc.ec            .        .    -0.0026     .        .
oc.er            .        .        .    -0.0037     .
oc.hp            .        .    -0.0049     .        .
income           .    -0.0511     .        .        .
```

Similarly to what we found using CV-min selection with `cv.glmnet`, here the matrix of coefficients selected by AICc has mostly zero elements. This is noisy data and it is difficult to find a useful signal in the inputs.

The coefficients on the results from `dmr` should be similar to what you get using the same penalties in `glmnet` with `family="multinomial"`. A direct comparison is difficult because `dmr` fits a different λ_m for each outcome class whereas `glmnet` uses a single penalty for all segments. Indeed, the predictive performance for `dmr` is often better than what you get from `cv.glmnet` because of this class-specific penalization. Note that the intercept values you get from `dmr` can be wildly different from those found using `glmnet`. However these differences between intercepts cancel each other out in the multinomial logit link function and the predictions will end up being comparable.

QUICK REFERENCE

This chapter has introduced the ideas behind classification using regression models. Later in the book we will introduce other powerful tools for classification, including the classification trees and forests of Chapter 7. The classification forests, in particular, will be preferable to either multinomial logistic regression or distributed multinomial regression in most settings. However, logistic Lasso regression is a workhorse of industrial classification applications that provides appealing speed and robustness even when you are working with very high-dimensional inputs.

Key Practical Concepts

- With *numeric* data matrix x with label vector y, and unlabeled data xtest, you can run *K*-NN classification with K neighbors using

  ```
  knn(train=x, test=xtest, cl=y, k=K)
  ```

  It is a good idea to first scale both xtrain and xtest by dividing by variable standard deviations. For example,

  ```
  xs <- scale( rbind(xtrain,xtest) )
  knn(train=xs[1:nrow(x),], test=xs[-(1:nrow(x)),], cl=y, k=K)
  ```

- Use logistic regression to estimate probabilities for binary classification problems, and use thresholding on probabilities to make classifications.

  ```
  yhat <- phat > threshold
  ```

- Use the table function on predicted classes yhat and observed classes y to calculate the confusion matrix for any classification rule.

  ```
  table(pred=yhat, actual=y)
  ```

- Given model matrix x and multilevel factor response y, fit CV Lasso multinomial logistic regression with the glmnet library.

  ```
  netfit <- cv.glmnet( x, y, family="multinomial")
  ```

- Alternatively, you can use a parallel cluster cl and the distrom library to fit fast distributed multinomial regression.

  ```
  dmrfit <- dmr( cl, x, y )
  ```

  The dmr function returns a list of gamlr regressions, one for each level of y. You can call coef and predict on dmrfit the same as you would call them on a fitted gamlr object.

5 CAUSAL INFERENCE WITH EXPERIMENTS

This chapter introduces concepts of causal inference and experimentation, and shows how you can use regression modeling to analyze treatment effects in experiments and near-experimental designs.

● **Section 5.1 Notation for Causal Inference:** Be able to talk about counterfactual estimation problems in terms of *potential outcomes* and average treatment effects.

● **Section 5.2 Randomized Controlled Trials:** Analyze an experiment where the treatment is assigned completely at random (e.g., an *AB trial*).

■ **Section 5.3 Regression Adjustment:** Use regression techniques to adjust for imperfect randomization and model heterogeneous treatment effects.

■ **Section 5.4 Regression Discontinuity Designs:** Estimate treatment effects in the situation where a treatment is assigned according to a threshold on a *forcing* variable.

◆ **Section 5.5 Instrumental Variables:** Understand how instrumental variables (IV) allow you to estimate treatment effects under endogeneity. Apply two-stage least squares IV estimators in an intent-to-treat setting.

◆ **Section 5.6 Design of Experiments:** Use ideas from probability to design your own experiments, and understand how *reinforcement learning* uses active experimentation to generate data for training ML models.

Every method we have discussed so far is able to detect patterns in past data. These patterns will be useful for predicting the future, *assuming that the future looks mostly like the past.* As the saying goes, "Correlation is not causation." But correlation might be all that you need. If people who rent the movie *Frozen* also tend to like the movie *Sing*, then you can reliably use this information for future recommendations. Both preferences are likely caused by a third unseen signal—that these people have small children who like cartoon musicals—but that doesn't lessen the usefulness of the discovered pattern.

However, when you are analyzing business and economic systems, you often need to dig deeper and get at causation. You need to be able to predict a future that will be different from the past *because you are going to take actions that make it different.* A decision that changes your product, marketing, or pricing creates a new data generating process that can break the correlation patterns that you've seen in the past. Suppose that you are a hotelier considering offering a discount to increase business. This price change is an action, and you need to know how sales will change *because* of that action.

In the past, hotel room prices have moved up or down according to projections of demand. For example, rooms are more expensive during holidays because you anticipate higher demand. This will lead to a correlational pattern where prices are high when sales are high—during holidays there are no vacancies, and the prices are very high. Of course, sales are not high *because* prices are high. Rather, the two are (like viewership of *Frozen* and *Sing*) co-dependent upon a third variable—in this case, the underlying demand for hotel rooms. If you act to change prices and break the past dependence structure, then this correlational pattern disappears. In this scenario, we would say that the observed relationship between prices and sales is "confounded" by unobserved underlying demand.

Price optimization is a setting that requires counterfactual prediction: prediction for scenarios that have not happened yet, but which might. For example, you might be considering charging a new price p_1 instead of the planned or current price p_0. Because of the confounding issue described above, you can't look at past data to understand the implications of this decision. The only way to really predict what will happen is to run an experiment where you move prices independently of demand and see what happens. The classic way to do this is to randomize prices, say across days or across customers. This is the purest form of experimentation—a randomized controlled trial (RCT)—and it is the gold standard for estimating counterfactuals.

Counterfactual analysis and causal inference—the statistics of measuring *why* things happen—is a big topic area and we are going to talk about only the most common tools and best practices. Further reading can be found in the texts by Imbens and Rubin (2015), Morgan and Winship (2015), Pearl and Mackenzie (2018), and Pearl (2009). This current chapter focuses on counterfactual analysis based on *experimental data*: situations where you know that your treatment of interest (e.g., price) has been changed across observations that are otherwise comparable (e.g., different groups of days with the same underlying demand). We'll start by introducing the notation of "potential outcomes" and then dive into analysis of data from randomized controlled trials. We will also cover some more complex settings where the treatment has not been directly randomized but you still have experimental variation in your treatment across comparable groups of observations.

Looking forward, the next chapter deals with "observational data" where there has been no experiment. In such settings you need to explicitly model confounding influences (such as the holiday demand spike in our hotel pricing example above). Between the two chapters, we hope to give you a primer on the state-of-the-art for counterfactual analysis. This type of analysis plays a huge role in how data is used in economics and business.

● 5.1 Notation for Causal Inference

As is often the case in science, understanding *notation* is a crucial part of understanding causal inference. For counterfactual prediction, we need a notation framework that is able to describe both events that have happened and events that *would* have happened under different inputs.

The language of experiments is built around the notion of "treatments" applied to "units," and the observed response for those units under this "treatment status." A treatment variable, say d, is a special input to your models. It is special because it can be changed independently from all other upstream influences on the response of interest. The notion of independence is the key property of treatments in a counterfactual analysis: you want to know what will happen if you *act* to change the treatment variable.

Potential Outcomes Notation

One powerful tool for describing counterfactual analysis is the *potential outcomes* notation wherein each unit (e.g., a subject in a clinical trial) is modeled as having a different possible response for each treatment level:

- $y_i(D)$ is the potential response for unit i under treatment status D.
- d_i is the observed treatment status for unit i, and $y_i = y_i(d_i)$ is our shorthand for the observed response.

To understand what is going on, imagine that everyone in a pharmaceutical trial has two potential outcomes: how they will respond to a placebo (say, $y(0)$) and how they will respond if given some drug treatment (say, $y(1)$). You don't know both of these potential outcomes, because you only get to observe one of them. If a person is assigned to the treatment group, then $d = 1$ and we get to observe their outcome under treatment. If a person is assigned to the control group, then $d = 0$ and we observe their outcome without treatment.

Binary Treatment Effects

Treatment variables can be discrete or continuous. For example, in this pharmaceutical trial example we have $d_i = 1$ for subjects i who are given a new drug and $d_i = 0$ for those receiving a placebo or control dose. Price is a common continuous treatment variable: as a business you decide to "treat" your potential customers to price d_t at time t, and they will choose to buy or not buy your product at this price. You can also have multiple treatments of all different sorts; for example, television marketing campaigns for consumer goods are often accompanied by price promotions so that you have a discrete marketing treatment (show or don't show ad) and a continuous price treatment (discount size). In the analysis of experiments we often think about just two treatment levels: $d = 1$ or $d = 0$ corresponding to treatment and control respectively. In this chapter we will focus on such binary treatment variables; however, everything we discuss can be extended to comparisons between multiple treatment levels.

Under a binary treatment, each individual unit has a *treatment effect* (TE) that represents the causal impact of the treatment:

$$\text{TE}_i = y_i(1) - y_i(0) \tag{5.1}$$

Here, $y_i(1)$ is the response for individual i if they are treated, and $y_i(0)$ is their response in an alternative untreated world. Of course, in most settings you only ever get to see $y_i(d_i)$ for $d_i = 1$ or 0, and thus Equation 5.1 is partially unobservable.

Average Treatment Effect

A common target of estimation is the average treatment effect, or ATE. This is the average impact of the treatment on the response across a population of units or individuals. Using the potential outcomes notation, we can write the ATE as

$$\text{ATE} = \mathbb{E}[y(1) - y(0)] \tag{5.2}$$

Since we only ever observe one of $y(0)$ or $y(1)$ for a given individual, we need to estimate the ATE without ever observing $y(1) - y(0)$ for the same individual. The key property that allows us to do this is having the potential outcomes, $y_i(0)$ and $y_i(1)$, be independent from the observed treatment status d_i. This is the assumption of *independent treatment assignment,* which we write as

$$y_i(D) \perp\!\!\!\perp d_i \tag{5.3}$$

In the context of our clinical trial example, this means that assignment to the treatment or control group is independent of what the potential outcomes are. If we randomly allocate people to treatment and control, say by flipping a coin, we know that their treatment status has nothing to do with their potential outcomes and Equation (5.3) holds true. The ATE is the simple difference between the average of outcomes in treatment and control groups.

$$\text{ATE} = \mathbb{E}[y|d = 0] - \mathbb{E}[y|d = 1] \tag{5.4}$$

In contrast, suppose you had a situation where only sick people got the treatment and healthy people got the control. Their treatment status, d, would be correlated with their potential health outcomes (presuming that $y(0)$ and $y(1)$ are expected to be worse for sick people). If you look at the difference in average outcomes between the treatment and control groups for this nonexperiment, then that difference will conflate the effect of the treatment with generally worse expected outcomes for sick people. The difference in means between treatment and control would not be a good estimator of the average treatment effect.

Conditional Average Treatment Effect

You can also model the effects as being conditional on covariates, say $\mathbf{x}$, such that Equation (5.3) becomes the assumption of *conditional* independence of treatment assignment,

$$y_i(D) \perp\!\!\!\perp d_i|\mathbf{x}_i \tag{5.5}$$

In causal inference and in the context of (5.5), these covariates are often called *control variables* or *controls* for short. By conditioning on them (i.e., controlling for their influence) you are able to model the causal impact of d on y.

In such settings, you will often estimate the conditional average treatment effect (CATE) such that the treatment effect depends upon the value of the controls:

$$\text{CATE}(\mathbf{x}) = \mathbb{E}[y(1) - y(0)|\mathbf{x}] \tag{5.6}$$

Analogous to the comparison in Chapter 1 between the marginal and conditional expectation, the CATE is a *function* of the covariates and the ATE is a simple number. We will dive into the practical analysis of experiments, and CATEs and ATEs, in the next two sections.

Other Languages for Causal Inference

The potential outcomes notation can get a bit messy as you move beyond basic experiments. For more complex settings, Pearl (2009) developed a powerful framework for causal inference that is based on directed graphs where causal relationships are represented through arrows between variables. Pearl advocates a comprehensive theory of causality that goes beyond the basic counterfactuals we discuss in this book. However, the language of directed graphs is useful and many people find it more intuitive than the potential outcomes notation. We will see a couple very basic versions of these graphs in our discussion of instrumental variables, and again in the next chapter on conditional ignorability.

Another tradition is to work through structural equations, where you describe your model through a set of equations specifying how inputs cause outputs. The output from one structural equation can be the input in another equation in the set, and each equation stands alone as representing a single causal relationship. We will use some simple structural equation models in the next chapter when doing counterfactual inference on observational data. Causal inference is a rich and active field (indeed, the Nobel Prize in Economics was awarded for it in 2021). These different notation frameworks are all useful and complementary tools for describing causal problems.

5.2 Randomized Controlled Trials

The gold standard for measuring the effect of an action is a randomized controlled trial (RCT) where units are randomly allocated to different treatment states and you measure how these random groupings differ after treatment. "Try it and see what happens" was at the core of the enlightenment and scientific revolution that began in the 17th century. The procedure of experimentation was combined with the formalism of frequentist statistics in the beginning of the 20th century, allowing scientists to put precise probabilities on how the results of an experiment would extrapolate to future experience. Into the 21st century, heavy experimentation by technology companies has made RCTs an essential part of business optimization.

Many readers will be familiar with the notion of an AB trial, which is Silicon Valley's label for a simple RCT wherein the experimental subjects are randomly assigned to treatment status. For example, you might randomize your website users into groups A and B; those in A, the control group, see the current website, and those in B see a new layout. This might seems simple but there are challenges to making AB testing work in practice. You can introduce subtle bias if certain types of customers are more likely to land on the page that triggers the treatment (this is often tested through an AA trial, where you give each group the same treatment so that any differences between groups are due to bias in treatment assignment). Or you can have dependence between your units if, for example, the customers are bidding against each other to buy the same products. In this section we will give you the basic tools to deal with issues like this when analyzing AB experiments.

Note that the term "control" here has a different meaning from how we used it after Equation (5.5) to refer to covariates that you condition on as controls. A control group in an RCT is a sample of subjects that do not receive any treatment, whereas control variables are those you condition on to get conditional ignorability. In both cases, the control group or control variables are necessary to understand how subjects would behave without any treatment and to model a counterfactual. The next chapter is dedicated to a deeper analysis of how control variables can be used to obtain causal treatment effect estimates even when you are unable to run an experiment.

Average Treatment Effects in an AB Trial

Recall our discussion of independent treatment assignment around Equations (5.3) and (5.4). The simplest way to get independent treatment assignments is through randomization: your allocation to group A or B is a function of a random draw that has nothing to do with the characteristics of the individual. If your treatment assignment is randomized in this way, then (5.4) says that the ATE is equal to the difference between treatment group expected responses. Thus, estimation for the ATE becomes simply estimation for the difference in means between two groups. This is material you learn in your first statistics class. Say $\bar{y}_0$ and $\bar{y}_1$ are the sample means for the n_0 and n_1 users in groups A ($d_i = 0$) and B ($d_i = 1$), respectively. Then your ATE estimate is

$$\widehat{\text{ATE}} = \bar{y}_1 - \bar{y}_0 \qquad (5.7)$$

As we did in Chapter 2, we can rewrite this difference in means as a parameter in the regression model,

$$\mathbb{E}[y_i | d_i] = \beta + \gamma d_i \qquad (5.8)$$

Here, γ is the ATE: the difference between treatment and control expected response. We will often use Greek gamma γ to denote our treatment effect variables, in contrast to the usual β coefficient notation, as a convention to highlight that this is interpreted as a causal treatment effect. Equation (5.8) is our first example of representing data from experiments using a regression model. We will take this approach throughout, and you will find that regression modeling is a great way to simplify your analysis of experiments. In this case, you can fit (5.8) using `glm` and use either the usual standard errors or a bootstrap to quantify uncertainty.

Example 5.1 **Oregon Health Insurance Experiment** As a running example in this chapter we're going to look to a large-scale health policy experiment. In 2008, the state of Oregon gained funding to expand its coverage for Medicaid—the U.S. social program that provides health insurance to people who cannot afford private insurance. Since demand was (correctly) expected to outstrip supply, the state worked with researchers (see Finkelstein et al., 2012) to design a lottery that *randomly* allocates eligibility for Medicaid enrollment among the state's low-income population. This led to the Oregon Health Insurance Experiment (OHIE), a randomized controlled trial for measuring the treatment effect of medical insurance.

Although this example deals with health policy rather than business decisions, it shares many of the classic properties of the experiments we encounter in technology companies: the treatment effects are small and hard to measure, the sample size is very large, and there are possible issues of bias in treatment assignment and dependence between units. The impact of insurance on people's behavior (and on payer costs) is also a big issue in designing the menu of employee benefits for large companies. The OHIE contains a rich set of material for understanding how health insurance works in practice.

There are many outcomes of interest here. Since the people in each treatment group were tracked for only 12 months in our data, you don't get to observe long-term differences between the two groups. This makes it impossible to draw conclusions about the effect of insurance access on long-term public health. However, you can observe how Medicaid changes the use of health services—this is important both for estimating the cost of expanded public insurance and for modeling the downstream public health improvements. For example, the researchers found a small increase in hospitalization for those selected in the Medicaid lottery (hereafter the *treated* or *selected* group) but no increase in usage for emergency room (ER) services (indeed, the point estimate shows slightly *decreased* ER usage). Results like this allow projections of cost and utilization changes as inputs to health policy.

The full data from the OHIE is available at `nber.org/oregon/4.data.html`. We have cleaned the data (the cleaning script is available on the book website) to create a simplified dataset containing:

- `person_id`: the identification key for individuals.
- `household_id`: the identification key for household (some individuals are from the same household).
- `numhh`: the number of people in each household who were part of the lottery.
- `selected`: a binary variable that is 1 for those selected to be allowed to apply for Medicaid, 0 otherwise. This is the variable that is randomized through the lottery.
- `medicaid`: a binary variable that is 1 for those who enroll in Medicaid, 0 otherwise. Not all those who were selected ended up actually enrolled; they might not have bothered applying, or they could have been found ineligible for a variety of reasons (e.g., if their income was higher than the state expected).
- `weight`: an estimated population weight for each observation, as necessary to extrapolate from the sample to the full Oregon population. (See the box on survey sampling.)
- `doc_num`: the number of times each patient saw a primary care physician (PCP; i.e., a family doctor or GP) in the 12-month study period.

Our response of interest will be *primary care usage* as measured through the variable `doc_num`, a count of PCP visits. This information was collected in a 12-month follow-up survey that gathered information from about 23,441 of the original 75,000 people from the full lottery. See the box on survey sampling adjustment for discussion on how to extrapolate from the experiment results to the full population.

ATE Estimation

The treatment effect on primary care usage is important because this is an early signal of increased engagement with health care. Primary care usage is generally viewed as a *good thing*: PCP visits are a relatively low-cost form of health care and they can prevent the need for expensive acute care from hospitalization or via the ER. The treatment of interest is (for now) the `selected` variable, so we will be investigating the treatment effect of being allowed to apply for Medicaid on PCP visits. Later, in our section on instrumental variables, we will consider the treatment effect of actual Medicaid enrollment on PCP visits (the reason we need to defer this analysis is that the enrollment is not random: it might be correlated with unobserved influences such as baseline health or income).

Reading the data into R as the `ohie` data frame, we see that approximately 50% of people in the lottery were randomly selected to be able to apply for Medicaid.

```
> ohie <- read.csv("OHIEresults.csv")
> dim(ohie)
[1] 23441     7
> head(ohie,3)
```

```
  person_id household_id numhh medicaid selected weight doc_num
1         1       100001     1        0        1      1       0
2         2       100002     1        1        1      1       0
3         5       100005     1        0        1      1       0
> table(ohie[,"selected"])
   0    1
11790 11651
```

The standard ATE estimate is available as a difference in means, as in Equation (5.7).

```
> ybar <- tapply(ohie[,"doc_num"], ohie[,"selected"], mean)
> ( ATE = ybar['1'] - ybar['0'] )
     1
0.2489679
```

Alternatively, you can get the same value by estimating γ from (5.8).

```
> fitATE <- glm(doc_num ~ selected, data=ohie)
> coef(fitATE)["selected"]
  selected
0.2489679
```

In either case, we see that being allowed to apply for Medicaid causes an average of 0.25 extra PCP visits in the following year.

Uncertainty Quantification

The glm summary gives you the standard error for this estimated ATE.

```
> summary(fitATE)
...
Coefficients:
            Estimate Std. Error t value Pr(>|t|)
(Intercept)  1.82536    0.02690  67.867  < 2e-16 ***
selected     0.24897    0.03815   6.526 6.89e-11 ***
```

The standard error of 0.0382 implies a 95% confidence interval for the ATE from 0.174 to 0.324 ($0.249 \pm 1.96 \times 0.0382$). Alternatively, you can use the bootstrap.

```
> library(parallel)
> library(boot)
> getATE <- function(data, ind)
+    coef(glm(doc_num ~ selected, data=data[ind,]))["selected"]
> ( bootATE <- boot(ohie, getATE, 1000,
+            parallel="snow", ncpus=detectCores() ) )
...
Bootstrap Statistics :
     original         bias std. error
t1* 0.2489679 -0.002080427  0.03856918
```

The standard error is nearly unchanged at 0.0385. Note that you may have gotten slightly different results due to the random sampling in the bootstrap.

The bias measured by the bootstrap is tiny, and indeed this estimator should be unbiased. However, it is a good default practice to build your bootstrap confidence intervals around the bias corrected procedure of Chapter 2. Recall that you do this by calculating the bootstrap sample of errors, $e_b = \hat{\gamma}_b - \hat{\gamma}$ for each bootstrap draw b, and then calculating percentiles on the bias corrected ATE estimates $\hat{\gamma} - e_b$. As described in Chapter 2, a quick bit of algebra shows that $\hat{\gamma} - e_b = 2\hat{\gamma} - \hat{\gamma}_b$, so that you can define the getCI function to get bias-corrected CIs from any boot object.

```
> getCI <- function(bo, p=c(.025,.975)) quantile(2*bo$t0 -
bo$t, p)
> getCI(bootATE)
     2.5%        97.5%
0.1766459  0.3239622
```

Again, the results are practically unchanged from what you get using the standard errors from glm. The 95% CIs are all above zero, so we have measured a significant positive effect for Medicaid eligibility on PCP visits. Oregon can plan for this range of increased PCP usage when it expands Medicaid eligibility to a wider population, and models that condition on PCP access when predicting public health can use this information to project the societal benefits of increased access to health insurance.

Survey Sample Weighting

The OHIE data contain the weight variable that can be used to map from the sample of individuals who responded to the survey to the future treatment population (all Oregonians who are eligible for Medicaid). The weights are higher for patients from demographic groups that are underrepresented in the survey data relative to their prevalence in the state population. Some patients are weighted almost four times higher than the baseline patient.

```
> range(ohie$weight)
[1] 1.000000 3.892884
```

If you want to extrapolate from your sample to a population with different demographics, you need to adjust for such underrepresentation because individual subjects do not all respond the same way to treatment. For example, perhaps young people who are healthy and less likely to seek a PCP are also harder to reach for a phone survey (and are thus underrepresented). You can apply this re-weighting by using the `weights` argument of `glm`. In this case, the estimated ATE increases by about 0.02.

```
> glm(doc_num ~ selected, weights=weight, data=ohie)
...
(Intercept)    selected
     1.9142      0.2682
```

Any of our analyses in this chapter can be repeated using this `weights` argument.

This sort of re-weighting, to map from the sample to the population of interest, is a standard step in many survey analyses. For example, political pollsters are always battling to figure out how their sample of survey respondents maps to the characteristics of the future voting population. An interesting contemporary overview of this area by Gelman et al. (2016) tackles the problem of using abundant survey data from nontraditional venues—e.g., via the Microsoft Xbox gaming platform—for insight about voting intentions of the wider population. As pollsters' recent lack of success demonstrates (e.g., Trump, Brexit), the sample-to-population mapping problem is a tricky one.

■ 5.3 Regression Adjustment

In a perfectly randomized trial, the probability of a unit's being in the treatment group vs. control is fully independent from the characteristics of that unit. In this situation, the independence condition in (5.3) is satisfied and it is hard to do better than a simple difference of means as your estimate of the ATE. Unfortunately, perfect randomization is not always possible. In an AB trial, for example, you might be testing a new website feature for communication between users. If one user is randomly assigned to this treatment, then you might also want to include everyone that they want to communicate with in the same treatment (otherwise you will end up with a strange one-sided communication experience). Users with big networks will be overrepresented in the treatment group because there is a higher probability that they are in communication with someone who was randomly assigned to the treatment group. If these big network users behave differently from those with a smaller network, then your estimated treatment effect can be biased.

Issues like this usually lead to small, practically ignorable, imperfections in website trials. But not always, and you might end up with a treatment group that has a different mix of key characteristics from the control group. Fortunately, so long as you know the factors that are causing a lack of balance between the groups, you can use basic regression techniques to control for these factors and recover solid ATE estimates. That is, you place conditions on these controls **x** to satisfy the conditional independence assumption of (5.5). Our use of regression models to analyze experiments makes this easy: you just add the controls to the regression.

Linear Regression Adjustment via Interaction

To adjust our ATE estimate to account for these controls, we need to allow **x** to impact the expected response for units in *both* treatment and control groups. You can express this through the interaction model,

$$\mathbb{E}[y|d, \mathbf{x}] = \mathbf{x}'\beta + d\mathbf{x}'\gamma \tag{5.9}$$

Here, as we often do, we've specified that the first dimension of **x** is the intercept so that, for example, $\mathbf{x}'\gamma = \gamma_0 + x_1\gamma_1 \ldots x_K\gamma_K$. Also, $d\mathbf{x}'\gamma$ will be 0 for the control group ($d = 0$) and $\mathbf{x}'\gamma$ for the treatment group ($d = 1$).

The model in (5.9) gives you an expression for the CATE—the conditional average treatment effect given **x**—available as $\mathbf{x}'\gamma$. You can then calculate the ATE as the average of the CATEs:

$$\text{ATE} = \mathbb{E}[\mathbf{x}'_i\gamma] \tag{5.10}$$

where this expectation is averaging over the distribution of **x** in your population. You can estimate this ATE by estimating the parameters of (5.9) and averaging over the $\mathbf{x}_i$ variables in your sample:

$$\widehat{\text{ATE}} = \bar{\mathbf{x}}'\hat{\gamma} \tag{5.11}$$

where $\bar{\mathbf{x}}' = (1/n)\sum_{i=1}^{n} \mathbf{x}_i$ is the sample average for your controls: $\bar{\mathbf{x}} = [1\,\bar{x}_1 \ldots \bar{x}_K]$.

In practice, it is often easier to predict the potential outcomes for each subject in your sample and average the difference.

$$\widehat{\text{ATE}} = \frac{1}{n}\sum_i [\hat{y}_i(1) - \hat{y}_i(0)] \tag{5.12}$$

Uncertainty for this ATE estimate can be obtained via bootstrapping. For a linear regression adjustment model as in (5.9), this average of differences is the exact same as (5.11). However, the expression in (5.12) is more general and also works if you are using, for example, logistic regression to analyze your experiment.

Example 5.2 OHIE: Adjusting for Household Size The Oregon Health Insurance Experiment has an issue of imperfect randomization. Each person selected in the lottery could apply for Medicaid for all of their family members, and thus the entire household has been 'treated' with eligibility to apply for Medicaid. This leads to people in larger households having a higher chance of being selected. The imbalance shows up clearly in the data (recall that there are around 11,700 people in each treatment group).

```
> table(ohie[,c("selected","numhh")])
    numhh
selected    1    2  3+
       0 8805 2979   6
       1 7655 3944  52
```

If health care consumption changes for individuals depending upon family size, then the ATE estimate that we obtained above as $\bar{y}_1 - \bar{y}_0$ will be biased toward the behavior of people in larger households.

Linear Regression Adjustment for Household Size

We have in our data the variable numhh, which is a factor taking the levels 1, 2, or 3+ for households with three or more people. We can write the regression model from (5.11) as

$$\mathbb{E}[y|d, \text{numhh}] = \beta_0 + d\gamma_0 + (\beta_1 + d\gamma_1)\mathbb{1}_{[\text{numhh}=2]} + (\beta_2 + d\gamma_2)\mathbb{1}_{[\text{numhh}=3+]} \qquad \textbf{(5.13)}$$

Recall that y is the doc_num count of PCP visits and d is selected. You can fit the model with glm by specifying an *interaction* between selected and numhh.

```
> fitAdj <- glm(doc_num ~ selected*numhh, data=ohie)
> coef(fitAdj)
    (Intercept)         selected         numhh2       numhh3+
      1.9031232        0.3294045     -0.3042645    -1.7364566
  selected:numhh2    selected:numhh3+
       -0.1516405            0.8693134
```

You can see that in the control group the members of larger households tend toward fewer PCP visits, especially in the 3+ households. The estimated CATEs given household size are 0.33 extra PCP visits for single person households, 0.18 extra visits for members of a dual person household (0.33-0.15), and 1.2 extra visits for members of households with three or more people (0.33+0.87).

Use the predict function to calculate $\widehat{\text{ATE}}$ as $(1/n)\Sigma_i[\hat{y}_i(1) - \hat{y}_i(0)]$.

```
> mean(
+    predict(fitAdj, data.frame(selected=1, numhh=ohie$numhh)) -
+    predict(fitAdj, data.frame(selected=0, numhh=ohie$numhh)) )
[1] 0.2867704
```

This is about 0.04 more PCP visits than we had for our original, unadjusted, ATE.

Bootstrapping the ATE Estimate

To quantify uncertainty for this new adjusted ATE, you can use a bootstrap. Since we now recognize that many individuals come from the same household, we should use a block bootstrap to account for potential dependence between the individuals. To do this, we will first break ohie into a list of data frames, one for each household. We will also introduce a new function, rbindlist from the data.table package. This is faster than the rbind function that we used to re-combine data frames when introducing the block bootstrap in Chapter 2.

```
> library(data.table)
> ohieHH <- split(ohie, ohie$household)
> system.time(rbindlist(ohieHH))
   user system elapsed
   0.08   0.00    0.08
> system.time(do.call("rbind",ohieHH))
   user system elapsed
   1.72   0.00    1.73
```

Both of the last two lines above transform ohieHH back to the original single data frame, but rbindlist takes 0.08 seconds while calling rbind takes 1.72 seconds on this author's laptop. Over many bootstrap samples, that will make a big difference.

To run the bootstrap you first define a function to reproduce your adjusted ATE and then apply the boot package.

```
> getAdjATE <- function(data, ids, binder){
+   data <- binder(data[ids])
+   fit <- glm(doc_num ~ selected*numhh, data=data)
+   mean(
+     predict(fit, data.frame(selected=1, numhh=data$numhh)) -
+     predict(fit, data.frame(selected=0, numhh=data$numhh)) )
+ }
> (bootAdjATE <- boot(ohieHH, getAdjATE, binder=rbindlist,
+           1000, parallel="snow", ncpus=detectCores()))
...
      original        bias std. error
t1* 0.2867704 0.002861392 0.03735892
> getCI(bootAdjATE)
    2.5%     97.5%
0.2114019 0.3592275
```

Being selected causes an extra 0.21 to 0.36 PCP visits in 12 months according to our 95% CI. Recall that, due to the Monte Carlo randomness in bootstrap sampling, the results you get when running this code will differ slightly.

Alternative UQ for Linear Regression Adjustment

Note that, since we are using linear regression analysis, you could also isolate the ATE as a single regression parameter by shifting the covariates to have a mean of zero. If you have done this, then Equation (5.11) becomes simply $\widehat{\text{ATE}} = \hat{\gamma}$. You can do this in R by first creating and then shifting the model.matrix for regression onto numhh.

```
> x <- scale(model.matrix( ~ numhh, data=ohie)[,-1],
scale=FALSE)
> colMeans(x)
       numhh2         numhh3+
 2.677399e-17  -1.355010e-19
> coef(fitx <- glm(doc_num ~ selected*x, data=ohie))["selected"]
  selected
0.2867704
```

The ATE estimate is exactly the same as what we found using the average for $\hat{y}_i(1) - \hat{y}_i(0)$ above. We can also use the sandwich package, as we did in Chapter 2, to obtain clustered standard errors as an alternative to running a block bootstrap.

```
> library(sandwich)
> library(lmtest)
> coeftest(fitx, vcov = vcovCL(fitx, ohie$household) )
...

               Estimate  Std. Error  z value   P(>|z|)
selected       0.286770   0.038815    7.3882  1.488e-13 ***
```

The resulting standard error is just slightly larger than what we found using the block bootstrap (0.0388 vs. 0.0374).

....

Regression adjustment when estimating your ATE is necessary whenever you know that certain variables (like numhh here) have influenced the probabilities of treatment assignment. In addition, analysts sometimes use regression to adjust for covariate imbalance even when the experiment has been perfectly randomized. For example, you might have found more elderly people in either treatment group and wish to adjust your ATE estimate for the influence of age even though you know that this imbalance occurred through pure chance. However, we tend to advise against these adjustments unless you have small sample sizes and know of a few factors that have a large influence on the response (in which case you should consider the sort of stratified or blocked design discussed in Section 5.6). The extra complexity of regression adjustment is often not worth the effort unless you have good reason to suspect that your treatment assignment is not random.

Although we have used linear regression methods throughout this section, you can also use other generalized linear models to analyze experiments and adjust for controls. The only difference is that instead of having a simple expression like (5.11) for your adjusted ATE estimate, you need to work with the full average difference in predicted outcomes as in Equation (5.12). This is already how we calculated the adjusted ATE in R, so you don't need to change anything else other than your regression model.

Example 5.3 OHIE: Logistic Regression As a quick illustration, we will use logistic regression to analyze the OHIE results for a binary target of interest: whether or not someone visited a PCP at all in the 12-month study period. This is available as the logical variable doc_num>0. We will apply the same functions that we used above to estimate the adjusted ATE and its bootstrap confidence interval, changing only the response variable and adding family="binomial" to glm and type="response" to predict.glm.

```
> getAdjATEbin <- function(data, ids, binder){
+   data <- binder(data[ids])
+   fit <- glm( doc_num > 0 ~ selected*numhh,
+         data=data, family="binomial")
+   mean(
+     predict(fit, data.frame(selected=1, numhh=data$numhh),
+         type="response")-
+     predict(fit, data.frame(selected=0, numhh=data$nunhh),
+         type="response"))}
> (bootAdjATEbin <- boot(ohieHH, getAdjATEbin, binder=rbindlist,
+           1000, parallel="snow", ncpus=detectCores()))
...

      original         bias   std. error
t1* 0.06362671 -3.454849e-05  0.006537611
> getCI(bootAdjATEbin)
   2.5%    97.5%
0.0515531 0.0759382
```

The probability of visiting a PCP increases by around 0.064 (with a 95% CI from 0.052 to 0.76) due to the ability to apply in Medicaid.

5.3.1 High-Dimensional Heterogeneous Treatment Effects

In the regression adjustment above, we measured different treatment effects depending upon household size. This produced a CATE function, providing the average treatment effect conditional on different levels of our covariate numhh. This phenomenon, where the influence of the treatment (i.e., a policy variable that you control) varies as a function of who or what is being treated, is referred to as *heterogeneous treatment effects* (HTEs). Whenever you find it useful to estimate a CATE you are modeling HTEs: the conditional average treatment effect is the main outcome of interest in an HTE analysis. In our regression-adjustment analysis above, we modeled the heterogeneity in treatment effects due to household size. Now, we will consider how to model and estimate HTEs when you have many potential sources of heterogeneity rather than a single known source.

As a first point to make clear, *heterogeneous treatment effects exist.* Almost any practitioner would agree that their treatment—medicine, advertisement, web service—has a different effect on different individuals. For example, people shopping for clothing on a website are more likely to buy when pictures are bigger, while those shopping for car parts prefer more items per page with smaller pictures. You don't need to know *why* this happens for it to be useful in website design. However, to consider modeling many different sources of heterogeneity, you will need to make use of the high-dimensional regression techniques that we introduced in Chapter 3.

When you have an RCT, modeling HTEs is easy: just run a regression that interacts the treatment variable with covariates. The model is exactly the same as we specified in Equation (5.9), which we can rewrite to allow for different GLMs by adding a link function:

$$\mathbb{E}[y \mid d, \mathbf{x}] = f(\mathbf{x}'\beta + d\mathbf{x}'\gamma) \tag{5.14}$$

Again, note that the first element of $\mathbf{x}$ is the intercept. Since the treatment (d) has been randomly assigned, you can use any of your usual regression tools for estimating the model (when d is not randomly assigned, as in our next chapter, you need to take special care in estimating the model to isolate the treatment effect).

For high-dimensional controls, you should look to the Lasso regression techniques that we introduced in Chapter 3. Once you have an estimated model, you can obtain CATEs by comparing predictions for treatment vs. control under different values for $\mathbf{x}$:

$$\text{CATE}(\mathbf{x}) \approx \widehat{\mathbb{E}}[y \mid d = 1, \mathbf{x}] - \widehat{\mathbb{E}}[y \mid d = 0, \mathbf{x}] \tag{5.15}$$

In the special case of linear regression, with the link $f(z) = z$, you can simplify to write $\text{CATE}(\mathbf{x}) \approx \mathbf{x}'\hat{\gamma}$.

Example 5.4 HTEs for the OHIE Experiment For our Oregon health insurance experiment, we have a set of 27 covariates from a survey on subject demographics carried out 12 months after the Medicaid lottery. The data include categorical responses (e.g., `edu_12m` is education-level categorization) and continuous responses (e.g., `hhinc_pctfpl` is the household income as a percent of the federal poverty line in 2009; this is, for example, 10,830 for a single person household). The data also include many `NA` values indicating non-response, or "missing data." To deal with this data, you can call the `naref` function from `gamlr` with `impute=TRUE` to set `NA` as the reference level for factors and, for numeric variables, *impute* a value for the missing observations. See Chapter 3 for details on how `naref` works to impute missing values.

```
library(gamlr)
> rawsurvey <- read.csv("OHIEsurvey.csv")
> survey <- naref(rawsurvey, impute=TRUE)
> dim(survey)
[1] 23441   32
```

Since there are many variables here (and many factor levels for those variables), we will use `gamlr` to run a linear Lasso regression for the model in Equation 5.14. The first step is to create a sparse model matrix. We do this by combining our earlier `numhh` and `selected` variables with the survey data (minus the `personid` column).

```
> Xohie <- sparse.model.matrix(~ selected*.,
+   data=cbind(ohie[,c("selected","numhh")], survey[,-1]))[,-1]
> dim(Xohie)
[1] 23441   183
```

As a key step, when you run the regression you should use the `free` argument to remove any penalization from `selected` and `numhh` and their interaction coefficients. That way, you are not putting any regularization on the terms that are necessary to condition upon to deal with the imperfect randomization. To put it another way, by leaving these variables unpenalized you are shrinking toward the model that we fit when calculating our regression adjusted ATE.

```
> free <- c("selected","numhh2","numhh3+",
+     "selected:numhh2","selected:numhh3+")
> htefit <- gamlr(x=Xohie, y=ohie$doc_num, free=free)
> gam <- drop(coef(htefit))
> gam <- gam[grep("selected", names(gam))]
> gam <- gam[gam!=0]
> length(gam)
[1] 42
```

The AICc Lasso finds 42 nonzero terms in $\hat{\gamma}$. For illustration, we can pull out those related to race.

```
> gam[grep("race", names(gam))]
   selected:race_hispYes      selected:race_whiteNo
        -0.07961591           -0.09998782
selected:race_amerindianYes    selected:race_asianYes
        -0.16110224           -0.18426221
   selected:race_pacificYes
        0.25377131
```

People of Pacific Islander descent see an extra 0.25 PCP visits in their treatment effect relative to the baseline (from looking at the list of nonzero race coefficients, the baseline here is non-Hispanic whites). You can also look at treatment effects for individuals. To do this, create two new model matrices that are the same as for the training data but with `selected=0` everywhere for control and `selected=1` for treatment. The difference between predictions for these two inputs will give you $\hat{y}_i(1) - \hat{y}_i(0)$, the individual estimated treatment effect.

```
> Xcntrl <- sparse.model.matrix(~ selected*.,
+   data=cbind(selected=0, numhh=ohie$numhh, survey[,-1]))[,-1]
> Xtreat <- sparse.model.matrix(~ selected*.,
+   data=cbind(selected=1, numhh=ohie$numhh, survey[,-1]))[,-1]
> survey[1,]
   person_id      smk_ever       smk_curr smk_quit     female
        1              1 Yes not at all      <NA>       Male
```

```
 birthyear.x  birthyear.miss  employ hhinc_cat
1      1978                0      No        $0
 hhinc_pctfpl.x  hhinc_pctfpl.miss  race_white
1             0                  0         Yes
...
> predict(htefit, Xtreat[1,,drop=FALSE]) -
+   predict(htefit, Xcntrl[1,,drop=FALSE])
1 x 1 sparse Matrix of class "dgCMatrix"
    seg95
1 0.5589697
```

The first person in the sample, a 31-year-old white male smoker with no employment, has an estimated treatment effect of 0.56 extra PCP visits.

■ 5.4 Regression Discontinuity Designs

In this section, we take a break from RCTs to discuss a common *near experimental* design. In a regression discontinuity design (RDD) the treatment allocation is determined by a threshold on some "forcing variable." Each unit in the sample has a value for this forcing variable, and those whose value is greater than the threshold receive the treatment and those less than or equal to the threshold receive the control. Subjects that are close to the threshold, on either side, are assumed similar enough that the comparison of their outcomes can be interpreted as the causal effect of treatment.

As an example of an RDD, Hahn et al. (1999) evaluate the causal effect of a discrimination law that applies only to firms with more than 15 employees. Here, the number of employees is the forcing variable and the authors compare firms on either side of the 15 employee threshold. Another common example has that student grade thresholds determine access to education programs; you can analyze the outcomes for students on either side of that threshold to determine the treatment effect of these programs. Similar situations arise all over the place: income thresholds influence availability of social assistance or tax breaks and age thresholds determine eligibility for all sorts of perks or programs.

The nice thing about RDD is that you know the only confounding variable that you need to control for: the forcing variable. Recall our earlier discussion on conditional treatment assignment independence (i.e., the condition in Equation 5.5). If the treatment assignment is independent from the potential outcomes conditional on some known control variables, then you can recover the causal treatment effect by controling for (i.e., include in the regression) those control variables. In an RDD the treatment is fully determined by the forcing variable so you just need to control for that variable. In the examples just given, you'd need to control for a firm's number of employees, a student's grade, a person's income, and a child's age.

A regression discontinuity analysis requires an assumption about how the response varies with the forcing variable near the treatment threshold. You must assume that if the threshold were to move slightly, subjects switching treatment groups would behave similarly to those near them in their *new* treatment group. This is a *continuity* assumption. It means that you can look at the relationship between the forcing variable and the response on one side of the

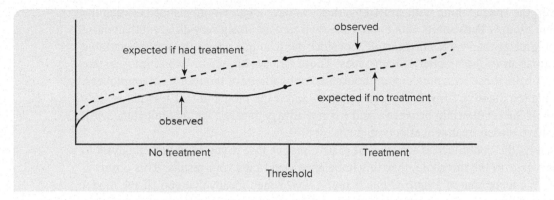

FIGURE 5.1 Illustration of the RDD continuity assumption. Solid lines are the observed mean response (*y* axis) given the forcing variable (*x* axis), and dashed lines show the unobserved mean response for each group.

threshold and extrapolate to the other side. Figure 5.1 shows observed (solid line) and unobserved (dashed line) expected response functions for each of two treatment groups. The RDD continuity assumption implies the behavior that you see around the treatment threshold (where the solid line jumps). Even though there is a discontinuity (i.e., a jump) in the observed mean response, the underlying treatment group functions are each continuous around this point (i.e., each group mean response is smooth over the transition from solid to dashed). This allows you to compare the counterfactual response across the two treatment groups.

The RDD Model

To make things more precise, we'll make use of the potential outcomes notation. Recall that $y_i(D)$ is the potential outcome for unit i under treatment D, where $D = 0$ for control and $D = 1$ for treatment. The *observed* treatment status is d_i, such that $y_i(d_i)$ is the observed response for this unit. In an RDD we add the forcing variable r_i, and for simplicity *we specify that the treatment threshold is always zero.* You can always make this fit your situation by shifting your original forcing variable. For example, in the Hahn et al. (1999) study mentioned above you would set r equal to the number of employees minus 15. Thus $r_i \leq 0$ implies that $d_i = 0$ and $r_i > 1$ implies that $d_i = 1$. We can write this using indicator variables:

$$d_i = \mathbb{1}_{[r_i > 0]} \tag{5.16}$$

The assumption of conditionally independent treatment assignment is then

$$[y_i(0), y_i(1)] \perp\!\!\!\perp d_i \mid r_i \tag{5.17}$$

Finally, the crucial continuity assumption says that the expected potential outcomes are the same for those right above and right below the threshold. Taking ϵ to denote a "very small value," this continuity assumption can be written

$$\mathbb{E}[y_i(D)|r = -\epsilon] \approx \mathbb{E}[y_i(D)|r = 0] \approx \mathbb{E}[y_i(d)|r = \epsilon] \tag{5.18}$$

Localized Linear Regression

As detailed in our section on regression adjustment, you can estimate the treatment effect under the assumption in (5.17) by fitting a regression model that interacts the treatment status, *d*, with the single control variable—the forcing variable *r*. Our usual model is then written

$$\mathbb{E}[y|d, r] = \beta_0 + \beta_1 r + d(\gamma_0 + \gamma_1 r) \tag{5.19}$$

However, the special thing with an RDD is that you have a known imbalance between the two treatment groups. Those units with r much less than zero are likely very different than those with r much greater than zero. For example, consider our example where the forcing variable is a transformation of the number of employees. Those firms with one or two employees are very different from those with hundreds or thousands (or hundreds of thousands) of employees. If you include the massive firms in the treatment set, and if the model in (5.19) is not exactly correct (e.g., if the relationship between y and r is not always linear), then this imbalance will lead you to have biased treatment effect estimates.

Fortunately, the continuity assumption of (5.18) implies that if you limit your analysis to units that are *near* to the threshold, then this imbalance won't bias your results. This observation leads to the technique of *localized linear regression,* which means that you fit the model of (5.19) within a "local" *window* of the threshold. Using δ to denote the chosen window size, this implies that you would fit

$$\mathbb{E}[y|d, r \in (-\delta, \delta)] = \beta_0 + \beta_1 r + d(\gamma_0 + \gamma_1 r) \tag{5.20}$$

This is the same model as in (5.19) except that we are limiting it to units that have r between $-\delta$ and δ.

Because of the special structure of an RDD, you will typically report the conditional average treatment effect (CATE) at $r = 0$ rather than an ATE that averages over different values for r. The treatment and control units are assumed most comparable at $r = 0$ (i.e., this is where you think the potential outcomes across treatment groups are most similar), so this is the treatment effect that is most robust to misspecification in your regression model. The CATE is easy to find as

$$\mathbb{E}[y|d = 1, r = 0] - \mathbb{E}[y|d = 1, r = 0] = \beta_0 + 0\beta_1 - (\beta_0 + 0\beta_1 + \gamma_0 + 0\gamma_1) = \gamma_0 \tag{5.21}$$

Thus the CATE is equal to γ_0. Figure 5.2 illustrates that this is the difference between the intercepts in the treatment and control group regression lines.

The fact that you trust only a single CATE in an RDD is a limitation of the design. You can't extrapolate results from RDD to estimate the treatment effect at values of r away from zero. However, if you understand this limitation, then RDD quasi-experiments are a useful way to estimate causal treatment effects when you don't have randomized controlled trial.

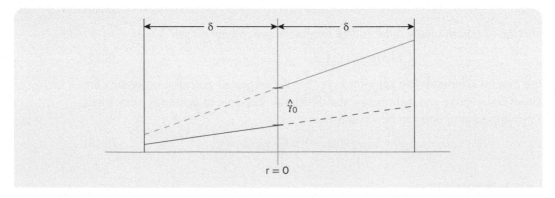

FIGURE 5.2 Illustration of Equation (5.20) where straight lines are fit to the left and the right of the threshold within a chosen window size, δ. The distance between lines at the discontinuity (the jump) is the difference between the intercepts for each group's regression line. This jump is γ_0, your CATE at $r = 0$.

Example 5.5 **Digital Marketing RDD** In an ad auction, such as the auctions that determine which ads show at the top of search engine results, the advertiser bids a certain amount for their ad to be shown. These bids are combined with information from the ad platform (i.e., the search engine provider) about the likelihood that each ad will be clicked by the user. The platform gets paid only if the ad is clicked. There are a number of formulas for combining bids with click-probabilities (see Varian 2009 for details). The end result is a *rank score* that determines the order of ad priority in the auction. The ad with the highest rank score is shown first.

In our example, the response variable y is a version of *ad revenue*—whether or not the ad was actually clicked, multiplied by the cost-per-click (CPC). You can imagine the CPC as the second-highest bid in the auction (this data is simulated, so it is nobody's real revenue). The treatment that you're considering is the specific *position* effect of an ad showing up in the "mainline" ($d = 1$)—above the main search results—instead of on a sidebar ($d = 0$). The search platform has a reserve price for mainline ads: if the highest rank score *is not* above this reserve, then no ads are in the mainline and this ad is shown on the sidebar. If the rank score *is* above this reserve, then it is shown in the mainline. Thus, the reserve price acts as a treatment allocation threshold for mainline positioning. You define the forcing variable as the rank score minus reserve price, such that the treatment threshold occurs at $r = 0$.

The data are in `RD.csv`:

```
> dat <- read.csv("RD.csv")
> head(dat)
  score        treat              y
1  -2.4030060   0.22426257
2  -9.7101060   0.22021732
3  -7.8246060   0.03316775
4 -11.8908060   0.23014707
5  -3.5631060   0.01581510
6 -11.3598060   0.22630121
```

The `score` column is our forcing variable r: the rank score minus reserve price so that the treatment threshold is 0. The `treat` column is our d variable: it consists of 1s for the treated ads (those that show in the mainline results) and 0s for the ads that show on the sidebar. The relationship between treatment allocation and the forcing variable is plotted in Figure 5.3.

Assuming that conditional expected revenue is smooth around this threshold, we have an RDD for estimating the treatment effect of ad position on revenue. For illustration, we will choose a window size of three rank score units on either side of the threshold (i.e., on either side of the reserve price in the auction).

```
> delta <- 3
> window <- which(dat$score > -delta & dat$score < delta)
```

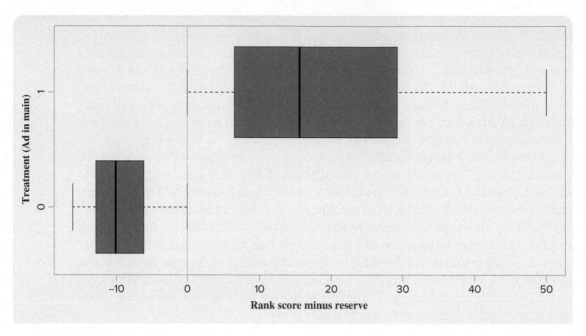

FIGURE 5.3   Forcing variable (rank score minus reserve) and treatment status (whether or not the ad is shown in the main line, instead of the sidebar) in the digital marketing RDD example. Notice that all and only ads with rank score greater than reserve are shown in the main line ($d = 1$).

You can then apply `glm` to fit a linear regression that interacts the treatment status and forcing variable, using the `subset` argument to restrict your data to the window of three rank score units on either side of zero.

```
> summary(linfit <- glm(y ~ treat*score, data=dat, subset=window))
...
              Estimate   Std. Error   t value   Pr(>|t|)
(Intercept)   0.0820048   0.0011768    69.682   < 2e-16 ***
treat         0.0119216   0.0017396     6.853   7.3e-12 ***
score         0.0006188   0.0006627     0.934     0.35
treat:score   0.0007242   0.0010020     0.723     0.47
```

Your estimate for the CATE at $r = 0$ is $\hat{\gamma}_0$, the coefficient on `treat`. We have estimated that expected revenue increases by 0.012 due to the ad being shown in the mainline rather than the sidebar. This implies an approximately 15% lift (i.e., increase) in revenue due to the placement in the mainline vs. the sidebar (0.012/0.082). The analysis is illustrated in Figure 5.4. The gap between the ends of the blue lines at the $r = 0$ threshold corresponds to your $\hat{\gamma}_0 = 0.012$.

The standard error on $\hat{\gamma}$ from `glm` is 0.0017, indicating a highly significant (small p-value) treatment effect. It is a good practice to allow for heteroskedastic errors on either side of the treatment threshold (i.e., allow for nonconstant error variance). We can calculate those as described in Chapter 2 via the `sandwich` package.

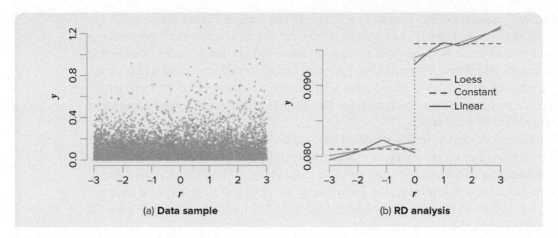

(a) **Data sample**   (b) **RD analysis**

FIGURE 5.4 Illustration of the digital marketing RDD analysis. In (a) you can see a sample of the response y values on either side of the treatment threshold at zero. In (b) you can see a zoomed-in view, with the conditional means for y estimated using localized *linear* regression, the *constant* difference-in-means model, and the *loess* weighted least-squares smoother. In each case, the estimation used observations with scores ± 3 units on either side of zero.

```
> library(sandwich)
> library(lmtest)
> coeftest(linfit, vcov=vcovHC(linfit))
 ...
              Estimate  Std. Error  z value   Pr(>|z|)
(Intercept) 0.08200480  0.00103483  79.2448  < 2.2e-16  ***
treat       0.01192160  0.00178763   6.6689  2.577e-11  ***
score       0.00061878  0.00057625   1.0738     0.2829
treat:score 0.00072424  0.00103718   0.6983     0.4850
```

In this case, the HC standard error (0.00179) is very similar to the original result from `glm` (0.00174).

Alternatives to Localized Linear Regression for RDDs

In the literature on RDDs, a couple of alternative approaches are common. One simple method is to just compare the mean response on either side of the $r = 0$ threshold. This is equivalent to fitting the basic "difference in means" model,

$$\mathbb{E}[y|d, r \in (-\delta,\delta)] = \beta_0 + d\gamma_0 \tag{5.22}$$

The treatment effect is still γ_0. Fitting this model in R we find a larger treatment effect estimate.

```
> summary( meandiff <- glm( y ~ treat, data=dat, subset=window) )
              Estimate  Std. Error  t value  Pr(>|t|)
(Intercept) 0.0810461   0.0005752   140.91   <2e-16 ***
treat       0.0148498   0.0008702    17.07   <2e-16 ***
```

The estimated treatment effect is now $\hat{\gamma}_0 = 0.015$. If you look at Figure 5.4 you can see why the treatment effect increased. The correlation between the rank score and the revenue is positive, which makes sense because rank score is intended to rank ads in order of expected revenue. The simple difference in means doesn't account for this dependence, and so the observations at the edge of your window (those near ± 3) bias the treatment effect to seem larger. The localized linear regression approach corrects for this bias and will make your results less sensitive to the choice of window size.

Another common strategy is to fit a *weighted* least-squares regression line on either side of the threshold, with weights on observations that are decreasing with distance from the threshold. This can make your inferences even less sensitive to the choice of window size; however, it introduces new parameters to tune (e.g., the decay rate in weights) and in practice we have not found any big advantages to the more complicated approach. The loess smoother in Figure 5.4 is an example of a weighted least-squares fit.

Choosing the Window Size

Finally, any RDD analysis is sensitive to the size of the local analysis window. We chose $\delta = 3$ here because the moving average (loess) mean estimates on the right of Figure 5.4 appear to be mostly linear in this window, but that is just a rough eye-ball decision. Moreover, looking at the left of Figure 5.4, there is no clear signal from the data that you can use to judge linearity (or anything else: until you take a moving average the noise in this data overwhelms any apparent discontinuity).

The best practice is to calculate the RDD treatment effect estimate for a range of windows. Figure 5.5 shows results for this example, and it is typical of what we see in other applications. After an initial high-variance region, where the window size is too small for you to estimate a reliable linear regression, the results settle down around $\hat{\gamma} = 0.012$. Moving to a wider window leads to lower uncertainty around the estimate, but this is at the expense of more restrictive

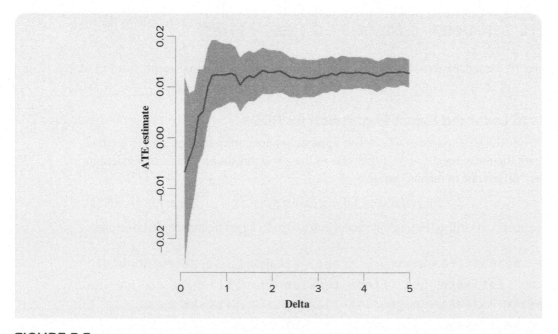

FIGURE 5.5 RDD inference for the ATE—mean and 95% CI—as a function of the window size δ.

linearity assumptions (you are assuming that the function is nearly linear for longer away from the threshold). In practice, this window-length selection is more art than science, and you should make sure that results are stable within a range of plausible values.

. . . .

RDDs are a common and useful tool in data analysis, and our coverage of the topic has been relatively brief. For more detail, you can look to Imbens and Lemieux (2008) and references therein. One particular situation is important to flag: it is possible to use similar tools for analysis when the treatment threshold is not strict (as you had here) but rather *fuzzy*: $r_i > 0$ changes the *probability* of treatment, but treatment allocation is not deterministic on either side of the threshold. These fuzzy RDDs turn out to be a special case of the instrumental variables design that we cover in the next section.

5.5 Instrumental Variables

In business and economic systems, you have a large set of inputs that all combine to generate your outcome of interest. As has been highlighted throughout this chapter, understanding causation in such systems requires randomization—you need to have events that *look like* experiments. Thus far, we've considered analysis around the treatment effect of policies that have been themselves randomized. But it is common that you want to know the treatment effect for a policy that has not been *directly* randomized but rather has been *indirectly* randomized through experiments on variables that influence policy selection. These indirect randomizers, or upstream sources of randomization, are called *instrumental variables* (IVs) and they form the basis for much of applied econometrics.

One intuitive IV example is the "intent-to-treat" setup. Harding and Lamarche (2016) describe a utility company looking to measure whether households respond to various prices for electricity and how this response changes when they have technology, such as a smart thermostat, which makes it easier for a household to change the AC settings in response to varying prices. In this experiment design, households are randomly offered a free smart thermostat (plus professional installation). However, not every customer who gets the offer will actually have the thermostat installed. Some may not want to bother, and others may have an old AC system that will not work with the new smart thermostat. Also, some households from the control group may go to their local hardware store and purchase a smart thermostat even if they were not randomly given one for free. All of this means that the randomized offer is one step removed from the treatment of interest: the treatment of getting a smart thermostat.

This can cause problems if the customers' *selection into treatment* is correlated with unobserved factors that also influence the response. For example, it could be that wealthier households are less worried about cost and don't want to bother with the installation or that poorer households tend to have older AC units that don't work with a smart thermostat.

In this setting, you need to recognize the randomized offer as the *instrument* and use an IV analysis to properly estimate the treatment effect of thermostat installation. You are able to take advantage of the randomization of the thermostat offer by tracking how it changes the *probability* that a user installs the thermostat. If they are not assigned a free thermostat offer, then the probability they install a new thermostat is small. If they are assigned to the thermostat offer group, then the probability they use the smart thermostat is much higher. An IV analysis models how this *change in probabilities* affects the customer outcomes (e.g., response to pricing). By connecting the response to the portion of treatment that is directly controlled by randomization (i.e., the treatment probabilities dictated by the IV), you can recover how the response changes that randomized component of treatment status. This allows you to model counterfactuals dependent upon whether the customer actually uses the thermostat.

5.5.1 Endogeneity

We'll use some math to make this more precise. First, we need to explain the general problem of *endogeneity*. In the general IV model, you have some treatment variable p and a response-of-interest y. You may or may not have observable covariates $\mathbf{x}$ that directly influence the response, and you always have the *instrument z,* which affects the response *only* through its influence on the treatment. In addition, there are *unobserved* factors or errors, say e, that have influence over both the treatment and response. The graph of this model is shown in Figure 5.6a. This graph makes clear the two crucial features of the instrument z: it only acts on y through p, and it is completely independent from the unobserved error e.

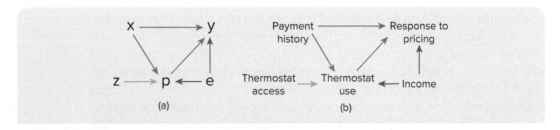

FIGURE 5.6   Diagram of a simple instrumental variables model. In each, the arrows are read as "*start has a causal impact on end.*" On the left, z is the IV, p is the policy (treatment) variable, x is an observed covariate, y is the response, and e is an unobserved variable that affects both treatment and response. On the right, you have these variables realized as components of the electric utility intent-to-treat example from Harding and Lamarche (2016).

Figure 5.6b connects these variables to the example electric utility experiment. The outcome of interest is response to pricing (i.e., how much they change electricity demand when prices rise or fall). The electric utility does not have access to their customers' incomes, but we can imagine that income affects both thermostat use and response to pricing. The instrument is randomized thermostat access (i.e., whether the customer got a thermostat offer in the randomized controlled trial) and this randomization affects the response *only* by changing the likelihood of the customer using the thermostat. Finally, you have the customer's payment history as a covariate—you can use this to model a treatment effect that depends upon payment history.

You can write a version of this causal model as a regression:

$$y = g(\mathbf{x}, p) + e, \ \text{cov}(e, p) \neq 0 \tag{5.23}$$

where $g(\mathbf{x}, p)$ is a function of the observed covariates, $\mathbf{x}$ and the treatment, p. Here, $g(\mathbf{x}, p)$ is a *structural* function. You are imagining that this represents how p acts causally on y (perhaps also as a function of $\mathbf{x}$; if it is easier for now, just ignore $\mathbf{x}$ everywhere). The important distinction between Equation (5.23) and the usual regression model is the statement that the error and policy p (or treatment) are correlated: $\text{cov}(e, p) \neq 0$. This implies that, in contrast to the usual statistician's regression, the error term is *not expected to be zero* given the treatment variable: $\mathbb{E}[e|p] \neq 0$. That is because the "error" influences policy selection, and hence policy realization gives you information about the error term.

In this setup we refer to the policy variable as *endogenous* to the response. It is jointly determined with the response as a function of unobserved factors or errors. In contrast, in our usual regression models (i.e., if you removed p from Equation 5.23), $\mathbf{x}$ is assumed to be *exogenous,* which means $\text{cov}(e, \mathbf{x}) = 0$. In the setting of Equation (5.23), however, applying off-the-shelf regression when learning your model will cause you problems. Consider the use of regression to estimate the conditional expectation for y:

$$\mathbb{E}[y|\mathbf{x}, p] = \mathbb{E}[g(\mathbf{x}, p) + e|\mathbf{x}, p] = g(\mathbf{x}, p) + \mathbb{E}[e|p] \tag{5.24}$$

Thus, standard regression techniques here will recover the true structural relationship, $g(\mathbf{x}, p)$, *plus a bias term:* $\mathbb{E}[e|p]$. This issue is referred to by social scientists as "omitted variable bias," and it haunts them whenever they need to work with treatment assignment that is not fully randomized. Note that we are assuming here that $\mathbf{x}$ has no influence on e so that $\mathbb{E}[e|\mathbf{x}, p] = \mathbb{E}[e|p]$. This is not necessary for any of the methods we'll discuss, but it makes notation and intuition easier.

Equation (5.24) gets to the heart of what differentiates counterfactual inference from common statistical or "predictive" inference. To the machine learner, in a setting where you want to predict a future that looks mostly like the past, $\mathbb{E}[e|p]$ is not a bias. Any patterns that help you predict e given p can be used to refine future predictions. But in a policy setting, you are planning an act to *change p*—you are planning to give away thermostats or change prices. This means that, in the future, you will have broken the relationship between p and e. The pattern for $\mathbb{E}[e|p]$ observed in past data will no longer exist, and any inference that confuses this term with g is rightly considered a bias. That is, when comparing counterfactual policies p_1 and p_0, you want to know $g(p_1, \mathbf{x}) - g(p_0, \mathbf{x})$, and adding to this $\mathbb{E}[e|p_1] - \mathbb{E}[e|p_0]$ will lead to incorrect conclusions and poor policy choices.

Example 5.6 Air Travel Demand: Simulation for Effect of Endogeneity A classic example of this endogeneity problem occurs in demand analysis. Consider air travel. During holidays and periods of peak demand, two things are true: flights are booked, and prices are high. Of course, it is not true that flights are booked *because* prices are high. Rather, both prices and sales are responding to changes in the underlying consumer demand. Airlines are good at tracking this demand and changing ticket prices to maximize profits.

If you look at air travel and you regress prices on sales, you will find a *positive* relationship: sales increase with higher prices. This is the economist's dreaded "upward sloping demand curve." Such results are troubling because it is unlikely that they describe any real economic system. But it is easy to see how this happens. Consider a simple linear demand system where demand shocks e and prices p respectively increase and decrease sales, y. We will use this data to simulate the problem of endogeneity.

The function yFun randomly generates sales based upon a given demand shock and price.

```
> yFun <- function(e,p){
+    y = 2 + 10*e-3*p + rnorm(length(e),0,.1)
+    y[y<0] <- 0
+    return(y) }
```

To use this function you need to generate some independent demand shocks. Notice that these are drawn from a Gamma distribution that depends on fixed parameters and does not depend on any other elements of our simulation.

```
> e <- rgamma(100,1,1)
```

We will draw two separate price sets. In the first, observed case, imagine that you have past data from a price setter (airline) who was able to execute targeted price discrimination—they charged prices that were positively correlated with the demand shocks. In our simulation we do this by setting prices to be equal to e plus a random error z.

```
> z <- rgamma(100,1,1)
> pObserved <- e + z
```

In the second case, imagine that you were able to run an experiment where prices are completely randomized. Here we simulate these prices by drawing from a Gamma distribution. Notice that these prices do not depend on the demand shocks e nor on any other variables in our model.

```
> pCounterfactual <- rgamma(100,2,1)
```

Finally, we feed the demand shocks and both of these sets of prices through the sales function.

```
> yObserved <- yFun(e, pObserved)
> yCounterfactual <- yFun(e, pCounterfactual)
```

The results are shown in Figure 5.7. The left panel shows that when prices are correlated to the demand shocks, meaning they are endogenous, we obtain a positive correlation between prices

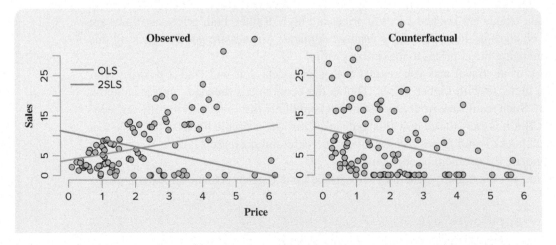

FIGURE 5.7   Illustration of the simulated air-travel demand system. On the left, prices were determined endogenously (jointly) with the unobserved demand shocks. On the right, prices are determined randomly independent of demand. The orange lines are OLS fit to each dataset. On the left you also see the 2SLS fit line, which matches up closely to the OLS fit to fully random prices on the right.

and sales. If you were to estimate this relationship with a simple linear, or OLS, regression you would erroneously predict an upward-sloping demand curve. In the right panel, random price variation allows OLS to pick up the correct (downward-sloping) demand relationship. In the left panel, we also show the results of a two-stage least squares (2SLS) IV analysis. This IV analysis was able to recover the correct price/sales relationship by taking advantage of the available instrument, z, the source of random variation in prices.

5.5.2 Two-stage Least Squares (2SLS)

Two-stage least squares (2SLS) is a simple procedure for recovering causal effects from IV variation. Recall the regression equation in Equation (5.23) and take expectation of both sides of this equation after conditioning upon the instrument z (and as usual conditioning on the controls, $\mathbf{x}$). Taking the conditional expectation yields

$$\begin{aligned} \mathbb{E}[y|\mathbf{x}, z] &= \mathbb{E}[g(\mathbf{x}, p) + e|\mathbf{x}, z] \\ &= \mathbb{E}[g(\mathbf{x}, p)|\mathbf{x}, z] + \mathbb{E}[e|\mathbf{x}, z] = \mathbb{E}[g(p, \mathbf{x})|\mathbf{x}, z] \end{aligned} \tag{5.25}$$

Notice that $\mathbb{E}[e|\mathbf{x}, z]$ went away in this calculation. Since e is independent of z (a key feature of an IV) and $\mathbf{x}$ (by our usual regression assumptions) we have $\mathbb{E}[e|\mathbf{x}, z] = \mathbb{E}[e]$. And under the standard assumption of zero-mean errors, $\mathbb{E}[e] = 0$. Equation (5.25) shows us that y has a conditional distribution with mean equal to the average of $g(\mathbf{x}, p)$ given z and $\mathbf{x}$.

Making life even simpler, consider a linear treatment model such that $g(\mathbf{x}, p) = \gamma p + \mathbf{x}'\beta$. Then Equation (5.23) becomes

$$y = \gamma p + \mathbf{x}'\beta + e. \tag{5.26}$$

Combining this with Equation (5.25) yields

$$\begin{aligned} \mathbb{E}[y|\mathbf{x}, z] &= \mathbb{E}[\gamma p + \mathbf{x}'\beta + e|\mathbf{x}, z] \\ &= \mathbb{E}[\gamma p + \mathbf{x}'\beta|\mathbf{x}, z] = \gamma \mathbb{E}[p|\mathbf{x}, z] + \mathbf{x}'\beta. \end{aligned} \tag{5.27}$$

This is the key equation for 2SLS and it means you can estimate γ with the two-step procedure in Algorithm 5.1.

Algorithm 5.1 Two-Stage Least Squares (2SLS)

- **Stage 1:** Fit the expectation $\mathbb{E}[p|\mathbf{x}, z]$ using OLS for p on $\mathbf{x}$ and z. For each observed $(p_i, \mathbf{x}_i, z_i, y_i)$ tuple, this provides the *predicted* policy:

$$\hat{p}_i = \hat{\mathbb{E}}[p|\mathbf{x}, z] \tag{5.28}$$

- **Stage 2:** Run a regression for the response regressed onto the predicted policy and covariates.

$$\mathbb{E}[y|\hat{p}, \mathbf{x}_i] = \alpha + \hat{p}_i\gamma + \mathbf{x}_i'\beta \tag{5.29}$$

You can then interpret $\hat{\gamma}$ as the *causal* effect of p on y.

Example 5.7 Simulated Air Travel Demand: 2SLS Let's revisit Example 5.6 using the simulated airline demand data. Recall that the observed prices were set as the sum of demand shocks and an independent random error: pObserved = e + z. Treating the z term as an observable instrument, you can run 2SLS. Stage 1 regresses the observed prices onto the instrument.

```
> pReg <- lm(pObserved ~ z)
```

Then, calculate the predicted values for p and run Stage 2 which regresses observed sales onto the predicted values, $\hat{p}$.

```
> pHat <- predict(pReg, data.frame(z=z))
> lin2SLS <- lm(yObserved ~ pHat)
> summary(lin2SLS)
Coefficients:
         Estimate Std.  Error t    value  Pr(>|t|)
(Intercept)  -2.2023   1.7697   6.726   1.17e-09 ***
phat         -2.2023   0.8168  -2.696   0.00825 **
```

The procedure recovers an estimate of γ within one standard deviation of the true value (-3).

```
> summary(lm(yObserved ~ pObserved))
...
Coefficients:
         Estimate Std.  Error t    value  Pr(>|t|)
(Intercept)   1.3751   1.0701   1.285   0.202
pObserved     3.0502   0.4503   6.774   9.37e-10 ***
```

This succeeded despite the fact that naive regression of sales on price yielded a completely different (wrong) model. Due to random variation in generating your simulated samples here, you may find that the 2SLS answer ends up further from the truth when you run it yourself. You should repeat the simulation and estimation exercise several times to get a feel for the amount of variation. This variation should also feed some skepticism whenever you see 2SLS estimates based on small sample sizes–this procedure is unbiased but it has high variance.

Example 5.8 Oregon Health Insurance Experiment: 2SLS Our OHIE example is actually an intent-to-treat setup. Although *access* to Medicaid insurance was randomized through the state's lottery, not all of those who became eligible for Medicaid took advantage of this and enrolled. For some people the enrollment process was just too inconvenient, and others likely had alternative insurance available. Thus, the earlier results describe not the treatment effect of enrolling in Medicaid but rather the indirect effect of expanded access. You can refine these results through an IV analysis.

Recall the setting of this OHIE example. The response of interest y is the count of PCP visits in the 12-month study period. In our earlier analysis, the treatment of interest was access to Medicaid health insurance. Now, this access to insurance will be the instrument $z = 1$ for those selected for enrollment and $z = 0$ otherwise. The new treatment, *p*, is whether the patient actually *enrolls* in medicaid. Since the z is randomized (assigned in a lottery) and it only affects PCP visits through its influence on Medicaid enrollment, this satisfies the definition of an instrumental variable. You can look at how the change in enrollment *p* changes with the lottery access z and infer the treatment effect of enrollment on PCP visitation.

Two-Stage Least Squares with glm

In the simulated IV analysis shown in Example 5.6 earlier, z was perfectly randomized. But in the OHIE analysis, you need to control for the household size, numhh, since people from larger households were more likely to obtain eligibility (any household member selected in the lottery makes all members eligible). As shown in Algorithm 5.1, this just means you need to include numhh in both the first- and second-stage regressions. You can run everything via calls to glm.

```
> stage1 <- glm( medicaid ~ selected + numhh, data=ohie)
> pHat <- predict(stage1, newdata=ohie)
> stage2 <- glm( doc_num ~ pHat + numhh, data=ohie)
> coef(stage2)["pHat"]
  pHat
0.952369
```

The estimated treatment effect, $\hat{\gamma}$, is the coefficient on phat: 0.95. This implies that enrollment in Medicaid causes an extra 0.95 expected PCP visits than if you don't enroll in Medicaid. Compare this to the earlier analysis, which found that being *eligible* for Medicaid enrollment led to only around 0.29 extra PCP visits. The earlier analysis gave an attenuated version of the IV results because eligibility is one step removed from actual enrollment and because those who are unlikely to enroll, even if eligible, are also less likely to visit a PCP.

Bootstrapping UQ on 2SLS

One important thing to note is that the standard errors output by glm for the coefficient on pHat are *incorrect*. This is because your second stage regression doesn't know that the input pHat is already the result of a model fit to the same data. However, we can bootstrap the whole procedure to get the correct standard errors. As before, we will use a block bootstrap on households to account for dependence between members of the same household. We'll use rbindlist from the data.table package again to make this fast and apply our getCI function to get the bias-corrected 95% confidence interval.

```
> getIV <- function(data, ids, binder){
+   data <- binder(data[ids])
+   stage1 <- glm( medicaid ~ selected + numhh, data=data)
+   pHat <- predict(stage1, newdata=data)
+   stage2 <- glm( doc_num ~ pHat + numhh, data=data)
+   coef(stage2)["pHat"]
+ }
```

```
> ( bootIV <- boot(ohieHH, getIV, 1000, binder=rbindlist,
+          parallel="snow", ncpus=detectCores() ) )
...
     original        bias std. error
t1* 0.952369 -0.0003580791  0.1280578
> getCI(bootIV)
    2.5%    97.5%
0.7131185 1.2179021
```

You get a standard error of 0.128 and 95% CI for the treatment effect of Medicaid on increased PCP visits is from 0.7 to 1.2. Again, your results will vary due to Monte Carlo variation.

Using AER for IV Analysis

You can also use the AER package to go through all of the IV analysis steps for you and provide the correct standard errors. It contains the function ivreg, which has syntax basically the same as for glm except that you use a pipe, |, to separate the first and second stage inputs. The policy variable p (our medicaid indicator) is listed before the pipe, along with the numhh covariates, as the input of primary interest. After the pipe, you list all of your instruments (you have only one, z, the selected flag) and again the covariates that you need to control for because they are connected with imperfect randomization. The function automatically detects numhh in both sets of inputs and thus knows it should be treated as a covariate rather than an instrument.

```
> library(AER)
> aerIV <- ivreg( doc_num ~ medicaid + numhh | selected + numhh,
data=ohie)
> summary(aerIV)
...
          Estimate Std. Error  t value Pr(>|t|)
medicaid   0.95237    0.12575    7.573 3.77e-14 ***
```

The estimate for $\hat{\gamma}$ is 0.95, exactly as we found above. The standard error is very close to the bootstrapped standard error, even though ivreg hasn't accounted for the potential dependence within households. You can update your analysis to account for this dependence by applying vcovCL to get clustered standard errors (refer to Chapter 2; this allows for correlation between errors within a household).

```
> VCL = vcovCL(aerIV, ohie$household)
> coeftest(aerIV, vcov = VCL)
...
          Estimate Std. Error t value  Pr(>|t|)
medicaid  0.952369   0.127737  7.4557 9.251e-14 ***
```

The dependence makes very little difference here, adding only about 0.002 to the standard error.

Notice that in our IV regressions we have numhh entering additively, rather than in interaction with the treatment as we did in our earlier regression adjustment. 2SLS is very sensitive to how you specify the regression, and things get more complicated if you want to model heterogeneous treatment effects. You also cannot easily swap in logistic regression instead of OLS. Fortunately, even if the regressions in Algorithm 5.1 are misspecified, Angrist et al. (1996) describe how you can interpret $\hat{\gamma}$ as a *local average treatment effect*: the average treatment effect among individuals who are switched between treatment groups because of their instrument's realization (i.e., those who do or do not enroll in Medicaid because of the lottery outcomes).

The Wide World of IV Analysis

Instrumental variable analysis is a big topic. Models of the type illustrated in Figure 5.6 are dominant in applied econometrics. The "mostly harmless" text of Angrist and Pischke (2009) is a great reference for those looking for a deeper understanding, as are the texts by Imbens and Rubin (2015) and Morgan and Winship (2015). IV methodology originated in the 1930s and 40s, with work by Jan Tinbergen and Trygve Haavelmo (and others) on measurement of the parameters of economic *systems*. These are systems where variables like price and sales are jointly determined from underlying demand levels. At the same time as statisticians were developing the rules of randomized experimentation, these economists were trying to understand how to do social science in settings where randomization is impossible (e.g., they could not randomize the income of individuals in an economy). Due to this heritage, econometric theory is often focused on IV setups where the instruments, *z*, are not explicitly randomized. The "exclusion structure" in Figure 5.6 can hold without randomized instruments—you just need the instrument to be *independent* of the response conditional on the treatment. For example, demand analysis often relies on assuming that factors affecting the supplier's *cost* of goods are instruments for the sales *price*. For example, weather conditions in the North Atlantic (making it easier or harder to fish) have been proposed as instruments for the price of fish in New York City (Angrist et al., 2000). IV analysis with weather instruments can be used to infer the treatment effect of price on sales.

These nonrandomized-instrument examples are open to questions around the validity of the instrument. Is it really that the weather at sea is far enough removed from the weather in NYC to not directly affect fish sales? The answer in this case is probably yes, so long as you condition on the right things, and the cited Angrist et al. paper is a nice example of demand analysis. But this criticism has led practitioners to view IV analysis with skepticism. However, this skepticism is misplaced in cases where the instrument has been explicitly randomized, as in the intent-to-treat examples. When the instruments are explicitly randomized, you have a clear view of all of the dependencies involved and can be much more confident that the IV model and exclusion structure hold true.

As a final point on the importance of IV models and analysis, note that when you are on the *inside* of a firm—especially on the inside of a modern technology firm—*explicitly randomized instruments are everywhere*. The algorithms and processes used by firms are constantly being randomized. This is the pervasive strategy of AB experimentation. But it is often the case that decision makers want to understand the effects of policies that are not themselves randomized but are rather downstream of the things being AB tested. For example, suppose an algorithm is used to predict the creditworthiness of potential borrowers and assign loans. Even if the process of loan assignment is never itself randomized, if the parameters in the machine learning algorithms used to score credit are AB tested, then those experiments can be used as instruments for the loan assignment treatment. Such "upstream randomization" is common, and IV analysis is your key tool for doing counterfactual inference in this setting.

◆ 5.6 Design of Experiments

There are many different ways to design an experiment. A completely randomized design, as in an AB experiment, is just the simplest design. In some cases, you can reduce the variance of your estimates through some careful planning to make the experiment as efficient as possible. To close this chapter we will describe a few useful options here. Note that this is only scratching the surface of the field of experiment design. For further reading you can look to Morris (2010) for statistical design of experiments, Santner et al. (2003) for a focus on computer experiments, and Sutton and Barto (2018) for a thorough treatment of reinforcement learning. Note that all of these texts require more mathematics than this book.

5.6.1 Block Design

When you know in advance that external factors have a large influence on either the response or on the treatment effect, you can reduce the variance of your ATE estimates by randomizing within *blocks* of experimental units that share similar properties. Often also referred to as *stratification*, the strategy is to break your full sample into subgroups of similar units and then apply a completely randomized treatment assignment *within* each subgroup. The process is illustrated in Figure 5.8. This sampling design reduces the potential for imbalance across treatment states, and will give you treatment and control groups that are as comparable as possible.

As an illustrative example, suppose that you have a website where people see advertisements and make purchases. You want to compare the effectiveness of a new ad campaign, with total purchase revenue (i.e., spending) as the outcome of interest. You suspect that customers with different baseline levels of spending will behave differently. Moreover, you worry that if you get too many heavy spenders in one of the two treatment groups it could bias your estimate

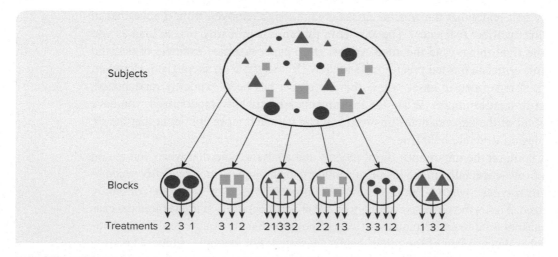

FIGURE 5.8   In a block design, subjects are divided into groups with others who share similar characteristics. The randomization to treatments happens within the block. In this case we have three hypothetical treatment states.

of the treatment effect. You can use a block design in order to reduce the estimation variance due to variability in past customer spending.

To do so, you first sort your website users into bins determined by their recent spending amount. For illustration, let's say you sort them into those whose past month's spending was in the bottom 25th percent, the 25–50th percent, the 50–75th percent, and the top 25th percent. You would then randomly assign subjects to either control (status quo, $d = 0$) or the new ad campaign (treatment, $d = 1$) *within each block*. You can then use standard regression techniques to obtain the ATE. Say that you have binary group membership variables $a_{i1} \ldots a_{i4}$, where $a_{ik} = 1$ if customer i comes from the kth spending group. The regression model is then

$$\mathbb{E}[y_i|d_i, \mathbf{a}_i] = \sum_{k=1}^{4} a_{ik}(\beta_k + d_i\gamma_k) \tag{5.30}$$

and the estimated treatment effect is

$$\widehat{\text{ATE}} = \frac{1}{4}\sum_k \hat{\gamma}_k \tag{5.31}$$

The ATE is a simple sum here because there is equal probability for each of our four blocks. More generally, the ATE estimate would be $\Sigma_k \text{p}(a_k)\hat{\gamma}_k$. This is just regression adjustment, but the procedure of pre-stratifying (or blocking) units into groups will lead your ATE estimates to have a smaller variance than if you just randomly assigned treatments regardless of previous spending.

An extreme version of this strategy is a *paired* samples design. Subjects are matched on some characteristics (i.e., age, gender, and income level for human pairs) and then assigned to one of two treatments (or you can use trios instead of pairs if you have three treatments, etc.). In this design each pair serves as a block.

5.6.2 Factorial Design

Another common design is a *factorial design*. These are used when you have multiple, potentially interacting, treatments. Figure 5.9 shows a stylized example of such a factorial design. There are 12 different treatment groups randomized so as to understand the interactions between different levels for two different treatments: (1,2,3,4) and (A,B,C). Individuals assigned to factor level 2 are further randomized to receive one of A, B, or C. Likewise individuals randomized to factor level B are also further randomized to receive either 1, 2, 3, or 4. This enables you to compare the impact of levels 2 vs. 3 or levels B vs. C while also measuring the effect of interaction between treatment factors.

As an example in the literature, remember how Harding and Lamarche (2016) describe an application where an electric utility wanted to know how pricing and technologies affect energy usage. The electric utility assigned households to one of three pricing strategies for electricity and also provided households with one of three different technologies to help them manage their usage (a website, a tablet, or a programmable thermostat). Here, we have two treatment factors (pricing strategy and energy technology), each with three levels. This leads to nine total treatment combinations. And since a factorial design was used, the electric utility can examine how pricing strategy or electric technology affect energy usage and they will also know how they interact. They will know whether the change in energy use for the different technologies depends on pricing strategy. The authors of this study reported to the electric utility that individuals respond more to prices when they have technology available which allows them to pre-program automated responses to price changes.

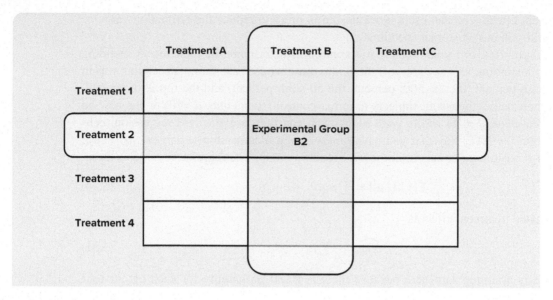

FIGURE 5.9   Stylized example of a factorial design.

5.6.3 Sequential Design

A very rich area of research concerns how you sequentially choose the data that you want to use for estimation. Simple examples include "early stopping rules," where you iteratively add subjects to your experiment and stop when your most current estimate of the ATE has a standard error below some prefixed threshold.

More complex sequential design algorithms are deployed in many engineering disciplines. For example, in aerospace it is common to run a physics simulator to test design ideas. The simulator maps from design parameters to performance variables such as stability and drag. These simulators can be expensive to run, so engineers spend care to design their *computer experiments* to be as efficient as possible. The data from these experiments is used to train statistical "response surface" models that map from the design parameters to the performance response (Gaussian processes, which we discuss in Chapters 1 and 7, are a common response surface model). Algorithms such as those in Santner et al. (2003) are designed to automatically specify the inputs for each subsequent simulator run so as to maximize the amount of new information. One simple strategy is to run the simulator next in the part of the design space where your predictive variance is highest (i.e., where you have the most uncertainty on how the design with those parameters will perform).

Reinforcement Learning

More recently, the area of sequential design of experiments is booming under a new name: *reinforcement learning* (RL). This is the general framework of ML algorithms actively choosing the data that they consume for training. RL is sometimes used to denote specific algorithms, but we are using it to refer to the full area of active data collection. That is, RL refers to algorithms that interact with the data generating system to generate *new* data for evaluation rather than just taking whatever you happen to observe. We also refer to this as *active experimentation*.

The general problem can be formulated as a reward maximization task. You have some policy or action function, $d(x_t; \Theta)$, that dictates how the system responds to an event at time t with characteristics x_t. The event could be a customer arriving on your website at a specific time, a scenario in a video game, and so on. After the event, you observe response y_t, and the reward is calculated as $r(d(x_t; \Theta), y_t)$. During this process you are accumulating data and *learning* the parameters Θ, so you can write Θ_t as the parameters used at event t. The goal is that this learning converges to some optimal reward-maximizing parametrization, say Θ^*, and that this happens after some T events where T is not too big—i.e., so that you minimize *regret*:

$$\sum_{t=1}^{T} \left[r(d(x_t; \Theta^*), y_t) - r(d(x_t; \Theta_t), y_t) \right] \tag{5.32}$$

This is a general formulation. We can map it to some familiar scenarios. For example, suppose that the event t is a user landing on your website. You would like to show a banner advertisement on the landing page, and you want to show the ad that has the highest probability of getting clicked by the user. Suppose that there are J different possible ads you can show, such that the action $d_t = d(x_t; \Theta_t) \in \{1, \ldots, J\}$ is the one chosen for display. The final reward is $y_t = 1$ if the user clicks the ad and $y_t = 0$ otherwise.

This specific scenario is a *multi-armed bandit* setup, so-named by analogy to a casino with many slot machines of different payout probabilities (the casino is the bandit). In the simplest bandit problem there are no covariates associated with each ad and each user, such that you are attempting to optimize toward a single ad that has highest click probability across all users. That is, the parameters of interest are $\Theta = \theta_j = p(y_t = 1 \mid d_t = j)$, the generic click probability for ad j, and you want to set d_t to the ad with highest θ_j. There are many different algorithms for bandit optimization. They use different heuristics to balance *exploitation* with *exploration*. A fully exploitative algorithm is greedy: it always takes the currently estimated best option without any consideration of uncertainty. In the simple advertising example, this implies always converging to the first ad that ever gets clicked. A fully exploratory algorithm always randomizes the ads, and it will never converge to a single optimum. The trick to bandit learning is finding a way to balance between these two extremes.

Thompson Sampling

A classic bandit algorithm, and one that gives solid intuition into RL in general, is Thompson sampling (Thompson, 1933). Like many tools in RL, Thompson sampling uses Bayesian inference to model the accumulation of knowledge over time. The basic idea is simple: at any point in the optimization process you have a probability distribution over the vector of click rates, $\theta = [\theta_1 \ldots \theta_J]$, and you want to show each ad j in proportion to the probability that θ_j is the largest click rate. That is, with $y^t = \left\{ y_s \right\}_{s=1}^{t}$ denoting observed responses at time t, you want to have the following such that an ad's selection probability is equal to the posterior probability that it is the best choice:

$$p(d_{t+1} = j) \propto p(\theta_j = \max \{\theta_k\}_{k=1}^{J} | y^t) \tag{5.33}$$

Since the probability in Equation 5.33 is tough to calculate in practice (the probability of a maximum is not an easy object to analyze), Thompson sampling uses Monte Carlo estimation. In particular, you draw a sample of ad-click probabilities from the posterior distribution at time t,

$$\theta_{t+1} \sim p(\theta | y^t) \tag{5.34}$$

and set $d_{t+1} = \text{argmax}_j\ \theta_{t+1j}$. For example, suppose that you have a Beta(1, 1) prior on each ad's click rate (i.e., a uniform distribution between zero and one). Following our Beta-binomial Bayesian updating example from Chapter 2, the posterior distribution for the jth ad's click rate at time t is

$$P(\theta_j | d^t, y^t) = \text{Beta}\left(1 + \sum_{s=1}^{t} \mathbb{1}_{[d_s = j]} y_s,\ 1 + \sum_{s=1}^{t} \mathbb{1}_{[d_s = j]}(1 - y_s)\right) \tag{5.35}$$

where $y_s = 1$ if the user clicked the add at time s and $y_s = 0$ otherwise. A Thompson sampling algorithm draws θ_{t+1j} from the posterior distribution in Equation (5.35) for each j and shows the ad with highest sampled click rate (the biggest drawn θ_{tj}).

Why does this work? Think about scenarios where an ad j would be shown at time t—in other words, when the sampled θ_{tj} is largest. This can occur if there is a lot of uncertainty about θ_j (so that you can randomly sample a large value from the posterior) or if the expected value of θ_j is high. Thompson sampling balances between exploration and exploitation by mixing high-risk high-reward treatments (i.e., when a θ_j with high uncertainty is randomly sampled to have a large value) with lower-risk rewards (i.e., when θ_j with low variance but high expectation is the largest sampled value). It is a very simple algorithm, and fairly inefficient (it can take Thompson sampling a very long time to converge to a solution), but this gives you the basic intuition to how RL works.

QUICK REFERENCE

This chapter introduces the theory of causal inference and how you can estimate causal treatment effects through experimentation. RCTs (and quasi-experimental designs like RDD) play a major role at many companies, and understanding how to analyze the results will be a key skill. In the next chapter we will move to the more difficult task of causal inference when you do not have an experiment.

Key Practical Concepts

- In potential outcomes notation, $y_i(1)$ is the response for individual i if they are treated, and $y_i(0)$ is their response in an alternative untreated world. The average treatment effect is

$$\text{ATE} = \mathbb{E}[y_i(1) - y_i(0)] \tag{5.36}$$

- When you have an experiment where treatment d is assigned at random, then the treatment effect on response y is the coefficient on d in a simple linear regression.

```
glm( y ~ d )
```

  You can use any of the methods of Chapter 2 to quantify uncertainty.

- When you have imperfect randomization, and data frame x contains controls that influence treatment assignment, then you can obtain *conditional* ATEs by estimating a regression model that interacts d with controls.

```
fit <- glm( y ~ d*., data=data)
```

  The ATE is then available by predicting for all of the rows of x both with d=1 and with d=0, and then taking the average of the difference.

```
mean( predict(fit, data.frame(d=1, x))
   - predict(fit, data.frame(d=0, x)) )
```

  Use the bootstrap to quantify uncertainty for the regression adjusted ATE.

- With many sources of treatment heterogeneity, you can estimate HTEs running a gamlr Lasso regression on a model matrix interacting the treatment with these sources of heterogeneity. For example,

```
dx <- sparse.model.matrix( ~ .*d, data=x)[,-1]
hte <- gamlr( dx, data$y, free="d")
```

  We have left the baseline treatment effect unpenalized via the free argument.

- A regression discontinuity design has forcing variable r defined such that treatment is d=0 for $r \le 0$ and d=1 for $r > 0$. You choose a local window around r=0 and estimate linear models for both treatment and control using an interaction regression.

  ```
  window <- which(r > -delta & r < delta)
  rddfit <- glm(y ~ d*r, subset=window)
  ```

  The fitted coefficient on d is your estimated treatment effect at r=0.

- Given instrumental variables z, run a two-stage least squares IV analysis with ivreg from the AER library.

  ```
  ivfit <- ivreg( y ~ d + . | z + ., data=x)
  ```

6 CAUSAL INFERENCE WITH CONTROLS

This chapter introduces the concept of *conditional ignorability,* and shows how you can use regressions for response and treatments as functions of controls to create powerful ML-based estimators for treatment effects.

■ **Section 6.1 Conditional Ignorability:** Understand how you can estimate treatment effects under the assumption of conditional ignorability, and use this assumption to build treatment effect estimators based upon the results of *residualizing* against controls.

■ **Section 6.2 Double Machine Learning:** Apply ML tools to predict the treatment and response from high-dimensional controls, and use cross-fitting to obtain treatment and response residuals that can be regressed on each other to obtain treatment effect estimates with known standard errors.

◆ **Section 6.3 Heterogeneous Treatment Effects:** Use the residuals from double ML to estimate heterogeneous treatment effects (HTEs), and study high-dimensional HTEs in estimation of a *demand system.*

◆ **Section 6.4 Using Time Series as Controls:** Understand how conditional ignorability applies in the context of multiple time series where one of those series receives a treatment at a point in time. Use diff-in-diff and synthetic controls methods to estimate the treatment effect on the treated time series.

L ife is easy if you have an experiment. Explicit randomization allows you to model the effect of moving the treatment variable *independently* from the other covariates. This is the key to counterfactual modeling: since you will be acting to apply treatment, you need to know how the response changes with *independent* movement in this variable. Even if you don't have perfect randomization, you can estimate counterfactual treatment effects by conditioning on a small number of known controls (i.e., through regression adjustment).

Unfortunately, life doesn't always give you experiments. In business, it is typical that you will be asked to make a decision about future actions based upon historical data without the benefit of explicit randomization. This is referred to as *observational* data, as opposed to experimental data. Instead of running an experiment where you get to set the treatment (or know exactly how the treatment was assigned), you are stuck simply *observing* what happened. In such settings, counterfactual estimation depends upon the assumption of *conditional ignorability:* that you have tracked and can *control* for all the factors that influence both treatment status and the response of interest.

The process of choosing controls is subjective and labor intensive. Applied economics discussions are dominated by debates over whether all of the important factors have been controlled. Some of this subjectivity and debate is unavoidable: causal inference without experiments is hard. But there are basic recipes and best principles that will help you stay within the bounds of believability. There are also ways that you can use tools from machine learning to help with parts of the process; this will be increasingly important as you look to automate and accelerate business decision making.

This chapter outlines the main tools for counterfactual analysis with observational data. In the next section, we describe the conditional ignorability assumption and explain how it works with familiar low-dimensional regression models. We then describe how ML tools can be used to manage estimation when you have high-dimensional sets of controls. These techniques will be extended for modeling of heterogeneous treatment effects in observational data, an idea we illustrate in the context of consumer demand estimation. Finally, we describe the methods of synthetic controls, where you use relationships across multiple time series in order to estimate treatment effects.

■ 6.1 Conditional Ignorability

Conditional ignorability implies that you observe all of the variables that influence *both* the treatment and the response. Whenever you hear a causal statement that includes "after controlling for other factors," there is an implicit assumption of conditional ignorability. For example, from *Forbes* on October 26, 2020:

> a recent study of 917 retail companies . . . found that the business model accounts for 5.1% of a firm's return on investment, after controlling for other factors.

This quote is based upon the research in Sohl et al. (2020) which indexed retail firm business models as traditional brick-and-mortar channels, a discount channel (e.g., outlet stores or a no-frills grocer), and an online channel. They then attempted to infer the causal effect on their profits relative to investment in assets, using control variables that include the firm's industry, size, past growth, and product diversity.

In practice, conditional ignorability usually requires a leap of faith. In most settings, it is unrealistic that you have managed to observe *all* factors influencing both the treatment and the response (both business model and return on investment). Instead, you hope that you have controlled for enough of the main factors so that your results are sufficiently accurate to be useful in practice.

We have already seen and been working with the assumption of conditional ignorability. This assumption was the basis for our 'regression adjustment' methods in the previous chapter. Recall the potential outcomes notation from Section 5.1. The response in subject i for treatment status D is denoted $y_i(D)$, and the observed treatment status is d_i such that $y_i(d_i) = y_i$ is the observed response. Restating Equation (5.5), conditional ignorability says that all of the potential outcomes are conditionally independent from the observed treatment status given the control variables, $\mathbf{x}_i$:

$$y_i(D) \perp\!\!\!\perp d_i \mid \mathbf{x}_i \tag{6.1}$$

That is, after conditioning on all of the information in **x**, the potential outcomes across all treatment levels are unrelated to the treatment status you have actually been assigned.

In the special case of binary treatments, Equation (6.1) takes a familiar form,

$$\{y_i(1), y_i(0)\} \perp\!\!\!\perp d_i|\mathbf{x}_i \tag{6.2}$$

such that the treatment effect $y_i(1) - y_i(0)$ is independent of treatment status. After assuming the conditional ignorability condition in Equation (6.1), you can *control* for the factors in **x** simply by including them in your regression model. Life gets more difficult when **x** is very high dimensional or if you don't know the form of its influence on d and y, but in later sections we will show how tools from ML can be used to help.

Example 6.1 OJ Sales: Controls Consider the Dominick's orange juice (OJ) sales data from Chapter 1. The data include weekly prices and sales (in terms of number of cartons) for three OJ brands—Tropicana, Minute Maid, and Dominick's—at 83 Chicagoland stores, as well as an indicator, ad, for whether each brand was advertised (in store or flyer) that week.

```
> oj<-read.csv("OJ.csv",strings=T)
> head(oj, 3)
  sales price      brand ad
1 8256  3.87  tropicana  0
2 6144  3.87  tropicana  0
3 3840  3.87  tropicana  0
```

For purposes of illustration, we will revisit this example to estimate a single shared price-sales elasticity. This is the causal treatment effect of price on sales in a log-log regression model.

Simple Linear Regression

To start, we can fit a simple model that regresses log price on log sales without any controls: $\mathbb{E}[\log(\text{sales})] = \alpha + \gamma\log(\text{price})$.

```
> baseFit <- glm(log(sales) ~ log(price), data=oj)
> coef(baseFit)
(Intercept)   log(price)
  10.423422    -1.601307
```

This yields an estimated −1.6 elasticity: sales drop by 1.6% for every 1% increase in prices. For this elasticity to be interpreted *causally* you need to have treatment status (price) be independent from the potential outcomes (the amount of OJ each customer would buy at different price points). That is, you need assume that there are no other factors that jointly influence both price and sales. That's clearly false. As a start, you *know* that there are different brands of OJ here and some are more valuable than others. For example, we expect Tropicana to sell more volume than Dominick's would at the same price point, and the brands have been priced according to this expectation.

OLS when Controlling for Brand

To address this, we can include the brand identity in our regression model as a control variable. The new model is then $\mathbb{E}[\log(\texttt{sales})] = \alpha_{\text{brand}} + \gamma\log(\texttt{price})$, where α_{brand} is a different intercept term for each different OJ brand. We would say that this model *controls* for brand when estimating the elasticity. Fitting this model, the elasticity estimate nearly doubles to −3.14.

```
> brandFit <- glm(log(sales) ~ brand + log(price), data=oj)
> coef(brandFit)
 (Intercept)  brandminute.maid   brandtropicana   log(price)
  10.8288216         0.8701747        1.5299428    -3.1386914
```

What happened here? The premium brands, Minute Maid and Tropicana, had equivalent sales to Dominick's at higher price points. So if you don't control for brand, it looks as though prices can rise without affecting sales for those observations. This dampens the observable relationship between prices and sales and results in the (artificially) low elasticity estimate of −1.6. When you include brand in the regression, you see positive sales effects for both Minute Maid and Tropicana. The model attributes the higher sales to these brand effects, and you recover the more realistic −3.14 elasticity.

Calculating Treatment Effects Using Residuals

More mechanically, *how* does adding covariates in a regression allow you to control for their influence when estimating treatment effects? Linear regression (OLS) coefficients represent the *partial* effect for each input after its correlation with the other inputs has been removed. To see this, consider an alternative stagewise algorithm that first regresses log(price) onto brand and then uses the *residuals* as inputs to predict log(sales).

```
> pricereg <- glm(log(price) ~ brand, data=oj)
> dhat <- predict(pricereg, newdata=oj)
```

```
> dtil <- log(oj$price)-dhat
> coef( glm( log(sales) ~ dtil, data=oj) )
(Intercept)        dtil
   9.167864 -3.138691
```

The coefficient on `dtil`, the residuals from regression of `log(price)` on `brand`, is exactly the same as what you get on `log(price)` in the multiple linear regression for log sales onto `log(price)` and brand. This a useful way to understand what OLS is doing: it is finding the coefficients on the part of each input that is *independent* from the other inputs.

So it's that easy! If you have conditional ignorability, then you just include the controls **x** (here, the brand factors) in your regression and you can recover treatment effects. So long as the dimension of your controls, say p, is much smaller than the number of observations, say n, you can use likelihood maximization techniques or OLS to estimate the model $\mathbb{E}[y|d, \mathbf{x}] = d\gamma + \mathbf{x}'\boldsymbol{\beta}$ and recover a causally interpretable $\hat{\gamma}$ estimate. In the language of statistics, you are able to "identify" γ as the effect of the independent part of d (i.e., the residuals $d - \mathbb{E}[d|\mathbf{x}]$) on y. That is the reason for this common practical advice: "If you need to adjust for confounders, just include them in the regression." The bias that an omitted confounder creates in your treatment effect estimate can be corrected by including that confounder as a variable in your regression model. The vast majority of observational studies—in economics, medicine, business, or elsewhere—make do with such standard regression techniques. Logistic regression doesn't have the same mechanical "regression on residuals" interpretation as OLS, but it works in roughly the same way: if you want to control for a confounder, you just add it as an input.

The problems get more complicated when you have many possible confounder variables to control for, such that p is not much smaller than n (or perhaps even $p > n$). We know from Chapter 3 that in this situation the standard maximum likelihood methods and OLS don't work well. Unfortunately, it is almost always the case that you have many confounders! There are a vast number of possible external influences in almost any observational study. The *only* reason that analysts are able to use low-dimensional OLS techniques is because they have *selected*— through the basis of intuition, experience, and a variety of subjective tools—a smaller dimensional **x** that contains the "important" confounders.

In practice, you have no way to know whether this is the right set of confounders. Hand-picking of controls is massively time consuming, unstable, and hard to replicate. Results will always be subject to skepticism around the analyst's choices and motivations. Whenever your analysis is premised on conditional ignorability, you are always susceptible to skeptics suggesting additional controls until the model is nearly saturated and you can't measure anything. Thus, almost all observational treatment effect estimation problems are high-dimensional problems when viewed from a high level, and we already know that standard OLS regression techniques are an imperfect tool for high-dimensional problems. You will need to adapt our ML tools, like Lasso, for causal inference under the conditional ignorability model.

6.1.1 Residualization

In Example 6.1, we showed that you could get the same estimated treatment effect (OJ sales-price elasticity) by (a) controlling for brand by simply including it in your regression *or* (b) controlling for brand by using it to first estimate log price, and then using the *residuals* in your regression. In equations, we showed that you can estimate the treatment effect of d on y by using OLS to estimate γ in *either* the multivariate regression

$$\mathbb{E}[y] = \alpha + d\gamma + \mathbf{x}'\boldsymbol{\beta} \tag{6.3}$$

or the simple regression

$$\mathbb{E}[y] = \alpha + (d - \hat{d})\gamma \tag{6.4}$$

where $\hat{d}$ is your estimate of $\mathbb{E}[d|\mathbf{x}]$. This works because $d_i - \mathbb{E}[d|\mathbf{x}_i]$ is the "portion of d_i that is independent from the controls." Under the assumption of conditional ignorability in (6.1), every observation of change in d_i that is *independent* from the controls is effectively a *mini-experiment*: you can track how y_i changes with the $d_i - \mathbb{E}[d|\mathbf{x}_i]$ residual errors and this gives you an estimate of how y changes with independent change in d. That is, it gives you an estimate of the treatment effect.

This is the technique of *residualization* (sometimes called "partialling out" in the economics literature). It will play a crucial role in this chapter. Through residualization, you gain flexibility in the types of regression techniques that you can use to estimate treatment effects under conditional ignorability. For example, you cannot use OLS to estimate (6.3) if the number of controls in $\mathbf{x}$ is larger than the number of observations that you have. Chapter 3 showed that you can use tools like the Lasso to estimate regressions with more covariates than observations. However, regularization penalties can cause bias in your treatment effect estimation if they are applied in the same way we would for a prediction task.

For example, if one of the confounders x_j is highly correlated with d, then the Lasso algorithm might give x_j a zero coefficient because that is convenient for minimizing the penalized deviance. But then your estimate of γ will be polluted by the influence of x_j because you have no longer controlled for that confounder. In contrast, you are fine to use a Lasso to estimate $\mathbb{E}[d|\mathbf{x}]$. This is a pure prediction problem: you just want to get the best possible prediction $\hat{d}$. You then use that prediction to calculate residuals to use for the second-stage OLS estimation of Equation (6.4). This second-stage problem is always a simple linear regression with a single input, so OLS will always be fit for the purpose.

Double Robustness

The key here is that we have broken treatment effect estimation into two problems: predict the treatment given the controls, and then estimate a regression for the response given the residuals from the treatment prediction. We have turned the tough part of controlling for confounders into a simple prediction problem (treatment prediction). Since we are now back in the domain of prediction problems, all of the tools from Chapter 3—cross-validation, information criteria, and regularization—can be deployed to deal with high-dimensional confounder adjustment.

We can go one step further to make our treatment effect estimates *doubly robust*. Suppose that you don't capture all the confounding information in $\mathbf{x}$ when estimating $\hat{d} = \mathbb{E}[d|\mathbf{x}]$, perhaps because your model selection criteria produced an underfit prediction model (e.g., if your selected Lasso penalty is too large). In that case, your estimate of γ from Equation (6.4) can still be polluted by these confounders.

You can make your estimation robust to these sorts of errors by also residualizing the response. That is, you estimate $\hat{y}_i \approx \mathbb{E}[y|\mathbf{x}_i]$—again, using whatever prediction tool you wish—and calculate the residuals $y_i - \hat{y}_i$. These *response residuals* are then regressed onto the *treatment residuals* in a final OLS estimation of the model

$$\mathbb{E}[y - \hat{y}] = (d - \hat{d})\gamma \tag{6.5}$$

The fitted $\hat{\gamma}$ is your "doubly robust" estimate of the treatment effect. It is robust to mistakes that you make in *either* of the two prediction problems: fitting $\hat{d} = \mathbb{E}[d|\mathbf{x}]$ and $\hat{y} = \mathbb{E}[y|\mathbf{x}]$. Note that you need to do a good job of at least one of these two prediction problems, and that if you get them both wrong the estimates can still be polluted by the influence of confounders.

Example 6.2 OJ Sales: Double Residualization We can apply this double residualization procedure to the OJ elasticity estimation problem of Example 6.1. Recall that we already estimated the treatment residuals, say $\tilde{d}_i = d_i - \hat{d}_i$, and used them to estimate the single residualization model of Equation (6.4).

```
> pricereg <- glm(log(price) ~ brand, data=oj)
> dhat <- predict(pricereg, newdata=oj)
> dtil <- log(oj$price)-dhat
> coef( glm( log(sales) ~ dtil, data=oj) )
(Intercept)        dtil
   9.167864  -3.138691
```

To turn this into a double residualization, we estimate the conditional expectation of the response (log unit sales) and use that to calculate response residuals, say $\tilde{y}_i = y_i - \hat{y}_i$.

```
> salesreg <- glm(log(sales) ~ brand, data=oj)
> yhat <- predict(salesreg, newdata=oj)
> ytil <- log(oj$sales) - yhat
```

Note that `salesreg` here regresses log sales onto only the brand factors (it does not use the treatment as an input). Finally, use OLS to estimate regression $\tilde{y}$ onto $\tilde{d}$.

```
> coef( glm( ytil ~ dtil -1 ) )
   dtil
-3.138691
```

The resulting treatment effect is exactly the same as what we got in the single residualization procedure which is also the same as what we got for the original OLS regression of log sales onto log price and brand. Note that in this simple example, where we use OLS for the residualization steps, all the methods give the same answer. But if **x** was high dimensional and we'd used, say, a Lasso for the residualization steps, then the latter double residualization estimate for $\hat{\gamma}$ would be more robust (have less chance of bias) than what you get from the single residualization procedure.

Notice that there is no intercept in Equation (6.5) or in the `glm` we just ran. Since $\tilde{y}$ and $\tilde{d}$ both have a mean of zero, you don't need one. You can include an intercept but its estimate will be practically zero.

```
> coef( glm( ytil ~ dtil) )
  (Intercept)           dtil
-4.652687e-13 -3.138691e+00
```

This technique of double residualization is quite flexible. It opens up the option of applying a wide variety of ML techniques—everything from the Lasso to the forests of Chapter 7 to the deep neural networks of Chapter 10—for use in obtaining robust treatment effect estimates under the assumption of conditional ignorability. We will build on it throughout this chapter.

6.1.2 Linear Treatment Effect Models

To build intuition for how this all works, it is helpful to think about the models that inspire double residualization. A *linear treatment effects* (LTE) model is a set of equations that describes how **x** and *d* influence *y* *and* how **x** influences *d*. We will use a general form of the LTE model:

$$y = d\gamma + m(\mathbf{x}) + \varepsilon, \ \varepsilon \perp\!\!\!\perp d, \mathbf{x} \tag{6.6}$$

$$\mathbb{E}[d|\mathbf{x}] = h(\mathbf{x}) \tag{6.7}$$

We are using $m(\mathbf{x})$ and $h(\mathbf{x})$ to denote any generic functions of **x**. This will be useful later when we consider alternative ML tools in our causal inference. If you want to make things more concrete, imagine $m(\mathbf{x}) = \mathbf{x}'\boldsymbol{\beta}$ and $h(\mathbf{x}) = \mathbf{x}'\boldsymbol{\theta}$ as the form of this model that assumes linear regression relationships.

Equations (6.6)–(6.7) are an example of a *structural equations model*. That means that each equation in the set describes a causal relationship between variables, and the full set of equations defines a model for the *system* through which the variables change with each other. In this case, Equation (6.6) is our usual linear regression model that assumes the inputs, *d* and **x**, are independent of the errors ε. Note that $\varepsilon \perp\!\!\!\perp d, \mathbf{x}$ here is just expressing the conditional ignorability assumption of (6.1). The model for our treatment assignment, Equation (6.7), says that *d* also depends upon **x**. Crucially, Equation (6.7) says that *d does not depend upon y*.

Causal Graphs

Recall in Chapter 5 that we discussed the graphical models of Pearl (2009) as an alternative language for representing causal relationships. See Morgan and Winship (2015) for an overview that connects various approaches to causal modeling. Figure 6.1 shows two different causal graphs, both of which satisfy the conditional ignorability of (6.1) and are consistent with the LTE model in (6.6)–(6.7). In these pictures, the *direction* of the arrows indicates causation. In Figure 6.1a **x** directly causes *d,* whereas in Figure 6.1b both **x** and *d* are caused by a shared underlying and unobserved confounder *u*.

In either case, a crucial fact is that it is impossible to follow the arrows from one variable back to the same variable. For example, you cannot trace the arrow from *d* through a path back to *d*. This means that each graph is *acyclic,* and graphs of this type are referred to as DAGs: directed acyclic graphs. You can do causal inference for models that do not have this acyclic property, but it will require additional assumptions about how the different variables act upon each other. The fact that your model can be represented as a DAG means that you can break it up into smaller causal relationships, such as Equations (6.6) and (6.7). This breaking up allows

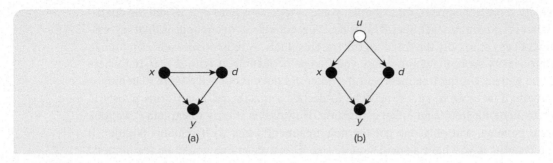

FIGURE 6.1   Graphical representations of conditional ignorability. In both graphs, both **x** and d act causally on y. In Figure 6.1a **x** causes both d and y, whereas in Figure 6.1b both **x** and d are caused by the same underlying and unobserved confounder u.

us to solve the causal estimation problem by applying ML prediction tools for estimating each constituent dependence relationship.

Residualization and LTE Models

Let's revisit double residualization using the LTE model of Equations (6.6)–(6.7). This provides another way to understand why double residualization works. You can rewrite the treatment equation of (6.7) as

$$d = h(\mathbf{x}) + \nu \tag{6.8}$$

where ν is the residual treatment error with $\mathbb{E}[\nu] = 0$. Plugging (6.8) into (6.6) yields

$$\begin{aligned} y &= [h(\mathbf{x}) + \nu]\gamma + m(\mathbf{x}) + \varepsilon \\ &= \nu\gamma + [h(\mathbf{x})\gamma + m(\mathbf{x})] + \varepsilon \end{aligned} \tag{6.9}$$

Since both ν and ε have expectation of zero, this means that $\mathbb{E}[y|\mathbf{x}] = h(\mathbf{x})\gamma + m(\mathbf{x})$. Rearranging (6.9) and recognizing $\nu = d - \mathbb{E}[d|\mathbf{x}]$, we then get

$$\begin{aligned} y - [h(\mathbf{x})\gamma + m(\mathbf{x})] &= \nu\gamma + \varepsilon \\ \Rightarrow y - \mathbb{E}[y|\mathbf{x}] &= (d - \mathbb{E}[d|\mathbf{x}])\,\gamma + \varepsilon \end{aligned} \tag{6.10}$$

Since both ν and ε have expectation of 0, then $\mathbb{E}[y|\mathbf{x}] = h(\mathbf{x})\gamma + m(\mathbf{x})$. Then, $y - \mathbb{E}[y|\mathbf{x}] = \nu \times \gamma + \varepsilon$, and since $\nu = d - \mathbb{E}[d|\mathbf{x}]$, then $y - \mathbb{E}[y|\mathbf{x}] = (d - \mathbb{E}[d|\mathbf{x}])\gamma + \varepsilon$.

Thus the LTE model *implies* that γ can be recovered by regressing residuals $y - \mathbb{E}[y|\mathbf{x}]$ onto treatment residuals $d - \mathbb{E}[d|\mathbf{x}]$.

Residualization with a Binary Treatment

In our OJ elasticity example we had a continuous treatment (log price) and used a linear regression model for treatment residualization. Another common setup is that you have a binary treatment variable, and instead use logistic regression to predict the treatment. Applying the logit link in our LTE model, we get

$$y = d\gamma + m(\mathbf{x}) + \varepsilon, \ \ \varepsilon \perp\!\!\!\perp d, \mathbf{x} \tag{6.11}$$

$$p(d = 1|\mathbf{x}) = e^{\mathbf{x}'\theta}/[1 + e^{\mathbf{x}'\theta}] \tag{6.12}$$

In this model, the estimated probability that d_i is equal to one, say $\hat{d}_i$, is often referred to as the *propensity score*. There are a number of algorithms for how you can use this propensity score in causal estimation.

In propensity score adjustment, for example, you can regress y_i onto $d_i - \hat{d}_i$ and the coefficient on the latter is your treatment effect. This is basically equivalent to our approach of regressing the OJ log(sales) onto only the fitted log(price) residuals. Another approach, common in medicine, is propensity score matching where you find pairs of subjects with $\hat{d}_i \approx \hat{d}_j$ but where $d_i \neq d_j$ (say, one patient got the treatment and the other did not). Propensity score matching is highly sensitive to how close $\hat{d}_i$ and $\hat{d}_j$ need be to declare a match and it performs poorly in general as a technique for treatment effect estimation. However, it is easy to explain ("we took pairs of similar patients, and only one got the new treatment") and so it remains popular. It also has some benefits if you have a small sample size. However in this book, we recommend that you use propensity scores in the same doubly robust procedure that we use for continuous treatment variables.

The Assumption of Linearity

The LTE models of this chapter are a powerful framework for understanding treatment effects. However, one thing to keep in mind is that we are restricting our attention to the *linear* effect of the treatments on the response. This is what defines a linear treatment effects model, and it implies that our response equation will always look something like Equation (6.6). That is, a treatment d will always affect y in an additive manner. This model is quite flexible. For example, you can transform the response and treatment with logs to estimate elasticities, and you can construct **d** to represent heterogeneous treatment effects. But it means that we will not, for example, be measuring the treatment effect on the log-odds as would be the case if we used logistic regression as the model for a binary response variable. It is totally possible to apply more complex response models beyond (6.13), however there are pitfalls in applying the simple *stagewise* estimation techniques that we will introduce in the next section. If you find yourself estimating a more complex response model, it is good practice to compare your results to what you get when estimating the same treatment effect in an LTE model.

■ 6.2 Double Machine Learning

The LTE models imply a simple and mechanical approach to estimation of treatment effects: you predict the treatment(s) from the controls and the response from the controls, and then regress response residuals onto treatment residuals to estimate your treatment effect. The key here is that we are breaking the causal treatment effect estimation problem into a series of prediction problems. In this chapter we will use Lasso algorithms for these prediction problems, but in the future you can also apply tools like trees and forests from Chapter 7 or even the deep neural networks from Chapter 10. Because you can use arbitrary ML tools for your residualization, these procedures are referred to as *double machine learning* in the statistics and economics literature.

One issue with the double residualization recipe that we've outlined thus far is that, in the case where you use a Lasso or other ML technique for your residualization steps, the standard errors output with the final OLS residuals-on-residuals regression are invalid. The glm function that you call for this final regression is unaware of the fact that you have already used the data sample to estimate $\hat{y}$ and $\hat{d}$, and so its standard error estimates will be smaller than they should be. Because you have optimized to the training data, the in-sample residuals $\tilde{y}$ and $\tilde{d}$ will tend to be smaller than the true errors, $y - \mathbb{E}[y|\mathbf{x}]$ and $d - \mathbb{E}[d|\mathbf{x}]$. When you use $\tilde{y}$ and $\tilde{d}$ in the final regression, your data look less noisy than it would be if you had the true errors.

To fix this issue, the double ML algorithm paper of Chernozhukov et al. (2017) provides a *cross-fitting* algorithm that uses *out-of-sample* errors to calculate the treatment and response residuals. Before introducing the algorithm, we will generalize our LTE model to allow for *multiple treatment effects*. If you have multiple treatments in a vector **d**, you can write the multivariate LTE as

$$y = \mathbf{d}'\boldsymbol{\gamma} + m(\mathbf{x}) + \varepsilon, \quad \varepsilon \perp\!\!\!\perp \mathbf{d}, \mathbf{x} \tag{6.13}$$

$$\mathbb{E}[\mathbf{d}|\mathbf{x}] = h(\mathbf{x}) \tag{6.14}$$

We will use this multivariate treatment model throughout this section because it allows us to work with more complicated treatment models (and to explore heterogeneous treatment effects). However, if you find the notion of a vector **d** confusing, you should feel free to work through the algorithm while ignoring this complexity and imagining a single treatment variable.

Cross-fitting

To apply cross-fitting, you split your observations into *B folds* exactly as in cross-validation. For each fold, you use all of the data *except* that fold to train your residualization prediction models: $\hat{y} \approx \mathbb{E}[y|\mathbf{x}]$ and $\hat{d}_k \approx \mathbb{E}[d_k|\mathbf{x}]$ for each treatment dimension $k = 1, \ldots, K$. You then calculate out-of-sample residuals on the left-out fold. After cycling through all B folds, you have out-of-sample residuals for the entire dataset. The full procedure is outlined in Algorithm 6.1.

Although the cross-fitting takes a bit more time than using in-sample errors, Algorithm 6.1's use of out-of-sample residuals results in a more robust treatment effect estimate with better theoretical properties. It also allows you to use familiar tools (e.g., the heteroskedastic-robust variance calculations from the `sandwich` library) to calculate the standard errors on $\hat{\gamma}$.

Algorithm 6.1 **Double ML**

Suppose that you have length-J control vectors $\mathbf{x}_i$, length-K treatment vectors $\mathbf{d}_i$, and response y_i. Split the data into B random and roughly equally sized folds.

1. **Residualization:** For $b = 1 \ldots B$:
   - Use your ML tools of choice to obtain prediction functions for the response and treatments given **x**,

   $$\hat{y}_i \approx \mathbb{E}[y|\mathbf{x}_i], \ \hat{d}_{i1} \approx \mathbb{E}[d_1|\mathbf{x}_i], \ \ldots, \ \hat{d}_{iK} \approx \mathbb{E}[d_K|\mathbf{x}_i] \tag{6.15}$$

   training on all of the data *except* observations from fold b.
   - Calculate out-of-sample residuals for these fitted prediction functions,

   $$\tilde{y}_i = y_i - \hat{y}_i, \ \tilde{d}_{i1} = d_{i1} - \hat{d}_{i1}, \ \ldots, \ \tilde{d}_{iK} = d_{iK} - \hat{d}_{iK} \tag{6.16}$$

   for all of the i in fold b.

2. **OLS:** Collect all of the OOS residuals from the residualization stage and use OLS to fit the final stage regression

$$\mathbb{E}[\tilde{y}] = \tilde{d}_1 \gamma_1 + \ldots + \tilde{d}_K \gamma_K \tag{6.17}$$

The resulting $\hat{\gamma}$ estimate is unbiased for the true γ in (6.13) and the usual techniques for calculating standard errors for OLS can be applied to quantify uncertainty about $\hat{\gamma}$.

Double ML via `gamlr`

Conveniently, there is also a `doubleML` function in the `gamlr` package that can be used to execute Algorithm 6.1. The `doubleML` function takes arguments x, d, y, and the number of folds. The data input can be the same as you use for `gamlr` (e.g., you can supply sparse or dense matrices for x or d). You can also use the `family` argument to set the regression family the treatment Lasso regressions (i.e., a `gaussian` default or `binomial` for logistic regression; family can also be a vector of different families for each treatment regression). See `help(doubleML)` for details.

Example 6.3 **Retirement Savings: Double Machine Learning** To illustrate double ML in an example with high-dimensional controls, we will investigate the relationship between financial savings plans and household wealth. The 1991 Survey of Income and Program Participation (SIPP) consists of 9915 observations of household finances for households with at least one working age member. Similar data has been analyzed in a number of economics articles that investigate the relationship between tax-advantaged savings plans, in particular the 401(k) plans that are offered by many employers in the U.S. and employee savings. This particular dataset is taken from Chernozhukov and Hansen (2004), where they investigated the treatment effect of 401(k) plan participation on total household wealth (see Poterba 2003 for an earlier analysis of similar data). It is included as part of the `hdm` package (Chernozhukov et al., 2016), which is an R package containing a number of different useful algorithms for causal inference.

We will be estimating the treatment effect of 401(k) participation on total household wealth. You can load the data from the `hdm` package (which you will need to install before running the code below). As a first step, we will break the dataset into the response y equal to "total wealth" or `tw`, the treatment d equal to a binary indicator `p401` that is 1 for those who participate in a 401(k) plan and 0 otherwise, and a set of controls **x**.

```
> library(hdm)
> data(pension)
> y = pension$tw
> d = pension$p401
> x = pension[, c("i1","i2", "i3", "i4", "i5", "i6", "i7","inc",
+      "a1", "a2", "a3", "a4", "a5","fsize",
+ "hs", "smcol", "col", "marr", "twoearn","db","pira","hown")]
> x[,"inc"] <- x[,"inc"]/1e4
```

Note that in the last line here we convert household income (`inc`) to be measured in units of $10,000 to avoid numeric overload when computing quadratic and cubic transformations. You can type `help(pension)` to get a full description of the variables. Items `i1` to `i7` are household income categories (which we include in addition to raw income), `a1` to `a7` are categories for the age of the reference household member, and the remaining variables represent demographic information such as whether the household member has completed high-school (`hs`), owns a house (`hown`), participates in an IRA savings plan (`pira`), or has a deferred benefits pension plan (`db`).

It should be intuitive that you need to condition on a bunch of household characteristics in order to estimate the influence of 401(k) participation on wealth. For example, the underlying incomes and employment status of the households will influence their total wealth *and* the probability that they are participating in a 401(k) plan. People with higher incomes are more likely to save money and to work at an employer who offers a 401(k) plan. Note that in 1991 such plans were not nearly so prevalent as they are today, so that potentially if we control for enough confounding variables (such as income) we will be able to observe independent random variation in plan participation across households. This is our conditional ignorability assumption: after conditioning on the information in **x**, the decision for a household to participate in a 401(k) plan is independent of their expected total wealth (with or without the plan).

OLS Analysis

Before turning to Lasso methods, we will use OLS to explore the treatment effect. What variables you condition on can have a big impact on your estimated treatment effect. Using OLS and conditioning on income class alone yields an estimated treatment effect for 401(k) participation of $15,031.

```
> ols <- glm(y ~ d + .-1, data=x[,1:7])
> summary(ols)
...
    Estimate  Std. Error  t value  Pr(>|t|)
d      15031        2396    6.274  3.66e-10 ***
```

Alternatively, we can consider a much larger set of controls by conditioning on all of the variables in **x** and *their three-way interactions*. This allows complex relationships such as, say, the impact of home ownership on 401(k) participation and total wealth being dependent on the interaction between age and income. To create the design matrix for these three-way interactions, and to fit the model, we will need to use sparse matrices and the gamlr package.

```
> library(gamlr)
Loading required package: Matrix
> xbig <- sparse.model.matrix( ~ .^3 -1, data=x)
> dim(xbig)
[1] 9915 1793
```

Our new matrix of controls is called xbig, and it is pretty big: 9915 rows and 1793 columns. Chances are that if you try to create this as a dense matrix you will run out of working memory on your computer. You can use gamlr to fit the OLS solution for this giant set of controls by asking it to use a penalty of zero (i.e., by setting lambda.start=0).

```
## takes a long time to run! 20 min on an Intel i-7 laptop
> olsbig <- gamlr(cbind(d,xbig), y, lambda.start=0, maxit=1e6)
> coef(olsbig)[2,,drop=FALSE]
1 x 1 sparse Matrix of class "dgCMatrix"
    seg1
d 9994.922
```

The resulting treatment effect estimate is $9995, about 50% smaller than we found when conditioning on income alone. If you ran this code on your computer, you might have noticed that it took a very long time to execute (about 20 minutes on an Intel i-7 powered laptop). Notice that when calling `gamlr` we had to increase the maximum number of optimization iterations `maxit` from the default of 100k to 1 million. This is due to how long it takes OLS to converge. In addition, with the number of variables (1794) equal to almost 20% of the sample size, this is a moderately high-dimensional estimation problem and OLS will have a high sampling variance. For these reasons, OLS is not the right tool for this job.

Step-by-step Double Residualization

Before moving to the easy-to-use `doubleML` function, it is worthwhile to go through the process of double residualization in detail. To apply double residualization here, we will be using the binary-treatment LTE model of (6.11)–(6.12). Our first task is to fit a logistic regression Lasso to predict *d*, an indicator for whether the household participates in a 401(k) plan, and use this Lasso to predict and then residualize the treatment variable *d*.

```
> dfit <- gamlr(xbig, d, family="binomial")
> dhat <- predict(dfit, newdata=xbig, type="response")[,1]
> dtil <- d-dhat
```

Notice that we take $\hat{d}$ as the first column of predictions from `gamlr`; this is just to convert to a vector from the single-column `Matrix` format output by `predict.gamlr`.

The treatment regression path plot and fitted values are shown in Figure 6.2. Notice that there is a lot of variation in fitted probabilities of 401(k) participation, $\hat{d}$. If the controls gave a much more accurate prediction of 401(k) participation (i.e., if $\hat{d}_i \approx 0$ when $d_i = 0$ and $\hat{d}_i \approx 1$ when $d_i = 1$) then we would have little residual variation to use for our final residuals-on-residuals regression. In this case, we have a lot of residual variation even after conditioning on all of the variables and transformations in `xbig`. That means there is a lot of leftover variation that can be used to *identify* the treatment effect on total wealth.

The next task is to residualize the response (total wealth) conditional on the controls. As always, we do this by subtracting the predicted values from the observed values.

```
> yfit <- gamlr(xbig, d)
> yhat <- predict(yfit, newdata=xbig)[,1]
> ytil <- y-yhat
```

The Lasso regularization path and the fitted values are shown in Figure 6.3. Again, there is a lot of residual variation after conditioning on controls.

The final step is to regress the residualized response, $\tilde{y}$ or `ytil` in the code, on the residualized treatment, $\tilde{d}$ or `dtil`.

```
> glm(ytil ~ dtil -1)
Coefficients:
 dtil
10117
```

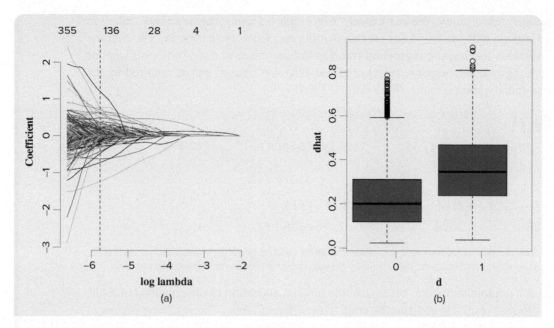

FIGURE 6.2   Lasso regularization path and fitted values $\hat{d}$ for predicting 401(k) participation given the controls **x**.

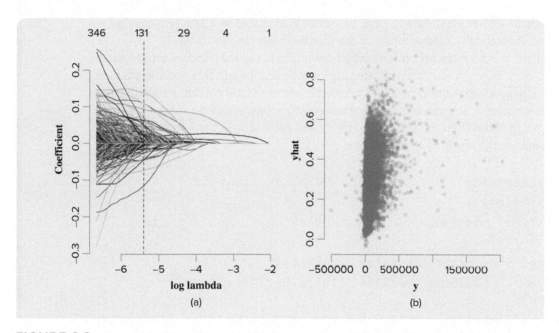

FIGURE 6.3   Lasso regularization path and fitted values $\hat{y}$ for predicting total wealth given the controls **x**.

The resulting coefficient on `dtil`, the treatment residuals, is our treatment effect estimate $\hat{\gamma} = 10{,}117$. This is just a bit larger than our OLS estimate that used the same controls `xbig`.

Cross-fitting with `doubleML`

This *in-sample* double residualization can be improved upon using the cross-fitting double ML procedure of Algorithm 6.1. Using this algorithm also allows us to get valid standard errors for

$\hat{\gamma}$ and thus quantify uncertainty. We can execute Algorithm 6.1 using the `doubleML` function from `gamlr`. Here we will use five folds for cross-fitting and `family="binomial"` so that the treatment regressions use logistic regression (the `family` argument to `doubleML` only applies to the treatment regressions; response regressions use `family="gaussian"` as required by the linear response specification in our LTE model).

```
> set.seed(1)
> dml <- doubleML(xbig, d, y, family="binomial", nfold=5)
> summary(dml)
...
   Estimate  Std. Error  t value  Pr(>|t|)
d      9808        2008    4.883  1.06e-06 ***
```

---

[*] Note that, even with the same seed, you may get different results for different operating systems and versions of R. You should at least be able to replicate your own results by running the same code twice on your own machine.

Note that we set a random seed here: because of the random allocation of observations to folds, you will get different results if you run the code with different seeds. The resulting treatment effect estimate, $\hat{\gamma} = 9808$, is slightly smaller than the result from the full OLS regression. Theoretically, this cross-fit double ML estimate should be better than the result from the full OLS regression (lower sampling variance) and from the double residualization procedure that used in-sample residuals (lower bias). In any case, the result is available in a few seconds *and* we have available a theoretically valid estimate of the standard error: $se(\hat{\gamma}) = 2008$.

When you are using double ML, it is usually a good idea to use the standard error estimate that allows for error heteroskedasticity (nonconstant error variance). In this specific example, we don't have any good reason to expect homoskedastic errors in total wealth. Following what you learned in Chapter 2, you can obtain a heteroskedastic robust sampling variance estimate with the `vcovHC` function from the `sandwich` library and can use `coeftest` from the `lmtest` library to summarize the resulting standard error.

```
> library(sandwich)
> library(lmtest)
> coeftest(dml, vcov=vcovHC(dml, "HC0"))
...
   Estimate  Std. Error  t value  Pr(>|t|)
d    9807.8      2316.2   4.2344  2.313e-05 ***
```

The robust standard error is about 15% larger, at $se(\hat{\gamma}) = 2316$. Looking at a range of two standard errors around $\hat{\gamma}$, this implies a 95% confidence interval from around \$5200 to \$14,400 for the increase in total wealth due to 401(k) participation.

```
> 9808 + c(-2,2)*2316
[1] 5176 14440
```

This interval includes the estimates of $\hat{\gamma}$ obtained both through the full OLS estimation and in-sample double residualization.

Comparison with Naive Lasso

Before leaving this example, note that you could also have ignored all the information in this chapter and simply fit the same sort of "naive" Lasso regression that you used for prediction in Chapter 3. You don't do any of the first-stage treatment prediction and calculation of residuals, and instead simply put d into a regression to predict y along with all the controls $\mathbf{x}$. In general, this *will not work well* for estimation of treatment effects. Depending on the structure of correlation between d and the controls, the Lasso can easily pollute $\hat{y}$ with the influence of elements of $\mathbf{x}$. However, in this specific example the naive approach gives a decent answer.

```
> naivefit <- gamlr(cbind(d,xbig), y, lmr=1e-3, free=1)
> coef(naivefit)[2,,drop=FALSE]
1 x 1 sparse Matrix of class "dgCMatrix"
    seg68
d 9948.092
```

Note that we left the treatment coefficient unpenalized in this Lasso (free=1) to reduce bias on this estimate. The resulting coefficient on d is similar to our previous estimates, and well within the range of our 95% confidence interval. You will not always be this lucky, however, and in general Algorithm 6.1 is a better procedure for estimating treatment effects in an LTE model.

◆ 6.3 Heterogeneous Treatment Effects

In the previous chapter, we talked about the modeling of *heterogeneous treatment effects:* treatment effects that change depending upon characteristics of the treated unit. Analyzing these HTEs is useful for many practical applications of counterfactual inference where you don't want to assume that each treated person or unit will respond in the same way. Heterogeneous treatment effects can be analyzed using Algorithm 6.1 simply by treating each interaction term as a distinct treatment effect. If $d\mathbf{w}$ is the interaction between the treatment d and sources of heterogeneity $\mathbf{w}$, then your double ML procedure can iterate through separate treatment residualization steps for each dw_k term in $d\mathbf{w}$.

Example 6.4 **Retirement Savings: Heterogeneous Treatment Effects** Revisiting the impact of 401(k) participation on wealth, consider creating an additional treatment as p401*hown that is 1 if the household owns their home *and* is participating in a 401(k), and is zero otherwise. You combine this with the original p401 treatment variable to create a two-dimensional treatment.

```
> d2 <- model.matrix( ~ hown*p401-hown-1, data=pension)
> d2[c(1,6234),]
   p401 hown:p401
      1    0     0
6234  1    0
```

We can then run double ML by passing d2 to doubleML as the treatment argument. We will again use family="binomial" since both hown and p401k are binary variables (you can pass a vector of arguments to family if you want to use different link functions for different treatment dimensions). The code below takes advantage of doubleML's ability to parallelize across cross-fitting folds by taking a parallel cluster argument. We also specify lmr=1e-3 to allow the gamlr regularization paths to run to a smaller lambda than the default.

```
> library(parallel)
> cl <- makeCluster(detectCores())
> set.seed(1)
> dml2 <- doubleML(xbig, d2, y, family="binomial",
      nfold=5, cl=cl, lmr=1e-3)
> coeftest(dml2, vcov=vcovHC(dml2, "HC0"))
...
            Estimate Std. Error t value    Pr(>|t|)
dp401         6648.4     1988.8  3.3429   0.0008323 ***
dhown:p401    4399.6     3639.5  1.2088   0.2267553
```

---

[*] Note that, even with the same seed, you may get different results for different operating systems and versions of R. You should at least be able to replicate your own results by running the same code twice on your own machine.

We now have a heterogeneous treatment effect for 401(k) participation: the baseline treatment effect is around $6600 for nonhomeowners, and $11k for homeowners. However note that the interaction term dhown:p401 is not statistically significant: we do not have strong evidence upon which to estimate the heterogeneity here.

High-Dimensional HTEs

This approach to using double ML for HTEs—doing a separate residualization for each characteristic indexing heterogenity—works fine, but it will become unwieldy if you have many sources of heterogeneity. For example, it would be totally impractical if we wanted to use all of xbig as potential sources of heterogeneity. An alternative is to use Algorithm 6.1 to obtain the residuals for the single treatment, and then interact these with your sources of heterogeneity in the final residuals-on-residuals regression. That is, you run double ML to obtain $\tilde{y}$ and $\tilde{d}$ for a single treatment, and then estimate the HTE regression

$$\mathbb{E}[\tilde{y}] = \tilde{d}\gamma_0 + \tilde{d}w_1\gamma_1 + \ldots + \tilde{d}w_K\gamma_K \tag{6.18}$$

where $\mathbf{w} = [1 \; w_1 \ldots w_K]$ is the vector of characteristics which index change in the treatment effect (including an intecept for the baseline coefficient γ_0).

We can re-do our analysis of the impact of home ownership on the treatment effect by adding interaction with hown into the original single-treatment double ML analysis of Example 6.3. The residualized treatment and response from that analysis are available in the fitted dml object, with $\tilde{d}$ as dml$x and $\tilde{y}$ as dml$y.

```
> dtil <- dml$x
> ytil <- dml$y
```

Running the residuals-on-residuals regression while interacting with home ownership yields similar coefficients as we found in the HTE analysis of Example 6.4.

```
> dml3 <- glm( ytil ~ dtil*hown - hown - 1, data=pension)
> coeftest(dml3, vcov=vcovHC(dml3, "HC0"))
          Estimate   Std. Error   z value    Pr(>|z|)
dtil        6955.2       1952.7    3.5619   0.0003682 ***
dtil:hown   3938.6       3672.2    1.0725   0.2834816
```

With a small number of sources of heterogeneity (i.e., a low-dimensional **w**) this alternative procedure saves you from running a small number of residualization steps. However, when you have high-dimensional HTEs (i.e., a high-dimensional **w**) it not only saves time but also opens up the option of using tools like the Lasso for estimating the complicated conditional average treatment effects. To illustrate use of double ML in modeling high-dimensional HTEs, we will turn to the classic problem of estimating a demand system where product sales-price elasticity depends on the characteristics of each product. This is a common task in business analysis, and we will detail the general problem setup as well as illustrate the use of double ML for estimation.

6.3.1 Demand Analysis

Consumer demand estimation is a counterfactual inference problem where controlling for confounders is super important. Understanding of a full-demand system requires subtle economic modeling: you might want to think about the long-term impacts of price on consumer habits, the relationships between substitutes and complements, the influence of budgets and income, and temporal effects such as "stock-piling" (see, e.g., Deaton and Muellbauer, 1980; Berry et al., 1995). However, in many settings you can aim to recover the *local* effects of price changes (i.e., the short-term effects of small changes) using the LTE models and the counterfactual estimation techniques of this chapter.

As we detailed in Chapter 1, the elasticity can be measured as the coefficient in a log-log regression for sales onto price (i.e., regressing log sales on log price). We refer to a "high elasticity" when γ is large and negative, and a "low elasticity" when γ is small or even positive. Goods with elasticity above -1, which means that sales drop less than 1% per 1% price increase, are considered *inelastic*. In practice, this can mean that the good is currently viewed as very cheap and at higher prices γ will drop below -1 (i.e., that the elasticity changes with price and your current price is so low that customers are unaffected by small changes). You can also find low elasticity (γ near or greater than -1) for products that are addictive or viewed as absolutely necessary (drugs and gas tend to have low elasticity). More commonly, if you estimate $\hat{\gamma} > -1$ it just means you've not managed to get a good estimate of the true elasticity. We discussed this in the context of avocado demand in Example 1.11. The common source of such misestimation is that you have neglected to control for a confounding variable that drives both sales and prices.

Estimation for the Price Elasticity of Demand

Most business analysts are aware that they can't naively rely upon observational studies to determine consumer price sensitivity. Whenever possible, it is highly advisable to introduce random price variation to help estimation for the causal price effect. But there are many settings where experimentation can't happen or has not happened in the past. In that case, the common last-resort solution is a so-called conjoint analysis: asking focus group members to make choices among product options using pretend money. However, as you might expect, focus groups and funny money are a poor approximation of reality.

Instead, even if you can't run an experiment or if you don't trust focus groups, you might be able to use the methods of this chapter to estimate the price elasticity of demand. For conditional ignorability to hold in a demand analysis, you need to have available as controls **x** the universe of variables that can potentially affect both prices and sales. Ignoring supply-side issues like going out-of-stock (which should be controlled for if they occur), this **x** is going to consist of information relevant to consumers. But, more specifically, only those *demand signals* that are known to the price-setter need to be controlled for. It doesn't matter if consumer Jill hears a country song on the radio that makes her think of pickup trucks, causing her to head to her local dealership looking for a truck at any price. So long as *the dealership* doesn't know that Jill's demand has increased and raised prices, that country song effect is part of an error term on sales that is independent of price changes. In more basic terms, conditional ignorability in this setting assumes you know all of the demand signals that determine price; if you work for the store that is setting the prices, you should be able to collect all of these signals.

If you have all of the required demand signals for product i at time t in $\mathbf{x}_{it}$, then you can build an LTE model for estimation of sales price elasticity. Recalling that elasticity is the regression coefficient in a log-log regression, we can base our analysis on a log-log LTE model. Say that q_{it} is some measure of unit sales quantity and p_{it} price for product i at time t. For this illustration, we will consider how elasticity changes as a function of *product characteristics* $\mathbf{w}_i$. These product characteristics should also be part of your control variables, $\mathbf{x}_{it}$, such that $\mathbf{w}_i$ is a subset of the controls that does not vary in time.

Our LTE demand model is then

$$\log q_{it} = (\log p_{it})\mathbf{w}_i'\boldsymbol{\gamma} + \mathbf{x}_{it}'\boldsymbol{\beta} + \varepsilon, \ \varepsilon \perp\!\!\!\perp p_{it}, \mathbf{x}_{it}, \mathbf{w}_i \tag{6.19}$$

$$\mathbb{E}[\log p_{it}|\mathbf{x}_{it}] = \mathbf{x}_{it}'\boldsymbol{\theta} \tag{6.20}$$

This simple log-log LTE model is a powerful platform for demand analysis. You can apply double ML to get $\mathbf{w}_i\hat{\boldsymbol{\gamma}}$ as an elasticity function that tells you the sales-price elasticity given characteristics $\mathbf{w}_i$.

These will be *local* estimates of the elasticity—those that apply for prices near to what you have actually observed in the data—and you should be cautious about extrapolating beyond the range of prices in your data. However, such local demand analysis is extremely useful for product development, pricing, and marketing. The heterogeneous treatment effect modeling is crucial here because you will not expect to find that all products have the same sales-price elasticity. The features $\mathbf{w}_i$ that drive differences in elasticity will be important inputs to your pricing and product decisions. These features and the associated elasticity effects can be used to understand who your market is: what they like and what they don't want to pay for.

Example 6.5 Beer Demand Analysis As an example, we will consider data on sales of beer between 1989 and 1994 at a Chicago Dominick's grocery store. These data are, like our orange juice data of Chapter 1, obtained from the Kilts Center for Marketing at the University of Chicago Booth School of Business. The data are stored as a binary R data object which has the file suffix .rda. Objects like this are a convenient way to store data in a compressed format; they are created with the save function and read back into R with the load function.

Beer Data Wrangling

When we load the Beer.rda data into R, we find that there are two new data frames: sales and upc. (Note that you may have additional objects in your workspace.)

```
> load("Beer.rda")
> ls()
[1] "sales" "upc"
```

The first dataframe contains weekly total sales, q_{it}, in the units column, and the average price, p_{it}, for each of 287 different types of beer products. Each beer type has a UPC code, which is a unique product identifier.

```
> head(sales)
            upc   week  price  units
7723  1820000016   166   3.79      1
7724  1820000016   167   3.79      3
7725  1820000016   168   3.79      6
7726  1820000016   169   3.79      2
7727  1820000016   170   3.79      1
7728  1820000016   171   3.79      1
> dim(sales)
[1] 14894   4
```

There are 14,652 UPC-week observations. In the model of (6.19)–(6.20) we have that i indexes a unique UPC and t indexes the week.

The second data frame contains, for each UPC, the product size in beer volume (oz, for fluid ounces) and a short text description title.

```
> head(upc)
                           title   oz
1820000016      BUDWEISER BEER 6pk   72
1820000051         BUSCH BEER 6pk   72
1820000106  BUDWEISER LIGHT BEER 6pk   72
1820000157  O'DOUL'S NON-ALCH CA 6pk   72
1820000188      BUSCH LIGHT BEER 6pk   72
1820000202  BUDWEISER DRY BEER 6pk   72
> dim(upc)
[1] 242   2
```

These beers differ by a variety of characteristics including brand, package size, and beer type. All of these differences, in addition to weekly trends, need to be incorporated into the set of demand signal controls.

Note that this is another example of *panel data*: a collection of several time series. This type of data was introduced in Chapter 1 with an example of Hass avocado demand analysis. This beer example has similar goals, but with a much richer set of products (242 beers instead of a single type of avocado). As a first step, we order the data by week and UPC and then calculate lagged unit sales, log q_{it-1} for each log q_{it}, to allow for autoregression in the sales time series.

```
> sales <- sales[order(sales$upc,sales$week),]
> sales$lag <- unlist(tapply(sales$units, sales$upc,
+         function(x) c(NA,x[-length(x)])))
> sales <- sales[!is.na(sales$lag),]
> head(sales,3)
            upc  week  price units  lag
7724  1820000016   167   3.79     3    1
7725  1820000016   168   3.79     6    3
7726  1820000016   169   3.79     2    6
> tail(sales,3)
             upc  week  price units  lag
1575403  9893110006   351   5.99     2    1
1575404  9893110006   352   6.49     1    2
1575405  9893110006   353   6.49     1    1
```

In calculating these lags, note that we pre-ordered the data by UPC and then week. After calculating lags, we throw away the first week's observation for each UPC (since it has NA for its lag value). Visual inspection of the data shows that we have managed to line up the lags correctly across weeks.

We also standardize the treatment of interest to be *price-per-fluid-ounce*: lpoz.

```
> sales$lpoz <- log(sales$price/upc[as.character(sales$upc),
"oz"])
```

This standardizes prices according to the volume of beer sold.

To construct our set of controls, we will create x as a large sparse matrix of *fixed effect* dummy variables for the beer type (UPC) and week.

```
> library(gamlr)
> x <- sparse.model.matrix( ~ week + upc, data=sales)[,-1]
> dim(x)
[1] 14652 544
```

To allow a different elasticity for each beer, we could simply use the dummy variables for each of the 242 different UPCs our sources of heterogeneity. But this doesn't give you any information on the *drivers* of different elasticities, and it doesn't allow for similarities between different UPCs. If a Bud Light 6-pack of cans is modeled as having demand that is completely independent from a Bud Light 12-pack of bottles, then you don't learn about the "Bud Light" impact on elasticity separate from the pack-size impact. Instead, a modern data science solution would be to *featurize* the UPCs by creating variables that describe their different attributes. You should do this in a way that allows your models to find a *hierarchy* in the data. If you have a dummy variable for "Bud," another for "Light," and yet another for "Bud Light," then the model is able to shrink across brands and beer style. You can then also create individual dummy variables for each unique beer UPC to fill in the lowest level of the hierarchy—for example, if "Bud Light 18 pack cans American Flag special edition" behaves differently than every other Bud Light product.

Beer Title Tokenization

In a preview of Chapter 9, we will create hierarchical features by "tokenizing" the beer titles into dummy indicators for the presence of each word in the beer-description vocabulary.

```
> library(text2vec)
> ititle <- itoken(as.character(upc$title),
+   tokenizer = word_tokenizer,
+   id=rownames(upc))
> vocab <- create_vocabulary(ititle)
> vectorizer = vocab_vectorizer(vocab)
> w = create_dtm(ititle, vectorizer)
> dim(w)
[1] 242 196
```

Each beer is now represented as a binary vector encoding presence and absence of the 196 possible vocabulary terms.

```
> w[1:5,ncol(w)-0:4]
5 x 5 sparse Matrix of class "dgCMatrix"
           6pk BEER 12pk MILLER LIGHT
1820000016   1    1    .    .     .
1820000051   1    1    .    .     .
1820000106   1    1    .    .     1
1820000157   1    .    .    .     .
1820000188   1    1    .    .     1
> w[242,w[242,]!=0]
 ALE  HONEY  OREGON  RED 6pk
  1     1       1     1    1
```

These terms encode a natural hierarchy. For example, many beers will be sold in 6-packs, but few will be from Oregon brewing, and even fewer will be red honey ales. Finally, we use the UPC code row titles to match this beer-title representation to each of our sales observations (saving the original smaller matrix as wupc).

```
> wupc <- w
> w <- w[as.character(sales$upc),]
> dim(w)
[1] 14652 196
```

Average Price Elasticity for Beer

Now that we have all of our variables constructed, we can estimate some elasticities! Before turning to HTE modeling, let's first try to estimate a single elasticity (the average treatment effect for log price) across beers. First, note that fitting a regression without controls yields a suspiciously small elasticity.

```
> coef( margfit <- glm(log(units) ~ lpoz, data=sales) )
(Intercept)        lpoz
  -1.162593 -0.698301
```

This says that sales drop by only 0.7% per every 1% price increase. As discussed earlier, elasticities greater than −1 indicate a product that is practically *inelastic*: increased prices are straight profit. This happens when you have goods that are massively underpriced, which is unrealistic for *all* beer in a supermarket, or when you have done a poor job of estimating elasticities. The latter is almost certainly the case here: we have not controlled for any product characteristics or time dynamics.

Recall from the panel data analysis in Chapter 1 that you can solve a lot of confounder-pollution problems by conditioning on the fixed effects and including lags. We can do that here, but to deal with the high-dimensional set of controls (lags and fixed effects) we will use double ML instead of OLS. We will use doubleML with the default family="gaussian" link function for the treatement regression since log p is a continuous treatement variable. We also specify free=1 so that the lagged log sales coefficient is always unpenalized, and lmr=1e-5 so that the regularization paths run down to very small penalty values.

```
> set.seed(1)
> beerDML <- doubleML(cbind(log(sales$lag),x),
+       sales$lpoz, log(sales$units),
+       nfold=5, lmr=1e-5, free=1)
> coeftest(beerDML, vcov=vcovHC(beerDML,"HC0"))
...
    Estimate  Std. Error  t value    Pr(>|t|)
d  -3.005914    0.057804  -52.002   < 2.2e-16 ***
```

---

[*] Note that, even with the same seed, you may get different results for different operating systems and versions of R. You should at least be able to replicate your own results by running the same code twice on your own machine.

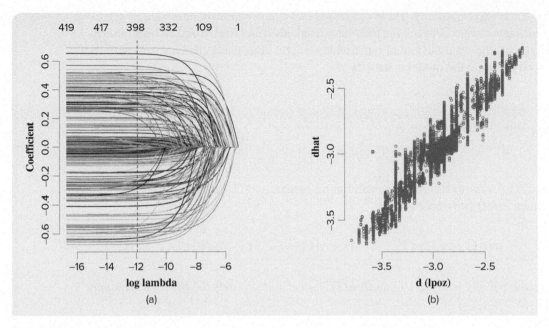

FIGURE 6.4 Lasso regularization path and fitted values $\hat{d}$ for predicting log beer prices.

The elasticity of $\hat{\gamma} \approx -3$ is much more realistic than what we found in the earlier analysis that did not include controls. Beer sales drop by 3% per every 1% price increase. This is in the range of values we would expect for beer (or, e.g., soft drinks as in Hoch et al., 1995).

To illustrate what is going on under the hood of `doubleML`, the regularization path and fitted values for one of the cross-fit treatment regressions are shown in Figure 6.4. In contrast to our previous 401(k) treatment example, we see here that **x** is strongly predictive of the treatment variable (`lpoz`): prices are a predictable function of product features and dates. The scatter in Figure 6.4b is the residual variation that we will use in our second-stage regression to estimate $\hat{\gamma}$.

Note that we could have also applied OLS methods here, and the resulting average elasticity estimate (the ATE of log price) is practically identical.

```
> beerOLS <- glm( log(units) ~ lpoz + as.matrix(x), data=sales )
> summary(beerOLS)
...
      Estimate  Std. Error  t value   Pr(>|t|)
lpoz  -3.193127   0.052151   -61.229   < 2e-16 ***
```

If you have a larger dataset, for example, with many stores rather than just a single store, then this OLS fit will become computationally impractical and you will need to use double ML.

Heterogeneous Beer Elasticities

Finally, to estimate UPC-specific elasticities we will apply the residual-interaction regression of Equation (6.18). We already have our residualized response and treatment from the double

ML estimation for average elasticity. These can be fed into a new residuals-on-residuals regression that includes interaction between the treatment residuals $\tilde{d}$ and the tokenized beer descriptions in **w**. First, pull the residuals out of our fitted `beerDML` object and interact them with the beer descriptions to create the model matrix `dw`.

```
> ytil <- beerDML$y
> dtil <- beerDML$x
> dw <- cbind(dtil, w*drop(dtil))
```

You can then use a Lasso to estimate the residual-on-residuals HTE regression. We leave the baseline treatment effect (γ_0) unpenalized.

```
> beerHTE <- gamlr(dw, ytil, standardize=FALSE, lmr=1e-4, free=1)
```

The AICc selected penalty leads to 103 nonzero HTE coefficients (plus the baseline treatment effect).

```
> gam <- coef(beerHTE)[-1,]
> sum(gam!=0)
[1] 103
```

Looking at some of the largest negative terms in $\hat{\gamma}$, we see that customers appear especially price sensitive for 30 packs of "genuine" beer (presumably corresponding to Miller Genuine Draft).

```
> head(sort(gam))
    30pk   GENUINE       GEN         6         d    LAGERNR
-4.448274 -3.617816 -3.550844 -3.305581 -3.188015 -2.598656
```

You can calculate the beer-specific elasticities by multiplying $\mathbf{w}'\hat{\gamma}$ for each beer's feature vector **w**. Using the `wupc` matrix of features for each UPC, we obtain this by using the `%*%` operator for matrix-vector multiplication.

```
> elastics <- drop( cbind(1,wupc) %*% gam )
> upc$elastics <- elastics
> head(upc,1)
                        title  oz   elastics
1820000016  BUDWEISER BEER 6pk  72  -3.554837
> tail(upc,1)
                            title  oz    elastics
79709636767  OREGON HONEY RED ALE 6pk  72   -3.321506
```

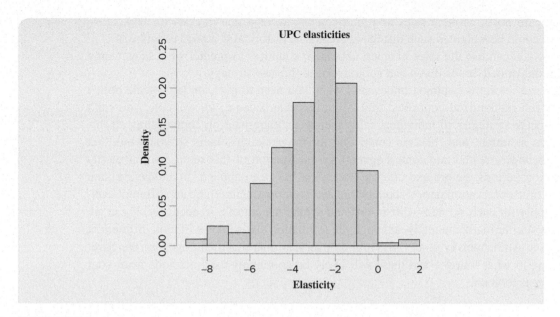

FIGURE 6.5 Estimated sales-price elasticities for each beer UPC in our Dominick's store.

For example, the first beer in our dataset (a Budweiser 6-pack) has an elasticity of -3.6 while the last beer (an Oregon Honey Red Ale) has an elasticity of -3.3.

The full set of estimated elasticities is plotted in Figure 6.5. The plot shows that we have estimated some elasticities close to, or even above, zero. Our LTE modeling approach here doesn't account for a number of more complex phenomena influencing demand, such as advertisement, seasonal availability, or the correlation between beer sales and the sales for other products in the store. It is also likely that, for at least a small set of beers, we have not controlled for all confounders that are correlated with both price and sales. As an exercise, you can explore this by adding to your controls interactions between the week indicators and the text features in $\mathbf{w}_i$.

◆ 6.4 Using Time Series as Controls

To conclude this chapter on controls, we will introduce a couple of strategies for causal inference in the common setting where you have a *panel* of multiple times series, and at some point in time a subset of those time series are treated with some policy. In the classic version of this setting you have a set of *units* of observation—for example, geographic regions, stores, or product classes—and some small number of these units are treated. For example, you might be rolling out a new sales strategy but only do so in a single geographic region, say the United States. You want to know the causal effect of this new strategy but simply comparing pre- and post-treatment U.S. sales could give you biased results. Other influential events have occurred over this same time period, including macroeconomic shocks and changes in the natural sales cycle. You don't want to conflate the treatment effect estimate with the effects of these other contemporaneous changes.

What if most of these other events also affect sales across the border in Canada (where the new sales strategy has not yet been tried)? You can use sales in Canada as a control: if, after the new strategy rollout, sales in the United States are growing faster than those in Canada, you have evidence that the new strategy is working. Even better, instead of just focusing on Canada, you can compare post-treatment sales to a multicountry average that tracks with U.S. sales. Each country could be weighted such that the aggregate is, historically, a good estimate of U.S. sales. That is, you can use the sales in other, untreated, countries to predict what sales would have been in the United States if you had not introduced the new strategy.

This general setting is common in business when you need to evaluate large-scale policy decisions. A full randomized controlled trial is not possible because, for example, you can't randomly allocate strategies to individual sales agents (they are paid on commission, so this would be seen as unfair, and they are competing for the same customers so you would get dependence between treated and control agents). In one version of this setup, you have only two observation periods: before and after the treatment has been applied. In another version you have multiple observation periods both before and after treatment. There are different techniques that apply for each version—diff-in-diff and synthetic controls, respectively. These are actually quite similar mathematically, although the estimation algorithms will look different at first glance; see Arkhangelsky et al. (2019) for an overview that ties them together. We cover each technique in what follows, and these will likely be commonly used methods from your business analysis toolbox.

6.4.1 Diff-in-Diff Analysis

A *difference-in-differences* (diff-in-diff, or DiD, for short) analysis applies when you have a number of *units* that are observed in two time periods: one before any treatment, and another after a subset of units have received treatment. The diff-in-diff framework consists of nothing more than some basic regression modeling along with a strong assumption of conditional ignorability.

The classic application of this framework has two markets, say Canada and the United States (to extend our example from above), with only one receiving some sort of new sales strategy. For example, suppose you want to see the effect of a free shipping promotion. You can model the trend in sales in both countries before and after treatment—free shipping—is rolled out *only* in the United States. If sales grow in the United States relative to Canada after treatment, then you have a positive treatment effect *if you assume that this difference is not because of external shocks that hit only one of the two countries.* This last assumption is the Achilles' heel of diff-in-diff analysis, and there is no way to get around it. It implies that, without treatment, your two time series would have continued to move in parallel. For this reason, diff-in-diff results are only as reliable as the two groups are truly comparable.

To introduce some notation, suppose that you have units i for $i = 1, \ldots n$ that are observed at times $t = 0$ and $t = 1$. Treatment versus control group membership is encoded as $d_i = 1$ if unit i is in treatment group, 0 otherwise. The treatment group units receive treatment only in the second time period, such that the actual treatment status is d_{it}: the interaction between the treatment group indicator and the time period indicator. For example, if unit i has $d_i = 1$ then in period $t = 0$ it has treatment status $1 \times 0 = 0$ and in period $t = 1$ it has treatment status $1 \times 1 = 1$. The control group units always have treatment status $t \times 0 = 0$.

The diff-in-diff regression model is then

$$y_{it} = \beta_0 + \beta_1 d_i + \beta_2 t + \gamma d_i t + \varepsilon_{it} \tag{6.21}$$

The treatment effect of interest is γ: the coefficient on the *interaction* between d_i and t. This model can be estimated using your usual regression tools (i.e., glm). Since the errors within the same unit (ε_{i0} and ε_{i1}) are possibly correlated, you will want to use the "clustered standard errors" techniques of Chapter 2 to calculate the standard errors on estimated $\hat{\gamma}$ (or use a bootstrap).

Because Equation (6.21) has a treatment group intercept term, $d_i\beta_1$, it is fine if the groups have different averages in the pre-treatment period. However, our conditional ignorability assumption here is that there is no factor other than the treatment that would cause the treatment group responses to *change* differently from those of the control group. We are requiring that nothing impacting the response has changed, other than treatment status, across observation periods. This is a strong assumption (e.g., what if something else changed in Canada, such as the Canadian economy getting weaker, between treatment periods). But it is an assumption that is often close enough to the truth to be useful.

Example 6.6 eBay Sponsored Search Marketing: Diff-in-Diff Analysis Our diff-in-diff example is taken from the paper by Blake et al. (2014), where researchers from eBay studied the effect of sponsored search marketing (SSM). *Sponsored* or *paid* search refers to the advertised links that you see around search results on, for example, Google or Amazon. Figure 6.6 shows an example web page returned after a Google search, dominated by paid search results. The research question is simple: "What is the effect of *paid search advertising?*" Or, to turn it around, what would happen to sales revenue if eBay stopped paying for SSM? Since a big website like eBay will show up anyway in the "organic" results (those which are not sponsored;

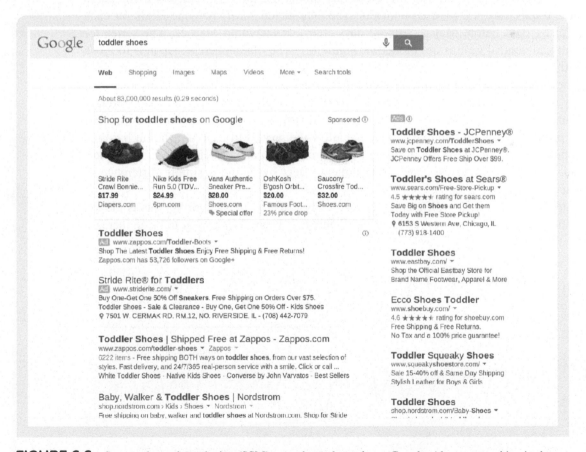

FIGURE 6.6   Sponsord search marketing (SSM) around search results on Google. Almost everything in the screenshot is sponsored—it has been paid for and has not risen *organically* through Google's relevance metrics. The only organic results are the bottom two listings in the main column, first for Zappos and second for Nordstrom.

e.g., see Zappos in both organic and paid results in Figure 6.6), do they get any benefit from also appearing in sponsored slots? And how big is the benefit? Is it worth the cost?

Questions about marketing return on investment (ROI) are generally tough to answer. The sponsored results get clicked and lead to conversions, but you have no idea if these users would have followed the organic result if there was no sponsored option. And you can't compare the pages where eBay ads don't appear to those where they do: the ads appear with the searches that eBay and Google think are most likely to lead to clicks. That is, the pages where ads don't appear will expect to see fewer clicks on eBay links for search-relevance reasons independent of the presence or absence of sponsored results.

Blake et al. managed to convince the leadership at eBay to run a large-scale experiment where SSM was turned off for a portion of users. This created a unique opportunity to measure the treatment effect of paid search (for a single company), something that had never before been reliably measured. In particular, eBay stopped bidding on any AdWords (the marketplace through which Google SSM ads are sold) for 65 of the 210 designated market areas (DMAs) in the United States for eight weeks following May 22, 2012. These DMAs are viewed as roughly independent markets around metropolitan centers ranging from Boston to Los Angeles. Google guesses the DMA on a browser and eBay can track users by their shipping address, allowing for DMA-specific treatment assignment and response tracking.

The data are in `paidsearch.csv`. Note that this is not the real data; it's a simulated version that obscures real revenue numbers. The data include *daily* revenue totals for each DMA, for 51 days before May 22 and 62 days after and including May 22. The series for treatment and control groups are plotted in Figure 6.7. The black line corresponds to those DMAs that are never treated (SSM is always on), and the red line is for those where SSM was turned off starting May 22 (marked with the dashed vertical). It is immediately clear that the daily revenues differ between treatment and control DMAs *before* May 22. The treatment DMAs have about 38% of the revenue of the control DMAs when SSM is on for both. This is not a problem for a DiD analysis, since we allow the groups to have a different baseline expectation (this is due to the $d_i \beta_1$ term in the DiD regression model). However, it illustrates that you wouldn't want to estimate the treatment effect by taking a simple difference in means across treatment groups.

Figure 6.8 shows the log difference between daily revenues in each group; this is the log of the ratio of the black line over red line from Figure 6.7. There does appear to be an increase

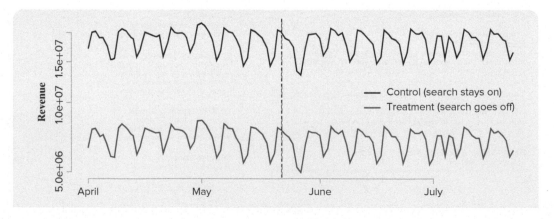

FIGURE 6.7 Daily revenue for treatment and control DMAs. The dashed line is May 22, when SSM (bidding on AdWords) was turned off for the treatment group.

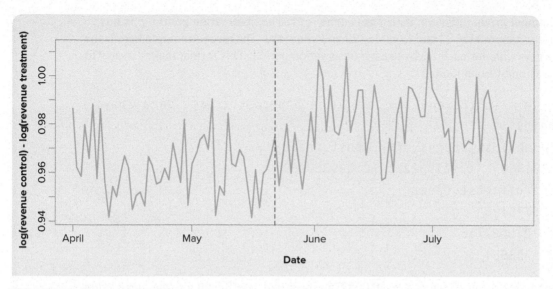

FIGURE 6.8   The difference in daily log revenue between treatment and control groups.

in the difference in the logs following May 22. Is it real (i.e., statistically significant), and what are the implications for the return on investment for SSM?

Assuming that nothing other than the SSM-turnoff changes between the treatment groups after May 22, you can answer these questions with basic regression modeling. After some initial data wrangling, we have the `ebay` data frame consisting of a row for each DMA in each of $t = 0$ and $t = 1$.

```
> ps <- read.csv("PaidSearch.csv")
> library(data.table)
> ebay <- as.data.table(ps)
> ebay <- ebay[,list(ssm.turns.off=mean(1-search.stays.on),
>    revenue=mean(revenue)),
>  by=c("dma","treatment_period")]
> setnames(ebay, "treatment_period", "post.treat")
> ebay <- as.data.frame(ebay)
> head(ebay)
> head(ebay)
  dma post.treat ssm.turns.off     revenue
1 500          0             1    75866.62
2 501          0             0  2162945.53
3 502          0             0    32718.68
4 503          0             0    36063.90
5 504          0             0   661015.85
6 505          0             1   371153.89
```

Our treatment group indicator, d_i, is `ssm.turns.off`. The observation period, t, is `post.treat`; it is zero before May 22 and 1 on May 22 and afterward. The revenue column here is the *average daily revenue* for each DMA in each observation period. This format makes it easy to run the regression of Equation 6.21.

```
> did <- glm(log(revenue) ~ ssm.turns.off*post.treat, data=ebay)
> coef(did)
  (Intercept) ssm.turns.off     post.treat
 10.963784366    0.011932272  -0.039359359
ssm.turns.off:post.treat
   -0.005775498
> 1-exp(-0.0057755)
[1] 0.005758854
```

Our estimated treatment effect is $\hat{\gamma} = -0.005775$, the fitted coefficient on the *interaction* between treatment group d_i and observation period t. Exponentiating shows that this corresponds to an approximately 0.58% drop in average daily revenue due to SSM having been turned off. You can use the `sandwich` library to get a standard error for $\hat{\gamma}$ that accounts for within-DMA dependence in errors.

```
> library(sandwich)
> library(lmtest)
> coeftest(did, vcov=vcovCL(did, cluster=ebay$dma))
                          Estimate Std.Error z value  Pr(>|z|)
ssm.turns.off:post.treat -0.0057755 0.0057018 -1.0129    0.3111
```

This says that the treatment effect—turning off paid search ads—is not statistically significant (p-value of > 0.3). Even if the result was statistically significant, the estimated effect size is so small that it is doubtful that paid search would have a positive ROI once the *cost* of the marketing is accounted for. A caution, however: this result is for a specific company and for situations where eBay links often occur in the top organic search results. There will likely be a positive ROI for digital marketing in other specific cases, especially when the advertiser is not well known or would not occur in the top organic results.

Analysis via Differences in Differences

Before moving on, we note that this DiD analysis is often presented as the analysis of differences between the pre- and post-treatment observations for each DMA. In this presentation, you first calculate the sample of pre-post *differences* for each DMA,

$$r_i = y_{i1} - y_{i0} \tag{6.22}$$

You then collect the average difference for the treatment and control groups, say $\bar{r}_1$ and $\bar{r}_0$, and use the difference between these averages as the ATE estimate:

$$\hat{\gamma} = \bar{r}_1 - \bar{r}_0 \tag{6.23}$$

This routine is the source of the "difference in differences" name. It gives the exact same answer as we found in our regression analysis.

```
> r <- tapply(log(ebay$revenue), ebay$dma, function(y) y[2]-y[1])
> d <- ebay[match(names(r),ebay$dma),"ssm.turns.off"]
> rBar <- tapply(r,d,mean)
> rBar[2]-rBar[1]
   1
-0.005775498
```

You can also apply the usual formula to get the sampling variance for a difference in means: $\text{var}(\hat{\gamma}) = \text{var}(\bar{r}_1) + \text{var}(\bar{r}_0)$.

```
> rBarVar <- tapply(r, d, function(r) var(r)/length(r))
> sqrt(sum(rBarVar))
[1] 0.00572258
```

The standard error is practically unchanged from our earlier regression analysis.

6.4.2 Synthetic Controls

In the eBay paid search example, we actually have a panel dataset: a set of daily revenue series for each DMA. We chose to collapse those time series into two observations for each DMA: average daily revenue before and after the treatment began on some DMAs. That allowed us to fit the simple diff-in-diff model of (6.21). But what if we had left the data as daily time series? We would have had time series for each of the 284 control group DMAs where the SSM marketing stayed on after May 22. Perhaps some of these control DMAs are closer comparators to the treatment group DMAs—their revenue moves more similarly to the treatment group's in the pre-treatment period before May 22. In the DiD analysis, we took a simple average of the control group DMA revenues to calculate the control revenue. But if some control DMAs are better predictors of the treatment DMAs, then we can do better by using a weighted combination of the DMAs to build the control revenue that we compare against treated revenue. For example, if the treated DMAs were all in the western U.S. then we would want to put more weight on the westerly DMAs in the control group.

This is the method of *synthetic controls*. To keep things simple, we will adopt a setup where you have a *single* treatment time series and a number of control time series. If your application involves multiple treatment units (as in the paid search example) you can adapt by averaging across them to get a single treatment series or you can analyze each treatment unit independently (i.e., do a synthetic controls analysis for each treatment series in turn, ignoring the others). The resulting data structure is a panel of time series, each corresponding to a unit of observation (e.g., store or region), where at some point in time the single treatment unit is treated with a policy. For example, you are tracking sales in all countries and at some point only the U.S. is treated with a free shipping policy. In a synthetic controls analysis, the pre-treatment relationship between the U.S. and all other countries is used to predict the *counterfactual* series for what would have happened post-treatment if you had not applied the treatment policy (e.g., free shipping). The difference between what is actually observed after treatment and the counterfactual series gives you an estimate of the treatment effect.

The Synthetic Controls Model

To add some notation, suppose that you have a treatment time series of interest, say $\mathbf{y} = y_1 \ldots y_T$. The treatment status is d_t, where $d_t = 0$ for untreated observations and $d_t = 1$ for the treated observations. There is some point t^* after which you *started* treatment, such that $d_t = 0$ for all $t \leq t^*$ and $d_t = 1$ for all $t > t^*$. You then have a number of control series, say $\mathbf{x}_1 \ldots \mathbf{x}_J$ where $\mathbf{x}_j = x_{j1} \ldots x_{jT}$. These control series are tracking the same outcomes as in your treatment series, but they are never treated. We've seen data structures like this before: this is just a panel of multiple time series. The special feature here is that one of the series in the panel receives treatment after time t^*.

The *potential outcomes* at each point t in the treatment time series are $y_t(1)$ for the treated outcomes and $y_t(0)$ for the untreated outcomes. Of course, you only get to observe one of these outcomes at each time point: $y_t = y_t(d_t)$. The treatment effects of interest are the differences between treated and untreated potential outcomes,

$$\gamma_t = y_t(1) - y_t(0) \text{ for } t = t^* + 1, t^* + 2, \ldots T \tag{6.24}$$

The trick of synthetic controls is to think about this estimation problem in terms of the *incomplete matrix,*

$$\begin{bmatrix} y_1(0) & y_2(0) & \ldots & y_{t^*}(0) & ? & \ldots & ? \\ x_{11} & x_{12} & \ldots & x_{1t^*} & x_{1t^*+1} & \ldots & x_{1T} \\ \vdots & & & \vdots & & & \vdots \\ x_{J1} & x_{J2} & \ldots & x_{Jt^*} & x_{Jt^*+1} & \ldots & x_{JT} \end{bmatrix} \tag{6.25}$$

The missing (?) values are the unobserved potential outcomes $y_t(0)$ for $t > t^*$. These are the untreated counterfactual responses for your treatment series after the treatment has been applied. If you can estimate these counterfactual outcomes, say as $\hat{y}_t(0)$, then you can subtract them from the observed responses $y_t = y_t(1)$ for $t > t^*$ to get the treatment effect at each time point as

$$\hat{\gamma}_t = y_t - \hat{y}_t(0) \text{ for } t = t^* + 1, t^* + 2, \ldots T \tag{6.26}$$

Given this data setup, the synthetic controls algorithm is straightforward. You fit a regression to predict $y_t(0)$ from $[x_{1t}, \ldots, x_{Jt}]$, the observations of the control series at time t, using the data where $t \leq t^*$. Looking at the matrix in (6.25), this corresponds to building a prediction model where you predict the top element of each column from the other elements in the same column. The training data is the set of complete columns. The recipe is outlined in Algorithm 6.2.

Algorithm 6.2 **Synthetic Controls**

- Build a regression model for $\mathbb{E}[y_t(0)|x_{1t}, \ldots, x_{Jt}]$, and estimate this regression using data from time periods $t = 1 \ldots t^*$.
- Use this regression to predict the untreated counterfactuals $\hat{y}_{t^*+1}(0), \hat{y}_{t^*+2}(0)$, etc., and estimate the treatment effect at each time point as

$$\hat{\gamma}_{t^*+s} = y_{t^*+s} - \hat{y}_{t^*+s}(0)$$

The original synthetic controls work of Abadie and Gardeazabal (2003) applied Algorithm 6.2 using a specific linear regression model with positive regression coefficients (weights) on the control series, and these weights were required to sum to one. However, you should feel free to use whatever regression model works best for prediction in your application. Since there are typically many control series (J) relative to the number of time periods (T), it will often make sense to use a regularized regression like the Lasso.

The conditional ignorability assumption that is required for all this to work is that the relationship between the control series and the treatment series holds after you have introduced treatment. That is, you need that the regression trained on data from times $t \leq t^*$ is accurate for out-of-sample prediction of $y_t(0)$ for $t > t^*$. As was the case for diff-in-diff analysis, this is a strong assumption that is difficult to verify in practice. But it is often close enough to true to be useful, and later in this section we will introduce a *placebo test* method that can help you check your analysis.

Example 6.7 **Basque Terrorism Data: Synthetic Controls** To illustrate the approach, we will revisit the data example from the original synthetic controls work of Abadie and Gardeazabal (2003). This example investigated the economic costs of terrorism in the Basque region of Spain. Beginning with a single killing in the summer of 1968, the terrorist group ETA began a campaign of killing and kidnapping that continued, with periodic cease fires, until 2010. The violence was high from the late 1970s through the early 1990s, with a peak of 92 people killed and 13 kidnapped in 1980. Almost 70% of the deaths occurred *in* the Basque country, and Basque business owners were common kidnapping targets.

Abadie and Gardeazabal ask the question: "How much did the ETA campaign harm the economy of the Basque country?" In addition to the obvious and tragic human cost of terrorism, the threat of violence will also deter investment and lower productivity. To answer this question, we can look at how the Basque region performed in comparison to the other regions in Spain (which experienced significantly less violence). For data, we have the GDP per capita (measured in 1986 $1000 USD) from 1955 through 1990 for each of the 17 regions in Spain. This data was obtained from the Synth package for R, which also implements the original estimators from Abadie and Gardeazabal. After some wrangling, it yields a matrix D of the form in Equation (6.25) with the treated, Basque, region in the first row and the 16 control region series below. We print the first four rows here.

```
> library(Synth)
> library(tidyr)
> data(basque)
> ## synthetic controls analysis
> ## wrangle the data
> D <- basque[,1:4] %>% spread(year, gdpcap)
> rownames(D) <- D$regionname
> D <- D[c(17,2:16,18), -(1:2)]
> D <- D[,1:35]
> D[1:5,1:4]
                                1955      1956      1957      1958
Basque Country (Pais Vasco) 3.853185  3.945658  4.033562  4.023422
Andalucia                   1.688732  1.758498  1.827621  1.852756
Aragon                      2.288775  2.445159  2.603399  2.639032
Principado De Asturias      2.502928  2.615538  2.725793  2.751857
Baleares                    3.143959  3.347758  3.549629  3.642673
```

Since the terrorism started midway through 1968, we will assume that the first treated year is 1969 (i.e., $t^* = 1968 - 1954 = 14$; results don't change if $t^* = 14$).

To estimate the synthetic controls, we first convert D from a data frame to a numeric matrix. You can then pull out the treatment series y as the first row and the control series x as the remainder of the matrix. We also calculate tstar (t^*).

```
> D <- as.matrix(D)
> y <- D[1,]
> x <- t(D[-1,])
> tstar <- 1968-1954
> y[tstar+c(-1,0,1)]
     1967      1968      1969
5.614896 5.852185 6.081405
```

We then train an AICc Lasso regression to predict the observed $y_t(0)$.

```
> fit <- gamlr( x[1:tstar,], y[1:tstar], lmr=1e-4)
> w <- drop( coef(fit) )
> w[w!=0]
  intercept          Baleares Castilla Y Leon    Valencia
  0.8324923        -0.1436622       0.5159924  -0.3581780
     Madrid    Murcia
  0.4263979 0.8928448
```

The regularization path plot for this regression is shown in Figure 6.9a and the nonzero coefficients are printed above. We see that the selected model for predicting untreated per-capita GDP in the Basque region has nonzero positive weights on Castilla Y Leon, the largest region bordering the Basque country, as well as on the Mediterranean region of Murcia and on the capital, Madrid. There are negative loadings on Valencia and the Balearic Islands, indicating

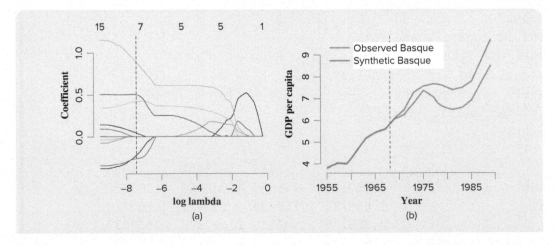

FIGURE 6.9 Synthetic controls analysis of the economic effects of Basque (ETA) terrorism. The Lasso path plot is in (a) with the AICc selected penalty marked, and (b) shows the synthetic (no terrorism) response against the observed economic performance. Per-capita GDP values are in 1986 $1,000 USD units.

that *after* controlling for Leon, Madrid, and Murcia, an *extra* increase in, say, Valencia's GDP tends to correspond to a decrease in GDP for the Basque country.

Given this regression fit, we can use it to predict the untreated potential outcomes for the Basque region's GDP, $\hat{y}_1(0), \ldots, \hat{y}_{t^*}(0), \ldots, \hat{y}_T(0)$.

```
> y0hat <- predict(fit, x)[,1]
```

The predicted values are shown in Figure 6.9b next to the observed time series. The introduction of treatment is marked with a vertical dashed line, you can see a clear break between the two series after 1968. The results indicate a cost of terrorism ($\hat{\gamma}_t$) as high as \$1,000 per capita in 1980. The gap between synthetic (i.e., predicted) counterfactual response and observed response after this point is your estimated treatment effect. Calculating each $\hat{\gamma}_t$ as $\hat{y}_t(0) - y_t$ for $t = t^* + 1, \ldots, T$ and taking the mean shows an estimated average treatment effect of around \$690 lower per-capita GDP annually due to the impact of Basque terrorism.

```
> gamhat <- (y - y0hat)
> mean( gamhat[-(1:tstar)] )
[1] -0.6921244
```

Placebos and Permutation Testing

What is the statistical significance of this result? You could apply a bootstrap to estimate a sampling distribution for the fitted counterfactual $\hat{y}_t(0)$ series, allowing you to put error bands around the synthetic series in Figure 6.9b. However, this would not give you any information on how realistic your assumption is that the control region GDPs did not deviate from the treatment series for reasons unrelated to ETA terrorism. Instead, in a synthetic controls analysis you have the nice option of using *permutation testing* to understand the statistical significance of your estimated treatment effects. Also called a "placebo test," these permutation methods repeatedly apply your same analysis algorithm to infer treatment effects for the *control* series. That is, you pretend that one of the control series is actually the treatment series and repeat your synthetic controls analysis. Since you know that the control series has not been treated (e.g., we are assuming that the terrorism impacts were largely isolated to the Basque region), the pretend treatment effects that you get out of such an analysis represent draws from the *null distribution*—the distribution of estimated treatment effects you would get if the true treatment has zero impact on the response.

Example 6.8 Basque Terrorism Data: Permutation Testing Permutation, or placebo, tests are a nice intuitive way to build confidence around your results in a synthetic controls analysis. Under this method, you compare the estimated treatment effects to results obtained using the same methods on *placebo* units: regions where you know that no treatment has been applied.

To facilitate this permutation testing, we create a simple function called synthc that executes Algorithm 6.2 by wrapping together the steps of Example 6.7.

```
> synthc <- function(D, tstar, treated, ...){
+   y <- D[treated,]
+   x <- t(D[-treated,])
```

```
+   fit <- gamlr( x[1:tstar,], y[1:tstar], ...)
+   y0hat <- predict(fit, x)[,1]
+   gamhat <- y - y0hat
+   ate <- mean( gamhat[-(1:tstar)] )
+   return(list(y0hat=y0hat, gamhat=gamhat, ate=ate ) )
+ }
```

This function takes the matrix D of time series (make sure it is a `matrix`, not `data.frame`) in the format of (6.25), with a row for each region and a column for each time period. The argument `tstar` indicates the last period before treatment, and `treated` is the row index of the treatment time series. For example using `tstar=14` (from 1968–1954) and `treated=1` recovers our analysis of Example 6.7.

```
> sc <- synthc(D, tstar=14, treated=1, lmr=1e-4)
> sc$ate
[1] -0.6921244
```

The output of `synthc` is a list containing `y0hat` as the predicted untreated outcomes $\hat{y}_t(0)$, `gamhat` as the estimated treatment effects $\hat{\gamma}_t$, and `ate` as the average treatment effect that you get taking the mean of $\hat{\gamma}_t$ for $t^* < t \leq T$. Note that `y0hat` and `gamhat` are fit for all time points even though only those after 1968 are evaluated as counterfactual predictions (we observe $y_t(0) = y_t$ for $t \leq t^*$).

If you run `synthc` for `treated` values greater than 1, you are doing a synthetic controls analysis that "pretends" an untreated control series (the placebo) is actually the treatment series. In this case, the placebo units are the 16 non-Basque regions of Spain. We can use the `parallel` library to execute these placebo analyses for each of the control series.

```
> library(parallel)
> cl <- makeCluster(detectCores())
> clusterExport(cl, c("D", "gamlr", "synthc"))
```

Note we exported our panel data matrix D and the functions we need to the cluster cl. We can now run all the placebo analyses using `parSapply`.

```
> getgam <- function(j){ synthc(D, 14, j, lmr=1e-4)$gamhat }
> G <- t(parSapply(cl, 1:nrow(D), getgam))
> rownames(G) <- rownames(D)
> G[1:4,1:3]
```

	1955	1956	1957
Basque Country (Pais Vasco)	0.044167208	0.0101789262	-0.023740491
Andalucia	0.007343847	-0.0012930165	-0.010210680
Aragon	-0.053050956	-0.0293610595	0.002545068
Principado De Asturias	-0.005668802	-0.0003661591	0.002851291

After transposing the result (and adding row names) the matrix G has the same format as our original panel data D, with a row for each region and a column for each year. The entries of G are the difference between synthetic and observed series for every region in Spain. The synthetic series are trained on data from 1955 to 1968. Only the first row of G contains actual treatment effect estimates (for years after 1968) corresponding to the Basque Country. The other rows are full of placebo effect estimates: draws from the null distribution of what the method would predict as the treatment effect in the case where no treatment was actually applied.

The estimated treatment effects from G are plotted in Figure 6.10a. The Basque (treatment) series is highlighted in red. You can see that it is indeed among the largest of the 17 estimated differences, giving us confidence that the underlying treatment effect is indeed significant. One placebo series showing a large difference corresponds to Madrid, the capital region of Spain. It is plausible that the relationship between Madrid and the rest of Spain is different before and after 1968, leading to the gap between observed and synthetic series for this region. For example, there was an attempted military coup in 1981, and Spain joined the European Union in 1986. Both of these events, and many others, changed the structure of the economy in Spain and the relationships between its regions. However, the permutation test shows that the Basque region's drop in economic performance after 1968 is among the largest deviations from what you would expect based on the pre-1969 relationship between regions.

We can use the results of the permutation test to calculate a *p*-value: the probability that an untreated series (i.e., a series from the null distribution) shows as big or larger a treatment effect estimate than what we obtained for the Basque region. Taking the average of the estimated treatment effects for each region (i.e., taking the post-1968 average for each line in 6.10a), we obtain the distribution of annual average GDP-per-capita treatment effects in Figure 6.10b. Only one of these average treatment effects (Madrid's) has an absolute value larger than that for the Basque region. This gives a *p*-value of 0.0625 (1/16) for a test of the two-sided hypothesis that the Basque region's economic performance was different after 1968 than what you would expect given the relationship between regions prior to 1968.

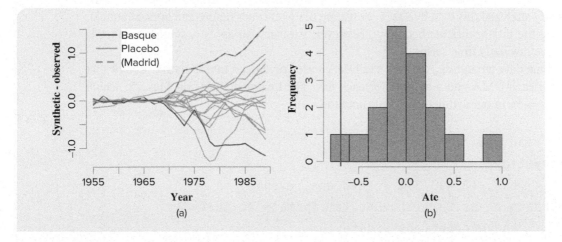

(a)

(b)

FIGURE 6.10 Permutation test of the synthetic controls analysis of the economic effects of Basque (ETA) terrorism. Figure (a) shows the estimated treatment effects when you apply Algorithm 6.2 for analysis of each region. Placebo results are plotted in gray, and the result for the Basque region is in red (we also highlight Madrid, which has a large placebo effect). Figure (b) shows distribution of the corresponding average treatment effects (the average value of each line in (a) for years after 1968). Again, the treated Basque region is marked with a red line.

```
> ate <- rowMeans(G[,-(1:tstar)])
> mean(abs(ate[-1]) > abs(ate[1]))
[1] 0.0625
```

Assumptions behind Synthetic Controls

Synthetic controls rely upon a strong assumption that the relationship between series would have remained stable if not for the treatment being introduced. As we see in Figure 6.10a, the placebo series all diverge from their pre-treatment expectations as time passes after treatment. In general, the assumption of a stable relationship between series gets less realistic as you go further into the future after treatment. There is no formal way to evaluate how far into the future you can trust the analysis. In practice, you eyeball plots like that in Figure 6.10a and decide when the placebo effects are so large that you can no longer trust the comparison.

Despite requiring strong assumptions, synthetic controls provide a way to get plausible estimates of causal treatment effects when you can only test policies on a small number of large aggregated units. One option to make the analysis more robust is to combine synthetic and observed controls; any additional control variables that you have just enter as extra covariates in the regression model of Algorithm 6.2. And there are a variety of other useful extensions of Algorithm 6.2 in the literature. For example, researchers from Google (Brodersen et al., 2015) created the causalInference package for R that implements synthetic control methods using Bayesian time series tools.

Example 6.9 **Paid Search Advertising: Synthetic Controls** To close the topic of synthetic controls, we can revisit the SSM effectiveness study of Example 6.6 where we tracked (simulated) eBay revenue before and after paid search ads were turned off in a subset of DMAs. We previously analyzed this data by first aggregating daily revenues before and after treatment, and applying the diff-in-diff methodology. However, we can also apply a synthetic controls analysis to the raw daily time series.

After some data wrangling, we have the DMA series organized into a matrix ebayD that has a row for each DMA and a column for each day. The treatment starts on May 22, which means that $t^* = 51$ in our synthetic controls notation.

```
> ps <- read.csv("paidsearch.csv")
> library(tidyr)
> ebayD <- ps[,-(3:4)] %>% spread(dma,revenue)
> ebayD$date <- as.Date(ebayD$date, format="%d-%b-%y")
> ebayD <- ebayD[order(ebayD$date),]
> row.names(ebayD) <- as.character(ebayD$date)
> ebayD <- t(ebayD[,-1])
> tstar <- 51
> ebayD[1:4,51:53]
```

```
      2012-05-21 2012-05-22  2012-05-23
500    70890.29    85870.94    67890.57
501 2495023.92 2456220.82  2355242.11
502    32875.46    43084.81    32837.05
503    37397.84    44031.41    35055.04
> dim(ebayD)
[1] 210 113
```

In this example, the treatment of getting SSM turned off was applied to multiple DMAs. To analyze the average impact, we will collapse all of those treatment group DMAs into a single time series of average revenue. We do this by matching the rows of ebayD with the treatment indicator ssm.turns.off from the ebay data frame that we analyzed in Example 6.6, and then averaging those series where ssm.turns.off=1.

```
> # Create a single average 'treatment' DMA series.
> d <- ebay$ssm.turns.off[match(rownames(ebayD),ebay$dma)]
> Y <- colMeans(ebayD[d==1,])
> ebayD <- log(rbind(Y,ebayD[d!=1,]))
> ebayD[1:4,51:53]
    2012-05-21 2012-05-22 2012-05-23
Y     11.65507   11.61958   11.58538
501   14.72981   14.71413   14.67215
502   10.40048   10.67093   10.39931
503   10.52937   10.69266   10.46467
```

After swapping the treatment DMA series for a single average treatment series, the final ebayD matrix has the same format as the panel matrix in (6.25) with the single treatment series in the first row and 142 control DMA series in the subsequent rows. Notice that we applied a log transform to the final matrix, so that we will again be calculating treatment effects on the log average daily revenue.

We can calculate the treatment effect of turning off paid search using the same synthc function we created for Example 6.8.

```
> ebaySC <- synthc(ebayD, tstar=51, 1)
> ebaySC$ate
[1] -0.02306891
```

The estimated average daily treatment effect of turning off SSM is −0.023, about four times larger (more negative) than what we found in Example 6.6 using DiD analysis. Some of the control DMAs are better predictors than others of the treatment DMA average. See Figure 6.11a for the Lasso regularization path in this regression, showing a variety of different coefficients on control DMAs (also, note that the regression coefficients are all positive

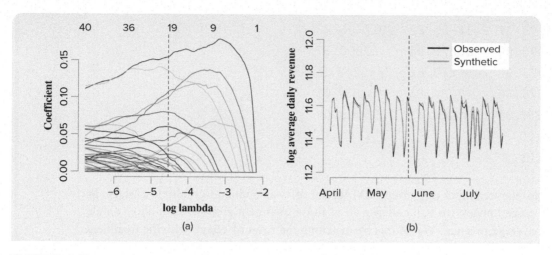

FIGURE 6.11 Synthetic controls analysis of the effectiveness of SSM for eBay. The Lasso path plot for the synthetic controls regression is in (a) with the AICc selected penalty marked, and (b) shows the counterfactual synthetic (SSM stays on) response against the observed log revenue.

this time). Because of this improved counterfactual prediction of the log revenue in treatment DMAs *if SSM stayed on,* synthetic controls analysis gives a different answer than what we got when comparing simple pre- and post-treatment averages between treatment and control groups (as we did in the DiD analysis).

However, the treatment effect of turning off SSM is still small and insignificant. The synthetic and observed series for treatment DMAs are shown in Figure 6.11b. It is hard to see much difference between the two lines after May 22. Indeed, the *p*-value for the average daily treatment effect is 0.47 for the test of whether the treatment DMA series diverged from its prediction given the control DMAs.

```
> library(parallel)
> cl <- makeCluster(detectCores())
> clusterExport(cl, c("ebayD", "gamlr", "synthc"))
> getATE <- function(j){ synthc(ebayD, 52, j)$ate }
> ate <- parSapply(cl, 1:nrow(ebayD), getATE)
> mean(abs(ate[-1]) > abs(ate[1]))
[1] 0.471831
```

Both DiD and synthetic controls analysis give the same answer: eBay was wasting money on paid search advertising (again, this doesn't say that all search advertising is useless but just that eBay's specific strategy was not worthwhile).

QUICK REFERENCE

All of the methods in this chapter, from basic low-dimensional OLS to synthetic controls, are best used in conjunction with available experimental evidence. Experimentation offers *unbiased* evidence of causal effects that can be complemented with observational studies on larger datasets. And any causal inference will likely be of little use without some domain structure (e.g., in beer pricing we saw that it is important to understand the potential outside influences on demand and to think about the price-per-oz as the treatment of interest). You should always try to ask yourself through what mechanisms the treatment can be acting on the response and use this information to guide your design of experiments, selection of controls, and modeling of heterogeneity. The ML and statistics tools of this and the previous chapter should be useful in your career as a data scientist, but you can't use them on autopilot without thinking about the structure of the problem at hand.

Key Practical Concepts

- Conditional ignorability is the assumption that your treatment assignment is independent of the response given a set of observed controls. With a data frame x containing control variables, you can estimate treatment effects under conditional ignorability by including these variables in OLS regression.

  ```
  fit <- glm( y ~ d + ., data=x)
  coef(fit)["d"]
  ```

  You can get the same answer through the process of *residualization*.

  ```
  yfit <- glm(y ~ ., data=x)
  ytil <- y - predict(yfit, data=x)
  dfit <- glm(d ~ ., data=x)
  dtil <- d - predict(dfit, data=x)
  ```

- When the set of controls is high dimensional, you can use the `doubleML` function to perform this residualization using out-of-sample prediction from cross-fit `gamlr` Lassos.

  ```
  xmat <- sparse.model.matrix( ~ ., data=x)[,-1]
  dml <- doubleML( xmat, d, y )
  summary(dml)
  ```

- You can interact the residuals from `doubleML` with sources of heterogeneity to estimate HTEs.

  ```
  dtil <- dml$x
  dx <- cbind(dtil, dtil*xmat)
  hte <- gamlr(dx, dml$y, free=1)
  ```

- In a diff-in-diff setup, you have treatment assignment d where units in the d=1 group are treated in period t=1 and those in the d=0 group are not. Every unit is untreated in period t=0. The treatment effect is the coefficient on the interaction between d and t in a linear regression to predict response y.

```
did <- glm( y ~ d*t )
coef(did)["d:t"]
```

Use standard errors that are clustered on each unit via the sandwich library.

- In a synthetic controls setup, you have time series y treated after time tstar, and a panel of contemporaneous untreated time series x. Estimate the treatment effect after tstar by predicting the untreated potential outcome based upon x, using a model trained on data up until tstar.

```
fit <- gamlr( x[1:tstar,], y[1:tstar] )
gamhat <- y - drop(predict(fit, x))
mean( gamhat[-(1:tstar)] )
```

To quantify uncertainty, use a permutation (i.e., placebo) test that repeats this analysis treating each untreated series as the response. The distribution of placebo treatment effect estimates is your null distribution for the null hypothesis that the treatment effect is zero.

7 TREES AND FORESTS

This chapter introduces tree-based models for flexible nonparametric regression.

- **Section 7.1 Decision Trees:** Use trees to make predictions, and apply the CART algorithm to find trees through a greedy deviance-minimizing search.

- **Section 7.2 Random Forests:** Stabilize and regularize your tree predictions by *bagging* and combining many CART trees together in a forest.

- **Section 7.3 Causal Inference with Random Forests:** Apply random forests as part of the double ML procedure for treatment effect estimation.

- **Section 7.4 Distributed Computing for Random Forests:** Understand the MapReduce framework for distributed computing algorithms, and how this applies for estimating *empirical Bayesian forests* on truly big data.

All of the regressions that we have worked with up until now are *parametric*. They place restrictions on how the inputs can influence the response, for example, forcing the relationship to act through a linear model. This is called *parametric analysis* because these models have parameters and you fit them to the data. *Nonparametric* regression algorithms make fewer assumptions about the relationship between $\mathbf{x}$ and y. These algorithms are designed to learn the true conditional expectation $\mathbb{E}[y|\mathbf{x}]$ as you observe more data, regardless of what this truth looks like. As you accumulate data, your predictions should get closer to the truth.

The most useful class of fully nonparametric regression models are *tree-based models*. In these models, you use hierarchical trees to partition the input space, such that, say, you split the data into one subset where $x_j \leq \tau$ and another where $x_j > \tau$ (i.e., partition on the jth dimension of $\mathbf{x}$). You then estimate a different expectation for y in each data split. If you split the input space into an increasing number of partitions as you accumulate data, then your conditional expectations $\mathbb{E}[y|\mathbf{x}]$ will get increasingly specific to each unique input $\mathbf{x}$. This chapter will introduce how to fit such *regression trees* and how to combine many trees into a *forest* that performs better at prediction than any single tree.

The main assumption that most nonparametric methods (including trees and forests) require is *independence* between observations. This is an important but often unmentioned requirement for fully nonparametric procedures. When it fails, these procedures will tend to be outperformed by parametric procedures that do account for dependence, even if they do so in a way that is somewhat misspecified. However, when you have independent data (or if you can use transformations and de-trending to remove dependence between observations), then nonparametric methods are a powerful technique for fitting complex conditional expectation functions.

Recalling what you've learned elsewhere in this book, you should expect that the flexibility gained through a nonparametric approach will lead to overfit unless it is combined with some type of regularization. Unfortunately, penalized deviance and CV-selection *do not* work for regularization of nonparametric regressions. For example, in tree models, you do not have regression coefficients that you can penalize. But even if you have a way to think about regularization, such as limiting the number of partitions you allow from the tree, the fits from a nonparametric regression are *unstable*. That means that small data jitter can lead to wildly different predictive performances, and this means that techniques like cross-validation do a poor job of estimating out-of-sample errors (and hence do a poor job of model selection). Fortunately, you can both stabilize and regularize with the technique called *bagging* (Breiman, 1996), where you fit many nonparametric regressions to different bootstrap samples of the data. That is, you bootstrap the regression function and use the bootstrap average for prediction. This strategy is also sometimes called *model averaging*; it is a necessary ingredient in practical nonparametric analysis. It is the technique that moves you from trees to forests.

When the dimension gets too big, the superflexibility of nonparametric models makes it hard to learn anything useful (even if you use bagging to help stabilize the regression). You should be cautious about using fully nonparametric regressions outside of settings where you have much more data than dimensions. That is, you can be nonparametric only when $p \ll n$ where p is the length of each observation vector $\mathbf{x}$ and n is your number of observations. A good rule of thumb is that you want $p < \sqrt{n}$ ("much less than") if you are going to be using trees and forests. In higher-dimensional problems, you will instead want to use *semiparametric* methods that combine targeted flexibility with parametric restrictions that encourage stability and dimension reduction. In Chapter 10 we'll introduce deep neural networks as a semiparametric method that plays a starring role in contemporary ML. However, there are a *ton* of real data applications where p is big but n is much bigger; in these settings, you should consider forests and other tree-based methods as your default prediction tool.

● 7.1 Decision Trees

A decision tree is a logical system for mapping from inputs to outcomes. Trees are *hierarchical:* you use a series of ordered steps (decision nodes) to come to a conclusion. Figure 7.1 shows a simple example for the process of deciding whether you bring an umbrella to work—each *node* implies a split on the forecast data available (from either a weather report or current conditions) and the final decisions—the *leaf nodes*—are based upon rain predictions conditional upon these splits. The tree nodes have a *parent-child* structure: every node except the root ("wake up") has a parent, and every node except the leaves has two children. The trick to building an effective decision tree is to have the sequence of decision nodes combine for good final choices.

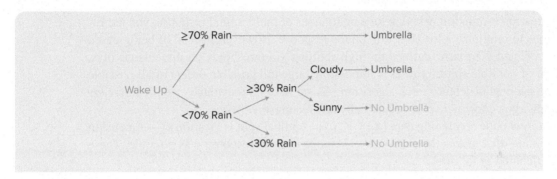

FIGURE 7.1   A cartoon decision tree, where you wake up and use the forecast probability of rain and a look at the sky to determine whether you should pack an umbrella.

A decision tree is a regression model. You have inputs **x** (forecast, current conditions) and an output of interest y (the amount or probability of rain). The decision (umbrella?) is made by combining the predictive distribution for y with the utility function, for example, on the competing inconveniences of carrying an umbrella and getting wet. The trees act like a game of mousetrap. You drop your observations in at the top, and each decision node bounces it either left or right. Finally, the observation ends up in a leaf node that contains the data subset defined by these decisions (splits).

The following is an example tree structure that uses our familiar regression notation:

$$x_1 < 10$$
$$x_2 < 2.5 \qquad \{\mathbf{x} : x_1 \geq 10\}$$
$$\{\mathbf{x} : x_1 < 10, x_2 < 2.5\} \qquad \{\mathbf{x} : x_1 < 10, x_2 \geq 2.5\}$$

The *prediction rule* at each leaf—the predicted $\hat{y}$—is the average of the sample y values that end up in that leaf. In this example tree, $\hat{y}$ for the bottom-left leaf would be the average of all y_i values such that $x_{i1} < 10$ and $x_{i2} < 2.5$. For example, if the response is a real number, then $\hat{y}$ is just a simple average. Suppose that x_1 is someone's years of work experience, x_2 is their college GPA, and their wage is the output y: the predicted response for people who end up in the $\{\mathbf{x} : x_1 < 10, x_2 < 2.5\}$ leaf is the average wage for those with less than 10 years work experience and a GPA below 2.5. If the response is categorical, such that each $\mathbf{y}_i$ is a vector of zeros and a one indicating the observed category, then the leaf average $\bar{\mathbf{y}}$ will be the proportion of observations in each category for that leaf.

To build such trees, you need an algorithm that takes previous [**x**, *y*] pairs and automatically constructs a useful set of splitting rules. The goal will be to minimize a *loss function*. The loss functions for trees look the same as the *deviance* functions that you've been using as objectives for the parametric regression modeling. For example, if the response is a real number, then you can fit your "regression" tree to minimize the sum-squared error $\sum_{i=1}^{n}(y_i - \hat{y}_i)^2$. For a classification problem, you can fit your tree to minimize the multinomial deviance $-2\sum_{i=1}^{n}\sum_{k=1}^{K}y_{ik}\log(\hat{y}_{ik})$. As a historical quirk, for classification most tree software implementations instead minimize "Gini impurity" $\sum_{i=1}^{n}\hat{y}_{ik}(1 - \hat{y}_{ik})$, a measure of the multinomial variance. Both Gini loss and multinomial deviance lead to similar fits, and both work fine for classification.

CART: Greedy Deviance Minimization

As in any regression estimation, whether for a continuous or multinomial response, you are fitting regressions to minimize a loss function on the response. However, instead of being based on $\mathbf{x}'\beta$, the predicted $\hat{y}$ are now defined through splitting via thresholds on dimensions of **x**. The full space of possible splitting rules is impossibly large (all possible orders of all possible splits), so you need an efficient search algorithm. As we've done previously, we'll use *greedy* forward search—you construct splits sequentially and recursively.

Given a *parent* node containing data $\{\mathbf{x}_i, y_i\}_{i=1}^{n}$, the optimal split is location x_{ij}—dimension j on observation i—that makes the *child* sets as *homogeneous* in response y as possible. These child sets are denoted as follows:

$$\text{left: } \{\mathbf{x}_k, y_k : x_{kj} \leq x_{ij}\} \text{ and right: } \{\mathbf{x}_k, y_k : x_{kj} > x_{ij}\}$$

Here, k can index any of your original n observations. For a regression tree with squared error loss, this means that you then want to minimize the function.

$$\sum_{k \in \text{left}}(y_k - \bar{y}_{\text{left}})^2 + \sum_{k \in \text{right}}(y_k - \bar{y}_{\text{right}})^2 \tag{7.1}$$

The classification and regression tree (CART) algorithm of Breiman et al. (1984) is the dominant method for fitting trees. It proceeds by iteratively choosing splits to minimize "node impurities." Breiman et al. use "regression" to refer to prediction of continuous responses and "classification" for multinomial responses. In the language of this book, these are all regression problems where your fitted response $\hat{y}$ is an estimate of the conditional expectation $\mathbb{E}[y|\mathbf{x}]$. All that differs is whether or not $\hat{y}$ can be interpreted as a probability that can then be used in classification tasks.

Algorithm 7.1 **CART**

For each node, beginning with the root containing the full sample:

1. Determine the single error minimizing split for this data sample—location x_{ij} that minimizes the loss across children, as in Equation 7.1.

2. Split this parent node into two children.

3. Apply steps 1 and 2 to each child node.

   This continues *recursively* until you reach a *stopping rule*. Each leaf is treated the same as we treated the root node: all the variables are potential candidates for splitting and you minimize the same loss function. The stopping rules are often the minimum size for a new leaf node (e.g., stop splitting when there are fewer than, say, 10 observations in your next leaf) or a minimum decrease in the loss function (deviance) due to a new split.

Using `tree` to Fit CART

To fit CART trees, you can use the `tree` library in R. The syntax is essentially the same as for `glm`.

```
mytree = tree(y ~ x1 + x2 + x3 ..., data=mydata)
```

There are a few other useful arguments, all of which adjust the stopping rules.

- `mincut` is the minimum size for a new child.
- `mindev` is the minimum (proportion) deviance improvement for proceeding with a new split.

In many applications, you will want to drop `mindev` from its default of `mindev=0.01` which stops splitting if there is a less than 1% improvement in loss. This is an overly high bar for many real-world applications. You can also specify `mindev=0` so that leaf size is the only stopping rule. To understand the results, you can call `print`, `summarize`, and `plot` (with `text` to get something readable) on the fitted object.

Example 7.1 Census Income Data: CART To illustrate CART, we'll look at income data from the Current Population Study (CPS), a regular survey conducted by the U.S. Census Bureau. The `hdm` package includes the `cps2012` data from a 2012 CPS survey. This is similar to the data used in Mulligan and Rubinstein (2008) which studied the impact of gender on wages. It contains data on incomes and respondent demographics. There are over 29k observations in this data set, so this is a setting where n is much larger than p (the number of demographic variables).

After the data is read into R we need to do some wrangling.

```
> library(hdm)
> data(cps2012)
> cps <- cps2012[,-c(1,17:23)]
> names(cps)[15] <- "pexp"
```

In creating the `cps` data frame here we removed the redundant first `year` column (everything is from 2012) and some trailing columns that contained transformations of continuous variables and reference levels for factors. The transformations (e.g., creating a variable x_i^2) are useful for linear regression models but unnecessary with trees (indeed, not needing to bother with such transformations is part of the appeal of using nonparametric regression methods). The final line renames our key "potential experience" variable to make the rest of the code more readable. This potential experience, `pexp`, is a heuristic for the number of years that a survey respondent could have been working full time. It is calculated as the subject's age minus 7 (no child labor here) minus their years spent in school (making the rough assumption that people don't work full time while getting educated).

Our response of interest is the nominal wage, which is the hourly wage for each subject in 2012 dollars. This is calculated as their annual earnings divided by the hours that they work in a year. It is recorded in the cps2012 data as log nominal wage (lnw) and we transform it to raw nominal wage by exponentiating it (you could also work with prediction on log scale if you wished; the tree methods will give different answers depending upon how you transform the response). The raw hourly wage response is renamed as hrwage.

```
> cps$lnw <- exp(cps$lnw)
> names(cps)[1] <- "hrwage"
> head(cps,3)
          hrwage female widowed  divorced separated nevermarried
1663459   6.75000     1       0         0         0            0
1663462   3.91875     1       0         0         0            0
1663463  12.68250     0       0         0         0            0
        hsd08 hsd911 hsg  cg  ad  mw  so  we pexp
1663459     0      0   0   0   0   0   0   0   22
1663462     0      1   0   0   0   0   0   0   30
1663463     0      0   1   0   0   0   0   0   19
```

The other variables in here (beyond hrwage and pexp) are all binary indicators for demographic categories. The education categories are whether the person's maximum educational attainment was less than the eighth grade (hsd8), between grades 9 and 11 (hsd911), high school graduation (hsg), college graduation (cg), or an advanced graduate degree (ad). The mw, so, we indicators are for the U.S. region where the subject lives: midwest, south, or west, respectively. The omitted categories determine the *reference* levels: our baseline subject here is a married male from the northeast who has some college but not a full four-year degree.

To start, we will fit a tree that predicts hourly wages from gender and potential experience. When we call the tree function, we will use mindev=1e-3 to allow for a more complex tree than what you get with the default mindev=0.01.

```
> library(tree)
> pexptree <- tree(hrwage ~ pexp + female, data=cps, mindev=1e-3)
> pexptree
node), split, n, deviance, yval
      * denotes terminal node
  1) root 29217 11020000 20.47
    2) female < 0.5 16690   8075000 23.00
      4) pexp < 12.75 4537    1031000 19.50 *
      5) pexp > 12.75 12153   6968000 24.30
```

```
   10) pexp < 29.25 9996    6230000 25.21 *
   11) pexp > 29.25 2157     691500 20.11 *
 3) female > 0.5 12527    2696000 17.11
  6) pexp < 31.25 11652    2636000 17.40 *
  7) pexp > 31.25 875       47160 13.30 *
```

The printed output for the `tree` object shows a series of decision nodes and the average hourly wage at these nodes, down to the leaves.

Visualizing CART

Trees are easiest to understand in a *dendrogram* plot—a diagram of internal splits, ending in leaf-node decisions. To get this in R you need two steps: first `plot` the tree outline and second add the `text`. We will plot the tree in gray so that it is easier to read the labels when they are superimposed.

```
> plot(pexptree, col="grey50")
> text(pexptree)
```

Figure 7.2a shows the resulting diagram. The value printed at each leaf node is $\hat{y}$, the predicted expected hourly wage at that leaf. This is simply the average of `hrwage` for observations allocated to that leaf. The vertical lines of the dendrogram have length that is proportional to the drop in deviance due to the partitioning implied by the associated node.

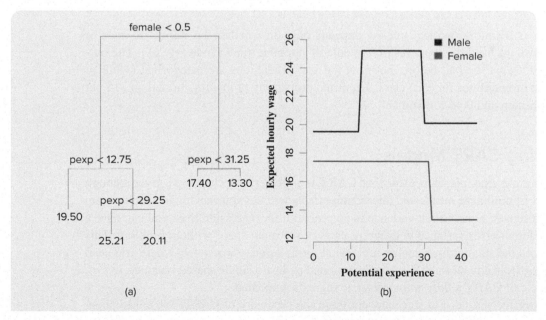

FIGURE 7.2   CART fit for predicting hourly wages from potential experience and gender. The dendrogram plot is in (7.2a) and in (7.2b) we show expected hourly wages as functions of experience for both men and women. Note that for the dendrogram an observation goes to the left child when the node statement is true and to the right when it is false. For example, the root node (`female<0.5`) splits men (`female=0`) to the left and women (`female=1`) to the right.

Since the input space is so simple here (one continuous input and one binary input), you can also visualize the fitted response surface. Figure 7.2b shows predicted $\hat{y}$ values for men and women as a function of their potential experience. We see that men have a higher expected wage during their prime working years (roughly 10–30 years experience), while for women their expected wage is flat until it drops near retirement age. Note that we didn't specify an interaction between gender and experience when we called `tree`, but the CART algorithm automatically detected that the impact of experience on wages depends upon gender. As a historical note, automatic interaction detection (AID) was an original motivation for building decision trees, and older algorithms have AID in their name (e.g., CHAID).

CART for Categorical Response

To illustrate how this works with a categorical response, we can also fit a tree to predict whether or not someone makes more than \$15/hour.

```
> probtree <- tree(factor(hrwage>15) ~ pexp + female, data=cps)
> probtree
node), split, n, deviance, yval, (yprob)
      * denotes terminal node
1) root 29217 40240 TRUE ( 0.4528 0.5472 )
  2) female < 0.5 16690 22070 TRUE ( 0.3740 0.6260 ) *
  3) female > 0.5 12527 17200 FALSE ( 0.5577 0.4423 ) *
```

The result is a simple two-leaf tree—$\hat{y}$ depends only on whether the subject is male or female—because we used the more restrictive default stopping rule (`mindev=0.01`). The output is similar to what we had before, but now the leaf predictions are categorical (`TRUE` or `FALSE`) and the probabilities for each class. The fitted probability of making more than \$15 per hour is 0.63 for men and 0.44 for women.

7.1.1 Pruning CART Models

Even in this simple example, it is clear that CART is a powerful technology: given enough data, trees will fit nonlinear means and interaction effects without your having to specify them in advance. Moreover, nonconstant variance is no problem: for regression trees you can have a completely different error variance in different parts of the input space without problem. This all contrasts with the standard parametric regression formulation, $y = \mathbf{x}'\beta + \varepsilon$, where you need to pick the design $\mathbf{x}$ in advance and ε is usually assumed to have a single shared variance, say σ^2. This is why we call CART a *fully nonparametric* regression method.

To avoid overfit, you need to somehow constrain the flexibility of CART. We talked about stopping rules already, but without looking at the data it is difficult to figure out the right place to stop. One approach for selecting the optimal stopping point is to apply our usual selection routine: build a *path* of candidate models and apply CV. Candidate CART models are ordered through a pruning process: fit an overgrown tree (deeper than you think will work well for prediction) and prune it backward by iteratively removing the leaf splits (those right above the leaf nodes) that yield the lowest in-sample error reduction. This reversal of the CART growth process yields a *pruning path* of candidate trees, and you can use cross-validation to choose the best model from this set (tools like AICc don't apply because there is no good estimate of degrees of freedom for trees).

Example 7.2 Census Income Data: Pruning CART To illustrate the process of pruning a CART fit, we include all of the other demographic variables to build a more complex tree to predict hourly wages.

```
> wagetree <- tree(hrwage ~ ., data=cps, mindev=1e-3)
```

The full (potentially overgrown) fitted tree is shown in Figure 7.3.

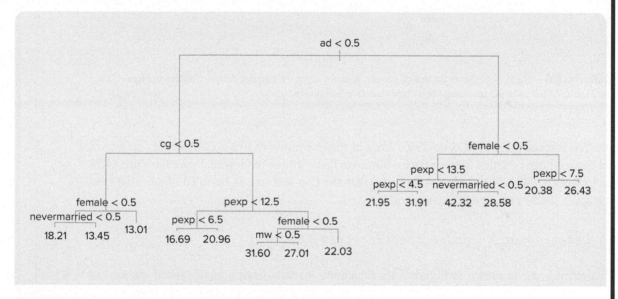

FIGURE 7.3   The unpruned CART model fit to predict hourly wages given all the demographic variables and potential experience.

The `cv.tree` function takes this fitted tree object and executes a CV pruning routine over *K* folds.

```
> cvwt <- cv.tree(wagetree, K=10)
```

The resulting object contains out-of-sample `deviance` for trees of each candidate `size` (number of leaf nodes) along the pruning path. You can visualize the OOS performance by plotting the `deviance` against the `size`.

```
> plot(cvwt$size, cvwt$dev)
```

The result is shown in Figure 7.4a.

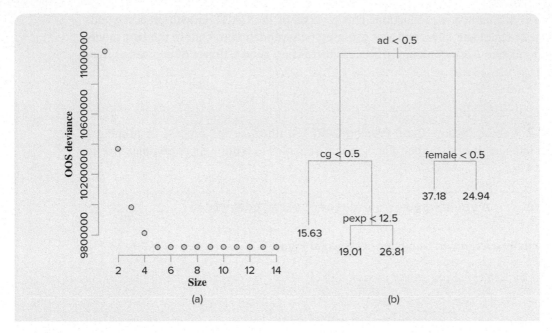

FIGURE 7.4 Figure 7.4a shows the out-of-sample deviance along the pruning path for the tree in Figure 7.3, and Figure 7.4b shows the resulting "best" tree with five leaf nodes.

You can see that the OOS deviance drops as the tree grows to five nodes and then it flattens out across more complex (deeper) trees. Since we favor simple models that give the same OOS performance, this CV experiment indicates that the five-leaf tree is best. To obtain that tree, you apply the `prune.tree` function with `best=5`.

```
> wagetreecut <- prune.tree(wagetree, best=5)
```

This pruned tree is shown in Figure 7.4b. Education matters: having an advanced degree (`ad` equal to one, reported as `ad>0.5` in the plot) or being a college graduate (`cg`) both lead to higher expected wages. Women with an advanced degree are still expected to earn only 2/3 of what men earn with advanced degrees.

■ 7.2 Random Forests

Trees seem great. And we will see that they play an important role in machine learning. Unfortunately, they have a number of limitations that reduce the usefulness of CART. Most importantly, the algorithm is so flexible that it is difficult to avoid overfit and choose a single "best" tree model. The CV routine that we just described does not work reliably in practice. The individual tree fits are very *unstable:* if you change the data slightly, you can get a very different model fit and out-of-sample predictive performance. When prediction rules are highly variable across the model path—here, the iteratively pruned trees—the CV estimates of OOS performance will vary dramatically across samples. This means that the model choice and predictions will have high variance, leading to a large average squared prediction error.

The solution to these issues is not to give up on trees, but rather to use *many trees* together to get a more stable and high-performing prediction algorithm. Breiman (1996) was among the first to highlight the problems of using CV selection on unstable models. As a fix he proposed the technique of *bagging,* which is a blend of the phrase "bootstrap aggregating." Recall the bootstrap from Chapter 2: you rerun your algorithm (e.g., regression) on multiple with-replacement samples of the data to mimic the sampling uncertainty for the fit on your original data. Following this logic, the *mean* fit across bootstrap samples is then an estimate of the *average* model fit. If you have a procedure that is unbiased but has high sampling variance, then the bootstrap mean will be a better model to use than the full-sample data fit. This is the premise behind bagging.

Bagging works best when the individual models are both simple but flexible so that you can quickly fit many *unbiased* (but overfit) models. CART trees are a perfect candidate. Indeed, the bagging of CART trees is the essence of the celebrated *random forest* (RF) algorithm of Breiman (2001). RFs fit CART trees on with-replacement samples of the data, and the resulting prediction rule is the *average* of the predictions from each tree in the bootstrap sample. The RF fitting procedure is outlined in Algorithm 7.2.

Algorithm 7.2 Random Forest (RF)

Say B is the bootstrap size (i.e., the number of trees in the forest).
For $b = 1 \ldots B$:

1. Sample with-replacement n observations from the data.

2. Fit a CART tree, say T_b, to this sample.

This results in a "forest" of trees $T_1 \ldots T_B$. The forest predictions are the average of individual tree predictions. If $\hat{y}_{fb}$ is the prediction for $\mathbf{x}_f$ from tree T_b, then the random forest prediction is $\hat{y}_f = \frac{1}{B}\Sigma_b\hat{y}_{fb}$.

Note that some RF algorithms use variations of CART in step 2 of Algorithm 7.2. For example, it is common to randomize the variables that are eligible to serve as a splitting variable at each node. This causes each tree in the forest to be more different from each other than if we applied the CART of Algorithm 7.1.

Example 7.3 Motorcycle Data: Random Forests To build intuition about random forests, we will start by visualizing a simple one-dimensional regression problem. The motorcycle data contained in the MASS package are 133 measurements of acceleration on a motorcycle rider's helmet in the moments after a head-on collision (this is data from crash-test dummies). Input x is time-since-impact and response y is acceleration. Figure 7.5 shows the data and CART fit. Even though this is a simple 1-D prediction problem, it illustrates the flexibility of CART: the tree is able to follow a nonlinear mean with highly variable errors (e.g., response variance at impact is low relative to the variability after whiplash).

Each tree in a random forest is fit to a resample of the data. Figure 7.6 illustrates this procedure: each bootstrap sample leads to a slightly different CART fit because the more heavily

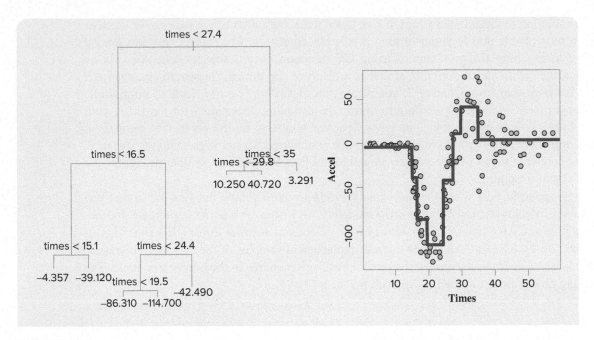

FIGURE 7.5 CART fit for the motorcycle data. The dendrogram on the left corresponds to the red prediction surface on the right.

weighted observations (those resampled more times) pull on the response surface. Figure 7.7 shows how the sampled CART fits accumulate and aggregate—for a forest with many trees, the average becomes a smooth (or mostly smooth) surface even though the constituent trees all imply jagged prediction surfaces. You can also build intuition by thinking about the distribution of trees in the forest as representing uncertainty about the conditional expectation

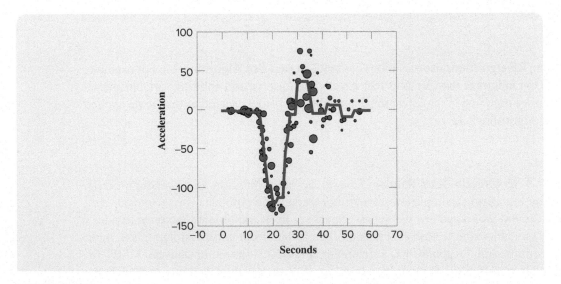

FIGURE 7.6 A single bootstrap draw of the CART fit for the motorcycle data. The points are sized proportional to the number of times they occur in this with-replacement sample draw, and the resulting CART fit is shown in red.

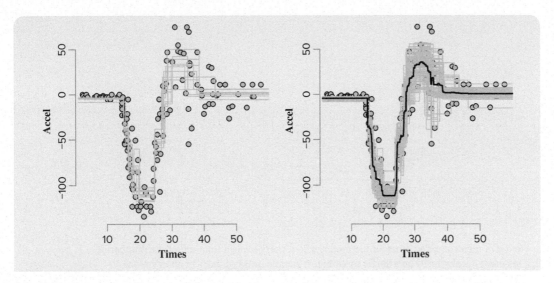

FIGURE 7.7 Bootstrap resampled CART fits for the motorcycle data. The left panel shows 10 fits, and the right shows 100 fits plus their mean in bold.

for y given the inputs (i.e., by thinking about the forest as a sampling distribution). Under this interpretation, Figure 7.7 shows that there is little uncertainty about $\mathbb{E}[y|x]$ at the edges of the time grid but large amounts of uncertainty during the backward-forward acceleration in the middle.

These figures illustrate how the mechanics of bootstrap aggregating act to regularize and avoid overfit: individual trees might be optimized to random noise in the data (i.e., spurious correlations or large idiosyncratic errors), but *by definition* this noisy overfit will not be repeated across many of the resampled CART fits (otherwise it is real structure and not just noise). The noise in the individual fits thus averages out after aggregation, and only the persistent structure survives. This is the massive power of model averaging: it can be used to stabilize and regularize arbitrary algorithms. This strategy features commonly in ML, under many names such as *ensemble learning, Bayesian model averaging,* or *bagging.* The basic idea is always the same: aggregate many models to eliminate the noise.

How Many Trees?

How many trees do you want in your forest? As for the original bootstrapping procedure, the answer is as many as you can get. There is no drawback from including more trees other than the time it takes to compute more CART fits. Each additional tree helps you get a better estimate of the true sampling mean. However, as with any sampling procedure, at a certain point there are diminishing returns for additional trees. Out-of-sample predictive performance tends to improve quickly with the first hundred or so trees and then flatten out as you add more. For example, Figure 7.8 shows that OOS performance for the motorcycle regression improves little beyond that of the 100 tree forest.

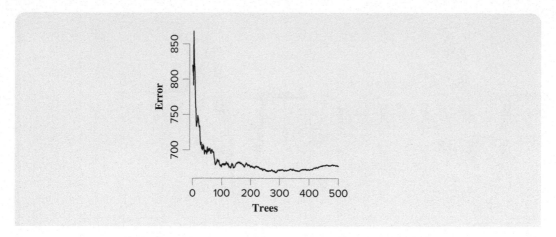

FIGURE 7.8 The OOS mean squared error for the motorcycle regression as a function of the number of trees in the forest. This error is calculated on a single random test sample of 33 of the 133 observations.

Example 7.4 California Home Values: Random Forests Fitting forests in R is easy with the `ranger` package, which uses essentially the same syntax as the `glm` and `tree` functions. To illustrate, we'll consider using census data to predict home prices in California. This is the same data that we used to illustrate Gaussian processes and spatial dependence in Example 1.12. The `CalCensus` data contain median home values for each of 20,640 census tract in California, along with

- Median income
- Latitude and longitude of tract centers
- Population and number of households
- Average room/bedroom numbers, occupancy, and median home age

We will be using trees and forests to predict the log median house value as a function of these census tract characteristics. This is a difficult prediction surface to characterize with a linear model: the covariate effects change nonlinearly in interaction with spatial location. In comparison to our early use of Gaussian processes to study this data, which estimated a smooth dependence function across the state of California, a CART fit will partition the state into different regression relationships for different regions. The random forest aggregate of CART fits will be able to recover a smooth but flexible relationship over the state.

After reading the data into R as the data frame `ca`, we can use `tree` to fit a CART model for predicting log median home values.

```
> ca <- read.csv("CalCensus.csv")
> library(tree)
> catree <- tree(log(medianHouseValue) ~ ., data=ca)
```

Figure 7.9 shows the fitted CART model. Income is a dominant input, and location becomes an important determining variable for low income tracts.

We will apply `ranger` to fit a 200-tree random forest.

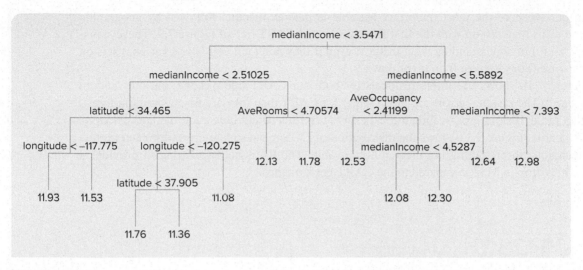

FIGURE 7.9   CART for California housing. Income and home prices (the leaf labels) are expressed in units of $10,000.

```
> library(ranger)
> carf <- ranger(log(medianHouseValue) ~ ., data=ca, num.threads=4,
+               num.tree=200, importance="impurity")
```

The num.threads argument here tells ranger that you want to fit each bootstrap resampled tree in parallel. In this case, we asked it to use four of the processors on our computer. Random forests are indeed a great big data technique: you can fit each tree in parallel, and if you have as many processors as trees in your forest then estimation is as fast as fitting a single CART model.

A disadvantage of moving from a tree to a forest is that you lose the single-tree interpretability of Figure 7.9. However, there are statistics of variable importance that can be used to gain some limited insight. With the argument importance="impurity", ranger tracks each T_b's predictive performance on the *out-of-bag* sample—the observations that were not included in the bth resample. These errors are paired with information about which variables are split upon in each tree. This yields a variable.importance statistic: the increase in error that occurs when that variable is *not* used to define tree splits. As usual, note that you may get different results due to variation in the samples used to fit each tree in the forest.

```
> sort(carf$variable.importance, decreasing=TRUE)
      medianIncome             latitude        longitude       AveOccupancy
        2343.5394            1073.9881        1050.4972          656.6070
         AveRooms    housingMedianAge         AveBedrms          households
         654.2630           259.8661          214.1165          172.7911
       population
         160.4347
```

In our RF here the most important variable is median income, followed by geographic location. This matches up with the first few splits in the CART tree of Figure 7.9. These statistics are useful in understanding what matters, even if they don't tell you how a variable acts on the response (does it make it go up or down?).

Figure 7.10 shows in-sample residuals for both our CART tree `catree` and our random forest `carf`. The residual errors are much larger for CART than they are for the random forest. We also ran a 10-fold cross-validation experiment to understand how each method performs out-of-sample. Figure 7.11 shows the distribution of OOS mean square errors for each regression technique in predicting log median home value. The RF is not overfitting: it provides a nearly 40% drop in MSE compared to the CART performance.

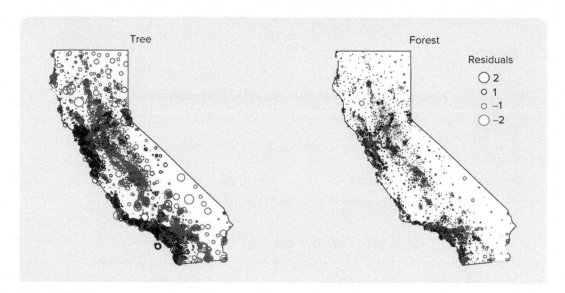

FIGURE 7.10 In-sample residuals for the California home values for CART (tree) and RF (forest) fitted regressions. These images were created using the `maps` package in R.

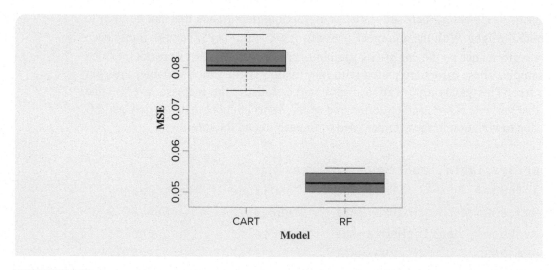

FIGURE 7.11 Out-of-sample performance over 10 random folds for the log median home value prediction.

Other Tree-based Models

Before moving onto some extensions of random forests, we note that RFs are not the only option for stable high-performing tree-based regression. The most important alternative class of tree-based algorithms, beyond random forests, are the gradient boosting machines (GBMs) of Friedman (2001). GBMs make use of the boosting procedure that we will introduce in Chapter 8 as the basis for partial least squares. They iteratively estimate a sequence of shallow trees, each trained to predict the residuals of the previous tree. This leads to a prediction rule that combines many simple (and stable) trees. In practice, RFs can be easier to work with because GBMs require a CV routine to choose when to stop boosting (whereas RFs are naturally regularized through the bootstrap averaging). However, there are many examples of successful industrial-scale GBM deployments, and if you find yourself working in a shop that prefers boosting over forests you don't need to worry.

■ 7.3 Causal Inference with Random Forests

In Chapter 6 we described how you can use prediction tools (like RFs) for use in causal inference through a process of *residualization*. The assumption of conditional ignorability allows you to recover the causal effect of treatment d on response y if you can properly control for the confounders $\mathbf{x}$. The double ML procedure does this through the following recipe:

1. Estimate $\hat{y} \approx \mathbb{E}[y|\mathbf{x}]$ and calculate residuals $\tilde{y}_i = y_i - \hat{y}_i$.
2. Estimate $\hat{d} \approx \mathbb{E}[d|\mathbf{x}]$ and calculate residuals $\tilde{d}_i = d_i - \hat{d}_i$.
3. Regress response residuals $\tilde{y}$ on treatment residuals $\tilde{d}$.

The estimated regression relationship in the third step here can be interpreted as a causal treatment effect. In Chapter 6 we used Lasso methods for the residualization steps. However, double ML can make use of any flexible ML methodology. Random forests are a perfect candidate for the two residualization steps.

Example 7.5 Census Income Data: Double ML We will revisit the census wage data from Examples 7.1 and 7.2, and investigate the treatment effect of gender (`female`) on the expected hourly wage.

To execute double ML, we first pull out `female` as the treatment variable and use `ranger` to predict this variable from the controls (all the other demographic variables). In Chapter 3 we used a cross-fitting procedure that provided out-of-sample residuals and allowed us to obtain theoretically valid standard errors. For simplicity, we will use in-sample residuals here and recover a point estimate of the treatment effect of gender on wages.

```
> d <- cps$female
> drf <- ranger(d ~., data=cps[,-(1:2)],
+               num.tree=400, min.node.size=1000)
> dhat <- predict(drf, cps[,-1])
> dtil <- cps$female-dhat$predictions
```

The result is our residualized treatment `dtil`. We repeat the same residualization via RF prediction on the response, `hrwage`.

```
> y <- cps$hrwage
> yrf <- ranger(y ~., data=cps[,-(1:2)],
+              num.tree=400, min.node.size=1000)
> yhat <- predict(yrf, cps[,-1])
> ytil <- cps$hrwage-yhat$predictions
```

Finally, we can do the residuals-on-residuals regression to recover the average treatment effect of being a woman on hourly wage.

```
> glm(ytil ~ dtil-1)
...
Coefficients:
   dtil
-6.154
```

We've estimated a roughly $6 decrease in hourly wages *due* to being a woman after you condition on experience, education, marital status, and location. That is around 30% of the average wage in this data.

Following the methods of Section 6.3 (and Equation 6.18 in particular), you can also estimate heterogeneous treatment effects using these treatment and response residuals. To do this, you re-run your residuals-on-residuals regression with the treatment residuals interacted with sources of treatment heterogeneity. For example, consider our original (noncausal) regression of wages onto experience and gender as shown in Figure 7.2. This CART fit suggested that the impact of gender on wages interacts with experience. It also found that there are distinct wage expectations for potential experience of roughly less than ten years (early career), from ten to thirty years (prime career), and thirty or more years (approaching retirement). We can use this insight to create factor variables to index heterogeneity in the treatment effect of gender on wages.

```
> pefac <- cut(cps$pexp, c(0,10,30,Inf),right=FALSE)
> head(pefac)
[1] [10,30)   [30,Inf) [10,30)   [10,30)   [10,30)   [10,30)
Levels: [0,10) [10,30) [30,Inf)
```

Via the cut function, we have sliced the pexp variable into bins of pexp < 10, $10 \leq$ pexp < 30, and pexp ≥ 30. Note that the right=FALSE argument says to keep the intervals open on the right and closed on the left.

When we interact this pefac variable with the treatment residuals in our residuals-on-residuals regression, we get a different treatment effect for each potential experience category. Note that in the formula below we remove the main effects for pexp and the intercept since they are unecessary in these residuals-on-residuals regressions (see Equation 6.18). We also remove the main effect for dtil so that the resulting coefficients are readable as a gender-wage effect for each experience category.

```
> coef(glm(ytil ~ dtil*pefac - pefac - dtil -1, data=cps))
   dtil:pefac[0,10)    dtil:pefac[10,30)   dtil:pefac[30,Inf)
          -3.518066           -6.971185            -5.686618
```

The result is that the counterfactual drop in hourly wages for women is \$3.50 early in their career, \$7.00 in their working prime, and \$5.70 late career. Again, you may get slightly different results due to the random variation in fitting a random forest.

Random forests are a great option to use as your residualization model in double ML. In addition, the tactic we used above to construct HTEs—using a simple CART tree fit to help guide construction of the sources of heterogeneity—is a useful trick when you want to transform a continuous variable like pexp into a discrete set of categories. There is also an active literature on causal inference algorithms that are specifically built around tree algorithms. Athey and Imbens (2016) propose the 'causal tree' algorithm as a simple extension of the usual CART algorithm. Instead of choosing splits to minimize prediction deviance, you choose the tree splits to *maximize* the squared difference between estimated treatment effects in each child node. These ideas are extended to forests in Athey et al. (2017), which describes a generalized random forest framework that includes ensembles of causal trees. The grf package implements these and other tree-based causal inference methods.

◆ 7.4 Distributed Computing for Random Forests

The RF algorithm is naturally parallelized: each CART tree can be fit in parallel, the same as we used parallel computing to speed up all of our bootstraps in Chapter 2. Indeed, ranger allows you to specify the num.threads argument to use multiple threads on your computer. However, this parellelization relies on copying a full bootstrap resample to each processor for each CART fit. That creates a lot of data copy overhead, and if you have really big data then it means you will need a lot of working memory for each processor. In industry, engineers have developed a number of work-arounds to deal with this issue of memory limits. One common strategy is to replace the with-replacement sampling of RFs with subsampling: each tree is fit to a without-replacement sample of size smaller than *n* (small enough to fit on a single core). This leads to what we call a *subsampling forest*, in which each tree has been fit to a small random data subset.

This is a bad idea. Subsampling forests tend to have sharply worse predictive performance than RFs. Understanding this gets to the heart of nonparametric analysis. Methods such as trees lead to increasingly complex surfaces as you give them more data. The idea of RFs is to take advantage of this nonparametric adaptivity while using bootstrap aggregation to avoid overfit. If you replace the bootstrapping with subsampling, then you are starving your nonparametric models (the trees) of the data that they need to perform well.

While working with eBay, one of us noticed a prediction performance decrease because of a switch from full RFs to subsampling forests. We also noticed that when you have a large dataset, the *tops* (or trunks—the first few splits) of the trees in a forest are mostly similar. For example, fitting CART to the California housing data down to a minimum leaf size of 3,500 observations results in the *trunk* shown in Figure 7.12. After fitting an RF to the same data (using the version of Algorithm 7.2 that doesn't randomly sample inputs for each split), a comparison across trees in the forest shows that they all have a trunk structure similar to that of Figure 7.12. In particular, that *exact* trunk occurs 62% of the time. The second-most common trunk, occurring 28% of the time, differs only in that it splits on median income again instead of on housing median age. Thus, 90% of the bootstrap sample consists of trees that split on income twice and then latitude. Moreover, 100% of trees have their first two splits on median income. Figure 7.13 shows the locations of these first two splits: each split-location is concentrated around the trunk split in Figure 7.12.

Algorithm 7.3 **Empirical Bayesian Forest (EBF)**

Given *K* distributed processing units,

- Fit a CART trunk down to *K* nodes—the trunk *branches*. If the data is massive (i.e., too big to fit on a single machine), then you can fit this trunk on a subsample. Since you are fitting only the first few tree splits, which correspond to dominant sources of response variation, you do not need big data to do a good job of estimation.
- This trunk then defines a mapper function in the MapReduce algorithm: `map` each observation to its allocated trunk branch and then `reduce` on each branch by fitting a full random forest. This returns the fitted EBF: a fixed trunk with RF models at each branch.

This trunk stability occurs with only 20,000 observations. The stability increases dramatically for the millions-plus observation datasets encountered in industrial big data settings. This all suggests an obvious distributed computing strategy for forests: since the trunks in the forest are all the same, just fit the trunk once and then use it to partition the data and facilitate parallelization. This is the empirical Bayesian forest (EBF) method proposed in Taddy et al. (2015) and outlined in Algorithm 7.2.

The result is a sort of hybrid CART-RF object, with fixed initial splits and a bootstrap sample of trees for deeper structure. Since the hypothetical (potentially infeasible) full sample

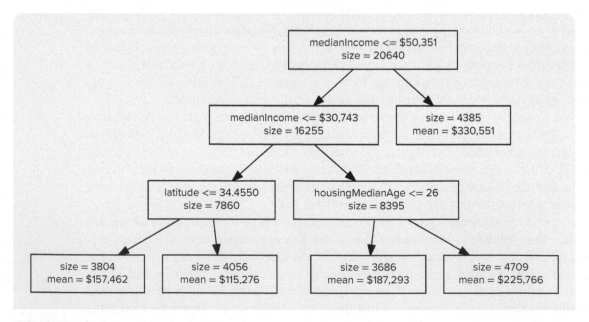

FIGURE 7.12 The trunk of the California housing tree that results when fitting with a minimum leaf size of 3500 (out of 20,640 total census tracts).

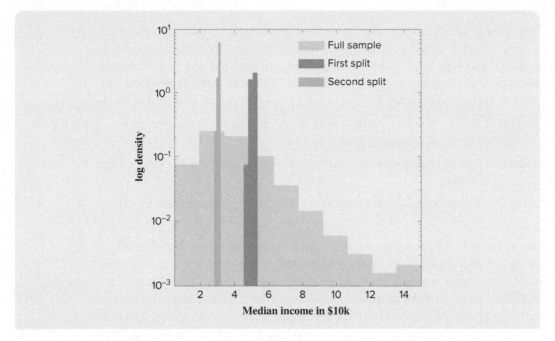

FIGURE 7.13   The distribution of median income and of the first two split locations for trees in the housing forest.

RF has the same trunk for most trees, this EBF will lead to similar predictions. In the California housing example, an EBF with the trunk of Figure 7.12 has 2% worse predictive performance than the full sample RF, compared with 10% worse for a subsampling forest of comparable computational cost. For large datasets the results are more dramatic; Taddy et al. (2015) show EBFs are 1% to 4% worse than a full RF on examples where the subsampling forests are 12% to 38% worse.

In massive data environments, simple efficient strategies like Algorithm 7.3 allow you to crunch more data faster (see the box "Distribution and Big Data"). And more data always wins: even though an EBF does a bit worse than a full RF on the same dataset, an EBF with more data will give better predictions than a small-sample RF. For prediction tasks, never reduce the amount of data you can work with to fit some fancy but computationally costly model—you're better off with a simple but flexible model fit to as much data as you can get your hands on.

Distribution and Big Data

The EBF in Algorithm 7.3 is designed for distributed data computing where data is analyzed on independent computers that do not need to talk with each other. The idea behind contemporary big data is to *shard* your data into many little pieces on many machines and then take advantage of massive bandwidth to allow communication between these machines during analysis. Systems such as Hadoop HDFS, Amazon's S3, or Microsoft's Azure Blob Storage split your data into little pieces (e.g., 64KB of a file) that are kept wherever is convenient. As the end user, you interact only with a map of where things are.

There are plenty of algorithms that have been developed to facilitate statistical analysis on these massive distributed datasets. Many fit within a framework known as *MapReduce* (MR), a simple but powerful recipe for algorithms that was popularized in 2004 by researchers at Google (Dean and Ghemawat, 2004). To use MapReduce, you need to be able to specify a *key* indexing data to subgroups that can be analyzed in isolation. You then proceed to

- `map`: Calculate and sort relevant statistics by key.
- Partition and pipe the outcome of `map` so that outcomes with the same key end up on the same machine.
- `reduce`: Apply a summarization operation within the subgroup defined by each key.

As a simple example, imagine the task of tabulating word occurrence by date across a large database of documents (e.g., books, magazines, newspapers). A `map` operation for each document outputs multiple lines, as in `date|word count`. For example, we have `2017/06/04|tacos 5` if the document uses the word `tacos` five times on June 4, 2017. The *key* in this example is `date|word`, for example, `2017/06/04|tacos`. The data is sorted and streamed so that each line with the same key ends up on the same reducer machine. The `reduce` operation then sums all lines with the same key (which are all on the same computer, so this is fast and easy).

This simple example can be extended into a number of more complex schemes. For example, in Algorithm 7.3 the shallow tree trunk defines how you map observations to computers and the reducer fits a random forest to each subset. Distributed machine learning algorithms like EBF can be fit using frameworks such as `Spark`, a layer built on top of a distributed storage system that makes it easier to incorporate machine learning and statistical algorithms. A technical guide to a framework like `Spark` is beyond the scope of this text, but there is abundant training material available if you do a quick Internet search. Those of you who are interested in engineering and large-scale data science might want to invest in learning the tools; you will find that these skills are in high demand in industry.

QUICK REFERENCE

This chapter started with single tree models and CART, but we learned that tree models are most useful when combined together in a forest. The technique of bagging averages across many fitted models and it yields a much higher performing prediction algorithm than any single model fit. Random forests are a workhorse of ML: they provide flexible prediction while avoiding overfit.

Key Practical Concepts

- With a data frame `data` containing response `y` along with input features, estimate a CART model using the `tree` library.

  ```
  datatree <- tree( y ~ ., data=data )
  ```

- Use `ranger` with `num.tree=B` to fit an ensemble of B trees in a random forest.

  ```
  datarf <- ranger( y ~., data=data, num.tree=200,
  num.threads=4)
  ```

  The `num.threads` argument is used to parallelize tree fits across your computer processors. You can also use the `min.node.size` argument to limit the depth of the trees in your forest and make the algorithm run faster. You can call `predict` on `rf` using the usual syntax to get predictions from this RF.

- Adding the `importance="impurity"` argument leads `ranger` to produce variable importance statistics ranking the input variables by their impact on predictive performance.

  ```
  sort( datarf$variable.importance, decreasing=TRUE )
  ```

- For categorical response `y`, run `ranger` with `prob=TRUE` to fit a forest with predictive probabilities at each tree leaf (see examples in Chapter 9).

8 FACTOR MODELS

This chapter introduces dimension reduction via factorization—modeling high-dimensional data as being generated by a low-dimensional set of underlying factors.

● **Section 8.1 Clustering:** Represent random distributions through mixture models. Use *K*-means to cluster observations according to a simple model with *K* mixture components.

■ **Section 8.2 Factor Models and PCA:** Represent high-dimensional data as the output of a *latent factor model* and understand how to reduce a huge number of variables into a smaller set of factors. Use principal components analysis (PCA) to estimate this low-dimensional factor structure.

■ **Section 8.3 Factor Regression:** Use your *unsupervised* estimates of factor models as inputs to regression models.

◆ **Section 8.4 Partial Least Squares:** Build *supervised* factors that explain dominant sources of variation in your inputs and in a response of interest.

n this chapter, you will learn how to estimate a low-dimensional *factor structure* to represent your high-dimensional data. Factors are latent—that is, unobserved—variables in the data generating process. You observe vectors **x** with dimension J, and model these as having been generated as a function of underlying factors ω with dimension K, where K is much smaller than J ($K \ll J$). Working with latent variables requires a number of new skills and ideas, but once you get the hang of it you will find that factorization is a powerful tool for simplification. Although it is a bit of an art, you can also build interpretations for the underlying factors and this is useful for how you describe and present your analyses.

All of the regression methods we've seen in the book so far have been examples of *supervised learning* where a "response" variable y dictates how you incorporate the **x** variables in your model. In contrast, for *unsupervised learning* there is no response or outcome. You have a high-dimensional **x**, and you try to model it as having been generated from a small number of underlying factors.

Why would you want to estimate this factor structure? As one example, you might have partially observed **x** and want to predict the unknown entries from those you get to see. For example, suppose that **x** is a vector where each element x_j represents the score from 1 to 10 for how much you liked "movie" j. A streaming video service like Netflix or Prime Video tries to predict x_j for movies you haven't seen from those you have watched and scored. Movies with a high expected score are recommended when you are deciding what to watch. Estimating a factor structure in this scenario gives you a representation of underlying preferences: the fact that people tend to like groups of similar movies will be represented in the factor model.

Another common problem is that you really want to predict y from **x**, but you have many observations of **x** without y. For example, you might want to predict the sentiment of people from the words in their tweets; you will have a massive bank of all tweets (lots of **x**) but for only a small percentage will you know whether they are expressing positive or negative sentiment (e.g., by hand-labeling the tweets using human readers). An unsupervised analysis will use all of the tweets to break them down into *topics*, and then you can easily sort these topics by sentiment on the subset of labeled tweets. In the next chapter we will adapt the factorization of this current chapter for text-as-data applications of this sort.

In this chapter, you'll learn about both unsupervised and supervised factorization. The unsupervised methods includes clustering, which is best understood as a simple and restrictive form of factorization, and principal components analysis. For supervised factorization we will learn about the method of partial least squares, a simple but powerful method for constructing a small number of factors that are especially useful in prediction.

● 8.1 Clustering

Cluster analysis is used to group similar observations into groups. This is used to, for example

- Break a corpus of documents into topics.
- Segment shoppers by preferences or price sensitivity.
- Group voters according to the issues that drive their votes.
- Find music listeners who tend to like the same genres or bands.

Clustering works by representing the data as the output of a *mixture model.*

8.1.1 Mixture Models

In a mixture model, you assume that each observed vector $\mathbf{x}_i$ is drawn from one of K different *mixture components,* the probability distributions $p_k(\mathbf{x})$ for $k = 1 \ldots K$. The parameters of these components, especially their means, define the clusters.

Figure 8.1 illustrates a mixture model. The single-dimensional variable x here could be customer spending levels, energy usage, travel times, or any other variable that has multiple modes (bumps). The modes here correspond to each underlying mixture component. The data that you actually observe has the *marginal* distribution drawn as the black curve, $p(x)$. In a mixture model, you assume that this marginal curve is actually generated by data that is clustered around each underlying mixture component, the colored $p_k(x)$ curves. We say that the data *clusters* are those observations that we estimate have been drawn from each underlying *component.* Note that even if the components are well defined, there will be ambiguity about the clusters: the colored distributions overlap in their tails, and it is not possible to determine exactly which component generated each observation. When we cluster data, we will typically assign each observation with the component that has highest probability of having generated that data point.

The marginal distribution for $\mathbf{x}$ can be represented as a linear combination of the mixture components:

$$p(\mathbf{x}) = \pi_1 p_1(\mathbf{x}) + \ldots \pi_K p_K(\mathbf{x}) \qquad (8.1)$$

Here, π_k is the probability for component k in the population. As illustrated in Figure 8.1, even if the individual components are simple distributions with a single mode, their mixture can yield all sorts of complicated distributions.

When you observe your data, you get to see only the marginal distribution for $\mathbf{x}$ (e.g., the black line, $p(x)$, in Figure 8.1). You don't observe the underlying mixture components and you don't know the clusters: Which observations have been allocated to which component. This is why we say that the mixture components are *latent.* They generate your data, but you don't get to directly observe how that data generation occurred. It begs the question: how do we estimate these latent distributions?

To fit the mixture components, we will specify a model and fit the parameters of this model to minimize the deviance. For example, in Figure 8.1 you can see that each component has a mean μ_k. These means are the expected value for an observation x_i given x_i belongs to cluster k. These are *conditional* expectations given cluster membership, which we write in general as

$$\mathbb{E}[\mathbf{x}_i | k_i] = \mu_{k_i}, \, k_i \in \{1 \ldots K\} \qquad (8.2)$$

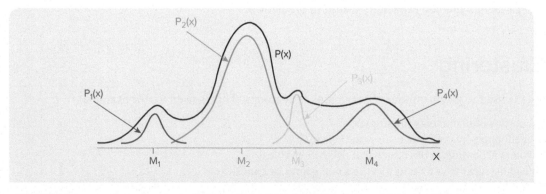

FIGURE 8.1 The unconditional distribution for x is the black function and the individual colored distributions represent the conditional distributions (the distributions for each individual mixture component).

where
- $\mathbf{x}_i$ is the vector of values for the ith observation
- k_i is the component which generated the ith observation
- K is the number of mixture components
- μ_{k_i} is the vector of means for component k_i

The normal-looking curves in Figure 8.1 for each $p_k(x)$ around these means suggest that each mixture component has a Gaussian distribution. This is an example of a Gaussian mixture model where each component distribution has the form

$$p_k(\mathbf{x}) = N(\mathbf{x}; \mu_k, \Sigma_k) \tag{8.3}$$

You will notice that we are working with multivariate $\mathbf{x}$ and multivariate Gaussian distributions here. The example in Figure 8.1 is univariate, which makes it easy to visualize. But you will usually have a number of different variables (dimensions) for each observation and your mixture model will need to account for all of them. For example, if each observation is a customer you might observe the dimensions of monthly spending and their tenure (how long they have been a customer). You want to estimate a mixture model that clusters customers jointly on these two dimensions, and to do so you could use a *bivariate* version of the multivariate Gaussian component model in Equation (8.3).

8.1.2 *K*-means

K-means is by far the most common algorithm that is used for clustering: for estimating the underlying μ_k mixture component centers and allocating each observation to its highest probability component. It is an *iterative least squares* algorithm: it iterates between choosing the mixture component membership for each observation, k_i, and then using the mean of the observations allocated to each component to estimate its mean, μ_k. The "least squares" element here is that it chooses each k_i by minimizing the squared distance between $\mathbf{x}_i$ and its assigned component mean. After you have run *K*-means, you will have a set of *cluster centers*—the estimated component means $\hat{\mu}_k$—and a cluster membership k_i for each observation. A bivariate example is illustrated in Figure 8.2.

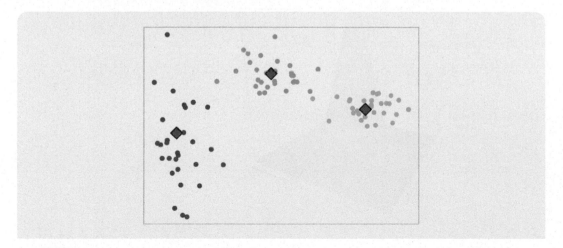

FIGURE 8.2   Illustration of a converged *K*-means procedure for $K = 3$ with two observation dimensions. The centers μ_k are marked and observations are colored according to the assigned cluster membership, k_i.

Algorithm 8.1 *K*-Means

To cluster observations $\{\mathbf{x}_i\}_{i=1}^n$ into K groups, initialize by *randomly* drawing $k_i \in \{1 \dots K\}$ for each i. Then, until convergence:

- Estimate

$$\hat{\mu}_k = \bar{\mathbf{x}}_k = \frac{1}{n_k} \sum_{i:k_i=k} \mathbf{x}_i$$

  where $\{i:k_i = k\}$ are the n_k observations that have $k_i = k$.

- For each i, update k_i to the component with center $\hat{\mu}_k$ closest to $\mathbf{x}_i$, by minimizing the sum of squared distances:

$$k_i = \operatorname{argmin}_k \sum_j \left(x_{ij} - \hat{\mu}_{kj} \right)^2$$

The *K*-means algorithm can be thought of as estimating a Gaussian mixture model with components as in (8.3), but where the $\mathbf{\Sigma}_k$ variance matrices are restricted to take the form

$$\mathbf{\Sigma}_k = \operatorname{diag}(\sigma_k^2) = \begin{bmatrix} \sigma_k^2 & 0 & & & \\ 0 & \sigma_k^2 & & \ddots & \\ & & \ddots & & \\ & \ddots & & \sigma_k^2 & 0 \\ & & & 0 & \sigma_k^2 \end{bmatrix}. \tag{8.4}$$

Recalling what you know about variance-covariance matrices, the diagonal entries here are the variances for each dimension of $\mathbf{x}$ and the off-diagonal entries are the covariances between dimensions. In the specification of (8.4), we have a single shared variance term for all dimensions (σ_k^2) and the dimensions are all *independent* from each other (zeros in the off-diagonal entries). A bivariate Gaussian distribution corresponding to this "shared-variance and zero-covariance" specification is shown in Figure 8.3.

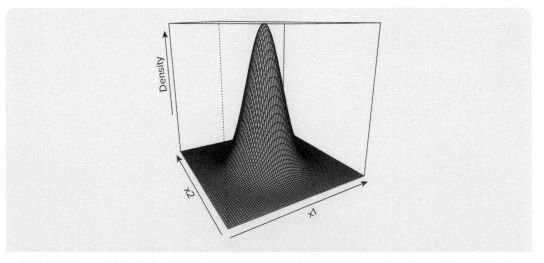

FIGURE 8.3 Graph of a bivariate Gaussian distribution with $\boldsymbol{\mu} = \mathbf{0}$, shared variance σ^2, and $\operatorname{cov}(x_1, x_2) = 0$. The height of the distribution is the likelihood (i.e., probability density) for an observation at that $[x_1, x_2]$ location.

The independence implied by the $\boldsymbol{\Sigma}$ in (8.4) is unrealistic for many applications. For example, if our data dimensions are customer spend and tenure then these two variables are likely related (older customers spend more?). However, the assumption of independence makes it much easier to fit a mixture model and this convenience is a big part of the popularity of K-means. This independence allows us to write (8.3), the conditional likelihood for an observation *given* its cluster membership k_i, as a product of univariate Gaussian distributions:

$$p(\mathbf{x}_i|k_i) = p_{k_i}(\mathbf{x}_i) = \prod_{j=1}^{J} N\left(x_j; \mu_{k_ij}, \sigma_{k_i}^2\right) \tag{8.5}$$

where J is the dimension of your observations (the length of $\mathbf{x}_i$), μ_{k_ij} is the mean for the jth dimension of mixture component k, and σ_k^2 is the common variance for all dimensions of component k. This likelihood implies the least-squares calculation in Algorithm 8.1.

Data Scaling for *K*-Means

The assumption of a single shared variance for each component, σ_k^2 for all dimensions of $\mathbf{x}$, is also restrictive. However, you can mitigate issues due to this assumption by making sure to transform all dimensions of $\mathbf{x}$ to have the same variance before running K-means. That is, you work with variables that have been divided by their *standard deviation* and fit K-means to the transformed $x_{ij} = (x_{ij} - \bar{x}_j)/\mathrm{sd}(x_j)$. These new units are also shifted to have mean of zero and are thus interpretable as units of *standard deviations from the pooled average*. This scaling is easy to do in R by applying the `scale` function to your X matrix of observations.

```
Xdot <- scale(X)
```

Example 8.1 **Uber Pickups: *K*-means** To illustrate the K-means procedure, we will consider clustering pickup locations for the Uber ride-hailing service. We have a sample of 60k Uber pickups in New York City from April to September 2014 (10k per each month). The data contain for each pickup the time and location that the pickup occurred. We'll read this information into R as the uber data frame.

```
> uber <- read.csv("uber.csv")
> head(uber)
          Date.Time        Lon       Lat
1 4/30/2014 17:10:00  -73.9423   40.7215
2 4/17/2014 16:41:00  -73.9928   40.7447
3 4/17/2014 21:04:00  -73.9930   40.7323
4 4/15/2014 16:00:00  -74.0081   40.7484
5 4/23/2014 16:00:00  -73.9602   40.7580
6 4/23/2014 10:51:00  -73.9866   40.7427
> dim(uber)
[1] 60000       3
```

We will be clustering pickup locations by applying *K*-means on the longitude (Lon) and latitude (Lat) columns. The centers of the estimated mixture model could be useful, for example, to guide where Uber locates physical hubs that provide supplies and support for drivers.

Applying *K*-means in R is easy with the kmeans function. You supply it with your data and specify a number of centers and then it iterates through Algorithm 8.1. Another useful argument is nstart which specifies the number of times that you want to re-run Algorithm 8.1 from a different *random* initialization (i.e., from a different random k_i start for each observation). *K*-means is the first *nonconvex* deviance minimization algorithm that we have encountered in this book. Nonconvexity says that the deviance surface is not a simple cup (e.g., like x^2) that has one single minimum; rather, it is a lumpy surface that can have multiple solutions where the k_i can converge in Algorithm 8.1. For this reason, it is often recommended that you run *K*-means multiple times from different random starts and use the solution that gives the lowest deviance (lowest sum squared error around the $\hat{\mu}_k$ centers).

We will apply kmeans on the raw longitude and latitude data using 3 random starts and 10 centers (i.e., assuming 10 underlying mixture components).

```
> hubs <- kmeans(uber[,2:3], centers=10, nstart=3)
```

Note that, contrary to our recommendation above, we did not scale the locations before giving them to kmeans. That is unnecessary here because longitude and latitude are a regular coordinate system. But you can try running the above code on scale(uber[,2:3]) instead and see how the results change.

The fitted kmeans object hub includes the centers element, which is a matrix containing the fitted component centers μ_k for $k = 1, \ldots, 10$. Using the maps package, we can produce Figure 8.4 showing the fitted centers on an outline of NYC area counties.

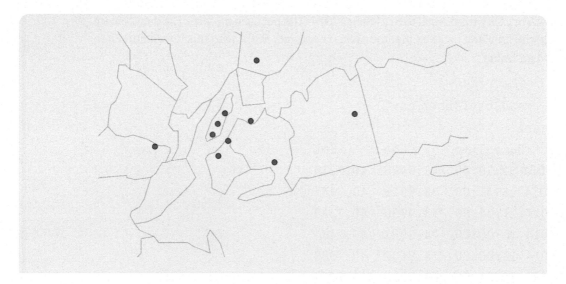

FIGURE 8.4 Fitted *K*-means component centers (red dots) for Uber pickup locations throughout the New York City area. Grey lines are county borders.

```
> library(maps)
> map('county', c('new york','new jersey'), col="grey60",
+     xlim=c(-74.4,-73.1), ylim=c(40.4,41))
> points(hubs$centers, pch=21, bg=2)
```

Interpreting these centers as potential driver hubs, we see that the algorithm has reasonably placed three hubs in Manhattan (moving north from downtown) and spaced the others out in the surrounding boroughs and suburbs. The `hubs` object also includes the fitted cluster membership for each observation, k_i, as the `cluster` entry. Your results will vary because of the random initialization of the K-means procedure (and with different runs the cluster numbering can change even if the members of each cluster remains the same).

```
> head(hubs$cluster)
[1] 7 4 1 1 4 4
```

Additional available information includes `tot.withinss`, the total sum squared error for the fitted mixture model. This is the deviance that K-means is fit to minimize, and it is obtained by summing the differences $(x_{ij} - \mu_{kj})$ across all observations i and dimensions j.

Mixture modeling is a rich topic, and there are many more sophisticated algorithms for fitting mixtures and clustering than the K-means procedure. Most algorithms improve upon the approach of Algorithm 8.1 by replacing the step that allocates each observation to a single k_i with a step that calculates the *probability* that each observation came from each component, say $p(k_i = k)$, given the most recent estimate of the mixture component parameters $\hat{\theta}_k$ (e.g., $\hat{\mu}_k$ and $\hat{\sigma}_k$). You then estimate updated parameters to maximize the *expected* likelihood

$$\sum_{i=1}^{n} \sum_{k=1}^{K} p(k_i = k) p(\mathbf{x}|\theta_k) \tag{8.6}$$

This is called the *expectation maximization* algorithm, and it is the basis for missing data imputation that we will see later in this chapter and the topic modeling that we will see in the next chapter.

Choosing the Number of Mixture Components

Before leaving behind the topic of clustering and mixture models, we can touch on the subject of how to choose K, the number of mixture components. The most important thing to understand is that this is a *subjective choice*. The "true" number of components for the underlying mixture model is not a well-defined target for estimation: the answer will be very sensitive to the assumed structure of the underlying mixture component distributions (e.g., a convenient Gaussian) and in most cases you will find that the number of useful components increases as you observe more observations. In practice, the number of components you use when clustering will be determined by your application. For example, in our Uber example we presume that Uber would have a budget for building driver hubs and that budget determines the number of centers that you are estimating.

■ 8.2 Factor Models and PCA

Mixture modeling is a special case of the more general *factor model* framework for unsupervised dimension reduction. Suppose that you have high-dimensional observation vectors $\mathbf{x}_i$ for $i = 1, \ldots, n$. A factor model treats each observation as a random draw around a mean that is constructed as a linear combination of *factor vectors* $\boldsymbol{\mu}_k$, for $k = 1, \ldots, K$. In an equation, a factor model has

$$\mathbb{E}[\mathbf{x}_i|\boldsymbol{\omega}_i] = \omega_{i1}\boldsymbol{\mu}_1 + \ldots + \omega_{iK}\boldsymbol{\mu}_K \tag{8.7}$$

where

- $\mathbf{x}_i$ is observation i which has length J
- $\boldsymbol{\mu}_k$ is the length J factor vector for "direction" k
- ω_{ik} are univariate factor values indicating how observation i depends on factor direction k

The language of factor models is motivated by linear algebra. We think about the underlying factor vectors as representing a direction or axis in J-dimensional space, and the factor values are coordinates along the corresponding axis. We will make the intuition clear through some examples.

You can also expand the model for each individual dimension of $\mathbf{x}$, writing:

$$\mathbb{E}[x_{ij}|\boldsymbol{\omega}_i] = \omega_{i1}\mu_{j1} + \ldots + \omega_{iK}\mu_{jK}, j = 1 \ldots J. \tag{8.8}$$

Equations 8.7 and 8.8 describe the same model. The ω_{ik} values are attached to each observation; they are like your original x_{ij} observations, in that they are specific for each observation i, but they are now unknown *latent* factors that need to be estimated. When you use a K that is much smaller than J, the estimated factors $\boldsymbol{\omega}_i$ provide a parsimonious representation for $\mathbf{x}_i$. The μ_{jk} direction elements are properties of the factor model and are shared across all observations. They are like regression coefficients that translate from ω_{ik} to the expected value for x_{ij}.

Mixture Models as Factor Models

To see the connection between this factor model and our mixture model of the previous section, rewrite the mixture model conditional expectation of (8.2) as

$$\mathbb{E}[\mathbf{x}_i|k_i] = \boldsymbol{\mu}_{k_i} = \sum_{k=1}^{K}\omega_{ik}\boldsymbol{\mu}_k \text{ where } \omega_{ik} = \mathbb{1}_{[k_i=k]} \tag{8.9}$$

such that $\omega_{ik} = 1$ if observation i is drawn from component k and is zero otherwise. Mixture modeling and K-means clustering use a restrictive version of the factor model where the factor values are forced to be all zeros except for a single one. It is a factor model where each observation is generated from only a single factor. In contrast, the general factor model of (8.7) allows for *mixed membership* where each observation is a combination of all of the underlying factor vectors. While clustering is intuitive and has some useful applications (e.g., when you need to tie each pickup to a single hub), the mixed membership approach of general factor models is going to be more useful in a wider variety of problems. When you encounter a clustering approach to an analysis problem, it is usually good to ask yourself if the problem would be better approached through factor modeling.

8.2.1 Principal Components Analysis

Principal components analysis (PCA) is an algorithm for estimating factor models. One way to think about PCA is as a greedy algorithm that iteratively estimates a series of factor values and directions. It starts by finding the initial ω_{i1} and μ_1 parameters that minimize the squared error loss $\Sigma_i \Sigma_j (x_{ij} - \omega_{i1} \mu_{1j})^2$. It then calculates the residuals, $\tilde{\mathbf{x}}_i = \mathbf{x}_i - \omega_{i1} \mu_1$, and finds the next factor parameters ω_{i2} and μ_2 that minimize squared error loss on these residuals. This process—fitting single factors for residuals then calculating remaining residuals—continues until you have K factors. Because of the greedy nature of this algorithm, the first factors will explain the most variation in $\mathbf{x}$ and the later factors contribute less.

Another way to think about PCA is as a decomposition of the observed variance of $\mathbf{x}$—the $J \times J$ variance-covariance matrix for your observed $\mathbf{x}_1, \ldots, \mathbf{x}_n$. The factor values $\boldsymbol{\omega}_i$ are the solution to the *eigenvalue decomposition* of this variance-covariance matrix. This is the way that most PCA algorithms are actually executed. From linear algebra, you can always find a *rotation* matrix that translates from the coordinate system of your covariance matrix (i.e., your original coordinate system for $\mathbf{x}$, where all the dimensions are correlated with each other) to a different coordinate system of J *independent* directions. That is, the eigenvalue decomposition finds new coordinates for your data (combinations of the original data dimensions) such that the data observations are all independent in the new coordinate system.

Visualizing PCA

This is all very abstract, and it helps to visualize how it works in low dimensions. Figure 8.5 illustrates PCA for a 2-dimensional dataset. The red line is the OLS fit for x_2 on x_1 (or vice versa; it's the same line). This line has a *length* spanning the range of observed data, and each data point can be mapped to a location on the line that is closest to its location in $[x_1, x_2]$ coordinates. The slope of the line is defined by a *rotation* vector, $\boldsymbol{\phi}_1$, and each point's mapped location on the line is its factor value, ω_{i1}. In particular, the rotations are defined such that $\omega_{i1} = \phi_{11} x_{i1} + \phi_{12} x_{i2}$. The factor value is a combination of the two original observations, and in general these rotation vectors allow you to calculate your factor values as a linear combination of the original variables. Looking at Figure 8.5 provides intuition about the usefulness of PCA. Because x_1 and x_2 are correlated here, the original points are scattered along the red line. Once you know ω_1, the nearest location on this line, you have a good idea of where x_1 and x_2 are located even if you don't know the specific coordinates.

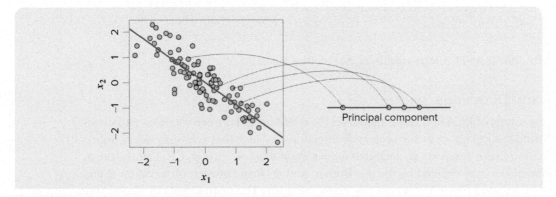

FIGURE 8.5 Illustration of PCA for two-dimensional data. PCA finds the line that fits through x_1 and x_2 and sets the factor value ω as the closest point on the line.

In finding this first principal component (PC), we've projected from 2D onto a new 1D axis (the red line). We described how principal component directions are all *independent* from each other. Visually, that implies that the second principal component direction must be *perpendicular* to the first: it is plotted as the blue line in Figure 8.6. This blue line is defined by the rotation vector $\boldsymbol{\phi}_2$, such that the factor values $\omega_{i2} = \phi_{21}x_{i1} + \phi_{22}x_{i2}$ are the location on the blue line that are closest to each observation. Figure 8.6 shows how subsequent PC directions decrease in importance: knowing where an observation lands on the blue line is much less informative than knowing where it lands on the red line. This decrease in importance is represented in the comparison of the lengths of the two lines: the first direction requires a much longer line to stretch through the data than the second factor direction. This means that the first factor values, ω_{i1}, will have a much higher *variance* than the second factor values, ω_{i2}.

Since we have only two dimensions, this is where the algorithm stops. There is a 1:1 mapping from $[x_1, x_2]$ to the new factor space $[\omega_1, \omega_2]$—every point can be perfectly re-created from its PC1 and PC2 factor values. Figure 8.6 shows that PCA has *rotated* the axes of the data, moving from the original coordinates to a space where most of the data variation is spread along the first coordinate and there is little spread along the second coordinate. In this example, we can summarize most of the variation in the data by keeping track of only the first principal component value, ω_1. In general, PCA will fit as many directions as you have data dimensions (or as you have observations, whichever is smaller). But the power of PCA is that you only need to keep track of the first several— enough to explain the dominant directions of variation in $\mathbf{x}_i$. Moreover, in the new coordinate space the factor dimensions ω_1 and ω_2 are independent from each other: the observations form a flat cloud around the red and blue lines in Figure 8.6 rather than the slanted cloud in the original x_1 and x_2 coordinates. We started with correlated variables, such that one dimension can be predicted from the observation in the other dimension. PCA removes this dependence.

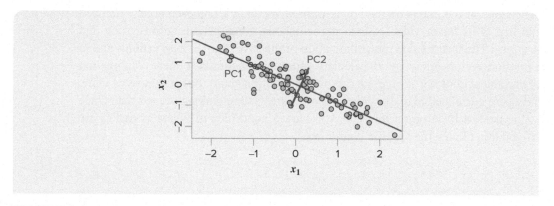

FIGURE 8.6   Two-factor PCA representation of the data from Figure 8.5.

Rotations and Directions

One confusing aspect of PCA and factor models is the relationship between rotations and directions. We started talking about factor vectors or directions, $\boldsymbol{\mu}_k$ such that $\mathbf{x} \approx \omega_1\boldsymbol{\mu}_1 + \ldots \omega_K\boldsymbol{\mu}_K$. And we now have factor rotations $\boldsymbol{\phi}_k$ such that $\omega_k = \mathbf{x}'\boldsymbol{\phi}_k = x_1\phi_{k1} + \ldots x_J\phi_{kJ}$. Evidently, the $\boldsymbol{\mu}_k$ are the inverse of the map defined by the $\boldsymbol{\phi}_k$. Both $\boldsymbol{\mu}_k$ and $\boldsymbol{\phi}_k$ map between observation $\mathbf{x}_i$ and the factor value ω_{ik}, and if you know one you know the other. The main targets of interest are the values, $\boldsymbol{\omega}_i$, and the PCA rotations allow you to calculate these values as a linear combination of the original inputs.

Performing PCA in R

There are a number of functions in R that will do PCA for you. A good robust option is the prcomp function. You give it a numeric matrix X, with n rows and J columns, and it will fit the matrix of rotations $\Phi = [\phi_1 \ldots \phi_D]$ where D is the minimum of n and J (you can't fit more PCs than you have either observations or dimensions). Below is a template for how you can call prcomp.

```
pca <- prcomp(X, scale=TRUE)
```

Note that we specified scale=TRUE here to tell prcomp to fit PCA on a scaled version of X where each column has a standard deviation of one. The columns are also shifted to have a mean of zero by default. You will *almost always* want to scale and shift your data in this way before performing PCA. The exception is if the columns of X are all in the same units and you want the higher variance columns to have a bigger influence on the fitted factor model.

The fitted pca object returned by prcomp contains estimated rotations Φ as the rotations element. You can use these to calculate the factor values or PCs by multiplying them with the scaled data matrix (prcomp just applies this same scale function when scale=TRUE). Below is a template for one way to do this.

```
w <- scale(X)%*%pca$rotation
```

Alternatively, calling predict.prcomp does the same thing.

```
w <- predict(pca)
```

Example 8.2 European Protein Consumption: PCA To illustrate PCA, we will start with a small and intuitive example. We have data on protein consumption by country, in grams per person per day for 25 European nations (note that some of the countries no longer exist; this is old data).

```
> food <- read.csv("protein.csv", row.names=1)
> head(food,4)
         RedMeat WhiteMeat Eggs  Milk Fish Cereals Starch Nuts Fr.Veg
Albania     10.1       1.4  0.5   8.9  0.2    42.3    0.6  5.5    1.7
Austria      8.9      14.0  4.3  19.9  2.1    28.0    3.6  1.3    4.3
Belgium     13.5       9.3  4.1  17.5  4.5    26.6    5.7  2.1    4.0
Bulgaria     7.8       6.0  1.6   8.3  1.2    56.7    1.1  3.7    4.2
```

We can apply `prcomp` to fit PCA and access the resulting rotations.

```
> pcfood <- prcomp(food, scale=TRUE)
> round(pcfood$rotation, 1)
           PC1  PC2  PC3  PC4  PC5  PC6  PC7  PC8  PC9
RedMeat   -0.3 -0.1 -0.3 -0.6  0.3 -0.5  0.2  0.0  0.2
WhiteMeat -0.3 -0.2  0.6  0.0 -0.3 -0.1  0.0  0.0  0.6
Eggs      -0.4  0.0  0.2 -0.3  0.1  0.4 -0.4 -0.5 -0.3
Milk      -0.4 -0.2 -0.4  0.0 -0.2  0.6  0.5  0.1  0.2
Fish      -0.1  0.6 -0.3  0.2 -0.3 -0.1 -0.1 -0.4  0.3
Cereals    0.4 -0.2  0.1  0.0  0.2  0.1  0.4 -0.7  0.2
Starch    -0.3  0.4  0.2  0.3  0.7  0.1  0.2  0.1  0.1
Nuts       0.4  0.1 -0.1 -0.3  0.2  0.4 -0.4  0.2  0.5
Fr.Veg     0.1  0.5  0.4 -0.5 -0.2  0.1  0.4  0.1 -0.2
```

The rotations matrix here is $\mathbf{\Phi}$. Each column is $\boldsymbol{\phi}_k = [\phi_{k1} \ldots \phi_{kp}]'$, the coefficients that translate from dimensions of $\mathbf{x}$ (here, protein types) to the kth PC direction. Note that, since we had `scale=TRUE`, these rotations apply to standard deviations in the original variables. For example, the entry for `PC1` and `RedMeat` indicates that a country's red meat consumption being one standard deviation above the mean contributes -0.3 toward the first PC direction (i.e., in the calculation for ω_{i1} for that country).

Calculating Factor Values

If you want to get the PC (i.e., factor) values—the $\boldsymbol{\omega}_i$ values—you apply `predict` to the fitted `prcomp` object. You can either provide a new $\mathbf{x}$ that you want mapped to $\boldsymbol{\omega}$ or you can call it without providing any `newdata` and it will return the matrix of PC values for $\mathbf{X}$, the data you used to fit PC rotations.

```
> round( predict(pcfood, newdata=food["France",]),2)
          PC1  PC2 PC3   PC4  PC5   PC6  PC7   PC8  PC9
France -1.49 0.79   0 -1.96 0.25 -0.9 0.95 -0.02 0.54
> head( round(wfood <- predict(pcfood),1))
                PC1  PC2  PC3  PC4  PC5  PC6  PC7  PC8  PC9
Albania         3.5 -1.6 -1.8 -0.2  0.0 -1.0 -0.5  0.8 -0.1
Austria        -1.4 -1.0  1.3 -0.2 -0.9  0.2 -0.2 -0.3 -0.2
Belgium        -1.6  0.2  0.2 -0.5  0.8 -0.3 -0.2 -0.2  0.0
Bulgaria        3.1 -1.3  0.2 -0.2 -0.5 -0.7  0.5 -0.8 -0.3
Czechoslovakia -0.4 -0.6  1.2  0.5  0.3 -0.8  0.3  0.0 -0.1
Denmark        -2.4  0.3 -0.8  1.0 -0.8 -0.2 -0.2 -0.6  0.5
```

We are rounding the output here to make it compact. Note that you can get the same results by applying the projections yourself as $\mathbf{X\Phi}$ (after scaling $\mathbf{X}$).

```
> w <- scale(food)%*%pcfood$rotation
> all(w==wfood)
[1] TRUE
```

Interpretation of the PC directions is a tricky game—as much art as science. Absent any outside context, these factors are defined only in terms of their linear algebra interpretation: they are values in the directions that explain the most amount of variance possible. But it is often desirable to build a *story* around the factors. Indeed, the potential of interpretable low-dimensional factor structure is a driving motivation behind the use of PCA in many social science applications. If you are going to get into this story-building business, then there are two routes: bottom up and top down.

Interpreting the PC Rotations

For a bottom-up interpretation, you can look at big individual φ_{kj} rotations to try to understand the main drivers in the map between ω_{ik} and x_{ij}. In the protein consumption PCA, each country's factor value in the kth PC direction is

$$\omega_{ik} = \phi_{k\text{redmeat}} x_{i\text{redmeat}} + \phi_{k\text{whitemeat}} x_{i\text{whitemeat}} + \dots \phi_{k\text{nuts}} x_{i\text{nuts}}$$

This factor value represents a diet—a latent pattern summarizing one identifiable style of protein consumption. Since the x_{ij} are scaled to units of standard deviation, each ϕ_{kj} tells you the amount that a country will load in the direction of diet k per one standard deviation extra consumption of protein j. Consider rotations for the first two PCs.

```
> t(round(pcfood$rotation[,1:2],2))
    R.Meat W.Meat  Eggs  Milk  Fish Cereal Starch Nuts Fr.Veg
PC1  -0.30  -0.31 -0.43 -0.38 -0.14   0.44  -0.30 0.42   0.11
PC2  -0.06  -0.24 -0.04 -0.18  0.65  -0.23   0.35 0.14   0.54
```

We see that a country loads high in PC1 if it consumes a lot of cereals and nuts; conversely, you load low in PC1 if you consume expensive proteins such as meat, eggs, and milk. The second PC is a Mediterranean diet: consumption of lots of fish and olives (a source of fruit and vegetable protein) pushes a higher ω_{i2} value.

Interpreting Factor Values

For a top-down interpretation, look at the fitted ω_{ik} and use domain knowledge about observation i to build a narrative. Figure 8.7 shows PC values plotted against each other for the first four directions in the protein consumption PCA. You see that PC1 provides a mostly western versus eastern representation of countries, while PC2 is more specific than a Mediterranean diet—it is an Iberian diet, identified by especially high values for Spain and Portugal.

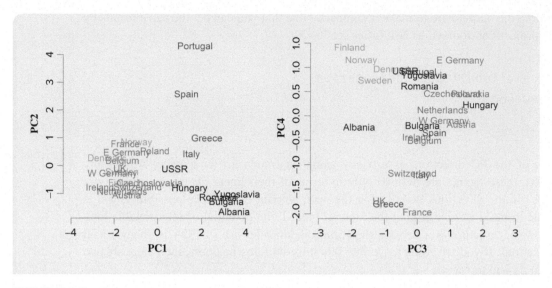

FIGURE 8.7   Protein consumption PC values ω_{ik} for the first four PC directions. The countries are colored according to a 4-means clustering on the PC values.

As an aside, note that the countries in Figure 8.7 are colored according to a 4-means clustering on the factor values ω.

```
> grpProtein <- kmeans(wfood, centers=4, nstart=20)
```

We use all 9 factor directions here, but since we *did not* scale wfood before calling kmeans, the clustering will be dominated by the higher variance PC directions (the first few). This general strategy—fitting PCA and then clustering on either all or a subset of the factor values—is a good option if you really do need to cluster your observations into separate groups. The *K*-means algorithm does poorly when you give it data consisting of many correlated variables. Running PCA beforehand translates to factor values where most of the variation is concentrated in the first few dimensions. This gives you a better chance of finding a useful clustering. In Figure 8.7 we see that *K*-means has clustered together the Nordic countries, the western Mediterranean countries (excluding France), and the USSR and its satellite nations (again, this is old cold war era data). The remaining countries are grouped together in a broad northern European cluster.

How Many Factors?

Once you've fit all the PC directions, the next question is, how many do you need? This is not a question that is easily answered. Unless you are using the factors in a concrete downstream prediction problem (in which case the usual CV tools can be applied), the decision of how many factors is "best" will be dependent upon some strong modeling assumptions. As a rough heuristic, it is common to look at the variance of each ω_k and see how quickly it is decreasing with k. If there is a big drop-off in the variance after a certain k, then perhaps you only need to keep PC1 through PCk. When you summarize the fitted prcomp object, it prints the running tally of variance across factors.

```
> summary(pcfood)
Importance of components:
                        PC1      PC2      PC3      PC4      PC5
Standard deviation    2.0016   1.2787   1.0620   0.9771   0.68106
Proportion of Variance 0.4452  0.1817   0.1253   0.1061   0.05154
Cumulative Proportion 0.4452   0.6268   0.7521   0.8582   0.90976
...
```

Since the sum of variances will be equal to the total variance across all x_{ij}, the summary also reports the *proportion* of variance explained by each PC direction. Each PC's contribution to this total variance is decreasing with k. You can also plot the prcomp object to get the *screeplot*, a visual representation of the variance for each PC direction.

You might make judgments about how many PCs are influential based upon these summaries, but we caution against reading too much into a screeplot. For example, in Figure 8.8a, it appears that the first PC explains most of the variation. However, we found above that PC2 has a clear interpretation in terms of the Mediterranean/Iberian diet. The choice of how many PCs to track is totally subjective, and you should feel free to use as many PCs as make sense given what you can interpret or use in exploratory analysis.

Calculating PCA Step-by-Step

Before leaving this example, we will show how you can go through the steps of PCA yourself instead of relying on prcomp. This may be useful when X is a large sparse matrix, because prcomp will convert it from sparse to dense matrix storage and this can fill up your working memory.

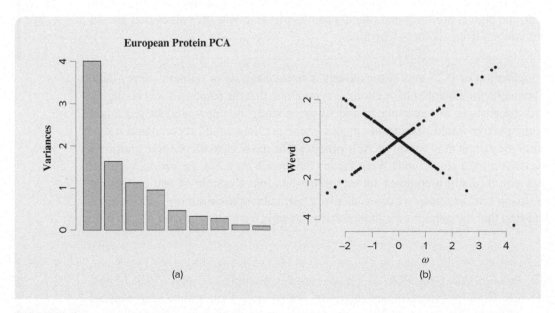

FIGURE 8.8   Panel (a) shows the variance for each PC direction's factor values, ω_k, in the European protein consumption PCA. Panel (b) plots the fitted factor values from prcomp to those obtained by applying eigen to the variance-covariance matrix.

First, you need to scale the data matrix such that each column has a standard deviation of one and a mean of zero.

```
> X <- as.matrix(scale(food))
```

If you were working with a large sparse matrix here, you might want to avoid the `scale` function (which converts to dense format) and instead just divide each column of the matrix by its standard deviation. You can skip centering in that situation, so as to avoid replacing your convenient zero entries (and making the matrix dense). Once you have the scaled data **X**, you can calculate the covariance matrix as

$$\mathbf{S} = \tfrac{1}{n}\mathbf{X}'\mathbf{X} + \bar{\mathbf{x}}\,\bar{\mathbf{x}}' \tag{8.10}$$

where $\bar{\mathbf{x}}$ is the column means vector (which will be all zero if **X** has been shifted to have zero means, but we include it here for completeness).

```
> xbar <- colMeans(X)
> XX <- crossprod(X)
> S <- XX/nrow(X) - tcrossprod(xbar)
```

Finally, you can call `eigen` on the variance matrix **S** to obtain the eigenvectors (rotations) **Φ**, and project **XΦ** to obtain the factor values.

```
> evd <- eigen(S, symmetric=TRUE)
> wevd <- X%*%evd$vectors
```

Figure 8.8b shows the `wevd` values obtained here plotted against the `wfood` values obtained using `prcomp`. The values are exactly the same up to a plus or minus sign; since the underlying factors are latent, the sign is arbitrary and one algorithm will give you PC values that are −1 times the values you get from another algorithm.

· ·

One common application of PCA and factor models is in the analysis of opinion survey data. When you ask someone for a number of opinions, it is common that the responses will be highly correlated across dimensions. For example, in a focus group study for a new product you might ask how much the person would pay for this product, whether they would recommend it to a friend, or whether they think they would use this product. The answers to all of these questions are going to be driven by a single underlying factor: *how much they like the product*. Factor modeling allows you to distill a complex set of survey data into a couple of key underlying opinion factors. In our next example, we consider a very particular opinion survey—the votes of legislators—and find that the opinions are indeed driven by only a couple of underlying factors.

Example 8.3 **Roll-Call Vote Data: PCA** As a more complex example, consider a PCA of how members of the U.S. Congress vote. In particular, you are going to look at the Congressional Record for *roll-call votes*—those votes where attendance is taken and every individual's vote is added to the Congressional Record. These are archived on the website `voteview.com`, and the R package `pscl` has tools for extracting and manipulating this data. The set of votes that we are going to look at come from the 111th Congress covering 2009 to 2010, the first two years of Barack Obama's presidency. There were 445 voting members in the U.S. House of Representatives for this Congress, and we have recorded their votes on 1,647 questions as -1 for nay, $+1$ for yea, and 0 for those who abstained or were absent. This leads to a large 445×1647 matrix with rows $\mathbf{x}_i$ representing the voting record for politician i.

```
> votes <- read.csv("rollcall-votes.csv")
> votes[1:6,1:5]
                    Vote.1  Vote.2  Vote.3  Vote.4  Vote.5
BONNER (R AL-1)         -1       1      -1       0       0
BRIGHT (D AL-2)          1      -1       1       1       1
ROGERS (R AL-3)         -1       1      -1      -1      -1
ADERHOLT (R AL-4)       -1       1      -1      -1       1
GRIFFITH (D/R AL-5)      1      -1       1       1       1
BACHUS (R AL-6)         -1       1      -1       1       1
```

There is intuitive support for a low-dimensional factor structure in this setting. Although the votes are on different issues, the individual voters are aligned upon partisan and ideological axes—e.g., Republican versus Democrat or conservative versus liberal. If you believe that all votes are in expectation partisan or ideological, then the vote for member i on issue j could be predicted as

$$\mathbb{E}\left[x_{ij}\right] = \mu_{1j}\omega_{i1}$$

where ω_{i1} is the member's value along, say, a traditional left-right ideological axis that is translated to votes via the single direction $\boldsymbol{\mu}_1$. This is precisely the sort of model that PCA can estimate.

After reading the vote data into R, you can run PCA using prcomp.

```
> pcavote <- prcomp(votes, scale=TRUE)
> plot(pcavote)
```

Figure 8.9 shows the screeplot for the resulting variances attributed to each PC direction. Notice that there are huge drops in variance from 1st to 2nd and 2nd to 3rd PCs. The political science literature (e.g., Poole, 2005) finds that a single component is able to explain the vast majority of variation in how politicians vote. A second dimension has been useful to understand voting at a few specific points in time, for example, during the Civil War in the 1860s or Civil Rights Movement of the 1960s when racism created a divide across party lines. We can ask the question of our data: *Is there an interpretable second dimension to the political space of 2009 to 2010?*

The first two PC directions are plotted in Figure 8.10. These are the $\boldsymbol{\omega}_i = [\omega_{i1}, \omega_{i2}]$ for each individual politician i. With the Republicans in red and Democrats in blue (and independents in green), you can see a clear partisan divide on the first principal component. Our intuition is supported by data: most voting behavior is driven by a single-partisan factor. The second

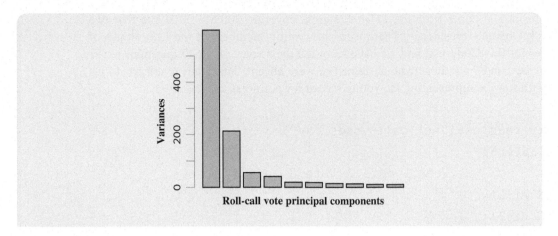

FIGURE 8.9   PC direction variances for the roll-call vote data.

direction is orthogonal to party (which is necessary if PC1 aligns with party). This dimension matters little for most politicians, but a small group of politicians have large negative ω_{i2}. What does it mean?

Interpreting the Vote Factors

Let's start with a top-down interpretation exercise. Looking at factor values for individual politicians, we find that the extremes of PC1 range correspond to ideological extremes. That is, the PC1 direction doesn't just capture party membership but also represents the spectrum of liberal-conservative beliefs within each party. For example, the most negative ω_{i1} correspond to far-right (very conservative) Republicans, and the largest positive values are all liberal Democrats.

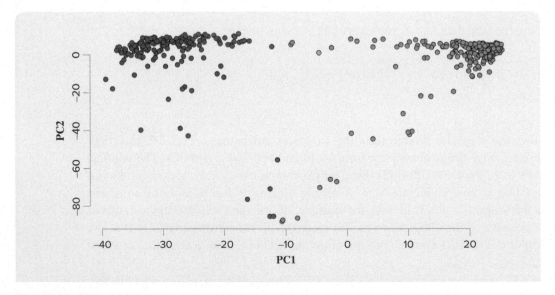

FIGURE 8.10   Politician values in the first two PC directions for roll-call voting, with Republicans in red and Democrats in blue. Inconveniently, the Republicans are on the left and Democrats are on the right—PC value signs are arbitrary, and you would get the same fit quality if you multiplied each ω_{i1} by minus one.

```
> votepc <- predict(pcavote)
> votepc[order(votepc[,1])[1:3],1]
   BROUN (R GA-10)      FLAKE (R AZ-6)   HENSARLIN (R TX-5)
        -39.37394           -38.25067           -37.58706
> votepc[order(-votepc[,1])[1:3],1]
EDWARDS (D MD-4)    PRICE (D NC-4)   MATSUI (D CA-5)
        25.29151          25.15912          25.12481
```

In contrast, looking at the individuals with large (negative) values for PC2, there is no obvious pattern. Indeed, it is not clear that this group of people would ever be able to agree on any issue of political substance!

```
> head(sort(votepc[,2]))
      SOLIS (D CA-32)   GILLIBRAND (D NY-20)    PELOSI (D CA-8)
          -88.31351             -87.58872          -86.53586
    STUTZMAN (R IN-3)         REED (R NY-29)    GRAVES (R GA-9)
          -85.59217             -85.53636          -76.49658
```

Moving to a bottom-up interpretation, Figure 8.11 plots the distribution of PC1 rotations across specific votes. Looking in detail at votes with large positive or negative rotations, we find they correspond to bills that were extreme enough to cause members of each party to vote with the opposition. For example, a vote for a specific set of Republican amendments to the Affordable Health Care for America Act indicates a negative (more conservative) PC1. This bill included cuts in care that made many in the GOP uncomfortable; only the most fiscally conservative or

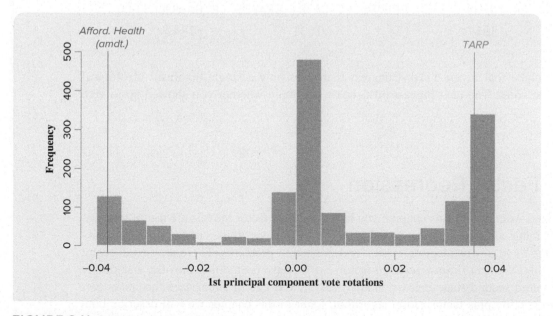

FIGURE 8.11   PC1 rotations ϕ_{1j} for votes.

libertarian members voted "yea." On the other end, a vote for the Targeted Asset Relief Program (TARP)—the controversial bail-out for financial institutions—is a push in the direction a positive (more progressive) PC1. This all supports an interpretation that PC1 can be used to the traditional liberal–conservative ideological axis.

For PC2, we look at the large $|\phi_{2j}|$ rotation elements to discern a pattern.

```
> phi <- pcavote$rotation[,1:2]
> phi[order(abs(phi[,2]), decreasing=TRUE)[1:5],2]
  Vote.1146    Vote.658   Vote.1090   Vote.1104   Vote.1149
0.05605862  0.05461947  0.05300806  0.05168382  0.05155729
```

After looking them up, we find that these votes all correspond to near-unanimous symbolic action. For example, 429 legislators voted "yea" for H.R. 1146, "Supporting the goals and ideals of a Cold War Veterans Day."

This solves the mystery: the members who get pushed toward negative PC2 were *absent* for these votes. They voted 0 when all others voted +1 (which will lead to negative values for the absent voters when you fit the PCA with `scale=TRUE`). Thus, PC2 represents attendance: those with big negative values in PC2 have terrible attendance records, some because they have perhaps more important things to do and others because they were elected only in by-elections midway through the congressional session. Here are the members with the highest number of absences:

```
> sort(rowSums(votes==0), decreasing=TRUE)[1:6]
  SOLIS (D CA-32) GILLIBRAND (D NY-20)    REED (R NY-29)
             1628                 1619              1562
STUTZMAN (R IN-3)      PELOSI (D CA-8) GRAVES (R GA-9)
             1557                 1541              1340
```

We can conclude that in the 111th Congress there was only a single dominant ideological factor driving votes. The next biggest influence was simply whether you showed up to vote regularly.

■ 8.3 Factor Regression

In the previous examples of this chapter, you have seen how factor models are useful for clustering, explaining, and compressing data. One of the most powerful uses of fitted factors, however, is as *inputs* to downstream regression and prediction problems. There are two different ways to do this. You can fit *unsupervised* factors, as we have been doing thus far, and simply feed those into a second-stage regression analysis. Or, you can fit *supervised* factors as part of a joint prediction plus factorization algorithm. Later in this chapter we will describe both approaches to factor regression.

8.3.1 Principal Components Regression

The concept of principal components regression (PCR) is simple: instead of regressing y onto $\mathbf{x}$, use a lower-dimension set of principal components as covariates. This is a fruitful strategy especially if you have far more unlabeled $\mathbf{x}_i$ than labeled $[\mathbf{x}_i, y_i]$ pairs. You can use *unsupervised* learning (PCA) on a massive bank of unlabeled data and use the results to reduce dimension and facilitate *supervised* learning on a smaller set of labeled observations.

The two-stage PCR algorithm is straightforward: you run PCA and then run a regression procedure.

```
mypca = prcomp(X, scale=TRUE)
v = predict(mypca)[,1:K]
reg = glm(y~., data=as.data.frame(v))
```

The number of PCs to include in the regression (K) can be selected using any of our usual variable selection tools. You can look at coefficient significance as a guide or choose K to minimize AICc. It also often makes sense to replace glm in the code above with a routine like gamlr that provides a path of estimated coefficients along with model selection tools.

It is also possible to perform a cross-validation experiment and choose K to minimize OOS error. An important practical point: whereas we have previously cautioned that you need to do all estimation *inside* the CV loop (e.g., perform PCA each time you leave out a fold), it is actually fine to obtain your PCs using the full dataset (or perhaps an even larger dataset, if you observe only the "labels" y for a subset of observations). You then apply CV as though the fitted PCs are any other regression inputs. So long as the random errors in your test y sample are not allowed to influence the model fit (i.e., so long as you are fitting an unsupervised factorization like PCA), the result of your trained model on left-out data remains a good estimate of OOS performance.

When considering PCR for an application, you should remember PCA will be driven by the *dominant* sources of variation in $\mathbf{x}$. If the response is connected to these dominant sources of variation, PCR works well. If it is more of a "needle in the haystack response," driven by a small number of inputs, then PCR will not work well.

Example 8.4 Equity Returns: PCR To illustrate factor regression, we will consider the classic problem of predicting asset price returns. The massively influential Fama-French model in financial asset pricing holds that equity returns are driven by a small number of factors (Fama and French, 1993). This insight motivates the currently dominant strategy of *passive* asset management, where investors hold an *index* of assets (stocks) where that index is designed to have certain risk properties based upon the factor structure in the market. We saw an example of this type of modeling in the preface, where we introduced the CAPM model that considers each individual stock's returns as a function of an overall market average return.

Recall that a stock's return is defined as the current price minus the previous price divided by the previous price. We will consider a set of monthly returns from 2010 through 2017 for stocks in the S&P500 index (this is a transformation of the data used in the Introduction). The returns in returns.csv have been adjusted by subtracting the concurrent return on U.S. Treasury Bills ("T-Bills," U.S. government debt) and represent returns in excess of the "risk free rate"—the rate of return you could have gotten by investing in bonds that have a near zero probability of default.

```
> R <- read.csv("returns.csv", row.names=1)
> head(R[,1:4],3)
              SP500            A           AA          AAP
2010-01  -0.03697270  -0.10134330  -0.21379807  -0.02894450
2010-02   0.02851214   0.11886911   0.04359901   0.03071968
2010-03   0.05879762   0.08913278   0.06667784   0.02487266
```

The first column of the data frame R is the monthly return on the aggregate S&P500 index. We will pull this out as a separate vector, and also pull out y as the returns on the Chevron Corporation (CVX). We will treat the Chevron returns as the target of prediction given the remainder of the stock returns.

```
> sp500 <- R[,"SP500"]
> ind <- which(colnames(R)=="CVX")
> y <- R[,ind]
> R <- R[,-c(1,ind)]
> dim(R)
[1] 84 499
```

This leaves us with a wide matrix of inputs R consisting of 84 monthly observations on 499 stock returns.

The first step of PCR is to calculate the principal components of R. However, printing the first few returns for some tech giants exposes an issue.

```
> round(R[1:3,c("AMZN","GOOG","AAPL","MSFT","FB")],4)
            AMZN     GOOG     AAPL     MSFT  FB
2010-01  -0.0712  -0.1487  -0.0921  -0.0790  NA
2010-02  -0.0594  -0.0094   0.0619   0.0186  NA
2010-03   0.1427   0.0725   0.1445   0.0175  NA
```

There are missing values! In particular, a number of the stocks are either listed or de-listed during our observation period. For example, Facebook (FB) had its initial public offering (IPO) on May 18, 2012 (and lost 23% of its IPO value over the rest of that month).

```
> R[27:30,"FB",drop=FALSE]
                  FB
2012-03          NA
2012-04          NA
2012-05  -0.22767548
2012-06   0.04860617
```

Facebook returns before that IPO month are NA.

Dealing with Missing Values

PCA doesn't work when you have missing values. For example, `prcomp` will return an error. However, it turns out that you can use a version of PCA to replace those missing values. The `missMDA` package of Josse and Husson (2016) provides the `imputePCA` function that performs an iterative *expectation maximization* algorithm (which we discussed earlier in the context of mixture models) that alternates between imputing (predicting) each missing value, performing PCA based upon those imputed values, and then updating the imputed missing values based upon the fitted PCs. This repeats until the estimated PCs converge (i.e., stop changing as you update the imputed values). The result is a completed data matrix with no missing values, and the imputed values are predicted from the nonmissing entries in a way that minimizes the impact on future factor modeling.

To use the `missMDA` package, you apply `imputePCA` on your original data matrix and use the argument `npc` to specify the number of principal components used to predict the missing values. The resulting object contains the `completeObs` entry that has replaced the `NA` entries with imputed values. Here, we apply `imputePCA` with `npc=4` to create the completed (no `NA` values) returns matrix `Ri`.

```
> library(missMDA)
> Ri <- imputePCA(R,npc=4)$completeObs
> round(Ri[1:3,c("AMZN","GOOG","AAPL","MSFT","FB")], 4)
            AMZN     GOOG     AAPL     MSFT      FB
2010-01  -0.0712  -0.1487  -0.0921  -0.0790 -0.0210
2010-02  -0.0594  -0.0094   0.0619   0.0186  0.0494
2010-03   0.1427   0.0725   0.1445   0.0175  0.0791
```

This `missMDA` package will likely come in handy in your business analyses because missing values appear in many factor modeling applications. For example, missing values are common in survey data—a classic application for factor modeling.

Calculating Equity Return Factors

Given the completed returns matrix, we can apply `prcomp` to perform PCA.

```
> retpc <- prcomp(Ri, scale=TRUE)
> w <- predict(retpc)
> phi <- retpc$rotation
```

We've extracted the fitted PC values ω_t for each month t as the rows of w, and the fitted PC rotations ϕ_k are the columns of `phi`. Note that we used `scale=TRUE` in `prcomp`, as is our usual best practice. Since this data is all measured in the same units (dollar returns), you could have instead run `prcomp` without this scaling if you wanted the stocks with more volatility (higher variance) to have bigger impact on your fitted PCs (it doesn't significantly impact the results in this case). Rotations for the four factor directions are plotted in Figure 8.12. Notice that the big tech firms—Amazon, Google, Apple, Microsoft, and Facebook—are clustered near each other in all four directions.

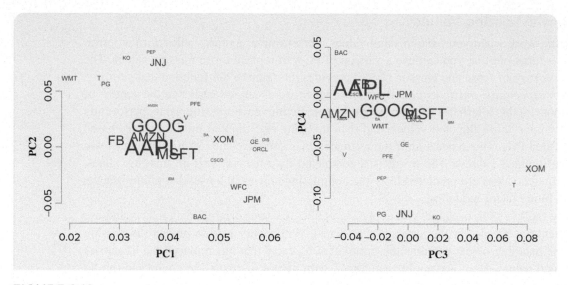

FIGURE 8.12 Rotations in the first four PC directions for some large stocks in our PCA of returns. The points are labeled by the stock ticker symbol and sized according to each company's market capitalization at the end of 2017.

Standard asset pricing theory predicts that the most dominant source of variation in equity returns is a single underlying 'market' factor that represents the change in investor expectations about average future returns. This is the logic behind the capital asset pricing model (CAPM) we discussed in the Introduction. This market factor is often taken to be represented by a broad market index like the S&P500. Indeed, Figure 8.13 shows that the first PC direction values, ω_{i1}, correlate closely with the S&P500 returns over the same period.

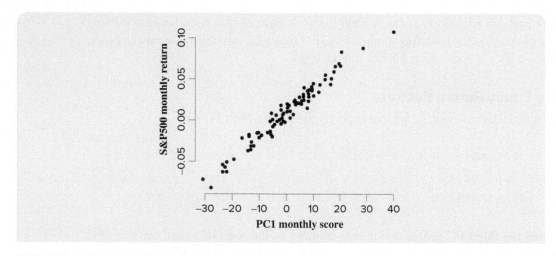

FIGURE 8.13 The first PC value plotted against returns for the S&P500 index. The most important (first) factor direction in returns data correlates closely with returns for this aggregate market index.

Factor Regression for Returns

Turning to our regression problem, we can fit the Chevron returns as a linear function of the fitted PC values ω_t for each month. Here, we regress y onto the values for the first four PC directions.

```
> fit <- glm(y ~ PC1 + PC2 + PC3 + PC4, data=as.data.frame(w))
> summary(fit)

Call:
glm(formula = y ~ PC1 + PC2 + PC3 + PC4, data = as.data.frame(w))

Deviance Residuals:
      Min         1Q      Median        3Q         Max
-0.061904  -0.020657  -0.000887  0.019243  0.060273

Coefficients:
               Estimate  Std. Error  t value  Pr(>|t|)
(Intercept)   0.0070588   0.0031821    2.218   0.02940 *
PC1           0.0031920   0.0002495   12.795   < 2e-16 ***
PC2          -0.0000710   0.0005266   -0.135   0.89310
PC3           0.0064689   0.0008087    8.000  8.74e-12 ***
PC4          -0.0027530   0.0009120   -3.019   0.00342 **
```

The first, third, and fourth PC directions are highly significant, while PC2 is not. Fitting a gamlr Lasso to the full set of PCs with 10-fold CV selects a model that includes these three significant directions.

```
> library(gamlr)
> set.seed(0)
> alasso <- cv.gamlr(w, y, nfold=10)
> B <- coef(alasso)[-1,]
> B[B!=0]
          PC1             PC3             PC4
   0.0024715261  0.0041337158  -0.0001193478
```

---

[*] Note that, even with the same seed, you may get different results for different operating systems and versions of R. You should at least be able to replicate your own results by running the same code twice on your own machine.

Our analysis here indicates that Chevron returns are explained by three underlying market factors.

For comparison, we can also perform a regression that includes both the PC factor values and the original 499 stock returns. This is not a standard strategy in practice—if you are doing PCR, it is likely because you have only a subset of labeled data and need to use an unsupervised technique to reduce the input dimension. However it gives a illustrative performance benchmark for this example.

Using cv.gamlr with the same folds as we used for our PCR (note also that we set the seed above, so you can replicate this same CV experiment exactly), we select a model that has coefficients on several other stock returns and doesn't use any of the fitted PC directions.

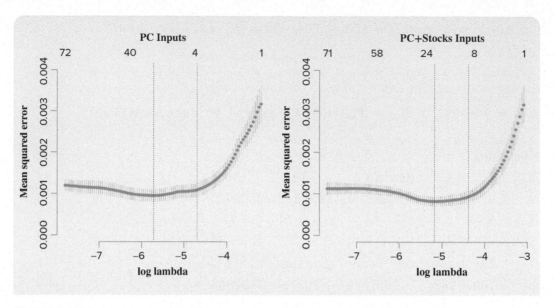

FIGURE 8.14   Comparison of OOS error rates for each factor regression approach to predicting Chevron returns: a PCR model including only the PC factors, and a hybrid model that used both the PCs and the original returns for the 499 other stocks as inputs.

```
> blasso <- cv.gamlr(cbind(w,Ri), y, foldid=alasso$foldid)
> B <- coef(blasso)[-1,]
> round(B[B!=0],5)
    AES     APC     CBS     COP     CTXS
0.00862 0.00734 0.05330 0.23541 0.00062
    FLR      GE     HES       L      XL     XOM
0.00117 0.01427 0.01461 0.10954 0.00797 0.29331
```

This is a basket of stocks with returns that appear to co-move with Chevron's over this time period. We can compare the OOS error rates for this model to those from our PCR above. The cross validation results for each are shown in Figure 8.14. Both show roughly similar OOS error rates across their Lasso path.

◆ 8.4 Partial Least Squares

Combining high-dimensional inputs into a few factors (or "indices") that predict a response y is an appealing idea. This strategy can lead to more interpretable model fits than, say, a high-dimensional Lasso onto raw inputs. And the underlying factor structure is often suggested by theory, as was the case in our asset pricing example. However, techniques that rely on unsupervised factorization (such as PCR) will work only if the dominant directions of variation in **x** are related to y. Unfortunately, in practice it is often the case that variation in **x** is dominated by influences that are unrelated to the response y. The response is not driven by the first few PC directions, and it is inefficient to try to use PCA as a middle-man between y and $\mathbf{x}$.

Is there a way to construct low-dimensional factors ω that are forced to be relevant to the response y? The answer is yes; this is referred to as *supervised factor modeling,* and it is a very useful business analysis technique. There is a big world of supervised factor modeling, and indeed there are several algorithms for supervised adaptations of PCA (e.g., Bair et al., 2006). We'll consider the simple but powerful method of *partial least squares* (PLS), a supervised factorization strategy that has its roots in 1970s chemometrics (measurement in chemistry; Wold, 1975) but has been reinvented and rediscovered many times since.

Marginal Regression

To understand PLS, start with the more basic algorithm of *marginal regression* (MR). In this scheme, you run a simple linear regression for y onto each input dimension x_j and then use the resulting regression coefficients to map from $\mathbf{x}$ to a univariate factor v. In detail, if $\hat{\phi}_j$ is the OLS estimated coefficient for regressing y on x_j, then the MR factor for observation i is $v_i = \Sigma_j x_{ij} \phi_j$. The full recipe is shown in Algorithm 8.2. The result is that the MR factors v_i aggregate the independent effect of each input variable on y. This factor direction will be dominated by x_j dimensions that both (a) have a big effect on y and (b) move consistently in the same direction with each other (since their influence on the factor is additive). That is, marginal regression constructs a single factor that is connected both to y and to a dominant direction of variation in $\mathbf{x}$. It yields a *supervised factor.*

Algorithm 8.2 **Marginal Regression (MR)**

- Estimate $\mathbb{E}[y] = \alpha + \phi_j x_j$ for each dimension $j = 1, \ldots, J$.
- Set your single MR factor $v_i = \Sigma_j x_{ij} \hat{\phi}_j$ for each observation i.
- Estimate the MR factor regression $\mathbb{E}[y] = \beta_0 + \beta_1 v$.

Example 8.5 Equity Returns: Marginal Regression Using the fact that $\hat{\phi}_j = \mathrm{cor}(x_j, y)/\mathrm{sd}(x_j)$ in OLS for a simple linear regression, we can perform marginal regression in three lines of R code.

```
> phi <- cor(Ri, y)/apply(Ri,2,sd)
> v <- Ri%*%phi
> fwd <- glm(y ~ v)
```

This code fit marginal regression for predicting Chevron returns from other stock returns. The resulting MR factor, v, is plotted in Figure 8.15a against the first PC direction from the PCA of Example 8.4. They are practically identical. This again supports the CAPM theory: the individual stocks are all tied to each other and to Chevron returns through a dominant underlying market factor. Figure 8.15b shows the fitted values from fwd against the observed Chevron returns.

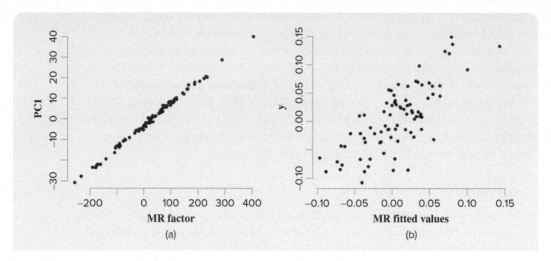

FIGURE 8.15 Marginal regression for predicting Chevron returns from other stock returns. Panel (a) shows the MR factor against the first PC direction from the PCA of Example 3.1, and panel (b) shows the MR fitted values against the observed Chevron returns.

PLS as Boosted Marginal Regression

Partial least squares is an extension of marginal regression. Instead of stopping after running the single MR, you iterate: take the *residuals* from the first MR and repeat a second MR to predict these residuals. You can then take the residuals from the second MR and repeat, continuing until you reach the minimum of J and n. To understand why this works, remember that residuals are the leftover variation in y that was not explained by your fitted model. When we fit the next model to the residuals from the previous model, we are getting a new combination of the x_j's to explain what wasn't explained from the previous combination. In this way, we are combining the x_j into latent factors while simultaneously making sure that these factors are correlated to y.

Another way to think about PLS is that it provides a *path* of models between marginal regression and the OLS fit. If $J < n$ (such that OLS estimation is possible) then the PLS(J) fitted values $\hat{y}_i^J$ will be the same as the fitted values you would get running OLS for y on $\mathbf{x}$. The implied coefficients on each x_{ij}, available as $\Sigma_k \beta_k \phi_{kj}$ in the notation of Algorithm 8.3, also match the OLS coefficients. Thus, PLS provides a path of models between MR and OLS.

Algorithm 8.3 Partial Least Squares (PLS)

Run MR of Algorithm 8.2 for y on $\mathbf{x}$. Store the MR factor as the PLS(1) factor $\mathbf{v}^1$ and the MR fitted values as the PLS(1) fitted values $\hat{y}_i^1$. Then, for $k = 2 \ldots K$,

- Calculate the PLS($k - 1$) residuals $\bar{y}_i^{k-1} = y_i - \hat{y}_i^{k-1}$.
- Run MR for the residuals $\bar{y}^{k-1}$ on $\mathbf{x}$. The MR rotations are the PLS(k) rotations $\hat{\phi}_k$ and the MR factors are the PLS(k) factors $v_i^k = \Sigma_j x_{ij} \hat{\phi}_{kj}$.
- Set the PLS(k) fitted values $\hat{y}_i^k$ as fitted values from OLS estimation of

$$\mathbb{E}[y] = \beta_0 + \beta_1 v^1 + \ldots + \beta_k v^k \tag{8.11}$$

This yields PLS rotations $\mathbf{\Phi} = [\boldsymbol{\phi}_1 \ldots \boldsymbol{\phi}_K]$ and factors $\mathbf{v}_i = \begin{bmatrix} v_i^1 \cdots v_i^K \end{bmatrix}$.

The full PLS recipe is in Algorithm 8.3. The notation is a bit complex but it is really a very simple algorithm. You are just running marginal regression on the residuals after each PLS(k) fit and updating the fitted values. This general procedure of taking a simple algorithm and repeatedly applying it to residuals from previous fits is called *boosting*. That is, PLS is *boosted marginal regression*. Boosting (see Friedman, 2001) is a general and powerful machine learning technique. It is a useful way to add flexibility to simple methods, and you will find it as an ingredient in many ML algorithms.

Example 8.6 Equity Returns: Partial Least Squares The `textir` package has a `pls` function for running partial least squares. You give it inputs x, response *y*, and a number of PLS factors to fit *K*. We'll use `pls` to fit a three-factor PLS(3) to predict Chevron returns from the other stock returns.

```
> library(textir)
> retpls <- pls(x=Ri, y=y, K=3)
Directions 1, 2, 3, done.
> plot(retpls)
```

The last line here produces Figure 8.16 showing the fitted values for PLS(1), PLS(2), and PLS(3). Note that if you already have an R plot window open it needs to be made large enough to fit the three plots, otherwise you might get an error. Note that PLS(1) is just marginal regression, so the leftmost panel is a version of Figure 8.15b. In the rightmost panel, we see that PLS(3) achieves an *in-sample* correlation of 0.98 between fitted and observed Chevron returns.

You can use cross-validation to select the best *K* for PLS(*K*) prediction. Unlike PCR, in PLS the *y* values are used in construction of the PLS factors. This means that you can't simply dump the full-sample fitted PLS factors into `gamlr` and get a valid OOS experiment. In addition, there is no easy way to know the degrees of freedom for each PLS(*K*) fit, so you can't

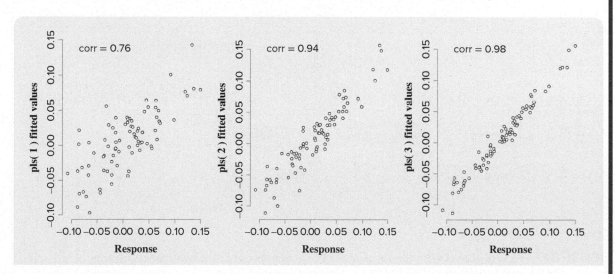

FIGURE 8.16 Fitted versus true values for PLS regressions with $K \leq 3$ to predict Chevron returns from the other stock returns. The in-sample correlations between fitted and observed values are printed on each plot.

apply tools like the AICc. You need to run a cross-validation routine where PLS is run on a data subset and you evaluate predictive performance on a left-out sample. We do that here for the prediction of Chevron returns using PLS(K) for $K = 1, \ldots, 5$.

```
> MSE <- matrix(nrow=10,ncol=5)
> for(i in 1:10){
+ train <- which(alasso$foldid!=i)
+ test <- which(alasso$foldid==i)
+ for(k in 1:ncol(MSE)){
+ plsi <- pls(x=Ri[train,], y=y[train], K=k)
+ MSE[i,k] <- mean( (y[test] - predict(plsi, Ri[test,]))^2 )
+ }
+ }
> colMeans(MSE)
          1             2             3             4             5
0.0014948610 0.0009513140 0.0008192589 0.0009018260 0.0008579738
```

Note that we are using the same CV folds that we used when applying `cv.gamlr` in Example 8.4, such that the results of this CV experiment are directly comparable to those shown in Figure 8.14. The distributions of OOS mean square errors for each PLS(K) specification are plotted in Figure 8.17a, along with the lowest OOS MSE achieved for each of the regressions from Example 8.4. We see that PLS(3) achieves mean OOS error as good as Lasso regression onto the original stock returns. Depending upon your application, it may be preferable to work with a couple of PLS factors as your predictors rather than working with a sparse regression onto the full set of stocks. Looking at the distribution of MSEs across CV folds, you could choose either PLS(2) or PLS(3) here depending upon your preference for simplicity. The rotations for the PLS(2) directions are shown in Figure 8.17b.

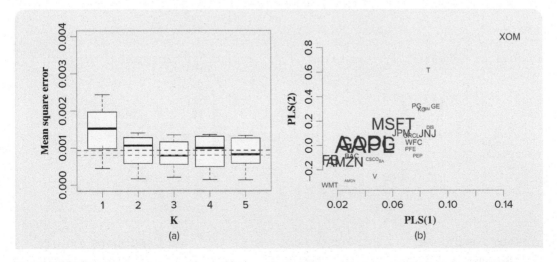

FIGURE 8.17 Panel (a) shows OOS prediction results for PLS as a function of K. The lowest mean OOS errors from Example 8.4 are marked for regression onto PCs (red) and regression onto PCs and **x** (blue). Panel (b) shows the PLS rotations for the first two directions for a selection of large companies (sized proportional to market value).

Note that the examples of this chapter, which focus on prediction for a single company's returns, are underselling the main usefulness of factor analysis in financial asset pricing. In a more complete treatment, such as that of Cochrane (2009), you will find that financial factor models play a central role in understanding the co-movement of prices and in designing portfolios of assets that reduce risk for the investor. The lesson of the analyses above should be that there are interesting factor structures that underlie asset prices and that the returns move together as a function of this underlying structure.

QUICK REFERENCE

Factor models allow you to reduce the dimension of your data and they are powerful tools for data analysis. PCA and PLS are two key methods for estimating factor structure, but there are many others. For example, in our next chapter we will learn about factor models that are specifically well suited to the modeling of text data. In general, factor modeling is often most useful as an intermediate step in a larger analysis framework and, in particular, to build low-dimensional inputs to a downstream regression model.

Key Practical Concepts

- For numeric data x, run *K*-means clustering with the `kmeans` function using `centers` to specify the number of mixture components and `nstart` to specify the number of random initializations. You will usually want to use `scale(x)` for data so that distance is measured in standard deviations.

```
mix <- kmeans( scale(x), centers=M, nstart=5)
mix$centers        # estimated mixture centers
head(mix$cluster)  # head of cluster assignments
```

- Use `prcomp` with `scale=TRUE` to estimate PCA on a numeric data matrix x.

```
pca <- prcomp(x, scale=TRUE)
pca$rotations      # fitted rotations
```

The factor values are available by calling `predict`, or equivalently by multiplying scaled data against the rotations.

```
predict(pca)[,1:2]                # First two PCA factors
scale(x)%*%pca$rotations[,1:2] # same thing
```

You can use bottom up (looking at rotations) and top down (looking at the factor values) to build interpretations for your fitted PCA.

- Use `imputePCA` from the `missMDA` package to impute missing data before running PCA. The `npc` argument sets the number of factors used to predict missing values, and the output contains the imputed data as `completeObs`.

```
xi <- imputePCA(x, npc=4)$completeObs
```

- Use the PCA factor values as inputs to a Lasso regression via `gamlr`.

```
w <- predict(pca)
fit <- gamlr( w, y )
```

- Use `pls` in the `textir` library to fit K supervised partial least squares factors.

```
plsfit <- pls(x, y, K=K)
plsfit$loadings          # n x K matrix of factor values
plsfit$directions        # J x K matrix of rotations
predict(plsfit, newdata=x)  # prediction
```

9 TEXT AS DATA

This chapter describes techniques for incorporating text data into your analyses and building models to understand meaning and sentiment in text.

- **Section 9.1 Tokenization:** Turn raw text into counts on tokens, and create document term count matrices to be used in downstream regression tasks.

- **Section 9.2 Text Regression:** Run Lasso regression models to predict meaning and sentiment from processed text data.

- **Section 9.3 Topic Models:** Build *latent Dirichlet allocation* (LDA) factor models for count data, and use these to estimate topics in text. Apply the same models on choice data as an input to building recommender engines.

- **Section 9.4 Word Embedding:** Work with token sequence data and build term co-occurrence matrices that represent how often tokens occur near each other in documents. Apply the Glove embedding algorithm to estimate vector representations for tokens in your vocabulary.

The modern business environment generates vast quantities of raw unstructured text. As the costs of storage drop and as more conversations and transactions move to digital platforms, we accumulate *corpora* (collections of text documents) that record communications including customer support chats and calls, product descriptions and reviews, employee reports, and social media conversations. For decision makers, this creates a new source of data on every aspect of their business. The information in text is a rich complement to the more structured variables contained in a traditional transaction or customer database.

Social scientists have also woken up to the potential to make use of text as data. See Gentzkow et al. (2017) for an overview of the use of text data in economics research. In finance, text from financial news, social media, and company filings is used to predict asset price movements and study the causal impact of new information. In macroeconomics, text is used to forecast variation in inflation and unemployment and estimate the effects of policy uncertainty. In media economics, text from news and social media is used to study the drivers and effects of political slant. In marketing, text from advertisements and product reviews is used to study the drivers of consumer decision making. In the political economy, text from politicians' speeches is used to study the dynamics of political agendas and debate.

To analyze text, you need to transform it into data that can be input to numeric regression and factorization algorithms. This is done by mapping from the raw text to either counts or sequences of words and phrases. We will begin this chapter by outlining this process of *tokenization,* the results of which are (very) high-dimensional *token* matrices that can be input to methods we've already covered in this book (e.g., Lasso regression). Indeed, working with text data is a great way to get more familiar with modern statistical learning techniques. It is messy but also interpretable (words have known meanings) and is high dimensional in a way that would stump classical statisticians: as you accumulate more text data, the size of the vocabulary—your model dimension—will also grow.

We will also cover a number of text-specific techniques, including topic modeling and word embedding. These tools are used to reduce the dimension of the high-dimensional text token matrices. They are useful for understanding themes and meaning in text, and to construct low-dimensional inputs to downstream regression tools like random forests. Understanding of such dimension reduction techniques is also a stepping stone into the deep learning methods of Chapter 10. The main message of this chapter is that with some standard data science tools you can tap into the information contained in messy unstructured text and use text as data in your business decisions.

● 9.1 Tokenization

Raw text—the language that humans read—is an incredibly rich object. It is much more than a sum of words. Meaning is built from ordered sequences of words that refer to each other, often separated across sentences or paragraphs. In business analysis, we can mostly ignore this complexity and rely on *counts* for language *tokens:* words, phrases, or other basic elements. A huge amount of information is contained in these simple counts. The lesson of the past 30 years has been that, for prediction and classification with text, it is difficult to make effective use of any statistics other than simple word and phrase counts. This is changing with the rise of deep learning techniques (see Chapter 10) and in the last section of this chapter we will consider analysis for ordered sequences of tokens. However, for practical data science many text-as-data applications will continue to focus on word and phrase counts. This token-count-based learning is just too quick and effective to be made redundant.

Consider a little Shakespeare:

All the world's a stage,
and all the men and women merely players:
they have their exits and their entrances;
and one man in his time plays many parts.

Powerful and poetic. What the data scientist sees is more pedestrian. For example, you might just count some key terms and represent the snippet as a numeric vector **x**. After choosing which words to represent and combining some (e.g. man and men), we have

```
world stage men women play exit entrance time
  1     1    2    1    2    1      1      1
```

Breaking this line of Shakespeare down into parts is called *tokenization*. Here, the tokens are individual words. Assigning a numerical measure to each token and representing the document as a vector is called *vectorization*. In this example, our numeric measure is the count of how many times each token appears. When the tokens are individual words and the vectorization maps to simple word counts, this is called the *bag of words* representation. Notice that common words such as "all," "a," or "the" weren't counted. Common words that you remove during tokenization are called *stop words*. When we remove some vocabulary, this is called *pruning*. In the pre-processing step, you can strip words down to just the stem and this is called *stemming*. For example, here "players" and "plays" are mapped to "play" and "men" and "man" are mapped to "men."

This tabulation of word counts is the *bag of words (BoW)* text representation. The BoW term is often used even if the tokens are not words: for example, you can tokenize into word stems or common short sequences (e.g., "very good" or "very bad"). In any case, you proceed by first tokenizing and then counting. The resulting data is a vector of counts for each token. The combined data from many documents is represented as a sparse *document term matrix* (DTM): each row is a document, each column is a token, and the entries are the counts for a given token in a given document. This representation of documents completely ignores the order of words or phrases. By summarizing a document in terms of token counts, you are throwing away all information relevant to any more complex processes of document construction. The advantage of this approach is its simplicity: you can characterize relationships between language and outside variables (e.g., authorship or sentiment) on the basis of word presence or frequency in documents.

9.1.1 Tokenization and Vectorization with R

There are many possible algorithms for going from raw text to a summary token-count vector **x**. A basic recipe is to split your text up on spaces (such that spaces separate tokens) and then prune the tokens to remove both very *common* words (stop words) and very *rare* words. After pruning the vocabulary you can then count the remaining tokens (words or other elements). The reason for doing the pruning before analysis is computational and statistical efficiency: you want to store and model only the tokens that are important for the task at hand.

You should strive for a light touch in these pruning steps. Since you're going to be using regularization and selection techniques in the downstream regression models, you don't need to be overly worried about including too many tokens. Words that are junk for one purpose might be crucial for another. For example, overly common words like `if` or `but` are often classified as stop words and the frequency of `the` in a document likely says little about the author's sentiment, so maybe it can be dropped. However, in other applications these common words can indicate a specific author's writing style. The classic work of Mosteller and Wallace (1963) uses counts for common words to classify authorship for disputed *Federalist Papers*. Similarly, a common pruning step is to remove punctuation. This is probably fine for removal when analyzing news articles or literature, but it can lead you to lose important signals on meaning and sentiment in online corpora such as text chat or Twitter `:-)`.

Exclusion of rare words is a necessary evil—these words are likely rich in meaning (they are rare and hence not generic), but you observe so few of them that you cannot hope to learn much about this meaning. As you accumulate more data, you can generally keep certain rare words. Culling rare words is also an effective way to reduce the cost of computation. You will typically remove all words that are not in at least X documents, where X is some intuitive minimum threshold. It is good practice to make sure that the results don't change if you make small adjustments to this threshold.

In this section we will introduce some useful text analysis tools in R by working through an example of processing customer reviews. In particular, the `text2vec` library in R wraps together a number of useful functions for text analysis and parsing. In the next chapter we will introduce the Keras library that bridges between R and a suite of powerful tools for deep learning. Between Keras and `text2vec`, along with supporting packages for specific tasks such as stemming, R can be used as a powerful platform for text processing and modeling.

Example 9.1 Yelp Data: Tokenization and Vectorization Yelp is a company that facilitates customers posting online reviews and ratings for all sorts of businesses. Yelp sponsors regular data science competitions, and the data we will be analyzing is a sample of 60k reviews from one of their competition datasets. The file `Yelp60kReviews.json` contains the `text` from these reviews along with business and user IDs and additional review attributes (star rating and votes for the review from other Yelp users).

The reviews are accompanied by star ratings on a scale from 1 to 5. For example, here is a 5-star review:

Such a unique place & a great find. Our waitress was funny, knowledgeable, and did a fantastic job. The food was amazing. We will definitely return and recommend this restaurant to other couples!

And here is a 1-star review:

Awful. Nearly inedible. . . even for airport food. Don't push the "prompt service" button on the table. The waitress said that they ignore it. Keep walking.

Certainly the word "fantastic" is associated with a high star rating and "awful" is associated with a low rating. Later in this chapter we will explore using the review text to predict the star rating. This is an example of *sentiment prediction*—attempting to automatically parse text for positive or negative sentiment. Sentiment prediction is a common application problem in domains like marketing and customer support: if you can automatically process a text to under-stand what a customer likes or dislikes, then you can streamline your marketing or help them get the proper support. Before getting there, however, we will use the review text as the plat-form for illustrating the text tokenization and vectorization capabilities of R. In the remainder of this example, we will use text2vec and other tools to convert the corpus of raw review texts into various document term matrices that contain the counts of tokens for each review.

Reading JSON Data

The data are stored in json (JavaScript Object Notation) format, which is a flexible way to store data that includes a number of attributes (including unstructured data like raw text) for a set of observations. Every line of Yelp60kReviews.json is a json record for a single review. For example, here is the first line of the file:

```
{"review_id":"704a011xuJEZxwbbMDj86Q",
"user_id":"Ef1UydcpC77nsoqn92GnFQ",
"business_id":"oxv2UyI5yF6yawPU20tOxA",
"stars":1.0,"useful":1,"funny":0,"cool":0,
"text":
"We have no idea how the food is since we left after waiting
...
With all the choices in Old Town Scottsdale, GO SOMEWHERE
ELSE!",
"date":"2018-12-01 04:20:00"}
```

You can use the jsonlite library to read this into R as a data frame that contains each attribute within a column.

```
> library(jsonlite)
> reviews <- stream_in(file("Yelp60kReviews.json"))
opening file input connection.
 Imported 60000 records. Simplifying...
closing file input connection.
```

This creates a data frame where each row contains the information from a single review (includ-ing the review text).

```
> dim(reviews)
[1] 60000     9
> reviews[1,]
     review_id       user_id    business_id
1 704a011xuJEZ Ef1UydcpC77ns oxv2UyI5yF6y
```

```
   stars useful funny cool
1    1      1     0    0
   text
1 We have no idea how the food is since we left after waiting
...
With all the choices in Old Town Scottsdale, GO SOMEWHERE ELSE!
                date
1 2018-12-01 04:20:00
```

Tokenization with `text2vec`

The `text2vec` package has abundant documentation at `text2vec.org`. To use it for tokenization, you start by creating a "tokenization" via the `itoken` function. Below we call `itoken` on the review text to create the `tokYelp` tokenization. Note that we load the `Matrix` library after loading `text2vec`; this is always a good step because the `text2vec` stores data as sparse `Matrix` objects.

```
> library(text2vec) # see http://text2vec.org/
> library(Matrix) ## always load this when you load text2vec
> tokYelp = itoken(reviews$text,
+                preprocessor = tolower,
+                tokenizer = word_tokenizer,
+                ids = reviews$review_id)
```

The arguments we have passed to `itoken` define our chosen pre-processing steps and how the tokenization occurs: the argument `preprocessor = tolower` specifies that we will convert all the text to lowercase, and `tokenizer = word_tokenizer` specifies that we will be splitting the text into word tokens (a word here is simply any string of text surrounded by spaces). The final argument, `ids`, sets the row names of the final DTM that we create.

The next step is to set the *vocabulary* of tokens that will make up the columns of your DTM. We create the full potential vocabulary by calling the `create_vocabulary` function on `tokYelp`. You can pass to the `stopword` argument any words that you want dropped from the vocabulary. Here, we just pass a few words for illustration; the `stopwords` package includes a number of common stopword lists that you can use if you want to be more aggressive in stripping out tokens.

```
> vocab<-create_vocabulary(tokYelp, stopword=c("if","and","or"))
```

By default, this `vocab` will include every token (here, word) detected by `tokYelp` except those specified as stop words. The next step is to prune this vocabulary to remove the most common and most rare words.

```
> # prune vocab with settings for rare and common words
> vocab <- prune_vocabulary(vocab,
+             doc_proportion_max = 0.1,
+             doc_proportion_min = 0.001)
```

The inputs to prune_vocabulary define which tokens to remove. The argument doc_proportion_max = 0.1 says to remove all words in more than 10% of the documents (here, more than 6000 documents), and doc_proportion_min = 0.001 says to remove all words that occur in less than 0.1% of documents (here, 60 documents).

Now that we have our vocabulary of tokens, we call the vocab_vectorizer function to create the function that will count tokens, and then call create_dtm on our tokens and this vectorizer to create the DTM.

```
> vectorizer = vocab_vectorizer(vocab)
> dtm = create_dtm(tokYelp, vectorizer)
> class(dtm)
[1] "dgCMatrix"
attr(,"package")
[1] "Matrix"
> dim(dtm)
[1] 60000 4958
```

The resulting 60k row by 4958 column matrix contains the counts for each token in each document. This DTM is a sparse Matrix of the same type that we have used as input to gamlr in previous chapters. As we will see in the next section, you can now use this matrix in analysis as you would any other sparse matrix of input variables.

Looking at the nonzero elements of the first row of dtm, we see that our first review has been vectorized into a row of token counts.

```
> dtm[1,dtm[1,]!=0]
    returns     repeated     stepped     tortillas
          1            1           1             1
...
```

You can also look at the column totals for the rarest words (which are allocated to the first columns).

```
> colSums(dtm[,1:4])
  lackluster     pleasing     protect     anticipated
          60           60          60              61
```

Or by considering dtm>0 you can see counts for the number of documents containing the most common words (which are allocated to the last columns).

```
> colSums(dtm[,ncol(dtm)-3:0]>0)
restaurant told said  her
      5784 5259 5929 6000
```

Note that the most common word, "her," occurs in 6000 documents; anything more common was removed in our pruning step.

Using *n*-gram Tokenization

If you want to tokenize combinations of words, then you can create the vocabulary with the ngram argument set to the range of *n*-grams you want to consider. For example, ngram=c(1,3) would tokenize all single words, two word combinations, and three word combinations. Here we use ngram=c(1,2) to tokenize all "unigrams" and "bigrams." The other steps are the same as what we did above to create our single-word DTM.

```
> vocab2<-create_vocabulary(tokYelp,ngram=c(1,2))
> vocab2<-prune_vocabulary(vocab2,
+             doc_proportion_max = 0.1,
+             doc_proportion_min = 0.001)
> vectorizer2 = vocab_vectorizer(vocab2)
> dtm2 = create_dtm(tokYelp, vectorizer2)
> dim(dtm2)
[1] 60000 18039
```

If you run the code you will notice that the tokenization takes longer, and we see that the resulting DTM has 3.6 times more columns (more vocabulary tokens). Looking at our first review shows a number of bigrams have made it through the pruning step.

```
> dtm2[1,dtm2[1,]>0]
        were_leaving       food_would      another_15
                   1                1               1
           idea_how          us_what   and_proceeded
                   1                1               1
...
```

Although bigrams seem intuitively useful, we will often just stick with words (unigrams) to keep dimension smaller. In downstream regressions this usually works as well as higher-order *n*-gram tokenization.

Stemming in Tokenization

Stemming is another common step in text tokenization. For example, a stemmer might derive `tax` from `taxing`, `taxes`, `taxation`, or `taxable`. When you remove simple suffixes, such as `s` and `ing`, you are doing a basic sort of stemming. More sophisticated options are available, including the snowball stemmer from the `SnowballC` package of Bouchet-Valat (2020). To use a stemmer in tokenization, you need to define a new tokenizer function that takes in raw text, applies one of the `text2vec` tokenizers, and then applies a `SnowballC` stemmer on the output of that tokenizer. Below we define `stem_tokenizer` to apply the `wordStem` stemmer on the output from `word_tokenizer`.

```
> stem_tokenizer =function(x) {
+    tokens = word_tokenizer(x)
+    lapply(tokens, SnowballC::wordStem, language="en")
+ }
```

This new tokenizer is then applied with `itoken` to create a new stemmed tokenization of the Yelp reviews.

```
> tokStemYelp <- itoken(reviews$text,
+          preprocessor = tolower,
+          tokenizer = stem_tokenizer,
+          ids = reviews$id)
```

Given this new tokenization, we feed it into the same steps that were used to create our earlier DTMs. Note that if you don't have the `SnowballC` package installed, use `install.packages("SnowballC")` before running the code below.

```
> vocabS <- create_vocabulary(tokStemYelp)
> vocabS <- prune_vocabulary(vocabS,
+            doc_proportion_max = 0.1,
+            doc_proportion_min = 0.001)
> vectorizerS = vocab_vectorizer(vocabS)
> dtmS = create_dtm(tokStemYelp, vectorizerS)
> dim(dtmS)
[1] 60000 3819
> dtmS[1,dtmS[1,]>0]
   nope tortilla popular repeat proceed scottsdal somewher
      1        1       1      1       1         1        1
```

Notice that in the first review, for example, "scottsdale" is now "scottsdal." The resulting DTM has lower dimension than our original unigram DTM that we obtained without stemming. In general, stemming is a useful step to reduce dimension but you need to be careful: the stemmers can be overly aggressive and reduce terms with distinct meaning to a single root (e.g., "taxing" and "taxes" to "tax").

● 9.2 Text Regression

Once you have a DTM full of token counts, you can use it as you would any other numeric matrix of features. The tools you've learned from elsewhere in this book give you a powerful framework for text analysis after vectorization. A common task is that you want to use the text data to predict some outcome target in a *text regression*. The Lasso regularization and selection techniques from Chapter 3 are especially useful for dealing with high dimensional and sparse DTM model matrices. You have already been fitting text regressions in this book, for example, in the analysis of beer demand in Chapter 6. In this section we will expand on these techniques and give you some general best practices for text regression.

There are a number of transformations that can be applied to your DTM before running a text regression. For example, you can transform from raw token counts to *proportions* that are normalized by the document lengths. You divide each row of the DTM by row totals so that, for example, it doesn't matter how much the reviewer writes but just which words they choose when they do. Another common transformation is *term frequency inverse document frequency* (tf-idf) that divides the token counts by the log of one plus the number of documents where the token occurs. This will upweight counts of rare terms and downweight counts of common terms. Alternatively, you can just pass the original DTM to `gamlr` with the default `standardize=TRUE` for similar results (since the standard deviations on common terms will be larger their coefficients will be penalized more than the coefficients on rare terms; see Chapter 3).

One transformation that tends to work well replaces counts x_{ij} with the indicators $\mathbb{1}_{[x_{ij}>0]}$ so that the inputs track whether a term was used ever in the document. In the code below we will use this indicator transformation by passing `dtm>0` to `gamlr`; this replaces `dtm` with a binary *document token presence matrix* with 1 where the token occurs in the document and 0 where it does not. You can experiment with different transformations to see how results change (and, using `cv.gamlr`, run OOS experiments to see which works best).

Example 9.2 Yelp Data: Sentiment Prediction The DTM output from `text2vec` vectorization has the familiar sparse `Matrix` format that we use as input for `gamlr`. We can use the word matrix `dtm` created above as a regression input to predict star ratings. We will start by running a linear Lasso to predict star ratings.

To build our sentiment prediction (i.e., star prediction) model, we will start with a linear Lasso regression for star ratings onto the term presence matrix.

```
> library(gamlr)
> fitlin <- gamlr(dtm>0, reviews$stars, lmr=1e-3)
> yhat <- drop( predict(fitlin, dtm>0) )
```

The resulting Lasso path is shown in Figure 9.1a. The fitted star ratings using AICc selection, `yhat`, are shown against true ratings in Figure 9.1b. We can use these fitted values to find some reviews with high and low predicted star ratings.

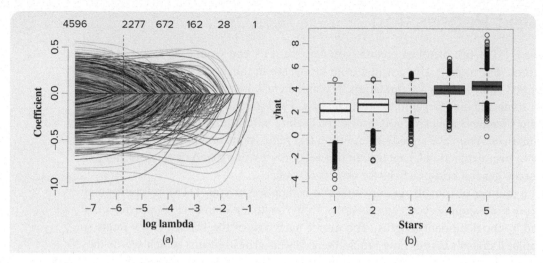

FIGURE 9.1   Review text Lasso for predicting star ratings. Panel (a) shows the Lasso path with AICc selection marked, and (b) shows the fitted values.

```
> l <- rowSums(dtm)
> reviews$text[l<10][which.max(yhat[l<10])]
[1] "Awesome group of people. Efficient, courteous service.
Would highly recommend them. Joe, Eddie, Patrick, Cheryl,
Thank you so much."


> reviews$text[l<10][which.min(yhat[l<10])]


[1] "They never have zesty sauce!!? Slow service and rude workers.
I have been here several times an i always get horrible customer
service. WILL NEVER GO HERE AGAIN. TERRIBLE!"
```

Note that l in this code is the number of tokens in the review (an indicator of review length), and via which.max and which.min, we have printed the modeled best and worst reviews with less than 10 tokens.

Investigating the regression estimate, we see that the AICc has selected a model that has around 60% nonzero coefficients.

```
> blin <- coef(fitlin)[colnames(dtm),]
> mean(blin!=0)
[1] 0.5935861
> head(sort(blin))
    racist      worst  poisoning   horrible       rude     rudest
-0.9217743 -0.8404234 -0.7716131 -0.6643645 -0.6429198 -0.6298581
> tail(sort(blin))
```

butt	thank	excellent	friendliest	awesome	thanked
0.3964892	0.4016954	0.4055354	0.4074772	0.4388107	0.5031916

These are the coefficients that determine how token presence translates to change in the expected star rating. It might not be immediately clear why "butt" should be a positive term, but in the reviews, it was often used in phrases like "works her butt off," "get your butt to the buffet early," and "saved my butt." The other most positive and negative coefficients make intuitive sense. For example, you expect to lose almost a full star if the review contains the word "racist," and to gain almost a 1/2 star if it contains "awesome."

Instead of treating `stars` as a numeric response, you can also view sentiment prediction here as a multinomial classification problem—predicting which star rating category is assigned to each review. We will use `dmr` to fit a distributed multinomial regression as a fast approximation of logistic multinomial regression (see Chapter 4). The syntax is similar as for our linear Lasso, but we now pass the star rating response as a factor variable. We also create a `parallel` cluster `cl` to allow `dmr` to distribute each underlying rating-specific regression to a different processor core.

```
> library(distrom)
> cl <- makeCluster(detectCores())
> fitdmr <- dmr(cl, dtm>0, factor(reviews$stars))
> phat <- predict(fitdmr, dtm>0, type="response")
```

The set of AICc selected fitted values, `phat`, is a matrix of probabilities across the 5 star ratings.

```
> round(phat[1:3,],2)
                           1    2    3    4    5
704a011xuJEZxwbbMDj86Q  0.72 0.19 0.04 0.03 0.02
4ndkbul5VnmW1SJ1HaJz5g  0.17 0.05 0.07 0.32 0.39
reP2C-WqAQ9AJWaAuUUwKg  0.08 0.02 0.05 0.07 0.78
```

We can use these fitted values to look at some short (less than 10 token) reviews with high probability for 1, 3, or 5 stars.

```
> reviews$text[l<10][which.max(phat[l<10,5])]
```

```
[1] "Awesome group of people. Efficient, courteous service.
Would highly recommend them. Joe, Eddie, Patrick, Cheryl,
Thank you so much."
```

```
> reviews$text[l<10][which.max(phat[l<10,3])]
```

```
[1] "It was okay. I was expecting a little more but this place
was just average. Hopefully they will tweak the menu and
upgrade the service and servers."
```

```
> reviews$text[l<10][which.max(phat[l<10,1])]
```

```
[1] "This place is terrible. The food is stale and the service
is even worse. I do not recommend this place, do not waste your
money or time going to this restaurant."
```

The short review with highest probability of 5 stars is again the review with nice feedback for Joe and crew. The review with highest 3 star probability feels that the restaurant was just "okay," while the restaurant for the review with highest 1 star probability is not recommended.

Looking at the estimated model, we see that AICc selected Lasso has around 20% nonzero coefficients.

```
> B <- coef(fitdmr)
> mean(B!=0)
[1] 0.1960879
> head(round(B,2))
6 x 5 sparse Matrix of class "dgCMatrix"
                   1      2      3      4      5
intercept      -1.29  -2.75  -2.66  -1.97  -0.57
lackluster       .     0.44   0.04     .    -0.18
pleasing         .      .      .       .      .
protect          .      .      .       .      .
anticipated      .      .      .       .      .
beats          -0.10    .      .       .     0.00
```

Recalling Chapter 4, these multinomial logistic regression coefficients can be interpreted in terms of the differences across coefficients on the same token for different classes. For example, adding the term "sucks" to a review increases the odds of 1 star over 5 stars by a factor of 2.3 and increases the odds of 1 star over 2 stars by a factor of 1.4.

```
> exp( B["sucks",1] - B["sucks",5] )
[1] 2.329074
> exp( B["sucks",1] - B["sucks",2] )
[1] 1.398993
```

■ 9.3 Topic Models

Text data is super high dimensional, and the DTMs we get through vectorization are super high dimensional (they will have many columns of tokens). In the previous section, we saw that we can use Lasso regularization methods to build regression models using text inputs. But it can also be useful to use *factor models* to reduce the dimension of this text data before trying to use it as an input to regression models. As we covered in Chapter 8, you can use methods such as principal components analysis (PCA) to estimate *latent* low-dimensional factors that summarize high-dimensional observations. In this section we will introduce a factorization strategy that works well for text data: *topic modeling.*

Unsupervised factor modeling—estimating factors for data vectors **x** without considering any connected response variable—is an especially useful strategy for text analysis because of the abundance of *unlabeled* text data. Labeled texts are those which are accompanied by attributes of interest. For example, our reviews are connected with their star rating attribute. In practice, it is common that you have a small amount of labeled texts and a massive amount of unlabeled text. For example, suppose that Twitter wants to build a classifier to predict abusive tweets. Their labeled subset would be a set of tweets that they have paid a human to read and classify as "abusive." Their massive bank of unlabeled data consists of all other tweets on their website. A successful strategy is to use the full set of text data, including both labeled and unlabeled texts, to estimate a factor model. The lower dimensional factor representation can then be used as input to a regression model to predict your response on the small labeled sample (e.g., to classify abusive tweets on the data human labeled tweets). This works nicely because when you have less data it always pays to reduce dimension if you can do it efficiently.

In our Yelp review example, we have all the labels we need because reviews are always accompanied by a star rating. However, using a factor model is still useful for dimension reduction because it allows us to use nonparametric regression techniques like the random forests of Chapter 7. If you can reduce the text data into a small set of factors, then you can use those factors as inputs to a random forest regression for flexible prediction of review sentiment (or any other attribute of interest).

The PCA approach of Chapter 8 can be applied to text data. However, it doesn't work very well. First, the `prcomp` function converts any matrix you give it to dense format before running PCA. With a large sparse text matrix, storing all of the zeros can exhaust the amount of working memory on your computer. For example, running `prcomp` on our Yelp `dtm` attempts to create a dense data set that occupies more than 2.2GB of memory (and it fails).

```
> pca <- prcomp(dtm, scale=TRUE)
  Error: cannot allocate vector of size 2.2 Gb
```

You can work around this computational constraint by calculating PCA step-by-step yourself, using the `eigen` function as we noted in Chapter 8. However, a bigger issue is that PCA uses a squared error loss to estimate its factors: it chooses the factors to minimize the squared distance between expected values from the factor model and the observation. When the observations are mostly zeros (as in a DTM), this approach to factorization can be inefficient and produce factors that are difficult to interpret (and less useful as inputs to a downstream regression). Instead, we will make use of a factor model that is specifically designed to work for term count data.

Latent Dirichlet Allocation

Prior to the 2000s, most text factorization relied upon versions of PCA under the label *latent semantic analysis* (LSA). However, this changed with the introduction of latent Dirichlet allocation (LDA) by Blei et al. (2003). Also known as *topic models,* an LDA factorization models the rows of each DTM as draws from a multinomial distribution. Recall that the multinomial distribution is what you get if you sample repeatedly from several categories with some fixed probabilities over getting a draw from each category. Since the DTM rows represent counts of tokens, and the multinomial is the random distribution for counts in token-categories, it is natural to model each document's token count vector using a multinomial. LDA tends to lead to a factorization of DTMs that is more interpretable (you can figure out what semantic topics each factor represents) and more efficient (you need fewer factors to summarize a document), and it has mostly replaced LSA for document summarization.

Introducing some equations, the LDA or topic model representation for document i has its length-J vector of token counts $\mathbf{x}_i$ drawn from a multinomial:

$$\mathbf{x}_i \sim \mathrm{MN}(\omega_{i1}\boldsymbol{\mu}_1 + \ldots + \omega_{iK}\boldsymbol{\mu}_K, l_i) \tag{9.1}$$

where $\mathrm{MN}(\mathbf{p}, l)$ denotes l draws from a multinomial distribution with probabilities $\mathbf{p}$. In Equation (1), the elements are

- $l_i = \sum_{j=1}^{J} x_{ij}$ is the document length (sum of word counts for document i).
- $\boldsymbol{\mu}_k$ is the vector of probabilities over tokens for *topic k.*
- $\boldsymbol{\omega}_k$ is the vector of probabilities over the K topics, and $\Sigma_k \omega_{ik}\boldsymbol{\mu}_{kj}$ is the probability of word j in document i.

Each $\boldsymbol{\mu}_k$ and ω_i are probability vectors, such that $\Sigma_j \boldsymbol{\mu}_{kj} = 1$ and $\Sigma_k \omega_{ik} = 1$.

One way to think about Equation (9.1) is to imagine a random "bag of words" document generation under this model. For each word in document i, the imaginary generation process is to

1. Choose a topic k with probability ω_{ik}.
2. Choose to use token j for that word with probability $\boldsymbol{\mu}_{kj}$.

In this way, the document can be summarized in terms of its topic probabilities ω_i. The individual ω_{ik} indicate the proportion of words in document i that come from topic k.

LDA as a Factor Model

Another way to think about LDA is to compare it to the linear factor models of Chapter 8. Recall our linear factor model from Equation (8.7):

$$\mathbb{E}[\mathbf{x}_i|\boldsymbol{\omega}_i] = \omega_{i1}\boldsymbol{\mu}_1 + \ldots + \omega_{iK}\boldsymbol{\mu}_K \tag{9.2}$$

where $\boldsymbol{\mu}_k$ is the length J factor vector for "direction" k and ω_{ik} are univariate factor values indicating how observation i depends on factor direction k.

The analogous topic model representation has the exact same structure in the expectation for the *proportion* of tokens in each document—that is, for $\mathbf{x}_i/l_i$. From the multinomial model in Equation (9.1), the expected value of this proportion vector is the vector of token probabilities:

$$\mathbb{E}\left[\frac{\mathbf{x}_i}{l_i}|\boldsymbol{\omega}_i\right] = \omega_{i1}\boldsymbol{\mu}_1 + \ldots + \omega_{iK}\boldsymbol{\mu}_K \tag{9.3}$$

Thus, topic models are simply a factor model for document term proportions. The main difference between our PCA approaches to factorization and this new LDA approach is that Equation (9.1) implies we will use a multinomial deviance to fit the factors whereas PCA minimizes the sums of squared errors. Also, the ω_i and μ_k are *probabilities* in LDA so that all of these vectors are forced to sum to one. Analogously to the terminology that we adopted in Chapter 8 on factorization, we refer to the ω_i factors as the *topic scores* for document i.

Computing LDA Topic Models in R

Topic model estimation is a computationally intensive task. However, since LDA is very useful, it is a problem that many have worked on and there are plenty of efficient algorithms available. The `text2vec` package contains an efficient implementation of LDA that we can use to fit a topic model for our Yelp reviews.

Example 9.3 **Yelp Data: Topic Modeling** To fit a topic model for the Yelp reviews, we can use the same `dtm` document term matrix that we created earlier. The `text2vec` package does topic modeling in two steps. You first create an untrained topic model using the `LDA$new` function, telling it how many topics you want to use, and you then use its `fit_transform` function to estimate the topic model that approximates the counts in your DTM. Here, we fit a 20 topic model:

```
> tpc <- LDA$new(n_topics = 20)
> W <- tpc$fit_transform(dtm)
```

As for any factor model, the choice of the number of topics K is subjective unless you are using the topics in a downstream regression task. When you are doing topic analysis to explore and understand a collection of documents, then you should experiment with different K and use the choice that leads to the most interpretable topics. When you are using the topics as inputs to regression, then you can use your usual model selection tools (e.g., cross-validation) to evaluate the performance of different numbers of topics.

There are a number of other arguments that can be passed to `LDA$new` which specify how the topics will be estimated. However, the default arguments work nicely for most applications. Note that, like our K-means clustering of Chapter 8, LDA is solving a *nonconvex* optimization problem and if you run this algorithm twice you might get slightly different answers.

After running this code, the `tpc` object has been updated to contain the fitted topic-word probabilities μ_k and the output `W` is the matrix of topic-scores: each ith row of `W` contains the document topic scores ω_i.

```
> dim(W)
[1] 60000 20
> round(W[1,],2)
 [1]  0.04  0.00  0.08  0.05  0.07  0.06  0.03  0.01  0.01  0.09
[11]  0.01  0.01  0.39  0.00  0.02  0.02  0.01  0.01  0.01  0.08
> sum(W[1,])
[1] 1
```

Our 4958 column DTM matrix has now been reduced to a 20 column topic matrix. Each row of this topic matrix is a vector of probabilities over topics.

Topic Interpretation via Lift and Probabilty

To interpret the fitted topics, you can look at the token probabilities within each μ_k (recall that the μ_k is a vector of probabilities over tokens). However, the largest probabilities within each μ_k will typically correspond to tokens that are generally common (high probability) and not high probability only within topic k. An alternative approach is to look at the topic-token *lift:* the probability for each token within a topic divided by the overall probability for that token,

$$\text{lift}_{jk} = \mu_{jk} / \frac{\sum_i x_{ij}}{\sum_i l_i} \tag{9.4}$$

This lift represents the increase in probability for a token in a given topic relative to its overall probability in the corpus.

The fitted `tpc` LDA object contains the function `get_top_words` which can be used to return the words with highest probability and/or lift within a topic. It takes the argument `lambda` which weights token probability against token lift when ranking the tokens. Setting `lambda=1` returns tokens ordered by their topic probability, setting `lambda=0` returns tokens ordered by their topic lift, and values between 0 and 1 rank tokens by a weighted combination of these two metrics. Looking at the 7th topic from our fitted model, the top words by topic probability are positive sentiment terms.

```
> drop( tpc$get_top_words(n = 5, topic=7, lambda=1) )
[1] "super"     "excellent" "awesome"   "happy"     "highly"
```

As with any algorithm that involves a random initialization, the results you get will vary from here and across runs. Looking instead at lift, we find that this topic is more specifically positive sentiment about Mexican restaurants.

```
> drop( tpc$get_top_words(n = 5, topic=7, lambda=0) )
[1] "mexico" "pastor" "queso" "asada" "taco"
```

Considering topic 19, the topic probability top words are all about communication.

```
> drop( tpc$get_top_words(n = 5, topic=19, lambda=1) )
[1] "called" "call" "told" "phone" "said"
```

When you change to `lambda=0` and rank on topic token lift, the top words are now clearly related to complaints and disputes.

```
> drop( tpc$get_top_words(n = 5, topic=19, lambda=0) )
[1] "collect" "liar" "cancellation" "fraud" "documents"
```

In each case, the probability ranking gave us generic information about the topic while the lift ranking gives us a specific subject matter.

Using `LDAvis` to Explore Topic Models

A really nice feature of using `text2vec` for our topic modeling is that the output feeds nicely into the `LDAvis` package (Sievert and Shirley, 2015), which offers a way to explore the topics interactively. To use this you need to first install the `LDAvis` and `servr` (Xie, 2020) packages. You can then run the following code:

```
> library(LDAvis)
> library(servr)
> tpc$plot()
```

This should launch an interactive `html` display in your web browser. Figure 9.2 shows a screenshot of the visualization we get for our Yelp topics. There is a ton of info on here, and you can explore hovering over and clicking the various objects. In the left panel the topics are represented in two dimensions (this is from another factor model fit to the topic scores) so you can see which topics tend to occur with each other in a document, and the right panel gives you a visual representation of the top words within a given topic (notice the `lambda` slider that allows you to toggle between ranking by probability or lift).

LDA Regression

Topics are fun for exploring documents and understanding the main sentiment themes. However, they are most *useful* as inputs to regression tasks. As mentioned earlier, a reduced-dimension

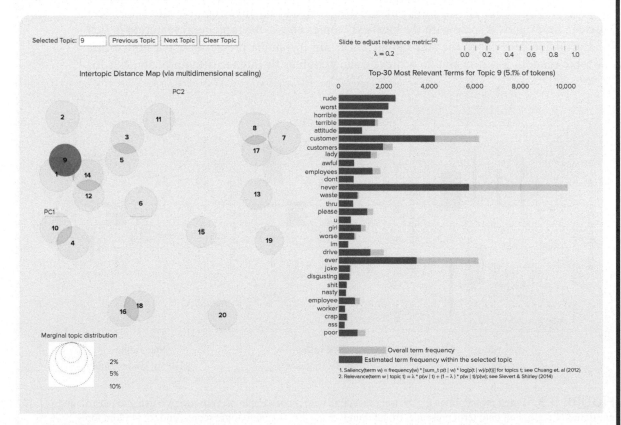

FIGURE 9.2   The interactive graphic from `LDAvis` for our Yelp review topic model.

representation for your text data allows you to fit nonparametric regression models like random forests (RF). Here, we will use the `ranger` function to build a forest that predicts the star rating probabilities given document topics. To run the regression, we first combine the star ratings (converted to a factor) with the topics in a data frame. We then run `ranger` as in Chapter 7 but with the argument `prob=TRUE` to get a model that predicts the probabilities across star ratings for each review.

```
> library(ranger)
> wdat <- data.frame(stars=factor(reviews$stars),W)
> topicRF <- ranger(stars ~ ., data=wdat, num.tree=100, prob=TRUE)
```

You can call the predict function to get the fitted probabilities, and we find a 71% predicted probability that our first review has a 1 star rating.

```
> pwRF <- predict(topicRF, wdat)$predictions
> round(pwRF[1,],2)
   1    2    3    4    5
0.71 0.08 0.07 0.10 0.05
```

The fitted probabilities for the true star rating—$\hat{p}_k$ when the true rating is k stars—are shown in Figure 9.3b. As we might have expected from our investigation into the "great Mexican food" and "dispute with the business" topics above, the topic representation is rich in information relevant to the star rating. These are in-sample predictions, but notice that our topic random forest is able to achieve a much tighter fit (higher fitted probabilities for

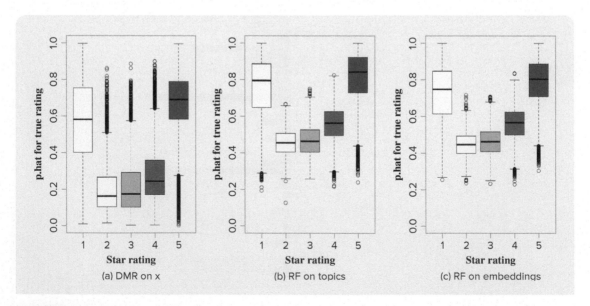

(a) DMR on x   (b) RF on topics   (c) RF on embeddings

FIGURE 9.3 Fitted probabilities for the true star rating across our sample of Yelp reviews, using (a) distributed multinomial regression onto term presence, (b) random forest regression onto topic scores, and (c) random forest regression onto the document average embedding.

the true class) compared to the multinomial logistic regression obtained by using `dmr` to regress star ratings onto the full token presence matrix. This tighter fit (lower deviance) is obtained using only the 20 topics instead of the original roughly 5k tokens. The dimension reduction of LDA, combined with the automatic interaction detection of an RF, is a powerful tool for production.

9.3.1 Collaborative Filtering with LDA

We will take a brief departure from text data to introduce another application area for LDA. *Collaborative filtering* is the task of predicting a person's future choices from their and others' past choices. Collaborative filtering is a key ingredient in building *recommender systems* that make suggestions for choices to customers. For example, the recommendations that you get for products on Amazon (people who buy this also buy), movies on Netflix (watch more like this), or for music on Spotify (suggested artist) are all using some form of collaborative filtering.

It turns out that LDA is a great technique for collaborative filtering. The data here are *counts* for *choices*. For example, if you have a streaming music service then your choices can be the artists that someone can listen to and the counts are the number of times that they stream that artist. Compared to text data, the choices (artists) play the role of tokens and the customer's streaming history creates your count vector $\mathbf{x}_i$.

Using LDA to model this choice data creates topics defined by the probabilities over choices ($\boldsymbol{\mu}_k$ for choice topic k). The factor scores ω_i represent how customer i's choices are weighted on these different choice topics. For example, in our streaming music example the $\boldsymbol{\mu}_k$ topic-choice probabilities could represent musical *genres* with high probabilities on artists within those genres. The factor scores ω_i represent the user's preferences across the genres. A recommender system built on top of LDA analysis could look at the genres k with high probability for a user (high ω_{ik}) and recommend artists that they have not previously streamed from that genre (artist j where μ_{kj} is big but $x_{ij} = 0$).

Example 9.4 last.fm Playlist: Topic Modeling To illustrate the use of LDA in factor modeling, we will look at data from last.fm, a now defunct online radio service. For each of 15k users, we have the playlist of their recent listening session. These data were made available by the `igraph` open source software for network analysis (Csardi and Nepusz (2006)).

Reading the data into R, we have in `lastFM` a four column data frame containing the user ID, the artists they have streamed, and their gender and country. Our first user is a woman in Germany with eclectic taste.

```
> lastFM<-read.csv("lastfm.csv",colClasses="factor")
> head(lastFM)
  user              artist sex country
1    1   red hot chili peppers   f Germany
2    1 the black dahlia murder   f Germany
```

```
3    1              goldfrapp    f Germany
4    1        dropkick murphys    f Germany
5    1              le tigre    f Germany
6    1              schandmaul    f Germany
```

To apply LDA, we need to get this data into a sparse count matrix of the sort that we can input to text2vec. Instead of a document term count matrix we are building a user artist count matrix, but the structure will be the same as our earlier DTMs. To build this matrix, we will use the sparseMatrix function from the Matrix library to create a simple triplet matrix from the observed choices. Recall from Section 3.2.3 in Chapter 3 on regularization that simple triplet matrices are defined by three vectors: the row id *i,* column id *j,* and value *x* for every nonzero entry. The sparseMatrix function allows you to define a matrix using these vectors.

```
> library(Matrix)
> fmX <- sparseMatrix(
+       i=as.numeric(lastFM$user),
+       j=as.numeric(lastFM$artist),
+       x=rep(1,nrow(lastFM)),
+       dims=c(nlevels(lastFM$user),nlevels(lastFM$artist)),
+
dimnames=list(levels(lastFM$user),levels(lastFM$artist)))
> dim(fmX)
[1] 15000 1004
```

The result is a 15k by 1004 dimensional matrix with a row for each user and a column for each artist. This is a sparse matrix.

```
> fmX[1:2,2:5]
2 x 4 sparse Matrix of class "dgCMatrix"
     [unknown] 2pac 3 doors down 30 seconds to mars
1         .    .         .                    .
1000      .    .         .                    .
> fmX[1, fmX[1,]!=0]
       dropkick murphys         edguy         eluveitie
                      1             1                 1
...
the black dahlia murder  the killers the rolling stones
                      1             1                 1
```

Notice the column for [unknown], which is presumably used when the user streamed an artist that we don't recognize. The nonzero elements of each row are the counts of times that the user listened to that artist in their streaming session.

Now that we have this fmX matrix, we can use text2vec to fit LDA exactly as we did for text DTMs. We will fit a 10 genre (i.e., 10 topic) factor model.

```
> # run the topic model
> library(text2vec)
> fmLDA <- LDA$new(n_topics = 10)
> fmW <- fmLDA$fit_transform( fmX )
```

Looking at top choices within each factor both by probability (lambda=1) and lift (lambda=0) ranking shows that the factors do indeed look like musical genres. Looking first by probability, we can see topics for various rock and pop genres.

```
> fmLDA$get_top_words(n = 3, lambda=1)
      [,1]              [,2]                  [,3]
[1,] "the beatles"  "death cab for cutie"  "metallica"
[2,] "the cure"     "sigur ros"            "iron maiden"
[3,] "radiohead"    "modest mouse"         "in flames"
      [,4]              [,5]                  [,6]
[1,] "system of a down"  "air"              "pink floyd"
[2,] "linkin park"       "massive attack"   "queen"
[3,] "the offspring"     "portishead"       "the beatles"
      [,7]              [,8]              [,9]
[1,] "kanye west"      "coldplay"     "nine inch nails"
[2,] "amy winehouse"   "the killers"  "tool"
[3,] "michael jackson" "muse"         "rage against the machine"
      [,10]
[1,] "madonna"
[2,] "fall out boy"
[3,] "britney spears"
```

Again, due to random initialization for the LDA algorithm, your results may vary. Top artists by *lift* shows less mainstream artists that are popular within each genre.

```
> fmLDA$get_top_words(n = 3, lambda=0)
      [,1]           [,2]                       [,3]
[1,] "bauhaus"     "spoon"                    "after forever"
[2,] "buzzcocks"   "animal collective"        "amon amarth"
[3,] "lou reed"    "architecture in helsinki" "amorphis"
```

```
       [,4]                  [,5]                  [,6]
[1,] "adema"              "amon tobin"          "billy joel"
[2,] "bloodhound gang"    "boards of canada"    "buena vista social
club"
[3,] "for my valentine"  "boys noize"           "elton john"
       [,7]                  [,8]                  [,9]
[1,] "50 cent"            "arctic monkeys"      "44"
[2,] "a tribe called quest" "dirty pretty things"  "comeback
kid"
[3,] "cunninlynguists"    "feeder"               "converge"
       [,10]
[1,] "all time low"
[2,] "ashlee simpson"
[3,] "christina aguilera"
```

A recommender engine strategy would be to look at the user-genre probabilities ω_i to find their favorite genres and then recommend high lift artists within that genre. For example, looking at genre 6 you might be able to surprise listeners of classic rock singer-songwriters with a suggestion for the Cuban Buena Vista Social Club.

◆ 9.4 Word Embedding

Throughout this chapter, we have focused on a single text vectorization strategy: counting the tokens. This is a simple and powerful technique. However, natural language processing has increasingly started to work with text that is vectorized as a *sequence* of tokens. Instead of counting tokens and representing corpora as a DTM with a column for each token, these sequence tokenizers represent a document as a vector of token IDs. The first element of the vector is the ID for the first token in the document, the second element is the ID for the second token, etc. In our next chapter, on deep learning, we will explore the analysis of text sequences in detail. However, there are also some simple dimension reduction strategies that allow you to take advantage of this token-sequence data in your analyses.

Word embedding is the technique of using sequences of tokens (i.e. words) to estimate *vector representations* for each. The goal is to replace each token with a vector value such that, for example, *hotdog* becomes the location $[1, -5, .25]$ in a three-dimensional *embedding space* (this is just for illustration; embedding spaces are typically of higher dimensions). These representation are useful because you can now treat a token as a location in space and use this information to calculate distances between tokens to understand how they relate in meaning. Most importantly, you can use the token embedding vectors as data input for downstream regression tasks. In addition to containing token sequence information that is lost when we simply count tokens, the embeddings can lead to document representations that are much lower dimensional than a DTM representation.

Token Sequences and Co-occurrence Matrices

To understand how word embedding works, consider a document that has been vectorized as a sequence of token ids:

$$\mathbf{x} = [\,10, 201, 12, \ldots\,] \tag{9.5}$$

representing that the first word of the document is the 10th token in the vocabulary, the second word is the 201st vocabulary token, the third word is the 12th vocabulary token, and so on. The length of $\mathbf{x}$ is the number of words in the document (e.g., a single review) such that every document will be represented by a vector with a document-specific length. This representation is accompanied by a vocabulary key that maps from the values in $\mathbf{x}$ to the original tokens (e.g., say "10:sushi" if the 10th token is "sushi").

The deep learning techniques of our next chapter can take these sequence vectors as inputs to deep neural network regression models. However, you can also do word embedding without deep learning by making use of *term co-occurrence matrices* (TCM). To construct a TCM you look at sequences of words and, for each pair of tokens in your vocabulary, calculate how often they occur near each other. The definition of "near" is your *window size;* for example, with a window of 5 your TCM entry for a pair of tokens is the number of times that these tokens occur within 5 words of each other in the sequences. If you have J tokens in your vocabulary, then the TCM will be a $J \times J$ square matrix $\mathbf{C}$ with elements $c_{i,j}$ representing the number of times that tokens i and j occur in the same window in your token sequences (e.g., within 5 words of each other).

Given a corpus of documents represented as sequence vectors, you can calculate the TCM by setting a window size and then summing the term co-occurences across all of the sequence vectors. For example if token 10 is "hotdog" and token 201 is "bun," then with a window of 4 the TCM element $c_{10,201}$ will equal the total number of times "hotdog" and "bun" occur within 5 words of each other. This leads to $c_{i,j}$ elements that are large if those words tend to occur near each other and small if the words do not tend to appear together. Typically these TCMs will be sparse: most tokens pairs never occur in the same window. The structure of the TCM defines the relationships between tokens in your vocabulary, and embedding techniques are used to summarize this structure.

Token Embedding Algorithms

Popular embedding tools include the Glove algorithm of Pennington et al. (2014) and Word-2Vec algorithm from Mikolov et al. (2013). They are roughly similar techniques, each training token embedding vectors that can be multiplied with each other to approximate entries in the TCM. We will use the Glove functionality that is available in the `text2vec` library. Glove estimates word embedding vectors, say ν_j for token j, to fit the model

$$\log(c_{st}) = a_s + a_t + \nu_s' \nu_t + e_{st} \tag{9.6}$$

where c_{st} are the co-occurrence count entries in the TCM $\mathbf{C}$, the a_s and a_t are intercept terms to account for the overall prevalence of tokens s and $t,$ and e_{st} is the error term. This model is estimated using least squares over all combinations where $c_{st} > 0$. This means that Glove ignores the zeros in $\mathbf{C}$, which is useful for computational speed (because $\mathbf{C}$ will be sparse) and tends to lead to better results.

The dimension of your embedding space, say K, is the length of the embedding vectors ν_j. Thus the product $\nu'_s \nu_t$ in (9.6) is equal to $\sum_{k=1}^{K} \nu_{sk} \nu_{tk}$. Choosing this embedding dimension is similar to choosing your number of topics of factors: it is subjective, based upon interpretability of the resulting token vectors, unless you are using the embeddings in a downstream regression task (in which case you can use cross-validation to choose K if you wish).

The result of the Glove algorithm is a J (number of tokens) by K matrix of token embedding vectors. These embedding vectors have the property that words with similar *embedding values* tend to have similar meanings. This can be useful to analyze meaning in language. For example, the paper "Man is to computer programmer as woman is to homemaker?" (Bolukbasi et al., 2016) used a word embedding trained on news articles to estimate gender bias in how people describe jobs that are traditionally held by men or women. The most common use of word embeddings, however, is as an input to a downstream regression task. As we will see in our example below, you can average embedding vectors across the tokens in a short document to get a K-dimensional "document embedding." Similar to how we incorporated LDA topics into regression in Example 9.3, this document embedding can then be used as an input to a regression model to predict document attributes.

Example 9.5 **Yelp Data: Word Embedding** To illustrate word embedding, we will again turn to our Yelp reviews. The first step is to calculate the TCM containing token co-occurrence counts. The text2vec package includes the create_tcm function that can be applied to the same *tokenizer* and *vectorizer* functions that we used in Example 9.1 to create a document term count matrix. Instead of a DTM, creat_tcm counts token co-occurrences to create a TCM. Recall that the co-occurrences are counted within a *window* of nearby words. The default window size is 5 but you can change this with the skip_grams_window argument.

```
> tcm = create_tcm(tokYelp, vectorizer)
> class(tcm)
[1] "dgTMatrix"
attr(,"package")
[1] "Matrix"
> dim(tcm)
[1] 4958 4958
> mean(tcm==0)
[1] 0.9263996
```

The resulting 4958 × 4958 TCM matrix has a row and column for each token in our vocabulary. Notice that 93% of the entries in this matrix are zero: the large majority of tokens never occur within 5 words of each other.

To fit the Glove model of Equation (9.6), you first use the GlobalVectors$new function to create a Glove model that is ready to be fit to data. It has two main arguments: rank is the dimension K of the embedding space, and x_max determines the *weights* used in estimation. Recalling that Glove estimates (9.6) through least squares estimation. In fact, it uses a *weighted* least squares optimization where it minimizes $\Sigma_{s,t}\delta_{st}e_{st}^2$ over all token combinations where $c_{st} > 0$. The weights δ_{st} are set equal to $\min(c_{st}/\text{x\_max}, 1)$, such that larger c_{st} have a larger weight until $c_{st} > \text{x\_max}$ at which point they all have a weight of one. If you increase x_max then your embeddings will be more influenced by the largest c_{st}.

Here, we fit glove for a 20 dimensional embedding with x_max=10. Once you create the model, you optimize it to the TCM using the fit_transform function.

```
> glove = GlobalVectors$new(rank = 20, x_max = 10)
> vGlove = glove$fit_transform(tcm)
> dim(vGlove)
[1] 4958 20
> round(vGlove[1,,drop=FALSE],2)
            [,1] [,2]  [,3] [,4] [,5]  [,6] [,7] [,8]  [,9] [,10]
lackluster 0.09 0.09 -0.31 0.38 0.14 -0.46    0  0.1 -0.46 -0.14
           [,11] [,12] [,13] [,14] [,15] [,16][,17] [,18] [,19] [,20]
lackluster -0.76  0.11 -0.06 -0.16 -0.18 -0.09    0 -0.46  0.19  0.11
```

The resulting matrix of embeddings has 4958 rows (one for each token) and 20 columns (equal to K). Each token is now represented by a length-20 vector ν_j. Since Glove has a random initialization, you will get different results when you run the same code.

Cosine Similarity

We said above that words with similar embedding values have similar meanings. The *similarity* between words in the embedding space is measured in terms of their *cosine similarity:* the cosine of the angle between the two vector embeddings. We can use the sim2 function to calculate the similarity between tokens. You give it a full vocabulary embedding (our vGlove matrix) and the embedding vectors for other tokens that you want to find similar words for. For example, here we apply it to find the 5 most similar tokens for the token "upscale."

```
> sims = sim2(x = vGlove, y = vGlove["upscale",,drop=FALSE])
> sort(sims[,"upscale"], decreasing = TRUE)[1:5]
   upscale     trendy      chic    reminds     classy
 1.0000000  0.8568592 0.8080232  0.8032796  0.7674276
```

One interesting feature of word embeddings is that you can do algebra on the word embeddings. A common example has that the vector for France minus the vector for Paris plus the vector for Germany will end up with a vector similar to Berlin. The idea is that France minus Paris is the same relationship as Germany minus Berlin if Paris is to France as Berlin is to Germany. We can look in our review data for a similar answer to the analogy "pepperoni is to pizza as tofu is to X?"

```
> analogy <- vGlove["pizza",]-vGlove["pepperoni",]+vGlove["tofu",]
> sims <- sim2(x = vGlove, y = matrix(analogy,nrow=1))
> sort(sims[,1], decreasing = TRUE)[1:5]
    ramen       pho      thai      soup     fried
0.7988933 0.7816291 0.7753570 0.7421802 0.7222137
```

The algebra finds that pepperoni is to pizza as tofu is to ramen and pho.

Document Average Embeddings and Regression

These algebra examples are cute, but the real power of embeddings is when you use them as inputs to other ML tasks. To illustrate, we will calculate the *average* token embedding across the tokens in each Yelp review. To do this, we will matrix multiply wGlove by our count dtm matrix to get the sum of token vectors in each review and then divide by the number of tokens to get the average. Note that the columns of the dtm matrix correspond to the same columns in the vGlove matrix (they represent the same tokens).

```
> all(rownames(vGlove)==colnames(dtm))
[1] TRUE
> V = as.matrix( (dtm %*% vGlove)/rowSums(dtm) )
> dim(V)
[1] 60000     20
> round(V[1,],2)
 [1]  -0.01  0.21 -0.21  0.06  0.17  0.43  0.28  0.09  0.16 -0.04
[11]   0.28 -0.10  0.24  0.18 -0.17  0.06  0.29 -0.06  0.01  0.34
> V[is.na(V)] <- 0
```

The resulting matrix V has rows equal to the length-20 average embedding for each of our 60k reviews. Note that this resulted in some NA values in V since some of the reviews include zero tokens (after removing common and rare words in the original tokenization), such that the averaging operation involves dividing zero by zero (which is undefined). We replace the embeddings for these reviews with zero.

Finally, we can use V as an input to a random forest to predict star rating exactly as we did with the LDA representation of the documents.

```
> vdat <- data.frame(stars=factor(reviews$stars),V)
> gloveRF <- ranger(stars ~ ., data=vdat, num.tree=100, prob=TRUE)
```

The resulting fitted probabilities for observed star ratings are shown back in Figure 9.3c. We see that the fit obtained by RF regression onto average document embeddings is similar to that obtained by regression onto topics.

QUICK REFERENCE

The tools that you have learned elsewhere in this book can be combined with tokenization techniques to allow you to incorporate text data into your regression analyses. The raw token count data can be incorporated into Lasso regressions, while topic modeling and word embedding methods allow you to use transformed text as inputs to nonlinear regression methods like random forests.

Key Practical Concepts

- Use the `text2vec` library to tokenize raw text into a token-count document term matrix `dtm`.

  Define a tokenizer with `itoken`.

  Create vocabulary with `create_vocabulary`.

  Prune the vocabulary with `prune_vocabulary`.

  Define a `vocab_vectorizer` on this vocabulary.

  Create `dtm` via `create_dtm` as a sparse `Matrix` object.

- Use `dtm` as an input to text regression models. You can use `dtm>0` to have your inputs be the presence of tokens in documents rather than counts.

  ```
  fit <- gamlr( dtm>0, y )
  ```

- Fit a *K* topic model using the `text2vec` package.

  ```
  tpc <- LDA$new(n_topics=K)
  W <- tpc$fit_transform(dtm)
  ```

  Use `tpc$plot()` to launch the `LDAvis` interactive graphic to explore topics.

- Use the `get_top_words` function to see top words within each topic ordered by topic probability and lift (topic probability over average probability).

  ```
  # words ordered by lift
  tpc$get_top_words( n=5, topic=k, lambda=0 )
  # words ordered by probability
  tpc$get_top_words( n=5, topic=k, lambda=1 )
  ```

- Use the estimated document topics as inputs to a random forest for prediction of response y.

  ```
  tpcRF <- ranger( y~., data=data.frame(y=y, W), num.
  tree=B )
  ```

- Build a recommender engine: fit topic models to customer choice data, and use high lift and high probability elements within each topic to suggest new choices to customers with high score for that topic.

- Use `text2vec` to tokenize raw sequences of text into a square token co-occurrence matrix `tcm` with entries counting the number of times each pair of tokens occur near each other in the text, and estimate a Glove embedding model on this `tcm`.

```
glove = GlobalVectors$new(rank = K, x_max=10)
vGlove$fit_transform(tcm)
```

Increase `x_max` if you want larger co-occurrence counts to have a bigger influence on the embedding estimation.

- Use the `sim2` function to calculate cosine similarity between words in the embedding space.

```
sims <- sim2(x=vGlove, y = vGlove["upscale",,drop=FALSE])
sort(sims[,"upscale"], decreasing = TRUE)[1:5]
```

10 DEEP LEARNING

This chapter introduces deep neural networks (DNNs) and the Keras framework for building DNN models.

■ **Section 10.1 The Ingredients of Deep Learning:** Understand the technology and ideas behind DNNs and the common model architectures.

◆ **Section 10.2 Working with Deep Learning Frameworks:** Use Keras to implement an end-to-end DNN analysis.

◆ **Section 10.3 Stochastic Gradient Descent:** Understand the basics of the algorithms used to optimize DNNs and apply this optimization technique for fitting other models.

◆ **Section 10.4 The State of the Art:** Outline specialized DNN architectures and ideas for transfer learning where models trained on one objective are used to hot-start your learning for a different objective. Get big picture context for how DNNs are influencing the pursuit of *intelligent automation*.

● **Section 10.5 Intelligent Automation:** Understand the practical applications of automation through ML.

For our last chapter, we dive into a new paradigm that has taken the field of machine learning by storm. Deep learning makes use of deep neural networks (DNNs) which can process complicated inputs, like text and images and video, in a largely *automatic* fashion. You don't need to spend huge effort in feature construction and pre-processing with deep learning: you just set up a model architecture and get training. But the full framework of deep learning is much more than just DNN models. It is the combination of DNNs with efficient programming frameworks and scalable parallel "stochastic gradient descent" optimization algorithms. The super complex DNNs that you might read about in the news, built at the cost of millions (or hundreds of millions) of dollars by giant technology companies, might seem out of reach (or irrelevant) for someone working as a business analyst. However, this chapter will introduce you to the basic underlying technology and show that it can be applied in business analysis. And through techniques for transfer learning, you can even take the models trained by tech giants and adapt them for your own analysis tasks. Indeed, the real promise of deep learning is that it can automate a lot of the grunt work of the data scientist (data wrangling and feature construction) and free you up to think bigger about the problems you want to attack with data.

This chapter should be viewed as a very basic primer on deep learning. This is a big area of research and practice, and we are just touching the surface. For further learning on deep learning, there are a number of great references including Goodfellow et al. (2016) for a broad overview and Chollet and Allaire (2018) for a focus on R (the authors are the developers of the Keras framework that we will be using here). There is also the fantastic interactive Dive Into Deep Learning website by a collection of Amazon researchers (Zhang et al.) available at d2l.ai. And you will benefit by searching the Internet and finding the wealth of examples that people have coded and made publicly available, e.g., on GitHub. Hopefully many of you will end up coding your own DNN applications and putting them online for others to learn from.

■ 10.1 The Ingredients of Deep Learning

Neural networks are an old idea. We will go into detail on these models in the next section, but as a starting example you can think of replacing a single logistic regression model with multiple logistic regression models. These multiple models are "nodes" that sit side-by-side in a "layer." The same inputs feed into each of these regression nodes, and their output (which will be a probability between zero and one) is then used as input to another final regression model that predicts your target of interest.

Layers

The deep learning revolution took these shallow networks and stacked them. Instead of one layer feeding into a single final regression, each layer feeds into another layer, which can feed into another layer, an so on, until you combine outputs into a single prediction function. This stacking is what characterizes a DNN. As we will learn below, this innovation supercharged the flexibility of the neural network models. It also provides a modeling paradigm that is highly *modular*. You can take a layer that is optimized for one type of data (e.g., images) and combine it with other layers for other types of data (e.g., text). You can also use layers that have been pretrained on one dataset (e.g., generic images) as components in a more specialized model (e.g., a specific recognition task). This flexible and modular DNN modeling framework is the first ingredient for deep learning.

Software

The next key ingredient is software: deep learning frameworks. As you've learned from this book, the R software (or an equivalent, like Python) is crucial for good analysis because it allows you to abstract away from a lot of the math and build models by defining functions and supplying data to those functions. Deep learning frameworks go further by making it easy to define DNN models as a combination of different types of layers, and then automatically construct the right optimization algorithm for training whatever model you've defined. Frameworks like Keras and TensorFlow, which are what we will work with in this chapter, take a defined DNN, do the math (i.e., automatically calculate derivatives) as necessary to define the optimization routine, and efficiently implement that optimization on whatever hardware is available (whether on your laptop CPUs or on large distributed farms of specialized processing units). These frameworks abstract away the details so that the coder, whether business analyst or software engineer, can concentrate on the big picture of what inputs to use and what predictions they care about.

Stochastic Gradient Descent

Deep learning frameworks rely on a special class of optimization algorithms called stochastic gradient descent (SGD). Whether you were aware of it or not, most of the model fits in this book have relied upon the algorithm of gradient descent wherein you calculate derivatives (i.e., change in your model deviance relative to changes in parameters) and follow these derivatives to minimize the loss (i.e., to obtain minimal deviance or, equivalently, maximum likelihood). SGD algorithms do the same thing but, instead of using the full dataset to calculate the derivatives, they do so repeatedly on subsample mini-batches of data. This allows models to be fit to a *stream* of data and avoid having to do *batch* computations on the entire dataset. This enables training complex models on massive datasets. SGD algorithms also naturally avoid overfit since you are optimizing against noisy samples of data rather than the full dataset. Like regularization and bagging, techniques we saw in earlier chapters, SGD leads to more robust and generalizable model fits. This is crucial for working with DNN models, which can have hundreds of thousands (or millions) of degrees of freedom.

Hardware

The final ingredient to deep learning is hardware. DNN training with SGD involves massively *parallel* computations: many basic operations executed simultaneously across parameters of the network. Graphical processing units (GPUs) were devised for calculations of this type, in the context of video and computer graphics display where all pixels of an image need to be rendered simultaneously. Although DNN training was originally a side use case for GPUs (i.e., as an aside from their main computer graphics mandate), AI applications are now of primary importance for GPU manufacturers. There are also new processing architectures that are designed specifically for training DNNs. Field-programmable gate arrays (FPGAs) and tensor processing units (TPUs) are specialized chips that facilitate parallel computing of "vectors" of operations, in addition to other customizations appropriate for DNNs. Fleets of computers using these fancy chips are now available from the big cloud computing services. The result is that anyone with enough compute budget can use a deep learning framework to build and train a fantastically complicated DNN model on state-of-the-art hardware.

The remainder of this chapter will work through the first three ingredients in turn: an introduction to DNN models, step-by-step examples using deep learning frameworks, and a high-level overview of stochastic gradient descent. We will be working within the limitations of most readers' on-hand hardware, i.e., not going beyond your laptop, but the material covered will give you enough background to do so if you want to sign up for AWS or another service and start working with GPUs and other parallel processing tools. We close with some topics on the state of the art of deep learning, and introduce transfer learning as a way that you can take advantage of the newest and coolest DNN models without spending millions on computation.

10.1.1 Deep Neural Networks

Neural networks use simple ingredients to build complex models. Their simplicity is a strength because basic patterns facilitate fast training and computation. Linear combinations of inputs are passed through nonlinear activation functions called *nodes*. A set of nodes taking different weighted sums of the same inputs is called a *layer,* and the output of one layer's nodes becomes input to the next layer. This structure is illustrated in Figure 10.1. Each circle here is a node. Those in the input (bottom) layer typically have a special structure; they are either raw data or

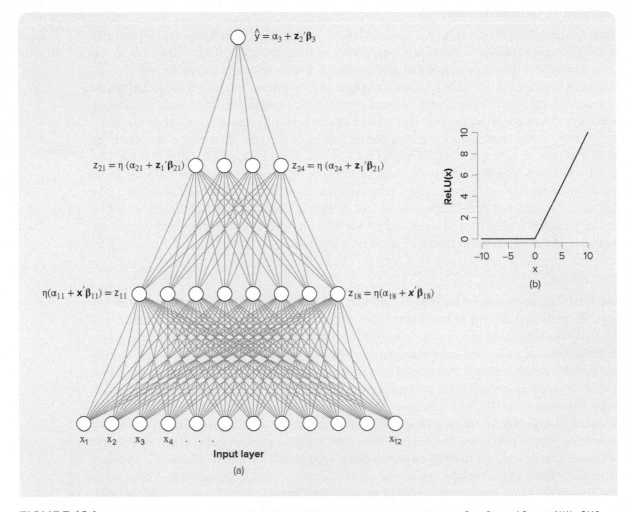

FIGURE 10.1   Panel (a) illustrates a 4 layer (two hidden) DNN, drawn using the tool at `alexlenail.me/NN-SVG`. The inputs are at the bottom and the output is at the top. Panel (b) shows a ReLU activation function which, for example, could be the activation $\eta(\cdot)$ used in the hidden layers of our example network on the left.

data that has been processed through an additional set of layers. The output layer predicts the outcomes of interest. This output could just be ŷ, the predicted value for some scalar variable *y*, but DNNs can be used to predict high-dimensional objects like a matrix of pixels. As in a generalized linear model, the output nodes have application-specific structure: linear links for simple regression, logistic links for categorical data, etc. The output is compared to observed response in a *loss function*. These loss functions correspond to a deviance, e.g., mean-squared error loss corresponding to a Gaussian deviance, or binomial loss and deviance for classification.

The picture in Figure 10.1a illustrates a simple 4 layer neural network. There are 12 inputs (bottom layer) that get processed in each of 8 nodes in the first hidden layer. Outputs of these 8 nodes are processed in each of 4 nodes in the next hidden layer, and finally combined together to a single prediction node. The first layer is called the input layer. Each node here corresponds to an input feature, say x_j just as we would write in standard regression notation (or x_{ij} for the *i*th observation of the *j*th input feature, but we'll ignore this observation indexing to avoid footnote overload here). And it looks like a standard regression equation when you combine these inputs to pass to each node in the next layer. The first node of the first hidden layer is passed $\alpha_{11} + \sum_{j=1}^{12} x_j \beta_{11j} = \alpha_{11} + \mathbf{x}' \boldsymbol{\beta}_{11}$, the second node is passed $\alpha_{12} + \sum_{j=1}^{12} x_j \beta_{12j} = \alpha_{12} + \mathbf{x}' \boldsymbol{\beta}_{12}$, and so on. There are 13 weights for each node in the first hidden layer (intercept plus 12 regression coefficients), so moving from the input to first hidden layer involves $13 \times 8 = 104$ parameters, or "weights" in the DNN lingo.

In each hidden layer node, the inputs are processed through an *activation function*. You can have different activation functions for different layers and applications, but in our diagram in Figure 10.1 we have the same function, denoted η, throughout. In most cases this would be the "rectified linear unit" or ReLU function, $\eta(v) = x \mathbb{1}_{[v > 0]}$. ReLU simply outputs the maximum of its input and zero, as shown on the right hand side of Figure 10.1. In the 1990s, people spent much effort choosing among different node activation functions. The evidence now is that you can use any simple and computationally convenient transformation and ReLU is by far the most common choice. If you have enough nodes and layers, the specific activation doesn't really matter so long as it is nonlinear.

Say $z_{1j} = \eta(\alpha_{1j} + \mathbf{x}' \boldsymbol{\beta}_{1j})$ is the output of node *j* in the first hidden layer (again, if we were indexing observations this would be output z_{1ij} for the *i*th observation). The "stacking" operation that gives DNNs their depth is to feed this output into an additional hidden layer. The first node of the second hidden layer takes inputs $\alpha_{21} + \sum_{j=1}^{8} z_{1j} \beta_{21j} = \alpha_{21} + \mathbf{z}_1' \boldsymbol{\beta}_{21}$, the second node takes $\alpha_{22} + \mathbf{z}_1' \boldsymbol{\beta}_{22}$, and so on. These are passed through the activation functions to output, for the *j*th node in this second hidden layer, $z_{2j} = \eta(\alpha_{2j} + \mathbf{z}_1' \boldsymbol{\beta}_{2j})$.

This process can repeat for many layers. In the example of Figure 10.1, we stop after two hidden layers and pass through an output layer. This output takes the four-dimensional output of our second hidden layer and processes it through a regression link function. For example, for a linear output we'd just have $f(z) = z$ so that $\hat{y} = \alpha_3 + \mathbf{z}_2' \boldsymbol{\beta}_3$. For a logistic output we'd have $\hat{y} = 1/(1 + \exp[-\alpha_3 - \mathbf{z}_2' \boldsymbol{\beta}_3])$. This choice depends upon the type of response you are targeting, and all of the lessons we have taken from our earlier work on generalized linear models apply here. For example, use an exponential output function if you talk about change in the response on a percentage scale (or, equivalently, if the variance of the response increases with its expectation). Use a logistic link if you have categorical data, and use a linear link as your default choice for a numeric response. DNN regression involves all the same considerations as our GLM regression, except now the hidden layers do the work of automatically wrangling and combining inputs into useful features for prediction. Those stacked hidden layers are what make DNNs so flexible and powerful.

10.1.2 Why Deep?

Neural networks have a long history. Work on these types of models dates back to the mid-20th century, e.g., including Rosenblatt's perceptron (Rosenblatt, 1958). This early work was focused on networks as models that could mimic the actual structure of the human brain. In the late 1980s, advances in algorithms for *training* neural networks (Rumelhart et al., 1988) opened the potential for these models to act as general pattern recognition tools rather than as a toy model of the brain. This led to a boom in neural network research, and methods developed during the 1990s are at the foundation of much of deep learning today (Hochreiter and Schmidhuber, 1997; LeCun et al., 1998; Hornik et al., 1989). However, this boom ended in bust. Because of the gap between promised and realized results (and difficulties in training networks on massive datasets) from the late 1990s, neural networks became just one ML method among many. In applications, they were supplanted by more robust tools such as random forests, high-dimensional regularized regression, and a variety of Bayesian stochastic process models (especially Gaussian processes).

What changed? A bunch of things. Two external events are of primary importance: we got much more data (big data), and computing hardware became much more efficient (GPUs). But there was also a crucial methodological development: networks went *deep*. This breakthrough is often credited to 2006 work by Geoff Hinton and coauthors (Hinton et al., 2006) on a network architecture that stacked many pre-trained layers together for a handwriting recognition task. In this pre-training, interior layers of the network are fit using an unsupervised learning task (i.e., dimension reduction of the inputs) before being used as part of the supervised learning machinery. The idea is analogous to that of principal components regression: you first fit a low-dimensional representation of **x** and then use that low-dimensional representation to predict some associated *y*.

This specific type of unsupervised pre-training is no longer viewed as central to deep learning. However, Hinton's paper opened many people's eyes to the potential for deep neural networks: models with many layers, each of which may have different structure and play a different role in the overall machinery. That is, a demonstration that one *could* train deep networks soon turned into a realization that one *should* add depth to models. In the following years, research groups began to show empirically and theoretically that depth was important for learning efficiently from data (Bengio et al., 2007). The modularity of a deep network is key: each layer of functional structure plays a specific role, and you can swap out layers like Lego blocks when moving across data applications. This allows for fast application-specific model development and also for transfer learning across models. An internal layer from a network that has been trained for one type of image recognition problem can be used to hot-start a new network for a different computer vision task.

Deep learning came into the ML mainstream with a 2012 paper by Krizhevsky, Sutskever, and Hinton that showed their DNN was able to smash current performance benchmarks in the well-known ImageNet computer vision contest. Since then, the race has been on. For example, image classification performance has surpassed human abilities (He et al., 2016), and DNNs are able to both recognize images and generate appropriate captions (Karpathy and Fei-Fei, 2015). The models behind these computer vision advances all make use of a specific type of *convolution* architecture. The raw image data (pixels) goes through multiple convolution layers (see Section 10.4 and Figure 10.11) before the output of those convolutions is fed into the more classical neural network architecture of Figure 10.1.

This is a theme of deep learning: the models use early-layer architectures that are specific to the input data format. For images, you use convolutional transformations to create "convolutional neural networks." For text data, you need a strategy to *embed* words into a vector space. And these different input architectures are then combined together in an overall architecture that predicts some target of interest. It is a highly modular design paradigm that allows you to mix

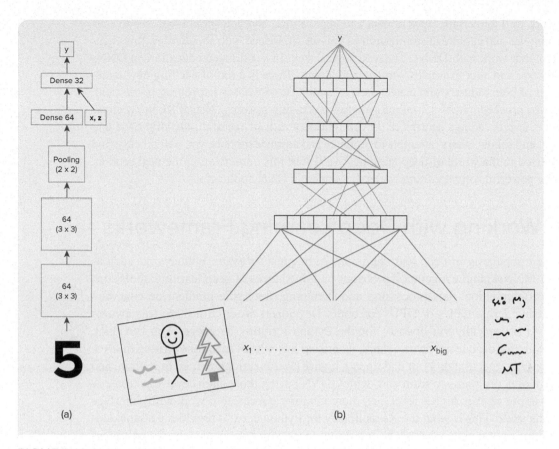

FIGURE 10.2   Panel (a) shows the simple architecture used in Hartford et al. (2017). Variables **x**, **z** contain structured business information (e.g., product IDs and prices) that is mixed with images of handwritten digits in the network. Panel (b) is a cartoon of a generic DNN, taking as input images, structured data $x_1 \ldots x_{big}$, and raw document text.

data types with great flexibility. For example, Figure 10.2 shows the simple architecture used in Hartford et al. (2017) for a task that mixed digit recognition with (simulated) business data.

One thing should be clear: there is a lot of *structure* in DNNs. These models are *not* just a version of nonparametric regression models used by statisticians, econometricians, and in earlier ML (e.g., our tree and forest models from earlier chapters). They are "semi-parametric." Consider the cartoon DNN in Figure 10.2. The early stages in the network provide dramatic, and often linear, dimension reduction. These early stages are highly parametric: it makes no sense to take a convolution model designed for image data and apply it to, say, consumer transaction data. The output of these early layers is then processed through a series of neural network nodes. These later network layers work like a traditional nonparametric regression: they expand the output of early layers to approximate arbitrary functional forms in the response of interest. Thus, the DNNs combine restrictive dimension reduction with flexible function approximation. The key is that both components are learned jointly.

We do not currently have many theoretical insights into when it is best to increase complexity by adding nodes to layers versus adding layers to the model. Indeed, tuning these parameters can itself be a target of machine learning. "AutoML" procedures experiment with different DNN configurations and model how the performance changes, and AutoML has become a standard step in production deep learning systems. You will typically find that there are architectures that people have found work well for certain types of data and applications, and you should feel free to start from these examples and explore customization as you see fit. Indeed, you should view this chapter as a *start* to your work with DNNs. The next several steps in a continued education on DNNs is to find and code and alter examples—to learn by doing. There is a ton of exciting new material coming out of both industry and academia. For a glimpse of what is happening in the field, browse the latest proceedings of neural information processing systems (NeurIPS), the premier ML conference, at proceedings.neurips.cc. If you follow threads of research, copying code and experimenting, and follow others' attempts to replicate and advance models, you will quickly find yourself immersed in the world of deep learning. We'll start this immersion in the next section, introducing the powerful software frameworks that underpin DNN applications.

◆ 10.2 Working with Deep Learning Frameworks

The success and popularity of deep learning is driven by great software. Frameworks such as TensorFlow or MXNet bundle together the various building blocks of deep learning: tools such as automatic differentiation, data processing and streaming, stochastic gradient descent, and parallel processing across CPUs or GPUs (or both). Developers work with these frameworks through their APIs, typically via libraries for the Python scripting language. You can think about the software for deep learning as a stack, where the lower level functions written in C++ and CUDA (for GPU functionality) sit underneath higher level functions written in Python, and the developer writes programs to train and deploy DNNs using those high-level functions. A great option is to put an even higher level (i.e., more intuitive and easier to work with) interface on the top of the stack. This is what the Keras library for Python does: it provides a simple language for defining neural network models, and it interfaces with your chosen back-end framework for the heavy lifting of model training and inference. Fortunately, the Keras and Rstudio creators have combined forces to create an R interface for Keras. You can get a full overview of the framework in the text *Deep Learning with* R (Chollet and Allaire, 2018), and we will use it as our access point to the deep learning stack. This *stack* is illustrated in Figure 10.3.

To work with Keras, you need to also define the back end framework that it sits on top of. We will be using TensorFlow. To get this all working, you need to go through the process of installing everything in your computing environment. For a production deployment, this will typically mean installation into multiple cloud instances and there are a huge variety of ways

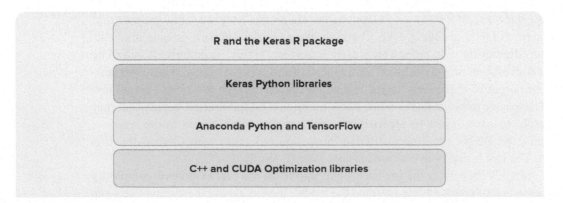

FIGURE 10.3   A diagram of the deep learning *stack* of software frameworks that we are using to build and estimate DNNs.

that you can set things up. But to work through the basics and get started, you can just install the necessary frameworks onto your laptop and use its CPUs for crunching numbers. There are detailed installation instructions at `keras.rstudio.com` and `tensorflow.rstudio.com`. If you are lucky, it can be as simple as entering the below commands into R.

```
> install.packages("devtools")
> devtools::install_github("rstudio/keras", force=T)
> devtools::install_github("rstudio/tensorflow", force =T)
> library(tensorflow)
> install_tensorflow()
> library(keras)
> install_keras()
```

If you are on a Windows machine, you will also need to install the Anaconda Python environment outside of R. And if you are unlucky, you might need to make some configuration adjustments in order to get everything connected right. This can unfortunately be frustrating. Common issues include not having a Python environment installed correctly. You can even get tripped up by simple things like having a space in the file path to where you have installed it. On Windows, you may also need to install Rtools from https://cran.r-project.org/bin/windows/ Rtools/rtools40.html. Fortunately, everything is well documented and if you get an error message, just copy the message into Google and you will likely find a fix for whatever issue you are encountering. The benefit of the wide usage of Keras and TensorFlow is that there is a ton of material online about how to use these tools.

Once you have things up and running, you can restart R and get started coding.

```
> library(keras)
> library(tensorflow)
```

Note that the second line here might be unnecessary, depending upon how you've installed TensorFlow, but it doesn't hurt to explicitly load the library. You may get some warnings when you run this code, e.g., telling you that you are only using CPUs and not able to access GPUs for computation. Don't worry about those warnings.

10.2.1 Vectorization

To introduce Keras and TensorFlow, we revisit the Yelp data from Chapter 9. To make this manageable on your laptop, we pulled a subsample of 60,000 reviews. Before setting up the DNNs, we will first work with Keras to quickly vectorize this text: convert from raw text to numeric vectors to feed into the DNNs.

Example 10.1 Yelp Data: Review Vectorization Recall that the Yelp data was stored in `json` format and we can use the `jsonlite` library to read this into R as a data frame that contains business and user IDs, the review text, and some additional attributes (star rating and review votes).

```
> library(jsonlite)
> reviews <- stream_in(file("Yelp60kReviews.json"))
```

Each row of `reviews` contains the information from a single review (including the review text).

```
> dim(reviews)
[1] 60000 9
> reviews[1,]
                review_id                      user_id
1 7O4aO11xuJEZxwbbMDj86Q EflUydcpC77nsoqn92GnFQ
              business_id stars useful funny cool
1 oxv2UyI5yF6yawPU20tOxA      1      1     0     0
                  text
1 We have no idea how the food is since we left after waiting ...
... With all the choices in Old Town Scottsdale, GO SOMEWHERE ELSE!
                  date
1 2018-12-01 04:20:00
```

In our previous text analysis work, we concentrated on a bag-of-words representation for text (see Chapter 9). In that case, we convert the text to a numeric input by creating a vector that is as long as the number of words (or tokens; refer to Chapter 9) in our training vocabulary. Each element of this vector corresponds to a word. Entries for the words in a review can be counts of the word in that review, or other statistics such as binary 0/1 for "this word occurs at least once." An advantage of working with DNNs is that we now have more flexibility in how we process the text. A useful alternative to bag of words is an integer representation for the text. In this case, we convert the text to a vector that is as long as the number of words in the largest review (or as long as we want to worry about; you can set a fixed maximum length and reviews will be truncated at that length for modeling).

Regardless of whether we want bag-of-words or integer representations, we can use Keras to create a *text vectorization* function that translates from the reviews to numeric vectors. Here, we will set a maximum review length of 300 tokens, and ask Keras to tokenize the text into 10,000 unique tokens. It will automatically split words on whitespace, and will overload the 10,000 unique tokens if that is not enough to cover the full vocabulary. It does this using the so-called hashing trick where words are assigned to random integers between 1 and 10,000; this algorithm is fast, but you can get collisions where two words end up assigned to the same number. This is not a big deal so long as you are using an index size (in this case, 10,000) that is around the same size as the actual vocabulary.

```
> max_tokens <- 10000
> max_length <- 300
> text_vectorization <- layer_text_vectorization(
+   max_tokens = max_tokens,
+   output_sequence_length = max_length)
> text_vectorization %>% adapt(reviews$text)
```

Note the use of the %>% pipe operator. This is common when working with Keras, and also with a number of R packages that use dplyr and related tools for data wrangling. You can understand it as forwarding the first object to the second function. In this case, we are applying the text_vectorization function to the cleaned and standardized text produced by the adapt function. The result is that our text_vectorization function has now been customized to vectorize the text of Yelp reviews. We can access the resulting word-to-index mapping with the get_vocabulary function.

```
> get_vocabulary(text_vectorization)
  [1] "the"        "and"        "i"
  [4] "to"         "a"          "was"
  [7] "of"         "for"        "it"
 [10] "is"         "in"         "my"
 [13] "they"       "that"       "this"
...
```

Note that Keras adds 1 to the index when it vectorizes. For example, "this" is the 15th word in the vocabulary and it will be assigned integer value 16 when we vectorize. We can apply our new text vectorization function to some short reviews to see the result.

```
> text_vectorization(matrix("this restaurant rules", ncol=1))[1,1:3]
tf.Tensor([ 16 125 2938 ], shape=(3,), dtype=int64)
> text_vectorization(matrix("this restaurant sucks", ncol=1))[1,1:3]
tf.Tensor([ 16 125 1663 ], shape=(3,), dtype=int64)
```

Each statement is now represented as a vector of three (the number of words in each review) integers followed by 297 zeros (padding out to 300, the maximum review length that we specified above). Notice that the results of vectorization are not our usual R vectors or matrices. Instead, they are now TensorFlow tensors, as denoted by tf.Tensor. These are special classes of arrays which are used by Keras and TensorFlow during the DNN training. If you try to feed R's basic matrix or vector representations into a model defined through Keras, it won't work.

10.2.2 An Architecture for Sentiment Prediction

Now that we have vectorized the text, we can use it for modeling. As an example, we will build a model to predict the review sentiment—whether it is positive or negative.

Example 10.2 **Yelp Data: Building a DNN Architecture** Our inputs are review text, and as a prediction target we will use a binary indicator for whether the review rating is higher than 3 (i.e., it is 4 or 5 star review).

```
> reviews$positive <- as.numeric(reviews$stars > 3)
```

We define the DNN model as a stack of layers. This is the key to Keras, TensorFlow, and deep learning in general. These frameworks allow you to define complicated models through combinations of building block layers—structures of nodes that represent basic algebra operations. Keras functions can take in specifications and return these layers as objects that TensorFlow understands and can manipulate. For example, we will define an `input` layer that expects a single string of review text.

```
> input <- layer_input(shape = c(1), dtype = "string")
```

The magic then happens when we use the pipe %>% operator to create a stack of hidden layers, the internal guts of the network, and connect these layers to our binary sentiment output.

```
> hidden <- input %>%
+    text_vectorization() %>%
+    layer_embedding(input_dim = max_tokens+1, output_dim = 32) %>%
+    layer_global_average_pooling_1d() %>%
+    layer_dropout(0.1) %>%
+    layer_dense(units = 16, activation = "relu")
> output <- hidden %>%
+    layer_dense(units = 1, activation = "sigmoid")
> starmod <- keras_model(input, output)
```

The `starmod` object that we create at the end is the Keras DNN model. It expects a single string of text as input, and processes this string through the layers defined in `hidden` and `output`.

There is a ton going on here and we will work through it line by line. The first bit, `input %>% text_vectorization()`, pipes the text string input layer into the text vectorization function we created earlier. These two layers translate from raw text to the length-300 integer vector.

The next layer is where most of the action is happening. This *embedding* layer maps from the 1×300 vectors of integers between 0 and 10,000 (our vector representation of the review) to a 300×32 dimensional matrix of real numbers. There is no great reason to choose 32 dimensions here; the size of these layers is something that you can only tune through out-of-sample experimentation. The `input_dim` argument is the size of our integer vocabulary—the `max_tokens` argument that we set to 10,000 when defining our text vectorization. Note that we tell this layer to expect integers up to 10,001; the extra dimension is necessary due to how Keras maps from the vocabulary tokens to their integer value. The `output_dim` is the size of our embedding space for the text.

This embedding layer provides a giant dimension reduction from the original 10,000 vocabulary size to a 32 dimensional space. This dimension reduction is encoded as a $10,000 \times 32$ matrix, where each row is the corresponding word's embedding in 32 dimensions. When this layer receives a vector of integers representing review text, each integer indexes an embedding. A vectorized review, which is input as a sequence of 300 integers, is then output as a 300×32 matrix with each row containing the corresponding embedding. The process is illustrated in Figure 10.4.

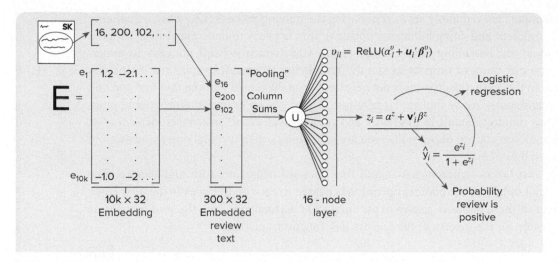

FIGURE 10.4 A diagram of our sentiment prediction network.

As we covered in Chapter 9 on text as data, there are dedicated algorithms like Word2Vec that can be used to train these embeddings. In a DNN, however, we can just train the embeddings as part of the larger network. Keras maintains the $10,000 \times 32$ embedding matrix as a set of model weights to be optimized, and during training it does the work of looking up each embedding to create the 300×32 matrix for each review. It then calculates how changes in the original embedding matrix impact the loss function, allowing us to optimize the embedding matrix to minimize prediction loss (i.e., to minimize deviance).

Our task is to predict overall review sentiment, not the sentiment of individual words in the review. Once we have the 300×32 matrix of embeddings for the words in the review, we need to somehow translate to a single vector representation for the review. There are many interesting ways to do this that account for the sequential ordering of the words in the review. Complex sequence models require massive amounts of data to be trained to the point where they are useful, but they have led to some fantastic recent advances in text understanding and, most impressively, automated text generation. See Section 10.4 for references. However, for a bulk of basic classification and regression problems, including sentiment prediction, modeling the order of words is not worth the extra complexity and effort. Aggregate statistics on the occurrence of the words, regardless of the order that they appear, will get you most of the available information for prediction.

In this case, we use a simple *pooling* operation to summarize the text content of a review. The operation defined by `layer_global_average_pooling_1d` takes the column averages of the 300×32 embedding representation of the review, producing a simple length-32 vector that summarizes average review content across these 32 latent embedding dimensions. This vector is then passed to each node in the next layer of the neural network. Although you might suspect that a lot of meaning is lost by simply averaging the value of words in a review, pooling operations like this work surprisingly well in practice. One thing to keep in mind is that the word embeddings are trained as part of a larger model in which this pooling takes place, and thus the embedding dimensions will be optimized to do a good job of predicting sentiment through a pooling operation. Figure 10.4 illustrates this pooling, with the output then passed to each node in the next layer of our neural network.

You'll notice that we applied a "dropout" operation between the 32 dimensional pooling output and the next layer. As described in Section 10.3.2, dropout is a strategy for training

DNNs where inputs are randomly set to zero during the training process (i.e., when calculating the deviance gradient and doing parameter updates). It is not easy to understand what dropout is doing without understanding the SGD of Section 10.3 (which is itself not easy to understand), but you can think of dropout as simply introducing independent noise that helps you avoid overfit. In this case, the dropout is not necessary; run the model without that line and you will get similar results. We've included it here just to give you an example of dropout in practice. If you are running models in the future and see your validation error rates increasing as you train (i.e., if you start to observe that you are overfitting), then try applying some dropout in the model to mitigate.

The last two layers represent a standard feed forward neural network architecture. The length-32 vector output of the pooling operation is passed to each of 16 nodes in the next layer, and the output of these nodes is passed to the final *sigmoid* function. This sigmoid function is just another name for the inverse of the logistic link function, such that

$$\text{sigmoid}(z) = \frac{e^z}{1 + e^z} \tag{10.1}$$

and we are treating the output of those 16 nodes exactly as we would 16 regressors in a logistic regression model.

You can call `summary` on the model to get a readout of the layers and their dimensions.

```
> summary(starmod)
Model: "functional_3"
```

Layer (type)	Output Shape	Param #
input_2 (InputLayer)	[(None, 1)]	0
text_vectorization (TextVectorizati	(None, 300)	0
embedding_1 (Embedding)	(None, 300, 32)	320032
global_average_pooling1d_1 (GlobalA	(None, 32)	0
dropout_1 (Dropout)	(None, 32)	
dense_2 (Dense)	(None, 16)	528
dense_3 (Dense)	(None, 1)	17

```
Total params: 320,577
Trainable params: 320,577
Non-trainable params: 0
```

Note the dimensionality of this model: it contains 320,577 parameters for us to optimize! With only 60,000 observations, we would obviously overfit without different strategies for regularization. Fortunately, when we train the model we have the nice properties of stochastic gradient descent to help avoid overfit. The application of dropout will also help, and we could have also added penalties (e.g., L2 ridge penalties) in any of our layers via the `kernel_regularizer` argument.

This architecture illustrates how Keras provides a building-block framework that allows you to define complex models with a few simple lines of code. But there is no magic here, and you can also write the model out mathematically. Write the vectorized text for the ith review as $\mathbf{k}^i$, a length-300 vector with elements k^i_t equal to the integer value for the tth word in the review. If we say $\mathbf{e}_k$ is the length-32 embedding vector for each vocabulary element $k = 0, \ldots, 10,000$, the whole model is

$$\mathbf{u}_i = \frac{1}{300}\sum_{t=1}^{300}\mathbf{e}_{k^i_t}, \quad v_{il} = \text{ReLU}(\alpha^v_l + \mathbf{u}'_i\boldsymbol{\beta}^v_l) \text{ for } l = 1\ldots16 \tag{10.2}$$

$$z_i = \alpha^z + \mathbf{v}'_i\boldsymbol{\beta}^z, \text{ and } \hat{y}_i = e^{z_i}/(1 + e^{z_i}) \tag{10.3}$$

10.2.3 Model Training

Once we've defined the DNN architecture, we need to train it. With Keras, you prepare for this by *compiling* the model. You set some key arguments for how the model will interact with data, and Keras then updates the model object with functions for reading data, comparing predicted values against observed targets, and optimizing model parameters (i.e., the DNN weights).

Example 10.3 Yelp Data: Model Training To begin training for our Yelp example, we will compile the `starmod` architecture so that Keras knows how we want to use data to estimate the model.

```
> starmod %>% compile(
+   optimizer = 'adam',
+   loss = 'binary_crossentropy',
+   metrics = list('accuracy')
+ )
```

Notice that our `starmod` object was modified in place here. After piping it to the `compile` function, it is now ready to train on data. The first two arguments here are key. The `optimizer` argument sets the specific optimization algorithm that will be used to update weights; we discus ADAM in Section 10.3 on SGD below. The `loss` argument sets the loss function that we will be training against. Recalling earlier chapters, this loss function corresponds to a deviance that we seek to minimize. In this case, the "binary-crossentropy" loss is just another way to say "binomial" loss, such that we will be minimizing the same deviance we minimize in logistic regression. The last argument, `metrics`, is optional and can include any measure of model fit that you want to track in addition to your loss function. In this case, we ask to track accuracy, which is the proportion of correct sentiment classifications using a 0.5 classification threshold (i.e., if $\hat{y} > 0.5$ we classify the review as positive).

Turning to the actual model training, we'll take a random sample of 50k reviews for training and leave out 10k to evaluate out-of-sample performance.

```
> train <- sample.int(6e4,5e4)
```

It's not really necessary to do this, because Keras automatically reserves some portion of the data for out-of-sample validation. In our training below, we tell Keras to reserve 20% of the data for validation. However, for purposes of illustration in this first example we also remove our own validation sample.

The way the SGD optimization here works (see more in Section 10.3 below), the model is fed small batches of data at a time and updates the weights based upon each small batch of data. We will specify a batch size of 512 observations; you can play around with the batch size to see what is most efficient (fastest training) in your computation setup. Unlike the full gradient descent methods that we have used elsewhere in this book, which completely optimize weights to minimize the loss on the full dataset, with SGD you move the weights only a small bit to improve performance for each new batch of data. For this reason, with SGD you can repeatedly feed the same data into your training algorithm and continue to improve the fit. For massive data implementations you don't bother with this and just always feed the model as much new data as you can afford to process. But for smaller samples, like our 60k reviews, you will want to take multiple passes through the data. In the language of Keras, each pass through the dataset is a training *epoch*. We'll use ten epochs here.

All this wraps together in the following command.

```
history <- starmod %>% fit(
+    x=reviews$text[train],
+    y=reviews$positive[train],
+    epochs = 10,
+    batch_size = 512,
+    validation_split = 0.2,
+    verbose=2
+ )
Epoch 1/10
79/79 - 1s - loss: 0.6693 - accuracy: 0.6372
79/79 - 3s - val_loss: 0.6393 - val_accuracy: 0.6660
...
Epoch 10/10
79/79 - 1s - loss: 0.2597 - accuracy: 0.9154
79/79 - 2s - val_loss: 0.2334 - val_accuracy: 0.9172
```

Notice that we have again modified the starmod object in place. As an aside, we've also modified the hidden and output objects (containing all the DNN layers that we used to create starmod), so that if you use these objects to create a new model then that model's parameters will be initialized at the values we've estimated for starmod. This is useful if you want to "hot start" a new model from values trained, say, on an older dataset.

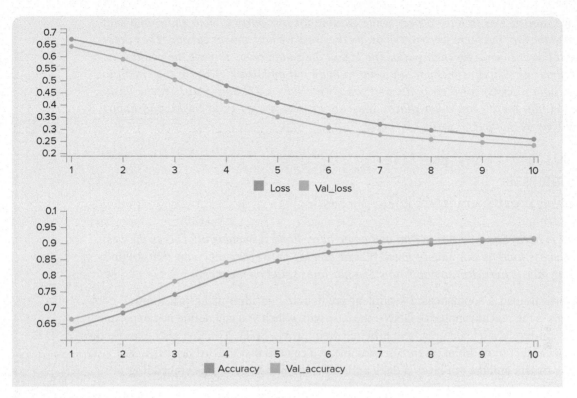

FIGURE 10.5 A diagram of our sentiment network training. Values along the *x* axis mark each training epoch. Blue lines are in-sample metrics, and the green lines mark out-of-sample performance.

Figure 10.5 shows how the fit metrics evolve during the SGD optimization. Both in-sample and out-of-sample fits are shown. We are able to get around 91% OOS accuracy on sentiment prediction. This can be confirmed by evaluating accuracy on our left-out 10,000 reviews (we are only printing a subset of the output below).

```
> evaluate(starmod, reviews$text[-train], reviews$positive[-train])
     loss accuracy
0.2521912 0.9100000
```

We can also look at predictions from the model for some individual reviews. You access the sentiment probabilities using the familiar `predict` function. (When reading the following reviews, keep in mind that they match the Yelp data in our dataset word for word. Typos, misspellings, and grammar errors appear here just like in the original reviews.) Note that, due to randomness in the fitting algorithm, you will get different loss and accuracy and probabilities when you run this code yourself.

```
> probs <- predict(starmod, reviews$text[-train])
> probs[1] # likely negative
[1] 0.3315065
> reviews$text[-train][1]
```

All we wanted was to have a beer while waiting for our party of 8 to show, one seat open at the bar, but there were two of us. So they said we had to wait outside. They don't have a liquor license for their patio. The guy at the counter was so rude, he could Cate less about us. Skip this place if you want to hang out and drink! They're too cheap to buy a liquor license for their patio, and you always have a 1/2 hour wait! Yes the Sushi is good, but there's are other places you can go with just as good Sushi, and happy employees & managers! I won't be back!

```
> probs[2] # likely positive
[1] 0.9117858
> reviews$text[-train][2]
```

Annie is here! She sold Annie Pho and came here. Food is wonderful! This is the best Vietnamese food on this side of town. Will be coming here every time now that Annie's smiling face is here. I'm so happy too. She has lotus salad on the menu.

We have trained a sophisticated sentiment prediction algorithm using just a few R commands. This is the real advantage of DNNs: the ease with which you can define and experiment with different model architectures, and efficient training via SGD. You can also explore the fitted model object to build intuition. For example, we can see that the 3rd layer is a 300×32 embedding matrix and the 4th layer is the length-32 column average of this embedding.

```
> starmod$layers[[3]]$output # 300 x 32
Tensor("embedding_2/Identity:0", shape=(None, 300, 32), dtype=
float32)
> starmod$layers[[4]]$output # 1 x 32 (just does a simple average)
Tensor("global_average_pooling1d_2/Identity:0", shape=(None, 32),
...
```

10.2.4 New Inputs and Outputs

The patterns we've used here can be applied to build models for all sorts of tasks, not just classification. For example, if we want to build a model to predict the star rating (instead of classifying for > 3 stars), we simply change the output target and the loss function (we use MSE now, corresponding to the standard Gaussian deviance for linear regression).

```
> linout <- hidden %>%
+    layer_dense(units = 1)
> linstarmod <- keras_model(input, linout)
> linstarmod %>% compile(optimizer = 'adam', loss = 'mse') # new loss
> linstarmod %>% fit(
+    reviews$text[train],
+    reviews$stars[train], # just raw star count now
```

```
+    epochs = 10,
+    batch_size = 512,
+    validation_split = 0.2)
```

Note that, depending on your operating system and R version, you may need to hit enter a couple of times to get the code to run. The training metrics and resulting predictions are shown in Figure 10.6. Notice that we could have used more training epochs here: the validation loss (OOS MSE) is still decreasing after 10 epochs and would likely continue to drop with more training.

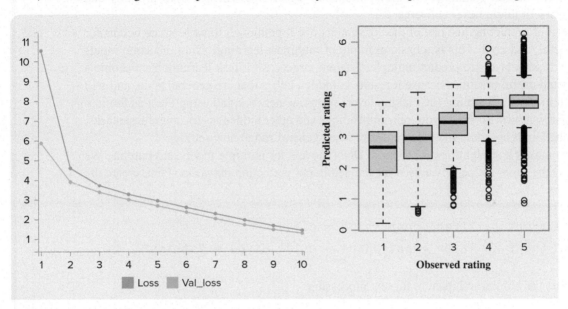

FIGURE 10.6   The left plot shows MSE for our star prediction model at completion of each training epoch. The right plot shows out-of-sample predicted versus observed star ratings.

Example 10.4 Yelp Data: Predicting Review Votes   As a more complex example, consider prediction for the number of votes that a review receives from other Yelp users. Each vote is a case where a user has said that a review is "funny," "useful," or "cool." We have counts of votes for each of these three categories.

```
> head(reviews[,c(1,4:7)])
            review_id stars useful funny cool
1 704a011xuJEZxwbbMDj86Q     1      1     0    0
2 4ndkbul5VnmW1SJlHaJz5g     4      3     0    2
3 reP2C-WqAQ9AJWaAuUUwKg     5      0     0    0
4 0dicquNuUuVyGzZ1pBd9_A     1      1     1    0
5 uuZIWZ54NRh7QekrfMp6DQ     1      3     4    2
```

The vote counts are correlated with the date that a review was published. Older reviews have had more time on the site to accumulate votes. So, to get a good model for how review text predicts the number of votes it will receive, we need to *control* for the publication date. As in any regression, we can do this by including the variable as an input. For this purpose, we convert the date to a numeric value.

```
> reviews$numdate <- scale(as.numeric(as.Date(reviews$date)))
```

Note that we've scaled the variable `numdate` to have a mean of zero and a standard deviation of one. For simple numeric inputs to DNNs it is always a good idea to do this normalization, otherwise the default parameters of the optimization algorithms will not work properly and your network fit might never converge.

Instead of predicting just one of the vote counts, we'll predict all three separate counts for funny, useful, and cool. This is a basic example of multitask learning: using the same inputs and DNN hidden layers to predict multiple different targets. Multitask learning has become a common and useful practice because it results in hidden layers that are generalizable, and will work well in transfer learning (i.e., taking layers from one network and using them as foundation for a new network). When you train embeddings and other hidden layers on multiple tasks, these embeddings are more likely to be useful when generalized to new settings.

Keras makes it straightforward to build DNN models for multiple inputs and outputs. We can follow the same recipe as we used for our sentiment prediction networks. First, create the input layers.

```
> date_input <- layer_input(shape = c(1))
> text_input <- layer_input(shape = c(1), dtype = "string")
```

Next, create the hidden architecture for text processing.

```
> text_hidden <- text_input %>%
+    text_vectorization() %>%
+    layer_embedding(input_dim=max_tokens+1, output_dim=32) %>%
+    layer_global_average_pooling_1d() %>%
+    layer_dropout(0.1) %>%
+    layer_dense(units = 16, activation = "relu")
```

This is unchanged from the `hidden` layer that we used in our earlier sentiment prediction network. The next step is to combine this hidden text processing architecture with the date input, and process both toward the vote count outputs. We'll do it first for the "funny" votes.

```
> funny_out <- layer_concatenate(c(text_hidden, date_input)) %>%
+    layer_dense(units = 8, activation="relu") %>%
+    layer_dense(units = 1, activation = "exponential", name="funny")
```

The first line here combines the output of the hidden text layers with the date input, and feeds these 17 variables (16 text dimensions and the single date dimension) to an 8 node hidden layer. The output of this 8 node layer is then combined together in a final layer that uses an "exponential" activation, such that $\hat{y} = e^z$ where z is a linear combination of the outputs of the 8 nodes in the penultimate layer. That is, our output layer takes the form of a familiar log-linear regression. We've given the output layer a name so that we can keep track when looking at fit and performance. Do the same thing for the two other vote categories.

```
useful_out <- layer_concatenate(c(text_hidden, date_input)) %>%
  layer_dense(units = 8, activation="relu") %>%
  layer_dense(units = 1, activation = "exponential", name="useful")
cool_out <- layer_concatenate(c(text_hidden, date_input)) %>%
  layer_dense(units = 8, activation="relu") %>%
  layer_dense(units = 1, activation = "exponential", name="cool")
```

Finally, we combine all the inputs and outputs together in a model object and compile it for training.

```
> votemod <- keras_model(list(text_input,date_input),
+                        list(funny_out,useful_out,cool_out))
> votemod %>% compile(optimizer = 'adam', loss= "poisson")
```

The full model is illustrated in Figure 10.7. You need to keep track of what order you set the inputs and outputs in their respective lists and make sure that you supply the training data in the same order. Note that we are using a Poisson loss function here, corresponding to the Poisson distribution deviance function, proportional to $\hat{y} - y \log(\hat{y})$. This is the same loss function that you'd use in a Poisson GLM, and it is commonly used for count data. You can run the same model here under MSE loss and get a slightly different fit (this is a good exercise for understanding the role of the loss function). You can also specify a vector of loss functions,

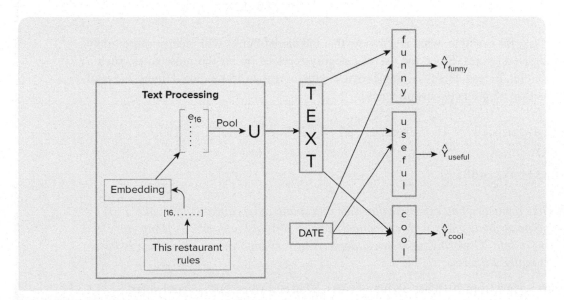

FIGURE 10.7 The architecture of our vote prediction network.

a different one for each output, and via the `loss_weights` argument, weight some objectives higher than others when training.

Fitting the data is the same as always; just remember to keep track of the order of inputs and outputs you've used to specify the model.

```
> votemod %>% fit(
+   x = list(reviews$text,reviews$numdate),
+   y = as.list(reviews[,c("funny","useful","cool")]),
+   epochs = 10,
+   batch_size = 512,
+   validation_split = 0.2,
+   verbose=2
+ )
Epoch 1/10
- val_loss: 2.6496 - val_funny_loss: 0.8502
- val_useful_loss: 0.8575 - val_cool_loss: 0.9418
...
Epoch 10/10
- val_loss: 0.4357 - val_funny_loss: 0.4147
- val_useful_loss: -3.2694e-01 - val_cool_loss: 0.3479
```

The training seems to have worked well, with a large reduction in validation losses from first to last epoch. We can take a look at the expected vote counts, imputing a normalized `numdate=0` to remove the influence of date on vote expectations.

```
evote <- do.call(cbind,
    predict(votemod, list(reviews$text,rep(0,6e4))))
```

We can then ask, for example, what is a review that the model thinks will receive more funny and cool than useful votes. Since the useful category receives by far the most votes, such a review is an outlier. Indeed, there is a single review with more than 15 predicted funny and cool votes and less than 15 predicted useful votes.

```
> which(evote[,1] > 15 & evote[,2] < 15 & evote[,3] > 15)
[1] 43857
> reviews$text[43857]
```

> *It looks like a unicorn had explosive diarrhea and splattered a rainbow on a cake, I say to my two poker buds giddy with excitement through a fit of laughter. . . . [long story] . . . If you're into IG worthy, uber sweet desserts at very high prices, this place is for you. Personally, I'll pass.*

In reality, this review from 2018 has 38 funny votes, 37 useful votes, and 38 cool votes.

◆ 10.3 Stochastic Gradient Descent

It is possible to get started in deep learning without understanding stochastic gradient descent. But if you run into trouble that you need to debug, or if you want to start building more complex customized models, you will be much better off if you have a base understanding of how SGD works. This section is heavy on mathematics, but working through the details of SGD will give you intuition for the entire deep learning paradigm.

First, we need to describe the *gradient descent* algorithms that R has been using to estimate almost all of the models that we have used in this book. SGD is simply a version of gradient descent that works well for estimation on massive datasets.

Gradient descent proceeds by taking the *gradient* (i.e., the derivative) of your optimization target at the current parameter estimates and then following that gradient to get new parameter estimates. Consider a minimization objective $L(\Omega; \mathscr{D})$, where Ω is the full set of model parameters and $\mathscr{D}$ is a set of data that you evaluate this objective against. This objective is defined by the loss function, which we know from earlier chapters is usually a penalized *deviance* function. For example, in a regression setting with Gaussian likelihood you have mean-squared-error loss,

$$L(\Omega; \mathscr{D}) = \frac{1}{n} \sum_{i=1}^{n} (y_i - \hat{y}(\mathbf{x}_i, \Omega))^2 \tag{10.4}$$

where $\hat{y}(\mathbf{x}, \Omega)$ could be $\mathbf{x}'\beta$ for linear regression, or it could be something more complicated (e.g., $\hat{y}$ is the output of a DNN).

Each iteration of gradient descent updates from current parameters Ω_t via

$$\Omega_{t+1} = \Omega_t - C_t \nabla L(\Omega; \mathscr{D})|_{\Omega_t} \tag{10.5}$$

where $\nabla L(\Omega; \mathscr{D})|_{\Omega_t}$ is fancy math to denote "the gradient (∇) of L evaluated at the current parameters (Ω_t)." The *gradient* is just the term for "full vector of first derivatives," so the thought experiment is that you change each parameter a little bit and the gradient tells you how the loss function changes in response.

The term C_t is a *projection matrix* that determines the size of the steps taken in the direction implied by this gradient. We have the subscript t on C_t because this projection is typically updated during the optimization. The version of gradient descent used by glm uses Newton's famous algorithm where C_t is the inverse of the matrix of second derivatives of L, while gamlr uses an adaptation of Newton's algorithm that updates each single parameter in turn rather than all at once (such "coordinate descent" is efficient when Ω_t is sparse). Figure 10.8 illustrates gradient descent and the role of C_t.

Both gradient descent and stochastic gradient descent make use of these same calculations. The difference is what data $\mathscr{D}$ they are calculating against. Notice that all of the gradient calculations involve sums over observations. When you have a huge number of observations (and a huge number of parameters), each gradient update is going to be extremely expensive. That is where SGD comes into play. The algorithm has a long history, dating back to the Robbins and Monro (1951) algorithm proposed by a couple of statisticians in 1951, but it can be summarized as a simple adjustment to gradient descent. Whereas gradient descent calculates each update using the full data sample (i.e., summing over all n observations in a so-called batch update), SGD uses a small subsample mini-batch for each gradient update. That is basically all there is to it. But this simple adjustment allows for faster parameter updates and, in many situations, faster overall convergence to a model fit that performs well out-of-sample.

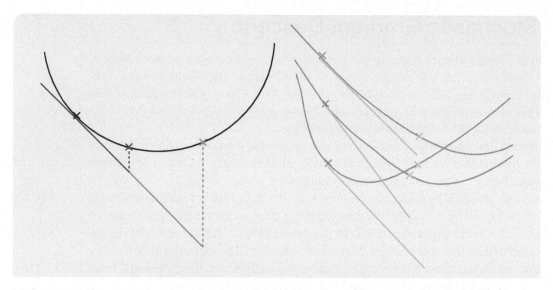

FIGURE 10.8   Simple 1D illustrations of gradient and stochastic gradient descent. In the left plot, the current parameter value and its loss are marked with a black cross. Two different gradient descent updates are shown, corresponding to two different values for the projection matrix C_t (in this case C_t is just the univariate step size). On the right we show three different loss functions (gray) and gradients (gold) for different hypothetical SGD mini-batch calculations. Even though each loss has a different shape, with a different gradient at the current value, the updated parameter values (x axis location of the gold crosses) are roughly similar.

To understand why SGD works, it is helpful to think of each gradient calculation in SGD as an *estimate* of the gradient that you would calculate if you used a lot more data from the same population that provided your subsample. The SGD gradients will have estimation error; they will be noisy versions of the population gradient. But so long as each subsample is a random draw from the population of observations, the SGD updates will move the parameters *on average* in the right direction. Because the SGD algorithm updates are noisy, it will take more iterations of SGD to minimize the in-sample deviance than it would for gradient descent, which uses the full sample to calculate gradients for each iteration. However, gradient updates using the full dataset require much more computation than gradient updates using a subsample, and thus SGD can get your model to a good fit with less overall computation than would be required with gradient descent.

The paradigm shift here is that we are thinking about computation budget rather than amount of data as the limitation on quality of estimation. In small data settings, traditional statistics views sample size as the binding constraint on model performance. In contrast, for applications where deep learning is deployed, you will typically have practically unlimited data (or even streaming data that is constantly being fed into your systems). The binding constraint is then the amount of computation rather than the amount of data available, and as nicely explained in Bousquet and Bottou (2008), SGD allows you to process as much data as possible under a fixed computation budget. Recall discussions in earlier chapters about in- versus out-of-sample fit. We care about how our models fit new out-of-sample data. Whereas gradient descent might be the fastest way to optimize in-sample fit on a given dataset, what you really want is to feed your models as much data as you can possibly process. Although our examples in this chapter work with small datasets that you can load into R, production deep learning applications stream through the data only in small chunks and avoid ever loading a full dataset into memory (e.g., Keras has a notion of "generator" functions that facilitate this). SGD algorithms are the key to training models against truly massive amounts of data.

This is related to an important high-level point about SGD: the nature of the algorithm is such that engineering steps taken to improve *optimization* performance will tend to also improve *estimation* performance. The same tweaks and tricks that improve performance of each SGD update will lead to fitted models that generalize better when predicting new unseen data. The "train faster, generalize better" paper by Hardt et al. (2016) explains this phenomenon within the framework of algorithm stability. For SGD to converge in fewer iterations means that the gradients on new mini-batches are approaching zero more quickly. That is, faster SGD convergence means by definition that the model fits are generalizing better to unseen data. Contrast this with full-sample gradient descent: faster convergence implies only quicker fitting on the current sample, potentially overfitting for future data. Adoption of SGD has made it easy for deep learning to evolve from a scientific to an engineering discipline. Faster is better, so the engineers tuning SGD algorithms for DNNs can just focus on convergence speed.

On the topic of tuning SGD, real-world performance is sensitive to the choice of C_t, the projection matrix in Equation 10.5. For computational reasons, this matrix is usually diagonal (i.e., it has zeros off of the diagonal) such that entries of C_t dictate the *step-size* in the direction of each parameter gradient. Different flavors of SGD use different rules for setting the diagonal elements of $C_t = [\gamma_{1t} \ldots \gamma_{pt}] I$, with p the dimension of Ω. Commonly, each γ_{jt} is chosen to approximate $\partial^2 L / \partial \omega_j^2$, the second derivative of the loss function, which yields C_t with the same diagonal entries as for the projection matrix used in Newton's algorithm. This is the approach of the ADAGRAD class of algorithms (Duchi et al., 2011), and most deep learning systems combine ADAGRAD with heuristics that have been shown empirically to improve performance. This includes the ADAM algorithm (Kingma and Ba, 2015) that we use in all of our examples in this chapter.

Back Propagation

It is often stated that neural networks are trained through a "back-propagation" algorithm, which is not quite correct. Rather, they are trained through variants of gradient descent. Back-propagation (Rumelhart et al., 1988), or back-prop for short, is an efficient method for calculating gradients on the parameters of a network. In particular, back-prop is just an algorithmic implementation of the chain rule from calculus. Consider our example network in Figure 10.1 compiled with linear output and SSE loss, such that $L = \Sigma_i(y_i - \alpha_3 - \mathbf{z}'_{2i}\boldsymbol{\beta}_3)^2$. Given observations $i \in \mathscr{D}$, the gradient with respect to a coefficient in the output layer, say β_{3j}, is

$$\frac{\partial L}{\partial \beta_{3j}} = \sum_i 2(y_i - \alpha_3 - \mathbf{z}'_{2i}\boldsymbol{\beta}_3) z_{2ji} \tag{10.6}$$

Moving a layer down, we have that $z_{2ji} = \text{ReLU}(\alpha_{2j} + \mathbf{z}'_{1i}\boldsymbol{\beta}_{2j})$. The gradient calculation for a single weight at this layer, say, β_{2jk}, is

$$\frac{\partial L}{\partial \beta_{2jk}} = \sum_i \frac{\partial L}{\partial z_{2ji}} \frac{\partial z_{2ji}}{\partial \beta_{2jk}} = \sum_i 2\beta_{3j}(y_i - \alpha_3 - \mathbf{z}'_{2i}\boldsymbol{\beta}_3) z_{1ki} \mathbb{1}_{[z_{2ji}>0]} \tag{10.7}$$

The point to see here is that the same top level residuals, $(y_i - \alpha_3 - \mathbf{z}'_{2i}\boldsymbol{\beta}_3)$, are propagated down through gradient calculations at all levels of the network. Once you have a vector of residuals, the directed structure of the network allows you to calculate all the necessary gradients in parallel through efficient matrix algebra operations. This recursive application of the chain rule, and the associated numerical matrix (or tensor) algebra recipes, is the basis for the automatic differentiation functionality that plays a huge role in our deep learning frameworks. To put it another way, deep learning frameworks take advantage of this structure automatically so that you never need to worry about doing the math in Equations (10.6) and (10.7). This *automatic differentiation* technology is a key part of the success of deep learning.

10.3.1 SGD in Keras

All of our Keras examples use SGD. However, SGD can work with any model you want to train against data. It is not specific to DNNs, and applying SGD on other models can help build your intuition for how it works. Recall our sentiment prediction example where we used DNNs to predict whether a review was positive (>3 stars). In earlier chapters we have combined bag-of-words vectorization with logistic regression for similar purposes (e.g., spam prediction). We'll use that approach here, illustrating the use of SGD beyond DNNs and benchmark our earlier DNN performance against a more traditional generalized linear model approach.

Example 10.5 Yelp Data: SGD for Linear Regression For text vectorization we will use the same Keras functions that we used earlier but will now use them to obtain a bag of words rather than integer vectorization. To illustrate how this works, consider a set of four short text snippets.

```
> shorttext <- c("all world is a stage","all world","world","all")
```

Applying the same `layer_text_vectorization` function but with `output_mode = "binary"` yields our bag-of-words representation.

```
> lilbow <- layer_text_vectorization(output_mode = "binary",
                                      max_tokens = 5)
> lilbow %>% adapt(shorttext)
> lilbow(matrix(shorttext, ncol = 1))
tf.Tensor(
[[1. 1. 1. 1. 1.]
 [0. 1. 1. 0. 0.]
 [0. 1. 0. 0. 0.]
 [0. 0. 1. 0. 0.]], shape=(4, 5), dtype=float32)
```

Each row in this resulting matrix is a vector of binary indicators for whether the corresponding vocabulary element is present in that text snippet. That is, each column corresponds to a distinct token. For comparison, we can also build the integer vectorization.

```
> lilvec <- layer_text_vectorization(max_tokens=6,
                            output_sequence_length = 5)
> lilvec %>% adapt(shorttext)
> lilvec(matrix(shorttext, ncol = 1))
tf.Tensor(
[[3 2 5 1 4]
 [3 2 0 0 0]
 [2 0 0 0 0]
 [3 0 0 0 0]], shape=(4, 5), dtype=int64)
```

The columns in this matrix correspond to the sequence of words in each snippet. For example, the first word of each snippet is the first column and we see that three of the snippets begin with the third vocabulary element (*all*) and one begins with the second element (*world*). Comparing these two vectorization methods, note that the bag-of-words representation has storage requirements (number of columns) that increases with the size of the vocabulary, whereas the integer vectorization's footprint increases with the length of the snippets. With proper use of sparse data storage techniques (e.g., simple triplet matrices), however, each representation uses about the same amount of space. The integer representation encodes sequence information that is lost in the bag of words. This is essential if you want to use time series methods to process your text (like an LSTM model). In contrast, the bag-of-words representation is easier to incorporate into traditional statistics techniques like logistic regression.

We create a text vectorization layer for the review text.

```
> bow <- layer_text_vectorization(
            output_mode = "binary", max_tokens=3000)
> bow %>% adapt(reviews$text)
```

In the language of deep learning, logistic regression is just a single dense layer DNN with a "binary-crossentropy" activation function. We can compile this model using the same recipe that we've used to define the more complex networks.

```
text_in <- layer_input(shape = c(1), dtype = "string")
bow_out <- text_in %>% bow %>%
            layer_dense(units = 1, activation = "sigmoid")
logitmod <- keras_model(text_in, bow_out)
logitmod %>% compile(optimizer = 'adam',
                    loss = 'binary_crossentropy',
                    metrics="accuracy")
```

This is more complicated than, say, defining the regression via `glm` or `gamlr`. But those focused-function packages don't allow you to use the same basic building blocks to build complicated nonlinear models.

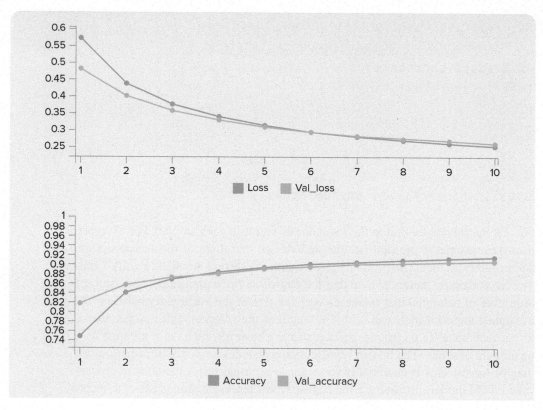

FIGURE 10.9 Loss and accuracy during SGD training for logistic regression prediction of review sentiment.

Running the model fit, we find that this logistic regression model is able to achieve higher than 90% accuracy (Figure 10.9).

```
> logitmod %>% fit(
+    reviews$text[train],
+    as.numeric(reviews$stars[train] > 3),
+    epochs = 10,
+    batch_size = 512,
+    validation_split = 0.2,
+    verbose=2
+ )
> logitmod %>% evaluate(reviews$text[-train],
+                    as.numeric(reviews$stars[-train] > 3))
     loss accuracy
0.2674044 0.9044000
```

That is nearly as good as the 91% accuracy that we got out of the earlier DNN! In this case, it turns out that the DNN we built in the previous section is probably not worth the effort (although, depending upon the application, that extra 1% accuracy could be worth a lot of value). The performance gap would widen if we gave the network a lot more data (more than 60k reviews). It might also improve if we replace the simple average pooling layer with something like an LSTM layer, although that would require *much* more data. You will find the DNNs are worth the extra effort if (a) you have a ton of data or (b) you are able to incorporate pre-trained layers, as we will discuss in our section on transfer learning below.

All we've done here is taken a standard logistic regression model and fit it using SGD. For example, you can access the regression intercept α and coefficients β.

```
> alpha <- as.matrix(logitmod$layers[[3]]$bias)
> beta <- as.matrix(logitmod$layers[[3]]$weights[[1]])
```

The most positive word is "awesome"; its presence increases the odds of a positive review by a factor of 1.6. The most negative word is "terrible"; seeing this in a review decreases the odds of a positive review by a factor of 0.6. Again, due to randomness in the stochastic gradient descent you may bet different 'top' words here.

```
> exp( c( max(beta), min(beta) ) )
[1] 1.6213649 0.6122096
> vocab <- get_vocabulary(bow)
# note the -1 index adjustment
> vocab[c( which.max(beta), which.min(beta) )-1]
[1] "awesome" "terrible"
```

10.3.2 Dropout

There is one more trick to DNN training we should talk about: *dropout.* This procedure, proposed by researchers at the University of Toronto (Srivastava et al. 2014), involves introduction of random noise into each gradient calculation. For example, Bernoulli dropout replaces each current parameter estimate ω with $w = \omega\xi$ where ξ is a Bernoulli random variable with $p(\xi = 1) = c$. The result is w equal to either zero or ω. Each SGD update draws new random dropout values and uses the "noised up" parameter values when evaluating the gradient.

Dropout is used because it has been observed to yield model fits that have lower out-of-sample error rates (so long as you tune c appropriately). Why does this happen? Informally, dropout acts as a type of implicit regularization (as opposed to explicit regularization, like adding a ridge or Lasso penalty on parameters, which is also often a good idea when fitting DNNs). By forcing SGD updates to ignore a random sample of the parameters, it prevents overfit in any individual parameter. More rigorously, you can derive that SGD with dropout corresponds to a type of "variational Bayesian inference" (Kendall and Gal, 2017). That means that dropout SGD is solving to find the posterior *distribution* over Ω rather than a point estimate. In practice, tuning the dropout rate (or deciding whether to include any dropout) is done by trying several values and choosing that which works best for out-of-sample prediction. A rule of thumb is that if you see your validation loss starting to increase during training, while the in-sample loss is still decreasing, then you can apply some dropout to fix the evident overfit.

◆ 10.4 The State of the Art

We close by taking a look at how deep learning is used in modern full-scale production AI systems. The models discussed here need to be trained on massive data using massive computer resources. However, through the ideas of transfer learning you can participate in the fun by downloading pre-trained models and adapting them into your customized analyses. This allows you to bring the full power of deep learning to bear on your business analysis work.

10.4.1 Specialized Architectures

As we've discussed throughout this chapter, DNNs work best when you use an architecture in the lower layers that is structured for processing specific types of inputs. Two common input types are text documents and images. In each case, the goal of the specialized processing layers is to produce *embeddings:* vector or matrix representations of the text or images that are rich in the information that you need for downstream tasks, e.g., text or image classification.

For text data, we've seen a few embedding techniques in this and previous chapters. A word2vec transformation (Mikolov et al., 2013) applies a factor model on the matrix of co-occurrence counts for words, e.g., within several words of each other, and our `hidden` layers in the sentiment prediction network map from a vocabulary of 10,000 words to 32 dimensional embedding representations. These techniques work well for many analysis applications. However, the most exciting recent advances in natural language processing, and in particular text generation, have been built on complex sequence models that seek to understand the relationships between words. For example, the GPT-3 model from OpenAI (Brown et al., 2020) is able to produce long and eerily human statements from a few short prompts. It is trained on hundreds of billions of words and is able, out of the box, to serve in all sorts of language processing tasks. At the time of writing, users had explored using GPT-3 for writing history, news, fiction, and even Keras code!

Models like GPT-3 are *autoregressive language models.* Like our autoregressive time series models in Chapter 1 on regression, they estimate a structure where observations (words and characters) occur in correlation with past observations. The original autoregressive neural networks are recursive neural networks (RNNs) where each element in a sequence provides information about the next element in the sequence. They are basically the neural network implementation of standard AR time series models. But models like GPT-3 are based on more complex sequence models that allow observations to have dependencies on both recent and long-past patterns. These sequence models are, for the large part, combinations and complications of the long short-term memory (LSTM) models of Hochreiter and Schmidhuber (1997). The LSTM models combine a basic autoregressive time series with an underlying "hidden" state. The probability of the next word in a sequence depends both on the previous word in the sequence and on the value of a smoothly moving underlying hidden state. You can think of this hidden state as a latent factor that influences the overall time series. See Figure 10.10 for illustration. This hidden state can be multidimensional, and each dimension of the hidden state can itself depend upon previous hidden states through another LSTM layer. Thus the LSTM models can be stacked and combined as nodes in a DNN, and this provides for massive complexity in a building-block fashion. The arrows in Figure 10.10 are obscuring a lot of complexity: relationships in an LSTM consist of combinations of inputs being fed through nonlinear activation functions. But the basic structure of an LSTM sequence is here, and you can imagine

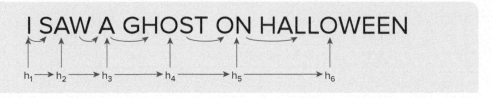

FIGURE 10.10   A cartoon of an LSTM sequence layer. Each word depends on the previous word *and* on the value of a hidden underlying state.

stacking multiple additional layers of hidden states to build a fantastically complex set of possible dependencies between words.

Even basic LSTMs require large amounts of data and they are expensive to train. For example, in our sentiment prediction DNN we could replace the pooling layer (which takes a simple average of the 32 dimensional embeddings for words in a review) with an LTSM layer, using the `layer_lstm` function, which would model the sequence of word embeddings through the review and return the hidden state at the end of the review. However, if you try this, you will notice that the resulting network doesn't work as well as the one that uses simple pooling. This is because we don't have enough data here to learn the complex sequence model, and also because the order of words is not especially relevant to the overall review sentiment.

For image data, the specialized architectures are based on convolutional neural network (CNN) models. These models for vision have a long history, but their use in modern neural networks really took off with the work of LeCun et al. (1989) and LeCun et al. (1995) which showed that the convolution weights could be learned automatically from data. Figure 10.11 shows a basic image convolution operation: a *kernel* of weights is used to combine image pixels in a local area into a single output pixel in a (usually) lower-dimensional output image. This operation would be a single node in a layer, and a full CNN has multiple layers of convolutions feeding into other convolution layers via nonlinear activation functions. Other tricks involve, for example, a *max pooling* layer constructed of nodes that output the maximum of each input matrix or the Capsule networks of Sabour et al. (2017) that replace the max-pooling with more structured summarization functions.

Like the LSTM architectures, CNN architectures require massive amounts of training data and fast parallel GPU computation for training. It is not the sort of thing that you can build on your laptop. However, one of the biggest benefits of the building-block structure of DNNs is the ability to take pieces of *pre-trained* networks and re-use them as part of your own models. So we can take advantage of CNNs and LSTMs even if we don't have terabytes of data and fleets of GPUs.

10.4.2 Transfer Learning

The idea behind transfer learning is simple: take layers from a DNN trained for one set of objectives, typically using huge amounts of data, and use those layers in another model with a different but related objective. This works well whenever the original DNN fit provides a dimension reduction that maintains much of the useful information from the inputs. In that sense it is related to earlier ideas of principal components regression or topic regression, where we used factor models trained on larger datasets to facilitate low-dimensional regression on smaller datasets. Transfer learning with DNNs replaces the unsupervised factor models with

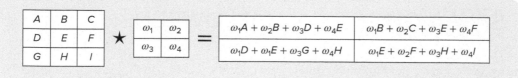

FIGURE 10.11 A basic convolution operation. The pixels *A, B*, etc. are multiplied and summed across kernel weights ω_k. The kernel here is applied to every 2×2 submatrix of the "image."

nonlinear low-dimensional representations—i.e., embeddings—that worked well for the tasks the DNNs were trained against. For example, you might use layers from a DNN trained for generic text generation as the basis for a particular text classification task. Presumably, if the original DNN found a language embedding model that is useful for classifying human text versus artificial jiberish, those same embeddings could be used as a low-dimensional text representation for predicting properties of the text (e.g., sentiment).

There are a large and growing number of DNN embedding models that you can download for free online. BERT is a language model from Google (Devlin et al., 2019) that they use to understand search queries and FastText from Facebook (Bojanowski et al., 2017). BERT provides word embeddings in nearly 300 languages. There are also a large number of image embedding models available. We will use one of the more recent models, the InceptionV3 model from Google, to illustrate how you can incorporate these pre-trained models into your work.

InceptionV3 is a fantastically powerful deep neural network architecture for computer vision (Szegedy et al., 2016). It has dozens of hidden layers and around 24 million free parameters. Google has trained the network on ImageNet data, a massive and growing collection of millions of images that have been labeled according to the objects they contain. Full details are available at `image-net.org`. The Inception V3 model has been trained for classification of photos into 1000 nonoverlapping image labels. It cost Google a ton of compute time to do this training (billions of processor operations). Fortunately, you can download the embedding model for free, directly through Keras, and use it as the foundation for your computer vision models.

```
inception <- application_inception_v3(
              weights = 'imagenet', include_top = TRUE)
```

The inception model—a stack of DNN layers, starting from an image processing input layer—is now loaded into R. Type `summary(inception)` to see the full stack of layers. The `imagenet` weights argument means that the model we get has been pre-trained on ImageNet classification tasks. The `include_top` argument means that we get the full architecture, up to the 1000 dimensional ImageNet classification layer (a set of probabilities over 1000 different image categories). For larger scale DNN applications, you will likely want `include_top=FALSE` so that `inception` ends at the higher dimensional embedding layers and you can customize on top of these. But given our small sample size, the 1000 dimensional top layer is plenty rich in information.

Example 10.6 Yelp Data: Image Classification For an image classification task, we will again turn to the Yelp reviews. This dataset also includes images uploaded by users, along with a classification into a basic five-type taxonomy: drink, food, inside business, menu, and outside of business. We start by reading in the metadata (in particular, labels) for a small sample of 5000 photos.

```
> library(jsonlite)
> pics <- stream_in(file("photos5k.json"))
opening file input connection.
 Imported 5000 records. Simplifying...
closing file input connection.
> pics$label <- factor(pics$label)
> table(pics$label)
  drink   food   inside   menu   outside
    313   2981     1357     45       304
```

We're limiting to 5000 photos to make this manageable on a standard laptop. If you download the full photos.json file from Yelp and the full set of photos, you can see significant improvements in performance by training on larger samples.

Reading images into Keras is not hard, but it requires some special pre-processing that depends upon the model you want to feed the pictures into. For full scale applications you will want to work with the Keras generator functions that read data from disk in chunks for SGD, rather than loading the full dataset into memory. But for our purposes we can write a simple function that loads the 5000 photos into R and processes them for Keras. Note that the photos are all jpeg files, stored in a folder called photos in the working directory. The following function reads a single photo, does some data processing to get it ready for input to inception, and returns the 1000 dimensional image representation (a set of probabilities across ImageNet categories).

```
> iv3gen <- function(id){
+    img <- image_load(sprintf("photos/%s.jpg",id),
                        target_size = c(299,299))
+    x <- image_to_array(img)
+    x <- array_reshape(x, c(1, dim(x)))
+    x <- inception_v3_preprocess_input(x)
+    inception %>% predict(x) }
```

We can test this image processor on an image of McDonald's breakfast lineup, shown in the top left of Figure 10.12. Note that for this code to work the relevant image file must be saved with the .jpg file extension on your computer.

```
> mcmuffin <- iv3gen("Z2HgD4BT3aMe9LTN5FAgkg")
> dim(mcmuffin)
[1]    1 1000
```

The result is a length-1000 vector representation of the image. In this case, the dimensions of this vector are interpretable as the probabilities that the image falls into each of the 1000 ImageNet categories. Keras provides a convenient function for decoding from these probabilities to the source categorizations.

Michael Neelon/Alamy

Moravka Images/Alamy

Portland Press Herald/Getty Images

Monkey Business Images/Shutterstock

FIGURE 10.12 A sample of ImageNet photos. InceptionV3 thinks the breakfast options in the top left photo are somewhere between a bagel and a cheeseburger, which seems about right. Our customized Yelp network classifies these images as (clockwise from top left) food, menu, inside, and inside.

```
> imagenet_decode_predictions(mcmuffin, top = 3)[[1]]
  class_name class_description      score
1 n07693725             bagel 0.71761292
2 n07697313       cheeseburger 0.14033426
3 n02776631            bakery 0.04470455
```

We see that the model views the breakfast sandwiches as related to both bagels and cheeseburgers, and that the overall presentation could be a shot of a bakery. Note that your results may vary due to randomness in the SGD fitting algorithm.

You won't always be able to interpret the output of pre-trained models in this way. Typically, the output will be abstract embeddings that are not directly interpretable. But in either case, the real usefulness of these pre-trained representations is that you can feed them into another neural network, and customize that new network for your specific prediction task. In our case, we want to predict the five-category Yelp classification. The first step is to process all of the raw `jpg` images into the 1000 dimensional Inception v3 representation. You can do that by processing each image through the `iv3gen` function provided above. We did the processing in advance and saved the results in a `csv` file for easy consumption.

```
> iv3feat <- read.csv("photos5k_iv3.csv",row.names=1)
> all(rownames(iv3feat)==pics$photo_id)
```

```
[1] TRUE
> iv3feat <- as.matrix(iv3feat)
```

The second line here confirms that the rows of this feature matrix match up with the rows of the photo metadata, and the last line converts from the dataframe into a numeric matrix for use with Keras. Our prediction target will be the Yelp photo classification, which we convert from character labels to integers from zero to four.

```
> levels(pics$label)
[1] "drink" "food" "inside" "menu" "outside"
> piclab <- to_categorical(as.numeric(pics$label)-1)
```

The model definition and fitting is now a straightforward application of the pattern we've used to fit all DNNs. Our simple network architecture passes the 1000 dimensional InceptionV3 embedding through a 32-node layer. The output of those nodes is passed into a "softmax" activation, which is just deep learning terminology for the inverse of a multinomial logit link function. Similarly, the categorical crossentropy loss function corresponds to a multinomial deviance, such that we are training the top layer of our network here the same as we would a five-category multinomial logistic regression.

```
> pic_in <- layer_input(shape = c(1000))
> pic_out <- pic_in %>%
+   layer_dense(units = 32, activation = "relu") %>%
+   layer_dense(units = 5, activation = "softmax")
> pic_mod <- keras_model(pic_in, pic_out)
> pic_mod %>% compile(optimizer = 'adam',
+                     loss = 'categorical_crossentropy',
+                     metrics="accuracy")
> pic_mod %>% fit(
+   x = iv3feat,
+   y = piclab,
+   epochs = 10,
+   batch_size = 10,
+   validation_split = 0.2,
+   verbose=2 )
...
Epoch 10/10
400/400 - 1s - loss: 0.1945 - accuracy: 0.9290
              - val_loss: 0.2904 - val_accuracy: 0.9160
```

We are able to achieve 91% out-of-sample accuracy, which is pretty decent for a five-category classification problem. We trained this image recognition machine on a laptop, using a small sample of photos. Of course, the heavy lifting here is being done by the pre-trained Inception V3 layers. That is the real promise of DNNs and transfer learning: you can easily take the output of one model—a super complex model trained on millions of observations—and adapt it for specific use cases where you have much less training data. As pre-trained models become more widely available, and as large companies invest in pre-trained general purpose models for their own internal data, this type of data science workflow will become increasingly standard.

We can investigate how the model performs on some specific photos. Figure 10.12 shows four pictures, and we can classify them, as ordered clockwise from top left.

```
> testpics <- rbind(iv3gen("Z2HgD4BT3aMe9LTN5FAgkg"),# mcmuffin
+                   iv3gen("_2p-dRCq5cLqfGoNiEVo2g"),# menu
+                   iv3gen("--8aLaOrf2gfOjA6kCC3WQ"),# inside bar
+                   iv3gen("_5w-wO4BmPKh9R3Eh7t31A"))#
eggspectation
> testpics <- pic_mod %>% predict(testpics)
> colnames(testpics) <- levels(pics$label)
> round(testpics, 2)
      drink food inside menu outside
[1,]   0.00 1.00   0.00 0.00    0.00
[2,]   0.06 0.07   0.01 0.83    0.02
[3,]   0.00 0.00   0.84 0.00    0.15
[4,]   0.00 0.00   0.56 0.01    0.42
```

The McDonald's breakfast items are certainly food, and it recognizes the menu and picture inside a bar with high confidence. It is wrong about the last picture being taken inside (this is the sign outside of Eggspecation in Montréal), but it is hard to tell and the probabilities are 0.56 inside and 0.42 outside.

10.5 Intelligent Automation

Intelligent automation is the practical application of AI alongside automation technologies to automate certain routine, low-level tasks. Economists describe a general-purpose technology as one which is uniquely useful *and* can be applied in a wide variety of settings with little or no customization. Deep learning is a general-purpose machine-learning technology. One of the hallmarks of a general-purpose technology is that it leads to broad industrial changes, both above and below where that technology lives in the supply chain. This is what we are observing with general-purpose ML. Below, we can see that chip makers are changing the type of hardware they create to suit these DNN-based AI systems. Above, deep learning has led to a whole new class of AI products: from chatbots to facial recognition to logistics to self-driving cars. It has also made ML into an engineering discipline. Model building is no longer a series of hypotheses and careful feature construction. You build reliable pipes for as much data as you can get, you use DNN architectures that are specified to work well on your types of data, and you train the thing for as long as you have computational budget.

As deep learning applications see commercial viability, and as money starts to flood in toward DNN-based automation, it is crucial that we take care in how this automation is implemented and understand the impact that it has on humans and the environment. Predictions of a robot-driven no-jobs future are unrealistic, but that doesn't mean that the new wave of AI applications will not have a major impact on how we live. There are many complex issues involved here, ranging from broad notions of fairness and privacy to specific demands for equal service levels for different groups of people. Smart people are devoting themselves to understanding the issues and mitigating harm. A number of academic and industrial science organizations have active research initiatives into fairness, accountability, transparency, and ethics in AI (e.g., Wortman, Vaughan, and Wallach, 2020).

Deep learning is susceptible to all of the same basic errors that people have been making since someone first drew a regression line through a cloud of points. You can create bias in your estimates through poor sampling, for example, relying on pictures of your employees to build a facial recognition tool that works only for people who look like the majority of your, say, mostly white employees. And you can mistake correlation for causation, potentially with tragic consequences. Work in eugenics (a nasty pseudoscience of race) by some early statisticians (including Karl Pearson and R.A. Fisher) is reprehensible. It also relies on bad causal analysis work that fails to recognize that racial correlations are completely confounded by unobserved societal factors. The mistakes here are obvious to modern analysts. However, the exact same basic causal analysis errors are in play whenever some naive start-up proposes a business idea around predicting, say, job performance from genetic data. More subtly, such errors are rife in proposals for automating judgment, for example, in complex health care recommendations or in setting bail for people charged in a crime.

There is nothing fundamentally new about DNNs: they are just regression machines that encode patterns of correlation. So all of the traditional pitfalls of data analysis still apply. Garbage in leads to garbage out: if you train on biased data then you get biased performance. However, the research process for deep learning introduces new issues. Because of the lack of a deep theoretical understanding of how and why they work, the development of DNN techniques relies heavily on testing predictive performance against industry benchmarks (e.g., benchmark image classification or text comprehension datasets). When those benchmarks come from a biased sample, such as image sets consisting of mostly white faces, then the resulting technology will inherit these biases. You can take the state-of-the-art architecture and train it on a new dataset, but if the definition of "state of the art" is driven by biased benchmarks then you will still end up underperforming for underrepresented groups. This is a driver behind the race and gender disparities in facial recognition technologies as documented by Buolamwini and Gebru (2018). Such disparities caused Amazon, IBM, and Microsoft to all pause or stop sales of facial recognition tools to law enforcement agencies in 2020.

Deep learning technology has created a boom in AI products and services, and many of these have had positive impact on our lives. But just because you can build a well-performing prediction algorithm doesn't mean that you are really moving forward. As we've emphasized throughout this book, what matters most is that you are able to use your data to make the right decisions in your applications. The same principles that we've emphasized throughout still apply: break your high-level application into prediction problems and causal questions that can be attacked with data; think carefully about what you can use as inputs, what outputs you are predicting, and how your loss function should be structured; and make sure that you have a strategy for out-of-sample validation that gives you honest feedback on model performance. These principles are just as important, if not more so, for black box DNNs as they are for simple linear regression.

QUICK REFERENCE

DNNs and the associated tools, such as SGD and frameworks like Keras, provide a powerful foundation for learning from data. This chapter gives you a primer on the large and rapidly changing world of deep learning. The core data science techniques of the rest of this book will suit your purposes for the bulk of your analysis needs. However, an understanding of deep learning will allow you to stay in touch with the state of the art and build the skills that you would need to go even deeper into machine learning.

Key Practical Concepts

- To work with DNNs in R, you need to make sure that you have installed `keras` and `tensorflow`. If you are using Windows, then you will also need to install the Anaconda Python environment. Crucially, you need to get Python and TensorFlow working properly and connected to R before the examples in this chapter will work. You cannot simply follow prompts from R and expect things to work.

- There is massive flexibility in Keras, but the basic recipe is that you use the %>% operator to chain together a series of model layers and to add information (rules for training, optimization to data) to the resulting DNN model. For example, for a simple text regression DNN:

```
## build input, hidden, and output architecture
    input <- layer_input(shape = c(1), dtype = "string")
    hidden <- input %>%
      text_vectorization() %>%
      layer_embedding(input_dim=maxlen+1, output_dim=32) %>%
      layer_global_average_pooling_1d() %>%
      layer_dropout(0.1) %>%
      layer_dense(units = 16, activation = "relu")
    output <- hidden %>%
      layer_dense(units = 1, activation = "sigmoid")
## combine layers into a model
    mod <- keras_model(input, output)
## compile for training
    mod %>% compile( optimizer = 'adam' )
## fit
    history <- mod %>%
       fit( x=x, y=y, epochs=10, batch_size=512 )
## predict
    probs <- predict(mod, reviews$text[-train])
```

A R PRIMER

This appendix is dedicated to getting you started in R. If you have no familiarity with this or other scripting languages, you should start here before attempting the rest of the book.

R or Python?

If you ask around on whether R or Python is the best software to use for data analysis, you might hear some strong opinions. What is all the fuss?

R was created in 1995 at the University of New Zealand–Auckland by two statisticians, Ross Ihaka and Robert Gentleman, for statistical computing. Python was created by the Dutch programmer, Guido van Rossum, in 1991 as a general-use programming language. This book uses R, which provides a comprehensive set of tools for modern business analytics. But we could have used Python instead. Both are great tools for working with data.

At most tech firms the analysts will know both languages and a number of others (inevitably you will need at some point to write an SQL query to pull data from a structured database). No language is the best for all purposes. Some tasks are easier to carry out in one or the other program. Since R was created for statisticians by statisticians, it can create highly customizable data visualizations and carry out sophisticated statistical methods with little coding. As you see in this book, you can fit complex statistical models in one or two lines of R code. Python is favored by many computer scientists for its readability and flexibility, and the ease with which you can work with unstructured data like text and images. Python is also the main language used for scripting in deep learning, and in Chapter 10 we use Python frameworks through an R interface to fit deep neural networks.

You can accomplish almost any task in either language. Sometimes it is easier to code in one, but faster to run in the other. Both R and Python rely on a large ecosystem of packages to expand their set of base capabilities. At the end of the day, they are both in high demand, and if you are working in data science, you will need to be flexible and willing to learn new tools to accomplish a variety of tasks. The good news is that once you get the hang of any computer scripting language, like R, you will much more easily be able to pick up on other languages.

A.1 Getting Started with R

You can run R in many ways. There is a dedicated graphical user interface (GUI) for whatever operating system you use. This is the program you will work with if you access R through the icons that arrive when you download and install R. We'll start out this way and then will utilize the built-in script editor throughout this book. You can also operate R directly through a *notebook* environment like that provided by Project Jupyter (see jupyter.org). You can find notebooks tuned specifically for R from R Studio, which is a company that produces a variety of R-friendly tools. This book does not cover using R Studio, but all of the commands we use will work there. Finally, since R works with just text commands, you can run it through any command prompt or terminal on your computer. For the purposes of this tutorial, we begin with interacting with R natively, through the GUI that comes with the download. Then, we will move on to using R's built-in editor functionality, for writing, executing, and saving code. Finally, we will use Markdown to publish code with its output in a document that can be viewed in a web browser.

A.1.1 Downloading R

Note that in order to download and install R, you will be getting the files from a CRAN mirror, which is one of the members of the Comprehensive R Archive Network where the open-source R code and supporting files are hosted. When you are prompted to choose a CRAN mirror, you are choosing the repository from which you will download the necessary R files. You can usually just pick the first one.

To download R:

1. Visit the homepage at http://www.r-project.org/.
2. Click Download R under Getting Started.
3. Choose a CRAN mirror from the list that is close to you.
4. On The Comprehensive R Archive Network page, click the link in the box that corresponds to your operating system (e.g., Download R for Windows or Download R for (Mac) OS X).
5. Follow the installations steps. The default installation settings are usually what you want, although you might click some customization options (e.g., putting an icon on your desktop if you want to access it that way).

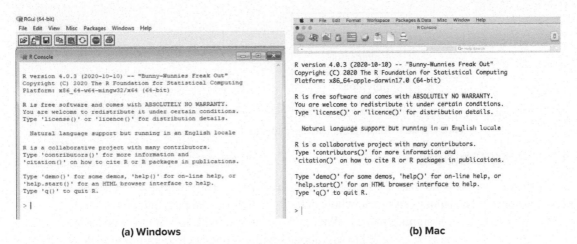

(a) Windows	**(b) Mac**

FIGURE A.1 R Graphical User Interface (GUI) on a Windows machine (a) and a Mac (b).

Once you have installed R, you can find the program and open it. Your screen should look similar to the pictures in Figure A.1. You can change appearance (colors, etc.) through either Edit -> GUI preferences in Windows or the Format menu on a Mac.

A.1.2 Arithmetic Operators

When you open R, the cursor should be flashing in the console window. There are several ways to interact with R, but let's start out with the most basic—typing commands directly into the GUI.

At its most basic, R is just a fancy calculator. Use the keyboard strokes in Table A.1 to accomplish basic mathematical computations.

The following commands demonstrate this basic functionality. Note that anything after a # is considered a comment and is ignored by R. Throughout the text, we sometimes use comment snippets to explain code routines. The > on your R GUI is called the command prompt since it is prompting you to give it a command. The R code in this text is contained in blue boxes. To follow along with this first part of the R tutorial, at your command prompt, type the command that follows the > in the blue code box, and hit Enter for a Windows machine or Return on a Mac. You should get the same output as shown here:

```
> 2*3 #multiplication
[1] 6
> 9/3 #division
[1] 3
> 27/9 #27/9
[1] 3
> 27/(3*3) #equivalent way to compute 27/9
[1] 3
> 27/(3^2) #another way to compute 27/9
[1] 3
```

Arithmetic Operators	
+	addition
-	subtraction
*	multiplication
/	division
^	exponent

TABLE A.1   Basic arithmetic operators in R.

A.1.3 Creating Objects

R's functionality goes way beyond that of a standard calculator. We need a way to store (at least temporarily) and refer to individual values and whole datasets so that we can pass them through functions. We use the idea of assigning names. When a name is assigned in R, this is known as defining an *object*. Names can be assigned to just about anything in R, such as an individual value, whole dataset, or function. R actually has two ways to assign object names, <- and =. The former is preferred because = is used both for function arguments and for variable name assignment, but people write fine code using either. This text uses the <- naming convention to create objects. Examine what happens with the following R code:

```
> 2*3 #ask R to calculate 2*3 and print the answer
[1] 6
> A<-2*4 #calculate 2*4 and store the answer as 'A'
```

Notice that when you executed the second line of code, R gave you only a cursor, seemingly without performing the computation. But R did exactly what you asked. It performed the calculation and stored the result as an object named A. To see what R has stored as A, simply type A into the console.

```
> A
[1] 8
```

You can define an object, store it, and print at the same time by wrapping the line in parentheses.

```
> (B <- 12)
[1] 12
```

We have defined only two objects so far—A and B, which isn't difficult to remember. However, it is not uncommon to have many objects defined in R as you are working on a project. To be reminded of the names of all defined objects, use either the ls or the objects command—these are identical.

```
> ls()
[1] "A"         "B"
> objects()
[1] "A"         "B"
```

And of course, to be reminded of what the object is defined as, simply type the name of the object.

```
> A
[1] 8
> B
[1] 12
```

When naming objects, make sure to start your names with a letter—R will not allow it to begin with a number. Note that R is case sensitive. You must reference objects with the *exact* spelling used when defining the object. You will want to choose object names that are short (to save on typing) but still make sense to you. We sometimes use "camel case" when creating object names, that is, dropping spaces or punctuation between words and capitalizing the first letter in all words except in the object name. For example, myObjectName.

If you get a + instead of > after hitting Enter or Return, you have left a parenthesis, quote, or bracket open. Close it on that line and hit Enter or Return and you should get the > on the next line. If you can't figure out what needs closing, hit escape to end the process and get the cursor again. To edit a previously executed line of code, use the Up and Down arrows on your keyboard to scroll through until you find the line you want to edit.

A.1.4 Data Types, Classes, and Structures

Up to this point, we have been working with numbers. There are actually many different object *classes* in R. For raw data entries, we have the following five classes:

- numeric
- integer
- character
- logical
- factor

Let's check the class associated with the data types we explored above.

```
> class(2)
[1] "numeric"
> class(2L)
[1] "integer"
> class("a")
[1] "character"
> class(TRUE)
[1] "logical"
```

Note that 2 is simply numeric, whereas the special symbol 2L tells R that this should be treated as an integer. You won't really need to worry about the distinction between integer and numeric values because R will convert integers to the more general numeric class when needed.

If your data is categorical, it can be treated as a factor in R. Factors in R are stored as a vector of integer values with a corresponding set of character values to use when the factor is displayed. The factor or as.factor commands are used to coerce the class of an object to be a factor. Both numeric and character variables can be made into factors, but a factor's levels will always be character values. You can see the levels for a factor using the levels command.

```
> C<-"c"
> cFactor<-as.factor(C)
> levels(cFactor)
[1] "c"
```

In the previous examples, our objects consisted of only one element. In the rest of this book, we work with large datasets, so we need to have a way to work with multiple elements all at once. Typically, a dataset will have several columns, each representing some variable, and many rows, with each row representing an observation of the variables. These datasets can have data all of the same type (homogeneous) or of several types (heterogeneous). After considering the data types and classes, R will assign a *structure*. R's basic data structures can be categorized by their dimensions (1, 2, or more than 2) and whether the data are homogeneous or heterogeneous. The most common are categorized in Table A.2.

R will assign these classifications when storing an object. It will inspect the data type(s) and then assign the structure. Let's explore a few of these. We will start small and demonstrate how to create datasets manually. To give R a dataset and store it, pick a name and use the c (combine, aka concatenate) command with your list of values in the parenthesis separated by commas.

```
> vec1<-c(2,4,6,8,10)
> vec1
[1]  2  4  6  8 10
```

vec1 contains numeric values, so the type should be of the numeric class. And since the data are all of the same type (homogeneous, which R calls "atomic"), it should be recognized as a vector.

```
> is.numeric(vec1) #is it class 'numeric'?
[1] TRUE
> is.atomic(vec1) #is it homogeneous?
[1] TRUE
> is.vector(vec1) #should be a vector - is it?
[1] TRUE
```

	Homogeneous	Heterogeneous
1-dimensional	vector	list
2-dimensional	matrix	data frame
more than 2 dimensions	array	

TABLE A.2 Table of common data structures in R.

Note, you can also use the `seq` function to create the same vector as `vec1`.

```
> vec2 <- seq(2,10,2) #seq(from,to,by)
> vec2
[1]  2  4  6  8 10
```

Another useful way to create a vector of numbers is to use the: operator.

```
> vec3<-c(1:10) #a:b indexes 'from a to b'
> vec3
 [1]  1  2  3  4  5  6  7  8  9 10
```

If you give R a list of words or numbers that are each in quotes, it will recognize the data type as character, and since the data are all of the same type (atomic), R will assign the structure of a vector.

```
> is.character(c("dog","cat","fish"))
[1] TRUE
> is.vector(c("dog","cat","fish"))
[1] TRUE
```

An important type of vector in R is a logical vector. There are many logical and other miscellaneous operators built into R. The common ones are outlined in Table A.3. Consider a vector of 4 values.

```
vec4<-c(10,20,5,17)
```

We can ask R, "Check each element of vec4 to see if it equals 10."

```
vec4==10
[1]  TRUE FALSE FALSE FALSE
```

Logical/Misc Operators	
==	equal to
!=	not equal to
<	less than
<=	less than or equal to
>	greater than
>=	greater than or equal to
|	OR
&	AND
a%in%b	a is contained in b

TABLE A.3   Logical operators in R.

The logical vector containing TRUE FALSE FALSE FALSE is returned since the first element of vec4 is 10 and the others are not. Operators can be combined to check several conditions. The following example says "Check each element of vec4 to see if it is greater than 15 or equal to 10."

```
> vec4>15|vec4==10
[1]  TRUE  TRUE FALSE  TRUE
```

The %in% operator allows us to check that the elements of one vector are contained in another.

```
> vec5<-c(5,10,17,20,30,40,5,17)
> vec4%in%vec5 #is each element of vec4 in vec5
[1] TRUE TRUE TRUE TRUE
> vec5%in%vec4 #is each element of vec5 in vec4
[1]  TRUE  TRUE  TRUE  TRUE FALSE FALSE  TRUE  TRUE
```

We use logical vectors a lot in this text. The ability to check a condition and take an action based on it is extremely useful.

We can create a matrix in R using the matrix command. Note that the matrix command assumes you are entering the values by column. If you are reading from left to right and want to enter the matrix values by reading through the rows, use the byrow=TRUE argument. The other important argument of this function is to specify the number of rows (nrow=) or the number of columns (ncol=).

```
> A<-matrix(c(1,2,3,4,5,6),nrow=2,byrow=TRUE)
> A
     [,1] [,2] [,3]
[1,]    1    2    3
[2,]    4    5    6
> B<-matrix(c(1,6,3,5,7,2),nrow=3)
> B
     [,1] [,2]
[1,]    1    5
[2,]    6    7
[3,]    3    2
```

And we can check the structure in R.

```
> is.atomic(A) #is it filled with same data type?
[1] TRUE
```

```
> is.matrix(A) #should be a matrix - is it?
[1] TRUE
> is.atomic(B) #same checks for B
[1] TRUE
> is.matrix(B)
[1] TRUE
```

Matrix Multiplication

The key thing to remember in matrix multiplication is that rows come first and columns second. A 2×3 matrix has 2 rows and 3 columns. If $\mathbf{A}$ is an $n \times m$ matrix and $\mathbf{B}$ is an $m \times p$, then $\mathbf{AB}$ is an $n \times p$ matrix. Notice that the number of columns of the first matrix need to be the same as the number of rows of the second matrix for matrix multiplication to be defined. Suppose $\mathbf{A}$ is a 2×3 matrix and $\mathbf{A}$ is a 3×2. We can compute $\mathbf{AB}$, but not $\mathbf{BA}$. Multiplying $\mathbf{AB}$ would result in a 2×2 matrix (since $(2 \times 3)(3 \times 2) = (2 \times 2)$).

As example multiplication, consider

$$AB = \begin{bmatrix} 1 & 2 & 3 \\ 4 & 5 & 6 \end{bmatrix} \begin{bmatrix} 1 & 5 \\ 6 & 7 \\ 3 & 2 \end{bmatrix} \tag{A.1}$$

To complete the multiplication above, do elementwise multiplication of the first row of $\mathbf{A}$ with the first column of $\mathbf{B}$ and then add these products (this is called a dot product), so that the resulting multiplication is

$$\begin{bmatrix} 1*1+2*6+3*3 & 1*5+2*7+3*2 \\ 4*1+5*6+6*3 & 4*5+5*7+6*2 \end{bmatrix} = \begin{bmatrix} 22 & 25 \\ 52 & 67 \end{bmatrix} \tag{A.2}$$

And this matrix multiplication can be done quickly in R.

```
> A%*%B
     [,1] [,2]
[1,]   22   25
[2,]   52   67
```

A common operation is that we will be working with matrices and vector. For example, we might have an $n \times p$ matrix of data X and a length-p vector of coefficients b. In matrix multiplication, the vector is treated as a *single column matrix*. Multiplying them together as X%*%b yields an $n \times 1$ vector with each element corresponding to the *inner product* between a row of X and b, say

```
(X%*%b)[i] = X[i,1]*b[1] + X[i,2]*b[2] + ... X[i,p]*b[p]
```

A.1.5 Calculations on Numeric Vectors and Matrices

Once you have a numeric named in R, you can do all sorts of manipulations and calculations.

```
> vec3 #remind me what vec3 is
 [1]  1  2  3  4  5  6  7  8  9 10
> vec3+5 #add 5 to e entry of vec3
 [1]  6  7  8  9 10 11 12 13 14 15
> vec3*2 #multiply e entry of vec3 by 2
 [1]  2  4  6  8 10 12 14 16 18 20
```

Notice that the calculations acted on the whole vector, not just one element of the vector. Most of the built-in capabilities in R are "vectorized" in this way.

The operator %*% is used to do matrix multiplication (see the nearby box "Matrix Multiplication" for a quick refresher on matrix algebra). Notice the difference in results when multiplying two vectors together using the usual * and the %*%.

```
> vec1 #what was vec1 again?
[1]  2  4  6  8 10
> vec2 #what was vec2 again?
[1]  2  4  6  8 10
> vec1*vec2
[1]    4  16  36  64 100
> vec1%*%vec2
     [,1]
[1,]  220
```

Using * multiplies each element of each vector by each other and returns a new vector of the same length. The other operation, vec1%*%vec2, computes the *inner product* (also known as the "dot product") that treats vec1 as a one-column matrix and vec2 as a one-row matrix. When you are using the matrix multiplication operator on two vectors of the same length, R assumes you want to compute the dot product.

```
> vec1
[1]  2  4  6  8 10
> vec2
[1]  2  4  6  8 10
> 2*2 + 4*4 + 6*6 + 8*8 + 10*10
[1] 220
```

```
> vec1%*%vec2
     [,1]
[1,]  220
```

Note that if you are trying to use the %*% operator on two vectors of differing lengths, you will get the `non-conformable arguments` error.

A.1.6 Built-in Functions

There are many built-in functions that perform basic calculations in R. For example

```
> mean(vec3) #calculate the mean (average)
[1] 5.5
> sd(vec3) #calculate the sample standard deviation
[1] 3.02765
> sum(vec3) #sum (add) the numbers
[1] 55
#five no. summary plus mean for numeric data
> summary(vec3)
   Min. 1st Qu.  Median    Mean 3rd Qu.    Max.
   1.00    3.25    5.50    5.50    7.75   10.00

#log of e entry, rounded to 2 places
> round(log(vec3),2)
 [1] 0.00 0.69 1.10 1.39 1.61 1.79 1.95 2.08 2.20 2.30

#e^every entry of the vector, rounded to 1 place
> round(exp(vec3),1)
[1] 2.7 7.4 20.1 54.6 148.4 403.4 1096.6 2981.0 8103.1 22026.5
```

Depending on how you were taught logarithms, you might have been introduced to logariths with a different base than $e \approx 2.7$ (e.g., base 10 is used to introduce logarithms in some schools). The convention in any statistical analysis, and in R, is that $\log(a) = b \Leftrightarrow e^b = a$.

Notice that there was only one entry in the `mean`, `sd`, `summary`, `log`, and `exp` functions, but there were two entries in the `round` function. Functions can take several *arguments* that allow the user to specify settings of a function. To find out what arguments are available, simply type `?functionName` into your R console and the help file for the function will pop up in a web browser tab. You can also call `help(functionName)` to get the same result. If you pull up the help file for the `round` function by typing `?round` into your console, you will find the arguments for this function—x and digits, where digits has a *default* of digits=0. Note that we didn't need to specify the digits= in the round(exp(vec3),1) example above. This is because the digits= argument comes second in the set of function arguments, so R assumes the second thing in the set we gave it is the second argument if not specified. So, round(log(vec3),1) is equivalent to round(log(vec3),digits=1).

Remember when we said that using these logical operators to return a logical vector is a powerful tool? They can be used inside many functions in R. The ifelse function is one such function. The following example creates a new vector based on the ifelse function which says "if the element of vec4 is 10, return 10, otherwise return 0."

```
> vec4 #what was vec4 again?
[1] 10 20  5 17
ifelseExamp <- ifelse(vec4==10,10,0)
ifelseExamp
[1] 10  0  0  0
```

The which function returns the position of an element when the logical vector is TRUE. This function will be useful when we want to pick out only certain elements of an object. The following example asks R to return the position of any element of vec4 that is 10. We know only the first entry of vec4 is 10, so it should return the position 1.

```
> which(vec4==10)
[1] 1
```

A built-in function that deserves special attention is the paste function. The paste function concatenates text. Notice how the c function behaves differently than paste.

```
> paste("I","am","learning","a","lot")
[1] "I am learning a lot"
> c("I","am","learning","a","lot")
[1] "I"         "am"        "learning" "a"         "lot"
```

The paste function concatenates the individual characters into one character string, while the c function combines the individual characters into one vector but maintains them as separate elements. We can check this using the length function, which checks the length of a vector (it counts the number of elements of the vector).

```
> length(paste("I","am","learning","a","lot"))
[1] 1
> length(c("I","am","learning","a","lot"))
[1] 5
```

Table A.4 lists some of the common functions you will use. Note that the functions discussed so far are built into base R. You can also write your own function or use a function that is contributed as part of a package. User defined functions and packages are covered in Section A.3.

Note that you will sometimes (often, when you are learning) get an error or warning message from R when you try to use a function. If you get an error or warning message, take a deep breath, read the error or warning, and try to figure out your error. Error messages usually provide some of your code truncated at the source of the error (usually a missing comma, misspelled argument, etc.). You should also feel free to google the error. There is usually someone

Task	Function	Explanation
Explore Data Structure	hcad()	shows first 6 rows of dataset
	str()	examines the data structure and type
	View()	pop-up with a spreadsheet-like view of data
	length()	number of elements in vector
	dim()	dimensions of a data frame/matrix
Combine	c()	combine or concatenate
	paste()	concatenates character vectors
	cbind()	bind vectors by column
	rbind()	bind vectors by rows
Calculations	sqrt()	square root
	log()	natural logarithm, base e
	exp(a)	e^a
	mean()	average
	var()	sample variance
	sd()	sample standard deviation
	summary(numeric)	5 no.summary plus mean
	summary(categorical)	count of each unique level
	*apply()	functions for avoiding loops when calculating
Formatting Numbers	round(x,a)	rounds elements of vector x to a places
	options(digits=n)	print n significant digits
	options(scipen=n)	large n turns off scientific notation
Ordering and Position	sort()	sort from least to greatest
	rev()	reverse order of elements
	order()	position in original vector for sorted values
	which()	gives position(s) of element(s) when a logical is true
Sequences	rep(x,n)	repeats x n times
	seq(from, by, to)	sequence
	a:b	integers from a to b
Read and Write Data	read.csv()	reads in a comma separated value file
	write.csv	writes a .csv file to a specified location
List of Objects	objects()	lists all objects currently stored
	ls()	lists all objects currently stored
Misc.	ifelse(cond,a,b)	if condition is TRUE, then a, otherwise b
	sample()	random sample
	Sys.time()	system time and date
Get Help	help(function) or ?function	pulls up help file
	help.search('topic')	searches help file for your topic

TABLE A.4   Common built-in functions in R.

who has posted a question about the error on a site like Stack Exchange and there are often good answers in the comments.

A.2 Working with Data

In Section A.1, we manually created data objects and performed basic calculations on them. Most often, you will be working with a dataset that is stored somewhere else. It will be called into your R session and stored as an object. You will then want to perform calculations on the values in the columns. You will need tools such as knowing how to refer to a specific column in a dataset, perform calculations on that column or a subset of that column, or create a graphical display. This section covers how to work with data in this way.

A.2.1 Reading in Data Files

Most of the time, you will not be hand-entering data into your R GUI. You will want to bring a dataset into R's working memory that is stored somewhere else, such as on a hard drive or a website. R can read mostly any data format, but in this book, we work mostly with .csv files containing *comma-separated values*. These are simple text files organized like a spreadsheet where the values (cell entries) are separated by commas. This format of data storage is called a *flat file* because it has only two dimensions: data observations (rows) and variables (columns). The data is stored in a simple text file, and in general you can choose any type of value *delimiter* (tabs, pipes [|], and spaces are alternatives to commas).

Usually, Microsoft Excel will be the default program to open and view a .csv file on your computer. If you open and view a .csv file this way, you won't see the commas that separate the values—the comma is simply the delimiter (separator/spacer) that is recognized by the program reading in the data. See the example in Figure A.2 of a .csv file opened using Microsoft Excel. The first row is a *header,* with column titles, and the remaining rows contain data entries. Note that you should beware of Excel making changes to your data (e.g., by automatically formatting numbers or by trimming rows). *Data that has been corrupted and re-saved by Excel is a common source of frustration when working through the examples in this book.* Mac users should note that our students have experienced problems when the Numbers application is the default for opening a .csv file. You may want to set that default to another program such as Excel.

R has the `read.csv` function for reading data from your `.csv` files into your workspace. A common newbie challenge is figuring out how to find your data. R has the concept of a *working directory,* and you can connect from there to where you store your data. One easy strategy is to create folders for storing both your data and analysis scripts.

	A	B	C	D	E	F	G	H	I	J	K	L	M	N	O	P	Q
1	id	name	description	neighborh	host id	host name	host since	host respons	host respoı	host accep	superhost	host listing	host total I	host has pr	host identi	neighborhc	neighborh
2	5065	MAUKA BB	Perfect for Neighbors		7257	Wayne	1/31/2009	within a day	100%	37% f		2	2 t		t	Hamakua	Hawaii
3	5269	Upcountry	The 'Auwai	We are loc	7620	Lea & Pat	2/9/2009	within a few	100%	95% f		5	5 t		t	South Kohı	Hawaii
4	5387	Hale Koa 5	This Wondı	IN a Farm I	7878	Edward	2/13/2009	within a few	100%	97% t		3	3 t		t	South Konı	Hawaii
5	5389	Keauhou V	It is less the	It is less tha	7878	Edward	2/13/2009	within a few	100%	97% t		3	3 t		t	North Konı	Hawaii
6	5390	STAY AT PF	\<b>The space\</b>\<br		7887	Todd	2/14/2009	within a few	100%	94% f		2	2 t		t	Koloa-Poip	Kauai
7	5434	Kauai Oceı	Hawaiian a	The resort	7984	Ahlea	2/16/2009	within an ho	100%	99% t		2	2 t		t	North Shor	Kauai
8	7896	Beachfront	GREAT VAL	Convenienı	21844	Caroline	6/16/2009	N/A	N/A	0% f		1	1 t		t	Kihei-Make	Maui
9	8833	Stay in the	Our condo	Close to thı	21349	Noah	6/13/2009	within a few	100%	98% f		1	1 t		t	North Konı	Hawaii
10	9877	Keolamaulı	The restful	Keolamaulı	33179	Kaye	8/22/2009	N/A	N/A	89% t		1	1 t		t	Hamakua	Hawaii
11	13238	Studio On I	The Studio	Located in	51647	Annie/Greį	11/5/2009	within a few	100%	100% f		2	2 t		f	North Shor	Kauai
12	13523	All Inclusivı	Property is	Quiet Beac	52931	Mark	11/10/2009	within a few	100%	100% t		14	14 t		t	Koolaupok	Honolulu
13	13527	Romantic C	Please notı	Kona Isle is	52967	Beth	11/10/2009	N/A	N/A	57% f		2	2 t		t	North Konı	Hawaii
14	13528	2BR Pacific	\<b>The spɛ	South Kihe	52969	Lisa	11/10/2009	within a few	100%	60% t		2	2 t		t	Kihei-Make	Maui
15	13653	Ocean Viev	Our Ocean	One block ı	53489	Maui Gardı	11/12/2009	within an ho	100%	100% t		8	8 t		f	Lahaina	Maui
16	13688	Oceanfron	Aloha and ı	Kehena Beı	53657	Iliahi J.	11/12/2009	within a few	100%	98% t		2	2 t		t	Puna	Hawaii
17	13799	Luana Kai C	\<b>The space\</b>\<br		54237	Donald	11/14/2009	within a few	90%	84% f		2	2 t		f	Kihei-Make	Maui
18	13899	DELUXE OC	This Luxury	Shopping n	54660	Dennis	11/16/2009	within an ho	100%	100% t		16	16 t		f	Lahaina	Maui

FIGURE A.2   Snapshot of the `HiListings.csv` file opened with Microsoft Excel.

To find your current working directory, use the `getwd` command:

```
> getwd()
[1] "C:/Users/first.last/Documents"
```

This is the way a pathname looks on a Windows machine. Your actual path returned by the `getwd` command might be a different path, but on a Windows machine, it will usually start with the `C:/`. To change the working directory to, say, the desktop, change the pathname in the `setwd` command. Note, if you aren't sure of the pathname to the location you want to set, go to that location, right-click a file, choose Properties (or Get Info for a Mac) and look at the path next to Location. Note that you must use forward slashes as separators. If you copy and paste the path and it has backslashes, you will need to change them to forward slashes.

```
> setwd("C:/Users/first.last/Desktop")
> getwd()
[1] "C:/Users/first.last/Desktop"
```

If you use `getwd` on a Mac, the pathname will look a bit different. It will not include the `C:`. For example

```
> setwd("/Users/first.last/Desktop")
> getwd()
[1] "/Users/first.last/Desktop"
```

Once you have your working directory set where you want and your data saved in that location, it's easy to call in your .csv file using the `read.csv` function and the name of the stored .csv file.

Example A.1 Hawaii Airbnb Listings: Reading Data In inside-airbnb.com is a project that scrapes Airbnb listings from the web for various locations and posts the data for public use. The `HiListings.csv` file contains data extracted from data downloaded on October 14, 2020.

The data are shown as opened in Excel in Figure A.2. Notice that `HiListings.csv` has column names. Pull up the help file for the `read` family of functions and look at the arguments that are options for the `read.csv` function.

```
> ?read.csv
```

The command above brings up the help page for the family of read functions. You will see that the `read.csv` function has `header=TRUE` as the default, meaning it assumes you have column names.

```
read.csv(file, header = TRUE, sep = ",", quote = "\"",
         dec = ".", fill = TRUE, comment.char = "", ...)
```

The rest of the arguments in the read.csv function are set up for a standard .csv file.

Note that there was a recent but major change in the way R handles character strings. For version 4.0.0 and higher, it assigns type as character for character strings, while previously, these were automatically assigned as a factor. If you want R to read character strings in as factors, use the stringsAsFactors=T argument, which can be shortened to strings=T.

Assuming this HiListings.csv file is in your working directory, running the following line of code will create an object in R called "aloha" and treat character data as a factor.

```
> aloha<-read.csv("HiListings.csv", strings=T)
```

If you want to call in a dataset that is not in your working directory, you can use the read.csv command and point R directly to where the file is stored by putting the entire pathname in the read.csv command, like this:

```
> aloha<-read.csv("C:/Users/first.last/Desktop/HiListings.csv")
```

An alternate way to call data in is to search for the file in a pop-up window by using file.choose instead of the path/file name, like this:

```
> aloha<-read.csv(file.choose(),strings=T)
```

The above code should prompt a pop-up window where you can navigate to your file and double-click it. However note that file.choose() can be slow and will sometimes produce strange warnings.

Make sure to give your dataset a name in R (here, we used aloha). If you don't define the read.csv statement as an object, R will read the data in and simply print it in the console (which is not very useful).

. . . .

Inspecting the Data

Once you have run the code to call in the data, it is important to look at it to make sure it was read in properly. In addition, you will want to know the data structure and how to refer to columns. A good workflow is to inspect the data, look for problems, and then clean the data (fix problems).

Example A.2 Hawaii Airbnb Listings: Inspecting the Data The following are all good ways to look at the data: str(aloha), head(aloha), and summary(aloha) functions. head will show the first 6 rows of each column. The str function gives the structure of the dataset, including the number of rows (obs.) and columns (variables) and each column name along with its data type and a preview. The following is a snippet of the str(aloha) output.

```
> str(aloha)
'data.frame': 22434 obs. of  54 variables:
$ id                   : int  5065 5269 5387 5389 5390 5434 ...

 ...

$ host.response.time   : Factor w/5 levels "a few days or more"
$ host.response.rate   : Factor w/64 levels "0%","1%","100%",..
$ host.acceptance.rate : Factor w/97 levels "0%","10%","100%",.
$ superhost : Factor w/2 levels "f","t": 1 1 2 2 1 2 1 1 2 ...
$ host.listings.count  : int  2 5 3 3 2 2 1 1 1 2 ...

 ...

$ reviews.per.month    : num  0.45 0.09 1.3 0.24 1.03 0.8 ...
```

We see that `aloha` is a `data.frame` with 22,434 rows and 54 columns. This `data.frame` class is *extremely important in R*. These `data.frame` obects allow you to store a table of heterogeneous data types in a convenient matrix-style format.

Each name output by the `str` function is a variable in the `data.frame`. The `id` is a set of whole numbers, so R assigned it as an integer. The `superhost` column contains t's and f's for true and false and since this column contains characters, the `strings=T` argument told R to make that a factor with 2 levels, numerically represented with 1 and 2. R assigned `host.response.rate` and `host.acceptance.rate` as factors, due to the characters in the columns (%). This would be problematic if we want to calculate numeric summaries, so this will need to be fixed. The `reviews.per.month` column contains decimal data, so R assigns it as numeric.

You may remember from Figure A.2 that the columns were named a bit differently in the Excel sheet than they are in R. For all the columns that have a space in the column name, R replaced the space with a period. For example, "host response time" in the Excel sheet became `host.response.time` in R. R will replace spaces and other special characters in the column names (%,@, etc.) with a period, and if the column name in the Excel sheet starts with a number, R will append an X to the front of that column label. This is why it is always important to look at how R stored column names and not rely on how it is named in the Excel sheet.

Applying `summary` to a whole dataset will give the five-number summary plus the mean for each column recognized as quantitative and will give the number of times each level of a factor (categorical variable) appears (it only prints up to six levels). To get a list of all levels of a categorical variable, apply the `summary` function to just that particular column, which we will see how to do soon. The output below contains a snippet of `summary(aloha)`:

```
> summary(aloha) #only a portion is shown below
      host.response.time host.response.rate host.acceptance.rate
a few days or more: 643     100%  :11644        100%   :8387
N/A               :3144     N/A   : 3144        99%    :2386
within a day      :3644     90%   : 1072        97%    :1479
within a few hours:5182     95%   :  571        98%    :1433
within an hour    :9821     80%   :  549        N/A    :1084
                            92%   :  547        95%    : 577
                            (Other): 4907       (Other):7088
```

```
        bedrooms                beds
Min.    : 1.000    Min.    : 0.000
1st Qu.: 1.000    1st Qu.: 1.000
Median : 2.000    Median : 2.000
Mean    : 1.802    Mean    : 2.415
3rd Qu.: 2.000    3rd Qu.: 3.000
Max.    : 17.000   Max.    : 38.000
NA's    : 3060      NA's    : 60
```

The `summary` function reported the five levels of `host.response.time` noted earlier from the `str` output along with their counts. So, the response time of "a few days or more" showed up 643 times. One of the levels in the data file was coded as N/A, which means it was missing from the Airbnb listing. R stores missing values as `NA`, which stands for "not available." And finally, we see that since `bedrooms` and `beds` are numerical, we get the five number summary plus the mean (and, again, the number of NAs).

A.2.2 Working with Data Frames

Most datasets will be organized so that each row is an observation and each column is a variable. When we read a `.csv` file into R that is formatted this way, R will assign the `data.frame`. A data frame looks the same as a matrix, but is a different way to store and treat the data in R.

R treats a `data.frame` as a list of lists: each column is an element of the data frame "list." Recall that a `list` is a flexible R object that can contain different types of data. In an R data frame, each list element is a column vector containing, say, numbers, characters, factors.

Referring to Columns and Rows

Knowing that a data frame is a list of columns will give you flexiblity in how you access information. Often, we will need to refer to a specific column, specific row, or specific row(s) of a certain column for a data frame.

There are four common ways to refer to a specific column.

1. `datasetName$columnName`
2. `datasetName[,i]` to refer to the *i*th column
3. `datasetName[['columnName']]` or `datasetName[[columnNumber]]`
4. `attach(datasetName)` and then refer directly to the column name

Way 1, using `datasetName$columnName`, allows you to refer to the column using $ before the column name. If we want to calculate the average for `accommodates` and `bedrooms` for a Hawaii Airbnb listing, use the mean function.

```
> mean(aloha$accommodates)
[1] 4.638718
> mean(aloha$bedrooms)
[1] NA
```

Notice that R returns 4.638718 for the average number of people a listing accommodates but gives NA for the average number of bedrooms, since there are missing values. A quick check of the help file using ?mean shows that the default to remove NAs is FALSE.

```
\R{mean(x, trim = 0, na.rm = FALSE, ...)
...
na.rm
      a logical value indicating whether NA values should
    be stripped before the computation proceeds.}
```

Change the na.rm (this stands for "remove NAs" in R) argument to TRUE by using the word TRUE in all caps or by just the first letter, T. In many functions in R, as long as it's not ambiguous, one can use an abbreviated version of the function argument. The following will all produce the same end result, yielding an average bedroom count of 1.801899.

```
> mean(aloha$bedrooms,na.rm=TRUE)
> mean(aloha$bedrooms,na.rm=T)
> mean(aloha$bedrooms,na=T)
> mean(aloha$bedrooms,n=T)
```

When you are just beginning or if the argument isn't too long to type, we recommend using the full argument name so that you can easily figure out the source if there is an error message or you can trace the process if you are re-using code.

Way 2, indexing, is often used if either you use the same data structure over and over and have the column number memorized (because you don't feel like typing out the column name!) or you are writing a loop and need the code to run over multiple rows and or columns. If using this method, start with the object name followed by square brackets to give the position. If you are indexing just a one-dimensional object (vector), put the position number in the square brackets. If you are indexing over a two-dimensional object, put the row number first, then a comma, then the column number. For higher dimensions, you will have a position for each dimension inside the square brackets.

Notice in the snapshot of HiListings.csv in Figure A.4 that the 2nd entry of the superhost column is f. The following are both equivalent ways to refer to the 2nd entry of the superhost column.

```
> aloha$superhost[2] #2nd entry of the superhost column
[1] f
Levels: f t
> aloha[2,11] #2nd row of the 11th column
[1] f
Levels: f t
```

If your column contains numbers, you will just get the numerical answer after the [1], but since superhost is a factor, it also gives us the levels.

Way 3 uses the double square bracket mechanism. The double square bracket will refer to one element of a list. And remember how we mentioned that a data frame is a fancy list of lists? Well, as a consequence, you can also refer to the 2nd element of the 11th element (list) of aloha using either of the following codes.

```
> aloha[['superhost']][2] #2nd element of list called superhost
[1] f
Levels: f t
> aloha[[11]][2] #2nd element of 11th list in aloha
[1] f
Levels: f t
```

You can think of the double square bracket convention as accessing one element of a list and the single square brackets as a subsetting mechanism. We use both in this book.

The fourth popular way to refer to a column in a data frame is to use the attach function so that you can refer directly to the column name without having to reference the name of the dataset. Once you have attached a dataset, R knows that is where to look for the columns. Notice below if we try to refer directly to the column name, without referring to the dataset name, we get an error, but after attaching, we no longer need to remind R which dataset this column is in.

```
> superhost[2]
Error: object 'superhost' not found
> attach(aloha)
> superhost[2]
[1] f
[]Levels: f t
```

Using this method to refer directly to the column names saves time typing the name of the dataset when you are referring to columns but can be problematic. You should always use detach to unattach a dataset before attaching another. Also, if you have an identical column name in the previously attached dataset and the newly attached dataset, R might "remember" the column from the previously attached dataset. Plenty of people recommend avoiding using attach because of these issues. We agree with this recommendation.

Data Cleaning

Now that we know how to refer to the data inside the data frame, we turn our attention to the formatting errors in our data and the missing values. Missing data is a pervasive problem with many modes of data collection and reporting. Sensors malfunction, people refuse to answer survey questions, certain data was not collected before a certain time, and so on.

Recall that R assigned the factor structure to the host response rate column, so if we want to run numerical summaries on this column, we'll need to fix these issues. Running summary(aloha$host.response.rate) shows us that there are two issues in this column—there are % signs on the values and there are 3,144 values coded as N/A. One way to get rid of unwanted characters is to use the `gsub` function which will replace instances of a certain set of characters (called "pattern" in the function arguments). The first three arguments are `pattern`, `replacement`, and `x`, so it is asking what to look for, what to replace it with, and where to look. The following code redefines the `aloha$host.response.rate` column without the % signs or the N/As using the `gsub` function on it. Notice, the arguments say to replace % or the N/As encountered with nothing (empty quotes) in the response rate column. The square brackets allow you to define more than one thing to replace.

```
> aloha$host.response.rate <-
+   gsub("[%N/A]","",aloha$host.response.rate)
> str(aloha&host.response.rate)
 chr [1:22434] "100" "100" "100" "100" "100" "100" "" "100" ""
```

Notice that upon checking the structure of the newly defined column, we have successfully gotten rid of the % signs and N/As, but the resulting vector is a character vector. We can change it to a numeric using the `as.numeric` function.

```
> aloha$host.response.rate <-
+   as.numeric(aloha$host.response.rate)
> str(aloha$host.response.rate)
 num [1:22434] 100 100 100 100 100 100 NA 100 NA 100 ...
```

We can clean the `host.acceptance.rate` column all in one line of code.

```
> aloha$host.acceptance.rate <-
+   as.numeric(gsub("[%N/A]","",aloha$host.acceptance.rate))
> str(aloha$host.acceptance.rate)
 num [1:22434] 37 95 97 97 94 99 0 98 89 100 ...
```

Cleaning up the `price` column takes a slight edit to our previous strategy. Since the $ comes at the beginning of the entries, we have to use two backslashes for it to find the $.

```
> aloha$price<-as.numeric(gsub("[\\$,]","",aloha$price))
> summary(aloha$price)
   Min. 1st Qu.  Median    Mean 3rd Qu.     Max.
    0.0   125.0   187.0   309.1   300.0  24999.0
```

There are four columns in this dataset that are dates, but are being treated as factors in R. Use the `as.Date` function to change these columns to the date format. The following code redefines the `first.review` and `last.review` columns as dates. The second argument in the function tells R the format of the reported date. `%m` denotes the month number, `%d` denotes the day number, and `%y` and `%Y` denote a 2-digit or 4-digit year, respectively.

```
> aloha$first.review<-as.Date(aloha$first.review,"%m/%d/%Y")
> aloha$last.review<-as.Date(aloha$last.review,"%m/%d/%Y")
> aloha$last.review[1]-aloha$first.review[1]
Time difference of 2589 days
```

Once you have date data formatted correctly, you unlock R's suite of capabilities for time and date data. You can see from the above output that computations can be made.

Let's now turn our attention to finding and dealing with NAs, R's notation for missing data.

```
> sum(is.na(aloha)) #total number of NAs in aloha
[1] 64638
> colSums(is.na(aloha)) #how many NAs in each column
...        host.response.rate   reviews.per.month ...
...                      3144                5615...
```

The `rowSums` function will calculate the number of NAs by row, also. Now that you have an idea of how many NAs there are, it's important to decide what to do with them. After asking why they are there, you can decide to leave them there, replace them, or remove them. After a quick Internet search on Airbnb's website, it seems that the `host.response.rate` is not reported if the host hasn't been contacted in over 30 days. Here, it wouldn't make sense to replace the missing values with a 0 since a 0% response rate is really bad and we don't know if a host is good or bad at responding since we are missing this information. So, these NAs should stay. It really is information that is not available.

In looking at the `reviews.per.month`, which appears to be an average number of reviews per month from renters, there are 5,782 NAs. We could take a look at the difference in time between the host's first and last review, as well as number of reviews, to get an idea of whether this data is really missing or whether these are hosts who have no reviews.

```
> rows<-which(is.na(aloha$reviews.per.month)) #row nums for NAs
> table((aloha$last.review-aloha$first.review)[rows])
< table of extent 0 >
> summary(aloha$number.of.reviews[rows])
   Min. 1st Qu.  Median    Mean 3rd Qu.    Max.
      0       0       0       0       0       0
```

It appears that after checking in two different ways, these hosts do not yet have any reviews. Depending on your data analysis, it might be reasonable to replace these NAs with 0s. This is called *imputing* values. Common values to impute are 0s or the average over the whole column. If we replace the NAs with 0, it is usually wise to create a new column so that we know which observations have been imputed. The following code creates a new column called `numRevsImputed` that is a copy of `reviews.per.month` and then imputes 0s for the NAs in the newly created column.

```
> aloha$numRevsImputed<-aloha$reviews.per.month
> aloha$numRevsImputed[is.na(aloha$reviews.per.month)]<-0
> summary(aloha$reviews.per.month) #original column
   Min. 1st Qu.  Median    Mean 3rd Qu.    Max.    NA's
  0.010   0.180   0.540   0.976   1.390  17.860    5615
> summary(aloha$numRevsImputed) #new column with 0's for NA's
   Min. 1st Qu.  Median    Mean 3rd Qu.    Max.
  0.000   0.000   0.270   0.732   1.020  17.860
```

Chapters 3 and 8 discuss approaches for imputing (replacing) these types of missing values. Here, for illustration, we will tend to either ignore or delete them. For example, you can use `na.omit` on `aloha` to remove all the rows with NAs in them. You will lose a lot of valuable data this way, though, so it is recommended that you look to the alternative imputation methods if you have a lot of missing data.

The Basics of Subsetting

We have already covered a few simple examples of calculating the mean for a certain column of data. It's easy to calculate the average review score for value, since that is a single column in `aloha`. If you want to know the average review score for hosts who have a large number of listings or for hosts who are superhosts, you will need to subset. Use single square brackets to specify certain rows on which to subset. When reading the following line of code, use "such that" or "only where" as words in place of the square brackets. Also notice the use of the logical operator == rather than a single equals sign and the quotes around the letter "t" which represents the word "true". If you are subsetting based on a numeric value, you won't need the quotes, but if you are subsetting based on a word or character, you need the quotes.

```
> mean(aloha$review.scores.value[aloha$superhost=="t"],na.rm=T)
[1] 9.640973
> mean(aloha$review.scores.value
+    [aloha$host.total.listings.count>9], na.rm=T)
[1] 9.179966
> mean(aloha$review.scores.value[aloha$superhost=="t" &
+    aloha$host.total.listings.count>9],na.rm=T)
[1] 9.44266
```

The first line of code above calculates the average review score for value for superhosts. It is read "calculate the mean review score for value only for superhosts." The second line takes the average for hosts that have more than the median number of listings, which is 9. And the third line calculates the average review score for value for hosts who both are superhosts and have more than 9 listings. You can use any of the logical operators to create any subset you want.

Another way to subset is to use the `subset` function. The `subset` function takes the name of the dataset as the first argument and the citerion for subsetting as the second argument.

```
> alohaSuperhosts<-subset(aloha,aloha$superhost=="t")
```

The above code creates a smaller data frame that keeps only the rows where the `superhost` column has a `t`. To compute the average review score for value for superhosts, use the following code.

```
> mean(alohaSuperhosts$review.scores.value,na.rm=T)
[1] 9.640973
```

As a side note, if your workspace is getting cluttered at this point in the tutorial you can use CTRL + L on a Windows machine or CMD + Option + L on a Mac to clear the console. To view the names of all defined objects, use `ls` or `objects`. To remove all objects, use `rm(list=ls())`.

A.2.3 Graphical Displays

R has a number of convenient plotting capabilities. One advantage of R is that it makes it easy to create professional graphs that are highly customizable. For example, you can quickly visualize the `aloha reviews.per.month` data with a histogram. The following code produces a histogram with customized axis labels and title suppressed (Figure A.3).

```
> hist(aloha$reviews.per.month,col="blue",
+    xlab="Average Number of Reviews per Month",
+    main="",cex.lab=1.25,cex.main=2)
```

The `ylab=` argument creates a customized y-axis label in a similar manner to the `xlab=` argument. The `cex.` arguments change the font size. Specifying the "`main=""`" argument tells R to leave the title empty.

Side-by-side boxplots as shown in Figure A.4 (used to compare a quantitative variable across the levels of a categorical variable) are easy to create with the `boxplot` command. Pay special attention to the ~ symbol in the boxplot command. This tilde symbol in R means "as a function of" or just simply "by." This notation is used a lot in this book when you begin to build models, such as regression models. The following code will create side-by-side boxplots to look at price (per night) of the rental by the neighborhood group (which is basically the islands of Hawaii). Also, since there are several expensive rentals, we took these out and looked at only the rentals whose prices are lower than 600 dollars per night. As an added touch, and to emphasize the capability for customization in R, we add a custom color for the boxes.

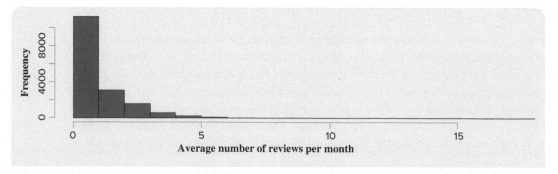

FIGURE A.3 Histogram of the average reviews per month column of the `aloha` dataset.

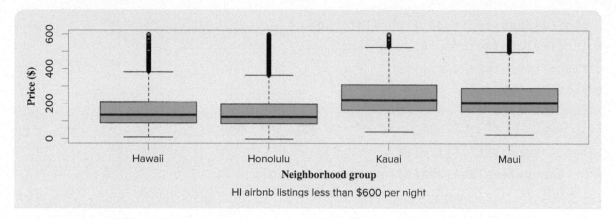

FIGURE A.4   Side-by-side boxplots of the `prices` that are less than $600 per night broken down by the categorical variable, `neighborhood.group`.

```
> boxplot(aloha$price[aloha$price<600] ~
+   aloha$neighborhood.group[aloha$price<600],
+   col="#00c3e3", #HI official water color according to Google
+   xlab="Neighborhood Group",
+   ylab="Price ($)",
+   sub="HI airbnb listings less than $600 per night",
+   cex.lab=1.25
+   )
```

To highlight the capability of plotting a scatterplot, we color code by a categorical variable. As a toy example, we plot the longitude and latitude of the listings, separated by `neighborhood.group`, which should reproduce something similar to a map of the Hawaiian Islands, color coded by the `neighborhood.group` (Figure A.5).

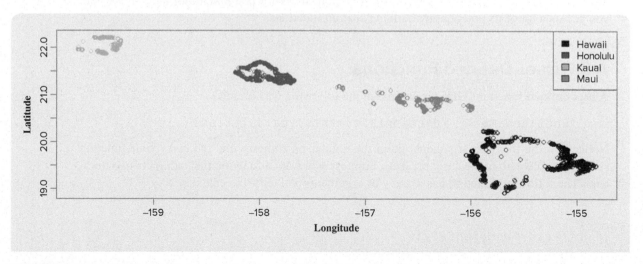

FIGURE A.5   Scatterplot of the `latitude` column against the `longitude` column, highlighted by `neighborhood.group`.

```
> plot(aloha$longitude,aloha$latitude,
+    col=aloha$neighborhood.group,
+ xlab="Longitude",
+ ylab="Latitude",
+ cex.lab=1.25
+ )
legend("topright",fill=1:4,
+    legend=levels(aloha$neighborhood.group))
```

It looks like all the rentals are near the beach!

Notice that when you call a new graphics window, the default is to overwrite the old one. To view two graphics windows at one time, use `win.graph()` for a Windows machine and `dev.new()` for a Mac to open a new graphics window. Your next plot command will then display to that new window.

If you want to put multiple graphs in one graphics window, use the `par` function. The following function would allow six graphs to be put on the same window, with two rows of three graphs.

```
par(mfrow=c(2,3))
```

Simply type that command and then the next 6 graphs you create will all be placed into that one graphics window.

A.3 Advanced Topics for Functions

There are many built-in functions to use in R, but they don't cover every scenario and there are many occasions that call for a customized function. Indeed R is a *functional* language where you access a lot of its potential by building custom functions.

A.3.1 User Defined Functions

A user defined function (UDF) is entered in the following way into R:

```
functionName <- function(arguments){calculation}
```

Notice that the function arguments go in the regular parentheses and the tasks your function should complete go in the curly brackets. Suppose you want a function that subtracts two numbers. The following function has x and y as arguments and tells R to calculate x-y.

```
subtract<-function(x,y){
   x-y
}
```

That could have all been written on one line, but it is customary to start a few spaces in on the next line after the first curly bracket. If your function has multiple lines inside the curly brackets, they all should be indented, with new routines being indented further than the last. Putting your code in this sort of outline format makes it more readable.

Notice, that if you copy and paste all three lines of our simple function, you will get a + instead of the cursor on the second and third lines, and then the command prompt and cursor appear on the next line after the end curly bracket.

```
> subtract<-function(x,y){
+    x-y
+ }
>
```

Remember, the + sign replaces the command prompt when R is waiting for the code to be closed out. It gives the + sign on the two lines after the open curly bracket and finally gives the command prompt after the closing curly bracket appears.

Now that you have stored a function in R, you can use it. Simply type the name of your function with the proper arguments in the parentheses. Notice, as with built-in functions, if you enter the arguments in the order they are listed when writing the function, you do not need to specify the argument name. If not specified, it will automatically make the first argument 'x' and the second 'y', since that's the way you entered them when the function was written.

```
> subtract(x=2,y=3)
[1] -1
> subtract(2,3)
[1] -1
> subtract(y=2,x=3)
[1] 1
> subtract(3,2)
[1] 1
```

It is often the case where a function is created to carry out a calculation that can be represented by an iterative process. Suppose you want to calculate the average for a variable in your dataset. One way to accomplish this is to use a *for loop* in the following way:

```
> mat1<-matrix(c(1,2,3,4,5,6,7,8,9),byrow=F,ncol=3)
> avgs<-c() #create empty vector to fill
> for(i in 1:ncol(mat1)){
+    avgs<-c(avgs,mean(mat1[,i]))
+ }
```

```
> mat1
     [,1] [,2] [,3]
[1,]    1    4    7
[2,]    2    5    8
[3,]    3    6    9
> avgs
[1] 2 5 8
```

Let's inspect this *for loop* code line by line. The second line of code creates an empty vector named "avgs" so that we have someplace to store our column averages. The next line begins the *for loop*. After the word "for," the counter goes in parenthesis. That line is read, "for i in 1 through the number of columns of the matrix. . ." Then the loop starts with i = 1 and combines (concatenates) the previous version of avgs with the mean of the column for the ith column. The process stops when the counter is done, here at the third column.

This loop can also be nested into a function in the following way:

```
> avgCols<-function(mat){
+     avgs<-c() #create empty vector to fill
+        for(i in 1:ncol(mat)){
+        avgs<-c(avgs,mean(mat[,i]))
+        }
+     print(avgs)
+ }
```

And then, to use the function, simply use the name of the function with a matrix name in the parenthesis. Let's define another matrix and use the avgCols function to calculate the column averages.

```
> mat2<-matrix(c(2,3,4,5,6,7,8,9,10),ncol=3)
> mat2
     [,1] [,2] [,3]
[1,]    2    5    8
[2,]    3    6    9
[3,]    4    7   10
> avgCols(mat2)
[1] 3 6 9
```

But look what happens if we compare the results of the function avgCols to the avgs object. They don't match!

```
> avgCols(mat2)
[1] 3 6 9
> avgs
[1] 2 5 8
```

Even though we defined something called avgs inside the function, it didn't overwrite the old avgs object. This is because the avgs inside the function only lives *inside the function*. When we ask R to print avgs, it only remembers the one that was created before (outside of) the function.

For loops are intuitive and tangible and beginning coders can get the hang of them fairly easily. For these reasons, they are widely used. However, care should be taken to avoid for loops when possible, especially for large data with intensive calculations, since this elementwise computation can greatly slow your analysis. Whenever possible, use a strategy that vectorizes the process. Remember that many of R's built-in functions already do this.

A.3.2 Avoid Loops: the `apply` Functions

An important set of functions that are worth a special mention are the *apply family of functions.

The apply function apply(X, MARGIN, FUN, ...) takes an array X, which is often a matrix. The margin should be set to 1 if the function is to be applied to the rows of X, and set to 2 if it should be applied to the columns. The third argument is the function that should be applied to the margin of x. The function also takes optional arguments for the function you want to apply, for example na.rm=T if the function is mean.

```
> apply(mat1,2,mean, na.rm=T)
[1] 2 5 8
```

lapply(X, FUN, ...) takes a list and returns a list object of the same length. Notice how it handles our matrix, mat.

```
> lapply(mat1,mean)
[[1]]
[1] 1

[[2]]
[1] 2

[[3]]
[1] 3

....
[[9]]
[1] 9
```

It treats the nine elements of the matrix as a list and returns a list with nine means. It took the mean of each individual number (so, of course, the mean is just the number itself). We could actually create a list and see how it works that way.

```
> a<-c(1,2,3)
> b<-c(4,5,6)
> c<-c(7,8,9)
> ourList<-list(a,c,b)
> lapply(ourList,mean)
[[1]]
[1] 2


[[2]]
[1] 8


[[3]]
[1] 5
```

`sapply(X, FUN, ..., simplify = TRUE, USE.NAMES = TRUE)` does the same thing as `lapply` except it simplifies the output, if possible, and returns a vector or matrix.

```
> sapply(ourList,mean)
[1] 2 8 5
```

`vapply(X, FUN, FUN.VALUE, ..., USE.NAMES = TRUE))` does the same thing as `sapply` except the `FUN.VALUE` argument allows the user to specify the type of output. If the output is not in the class specified, an error will be returned.

```
> vapply(ourList,mean,numeric(1))
[1] 2 8 5
```

And last, but not least, is the `tapply` function. Recall in section A.2.2 on subsetting, that it was a fairly lengthy command to calculate the mean on only certain rows of the `aloha` dataset. The `tapply` function allows for the application of a function to the rows or columns but separately for some specified categorical variable.

`tapply(X, INDEX, FUN = NULL, ..., default = NA, simplify = TRUE)` is called where `X` is the object to apply the function, `INDEX` is the column containing the categorical variable (factor) to break `X` up by, and `FUN` is the function to be applied.

```
> mean(aloha$review.scores.value[aloha$superhost=="t"],na.rm=T)
[1] 9.640972581
```

```
> mean(aloha$review.scores.value[aloha$superhost=="f"],na.rm=T)
[1] 9.202914798
> tapply(aloha$review.scores.value,aloha$superhost,mean,na.rm=T)
           f           t
9.202914798 9.640972581
```

The `tapply` function calculated the mean `review.score.value` for all levels of `superhost` with one line of code.

A.3.3 Packages

An R package is a collection of functions and/or datasets. A great advantage of using R is the availability of many contributed packages—currently almost 17,000 and climbing. The packages are free for anyone to use and any R user can contribute a package. And although *writing* a package is beyond the scope of this book, we *use* many packages. In order to use a package, it needs to be installed in your version of R and loaded into your workspace.

- Install a package using `install.packages("packageName")`
  Files for packages are on the CRAN. If prompted, choose a mirror close to you.
  Once you install a package, you never have to do it again.
- Use a package with `library(packageName)`
- Get help with a package using `help(package="packageName")`
- List dataset names in package `data(package="packageName")`

There are many packages that come with the base version of R and any of these can be loaded into the workspace by using the `library` command. If you get the command prompt after running the `library` command, your package is loaded and you are good to go.

We will be using the `rmarkdown` (Allaire et al., 2019) package in the next section. If you try to load it into your workspace right now, you will likely get an error.

```
> library(rmarkdown)
Error in library(rmarkdown) :
  there is no package called 'rmarkdown'
```

This means the package files have not yet been installed on your computer, so use `install.packages`.

```
> install.packages("rmarkdown")
```

If you haven't already chosen a CRAN mirror during your current session of R, it will prompt you to choose one. If R asks if you want to install into a personal library, click "Yes." Be warned: the `rmarkdown` package depends on (uses) many other packages and if these are not installed in your version of R, they will also be installed at the same time. Lots and lots of messages should appear on your screen as the `rmarkdown` package and all its dependencies are installed. Make sure you have a good Internet connection and be patient. Figure A.6 shows a small portion of what could show on your screen as the package is installing.

```
> install.packages('rmarkdown')
Installing package into 'C:/Users/name/Documents/R/win-library/3.4'
(as 'lib' is unspecified)
--- Please select a CRAN mirror for use in this session ---
also installing the dependencies 'highr', 'markdown', 'digest', 'Rcpp',
'knitr', 'yaml', 'htmltools', 'evaluate', 'base64enc', 'jsonlite', 'mime',
'tinytex', 'xfun'

  There is a binary version available but the source version is later:
         binary source needs_compilation
rmarkdown   1.13   1.14              FALSE

trying URL
'https://mirrors.nics.utk.edu/cran/bin/windows/contrib/3.6/highr_0.8.zip'
Content type 'application/zip' length 48757 bytes (47 KB)
downloaded 47 KB

trying URL
'https://mirrors.nics.utk.edu/cran/bin/windows/contrib/3.6/markdown_1.0.zip'
Content type 'application/zip' length 190005 bytes (185 KB)
downloaded 185 KB

trying URL
'https://mirrors.nics.utk.edu/cran/bin/windows/contrib/3.6/digest_0.6.20.zip'
Content type 'application/zip' length 223121 bytes (217 KB)
downloaded 217 KB
…..

*** arch - x64
** testing if installed package keeps a record of temporary installation path
* DONE (rmarkdown)

The downloaded source packages are in
        'C:\Users\lesli\AppData\Local\Temp\RtmpQZ2rjk\downloaded_packages'
>
```

FIGURE A.6   Portion of R GUI when installing `rmarkdown` package.

Once you install a package, the files are stored on your hard drive in your R folder. To use the package, use `library(packageName)` to load it in the workspace. The package does not need to be installed again in future R sessions. Here, you can load the package using `library(rmarkdown)` and you will be able to use it.

```
> library(rmarkdown)
```

Stay tuned . . . we'll show you how to use this package in the next section to produce an HTML report of your R code project.

A.4 Organizing Code, Saving Work, and Creating Reports

There are plenty of occasions where you will want to type code directly into your R console, like when you are typing `?functionName` or doing a quick, one-off calculation. However, if you are working on a nontrivial project, it is a good idea to keep track of your code in a way that makes it easy to edit, save, and share.

A.4.1 R's Script Editor

R has a convenient built-in script editor functionality. To start a new script file, click `File ->` `New Script` on a Windows machine or `File -> New Document` on a Mac. This will open a blank script editor. Simply type a line of code into the script editor. To run the code in your console, put your cursor anywhere on the line you want to run and hit `CTRL+R` for a Windows machine. For a Mac, use `CMD+Return`. You can run multiple lines at one time by highlighting the lines and then executing with `CTRL+R or CMD+Return`. You can quickly run all of the code in the script by doing `CTRL/CMD + A` and then `CTRL+R or CMD+Return`.

Simply save your script file with the name and in the location of your choosing by using the `File -> Save As...` menu options at the top left of your R console before closing R. You can open a previously saved script file from inside R using `File -> Open`.

You can use #'s to insert comments into your script file. R will ignore anything after a # so the comments won't create any problems when running your code and comments help to stay organized. Don't forget that you must open a previously saved script file from the R menu options. If you simply navigate to it and open it on your computer, it will likely be opened in a simple text editor and you will not be able to run the code without copying and pasting it.

A.4.2 Using Version Control

If you are working in a group, or simply trying to keep yourself organized, you may want to invest the time in learning how to use a *version control system* such as Git. These systems are similar to file-shares such as Dropbox, which store remote copies of your files on the Internet, but they come with a system for checking in and checking out changes. They also let you fork off different branches of files and then merge them back together when you want to consolidate. The most commonly used public Git system is GitHub. You can go to `www.github.com` for extensive documentation, and also free-tier versions of their software.

`GitHub` will have a bit of a steep learning curve if you have never worked with version control before, but it is well worth the investment if you are collaborating with other students or analysts and need to keep track of how your project is progressing. For R projects involving many different versions of analysis scripts, some form of version control will become essential if your project involves multiple collaborators. You can also choose to make your `GitHub` repository public, and many students do this to show potential employers their portfolio of data science work.

A.4.3 Creating a Report with `rmarkdown`

Markdown is a simple code for writing documents in plain text that can be converted to nice-looking HTML code and rendered as, for example, a webpage. For example, Table A.5 shows some of the commands that you can use in a markdown document to get different formatting.

To convert markdown code to a nice document, you need a program to *render* the code. The `rmarkdown` package uses the Pandoc (MacFarlane, 2019) rendering system to do this, and it has special capability that allows you to include and execute R-code as part of your documents. This is useful for producing reports that include R code analysis. We already installed `rmarkdown` in the previous section. To use it, you need to go outside of R and install Pandoc.

`*word*`	italic
`**word**`	bold
`***word***`	bold and italic
`#`	big header (H1)
`##`	smaller header (H2)
`###`	even smaller header (H3)
2 spaces at end of line	starts new line
` `	skip line

TABLE A.5   Some Markdown formatting commands.

Visit `pandoc.org` and click the install links and follow the instructions. You may need to restart your computer after installation so that everything works.

Once you have this all installed, you can start writing an *R Markdown* document. This is just a text file that you write using the markdown language. You can open the file in the R editor exactly as you would a usual R script. The difference is that now you are writing the script using markdown language. There are two different ways to do this:

- Write an R markdown document, with file ending `.Rmd`, that uses usual markdown language and contains R code in *code blocks* that are denoted like ```` ```R 2+2 ``` ````. An example script, say `SampMark.Rmd`, is below:

```
---
title: "A Super Simple Markdown Example"
---


### "the easier way to write reports"


This is how plain text looks.
Below we create an R code block.
```{R}
mean(c(1,2,3))
```

Enjoy!
```

- Alternatively, you can write a standard R script with lines for comments starting with `#'`, and put markdown language in the comments. For example, here is the `SampMark.R` script.

```
#' ---
#' title: "A Super Simple Markdown Example"
#' ---


#' ### "the easier way to write reports"
```

```
#' This is how plain text looks.
#' Below we create an R code block.

mean(c(2,3,4))

#' ***Enjoy!***
```

The difference between these two options is whether you have a markdown script containing blocks of R-code, or an R script that contains markdown in the comments. Either works, and you can work with these scripts in the R editor as you would any normal R script, however, rendering the .Rmd markdown script with blocks of R code might be more easily done using R studio.

If you save the code in your working directory as SampMark.R, then the following code in R will render the document.

```
> library(rmarkdown)
> render("SampMark.R")
```

This should produce an HTML version in your working directory folder. Simply navigate to it and double click to open. Your default web browser should open it and look like Figure A.7. If you need to make changes to the HTML document, simply edit the R script file, save the document, and render it again.

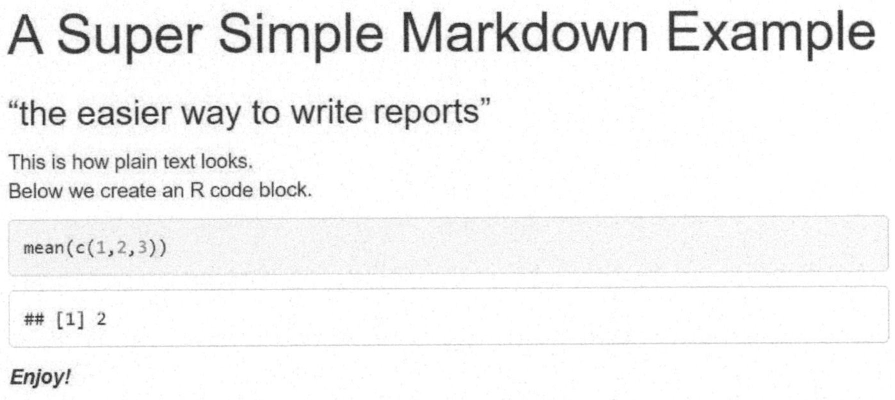

A Super Simple Markdown Example

"the easier way to write reports"

This is how plain text looks.
Below we create an R code block.

```
mean(c(1,2,3))
```

```
## [1] 2
```

Enjoy!

FIGURE A.7 R markdown script rendered as an HTML document.

A.4.4 Closing the Workspace

When you need to close out your R session, there are a few tips that should save headaches later. Make sure to save your script file before closing the R session. In order to close the script file

1. *Click in the script file* to make sure the cursor is in the script file
2. Then choose File -> Save or Save as
3. Close the R script

Once you have saved your R script, you can close out of R. You will get a message asking if you want to save your workspace. Saving the workspace will save only the objects created and not the actual commands in the R GUI. Saving all your objects can be problematic in later sessions if you accidentally use the same name for a new object and overwrite the old object. This can lead to coding errors. It is almost always best to say no to saving the workspace since you can always recreate your objects by quickly running your R script again in your next session.

BIBLIOGRAPHY

Abadie, A., and J. Gardeazabal (2003). The economic costs of conflict: A case study of the Basque country. *The American Economic Review 93*(1), 113–132.

Akaike, H. (1973). Information theory and the maximum likelihood principle. In *2nd International Symposiumon Information Theory*. Budapest: Akademiai Kiado.

Allaire, J., Y. Xie, J. McPherson, J. Luraschi, K. Ushey, A. Atkins, H. Wickham, J. Cheng, W. Chang, and R. Iannone (2019). *rmarkdown: Dynamic Documents for R*. R package version 1.14.

Angrist, J. D., K. Graddy, and G. W. Imbens (2000). The interpretation of instrumental variables estimators in simultaneous equations models with an application to the demand for fish. *The Review of Economic Studies 67*, 499–527.

Angrist, J. D., G. W. Imbens, and D. B. Rubin (1996). Identification of causal effects using instrumental variables. *Journal of the American Statistical Association 91*, 444–455.

Angrist, J. D., and J. S. Pischke (2009). *Mostly Harmless Econometrics*. Princeton University Press.

Arkhangelsky, D., S. Athey, D. A. Hirshberg, G. W. Imbens, and S. Wager (2019). Synthetic difference in differences. Technical report, National Bureau of Economic Research.

Athey, S., and G. Imbens (2016). Recursive partitioning for heterogeneous causal effects. *Proceedings of the National Academy of Sciences 113*, 7353–7360.

Athey, S., J. Tibshirani, and S. Wager (2017). Generalized random forests. *arXiv 1610.01271v3*.

Bair, E., T. Hastie, P. Debashis, and R. Tibshirani (2006). Prediction by supervised principal components. *Journal of the American Statistical Association 101*, 119–137.

Bengio, Y., Y. LeCun, et al. (2007). Scaling learning algorithms towards AI. *Large-scale Kernel Machines 34*(5), 1–41.

Benjamini, Y., and Y. Hochberg (1995). Controlling the false discovery rate: A practical and powerful approach to multiple testing. *Journal of the Royal Statistical Society, Series B 57*, 289–300.

Berry, S., J. Levinsohn, and A. Pakes (1995). Automobile prices in market equilibrium. *Econometrica 63*(4), 841–890.

Blake, T., C. Nosko, and S. Tadelis (2015). Consumer Heterogeneity and Paid Search Effectiveness: A Large-Scale Field Experiment. *Econometrica 83*(1), 155–174.

Blei, D. M., A. Y. Ng, and M. I. Jordan (2003). Latent Dirichlet allocation. *Journal of Machine Learning Research 3*, 993–1022.

Bojanowski, P., E. Grave, A. Joulin, and T. Mikolov (2017). Enriching word vectors with subword information. *Transactions of the Association for Computational Linguistics 5*, 135–146.

Bolukbasi, T., K. W. Chang, J. Y. Zou, V. Saligrama, and A. T. Kalai (2016). Man is to computer programmer as woman is to homemaker? Debiasing word embeddings. In *Advances in Neural Information Processing Systems*, 4349–4357.

Bouchet-Valat, M. (2020). *SnowballC: Snowball Stemmers Based on the C 'libstemmer' UTF-8 Library*. R package version 0.7.0.

Bousquet, O., and L. Bottou (2008). The tradeoffs of large scale learning. In *Advances in Neural Information Processing Systems*, 161–168.

Breiman, L. (1996). Heuristics of instability and stabilization in model selection. *The Annals of Statistics 24*, 2350–2383.

Breiman, L. (2001). Random forests. *Machine Learning 45,* 5–32.

Breiman, L., J. Friedman, R. Olshen, and C. Stone (1984). *Classification and Regression Trees.* Chapman & Hall/CRC.

Brodersen, K. H., F. Gallusser, J. Koehler, N. Remy, S. L. Scott, et al. (2015). Inferring causal impact using Bayesian structural time-series models. *The Annals of Applied Statistics 9,* 247–274.

Brown, T. B., B. Mann, N. Ryder, M. Subbiah, J. Kaplan, P. Dhariwal, A. Neelakantan, P. Shyam, G. Sastry, A. Askell, S. Agarwal, A. Herbert-Voss, G. Krueger, T. Henighan, R. Child, A. Ramesh, D. M. Ziegler, J. Wu, C. Winter, C. Hesse, M. Chen, E. Sigler, M. Litwin, S. Gray, B. Chess, J. Clark, C. Berner, S. McCandlish, A. Radford, I. Sutskever, and D. Amodei (2020). Language models are few-shot learners. In H. Larochelle, M. Ranzato, R. Hadsell, M. F. Balcan, and H. Lin (eds.), *Advances in Neural Information Processing Systems,* Volume 33. Curran Associates, Inc. (digital only).

Buolamwini, J., and T. Gebru (2018, 23–24 February). Gender shades: Intersectional accuracy disparities in commercial gender classification. In S. A. Friedler and C. Wilson (eds.), *Proceedings of the 1st Conference on Fairness, Accountability and Transparency,* Volume 81 of *Proceedings of Machine Learning Research.* New York: PMLR, 77–91.

Chernozhukov, V., D. Chetverikov, M. Demirer, E. Duflo, C. Hansen, W. Newey, and J. Robins (2017). Double/debiased machine learning for treatment and structural parameters. *The Econometrics Journal.*

Chernozhukov, V., and C. Hansen (2004). The effects of 401 (k) participation on the wealth distribution: An instrumental quantile regression analysis. *Review of Economics and Statistics 86*(3), 735–751.

Chernozhukov, V., C. Hansen, and M. Spindler (2016). hdm: High-dimensional metrics. *R Journal 8*(2), 185–199.

Chollet, F. and J. J. Allaire (2018). *Deep Learning with R.* Shelter Island, NY: Manning Publications.

Cochrane, J. H. (2009). *Asset Pricing.* Revised edition. Princeton University Press.

Croissant, Y. (2020). Estimation of random utility models in R: The mlogit package. *Journal of Statistical Software 95*(11), 1–41.

Croissant, Y., and G. Millo (2008). Panel data econometrics in R: The plm package. *Journal of Statistical Software 27*(2), 1–43.

Csardi, G., and T. Nepusz (2006). The igraph software package for complex network research. *InterJournal Complex Systems,* 1695.

Davison, A. C., and D. V. Hinkley (1997). *Bootstrap Methods and Their Application,* Volume 1. Cambridge University Press.

De Cock, D. (2011). Ames, Iowa: Alternative to the Boston housing data as an end of semester regression project. *Journal of Statistics Education 19*(3).

Dean, J., and S. Ghemawat (2004). MapReduce: Simplified data processing on large clusters. In *Proceedings of Operating Systems Design and Implementation,* 137–150.

Deaton, A., and J. Muellbauer (1980). An almost ideal demand system. *The American Economic Review 70,* 312–326.

Devlin, J., M. W. Chang, K. Lee, and K. Toutanova (2019). BERT: Pre-training of deep bidirectional transformers for language understanding. In *Proceedings of the 2019 Conference of the North American Chapter of the Association for Computational Linguistics (NAACL),* 4171–4186.

Duchi, J., E. Hazan, and Y. Singer (2011). Adaptive subgradient methods for online learning and stochastic optimization. *Journal of Machine Learning Research 12,* 2121–2159.

Efron, B. (1982). *The Jackknife, the Bootstrap and Other Resampling Plans.* SIAM.

Fama, E. F., and K. R. French (1993). Common risk factors in the returns on stocks and bonds. *Journal of Financial Economics 33*(1), 3–56.

Finkelstein, A., S. Taubman, B. Wright, M. Bernstein, J. Gruber, J. P. Newhouse, H. Allen, K. Baicker, and O. H. S. Group (2012). The Oregon health insurance experiment: Evidence from the first year. *The Quarterly Journal of Economics 127*(3), 1057–1106.

Friedman, J., T. Hastie, and R. Tibshirani (2010). Regularization paths for generalized linear models via coordinate descent. *Journal of Statistical Software 33*(1), 1–22.

Friedman, J. H. (2001). Greedy function approximation: A gradient boosting machine. *Annals of Statistics,* 1189–1232.

Gelfand, A. E., and A. F. Smith (1990). Sampling-based approaches to calculating marginal densities. *Journal of the American Statistical Association 85*(410), 398–409.

Gelman, A., J. B. Carlin, H. S. Stern, and D. B. Rubin (2014). *Bayesian Data Analysis*, Volume 2. *Boca Raton,* FL: Chapman.

Gelman, A., S. Goel, D. Rothschild, and W. Wang (2016). High-frequency polling with non-representative data. *Political Communication in Real Time: Theoretical and Applied Research Approaches,* 89.

Gelman, A., and J. Hill (2006). *Data Analysis Using Regression and Multi- level/Hierarchical Models.* Cambridge University Press.

Gelman, A., A. Jakulin, M. G. Pittau, Y. S. Su, et al. (2008). A weakly informative default prior distribution for logistic and other regression models. *The Annals of Applied Statistics 2*(4), 1360–1383.

Gentzkow, M., B. Kelly, and M. Taddy (2017). Text-as-data. NBER working paper 23276.

Goodfellow, I., Y. Bengio, and A. Courville (2016). *Deep Learning.* MIT Press.

Gramacy, R. B. (2007). tgp: An R package for Bayesian nonstationary, semiparametric non-linear regression and design by treed Gaussian process models. *Journal of Statistical Software 19,* 1–46.

Gramacy, R. B. (2015). lagp: Large-scale spatial modeling via local approximate gaussian processes in R. *Journal of Statistical Software* (available as a vignette in the laGP package).

Gramacy, R. B., and D. W. Apley (2015). Local Gaussian process approximation for large computer experiments. *Journal of Computational and Graphical Statistics 24*(2), 561–578.

Gramacy, R. B., and H. K. H. Lee (2008). Bayesian treed Gaussian process models with an application to computer modeling. *Journal of the American Statistical Association 103*(483), 1119–1130.

Gramacy, R. B., and M. Taddy (2010). Categorical inputs, sensitivity analysis, optimization and importance tempering with tgp version 2, an R package for treed Gaussian process models. *Journal of Statistical Software 33,* 1–48.

Hacking, I. (1975). *The Emergence of Probability.* Cambridge University Press.

Hahn, J., P. Todd, and W. Van der Klaauw (1999). Evaluating the effect of an anti-discrimination law using a regression-discontinuity design. NBER Working Paper 7131.

Harding, M., and C. Lamarche (2016). Empowering consumers through data and smart technology: Experimental evidence on the consequences of time-of-use electricity pricing policies. *Journal of Policy Analysis and Management 35*(4), 906–931.

Hardt, M., B. Recht, and Y. Singer (2016). Train faster, generalize better: Stability of stochastic gradient descent. In *International Conference on Machine Learning,* 1225–1234.

Hartford, J., G. Lewis, K. Leyton-Brown, and M. Taddy (2017). Deep iv: A flexible approach for counterfactual prediction. In *International Conference on Machine Learning,* 1414–1423.

Hastie, T., R. Tibshirani, and J. Friedman (2009). *The Elements of Statistical Learning* (2nd ed.). New York: Springer.

He, K., X. Zhang, S. Ren, and J. Sun (2016). Deep residual learning for image recognition. In *Proceedings of the IEEE Conference on Computer Vision and Pattern Recognition,* 770–778.

Hinton, G. E., S. Osindero, and Y. W. Teh (2006). A fast learning algorithm for deep belief nets. *Neural Computation 18*(7), 1527–1554.

Hoch, S. J., B. D. Kim, A. L. Montgomery, and P. E. Rossi (1995). Determinants of store-level price elasticity. *Journal of Marketing Research,* 17–29.

Hochreiter, S., and J. Schmidhuber (1997). Long short-term memory. *Neural Computation 9*(8), 1735–1780.

Hornik, K., M. Stinchcombe, and H. White (1989). Multilayer feedforward networks are universal approximators. *Neural Networks 2,* 359–366.

Hurvich, C., and C. L. Tsai (1989). Regression and time series model selection in small samples. *Biometrika 76*, 297–307.

Imbens, G., and D. Rubin (2015). *Causal Inference in Statistics, Social, and Biomedical Sciences.* Cambridge University Press.

Imbens, G. W., and T. Lemieux (2008). Regression discontinuity designs: A guide to practice. *Journal of Econometrics 142*(2), 615–635.

James, G., D. Witten, T. Hastie, and R. Tibshirani (2013). *An Introduction to Statistical Learning,* New York: Springer.

Josse, J., and F. Husson (2016). missmda: A package for handling missing values in multivariate data analysis. *Journal of Statistical Software 70*(1), 1–31.

Karpathy, A., and L. Fei-Fei (2015). Deep visual-semantic alignments for generating image descriptions. In *Proceedings of the IEEE Conference on Computer Vision and Pattern Recognition,* 3128–3137.

Kendall, A., and Y. Gal (2017). What uncertainties do we need in Bayesian deep learning for computer vision? *arXiv preprint arXiv:1703.04977.*

Kingma, D., and J. Ba (2015). Adam: A method for stochastic optimization. In *3rd International Conference on Learning Representations (ICLR).*

Krizhevsky, A., I. Sutskever, and G. E. Hinton (2012). Imagenet classification with deep convolutional neural networks. In *Advances in Neural Information Processing Systems,* 1097–1105.

LeCun, Y., Y. Bengio, et al. (1995). Convolutional networks for images, speech, and time series. *The Handbook of Brain Theory and Neural Networks 3361.*

LeCun, Y., B. Boser, J. S. Denker, D. Henderson, R. E. Howard, W. Hubbard, and L. D. Jackel (1989). Backpropagation applied to handwritten zip code recognition. *Neural Computation 1*(4), 541–551.

LeCun, Y., L. Bottou, Y. Bengio, and P. Haffner (1998). Gradient-based learning applied to document recognition. *Proceedings of the IEEE 86,* 2278–2324.

MacFarlane, John (2019). *Pandoc:* A Haskell library for converting from one markup format to another, and a command-line tool that uses this library. Available at pandoc.org.

Mikolov, T., I. Sutskever, K. Chen, G. S. Corrado, and J. Dean (2013). Distributed representations of words and phrases and their compositionality. In *Advances in Neural Information Processing Systems,* 3111–3119.

Morgan, S. L., and C. Winship (2015). *Counterfactuals and Causal Inference* (2nd ed.). Cambridge University Press.

Moro, S., R. Laureano, and P. Cortez (2011). Using data mining for bank direct marketing: An application of the crisp-dm methodology. In *Proceedings of the European Simulation and Modelling Conference.* EUROSIS.

Morris, M. (2011). *Design of Experiments: An Introduction Based on Linear Models.* New York: CRC Press.

Mosteller, F., and D. L. Wallace (1963). Inference in an authorship problem. *Journal of the American Statistical Association 58,* 275–309.

Mulligan, C. B., and Y. Rubinstein (2008). Selection, investment, and women's relative wages over time. *The Quarterly Journal of Economics 123*(3), 1061–1110.

Pearl, J. (2009). *Causality.* Cambridge University Press.

Pearl, J., and D. Mackenzie (2018). *The Book of Why: The New Science of Cause and Effect.* New York: Basic Books.

Pennington, J., R. Socher, and C. Manning (2014). Glove: Global vectors for word representation. In *Proceedings of the 2014 Conference on Empirical Methods in Natural Language Processing (EMNLP),* 1532–1543.

Poole, K. T. (2005). *Spatial Models of Parliamentary Voting.* New York: Cambridge University Press.

Poterba, J. M. (2003). Employer stock and 401(k) plans. *American Economic Review 93*(2), 398–404.

Robbins, H., and S. Monro (1951). A stochastic approximation method. *The Annals of Mathematical Statistics,* 400–407.

Rosenblatt, F. (1958). The perceptron: A probabilistic model for information storage and organization in the brain. *Psychological Review 65,* 386.

Rubin, D. B. (1981). The Bayesian bootstrap. *The Annals of Statistics,* 130–134.

Rumelhart, D. E., G. E. Hinton, R. J. Williams, et al. (1988). Learning representations by back-propagating errors. *Cognitive Modeling 5*(3), 1.

Sabour, S., N. Frosst, and G. E. Hinton (2017). Dynamic routing between capsules. In *Advances in Neural Information Processing Systems,* 3857–3867.

Santner, T. J., B. J. Williams, W. I. Notz, and B. J. Williams (2003). *The Design and Analysis of Computer Experiments,* Volume 1. New York: Springer.

Schwarz, G., et al. (1978). Estimating the dimension of a model. *Annals of Statistics 6*(2), 461–464.

Sievert, C., and K. Shirley (2015). *LDAvis: Interactive Visualization of Topic Models.* R package version 0.3.2.

Sohl, T., G. Vroom, and B. T. McCann (2020). Business model diversification and firm performance: A demand-side perspective. *Strategic Entrepreneurship Journal 14*(2), 198–223.

Srivastava, N., G. E. Hinton, A. Krizhevsky, I. Sutskever, and R. Salakhutdinov (2014). Dropout: A simple way to prevent neural networks from overfitting. *Journal of Machine Learning Research 15*(1), 1929–1958.

Sutton, R. S., and A. G. Barto (2018). *Reinforcement Learning: An Introduction.* Cambridge, MA: MIT Press.

Szegedy, C., V. Vanhoucke, S. Ioffe, J. Shlens, and Z. Wojna (2016). Rethinking the inception architecture for computer vision. In *Proceedings of the IEEE Conference on Computer Vision and Pattern Recognition,* 2818–2826.

Taddy, M. (2015). Distributed multinomial regression. *The Annals of Applied Statistics 9,* 1394–1414.

Taddy, M. (2017). One-step estimator paths for concave regularization. *Journal of Computational and Graphical Statistics 26*(3), 525–536.

Taddy, M. (2019). *Business Data Science: Combining Machine Learning and Economics to Optimize, Automate, and Accelerate Business Decisions.* McGraw Hill Professional.

Taddy, M., C. S. Chen, J. Yu, and M. Wyle (2015). Bayesian and empirical Bayesian forests. In *Proceedings of the 32nd International Conference on Machine Learning.*

Thompson, W. R. (1933). On the likelihood that one unknown probability exceeds another in view of the evidence of two samples. *Biometrika 25,* 285–294.

Train, K. E. (2009). *Discrete Choice Methods with Simulation.* Cambridge University Press.

Vapnik, V. (1996). *The Nature of Statistical Learning Theory.* New York: Springer.

Varian, H. R. (2009). Online ad auctions. *The American Economic Review 99,* 430–434.

Venables, W. N., and B. D. Ripley (2002). *Modern Applied Statistics with S* (4th ed.). New York: Springer.

Wasserstein, R. L., N. A. Lazar, et al. (2016). The ASA's statement on p-values: context, process, and purpose. *The American Statistician 70*(2), 129–133.

Wold, H. (1975). Soft modeling by latent variables: The nonlinear iterative partial least squares approach. In *Perspectives in Probability and Statistics, Papers in Honour of M.S. Bartlett.* Academic Press.

Wortman Vaughan, J., and H. Wallach (2020). A human-centered agenda for intelligible machine learning. In M. Pelillo and T. Scantamburlo (Eds.). *Machines We Trust: Getting Along with Artificial Intelligence.* Cambridge, MA: MIT Press.

Xie, Y. (2020). *servr: A Simple HTTP Server to Serve Static Files or Dynamic Documents.* R package version 0.17.

Zhang, A., Z. Lipton, M. Li, and A. Smola. Dive into deep learning. Available at d2l.ai.

Zou, H., T. Hastie, and R. Tibshirani (2007). On the "degrees of freedom" of the lasso. *The Annals of Statistics 35*(5), 2173–2192.

GLOSSARY

activation function a function used to process inputs in a deep neural network.

Akaike's information criterion (AIC) an information criterion using the in-sample deviance and model degrees of freedom.

architecture in deep learning, the structure of a model used.

autocorrelation a variable y, being correlated with itself. That is, it depends on other values of y.

autoregressive model a type of model in times series that includes a previous (lagged) version of y as an explanatory variable to account for the dependence on past observations (autocorrelation).

bag of words a representation of text when individual words or phrases are tokenized and the vectorization results in simple word counts.

balanced having the same number of observations at each combination of factors being considered.

Bayesian statistics the framework for formalizing subjective beliefs and updating those beliefs based on data.

bivariate dealing with the relationship between two variables.

block a set of similar subjects or observations.

boosting the process of repeatedly applying a simple algorithm to residuals from previous fits.

bootstrap an algorithm that uses resampling from the observed data to estimate a sampling distribution. The resamples are each the same size as the observed data and are taken with replacement.

boxplot also known as a box and whisker plot, a graphical display of the five-number summary, with a box to span the quartiles, whiskers extending to the max and min, and a line dividing the box representing the median.

candidate model a model that may be chosen during model selection.

causal inference the statistics of measuring the causal reason for an outcome.

CART (classification and regression tree) the dominant method for fitting trees.

clustering grouping similar observations into groups.

collaborative filtering a way of predicting a person's future choice based on their and others' past choices.

conditional distribution when there is more than one variable, say x and y, the marginal distribution of $y \mid x$ is the distribution of y, given the effects of x. That is the conditional distribution of $y \mid x$ is the probability of y at all possible values of x.

conditional ignorability the idea that all factors that influence treatment status and response of interest have been tracked and controlled for.

confusion matrix in classification, a table with predicted classes on one axis and actual classes on the other. In the body of the table, the number of true positives and negatives, and false positives and negatives are listed.

convex curving upward.

corpus a collection of documents used in text data analysis; plural is *corpora*.

correlation a measure of the association between two variables. For numerical data, Pearson's correlation measures the strength and direction of a linear relationship. Correlation closer to 0 indicates little correlation while correlation closer to $+1$ or -1 indicates a strong linear relationship.

covariance a measure that is closely related to correlation; used to obtain correlation by dividing the covariance by the standard deviations multiplied by each other.

cross-sectional data that is measured at one time point for several individuals.

cross-validation (CV) using out-of-sample experiments to select the best model.

data frame a list of lists that is a special way R stores data organized in rows and columns.

data generating process (DGP) the process that allows us to map from data samples to probabilities about the underlying, but unknown, mechanisms that generate them.

deep learning (DL) a technique that uses deep neural networks to process complicated inputs automatically.

deep neural network (DNN) a deep learning model with many layers of neural networks.

degrees of freedom the number of random observations your model could fit perfectly; in regression models this is the number of coefficients.

delimiter a character or symbol that separates strings of data from one another.

dendrogram a tree diagram.

deviance the distance between the observed data and the fitted model.

difference-in-differences (DiD) an analysis that applies when you have a number of units that are observed in two time periods, one before treatment and the other after a subset of units have received treatment.

discriminator something used to allow for clear distinguishing between groups.

document term matrix (DTM) in text analysis, a matrix with a row for each document and a column for each term.

dummy variable also called an *indicator variable;* representing membership in a category with the number 1, and lack of membership as a 0.

elasticity in economics, the proportion change in a variable in response to the change in another.

elastic net an elaborate name for the combination of ridge and Lasso penalties.

embedding in text analysis, a technique of using sequences as tokens to estimate the vector representations of each.

empirical Bayesian forest (EBF) a strategy based on the idea that the trunks in the forest are all the same. Thus, you fit the trunk once and then use it to partition the data and facilitate parallelization.

epoch each pass through the dataset when training a model in Keras.

Euclidean distance the straight-line distance between two points (see Pythagorean theorem for Euclidean distance in two dimensions).

factor modeling a process used to distill a complex set of data into a few key underlying factors.

factorization a set of methods to aid in dimension reduction.

false discovery rate (FDR) the proportion of false discoveries resulting from a procedure.

fitted value the estimate value based on the fitted model.

fixed effect fixed or nonrandom quantities in a model.

fold a subset resulting when a dataset is broken into evenly sized subsets for use in cross-validation.

forecasting extrapolating to make predictions of future *y* in time series analysis when certain conditions are met.

frequentist statistics based on the thought experiment of repeated draws from a fixed data-generating process.

Gaussian the dominant models for spatially dependent data and work by smoothing predictions across observations according to distances between their locations; *also*, another name for the normal distribution.

generalized linear model (GLM) a model that defines the relationship between a linear function and the response.

greedy search a search that, at each step, makes the locally optimal choice which reduces the complexity of the search.

heterogeneous consisting of parts all of different kinds.

histogram a graphical display for visualizing a quantitative dataset where the values are grouped together in equal intervals and the height of adjacent bars describes how many values fall within each interval.

homogeneous consisting of parts all of the same kind.

indicator variable also called a *dummy variable;* representing membership in a category with the number 1, and lack of membership as a 0.

information criteria (IC) theoretical approximations to what out-of-sample deviance you can expect when using your model to predict new data.

instrumental variable in causal inference, a variable that affects the response only through the policy (or treatment) variable and is independent of the unobserved errors.

iterative least squares an algorithm that iterates between choosing the mixture component membership for each observation, then uses the mean of the observations of each component to estimate its mean.

K nearest neighbors (K-NN) a way to classify observations with unknown labels as a function of their neighbors (nearby observations) with similar input features.

Keras framework a framework for working with deep neural networks in R.

Lasso regularization with the absolute value penalty.

latent Dirichlet allocation (LDA) in text analysis, models the rows of a DTM as draws from a multinomial distribution and yields an efficient factorization that is interpretable.

likelihood the probability of the data given the estimated model; the goal is to make this as big as possible.

linear regression a linear approach used in statistics to model the relationship between dependent and independent variables.

log penalty in regularization, the penalty on coefficients and has diminishing bias.

logistic regression an approach used in statistics to model a binary dependent variable.

logit in logistic regression, the logit link implies that you have a linear regression for the log odds: $\log(p/1 - p) = \mathbf{x}'\boldsymbol{\beta}$ where $p = \mathrm{p}(y = 1|\mathbf{x})$.

loop a sequence of computer commands that is repeated until a specified condition is reached.

machine learning (ML) a set of tools to automate model building, based on the idea that a computer can recognize patterns with little human intervention.

marginal distribution when there is more than one variable, say x and y, the marginal distribution of y is the distribution of y (ignoring any effect x has on it).

marginal regression an algorithm that runs a simple linear regression for dependent and independent variables, then uses the resulting regression coefficient to map $\mathbf{x}$ to a univariate factor.

matrix in R, a two-dimensional set of entries of the same data type.

maximum likelihood estimate (MLE) choosing the parameters of a model so that the likelihood is maximized.

mean squared error (MSE) average squared deviation of an observed y to its predicted value.

mirror in R, a repository containing the files for downloading R and its available packages.

modular the characteristic of models that can combine layers optimized for one type of data and combine them with layers optimized for other types of data.

multicollinearity also called *collinearity*; a predictor is said to exhibit collinearity if it can be predicted well from a combination of the other predictors in a model.

n-gram in text analysis, combining tokens in pairs (2-gram) or triples (3-grams), or any other n.

negative predictive value (NPV) the probability of actually not being in a category given that you were classified as not belonging to that category.

nonconvex the shape of a function that does not curve upward.

nonparametric quantifying uncertainty using results of a given procedure without assuming correctness of the underlying models.

notation a framework for describing causal inference.

null model a baseline model used for comparing to a proposed model. The null model in regression is typically the model that only contains an intercept.

ordinary least squares (OLS) a method for estimating the parameters in a regression by choosing them such that the sum of the squared deviations of an observed y to a predicted y is minimized.

overfit the quality of a model that is tuned so closely to specific features in the training data that it doesn't predict well on new data.

package a package in R is a set of functions and datasets that are not included in the base R console until they are called into the session.

panel data that is measured at several regular time points for several individuals.

parallel computing when many calculations are carried out simultaneously.

parametric depending on the assumption that an underlying model is correct.

partial least squares (PLS) a supervised factorization strategy that is an extension of marginal regression.

penalization a term used in regularization that is introduced to control coefficients and stabilize the system.

Poisson a statistical distribution used to calculate probabilities associated with the number of events in a certain interval (usually a time period). For example, the Poisson models the number of calls in an hour coming into a call center.

polynomial regression when the model fit to data in a regression is an nth-degree polynomial.

positive predictive value (PPV) the probability of actually being in a category given that you were classified in that category.

principal components analysis (PCA) an algorithm for estimating factor models by iteratively estimating a series of factor loadings and directions.

principal components regression (PCR) instead of regressing y onto x, use a lower-dimension set of principal components as covariates.

pruning a technique used to remove leaf splits (e.g., some vocabulary) before carrying out an analysis of text, thus yielding the lowest in-sample error.

Pythagorean theorem a formula used for a right triangle, the length of the hypotenuse, $c^2 = \sqrt{a^2 + b^2}$.

R open-source software environment for statistical computing and graphics. It compiles and runs on UNIX, Windows, and MacOS.

random forest a big data technique in which each tree in a sample is fit to a resample of the data.

random walk a model that says that the next value in a time series is a random change from the previous value.

reference level a level that is omitted from a model matrix and used as a baseline to compare the expected response of the other factor levels against.

regression modeling a response variable y with a set of inputs or covariates, x.

regression adjustment attempting to account for all potential confounders in a regression so that causal inference can be made.

regression discontinuity design (RDD) an experiment design in which the treatment allocation is determined by a threshold on some "forcing variable."

regularization a strategy that penalizes complexity so as to depart from optimality and stabilize a set of candidate models.

reinforcement learning (RL) a framework of machine learning algorithms that actively chooses the data consumed for training.

residual the difference between fitted values and observed values.

ridge a type of regression that is a regularization where the penalty function on coefficients is β^2; the penalty increases rapidly as β increases.

rotation matrix a matrix that translates from a covariance matrix's coordinate system to a different coordinate system of J independent directions.

scatterplot a graphical display to show the relationship between two quantitative variables with a dot plotted at each x,y pair.

screeplot a visual representation of the variance for each principal component direction.

seasonality a regular fluctuation in a times series variable that is predictable by season.

semiparametric a flexible model that incorporates parametric and nonparametric components.

sensitivity the probability of classifying something as positive if it really is positive.

sigmoid function an S-shaped function that is the inverse of the logistic link function.

softmax the multinomial logistic regression analog to the logit link in binary logistic regression.

specificity the probability of classifying something as negative if it really is negative.

stationary a way to describe a series that has the property of mean reverting, as such they are useful for predictions.

stemming In the pre-processing phase of text analysis, it is common to remove suffixes, such as "ing," from words to leave only their stem.

stop words common words to be removed from the vocabulary in text analysis; typically includes words such as "the" and "and."

supervised learning in machine learning, an approach that uses labeled datasets (i.e., y dictates how x variables are incorporated into a model).

tensor processing unit (TPU) specialized chips that facilitate parallel computing of vectors of operations for deep neural networks.

text regression a technique that uses text data to predict some outcome target.

time series data that is measured at several regular time points for one individual.

token in text analysis, the pieces of a character string that has been broken up by tokenization.

tokenization the process of breaking up character strings into pieces such as words, sets of words, symbols, and other elements.

topic the pieces that result after an unsupervised analysis breaks down text data.

topic model a factorization model for estimating factors for data vectors using unsupervised modeling.

training data the data used to fit a model.

unbalanced an unequal number of observations at each combination of factors being considered.

underfit a model that fails to capture the structure of the data, possibly due to missing key predictors. In other words, it is missing some of the signal in the data.

univariate concerning a single variable.

unsupervised learning a method in which there is no response or outcome dictating how variables are incorporated into a model.

user-defined function (UDF) a function that is created by the user, not a built-in function.

variance-covariance matrix a $k \times k$ matrix containing the variances of k random variables on the diagonal and the covariances of each pair on the off-diagonal.

vector in R, a one dimensional set of entries of the same data type.

vectorization in text analysis, the process of assigning a numeric measure to a token.

ACRONYMS

ACF autocorrelation function

AIC Akaike's information criterion

AR autoregressive

BoW bag of words

CART classification and regression tree

CV cross-validation

DGP data generating process

DiD difference-in-differences

DL deep learning

DNN deep neural network

DTM document term matrix

EBF empirical Bayesian forest

FDR false discovery rate

GLM generalized linear model

GP Gaussian process

IC information criteria

K-NN K nearest neighbors

LDA latent Dirichlet allocation

LSA latent semantic analysis

ML machine learning

NPV negative predictive value

OLS ordinary least squares

PCA principal components analysis

PCR principal components regression

PLS partial least squares

PPV positive predictive value

RDD regression discontinuity design

RL reinforcement learning

SGD stochastic gradient descent

TPU tensor processing unit

UDF user-defined function

INDEX